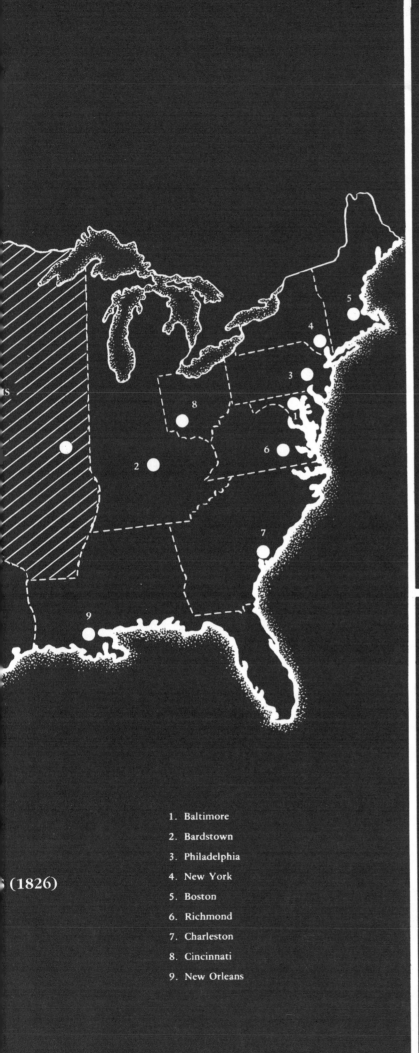

D1221049

(1826)

1. Baltimore

2. Bardstown

3. Philadelphia

4. New York

5. Boston

6. Richmond

7. Charleston

8. Cincinnati

9. New Orleans

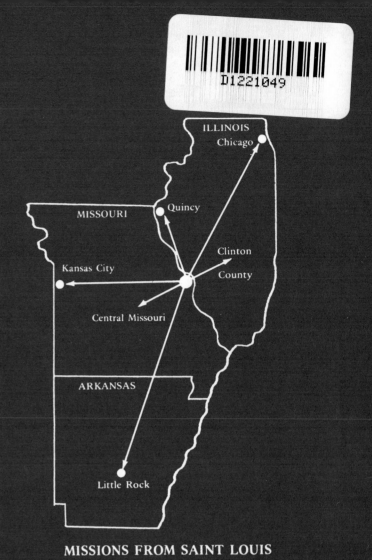

MISSIONS FROM SAINT LOUIS

IN THE 1830's

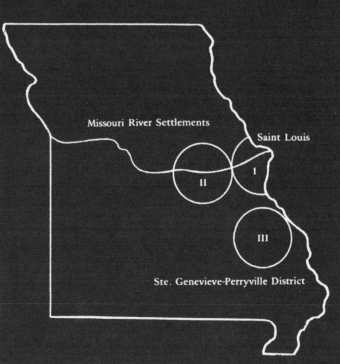

MISSOURI CENTERS OF CATHOLICISM

(AFTER 1840)

Designed by Edna Suermann.

Dream by the River

A statue of Saint Louis IX, patron of the City, the Archdiocese, and the Cathedral of St. Louis - the work of sculptress Angela Gregory. (Photograph by Claudia Voulgarakis.)

Dream by the River

Two Centuries of Saint Louis Catholicism

1766–1997

Third Revised Edition

William Barnaby Faherty, S.J.

IMPRIMATUR
Most Rev. Archbishop of St. Louis
Justin Rigali, D.D.

IMPRIMI PROTEST
E. Edward Kinerk, S.J.
Provincial, Missouri
Jesuit Province

Previous editions © 1973, 1981

Copyright © 1997 by The Archdiocese of Saint Louis. All rights reserved. No part of this publication may be reproduced or transmitted in any form or by any means electronic or mechanical, including photocopy, recording or any information storage and retrieval system now known or to be invented, without permission in writing from the publisher, except by a reviewer who wishes to quote brief passages in connection with a review written for inclusion in a magazine, newspaper or broadcast.

Published by The Archdiocese of St. Louis. St. Louis, Missouri 63108

Printed in the United States of America

Library of Congress Card Number: 81-80221

ISBN: 0-933150-21-0

Printed by Western Press, Inc., St. Louis, Missouri

Patrick Justice and Katie Orbin

To the Catholics of Saint Louis
and their chief Shepherd, Archbishop Justin Rigali
on the 150th Anniversary of the Archdiocese

(Photograph by Saint Louis Review)

A conception of the first church in Saint Louis by Sheila Harris.

Contents

Contents

The Cover

The Cover Photo by Ralph Frese shows reenactors following the route of merchant-explorer Louis Jolliet and missionary Pere Jacques Marquette when they discovered the Mississippi River in 1673. The missionary was the first to bring the Gospel to the tribes of the region.

Introduction

The temper of Catholicism in Saint Louis differs greatly from that of other American cities. Outstanding bishops, a remarkable clergy, many religious orders, significant lay leaders, varied nationalities, unnumbered organizations, and the unique spirit of the city itself combined to give a distinct flavor to Saint Louis Catholicism.

A blend of the east and west, of north and south, the city itself holds the urbanity of the eastern seaboard and the informality of the western plains: it provides a foretaste of the languid delta lands at the edge of the North; its industrial complex hums like a northern dynamo, out of place in the warm South. Saint Louis boasts a people obedient when authority speaks, but more concerned to go on their own way and get the job done, with little concern for those in charge; a people not easily understood: conservative in some things, progressive in others, with little logic in the divergence.

Saint Louisans built Eads Bridge across the Mississippi in the 1870's; but had not yet set up one way streets to expedite north-south traffic in the 1970's; they promoted the Jefferson Memorial Gateway Arch, the most distinctive monument of the contemporary world; but endlessly debated what to do with the Old Post Office, an historical and architectural landmark.

Just as Saint Louisans of all denominations had outlooks that differed from those of New Yorkers or Baltimoreans, so the unusual origins of Saint Louis gave to local Catholics a further differing attitude from their co-religionists elsewhere. On the eastern seaboard, Catholic immigrants found Boston or Philadelphia already stratified Anglo-American Protestant communities. Catholics began Saint Louis. They formed as much a part of the scenery as the trees, the streets, the buildings. During the forty years before Saint Louis became a part of the United States, few members of other denominations came to the city. When Saint Louis became American at the time of the Louisiana Purchase (1804), individuals of other religious affiliations arrived. Even twenty years later, they did not outnumber the Catholics. Since then, Catholics have usually numbered close to half the populace. In his book, *Inside U.S.A.*, social observer John Gunther forthrightly called Saint Louis a "Catholic city."[1]

In recent centuries men and women died in Paris, Munich, Warsaw, and Madrid for their Catholic faith. Even Rome itself went through periods of anti-Catholic rule. Against this background, the Saint Louis story shines with pure light.

St. Louis became the center of the French Empire in the Upper Mississippi Valley when the flag of France went down at Fort Chartres and Commandant Louis St. Ange de Bellerive crossed the river and set-up his headquarters at Laclede's trading post in 1765.

PART I

Saint Louis: Frontier Parish

Father Sebastian Meurin baptizes Mary Deschamps in May, 1766, "in a tent for want of a church" — as he recorded in the first church record of the Saint Louis parish (from a mosaic in the Cathedral of Saint Louis, photograph by Jack Zehrt).

This old bell, according to family tradition, was donated by Benito Vasquez, and blessed by Father Valentine, O.F.M. Cap., in 1772. It hung in the first church of Saint Louis. (Photograph by St. Louis Review.)

Chapter 1

The Dream of Pierre Laclede

Laclede's Post

The glamour of French achievement in the colonial Midwest has not dimmed with the years. Two groups divided the activity between them. They matched vigor and endurance, but differed in motives. Missionaries made up one group, especially Jesuits and Franciscans: men such as Jacques Marquette and Claude Allouez. Empire-builders made up the other group: men such as Jolliet, La Salle, Bienville, and Cadillac.

The founding of Saint Louis proved to be the last achievement of the French on the North American continent. In the twilight years of the French empire in America, the government of King Louis XV granted to Colonel Antoine Maxent and Pierre Laclede, French-born residents of New Orleans, exclusive right to trade west of the Mississippi along the Missouri River.[1]

Before Laclede and his fur traders moved upstream to establish a trading post, however, the French and Indian War ended in British victory. The Treaty of Paris, signed in 1763, the very year Laclede set out on his expedition, gave the former French territory east of the Mississippi to England. By a secret treaty, a few months previously, France had ceded the lands west of the river to her ally, Spain.

Unaware of this latter diplomatic move, Laclede moved upriver. His young associate, Auguste Chouteau,[2] and twenty-four hired men went with him. The *voyageurs* pulled a barge laden with provisions and equipment for a trading post. In November, Laclede approached Ste. Genevieve, the largest and oldest city on the west bank of the river, about eighty miles below the conflux of the Missouri. Now he was in the "Illinois Country" — as the French called the rich area lying on both sides of the Mississippi. While at Ste. Genevieve, Laclede received confirmation that the Treaty of Paris had given the east bank of the river to the English. This information played a significant part in the development of his plans.

Rich bottomland on the east bank stretched about seventy miles northward. On this prairie, the French had settled at Kaskaskia, a few miles south of Ste. Genevieve, and in a cluster of villages a few miles to the north, around Fort Chartres: St. Philippe, St. Anne, and Prairie du Rocher. They also had another settlement, Cahokia, forty miles upriver, on the east bank.

Commandant Neyon de Villiers invited Laclede and his men to winter at Fort Chartres, a rock bastion the French had built to anchor their empire in the Mississippi Valley. Laclede gladly accepted.

In December, the enterprising fur-trader scouted the west bank to the mouth of the Missouri. A little above and across from the French village of Cahokia, Laclede chose a terraced area as the site for his projected post. He marked the trees and returned to Fort Chartres. He invited residents of the neighboring villages to settle at his chosen spot.

When the winter of 1763-1764 continued mild, Laclede decided to start his work in early February. He sent his men up the river with the barge. Four days later, on the fourteenth of February, 1764, they reached the place he had chosen. The next morning they began to build log huts for themselves and a warehouse for the furs. A few days later Laclede came up from Fort Chartres. The men wanted to call the place Laclede. Instead, he suggested the name of the patron saint of the reigning monarch, Louis XV of France — the crusader king, Saint Louis IX.[3]

Laclede planned a village three blocks in depth to stretch along the river for a half-mile north and south. He named the central square at the riverfront the Place D'Armes. He set aside the block behind it for the headquarters of Maxent, Laclede and Company. The church would occupy the third square to the west.

Illinois French: Saint Louis' First Residents

By this time, the Illinois villagers on the east bank of the river had a few winter months to consider what it might mean to live on soil belonging to England. They remembered the tragic experiences of their Acadian brothers. Just ten years before, the British had driven the Acadians from their homes in Nova Scotia, split up families, and scattered them along the shores of North America. Many of these people had ended up in Louisiana. The story of this cold-hearted action of the British government, abetted by the Puritans of New England, made a deep impression on the French people of the prairies. The villages near Fort Chartres, St. Anne, and St. Philippe grew restless in the late winter. Prairie du Rocher, nestling under the Illinois bluffs about three miles away, remained more calm.

Commandant Neyon de Villiers of Fort Chartres planned to go down to Louisiana. He persuaded large groups of families, especially from the village of St. Anne, to go with him. Laclede induced a number of the Illinois French, including almost the whole town of St. Philippe, under the leadership of Joseph Labuschiere, to move to the site of his new post.

These Illinois French villages possessed an air of permanence unusual on the frontier. The people had a light-hearted, easy-going attitude, and also the ordinary amount of human cantankerousness evidenced by desertion, infidelity, and over-indulgence. "These French of the border were not saints," Illinois historian Clarence Alvord wrote. "The records of the courts, however, do not reveal an excessive amount of crime among the settlers."[4]

These people had no spontaneous desire to leave the homes with the wide verandas they had built up in a course of a generation. Many of them had been born in Illinois, most of the others in Canada. They had become mere pawns on the diplomatic chess table. Little wonder then that so many decided to move, some down to Louisiana, the rest to the area adjoining Laclede's trading post.

The migration of these Illinois French made Laclede's post a village. As the settlement began to take shape, more and more of the farmers from the Illinois side of the river moved across to the new settlement.[5]

The Illinois villages had stood in the midst of populous Indian settlements, mainly because the missionaries chose the sites to Christianize the Indians. No large concentration of Indian peoples, however, dwelt in the immediate vicinity of Saint Louis. But the Missouri and Mississippi rivers, joining a few miles above the village, offered easy access for the Indians. Laclede's men, too, could readily move along the waterways.

Another group of French had its part in the foundation of Saint Louis. Late in 1765, Louis Saint Ange de Bellerive, successor to De Villiers as Commandant at Fort Chartres, and last representative of the French crown in the upper Mississippi Valley, turned over Fort Chartres to the English at the orders of the French government. He crossed the river with his troops and set up the first civil administration in the city of Saint Louis.[6] He was to remain in authority until the first Spanish lieutenant governor arrived five years later.

The law that governed Saint Louis, and the other villages of the Upper Mississippi Valley, was the *coutume de Paris,* "the common law in the city of Paris and the district depending on it."[7] This most liberal of the many pre-Napoleonic legal codes of France gave every male over fourteen the right to vote on Trinity Sunday for town officials such as the notary, the syndic, and others. It created a climate of popular participation in local government.

During the next few years French settlers on the east bank continued to the west side, settling at Ste. Genevieve, at Saint Louis, and, a few miles to the south, at Clement Delor's settlement, later to be called Carondelet. Within a short time, a number of the people, who had gone down to the Bayou Country with De Villiers, came back upriver to Saint Louis. By 1770 the village was to have about five hundred inhabitants.[8]

Saint Louis' Pioneer Priests

During the Age of Absolutism, rulers of Western Europe took a disproportionate hand in the workings of the Church. They gained undue influence in the choosing of ecclesiastical administrators in their areas. They used religion as a force for national unity and for the extension of their empires. The royal patronage played a significant part in the amazing development of the Church in America. In French and Spanish America, for instance, Paris and Madrid, more than Rome, guided the development of the Church. So intertwined were structures of Church and state that they rose or fell together. When Paris sneezed, the Church in the Mississippi Valley automatically reacted. Paris sneezed in the 1760's.

Jesuits had been among the pioneers of the French empire in the middle valley. But in September, 1763, a royal courier had come to the Illinois country. He had announced the suppression of the Jesuit order in the Louisiana territory. The French government ordered the Jesuit priests to leave and put their residences up at public auction.[9]

Six of the seven Jesuits in the Illinois country accepted this decision of the king as an expression of God's will. But the fifty-six year old Sebastian Louis Meurin, the pastor at Kaskaskia, did not intend to leave without a fight. He had lived the dangerous life of a frontier missionary for twenty-one years. His extant letters show him to be a man hard to please.[10] Certainly the new action of the French government did not please him.

At the very time Laclede moved up the Mississippi, Meurin had gone down to New Orleans, protested to the superior council, and gained permission to go back to the Illinois country. The council placed certain restrictions upon his future activity. It required him to take up residence in Ste. Genevieve; it informed him that the Diocese of Quebec no longer included Louisiana; it ordered him to recognize no other ecclesiastical jurisdiction except that of the superior of the Capuchins in New Orleans.[11]

Father Meurin would be happy to live in Ste. Genevieve, and work under the distant jurisdiction of the Capuchin superior. But many of his former flock still lived on the other side of the river. Since he had long enjoyed the faculties granted by the bishop of Quebec, he would use these whenever the people on the east bank needed him. About the time Pierre Laclede began his trading post in Saint Louis, Sebastian Meurin started back upriver.

Two years later, in 1766, he visited Laclede's settlement. He baptized four children "in a tent for want of a church," as he wrote in the initial records of the parish of Saint Louis. He recorded the names of Mary Deschamps, Veronica Ride, a French-Indian, Antoine, and Constance Bissonet. The following May, Father Meurin returned. He baptised Helene Hebert, Pelagie Kiercereau, Marie Langevin, and Henri Francois Roy.[12]

At this time, Father Meurin asked the bishop of Quebec to send a missioner to assist him. During the following year (1768), a thirty-one year old *Canadien,* the newly ordained Pierre Gibault, came to the Illinois country, and took up residence at Kaskaskia.

A Spanish Governor Arrives

Saint Louis became part of the Spanish empire at a time of renewed vigor in the Spanish-speaking world. In 1759, five years before the founding of Saint Louis, Charles III, Spain's greatest king since the sixteenth century, took the throne. He chose enlightened ministers, reduced the public debt, increased the efficiency of the government, began public works, reorganized the army, rebuilt the navy, and put new spirit in the empire.

In view of the vast size of her dominions, one would hardly expect Spain to find enough capable administrators to man such a distant outpost as Saint Louis. Yet, she was to send a succession of good lieutenant governors to upper Louisiana.

The first lieutenant governor, Don Pedro Piernas, arrived in the village on February 17, 1770. Wisely, he accepted things as they were. He ratified all that St. Ange had done during his five years. He next urged the townspeople to build a church on the block designated for it in the original layout of Pierre Laclede.[13] Father Gibault came across the river to dedicate the church on June 24, 1770. The old cathedral records show regular visits by Father Gibault during the next two years. He baptized thirty French, eighteen Negroes, and sixteen Indians.[14]

Father Meurin, in the meantime, ran into difficulties with Philippe Rocheblave, Spanish commandant at Ste. Genevieve.[15] Rocheblave viewed Meurin's missionizing both banks of the river a transgression of the privileges of the Spanish empire. The priest left Spanish territory and took up residence at Cahokia, across from Saint Louis.

Occasionally, he crossed the Mississippi on sick calls. This he did at night, to avoid coming to the "official" attention of the Spanish authorities. During his last years, the old missionary served the people of Prairie du Rocher.

A Capuchin missionary, Father Valentine, Saint Louis' first resident priest, came in May 1772. He remained for three years. During this time he baptized sixty-four French, twenty-four Negroes, and nineteen Indians. He solemnized four marriages and officiated at the funerals of forty-two French, eleven Negroes, and nineteen Indians. One of these French was Louis St. Ange de Bellerive, who died at Christmas time, 1774. Father Valentine also blessed the new church bell, a gift of the lieutenant governor and his wife.[16]

Father Valentine never had the status of pastor; he seems rather to have functioned officially as chaplain of the small Spanish garrison. He did meet with Piernas and city residents, however, to plan a new church. The blueprints called for a structure of white oak timbers sixty feet long by thirty feet in width. Piernas assessed all inhabitants, white and Negro, over fourteen and not yet sixty, for construction materials. He named Pierre Baron the superintendent of construction. The participating citizens signed their names to the proceedings.[17]

The three principals, unfortunately, left shortly afterward. Lieutenant Governor Piernas finished his term, Father Valentine moved to New Orleans, and Baron died. Slightly over a year later, on January 28, 1776, the new governor, Francisco Cruzat, assembled the inhabitants in the government hall and resumed the plans.[18] In March of that year (1776) a Capuchin stationed at Ste. Genevieve, Father Hilaire, brought welcome news that Saint Louis would soon have a pastor of its own.[19] Before the builders had completed the new church, a German-born Capuchin, Father Bernard de Limpach, arrived.

Showing once again the close relationship of the Spanish government and the Church, Lieutenant Governor Cruzat formally installed the first pastor, Father Bernard, on Sunday, May 19, 1776. Cruzat summoned all prominent citizens to be present at this ceremony. Father Bernard signed the documents officially installing him as pastor of Saint Louis. Among the citizens who signed were Pierre Laclede, Joseph Labuschiere, and last of all, Lieutenant Governor Francisco Cruzat.[20]

The Town as Father Bernard Saw It

At the time of Father Bernard's arrival, Saint Louis stretched along the riverfront for many blocks, but was only three squares deep east and west. The blocks were three hundred feet north and south and two hundred and forty feet east and west with four lots of identical size in each. The first street bore the name *Rue Royale,* the second street *Rue d'Eglise,* and the third *Rue des Granges,* the street of the barns. In the central squares of the town, in ascending order west stood the *Place d'Armes,* the headquarters of Laclede, and the church square.

Several residences, including those of Pierre Laclede and Joseph Labuschiere, the largest in the village at the time, were of stone. Most, however, were of upright logs, pointed and driven into the ground, a bit apart, chinked with stone and lime mortar, and then covered with hand split lath and white-washed plaster. Every house had a porch at least on the front, one large central room and four small rooms on the corners opening into it, and a

large fenced-in rear yard with gardens, orchards, and outbuildings. Four identically-sized lots made up each block.

The land rose in terraces from the river. A fence followed the first ridge just beyond the *Rue des Granges* and marked the western limit of the village. Beyond this, on the southwest, common pasture land extended along Mill Creek. North of this section stretched the common fields, thin strips, one acre in width and forty or fifty in depth. Thus each tiller of the soil had access to his land from the edge of the village. No walls enclosed Saint Louis, even though it lay in the heart of the Indian country. In contrast, every settlement on the Anglo-American frontier at the time depended on a wall or stockade for security.

When Father de Limpach arrived in Saint Louis, he found the new church in process of construction. He held services in the temporary log shed that had served the people as a church. The church had all the vestments and sacred vessels needed for Divine Service, even a monstrance for Benediction and the increasingly popular Corpus Christi procession.

Early in the summer, Father Bernard blessed the new church, a structure of upright logs, with the roof extending over a five-foot wide porch — in the tradition of the French midcontinental structure. The building faced the *Rue d'Eglise.* When all pledges were in, seventy-eight families had contributed to the building.[21]

After High Mass on September 1, 1776, Lieutenant Governor Cruzat assembled the parishioners to discuss plans for a new parish house.[22] The assembly planned a two-story stone house, forty-five feet in length along the *Rue d'Eglise* and twenty-seven feet in depth. With a casualness to be customary in Saint Louis, the parishioners let out the bids for the building the following summer.

The records of Saint Louis' first church, as well as those of the Illinois villages, show that the priests performed the basic religious functions for all Catholics regardless of race. Negro and Indian slavery had existed in French Illinois before the founding of Saint Louis. Many of Saint Louis' original settlers brought Negro servants with them. In the early 1770's, for instance, the population of Saint Louis had consisted of 399 white persons and 198 Negroes.[23] During his twelve years in Saint Louis, Father Bernard baptized 410 white people, 106 Negroes, and 92 Indians.[24]

These church records attest at least a minimum of concern on the part of the French masters for the spiritual needs of the blacks. French law obliged every owner to have his slaves instructed in religion and prepared for baptism. The law, further, protected female slaves from molestation, disallowed separation of families by sale, and forbade extreme punishments. While some French colonists had Indian slaves, on the whole, their attitude towards the Indians was far more friendly than that of their English counterparts on the Atlantic coast. Similarly, the French were not as inclined to racism in their attitudes toward the Negroes. Further, the region of Saint Louis did not have the plantation economy or climate, such as in Lower Louisiana, that made extensive use of slave labor profitable.

Some blacks were free in infant Saint Louis, and many more were to gain their freedom as time went on. As early as September 1, 1767, three years after the founding of the village, for instance, Father Meurin had baptized Paul Gregory, a free Negro.[25] On June 2, 1770, an officer in the Spanish service, Lt. Louis Villars, had freed a Negro woman not yet in middle age.[26] Some slave owners, such as Claude Mercier,[27] freed their slaves in their wills. The Spanish authorities generally accepted the French slave system.

The Wide World Moves Up Close

The wider world of international politics began to close in on the little village of the Illinois country. Less than two months after Father Bernard came to Saint Louis, the English colonies on the Atlantic seaboard declared their independence of Great Britain. They hoped to win the French people of Canada to their side and sent representatives to discuss the matter. Bishop Briand of Quebec, however, demurred. Some of the colonial leaders, especially of the northern colonies, had spoken bitterly against the British government for giving freedom of religion to the Canadian Catholics a few years before. Bishop Briand worked on the principle that the "British lion you know is better than the colonial tiger you don't know." He not only supported the existing British government, he threatened excommunication to anyone who aided the American cause.[28]

Father Pierre Gibault was the only priest left on the east bank of the river. The year before, the grand old man of the middle valley, Father Sebastian Louis Meurin, had died. Father Gibault had buried him at Prairie du Rocher. On July 4, 1778, two years to a day from the Declaration of Independence, a colonial officer, George Rogers Clark, arrived in Kaskaskia with a small force of Virginians. Father Gibault sided with the Americans. He won over Gabriel Cerré, the civic leader of the community, to the American cause. Gibault prevailed on the inhabitants of the Illinois settlements to support Clark; he traveled to Vincennes and convinced the settlers on the Wabash that their future lay with the American colonies.[29]

These actions put Father Gibault in a difficult position religiously and politically. Bishop Briand opposed Gibault's action. The British commander at Detroit, Henry Hamilton, listed Father Gibault as a traitor to Britain.[30] Hamilton was not a gentle fellow. He offered a bounty to the Indians for the scalps of any white men they could kill. Father Gibault further suffered substantial financial losses for the many supplies he secured for the American forces. And lastly, he made himself an exile from his native land, Canada. He was never able to go back. Few men in the country so wagered their future on the American cause.

By 1780 British arrogance had fanned the little fire of the American Revolution into a world conflagration. England stood alone against the combined forces of Spain and France, with the active support of Holland and the sympathetic "armed neutrality" of Russia, Prussia, Austria, Sweden, and the rest of Europe.

The outpost of Saint Louis seemed beyond the limits of this great struggle. Yet, it felt the impact. In May, 1780, the British in the Great Lakes area planned a sweep through the Central Mississippi area. Among their special targets were to be Saint Louis and Cahokia. British General Patrick Sinclair in Michili-Mackinac sought the services of all the Indians of the north, especially the Sioux in Minnesota. He unleashed a thousand braves on the peaceful villages of the middle valley.

The American Colonel George Rogers Clark and the Spanish lieutenant governor at Saint Louis, Fernando de Leyba, conferred on problems of defense. The two worked well together.

In spite of sickness, de Leyba ordered the building of a stone fort on the ridge beyond the church. He planned a trench in the shape of a broad, short-stemmed wire staple entirely around the village. It stretched along the edge of Third Street and turned at right angles to the river on the north and south ends of town.[31]

With a thousand hostiles poised not far north, the people of Saint Louis celebrated the feast of Corpus Christi, May 25, 1780, with a procession of the Blessed Sacrament and a strawberry festival outside the trench-limits of the village. Fortunately, the Indians did not attack that day. Fanning out on both sides of the river, they killed a number of settlers on remote farms near Florissant and Spanish Lake. The next day they attacked Saint Louis and Cahokia simultaneously. The Spanish-French-American allies drove the Indians back. One month later, stung by criticism for his slowness in fortifying Saint Louis, and still depressed by the death of his wife the previous September, Lieutenant Governor de Leyba died. Former governor Francisco Cruzat returned to take over in Saint Louis.

Troubled Years on the American Side

As the thirteen sovereign colonies on the Atlantic seacoast moved from confederation to Constitution, they had little time to think about the distant settlements in Illinois. Neglect brought disorder. Disorder drove many *habitants* to the more organized Spanish dominions on the west bank. People who had refused Laclede's invitation in 1764, now left Kaskaskia, Cahokia, and Prairie du Rocher.

Confusion of church administration rivaled the political unrest. Between the outbreak of the Revolution in 1775 and the Peace of Paris in 1783, the few priests in the American colonies had no contact with the vicars apostolic of the London District, their nominal religious superiors. Finally in 1784, Rome appointed young America's outstanding priest, John Carroll, "Prefect Apostolic" — a title that traditionally went to the administrator of a territory in the early stage of missionary development.

The task of organizing the Church along the Atlantic coast challenged the great skill of John Carroll. He was able to give little time to Illinois and its problems — a land he hardly knew and one not yet clearly within his jurisdiction.

All the while, Father Gibault, now in Vincennes, still thought he had charge. The bishop of Quebec had appointed him vicar-general of the territory. Gibault had received no notice of any change.

A Carmelite Friar, Father Paul de St. Pierre, arrived in Kaskaskia in 1785.[32] This German-born priest had come to America as chaplain of one of the French regiments fighting against the British. After Yorktown, he offered his priestly services to John Carroll. Since Father Paul wished to work among the French, Carroll's vicar, Father Ferdinand Farmer, sent the former chaplain west. His coming aroused some jurisdictional suspicions on the part of Father Gibault.[33] Nonetheless, Father Paul served the people of Illinois energetically and devotedly.

A big question remained unanswered: did Church authorities in Baltimore or in Quebec have jurisdiction in the West? The arrival in Illinois of a French Sulpician, Father Pierre Huet de la Valiniere, in the summer of 1786, served to sharpen, not solve the issue.[34] De la

Valiniere could not live quietly. In Canada during the Revolution, he had supported the American cause. The British governor exiled him. When he arrived in the newly independent states, Bishop Carroll hesitated to assign him to a parish. Eventually, he sent him to the midwestern French with the powers of vicar-general.[35] He stirred up tornadoes wherever he went. He fought adventurer John Dodge, who preyed on the people of the Kaskaskia district. Carrying the case to Congress, De la Valiniere won.[36]

Thinking himself secure now in the estimation of his people, he began to flex his ecclesiastical muscles. Only two other priests worked in the vast area, Father Gibault and Father de St. Pierre. De la Valiniere turned on the latter. Within a year of his arrival in Illinois, he sent a letter to the congregation of Cahokia listing complaints against the pastor.[37] These complaints added up to nothing. The outraged parishioners defended Father de St. Pierre.

On November 6, 1787, Rome set up the diocese of Baltimore. In October of the following year (1788), it officially transferred the Illinois country from the jurisdiction of Quebec to that of Baltimore. A year after Carroll's consecration on August 15, 1790, Rome made his diocese coterminous with the American boundaries.[38]

In the meantime, religious matters had not gone smoothly in the Illinois country. The Kaskaskians had had enough of Vicar De la Valiniere. He left the Illinois country in 1789, going first to the Atlantic seaboard and eventually to New Orleans.[39] The vicar's letter to the people of Cahokia, and the general ecclesiastical confusion, drove Father de St. Pierre to more orderly Spanish Louisiana. He became pastor of Ste. Genevieve in 1789.

Father Gibault, likewise, was ready to move. Against the wishes of his ecclesiastical superior in Canada, he had supported the American Revolution. In return he had received little thanks from the colonial authorities. He had served the Church well in a most difficult post for almost twenty years. Now he received scant support from the overburdened ecclesiastical authorities in Baltimore. Gibault moved to the town of New Madrid, twenty miles below the conflux of the Ohio, on the west bank of the Mississippi, and became pastor in 1793.[40] He organized the parish of St. Isidore, built a fine church and a comfortable parochial residence of cypress timbers so plentiful in the area, and lived his remaining years in a reasonable comfort he so properly deserved after his long years of missionary endurance.

The Northwest Territory had no Catholic clergy. At this juncture, the Reign of Terror broke out in France, the first of many European upheavals during the next hundred years that indirectly aided the American Church. Many members of the Order of Saint Sulpice preferred exile in America to imprisonment or death in their native land. They began to arrive in March 1792 to the benefit of the Church in the West.

As a result, during the succeeding years, Bishop Carroll had a number of exceptional Sulpicians to send beyond the Alleghenies. Outstanding among them, Benedict Joseph Flaget, served in several Kentucky parishes and finally became bishop of Bardstown (Kentucky), the first episcopal see of the Trans-Allegheny United States. Father Michael Levadoux worked at Cahokia for some years; Father Gabriel Richard, destined to be the first priest elected to Congress, at Prairie du Rocher; Father Jean Francois Rivet at Kaskaskia and later at Vincennes. The Olivier brothers, Jean and Donatien, served various parishes. Father Pierre Janin devoted several years to the Catholic Indians in the Illinois country, and later crossed the river into Spanish Territory.[41]

STE. GENEVIEVE ACADEMY. In 1808, Irish-born Pastor James Maxwell headed a corporation that set up the first school chartered by the Territorial government in this building. President James Madison appointed Father Maxwell to the Territorial Legislature in 1812 and that body elected him president. He received his original appointment as Vicar General of Upper Louisiana from the King of Spain in 1794.

Chapter 2

River Valley Reunited

Saint Louis and the Trans-Mississippi

While religious affairs in the Trans-Allegheny United States were in turmoil, things were relatively quiet in Spanish Territory on the west bank of the Mississippi. In spite of his advancing age and growing infirmities, Father Bernard de Limpach carried on in Saint Louis. He extended his ministration to the farming community of Carondelet on the Mississippi about eight miles to the south, to Portage Des Sioux on the river a few miles above the mouth of the Missouri, and to St. Charles, a growing village on the left bank of the latter river, twenty miles west-northwest of Saint Louis. Father Bernard occasionally crossed the river to American territory, when Cahokia lacked a pastor.[1] In 1787, the venerable Capuchin asked his superiors to relieve him of the heavy duties of Upper Louisiana. Two years passed before they granted this request. In the autumn of 1789, he left for a less strenuous assignment in the lower valley.[2]

After the departure of Father Bernard, Father Francois le Dru came from Kaskaskia and served in Saint Louis until 1794. During this time, the Church records show that Fathers de St. Pierre and Gibault also conducted religious services on occasion in Saint Louis.[3] On his arrival Father Le Dru pointed out to the authorities the need of a new church. Lt. Governor Manuel Perez wrote Don Esteban Miro, the governor of Louisiana, about the matter. Perez insisted that the people had not refused to build a new church. They simply were too poor to do so. Perez suggested that revenues from trade with two or three tribes "of the Misury" should go for this purpose.[4] Nothing came of this proposal.

In the 1790's groups of Catholic Frenchmen came into Missouri. A few refugees of the Reign of Terror in France crossed the Mississippi. Some of these newcomers remained in Saint Louis. The majority went downriver to start life over, many at New Bourbon near Ste. Genevieve.

Several projects for French settlers in the Ohio Country proved abortive. Eventually many of these people moved to Upper Louisiana. From the French settlement of Gallipolis, in Ohio, Dom Pierre Joseph Didier, a Benedictine of the Congregation of Saint Maur, went west. The church records of St. Charles showed his name as early as 1792. At the same time he cared for the spiritual needs of the people at Florissant, twenty miles north-northwest of Saint Louis, in one of the richest farming areas of the region. Founded in 1786 under the patronage of St. Ferdinand, this village built a frame church in 1792. From December, 1793, to April, 1799, Dom Didier served Saint Louis. The parish records of the time show that he baptized three hundred and fifteen individuals — sixteen Indians, seventy-nine blacks, and two hundred and twenty whites. He solemnized seventy-four marriages and buried eighty-five whites, sixty-one blacks, and nine redmen.[5]

During Dom Didier's pastorate, Louisiana-born Zenon Trudeau served as lieutenant governor for seven years, until 1799. He proved a forward-looking and progressive leader.

At the start of Trudeau's term, an event of great promise for Saint Louis' future took place. Pedro Vial, a French explorer in the employ of the Spanish governor, crossed the plains from Santa Fe to Saint Louis. This trip showed the Spanish authorities that the two villages were closer than they had anticipated,[6] and led to the eventual opening of trade between them.

The lieutenant governor did not wholly approve the traditional Spanish restriction of immigration to persons of the Catholic religion. He was ready to wink at enforcement of this law, in order to lure Anglo-Americans from the other side of the river. The trickle of English-speaking people into the trans-Mississippi, destined to become a torrent, began in his day. All the settlements had a few Anglo-Americans, with the only sizable group concentrating in Cape Girardeau. Few of these were Catholic. Except in that region, the English-speaking newcomers were hardly noticeable in the larger French-speaking populace. Many of them scattered on farm lands along the Mississippi and Missouri rivers.

During Trudeau's term, a change in religious administration took place. During the earlier decades, the priests of Louisiana had served under the authority of the bishop of Havana. A vicar-general represented him at New Orleans. This situation changed in 1795. Luis Penalver y Cardenas arrived in the Crescent City as bishop of all Louisiana.

Bishop Penalver centered his attention on the lower valley. But he did not completely overlook his spiritual children to the north. In 1796, he sent an Irish priest, Father James Maxwell, to Upper Louisiana. Like so many of his fellow countrymen in those days, Maxwell had received his education at the Irish College of the University of Salamanca in Spain. He felt a call to the apostolate in America and came to Spanish Louisiana. The bishop appointed him vicar of the Illinois Country, and later on, pastor of Ste. Genevieve, in place of Father Paul de Saint Pierre who took an assignment in Lower Louisiana. Bishop Penalver asked Maxwell to make a report on the religious situation in Saint Louis. This Maxwell did. The condition of the log church was appalling, he reported. "Not only is it too small for the village, but its timbers are rotted and it cannot be kept from falling into ruins."[7]

Bishop Penalver never personally visited Upper Louisiana, but as a result of Maxwell's report, he asked the governor to defray one third of the cost of restoration of the church in Saint Louis. Since the faithful had become accustomed to miss Mass, the bishop feared that it would be difficult to get them to return to the habit.[8]

Trudeau also reported on the economic state of the

The mother church of the Mississippi Valley, the Cathedral of St. Louis IX, faced Jackson Square in New Orleans even back in the days of Bishop Du Bourg. A Spanish bishop had presided here in the 1790's.

region. The villagers of Saint Louis neglected their cultivated strips, failed to repair their fences, and let the cattle from the common pasture graze at will among the vegetables. They carried on what commerce existed, especially with the tribes of the Missouri. The people of Carondelet and Florissant, on the other hand, were industrious farmers. Some planters in the latter village were of American background. Trudeau suggested that the authorities "send them a priest of the Irish nation." Trudeau gave the population of Saint Louis itself as "948 persons of all ages and sexes" in 1798.[9]

Father Maxwell carried on an active apostolate in Ste. Genevieve and environs. He had the tough physique and buoyant temperament to cope with the frontier environment. During the next years he proved successful in his priestly work. The Spanish officials liked him; the people of Ste. Genevieve worked with him; those of Saint Louis and St. Charles knew and respected him greatly.

Maxwell regularly served a number of settlements within a radius of a hundred miles of Ste. Genevieve, such as New Madrid, Potosi, Old Mines, and Perryville. He planned an Irish colony in the Ozarks about sixty miles southwest of Ste. Genevieve just beyond Tam Sauk Mountain,[10] the highest point in the region. He sought land for his "Vale of Avoca" in the interior of Missouri. International changes thwarted his project. The day of the Irish in Upper Louisiana was still some years into the future. Maxwell's plan failed; but it attests the vision of the pioneer missionary.

The End of the Spanish Regime

The distance from Saint Louis to the southern-most point of the Spanish possessions in the Americas was seven times the mileage between Saint Louis and New Orleans. This incredibly vast empire belonged to a country much smaller in size than its one territory of Upper Louisiana. Its population hardly went above ten million. It is not surprising then that few Spanish people came to the newly added province of Louisiana, and even relatively fewer came to Saint Louis. Several Spanish soldiers, however, married local French girls. Eugenio Alvarez, for instance, married Josepha Crepeau; Benito Vasquez married Julie Papin. Many of their descendants remained in Saint Louis. Several participated in the fur trade in the Rocky Mountains. Vasquez Peak in central Colorado gained its name from one of these traders.

During the 1790's the Spanish from Saint Louis launched several expeditions up the Missouri River. These trips opened the way for the American exploration of Lewis and Clark in the succeeding decade. At the same time, the Spanish authorities in Louisiana kept a wary eye on the Anglo-Americans moving into the eastern half of the Mississippi Valley. Spanish policy fluctuated. At some times the Spanish officials excluded Anglo-Americans and restricted trade on the Mississippi; at other times, they encouraged trade and invited English-speaking settlers from the east bank. All the while they welcomed French settlers from Illinois into the Spanish empire. But the tide of empire definitely lay with the Americans.

Not all French — either in America or Europe — appreciated this fact. Official and unofficial delegates of the French revolutionary government moved secretly among the people to stir a desire for a new French empire in America. Some French-speaking residents of Louisiana listened attentively to talk of the glories of revolutionary

France. But the agitation remained on the level of mere talk, until Napoleon became First Consul of France. He dreamed of restoring France's oversea power. As part of his far-flung scheme, he demanded Louisiana from Spain in 1800. Spain had to grant his request in the secret Treaty of San Ildefonso. But Napoleon's plan caught on an unexpected snag in Santo Domingo. He quickly gave up his colonial designs.

At a fortunate time, President Thomas Jefferson sent representatives to Napoleon to negotiate the purchase of New Orleans and insure access to the gulf. The American commissioners found Napoleon quite willing to sell the entire Louisiana. In 1803, the United States doubled its size by purchase of the French territory on the west bank of the river. This area included all the lands above Texas draining into the Mississippi from the west.

Before the people of Upper Louisiana knew they belonged once again to France, they were on the verge of becoming Americans. This change put a great burden of decision on the few remaining priests of the area: Fathers Leander Lusson, pastor at St. Charles, Pierre Janin at Saint Louis, and James Maxwell at Ste. Genevieve. The Spanish authorities had paid them an annual salary and supervised the building and maintenance of the churches.[11] The change of administration would create an entirely new situation that would probably be temporarily difficult.

Lieutenant Governor Charles De Lassus expected the three priests to leave with him when he left Upper Louisiana.[12] Father Janin and Lusson decided to go. At the same time, Father Jean Olivier, pastor of Cahokia, went to New Orleans to become chaplain of the Ursulines. Thus the Saint Louis district had no priest.

Father Maxwell chose to stay at Ste. Genevieve, even though he had closer ties to Spain than the French-born priests. Since Father Gibault had died shortly before, Maxwell was the only priest in the former Spanish territory of Upper Louisiana. He thus became a tie between the "Old Regime" and the American Republic. With almost superhuman effort, Maxwell managed to visit as many Catholics of Missouri as he could. He kept alive in the people of the various settlements the hope of having their own pastor one day.

"Hurricane" in the Lower Valley

If a shortage of priests hindered the religious development of Upper Louisiana, a super-abundance of vicars-general, and the absence of a bishop, thwarted progress in Lower Louisiana. When Bishop Penalver had left New Orleans in 1801 to become archbishop of Guatemala, he had appointed Fathers Thomas Hassett and Patrick Walsh vicars-general. The Capuchin rector of the New Orleans cathedral, Fray Antonio de Sedella, known affectionately in New Orleans as "Pere Antoine,"* had not accepted this announcement gracefully. After all, with Fray Antonio around, what need was there of vicars? The King of Spain had appointed him pastor. His long pastorate had already seen the building of the cathedral and the presbytery. He had cared for the poor, and during frequent epidemics he stayed at his post. Many people in New Orleans revered

*A picturesque street in the French Quarter still bears his name. Edward F. Murphy wrote a novelized version of his life (Doubleday, 1947).

The famous "Pere Antoine," Fray Antonio de Sedella, O.F.M.Cap., pastor of the Cathedral of New Orleans by appointment of the King of Spain, greatly influenced the course of Saint Louis religious history in an indirect way. Because of Pere Antoine's power in New Orleans, Bishop Du Bourg decided to locate in Saint Louis in 1818.

him as a saint. Eventually, he became the most popular figure of his time in Louisiana. In short, he was a considerable person, and in any conflict, a strong adversary.

Pope Pius VII had approved a successor to Bishop Penalver. But the newly consecrated bishop, Francisco Porro y Peinado, had delayed his embarkation for America because the ownership of Louisiana hung in doubt. Then, in 1803, when Louisiana became a part of the United States, Bishop Porro y Peinado accepted the see of Tarragona in Spain.

Vicar Thomas Hassett notified Bishop Carroll of Baltimore of the ecclesiastical situation in America's new territory. He mentioned nothing of Fray Antonio and little of the actual spiritual condition of the area. His main concern seemed to be the livelihood of the priests since they no longer received a stipend from the Spanish government.[13]

Since a rescript of the Holy See in 1791 had given Carroll jurisdiction over all U.S. territories, the Baltimore bishop notified Rome on February 14, 1804, of the American purchase of Louisiana.[14] In response, the Office of the Propaganda asked him to nominate three priests so Rome could choose bishops for the area.

Two months later, Father Hasset died in New Orleans. In March, 1805, the surviving vicar, Patrick Walsh, issued a pastoral letter calling on all to recognize his spiritual authority.[15] Fray Antonio defied Walsh. The vicar withdrew the Capuchin's faculties, placed the cathedral under a quasi-interdict, and informed the Holy See of the pastor's insubordination.[16] The president of the Cathedral trustees notified Carroll on April 12, 1805, that they did not recognize Walsh's authority since the bishop who had appointed him had gone elsewhere.[17] In September, 1805, Propaganda authorized Carroll to appoint an administrator,[18] and wrote Father Patrick Walsh of this fact. The beleaguered vicar died a short time later.

Because of Fray Antonio's close connection with the Spanish government, Bishop Carroll followed the advice of the Office of Propaganda and conferred with James Madison, secretary of state to President Thomas Jefferson.[19] The Baltimore bishop feared that some international complications might result from the Capuchin's connivances. Privately, Madison expressed the hope that Carroll might be able to curb the anti-American influence of de Sedella. Officially, he answered that the administration did not think it wise to intervene in the selection of a bishop for the territory. He added that President Jefferson had perfect confidence in Carroll's wisdom and loyalty.[20]

Bishop Carroll appointed Father Jean Olivier, former pastor of Cahokia, and at the time chaplain of the Ursulines in New Orleans, as his vicar-general for Louisiana. The Office of the Propaganda urged Carroll to appoint Belgian-born Father Charles Nerinckx administrator-apostolic of Louisiana. The Kentucky missionary refused the difficult task. The Church in the lower valley waited in an uncertain calm.

Transition in the Upper Valley

In Upper Louisiana, in the meantime, the Creoles of Saint Louis and the other French settlements were trying to adjust to the fact that they belonged to the United States. The days of heavy immigration were still a few decades off. Those were the times of exploration and tentative settlement.

At that time, the white man's Missouri was by no means coterminous with later state boundaries. A thin line of population extended northward along the Mississippi from New Madrid to the conflux and up the Missouri another hundred miles. Some few pioneers farmed in the valley of the Meramec River that flowed into the Mississippi twenty miles south of Saint Louis. Traders had explored the West. But settlers had not yet filled those areas. In the next two years Lewis and Clark moved up the Missouri, Pike up the Mississippi. Later on, Pike went toward the Spanish borderlands of the Southwest. Anglo-Americans soon crossed the Mississippi in great numbers.

The regime of Spain had been benign. The rulers shared the Catholic faith of the populace. Now the Saint Louis French were to be part of a new country, an outgrowth of a nation that had fought France for over a hundred years. The new country spoke a different language. The majority of its citizens belonged to various Protestant groups. Yet the transition from French to American ways was to prove relatively easy.[21]

An important factor in this was the progressive legal code that had prevailed in colonial Saint Louis. This had provided an opportunity for all males over fourteen to participate in local elections,* and helped prepare them for American democratic practices. Other factors were the reluctant but eventual acceptance of the inevitable changes by so many French Saint Louisans, and the caliber of many newcomers of Celtic or Anglo-Saxon background. Such were William Clark, brother of George Rogers Clark, territorial governor and superintendent of Indian affairs; Joseph Charless, an Irish revolutionary of Welsh ancestry who began Saint Louis' first newspaper; Alexander McNair, first state governor who married into a French family; and business leaders John Mullanphy and John O'Fallon, both of Irish ancestry, the former a Catholic, the latter a Methodist.

One outstanding Frenchman came with the American regime. President Jefferson appointed Jean Baptiste Lucas commissioner of land claims. A member of Congress from Pennsylvania, Lucas had been born in Normandy, and had moved to the United States at the urging of Benjamin Franklin.

After the initial influx of Illinois-French to Saint Louis in the days of Pierre Laclede, a few *Canadiens* moved in, but no numerically significant group of French people arrived. One small but distinct and influential group, however, deserves mention at this time. Planter families from Santo Domingo fled a slave insurrection in the 1790's, settled for a while on the east coast, principally in the Philadelphia area, and, later on, such families as the Pauls, De Muns, Nidelets, and Garesches[22] moved to Saint Louis.

Among the newly arriving Irish, along with Mullanphy, O'Fallon, and Charless, Jeremiah Connor, Thomas Brady, and John McKnight took part in a variety of economical and social activities. A large majority of Irish and Irish-Americans were Catholics.

The Irish were at home in Saint Louis from the earliest days, as they were in no other city in the country. They were to profit both by their identity of faith with the French inhabitants and the fact that the Irish and the French mutually shared England's hostility at the time.

*Vide *supra*, p. 3.

As a result, the Celts and the Creoles regularly intermarried.

A wandering Irish priest, in fact, arrived in 1806. Dublin-born Thomas Flynn had received his education on the continent, and worked in parishes in France. At the outbreak of the French Revolution, he left France for the United States. For fourteen years, he labored among Catholics on the eastern seaboard. On his arrival in the West, the local church wardens installed him as pastor of Saint Louis. He remained a little more than a year. He left for Kentucky early in 1808.[23]

Upper Louisiana had welcomed individual priests of many religious orders after the expulsion of the Jesuits in 1763. The most surprising group came in the last weeks of 1808. Hardly anyone would have expected to find Cistercians of the Strict Observance on this frontier of Catholicism in the early United States.* Yet, the Trappists, one of the most rigorous of the contemplative orders, unexpectedly appeared in the Saint Louis area.

Refugees of the French Revolution, like Capuchin Flynn and Sulpician Flaget, the Trappists had come to America and founded a monastery in Kentucky. The austerity of the rule combined with the rough frontier surroundings to shatter the health of many of the community.[24]

Superiors thought that a temporary change might help. Perhaps mission work among the Indians might afford that healthy relief. Abbott Urban Guillet went westward to assess the situation. The Abbott, a lay brother, and a recently arrived priest, Father Joseph M. Dunand, set off on foot for the Mississippi. Unfortunately, the white-robed trio traveled in late fall. They reached Cahokia in December. A fierce winter swept in early. On Christmas Eve, Father Dunand crossed the Mississippi on a bridge of ice.[25]

Saint Louisans rejoiced at their good fortune of a Christmas Mass. Later on, Father Dunand was to observe that with the coming of the Americans, the Creoles had abandoned the practice of their religion. On that Christmas morning, however, he saw that the French kept some of the old fervor. "I found the church well filled, despite the rigor of the cold," he reported. "Everybody approached the Sacraments."[26]

Abbott Urban soon had two attractive offers of land for a monastery. One lay on the Missouri side, in the village of Florissant. The house once occupied by Francois Dunegant, first civil and military commandant of the village of St. Ferdinand, stood on this property. On the Illinois side, land-owner Nicholas Jarrot made an even more generous offer of four hundred acres.

Abbott Urban wrote to civil officials and to Bishop Carroll of Baltimore regarding the choice. He initially decided on Florissant. The Trappist community came from Kentucky to the former officer's home in Coldwater Creek Valley. After a year there, however, Abbott Urban accepted the other site, north of Cahokia on the Illinois side.[27] The Trappist priests moved across the river, but still missionized Saint Louis and other Missouri villages.

The Trappists were to stay only long enough to become a part of the lore of Southern Illinois. The four hundred acres they occupied included a large number of

Indian mounds, the relics of an earlier culture. Most of these mounds were conical in shape and relatively small. The largest was a quadrangle terrace, with a flat top of perhaps forty acres. From the Trappists' short stay there, the place gained the name Monks Mound.

Illness continued to hit the Trappists. In their few years in the West, fifteen monks died. Father Urban was not able to regularize the confused title to the land. Superiors recalled all but Father Dunand.[28]

Four Priests Carry On

The withdrawal of the Trappists did not leave the Illinois country stripped of priests. In Cahokia, Father Francois Louis Savine, the last of the Canadian missionaries to work on the Illinois-Missouri mission, had replaced Father Jean Olivier who had become chaplain of the Ursuline nuns in New Orleans. For several years Father Savine crossed over from Cahokia to serve Saint Louis, again without a resident priest.

In the Ste. Genevieve area, Father James Maxwell did more than carry on. He planned a school for boys. With twenty-one leading citizens, he set up a corporation and began construction of Ste. Genevieve Academy in 1808. On June 21 of that same year, the territorial government granted a charter to the new institution — the first chartered school in the region.[29]

During the year 1813, Father Maxwell assumed a new role. Louisiana had become a state the year before; the northern reaches of Jefferson's purchase became the Territory of Missouri. President Madison named the priest to the legislative council of the territory. The following January, the members of the council elected him president of that body.[30]

A little more than four months later the career of this distinguished Missourian ended abruptly. While he was on a sick call, his horse reared and threw him. Father Maxwell never recovered from the fall. His devoted people gathered for his funeral on May 30, 1814, in the church at Ste. Genevieve.

From his headquarters at St. Charles, and later Florissant, the one Trappist who remained in the West, Father Joseph M. Dunand, ranged up and down the Mississippi.[31] After Father Maxwell's death, he visited a colony of Anglo-American and Irish families in southeast Missouri. They had settled around the little village of Perryville in an area called "The Barrens," that lay ten miles from the southeast flowing Mississippi about twenty miles south and a little east of Ste. Genevieve. These Anglo-American families stemmed from Maryland and had lived for a time in Kentucky. In 1814 Father Dunand urged the parishioners to build a church.

Less in the public eye than either Fathers Maxwell or Dunand, Father Donatien Olivier, the brother of Jean Olivier, worked steadily and untiringly at Prairie du Rocher and Kaskaskia. Already fifty-three years of age on his arrival in Illinois in 1799, he was to continue his pastorate for twenty-eight years until the age of eighty-one, and then live on fourteen more years in retirement. Eventually he was to gain a reputation for holiness among people of all faiths. Governor John Reynolds of Illinois, who, as a young man in Kaskaskia, knew Father Olivier personally, was to write of him: "He acquired a great reputation for his sanctity and holiness, and some believed him to be possessed of the power to perform small miracles, to which he made no pretensions."[32]

---

*Trappist Thomas Merton interestingly described the wanderings of these Monks in his *Waters of Siloe* (New York: Harcourt, Brace and Company, 1949), pp. 64-82.

The first steamboat "Pike" came up the river to St. Louis on August 2, 1817. The first bishop to reside in St. Louis, Bishop Du Bourg, arrived less than a year later. (Sketch by Norbury Wayman.)

Michigan Territory
Winnebago

Iowa

Fox

IL

Ottawa
Chippewa

IN

OH

Sauk

Potawatomi

Missouri Territory

Missouri

Kickapoo

Wea
(Miami)

Delaware

St. Louis

Kaskaskia

KY

Osage

Tamaroa
Peoria
Cahokia

Michigamea
Piankeshaw
Shawnee
Delaware

Map by Mary Struckel
and Nancy Merz

TN

Quapaw

Chickasaw

Indian Country - 1818

Transplanted Tribes - Light   Nonremoved Tribes - BOLD

In 1818, St. Louis stood in the heart of Indian Country, with a number of tribes in their ancestral areas in Illinois, Iowa and Wisconsin and remnants of other tribes moving across the Mississippi River.

PART II

Louis W. V. Du Bourg: Promotional Prelate (1815-1825)

Above: *Bishop Louis W.V. DuBourg of Louisiana Territory located in St. Louis rather than at the Cathedral in New Orleans for various reasons. Among them, he wanted to be near the native tribes.*

Right: *Bishop Rosati began St. Mary's Seminary Church in Perryville, modeled after the Mother Church of Monte Cittorio in Rome. A new church in Ste. Genevieve followed the same plan.*

Chapter 3

A Prince-Bishop of the Old Regime

John Carroll, archbishop since Pope Pius VII raised Baltimore to the rank of archdiocese in 1808, still sought a qualified administrator for the Territory of Louisiana. He needed a bi-lingual priest, preferably of French background, since the administrator would have to reside in a predominantly French city. Carroll sought, at the same time, a man identified with the United States and sympathetic to its spirit and goals. The appointee had to possess, finally, enough administrative experience and diplomatic skill to cope with Fray Antonio and the trustees in New Orleans.

In 1812, the year Louisiana became a state of the Union, Archbishop Carroll decided on a likely candidate in the person of the Sulpician educator, Louis William Valentine Du Bourg. A native of the island of Santo Domingo, Du Bourg had gone to France with his family in 1768 at the age of two. He took his studies in Bordeaux and then enrolled in the seminary of St. Sulpice in Paris to prepare for the priesthood. Ordained in the autumn of 1788, he directed a preparatory seminary at Issy near Paris, and pursued advanced studies at the Sorbonne. The Reign of Terror drove him out of France a few years later, and he followed many of his friends to the Sulpician-staffed seminary in Baltimore, Maryland. On his arrival, he set about learning English in a systematic way. In 1795 Du Bourg joined the Society of St. Sulpice, a group of priests devoted to the education of clerical students. Soon afterward, Bishop Carroll became aware of his capabilities and appointed him president of Georgetown College. Du Bourg's friend and fellow Sulpician, Benedict Joseph Flaget, served as vice-president. On one occasion during these years Du Bourg was a dinner guest of President George Washington at Mount Vernon.[1]

Upon completion of his term as president of Georgetown College, Du Bourg and Flaget left for Havana to begin a college in that city. The Spanish government frustrated their efforts and they returned to the United States.[2] On the way back Bishop Du Bourg presumably visited New Orleans where a brother, Pierre Francois Du Bourg, had resided for a few years. Returning to Baltimore, Du Bourg started St. Mary's College that won its charter from the Maryland legislature in 1805. He opened the school to all students, day or boarders, without distinction of creed or nationality — a truly remarkable characteristic at that time.[3] In 1808, his friend Flaget went west as bishop of Bardstown, Kentucky, one of the four suffragan sees, along with Philadelphia, New York, and Boston, of the newly erected province of Baltimore.[4]

During these years, Du Bourg added other activities to his college duties. He built up a congregation of French-speaking Negro servants of French West Indian families who had arrived recently in Maryland. He established a fraternal society similar in structure to later St. Vincent de Paul societies.[5] He participated in the drive for a new cathedral in Baltimore. He counseled the widow Elizabeth Seton, foundress of America's first religious congregation.[6] He engaged in public controversy on matters of religion, especially with the Presbyterian Synod of Baltimore. He gave thought to the need of a periodical to give a Catholic slant on religious questions.[7]

Du Bourg had more qualities than one might hope for and Carroll chose him as the apostolic administrator of New Orleans. Of French background, he spoke the language of the vast majority of Louisiana's citizens as well as excellent English. He was one of the best educated men in the United States. An impressive personage, he could move easily in the company of prominent persons in Church and state. He had not yet proved his capacities as a popular leader; nor had he any experience in dealing with strong adversaries.

Even without Fray Antonio, Du Bourg would have had an almost insurmountable task. International diplomacy had shifted the Louisiana Territory from Spain to France to the United States with little regard for the feeling of the inhabitants. Scarcely a dozen priests, half of them advanced in age, had to serve fifty thousand people scattered across half a continent. Religious life did not flourish.

Du Bourg, further, did not have the prestige and power of the episcopal rank, although Archbishop Carroll's commissioning letter had repeated Rome's original words of four year's before: "with the rights of an Ordinary."[8] Several of Du Bourg's letters, further, seemed to suggest that Pope Pius VII had appointed him bishop, but because of the confusion of Napoleonic times, was not able to send him the essential documents.[9]

In his early months in New Orleans, Father Du Bourg presumably got along well with everyone. Fray Antonio did not object to Du Bourg's residing at the cathedral rectory. Du Bourg himself decided not to do so. He set up headquarters at the Ursuline convent. He did not want to be under the scrutiny of Fray Antonio's partisans or to be "officially" aware of the public scandals of the assistant pastors. Du Bourg credited the "pretended affection" the people had for Fray Antonio to the latter's condoning of evils.[10]

In a letter to Archbishop Carroll, Du Bourg referred to the people of New Orleans as a "rabble" and the Church in New Orleans as dissolute; he gave many indications of being loyal to the Bourbons in a pro-Bonaparte city; he deplored that, under the existing government, nothing could be done as long as "a certain individual lived." He frankly admitted his own deficiencies. After a few formalities (the admission of a lack of humility, of the spirit of prayer, and of fidelity to God's grace) he analyzed his failings well: timidity and uncertainty, wavering between extremes, and a lack of perseverance in any system. He admitted these failings. He knew that Louisiana would get a bishop. He deemed one indispensable. He asked Carroll to keep him from the burden.[11] In spite of these difficulties, he remained in New Orleans during 1813 and 1814.

Flaget Visits Missouri

With all his problems in Lower Louisiana, Administrator Du Bourg did not have time to visit the Missouri territory, many hundred miles upriver. Instead, in 1814, he asked his friend Bishop Flaget of Bardstown to attend to the spiritual needs of the people in the old settlements along the upper Mississippi. It was good that Flaget did so, not only for the spiritual welfare of the people of the area, but also for the religious history of the times. Bishop Flaget kept a journal. During his routines at home he listed sparsely the major events of the day and weather conditions. When he traveled, however, he tended to write at length of his experiences.[12]

Flaget set out in mid-May, 1814, and spent two weeks in Vincennes, a parish he had served in the nineties. He found that religious life had deteriorated. He started for the Mississippi accompanied by a group of French Rangers, special troops mustered for defense during the War of 1812. On arriving in Cahokia after four days' travel, he found things in good order. Father Savine was on hand. The congregation was free of debt. It had, in fact, a surplus of $200. Flaget heard confessions and confirmed 118 persons.[13] On June 30, the people of Cahokia conducted the bishop in procession to the banks of the Mississippi and a boatman took him across the river. The religious apathy of the people of Saint Louis depressed the visiting bishop. He thought religion was in an even worse condition there than it was at Vincennes. "The rich, the fathers, the mothers, and the children over 15 years, stayed away from the confessional and he could make no impression whatever on their callused hearts."[14] He administered confirmation and received gifts of a cross and a mitre from the ladies of St. Louis. The only source of joy Bishop Flaget records during this visit was the news of the downfall of Napoleon. He determined to have a *Te Deum* in honor of the event when he returned to Bardstown.[15]

On July 8 he departed for Florissant where Father Dunand and his people welcomed him with enthusiasm. His whole visit was quite happy. He crossed the Missouri and confirmed 103 persons in Dardenne, where he found a deep cleavage between two factions of the congregation. Flaget confirmed 54 persons at Portage Des Sioux and then went to St. Charles. Here he found religion in a sad state. The congregation at St. Charles did not seem to get along as well with Father Dunand as the people at Florissant did. So Flaget set out to restore peace to the community. He finally won from the people a promise not only to support their missionary, but also to build for him a suitable residence.

On August 3, the bishop returned to Saint Louis. His second visit only confirmed his earlier impression. He thought the religious situation in Saint Louis the most unhappy in the whole region he had visited. "This congregation is in a state of extreme indifferentism: my sojourn here will be almost useless."[16] He confirmed 72 persons and preached to the Anglo-Americans in the English language. They were so pleased with the sermon that they sent a deputation to express their satisfaction. Governor William Clark paid the bishop every possible courtesy and

invited him to his house and asked him to baptize three of his children as well as an orphan girl residing in his family. Mrs. Ann Lucas Hunt, the daughter of Judge J. B. Lucas, commissioner of land claims, was godmother on this occasion.

On August 14 the bishop left Saint Louis for Cahokia, Illinois, where he confirmed 58 persons. In late August he went to Prairie du Rocher where Father Donatien Olivier resided. The bishop confirmed 65 persons on September 1. In Father Olivier's other pastorate of Kaskaskia, the bishop found a superb church and an impressive congregation.[17] On September 21 he visited Ste. Genevieve where he preached against dancing to the great consternation of the people. He concluded his visit to the West side of the river with a two-week stay in the Anglo-American settlement of Perryville.

In retrospect, some villages pleased Flaget, some left him depressed. Of those that pleased him, all had a resident pastor among them. Cahokia had Father Savine, Florissant had Father Dunand, Prairie du Rocher and neighboring Kaskaskia had the devoted Father Donatien Olivier, and Ste. Genevieve had had Father Maxwell up to a few months before. Perhaps the steady work of their pastors had made these parishes so good. Or it might have been that the people who sought a pastor and took care of him had a deep religious spirit originally.

At the end of the first episcopal visitation of the middle valley, the picture looked uncertain. Priests were few, religious practice was spasmodic, the quality of faith uneven. The town that would be the central city of the mid-continent for years to come did not even have a resident priest. The expected flood-tide of Anglo-American newcomers might overwhelm the isolated French Catholic communities.

Obviously, the Church had to do something about the Upper Louisiana area. It was not to be the Church in general, however, that took the step that moved the Saint Louis region out of its spiritual doldrums. It was to be the work of one man, Louis W. V. Du Bourg, then administrator of Louisiana, who would move his headquarters for a time to Saint Louis and bring with him many devoted missionaries. A new day would dawn sooner than the pastor-less people of Saint Louis would have dared to dream.

A Bishop for American Louisiana

After the victory of General Andrew Jackson over the British at New Orleans in early 1815, and the presumed ending of the Napoleonic wars in Europe, Du Bourg decided to go to Rome to lay the matter of religion in Louisiana before the officials of the Propaganda, the Roman body in charge of affairs in mission countries. Napoleon's long detention of Pope Pius VII had severed the ordinary relations between the head of the Church and the bishops of the American dioceses. Du Bourg felt that a personal conference alone could resolve the Louisiana problems.

He realized, on the other hand, that once he had left New Orleans Fray Antonio would ride high. But Du Bourg had to hazard that possibility. He named Father Louis Sibourd as administrator during his absence. Volcanic de Sedella challenged Du Bourg's right to make such an appointment and declared that he would obey neither Sibourd nor the directive unless the administrator could show proof of his right to name a vicar-general. The debate was bitter.* Greatly worried, DuBourg left for Europe on May 4, 1815. He arrived at Bordeaux in early July, shortly after Napoleon had lost at Waterloo and had abdicated his throne. The Prussians reached Paris on July 3 and turmoil convulsed the country. Travel was not easy.

Du Bourg wrote to Rome explaining his delay and pressing for a solution to the administrative confusion in New Orleans. The Holy See now complied with his request. The Pope immediately sent word to Archbishop Carroll to advise the people of New Orleans that it had confirmed Sibourd's appointment as vicar-general, and named Du Bourg bishop of Louisiana and the Floridas. Du Bourg's consecration took place in Rome, in the church of Saint Louis of the French, on September 24, 1815. The trans-Mississippi at last had its own bishop.

It would have had two bishops right away, had Du Bourg had his way. He strongly and wisely advised that Rome divide the territory, with Saint Louis the see of Upper Louisiana and New Orleans that of Lower Louisiana. He even suggested bishops for the two sees, his friend Flaget for Upper Louisiana, and he himself for Lower Louisiana. He suggested Father (and Prince) Demetrius Gallitzin for the see of Bardstown that Flaget would vacate. Propaganda wrote to Archbishop Carroll and to Bishop Flaget, on December 23, 1815, asking their advice on this proposal.[18]

Archbishop Carroll never received this letter. He had died twenty days before, on December 5, 1815, in his eighty-first year. Flaget recognized the need of two bishoprics in the vast territory. Earlier he had seemed willing to go to Saint Louis; but now he did not want to abandon his work in Kentucky. Rome took no immediate action.

For the present, Du Bourg would have all of Louisiana, Lower and Upper.

Recruits for the Diocese of Louisiana

Now that he was bishop of the territory, Du Bourg had even greater responsibilities. He had to untangle affairs in New Orleans, and to staff the whole region. This he immediately set out to do. While in Rome, at the headquarters of the Congregation of the Mission,** he had met an impressive young priest. Father Felix de Andreis had successfully missionized parishes of his native Italy. He possessed the needed strength of character — if not the ruggedness of physique — for work in the far-off American west. Naturally, the acting Vincentian superior, Father Charles Dominic Sicardi, would not find it easy to fill Father de Andreis place in Italy. But Bishop Du Bourg wanted him to direct a seminary that he planned for the new country. Du Bourg enlisted the intercession of the papal secretary of state, Hercole Cardinal Consalvi. He brought the case directly to Pius VII himself. Acting Vicar-General Sicardi had to yield in the face of this array of pressure, and assigned Felix de Andreis to the trans-Mississippi mission.

While Du Bourg's recruiting activities continued in full

force in Northern Italy, a hopeful development took place out in Missouri. Newly ordained Henry Pratte returned from the seminary in Montreal to be pastor of his place of birth, Ste. Genevieve. Twenty-seven years old, he was the first native-born priest of Missouri. In the absence of Bishop Du Bourg, Bishop Flaget made the assignment.

Back in Europe, Father De Andreis, Bishop Du Bourg's first recruit, gathered personnel for the seminary he was to establish within the diocese of Louisiana. He enlisted the services of a promising young priest, a fellow Vincentian, the twenty-six year old Neapolitan, Father Joseph Rosati, who had given home missions in the Papal States for four years. While a pupil of De Andreis, Rosati had undertaken the study of English at his professor's suggestion. Now he would have an opportunity to put this new skill to work.

After receiving the blessing of Pope Pius VII, Father Rosati set out for Marseilles with a little band of volunteers on October 14, 1815. De Andreis remained in Rome for several weeks more to gather books, religious articles, and money, and to complete arrangements for the mission in America. Two months later he traveled up the Italian peninsula, accompanied by seminarians, F. X. Dahmen and Casto Gonzalez. The two bands joined at Toulouse and proceeded to Bordeaux to await the arrival of their new bishop. They enjoyed the hospitality of the archbishop of Bordeaux and helped in his jurisdiction while they marked time at the French port of embarkation.

Du Bourg also succeeded in his other recruiting venture. He won the consent of a number of priests and students in Milan to go with him to the American west. One of them left immediately in his company, Joseph Tichitoli. Others were to follow. Among these last, the youngest of the group, the seventeen-year-old Belgian, Leo De Neckere, and newly ordained Antoine Blanc were to become successive bishops of New Orleans. Michael Portier was to become bishop of Mobile.

The prospect of trouble in New Orleans still hung like a cloud over Bishop Du Bourg. On April 11, 1816, he wrote to the pro-prefect of Propaganda, Cardinal Dunagni: "The news that I received from New Orleans would almost make me give up the whole undertaking."[19] Du Bourg stated that when Fray Antonio had heard of his appointment as bishop, the friar had begun to take counter-measures. There was talk of a state law putting all church temporalities under the control of the trustees. Du Bourg was almost ready to quit.

"Unbearable it would be, indeed, your Eminence," Du Bourg wrote, "for the most courageous and fearless bishop, if he were obliged to settle in the city of New Orleans, or even in Lower Louisiana, almost entirely under the influence of that wretched religious. Nothing at all can be hoped there as long as that man is living."[20]

To forestall a premature confrontation that might jeopardize the episcopal dignity, Du Bourg hoped to stay away from New Orleans. He asked permission to set up his episcopal see in Saint Louis. He intended to visit tumultous New Orleans only when absolutely necessary. He wanted authorization to appoint a vicar-general to administer confirmation in the parishes along the lower Mississippi.

Since he had to establish a seminary and primary schools, they had to be under his immediate and constant supervision. "Now everything is against their being located in Lower Louisiana," he wrote, "whereas everything looks favorable to their happy development if they be in Upper

---

*The exchange of letters between Du Bourg and de Sedella make interesting reading; but they pertain more to the history of the church in New Orleans. Charles Souvay presented them in his article "Centennial of the Church in St. Louis," *The Catholic Historical Review* 4: 53-58.

**The Vincentians were reinstituted in 1815 after Napoleon's downfall. Thus at the time they were just getting reorganized.

Louisiana; in the one place morality is at an incredibly low ebb; it remains untainted in the other; in the one the air is unhealthy; it is pure and healthy in the other; in the one real estate and living are very high; they are cheap in the other."[21] What he did not say was that New Orleans had been the see of a bishop and had a cathedral. Saint Louis did not even have a resident priest. Its only church was a miserable shed of upright logs.

Ten days later Du Bourg advised De Andreis of the change of plans. The bishop's own uncertainty shows clearly in this letter. In one paragraph he speaks of his plans for Saint Louis as a temporary arrangement until he can go to New Orleans in proper style. He uses the example of a military leader. In conquering a country, the general may at first avoid the fortified cities, and establish himself in points of easier access. In the next paragraph, Du Bourg seems to think of Saint Louis as a permanent choice. "Many reasons convince me," he wrote, "that, even apart from the opposition to be met in New Orleans, the good of the diocese suggests that Saint Louis should have preference as the Episcopal city."[22] Further, Saint Louis stood near Indian country and would thus greatly appeal to prospective missionaries, and to benefactors of the missions.[23]

De Andreis and his little band in Bordeaux greeted the news with enthusiasm. They set about the study of English more intensely. They would need that language in Upper Louisiana much more than in the lower valley where so many Catholics spoke only French.

In May the cardinal prefect granted Du Bourg's requests. The letter, however, did not reach him by mid-June. So Du Bourg wrote again, repeating his previous suggestions, and further criticizing Fray Antonio. This time the bishop listed the people who warned him of the unsatisfactory situation in New Orleans. They included his own brothers, his vicar-general, and the Ursuline Sisters. In the meantime, Du Bourg had asked his friend and fellow Sulpician, Benedict Joseph Flaget, now the bishop of Bardstown, Kentucky, to sound out the attitude of the Upper Louisiana residents.[24]

On February 8, 1816, Bishop Flaget wrote an open letter to the people of the middle valley. He told them that they would probably have a resident bishop either in Saint Louis or Ste. Genevieve before the end of the year. This diocese, he believed, would comprise the territories of Missouri and Illinois, and for the time being, Indiana and Michigan. This was contingent, however, on the unanimous agreement of the people of these territories, to receive the bishop and his successors with due honor and to place in his hand funds for the upkeep of the seminary.

Bishop Flaget directed this letter to Father Donatien Olivier at Prairie du Rocher. He ordered him to notify all parishes, both on the east and west bank. The bishop suggested that every parish hold a meeting to select a delegate for a central meeting in Saint Louis on a date to be decided. These delegates were to deliberate: first, on the annual income they could promise their bishop; second, on the ways and means of securing this income; third, on the bishop's house, furniture, and servants; fourth, on a building for the seminary that must be near the church or on lands with sufficient revenue to educate a number of young men destined for the sacred ministry; and fifth, on the funds necessary to defray the costs of the bishop's coming to them. He even suggested that they might discuss what site would be more advantageous —

Ste. Genevieve or Saint Louis. Bishop Flaget anticipated a great increase in population in the area in the following ten years. Father Olivier added a footnote to the letter, asking each pastor to carry out Bishop Flaget's directives.[25]

Flaget had high hopes for Saint Louis as an episcopal see. "If the Holy Father were to send a Jesuit as a bishop," he wrote Archbishop Leonard Neale of Baltimore, "and give him five or six companions, I do not entertain the least doubt, but in less than twenty years it would be the most flourishing diocese in the United States."[26] He thought that the new bishop should open a college and seminary promptly. He suggested the Jesuits for two reasons: they had worked in that area in colonial times; he feared Rome might send him there, and thus hurt his work in Kentucky.[27]

When Flaget came to realize that Rome would not split the trans-Mississippi region and transfer him thither from Kentucky, he supported his friend Du Bourg even more strongly.

There was progress in Europe in the meantime. After seven month's separation, Du Bourg rejoined his band of volunteers in Bordeaux on the eve of the Feast of the Ascension, May 22, 1816. Several of the original group had returned to Rome during the long delay. New volunteers filled their places. Although the answer from the Congregation of the Propaganda had not yet reached him, Du Bourg made arrangements to send his men to America. They left Bordeaux, June 12, on an American brig, the *Ranger*. The bishop put De Andreis in charge and named him vicar for the Diocese of Louisiana. The group now consisted of De Andreis, two priests and a lay brother of the Congregation of the Mission, two secular priests, four seminarians, and three young laymen. Six hard weeks after sailing, the *Ranger* docked at Baltimore on July 26.

Saint Louis in 1816

All this ecclesiastical jockeying might have befitted a mature see like Lyons, Turin, Warsaw, or Munich. Saint Louis was hardly such. Only by comparison with the neighboring villages and hamlets could anyone rightly call Saint Louis a "city." Its population did not surpass several thousand.

The city along the river had not yet reached west beyond the fence enclosing the common pasture and fields on the far side of Third, the Street of the Barns (*Rue des Granges*). The tumbledown log building in the Church Square hardly befitted the chair of a bishop.

Formal Catholicity was low. Father Francis Savine came over from Cahokia once every few weeks for Mass and the Sacraments. The Creole population was Catholic for the most part, at least in name. Many newcomers, Irish and Santo Dominigan French, professed the faith.

Economically, most Saint Louisans still engaged in the fur trade or some related enterprise. Industry was an infant. The few skilled workers earned what were then quite high wages of $2 and $3 a day. Poor transportation greatly limited the market area. It was not until the following year, 1817, that the first steamboat tied up at the Saint Louis Levee.

By April, 1816, Missouri had advanced to the last stage of territorial status. Statehood stood on the near horizon. The large landholders, both Americans and Creoles, however, did not welcome this rapid progress toward statehood. It would surely bring heavy tax burdens to property-holders. Edward Hempstead, the territory's first representative to Congress, had been charged to work for the interests of this class.

But neither Du Bourg nor any of his European recruits saw this Saint Louis of 1816. Their arrival was still months into the future.

On Toward Saint Louis

De Andreis and his dozen companions received a warm welcome at Saint Mary's College near Baltimore. The rector, Father Simon Bruté, a fellow Sulpician of Du Bourg and Flaget, would naturally have liked to keep these zealous men. Nonetheless, he felt it his duty to urge them to start westward before the advent of bad weather. In two groups, they set out from Baltimore early in September. Incessant rains reduced the dirt roads to quagmires. The travelers had to fight their way through Appalachia.

At the Forks of the Ohio, newly incorporated Pittsburg normally bustled with river traffic. But with low water in the Ohio Valley — the rains had all been east of the mountains — the travelers had to delay the next stage of their journey. De Andreis helped out at Pittsburg's one small log church. During the month of enforced delay, the gentle priest readily won the hearts of the rough frontiersmen. Finally, on October 23, the travelers were able to move downstream by flatboat. The five-hundred mile journey to Louisville took almost a month. During these weeks, they vigorously maintained the regime of study and prayer.

In the meantime, Bishop Flaget had made several fruitless trips to Louisville to be on hand to greet them. When they finally arrived, on November 19, only his letter of invitation to Bardstown welcomed the travelers. Following Flaget's suggestion, De Andreis traveled forty miles south to Bardstown to find out what to do next. The bishop advised against continuing on to Saint Louis. First, winter had come to the mercurial midwest. Secondly, the Missouri Catholics knew little or nothing of the approaching band. Flaget thought it wiser to wait until some provision had been made in Saint Louis for their housing. They could stay through the winter at Bardstown's Saint Thomas Seminary and carry on their study of English and French.

This fourth halt in their progress toward Saint Louis left them three hundred miles from their goal, and over two thousand miles from their superior, Bishop Du Bourg, still in Europe.

Du Bourg Wins More Volunteers

Bishop Du Bourg was still busy, but not less unsure of his ultimate destination. Saint Louis, not New Orleans, now worried him. Shortly after he dispatched De Andreis' band from Bordeaux, he had written to the Propaganda that he did not intend to proceed to Saint Louis until assured of a favorable reception by the Catholics. When he had not yet started for his diocese by the end of the year, Rome demanded an explanation. From Lyons he assured authorities that he was spending his time profitably. He could report, in fact, that he had sent out a second band — this one for New Orleans.[28]

Nuns made up the majority of this contingent. On his travels in France, he had kept a promise to the Ursuline superior in New Orleans to seek postulants for the New Orleans diocese. When their general superior, Mother Marie Olivier, heard of the de Sedella troubles, she sought Pius VII's permission to recall her nuns to France. The Pope informed her that he had named Du Bourg bishop, that the new bishop would soon return to America, and that she need entertain no worry about the future of her American subjects. Nine of the aspirants Du Bourg gathered in France reached the Ursuline convent in New Orleans on the third day of 1817. Four clerics, destined to work in the lower valley, made up the remainder of the contingent.

While recounting this happy development, Du Bourg could also report to Rome that he had enlisted a dozen other volunteers to work in America. He had obtained free passage for them on a French ship. They did not weigh anchor, however, until mid-1817. In the meantime, Du Bourg continued begging for his diocese. Paintings in the "Old Cathedral" of Saint Louis and in the Cathedral of New Orleans were to attest the charity of French and Belgian Catholics and the eloquence of Du Bourg's pleas at this time.

The Band in Kentucky

Over the winter of 1816-1817, De Andreis' band remained at the Bardstown seminary. The leader took up again the task he had left in Rome, that of seminary professor. Rosati taught also. The seminary was a log house in the middle of a forest. The head of the seminary, kindly John B. David, had long worked in the west. Bishop Carroll had earlier considered him for the Louisiana bishopric. Rome was soon to name him coadjutor to Bishop Flaget.

The regimen at the Bardstown seminary was realistic. The young clerics studied theology and languages. They took the mission trail as often as necessary. They learned to adjust themselves to Kentucky fare, "cornbread badly baked, tough salt pork, potatoes, and water." Strong Rosati throve on the work and the diet. The frailer De Andreis found it much more difficult; but he kept high his resolve to work among the Indians beyond the Mississippi. He studied Indian languages and planned to translate the catechism. Kentuckians found it strange that he wore his cassock. They were not used to seeing their priests in such formal clerical garb. De Andreis told his friend Father Sicardi of curious folk coming from afar to see "a Roman priest dressed like a woman."[29]

The "Missourians-to-be" were still distant from their goal. But they were far from idle. They studied; they conditioned themselves for the rigors of the west; they learned western lore from veteran missionaries.

Chapter 4

Bourbon Bishop on the American Frontier

Du Bourg Embarks

Before he left France, Du Bourg recruited one last team of missionaries who were destined to bring rich benefits to both Upper and Lower Louisiana. He appealed to Saint Madelience Sophie Barat, the foundress of the Religious of the Sacred Heart, in January 1817, for nuns to work across the sea. She made no promise at that time; but, when the bishop returned in May, his cause had the support of an enthusiastic volunteer within the convent. Forty-seven year old Mother Philippine Duchesne had been pleading with her superior for an American assignment. She wanted to work among the Indians. A year later the unstoppable Mother Duchesne was to lead a group of four nuns to the New World.

Du Bourg also enlisted the help of the cardinal secretary of the Propaganda,[1] and even of Pope Pius VII himself[2] in getting Brothers of the Christian Schools for work in the American West. The superior general, Brother Gibaud, agreed to send three young men with Bishop Du Bourg, Brothers Aubin, Fulgence, and Antonin.[3]

By mid-1817 Bishop Du Bourg had finally completed

Father Charles de la Croix of Ghent, Belgium, answered the challenge of Bishop du Bourg to work in the New World. He began a mission among the Osage in western Missouri Territory, offered spiritual guidance to Mother Duchesne and undertook the building of St. Ferdinand's Church.

preparations for his return to America. On June 16 he wrote to the Propaganda: "At length the long wished for day is at hand: tomorrow we shall embark and, God willing, set sail for America."[4] King Louis XVIII of France provided a royal frigate, *La Caravane*, for the party. The vessel was not able to leave on schedule. But finally on July the first, it sailed from Bordeaux.

In all, Du Bourg had twenty-nine men in his company. In status they ranged from five priests to four workmen. As had been true with the *Ranger*, *La Caravane* soon resembled a floating monastery. During the sixty-five days at sea, Father Antoine Blanc, a future archbishop of New Orleans, preached a mission to the ship's officers and crew. Many sailors returned to the practice of their faith. A few newcomers joined the Church. Seven received Holy Communion for the first time. Bishop Du Bourg confirmed thirty-five others on the feast of Saint Bartholomew (August 24).[5] *

The frigate docked at Annapolis on September 4. Some of the party stayed for a time as guests of Charles Carroll, signer of the Declaration of Independence. Du Bourg went on with the rest to Baltimore, where he enjoyed the hospitality of his fellow Sulpicians at Saint Mary's Seminary. It was a true homecoming for the Bishop of Louisiana.

From Baltimore, Du Bourg sent word of his arrival to Bishop Flaget. He also had a favor to ask. Still concerned over his reception in Saint Louis, he wondered if Flaget would be willing to journey there to determine the general attitude. In his mind an index of the disposition of the Saint Louis Catholics would be their willingness to raise funds for the erection of a cathedral and for the support of the coming missionaries. He even hoped the people of Saint Louis would reimburse him for the expenses of the journey.

This amazing request puts Du Bourg in a bad light. In contrast, Flaget's willingness to undertake the thankless task shows the generous fibre of the Bardstown bishop. At the suggestion of Du Bourg, Flaget took along the two leaders of the advance band, De Andreis and Rosati. They rode out of Bardstown on October 2.

After nine days of hard travel, they reached Kaskaskia. The following Sunday, accompanied by the veteran Father Donatien Olivier, they crossed over to Ste. Genevieve. Here young Father Henri Pratte welcomed the party. Father De Andreis remained in Ste. Genevieve. Father Pratte accompanied the others northward.

Two more days of travel brought the party to Saint Louis. Their log seminary in the Kentucky woods seemed

---

*These manifestations of piety took added significance later. On its return voyage, *La Caravane* ran into a hurricane and nearly all the crew perished (*Annales de la Propagation de la Foi* 2, no. 1:18).

like a southern mansion in comparison with the tumble-down church and rectory they found in Saint Louis. Flaget wrote that the rectory had no doors, no windows, no floor, no furniture. Notwithstanding, the kindly bishop stayed there during the visit; he used a cot furnished by one of the neighbors. The others slept on buffalo robes.[6]

Flaget assembled the heads of families and spoke to them of the approaching arrival of their own bishop and the missionaries he was bringing with him. Since the bishop's residence among them would confer so many advantages on their city, they ought to cooperate in every way they could. He held several other meetings, and asked the citizens to express their opinions.

During one of these meetings a certain Mr. L.* arose and said, "I am far from disapproving the choice that Bishop Du Bourg has made of this city for the place of his ordinary residence. He is a Bishop and is, therefore, at liberty to fix his abode in whatever part of his diocese he may think proper to select. But, inasmuch as it concerns the inhabitants of Saint Louis, I see no particular reason why they should contribute to the expense that he consequently incurred. The expense of the diocese should be divided among the whole population. It is not just that it fall on us alone. We have a parish church. We will give our pastor a proper salary. This will be quite enough for our share. If the church is going to ruin, it is our duty to repair it, and though we have no pastor at present, let one be sent to us and we will cheerfully receive him. But as to the Bishop, we are not obliged to do anything because his permanent residence belongs alike to all."[7]

What Mr. "L" said was logical and just. The jump from a no-pastor situation to an episcopal see was a mighty one. The financial burden should have been prorated throughout the area. But the speaker might have given a less negative flavor to his remarks. Most of the residents seemed a bit more favorably inclined.

Two delegates from Saint Mary's of the Barrens, a settlement of thirty-six Maryland families in southeast Missouri, arrived at this time. They asked that the bishop locate the diocesan seminary in their parish. They would purchase 640 acres of land for this purpose.[8] Father Dunand, the circuit-riding Trappist, had urged them to do this so that they would always have a priest at hand.[9]

Flaget remained long enough in Saint Louis to make sure that the people were well disposed to the coming of a bishop. Then he left for Ste. Genevieve.

Flaget asked Father De Andreis to remain temporarily at Ste. Genevieve. He commissioned Father Henri Pratte to go to Saint Louis to supervise the preparations. Flaget returned to Kentucky with Rosati, gratified that his mission had succeeded.

Bishop Du Bourg to the West

Back at Bardstown, Rosati took over the classes in theology that De Andreis had previously taught. But the seminarians had greater interest in the imminent arrival of their bishop than in the textbooks.

Bishop Du Bourg and his band started from Baltimore by stagecoach on November 4, 1817. The inability of the horses to pull the heavily loaded vehicles over the almost non-existent roads made travel slow and difficult. During

much of the journey, the travelers sloshed along the muddy trail alongside the stage. The first pastor of Pittsburgh, Father William F. X. O'Brien, host to De Andreis a year before, provided accommodations for this newest band.

Soon Du Bourg pushed on down the Ohio to Louisville and thence overland to Bardstown. After almost a year and a half of separation, the reunion of Du Bourg and his volunteers was joyous. Reassured by Flaget that Saint Louis would be ready to receive him, Du Bourg wanted to set out immediately. The indefatigable Flaget, the veteran Kentucky missionary Stephen Theodore Badin, and a young seminarian recently arrived from Europe, Francois Niel, went with him.

At Louisville the four travelers boarded a new-fangled invention, called a steamboat. They hoped to reach Saint Louis by Christmas on their "floating furnace." Unfortunately, ice stalled the *Piqua* at the junction of the rivers. Shortly after Christmas Day, they pushed upstream. On the evening of December 28 the *Piqua* reached the landing near "Fenwick's Settlement," at the mouth of Apple Creek, in Southern Missouri. There Bishop Du Bourg first set foot on the soil of Missouri. He and his companions set up a cross and sang the thanksgiving hymn, *Vexilla Regis.*[10]

The Fenwicks and many of the Catholic settlers at "The Barrens," near Perryville, had been parishioners of Father Badin. The Kentucky-missioner left the boat at this point to pay a short visit to his old parishioners. Bishops Du Bourg and Flaget and young Father Niel continued upstream aboard the *Piqua.* They reached Ste. Genevieve on the last day of the year. Father De Andreis and forty townsfolk met the travelers at the landing and escorted them to the town with all the pomp and ceremony the little village could muster. Du Bourg thanked the people and won their affection.

In those days, the first of January was not a holy day in the United States. But the Feast of Circumcision in 1818 became memorable in the annals of Ste. Genevieve. The little town had its first Pontifical Masses — and the first Pontifical Mass of Bishop Du Bourg in his own diocese. Father Badin now rejoined the party. The four recrossed the river and proceeded northward on the Illinois side. After spending Sunday with Father Savine at Cahokia, the party prepared to move over to Saint Louis on January 5.

A mounted patrol of forty Cahokians escorted the episcopal party to the ferry. Across the Mississippi stood Saint Louis, the end of a long journey and the beginning of a new work for Bishop Du Bourg. As the ferry drew near to the landing at the foot of what came to be Market Street, most of the town's 2,500 residents roared a welcome. A joyous procession led the party to the "episcopal palace," the sorry-looking, small stone rectory built in 1777-1778. Father Pratte had been able to do little more than tidy up the place, install a few windows, and hang a door or two. But Bishop Du Bourg rejoiced at being in his new home at last.

He and Bishop Flaget changed into their full pontifical robes. Led by twelve altar boys, they processioned along the *Rue d'Eglise* to the log church of 1776, "a kind of miserable barn falling into ruins." Flaget conducted his friend to the makeshift episcopal throne for the official ceremony of installation. The crowd overflowed the church. With emotion in his heart and tears in his eyes, the kindly prelate of Bardstown commended Bishop Du Bourg to his people. Du Bourg took the opportunity to

---

*Who this Mr. L was has never been ascertained, but it was most likely Patrick Lee, the chief warden of 1817.

make an eloquent response. According to the testimony of De Andreis, Du Bourg's speech won his hearers. "Kindness, dignity and suavity of manner... dissipated in a great measure every prejudice, and captivated all hearts."[11]

Two days later Flaget and Badin went back to Kentucky.

Du Bourg in Saint Louis

What then, did the diocese look like on that January day when Du Bourg came? His responsibility included areas on the gulf coast and the entire Louisiana Purchase, a vast land of 885,000 square miles, four times as large as the kingdom of France, added to the United States by President Jefferson fourteen years before. Louisiana was the only state in this vast area. There were two main, but small cities, New Orleans and Saint Louis. The population of the latter had not yet reached four thousand. Other towns such as Ste. Genevieve and New Madrid in Missouri, and Kaskaskia, Cahokia, and Prairie du Rocher in Illinois, were on the Mississippi. There was only one organized English-speaking parish — that of Saint Mary's in southeast Missouri. Settlements did not go much beyond the waterways. In the interior, numerous Indian tribes roamed. A great westward expansion of the nation moved toward full tide.

The task would have challenged a Gregory the Great. Du Bourg had Gregory's vision, but not his organizing ability or his carry-through. Du Bourg did not plan a little farm; he wanted a big plantation. But he was incapable of visualizing what he needed to build it. He dealt with larger conceptions, rather than with the details for carrying them out. He thought big, planned big, talked big. On numerous occasions he over-reached himself to the point of appearing high-handed. Others had to hold the pieces together. Fortunately, he had enlisted men capable of doing this. He would recruit a few more.

The contrast between town and bishop was staggering. A village without a resident pastor, suddenly became the seat of a bishop — and an extraordinary one at that. One of the most intellectual men in the country at the time presided over a frontier settlement with only a few small schools. A man who spoke easily with popes, kings, and presidents, shepherded fur traders and *voyageurs*. He was a man of distinction; but he seemed to lack the common touch. A man so cautious and changeable that he shunned his assigned city, asked for another, and then hesitated to go to it until a fellow churchman paved the way; this man was bishop of the wild frontier.

Du Bourg's journey to the United States involved an unprecedented movement of personnel. When the bishop departed from France, he had already sent to America nine Ursuline aspirants, five priests, four clerics, and four brothers under the direction of Father De Andreis. Du Bourg was to bring along with him five priests, four subdeacons, nine clerical students, three Christian Brothers, four young men still in their classical courses, and four lay assistants — a total of twenty-nine men.[12] Mother Philippine Duchesne and four other Religious of the Sacred Heart would soon leave France for Saint Louis. A few years later Du Bourg would call west eleven Jesuits — two priests, seven novices, and two lay brothers — to work on the Indian mission.

A fellow Sulpician, Archbishop Ambrose Marechal, complained later that Du Bourg favored the dramatic entrance.[13] The Louisiana bishop seemed to believe that grandiose display could remove problems. Historian Louise Callan rightly concluded: "The Bishop's optimism was equalled only by his vivid imagination, which always bypassed the difficulties involved in the arrangements he proposed."[14]

Adequate preparations to deploy Du Bourg's total force of recruits would have taxed the resources of all the Catholics in the diocese. Instead, four small parishes had to bear the brunt of this for-the-moment staggering task.

Bishop Du Bourg began at once four main programs in Missouri: the building of an adequate church building and the strengthening of the organization of the Saint Louis parish; the founding of an academy for boys under the direction of the newly arrived priests of the diocese; the setting up of a school for girls under the guidance of the Religious of the Sacred Heart, soon to arrive from France; and the establishment of the seminary. A few years later he was to begin a venture for missionizing the Indians.

On January 7, 1818, two days after Bishop Du Bourg's arrival, the parishioners of Saint Louis met to discuss the site, the size, and the materials of the new church. They pledged over $6,000 for its construction. Three groups made up the eventual contributors: such Creole families as the Chouteaus, the Prattes, the Sarpys, the Robidoux, the Gratiots, the Papins, the Soulards, the Cabannes, and the Lisa; such recent Irish arrivals* as Jeremiah Connor, Thomas Maguire, Thomas Brady, and John Mullanphy; and Anglo-Americans Alexander McNair, Thomas H. Benton, William Carr, William Clark, Frederick Bates, and Theodore Hunt — many of whom were not Catholics.

Thomas Maguire collected over three thousand dollars and Jeremiah Connor another thousand. These combined figures totaled two-thirds of the original pledges. The contractors soon broke ground in the church square on the southwest corner of Second and Market Streets. The building was to face the river from Second Street, the *Rue d'Eglise*. A second subscription, a few months later, chiefly among Catholics, netted thirteen hundred dollars. Mr. P. Le Duc did most of the collecting.[15]

Even though he had more than his share of problems in the trans-Mississippi, Du Bourg had definite ideas on how to run the Church in the rest of the country, and sent his suggestions to Rome. He warned against members of a certain religious order and priests of a particular nationality. He universally condemned these latter. He did give a wise suggestion for the solution to eastern seaboard problems, namely to choose a bishop of American rather than European birth. Unfortunately, the little Catholic colony of Maryland did not have enough priests to man all episcopal posts in the growing country.

Frequently during the first winter, the old church was so cold that the bishop said Mass in the slightly warmer rectory. On Maundy Thursday, March 19, 1818, Bishop

---

*One of the earliest benevolent societies to organize in Saint Louis got underway shortly after Bishop Du Bourg's arrival. An organization of citizens of Irish background, the Erin Benevolent Society, started in October, 1819, with Jeremiah Connor as president, and Joseph Charless, Thomas Hardy, Robert Catherwood, Hugh O'Neill and the Timon and Ranken brothers among the active members. At first a mutual aid society for Irishmen in Saint Louis, it gradually came to show greater interest in the welfare of those Irish who at the time were not fortunate enough to get to the United States. Its inter-denominational makeup illustrates the ecumenic spirit of Saint Louis at the time.

Du Bourg ordained Francois Niel, one of the young seminarians who had come with him from France.[16] The following afternoon, the people gathered in the church for the *Tre Ore* service. This was only the second time Americans had taken part in this Good Friday devotion. The priests from France had inaugurated it the year before in Bardstown.

Nine days later, on March 29, Bishop Du Bourg laid the cornerstone of the new church. Father De Andreis, the vicar-general of the diocese, and Fathers Niel, Pratte, Dunand, Savine, and Donatien Olivier assisted him at the ceremony. On April 20, the vicar-general reported that the walls were six feet high. Some months later they reached a height of fifteen feet. After this initial surge of effort, construction moved as sluggishly as the Mississippi in August. The bishop ran out of money and called a halt to construction.[17]

In August 1818, Mother Philippine Duchesne and the Religious of the Sacred Heart arrived in Saint Louis. They had presumed they would be able to open a school for young ladies in the city. The citizens welcomed them warmly and wanted them to begin their school. Instead, Bishop Du Bourg sent them to St. Charles with a glowing tribute to its anticipated growth. The situation there was not suited; several years later, they had to move to an equally unsatisfactory location in Florissant.*

In early fall, Bishop Du Bourg announced that Father Niel and three other priests would open an academy for boys on November 16. The original announcement of the opening of the school set the tuition at $12 a quarter, payable in advance. The school offered classes in Latin, English, French, arithmetic, mathematics, and geography.[18]

The seminary began at two places: in Saint Louis and at Perryville in southeast Missouri. In conjunction with the Saint Louis Academy, Father De Andreis directed five or six seminarians. Some of these men taught in the academy; all pursued their priestly studies — some for the diocese, some for the Congregation of the Mission.

The other half of the seminarians, recruited by Bishop Du Bourg and Father De Andreis, studied at Perryville under the direction of Father Rosati. They lived in a residence near the church provided by Mrs. Sarah Hayden, a well-to-do widow, until workers completed the seminary buildings. The residence served as chapel, dormitory, studyhall, kitchen, and workshop. Father Rosati combined the multiple responsibilities of seminary director with that of pastor of the Catholics of the neighborhood. Originally Du Bourg had wanted his seminary in Saint Louis. The generosity of the people of Perryville, however, led him to build the permanent seminary there.[19]

The villages of Saint Louis, St. Charles, and Perryville had schools of various kinds under Catholic auspices. Ste. Genevieve, the oldest town in the state, had remained without a Catholic school since the death of Father Maxwell, except for a short period. Father Henri Pratte, the pastor of the parish there, completed the construction of Ste. Genevieve Academy, and asked Bishop Du Bourg to send a Christian Brother to teach there. The three brothers had spent some time in Bardstown after their arrival in the United States and were, at the time, studying the English language in Perryville. Du Bourg authorized Father Pratte to write Father Rosati, the Superior at Perryville, to send Brother Antonin, who had gained a greater proficiency in English than his fellows.[20]

Brother Antonin became the first Brother of the Christian Schools to teach in the United States, when he began teaching at Ste. Genevieve Academy on January 8, 1819. Since a rule of the Brothers forbade a member to assume sole charge of a school, Bishop Du Bourg sent the other two brothers, Aubin and Fulgence, to Ste. Genevieve before the end of the year.[21]

Church and College

As a result of the shortage of funds, the architects of the Saint Louis Church modified their original plans. They had intended a seventy-foot wide church with five arches separating the middle from the side aisles. Instead, they filled the arches with masonry and windows. These served as outer walls. The Bishop finally blessed the church on January 9, 1820. One hundred and thirty-four feet long, and forty feet wide, it was an architectural monstrosity.

Yet the first *Saint Louis Directory*, issued soon after, stated:

(The) Cathedral of Saint Louis can boast of having no rival in the United States for the magnificence, the value, and elegance of her sacred vases, ornaments and paintings, and indeed few churches in Europe possess anything superior to it. It is a truly delightful sight for an American taste, to find in one of the remotest towns of the Union a church decorated with the original paintings of Rubens, Raphael, Guido, Paul Veronese, and a number of others by the first modern masters of the Italian, French, and Flemish schools. The ancient and precious gold embroideries which the Saint Louis Cathedral possesses would certainly decorate any museum in the world. All this is due to the liberality of the Catholics of Europe who presented these rich articles to Bishop Du Bourg on his last visit to France, Italy, Sicily, and the Netherlands. Among the liberal benefactors could be named many princes and princesses, but we will only insert the names of Louis XVIII, the present King of France, and that of Baroness La Candale de Ghyseghem, a Flemish lady, to whose munificence the Cathedral is particularly indebted.[22]

Whoever wrote that statement for the *Directory* certainly over-reached himself. The Cathedral of Saint Louis in New Orleans surpassed the Church of Saint Louis. No one who knew art work ever claimed that among these fine paintings Du Bourg brought from Europe one could find a Rubens or a Raphael. Still, the collection was unique on the frontier.

The parish assembly authorized the trustees to sell the materials of the old church and to add the proceeds to the building fund of the new. According to an entry in the parish account book,[23] the sale brought only $110. The men of the parish elected six persons to act jointly with the building committee for the rental of the new pews. The men were John C. D. Lucas, Antoine Denjen — soon to be replaced by Francois Guyol — Francois Xavier Valois, Pierre Didier, Antoine Chenie, and Hugh O'Neill. They sold 95 pews for a promised $9,295. They eventually collected $6,786.38 of this. The drives and pew rentals did not reach the building cost of $24,000.[24]

A man of wide culture and broad tolerance, Bishop Du

---

*Mother Louise Callan, historian of the Religious of the Sacred Heart, rightly concluded that this unwise exile set back their educational efforts a quarter of a century. (See Louise Callan, R.S.J., *Philippine Duchesne* [Westminster: Newman Press, 1957], pp. 260-264.) In justification of Bishop Du Bourg's decision, this should be remembered: the wealthy Saint Louis Catholic individuals — Creole and Irish — who promised so much to Mother Duchesne did not bring to conclusion a project of more immediate need — the parish church.

Bourg promoted an orchestra and a choir, remarkable for the quality of music and the makeup of the musicians. It included Catholics and Protestants, men and women, whites and one black, the tenor Augustine, a member of the bishop's household.

The little academy and seminary continued during the delays and hesitations in the building of the church alongside it. At the start of the second year, Father Niel reasserted his and his associates' concern for the moral and literary improvement of the pupils. He stated in the *Missouri Gazette:*

A due sense of religion, the foundation of all morality, will by them be indefatigably cultivated, but without interference with the peculiar tenets of such as might be attached to persuasions different from that of their instructors.[25]

The policy of not demanding religious conformity — a policy Du Bourg had pursued at his earlier school in Baltimore — was truly unusual in the early nineteenth-century United States. At the same time, Niel announced the beginning of boarding facilities. These would be ready by the following November.[26]

The most noted alumnus of this early combined seminary-academy was Leo de Neckere, the youngest of Du Bourg's recruits. Belgian-born De Neckere soon joined the Vincentians. A few years after his ordination he was to rise to the position of bishop of New Orleans. Two other students, one in the academy, one in the seminary, were to hold important church positions later on. John Timon, a resident of Saint Louis, studied at the academy as a lay student for six months, and then joined the Vincentians.[27] Edmund Saulnier completed his seminary training at Saint Louis College. Both of these men were to enrich the history of the Saint Louis archdiocese.

In spite of the widespread failure of banks in the Mississippi Valley as a result of the depression of 1819, new quarters were ready for the students by mid-December.[28] The annual announcement in the *Missouri Gazette* for the fall term of 1820, bore the heading, "Saint Louis College," and announced enlarged boarding facilities.[29] In November of the same year, the school offered its first adult evening classes in the French language.[30]

During the same fall term, the saintly Felix De Andreis died on October 15, 1820. He had been the first professor of prominence of Saint Louis College, superior of the Vincentian Mission, and vicar-general of the Diocese of Louisiana. Even though he had lived in the city only a short time, the lengthy tribute to his memory in the *Missouri Gazette* gave evidence of the esteem the citizens of Saint Louis held for him.[31] De Andreis left Saint Louis two legacies: the memory of a saintly life and a remarkable recruit — Joseph Rosati.

After the death of Father De Andreis, the faculty of Saint Louis College consisted of four priests, including the president, Father Francois Niel, and four laymen. *The Saint Louis Directory and Register* described Saint Louis College:

It is a two-story brick building and has about 65 students who are taught the Greek, Latin, French, English, Spanish, and Italian Languages; mathematics, elementary and transcendent, drawing,

etc. There are several teachers. Connected with the College is an ecclesiastical seminary, at the Barrens in Ste. Genevieve county where Divinity, the oriental languages and philosophy are taught.[32]

The seminary department was to function only until 1822, when the Missouri legislature incorporated Saint Mary's Seminary in Perryville. The lay college, however, was to have a longer career.

The Indian Frontier

Du Bourg placed high among his reasons for locating in Saint Louis its proximity to the Indian country. From his arrival in the city, in spite of his many other ventures, he had looked to the possibility of work among the Indians. In 1819, Secretary of War John C. Calhoun had announced that the federal government would expend $10,000 a year for programs to help the Indians. These subsidies could go to any group, religious, educational, or philanthropic, that presented a workable plan for the improvement of the tribes.[33] Among the recipients of grants were Baptists, Quakers, the United Brethren of North Carolina, and the Methodists of South Carolina.[34] Bishop Du Bourg saw in this offer of the government the possibility of undertaking work among the Indians. It was to be a few years, however, before he could work out a satisfactory plan in cooperation with the government.

According to a first-issue article in the *Annales de la Propagation de la Foi*, a number of chiefs of the Osage, led by a natural orator, called by the French *Sans-Nerf*, visited Bishop Du Bourg in 1820, and requested a Black Robe. The bishop presented his guests with medals and crucifixes, and personally promised to visit their villages in the following fall.[35] The over-enthusiastic Du Bourg shared with many of his French contemporaries a romantic view of "the noble savage" popularized by the French writer, Jean Jacques Rousseau, two generations before. Du Bourg planned to take De Andreis with him to the Osage villages at the western extremity of the Territory of Missouri. Before Bishop Du Bourg could fulfill his promise, however, De Andreis died; and he himself had more than his share of pressing duties both in Saint Louis and New Orleans.

While he gave thought to prospective Indian Christians, Du Bourg did not neglect his fellow French-Americans. He knew how enthusiastically they celebrated the feasts of the Church, and especially of their own village patrons. He wanted to encourage this. The entire Church honored some of these saints, such as Saint Louis IX, patron of his two cathedrals. Other saints had local interest, or, as Bishop Du Bourg wrote, "illumined our America with the sanctity of their lives."[36] In September, 1821, he published in his superb Latin a special supplement of the priest's office that encouraged devotion to many saints honored in the region. He singled out three: St. Ferdinand, king of Spain, patron of the parish at Florissant; St. Genevieve of Paris, patron of Missouri's oldest village; and St. Landry, bishop of Paris, and patron of a town and parish in the Bayou country of Louisiana.[37]

Chapter 5

New Orleans Beckons

Du Bourg Looks South

With so many problems in Saint Louis and his lack of rapport with the people there,* Du Bourg had begun to look southward. He had come to see his problem in New Orleans not as residing in the person of De Sedella, but in those "two vicious subjects," the assistant pastors. He assigned Fathers Leopold Moni, Bertrand Martial, and Auguste Jeanjean to assist De Sedella at the Cathedral in New Orleans.

Things began to move smoothly. Father Martial seemed to function well as a peacemaker. Fray Antonio took a more favorable attitude toward the bishop. With his great capacity for taking a new tack, Du Bourg asked to have De Sedella as his coadjutor. Since the aged De Sedella could not travel extensively, Du Bourg also submitted the name of Louis Sibourd. He wanted two coadjutors; one for the city, De Sedella; one for the hinterland, Sibourd.[1] The Congregation of the Propaganda passed over the Sibourd recommendation because of the latter's age and its own inadequate acquaintance with his "prudence, zeal, and knowledge."[2]

Fray Antonio refused the honor. In a gracious letter to Du Bourg, he admitted that the people of New Orleans held him in warm esteem. But he insisted that he lacked the requisite qualities, and was too old to be a bishop (he was then seventy-one). He then brought up a problem Du Bourg had tried to avoid: the fact that New Orleans had a cathedral and had been an episcopal city.

If by residing in the capital, [Fray Antonio wrote] you should nominate a coadjutor for the remote parts of the diocese . . . you would have done nothing more prudent; but to put the Metropolitan in an inferior country, and the coadjutor in the capital is rather preposterous . . . It is not pleasant to see the Cathedral in Saint Louis set up by reducing this Church to a mere parish . . . It would seem absurd to see a coadjutor with an endowment and a titular with a small income.[3]

This letter, no doubt, greatly influenced Du Bourg's decision to go to New Orleans the following year.

In the meantime, a young Italian of great charm had come to Saint Louis in 1819. Angelo Inglesi volunteered his services for the Saint Louis diocese. The young man stated that he had finished many of his clerical studies in Europe. The Napoleonic Wars, however, had forced him to interrupt his course. According to his own story, he served both Napoleon and the Allies with distinction. He deeply impressed Du Bourg. With unseemly and uncanonical haste, Du Bourg advanced him in the clerical state. He ordained him in the Saint Louis Cathedral on March 20, 1820.

In November, 1820, Du Bourg left for New Orleans. By this time he had almost completed the church and had founded a "college" for boys in Saint Louis. The Religious of the Sacred Heart under Mother Duchesne at Florissant were carrying out their work of educating girls. Father Rosati was providing a training for the future clergy of the diocese in the seminary at Saint Mary's. Bishop Du Bourg had supplied priests for a number of parishes in Upper Louisiana. He was still laying plans for work among the Indians along the Missouri River. Du Bourg's plans anticipated Saint Louis development by twenty years. His presence in the city undoubtedly speeded up that religious growth immeasurably.

In 1821 Bishop Du Bourg sent Inglesi to Europe to gain funds for the diocese. Inglesi claimed eventually to have received large donations from the kings of France, Sardinia, and Holland, the Emperor of Austria, the Tsar of Russia, and other notable personages, who had gathered for a peace conference. Inglesi met with a group of laymen in Lyons, France, to discuss the possibility of a permanent international society for the financing of foreign missions. Bishop Du Bourg seems to have had such an idea as early as 1815. Now it was to become a reality in the Association for the Propagation of the Faith.[4]

Du Bourg asked Rome to make "his beloved son Angelo" his coadjutor.[5] Fortunately for the Church in America, Inglesi had momentarily gotten out of his "role" in Rome. He donned lay garb and appeared at several social functions in the company of the young ladies, or as the official Roman document from Cardinal Consalvi states: "he exhibited signs of levity and impropriety, both by taking part in dances and by a mode of dress in no way befitting an ecclesiastic."[6]

The priests of the diocese had not succumbed to Inglesi's glib words. When Du Bourg told Martial that he had asked for Inglesi as his coadjutor, the two men almost became estranged. "The opposition which manifested itself," Martial wrote, "so rent the Bishop's soul that he issued a circular letter to the priests to strike fear into them . . . He was sorry for it afterwards, when he beheld the effect it produced."[7] As an afterthought, Martial concluded: "Well, clever men can sometimes make frightful mistakes."[8]

When the full story of Inglesi came to Bishop Du Bourg's attention, he never quite got over it. His many letters to the Holy Father, to the Propaganda, and to friends showed that his misjudgment weighed heavily on his conscience. A short time later, for instance, Du Bourg wrote to the Vincentian, Father Philip Borgna, how the "notorious Inglesi magnetized me and Father De Andreis and all, both priests and lay people, who knew him."[9] He acknowledged his mistake. He deplored it. Totally discouraged, he said he was tempted "to ask his Holiness for permission to retire."[10] Only the fear of seeing the

---

*Historian Louise Callan speaks of "the hostility in Saint Louis toward Bishop Du Bourg," that was "due in part to the character and temperament of the prelate himself." See Louise Callan, RSCJ, *Philippine Duchesne: Frontier Missionary of the Sacred Heart, 1769-1852* (Westminster: Newman, 1957), p. 776, n 17.

diocese badly shaken prevented this.

Angelo Inglesi proved to be "the great imposter" of the mid-continent in the early nineteenth century. When his full story came out, it showed a magnificent mountebank. Before coming to Saint Louis, he had lived in Quebec. There he had married a French-Canadian Catholic girl in a Presbyterian Church, left her to pursue another, acted and directed plays, and finally fled Quebec one step ahead of his creditors. No one could verify his claim to early ecclesiastical studies, or his amazing war record. When he came back from Europe, he cut an imposing figure for a time in Philadelphia clerical circles. His death a few years later was to be his most edifying act. It came while he was caring for the stricken in an epidemic in the Caribbean area.

While Angelo Inglesi received the headlines, Father Henri Pratte, Missouri's first native-born priest, had continued his steady work as pastor of his native parish of Ste. Genevieve. He built a church at Old Mines, 60 miles to the west. Unfortunately, in 1822, he died of yellow fever at the age thirty-four.

Father Pratte's death indirectly resulted in the destruction of the first effort of the Christian Brothers in American education. Shortly afterward, Bishop Du Bourg gave in to the educational needs of his frontier diocese as he saw them. He separated the three recruits, even though such fragmentation was against the rule of the institute. He left Brother Antonin at Ste. Genevieve, sent Brother Aubin to Perryville, and Brother Fulgence to New Orleans. With little spiritual direction, and no identification as a community, the three young brothers were left entirely on their own resources. None of them proceeded to his final vows.[11]

The successor of Father Pratte as pastor of Ste. Genevieve, Francis Xavier Dahmen, C.M., had as many stories of Napoleon's campaigns as Angelo Inglesi. The only difference was this: Dahmen's reminiscences were true. Like so many Rhinelanders of the time, he had served as a cavalryman in the French Imperial armies. After Napoleon's defeat, he had joined the Vincentians at the age of twenty-six, and resumed clerical studies that the wars had interrupted. One of Du Bourg's first recruits, he had travelled with Father De Andreis from the Vincentian house at Monte Citorio to Bordeaux and on to the United States. A man of fine physique and cheerful disposition, given to action rather than study, he spoke French and German fluently. He preached well in both of those languages. His speech was rugged, his manner sometimes brusque and military.

He came to Ste. Genevieve in 1822, and was to remain for eighteen years. During this time, the total French character of the village gave way to wide-spread German immigration and free-holding farming supplanted the earlier slave-manned plantation system. Dahmen's German background and knowledge of the language helped him serve the newcomers well. Ste. Genevieve was to remain a small city but a strong center of Catholicism.

Trouble in River City

In leaving Saint Louis at this time, Du Bourg was leaving troubles. The Church had two problems: no money and too many languages. The congregation consisted of French- and English-speaking parishioners. Before Bishop Du Bourg's time, no priest used English in the Saint Louis Church. An excellent linguist himself, the bishop preached in both languages. He made a rule that provided an English sermon after Vespers every Sunday evening. Father De Andreis had tried to give this sermon when Bishop Du Bourg was out of town. He never quite succeeded in English.

The successor of Father De Andreis as pastor, Father Francois Niel, learned English well. A native of Ste. Antoine in South Central France, he had the distinction of being the first priest ordained in Saint Louis. He had given a sermon in French in 1820, condemning certain frivolities of the Creole population. This message did not leave his hearers undisturbed. On Palm Sunday several years later he was to preach a sermon on charity that brought praise beyond the Mississippi Valley.[12]

Du Bourg gave one of his best sermons on the Sunday before the Feast of Saint Louis the Ninth during the summer of 1822 — his last extended stay in the city.[13] The brick cathedral was incomplete, but the first city directory published the previous year had romanticized its furnishings.[14] The occasion also gave the bishop a chance to indulge his liking for pomp and splendor.

An article in the local *Enquirer* for September 2, 1822, described the ceremonial in a style so similar to Du Bourg's manner of preaching that the reader presumes it a paraphrase of his report of the occasion.

The Festival of Louis the Ninth of France, the titular Saint of our town, was solemnized at the Cathedral on Sunday, the 18th inst. under the auspices of Right Rev. Bishop Du Bourg. The ceremony was one of peculiar interest and novelty, particularly to a number of American inhabitants, who were politely invited by the Bishop to join in the festival. The character of Louis is one of equal pride and satisfaction to the soldier or to the Christian — for he may be truly ranked amongst the most chivalrous of the heroic age, and as one of the most pious and devout followers of the cross ... The citizens of the place generally felt a kind of local pleasure in participating with the reverend clergy on the occasion and doing honor to the memory of the man whose name has been conferred on the town of St. Louis.[15]

As a feature of the occasion, the bishop blessed the flags of the two volunteer companies, the "Guards" and the "Chasseurs." Captain William C. Kennerly and Captain Rene Paul marched into the sanctuary to present the colors to the bishop.

Du Bourg spoke on the seeming contradiction of cross and sword. "Is it possible," he asked, "to reconcile military valor with Christian humility?" He pointed to Moses, Joshua, David, Constantine, Theodosius, and Louis as examples of the reconciliation. He quoted the French writer Voltaire. Though a great enemy of formal religion, Voltaire had only praise for Louis the Ninth: "Prudent and firm in his councils; intrepid, yet cool in the heat of battles, compassionate as if he had ever been in misfortune. It was never given to man to exhibit brighter examples of real virtue."[16]

With this tribute to Saint Louis the crusading king, the bishop left Saint Louis the city a month later, with the church still unfinished and no satisfactory arrangements for the English-speaking members of the congregation. They wanted a sermon at High Mass every other Sunday. Father Niel hesitated to change the "immemorial custom" of the parish. But at least the predominantly Irish group still had an evening sermon.

The old and new rich families of Saint Louis did not act in any notable way to clear up the debts on the church, though they did meet their larger pledges more consistently than smaller donors.[17] As a matter of fact, the commissioners of the congregation, Auguste Chouteau, Pierre Chouteau, and Bernard Pratte, were personally liable for the debt of forty-five hundred dollars on the building. Even though they were relatively wealthy men,[18] the three commissioners were not ready to pay the outstanding debts out of their own pockets, or to try to raise the money from friends and relatives. After all, the transaction pertained to the entire Catholic community of Saint Louis and not exclusively to the three lay representatives. At a stormy parish meeting in the fall of 1822, the Chouteaus and Pratte resolved to seek authorization for the sale of what part of the church property was necessary to indemnify them for the amount they had advanced.[19]

At the request of the commissioners, Sheriff John K. Walker sold the southern part of the church block on September 16, 1823. Father Francois Niel, the parish priest, secured the four lots in the name of the bishop. The entire matter dragged on for some years. Eventually, Joseph Rosati, as successor to Bishop Du Bourg, paid this debt with money from the Association of the Propagation of the Faith in Europe, not from contributions of the parishioners in Saint Louis.[20]

Father Niel had a little more success with the Saint Louis College than he did with the reluctant parish. In February, 1823, he succeeded in getting the first prominent educator of another religious denomination to join the faculty.

Professor Elihu Shepard, a veteran of the War of 1812, and a teacher by profession, taught at Saint Louis College for several years. He left a history of the early years in Saint Louis and an autobiography. This latter book provides a first-hand look at activities of the school at the time. The list of students who attended Saint Louis College in the Shepard days includes the sons of prominent citizens and young men destined for fame themselves: the four sons of Governor Alexander McNair, three sons of Judge Silas Bent, a son of explorer and territorial governor, William Clark, and a son of Illinois' first territorial governor, U.S. Senator Ninian Edwards. Meriwether Lewis Clark became surveyor general of the United States, the Bent boys important fur traders in the early West, Ninian Edwards the attorney general of Illinois, and, incidentally, the brother-in-law of Mary Todd Lincoln.

The five thousand residents of Saint Louis, equally divided between French- and English-speaking people, voted for municipal incorporation on the first Monday in April, 1823. The vote won by a surprisingly close margin.[21] The new city fathers took two steps that affected Father Niel and the Church.

First, they wanted all cemeteries outside the city limits. This forced the lay committeemen of the Cathedral parish to explore the possibilities of a new site for the graveyard. William Stokes, a brother-in-law of John O'Fallon, offered four acres of ground on the St. Charles Road, a mile from the city limits. Father Niel agreed to move the graveyard to this site and authorized the sale of the adjoining burial lots.[22]

Secondly, the city fathers began to consider the opening of a public library and a public school.[23] Since they were not able to begin a school immediately, they agreed to pay Father Niel to educate poor boys of the city at Saint Louis College.[24]

During the next year, Father Niel prepared to return to France to beg funds for the College and the Cathedral. He turned over his pastoral duties and his general superintendence of the school to Father Edmund Saulnier.[25] He confided the day-to-day direction of the college to Dr. C. G. Brun, "whose learning and experience," he insisted, "entitle him to the confidence and the patronage of the public."[26] Niel left for France. He proved successful in his solicitations of funds for the Saint Louis institutions, but he never returned to America.

Indian Mission and School

Du Bourg had so many calls on his time and so many grand dreams, it is surprising that he did not forget his Osage children. In 1822, however, he had sent Father Charles de la Croix, to visit the tribe. A native of Ghent in Belgium, de la Croix had offered his services to Du Bourg, and came to America in 1817. Stationed at the bishop's farm near Florissant, he served as spiritual father for Mother Duchesne and the Religious of the Sacred Heart. In May, 1822, Father de la Croix visited the Chouteau trading post at the main village of the Osages near the western boundary of Missouri sixty miles south of the junction of the Kansas and Missouri rivers. In August of the same year, he returned to visit other Osage villages. He baptized many French-Indian children. Saint Louis fur traders, Paul Ligueste Chouteau and Pierre Melicour Papin, acted as sponsors in these baptisms.[27]

Bishop Du Bourg had long tried to get Jesuit priests to work among the tribes. As usual he tried all avenues of access. He asked the Holy Father to get in touch with the Jesuit general. He wrote the prefect of the Propaganda, Cardinal Fontana, suggesting some individuals of the society, such as a Father Louis Barat, then teaching at a seminary in Bordeaux.[28]

Finally in 1823, he saw the possibility of enlisting the services of a group of Belgian Jesuits in Maryland, several of them priests, the remainder novices who had heeded the call of Kentucky missioner Charles Nerinckx to come to America. The novitiate in Maryland faced a financial crisis and planned to move. In this eventuality, Du Bourg saw his chance.

He first petitioned Secretary of War Calhoun for a subsidy to locate three missionaries in strategic areas along the Missouri and the Upper Mississippi Rivers. President Monroe approved this three-man missionary project.[29]

In the midst of Du Bourg's negotiations with the government and the Jesuits, Archbishop Ambrose Marechal of Baltimore demurred. He needed the Belgian missionaries in his diocese. A momentarily chastened Du Bourg wrote to Marechal on March 6, 1823. He stated that he did not know any of the young Belgian Jesuits. He presumed that financial difficulties would force the closing of the novitiate in Maryland. Should the novices be dispersed, some would join another religious community; others would join the diocesan clergy. "In the last supposition," he stated, "I declare to you I want none of them . . . As to the priests already employed in your diocese . . . I am disposed to refuse their services."[30]

In spite of this promise to Marechal, the ebullient Du Bourg had already planned to invite the Belgian Jesuits — both priests and novices — to move to Missouri. He wrote that the government would defray two-thirds of the cost of a new project he had in mind.[31] No evidence exists to indicate that this enlarged subsidy existed anywhere but in Du Bourg's excessive imagination. Before he got full clearance from the Jesuit superior in Maryland, or told Marechal of his change of attitude, he proposed an elaborate plan to the secretary of war. With government aid, he hoped to set up a combined Indian school and missionary training center near the confluence of the Missouri and Mississippi Rivers. Here the Belgian Jesuit novices could complete their training; at the same time, they could teach a group of Indian boys the ways of civilized life. The interchange between the prospective missionaries and the future tribal leaders would prove mutually helpful. Du Bourg agreed to turn over to the Jesuits a substantial estate near Florissant as a site for the combined Indian school and seminary. In view of the extended plans, Du Bourg asked a greater subsidy of the government.[32]

Du Bourg wrote enthusiastically to his brother the same day. "If I had my choice, I could not have desired anything better; seven young men, all Flemings, full of talent and the spirit of Saint Francis Xavier . . . ."[33] This was only ten days after he had assured Marechal he would refuse their services.

Two days later, on March 19, 1823, before he had an answer from Calhoun, Bishop Du Bourg entered into an agreement with Father Charles Neale, superior of the Jesuits in the United States, relative to the Indian Missions of the West. By this agreement, the bishop of New Orleans gave to the Society of Jesus the exclusive care of all the missions already set up and those to be begun on the Missouri River and its tributary streams, the spiritual direction both of the white population and of the various Indian tribes, "together with all the churches, chapels, colleges, and seminaries of learning already erected, and which shall hereafter be erected.[34]

The bishop promised to give a valuable tract of land at Florissant and bound himself and his successors to support, encourage, and promote the missions and various establishments of the Jesuits, especially the seminary to be commenced immediately on the above-mentioned tract of land in Florissant.

The Jesuit superior, in turn, agreed to send immediately to Missouri two priests, seven novices, two or three lay brothers, and four or five Negro slaves to erect additional buildings and to cultivate the farm. The superior also agreed that at the expiration of two years he would send at least four or five missionaries to remote stations, especially in the vicinity of Council Bluffs, and to keep two Fathers at the principal residence at Florissant to direct the preparation of the young men destined for the Indian missions.

Four days later, on March 21, 1823, Calhoun informed Du Bourg that President Monroe approved the projected school. The Chief Executive thought the new plan an improvement over the initial suggestion. He was not, however, able to enlarge the original grant. The payments, as originally stipulated, would be forthcoming once the school was in operation and General William Clark, the western superintendent of Indian affairs, had so notified the government.[35]

The Jesuit vice-superior, Father Charles Felix Van Quickenborne, preached in New York, Philadelphia, and Baltimore, and collected a thousand dollars for the Missouri venture. Du Bourg, in the meantime, was trying to explain his inconsistent policies to Archbishop Marechal. Bishop Du Bourg's words might be translated freely thus: "The Belgian Jesuits have twisted my arm."[36]

Archbishop Marechal had this to say of Du Bourg's project and methods in a letter to Father Robert Gradwell, Jesuit rector of the English college in Rome:

Monsignor Du Bourg's project is regarded here by persons of experience as chimerical. They think, and not without reason, that the real purpose of the prelate is to make a little display in the newspapers of Europe and under pretext of the conversion of the Indians to make collections in Europe and elsewhere.[37]

Du Bourg did not follow Marechal's suggestion that traveling missionaries go inconspicuously in twos and threes. He realized the publicity value of a big missionary force moving down the Ohio on a flat-boat. A large crowd turned out for the public procession held on the occasion of their arrival in Saint Louis, May 31, 1823. The priests at the Cathedral and the college welcomed the Belgians at a dinner at the bishop's residence.[38]

The Jesuit group consisted of two priests, Father Charles F. Van Quickenborne and Father Peter Timmermans, three coadjutor brothers, Henry Reiselman, Charles Strahan, and Peter DeMeyer, seven novices — all missionary recruits of Father Charles Nerinckx — Felix Verreydt, Francis de Maillet, Judocus Van Assche, Peter J. Verhaegen, John Baptist Smedts, John A. Elet, and Pierre Jean De Smet, and three young Negro married couples. The Jesuits enjoyed the hospitality of Mother Duchesne in the village of Florissant until such time as the bishop's farm was ready for occupancy. The group soon lost two members: Brother Strahan returned to Maryland; Francis de Maillet left the novitiate and became a lay teacher at Saint Louis College. The remaining six novices took their first vows as Jesuits in August. The hard-working young Father Timmermans did not survive the first year. He died on May 31, 1824, the anniversary of his and the other Belgians' arrival in Missouri.

Father Van Quickenborne hardly seemed the type of man to guide this new enterprise in its early years. He was as changeable as Du Bourg, and severe. He deplored his difficult task; yet rejected the reasonable solutions of others.[39] He refused to take full responsibility for the success of the Jesuit mission; yet he undercut the efforts of everyone else.[40] Nonetheless, he held his little group of tough-minded Flemings together to build one of the most significant mission enterprises in the nineteenth century.

He opened the Indian school in May, 1824, without any clear idea of what its goals were to be. Two Sauk boys came first, then three "Hyaways" — as Van Quickenborne called the Iowa Indians. The Jesuit seminarians and the coadjutor brothers taught the young braves. The Saint Regis Indian Seminary, a joint project of government and Church, of Monroe and Du Bourg, Calhoun and Van Quickenborne, was under way.

Bishop Du Bourg had hopes for further Jesuit work in his diocese besides Indian missions. Recognizing the educational as well as the missionary traditions of the Jesuit order, Du Bourg wanted Jesuits to staff Saint Louis College. In November of the year of the Belgians' arrival, Du Bourg offered the American Jesuit superior in Maryland two blocks of land as a site for a college. He agreed to turn over the equipment of the existing school in Cathedral square. He concluded: "In the course of time a church will certainly be erected, which will be entirely under your control."[41] On two other occasions he repeated similar invitations.[42] At the moment, however, the Jesuits had their hands full with the Indian school.

Typically, Du Bourg does not seem to have discussed this important matter of asking the Jesuits to man Saint Louis College with Father Niel and his successor, Father Saulnier, the two men most intimately involved with running the existing Saint Louis College. Letters of Saulnier indicate he heard of these negotiations only indirectly.[43]

Chapter 6

Du Bourg Withdraws from Missouri

Rosati as Coadjutor

From his arrival in Missouri, Joseph Rosati had combined the heavy responsibilities of seminary director in Perry County with that of pastor of the Catholics in the neighborhood. After the death of Father De Andreis, he also held the post of superior of the Vincentians throughout the United States. During the early years, he devised the plans for Saint Mary's Seminary, superintended its construction and taught its important courses.

On November 26, 1822, the thirty-two-year-old Vincentian received a papal letter, conferring on him the title "Bishop of Tenagra" and the task of vicar apostolic of Mississippi and Alabama. Rosati made a careful investigation of the region assigned him. He found that Alabama had one city capable of supporting a pastor, namely Mobile. Mississippi had none. Natchez had only thirty Catholic families and was losing its pastor; Bay Saint Louis had only twenty. The creation of a diocese seemed premature and ill-advised.[1] Churchmen Du Bourg, Marechal, and Flaget joined Rosati in this opinion.

This bungling had resulted from the attempt of bureaucrats in Rome, with limited geographic knowledge, to set up the regional ecclesiastical administration in the United States. The creation of the diocese of Charleston (S. Carolina) in 1820 had cut Mississippi and Alabama adrift from the Archdiocese of Baltimore. Fortunately, Rome heeded the American bishops' protests and abandoned the hasty plan of creating the vicariate.

Instead, on July 14, 1823, Pope Pius VII appointed Rosati coadjutor to Bishop Du Bourg, and insisted he accept the position. The Pope also designated the time of his coadjutorship as three years. At the end of that term Rome intended to divide the Diocese of Louisiana. Bishop Rosati would then resign his position as coadjutor and become the bishop of the diocese that remained after Bishop Du Bourg had made his choice. If, however, at the time of the division, Bishop Du Bourg were no longer governing the Diocese of Louisiana, Bishop Rosati would administer the entire Louisiana Territory until the Holy See made final dispositions.[2]

The office of the Propaganda in Rome allowed Bishop Rosati to continue as superior of the house and seminary at Perryville and to function as the vicar-general for the Vincentians in the United States. Rosati accepted the coadjutorship and promised to receive consecration as soon as possible.[3]

During that same year, Bishop Rosati welcomed thirteen Sisters of Loretto to Perry County. At the request of Bishop Du Bourg, Father Charles Nerinckx selected the Sisters for this first effort of the eleven-year-old congregation beyond the borders of Kentucky. At the time of their arrival, the building intended for the Sisters was still under construction. As a result, the party stayed for a month at the home of the mother of one of the group,

Mrs. Sarah Hayden, who had provided accommodations for the Vincentians on their arrival several years before. In the fall of 1823, the Sisters began a school for girls. Father Nerinckx discussed by letter with Bishop Rosati the possibility of sending Sisters to Saint Louis at the request of some of the citizens to take care of the sick and orphans.[4]

Early in 1824, the ladies of Saint Louis formed a "Female Charitable Society," with Mrs. George F. Strother its first president and the wife of Governor McNair as vice-president. Father Francois Niel devoted his Palm Sunday sermon at the Cathedral to the new organization. He praised the charitable purposes of the society and the cooperation of Catholic and Protestant, French-speaking and English-speaking ladies in the venture.[5]

In the meantime, Bishop Rosati had spent most of the month of February (1824) in Ste. Genevieve waiting for the ice floes to diminish on the river. He planned to go to Louisiana for his consecration. On February 21 he finally left Ste. Genevieve, and arrived at Donaldsonville, Louisiana, on March 11. Two days later he paid a visit to Bishop Du Bourg who stayed at the home of one of his nephews, nine miles from Donaldsonville. Then Rosati made an eight days' retreat to prepare himself for the consecration. A large crowd greeted him on his return to Donaldsonville on March 24. A roll of cannon heralded his entrance into the town. Everywhere in the old French village, the Creoles joined in the festive ceremonies.

Bishop Du Bourg was the consecrating prelate. In the absence of other bishops, Father Louis Sibourd and Fray Antonio De Sedella acted as co-consecrators by papal dispensation. Father Aristide Anduzi, pastor of St. James, Louisiana, a close friend of Bishop Rosati, preached the sermon. During the days that followed the consecration, Bishop Rosati visited the various parishes in Louisiana and gained an acquaintance with the conditions in that part of the diocese.

In a letter to his brother, written four days after his consecration, Bishop Rosati stated:

I take comfort in the consciousness that far from desiring this dignity, I have done everything in my power to prevent its being bestowed upon me . . . . Anyhow one of the shoals of the episcopate I am safe from, being a bishop in such a country as this: for here there are neither honors, comforts, nor riches attached to the dignity . . . another motive urging me to imitate in my conduct the examples of the apostles, the office of whom I have been called to discharge.[6]

This was to be a recurring theme in Rosati's attitude toward bishoprics on the frontier: that they were a burden rather than an honor, a cross rather than a crown.

At Bishop Du Bourg's suggestion, Rosati visited as many towns and as many priests in Louisiana as he could. After a time outstate, he went to New Orleans and called on Fray Antonio. On Easter Sunday Rosati celebrated the Pontifical Mass in the Cathedral.

On his return journey, Rosati again stopped at Donaldsonville. Finally, on May 10, he boarded a steamboat, the "Dolphin," to return to Missouri. He arrived in Saint Louis in mid-May. The priests of the college warmly greeted him. He visited the Religious of the Sacred Heart at Florissant and the Jesuits at the St. Regis Seminary not far away. He appointed Father Van Quickenborne vicar-general of Upper Louisiana. Then he returned to Southeast Missouri.

Rosati had already opposed Du Bourg's recalling some of the Missouri priests to Lower Louisiana. Now he faced a new scheme of Du Bourg. The bishop wanted to transfer the seminary at the Barrens to Lower Louisiana. One year before, the Vincentian pastor at Opelousas, Louisiana, had discussed with Rosati the possibility of opening a preparatory seminary in the south. The pastor had already received a promise of land from a Mrs. Charles Smith at Grand Coteau. Rosati had vetoed the suggestion at the time.

At the time of Rosati's consecration, Du Bourg presented a new plan. In view of the eventual religious division of Louisiana Territory, he believed that New Orleans should have its own seminary. He had already secured the donation of a thousand acres. A zealous priest offered $4,000 for the erection of the buildings. Rosati looked over the place and found it desirable. But at this time Bishop Du Bourg had said nothing about suppressing the seminary in Perry County.[7]

The following summer Du Bourg asked Rosati to meet him in Assumption, Louisiana, and explained the total project. Du Bourg intended to buy a house and plantation next to the land already donated for the foundation of a seminary. The purchase could be made by an immediate payment of $3,000 and the obligation to pay a yearly interest of $1,200 to the owner. The man was then 74 years old, but in good health. In order to build the college and furnish it, Du Bourg would seek a loan from the State Bank at a seven percent interest and the annual payment of one-fifth of the principal. To produce a cash crop of sugar cane, Du Bourg would enter into partnership with a farmer who would care for the land. The profit would be divided evenly. Rosati listened with growing skepticism. He believed this complicated plan might expose the Church and the Congregation of the Mission to bankruptcy.[8]

Du Bourg exerted great pressure on Rosati to get him to agree to starting the seminary in Louisiana; Du Bourg insisted that a refusal was tantamount to bringing ruin upon the whole diocese. Thus Rosati agreed to consider a plan he in no way favored: to leave one or two priests with the boys of the lower classes in Missouri; and go himself with all the rest to Lower Louisiana to conduct the seminary and college to be built there.[9]

The following day Du Bourg resumed the conversation. Rosati, in turn, insisted that he had to consult the priests in Missouri before beginning the new venture. The delay proved wise. Rosati returned to Missouri. On November 25, 1825, four days after he arrived in Perry County, Rosati called together Fathers De Neckere, Dahmen, Permoli, and Odin. In a letter to the Vincentian Vicar-General Baccari in Rome,[10] the priests gave the reasons for their opposition to the plan: it would be risking too much to run into debt, as Du Bourg intended in his plans for a plantation; the qualified priests were too few for both dioceses; and lastly, it would be unjust to abandon the Missouri mission in favor of Louisiana. They would not act until they received Baccari's reply. In the mean-

time, Rosati asked Du Bourg to delay his plans for the proposed seminary until the means and the subjects were available. Du Bourg did so.

Jesuits At Florissant

Since the time Bishop Rosati had become coadjutor to Bishop Du Bourg, the Jesuit vice-superior in Missouri, Father Van Quickenborne, had served as vicar-general of Upper Louisiana. He also taught theology to the Jesuit seminarians, helped in the parishes of Florissant and St. Charles, supervised the Indian School, and gave spiritual direction to the Religious of the Sacred Heart, who, in the spring of 1825, had begun a school for Indian girls.

With his added duties as vicar-general, Van Quickenborne decided to do something about the seminary training at Florissant. The simplest solution would have been to advance the better trained scholastics to ordination, as Bishop Du Bourg wanted him to do.[11] All the young Jesuits had been seminarians in Belgium when they answered the call of Father Charles Nerinckx for the American mission. Instead, Van Quickenborne appointed John Elet and Peter Verhaegen to teach the other scholastics. When Van Quickenborne's health gave way under his many stresses, the Jesuit superior in Maryland sent Father Theodore De Theux west in October, 1825, to teach theology and assist Van Quickenborne in his wide duties.

De Theux brought with him an experience in the priestly ministry rivalled only by Bishop Du Bourg on his arrival in the diocese. A Belgian nobleman, De Theux had become a priest of the Diocese of Liege in his native land thirteen years before. He had administered the diocese and taught theology before hearing the call of the American missions from Father Nerinckx. After coming to America he entered the Jesuit order in Maryland in August, 1816. He did pastoral work in the vicinity of Washington for six years. Then the Jesuit superior sent him to Missouri.

De Theux had the non-democratic manner of his forebears, and a rigoristic moral outlook. He was as severe as Van Quickenborne, but much more consistent. While not easy of approach, he was a man of priestly dignity who impressed people with his stern but genuine virtues and a deep commitment to God.

At De Theux's arrival, Bishop Du Bourg sought the Florissant Jesuits for pastoral work in Saint Louis. "I would like to see your fathers in charge of the parish and village of Saint Louis," the bishop wrote to the Jesuit superior in Maryland, Father Francis Dzierozynski, on October 24, 1825. "Father De Theux would do well in that office, no less than Father Van Quickenborne."[12] Bishop Rosati became aware of this request of Du Bourg. The coadjutor wrote in his diary a month later: "The parish of that city, Saint Louis, is, according to the determination of the Bishop of New Orleans, to be administered by the Jesuit Fathers."[13]

The Jesuit Fathers were to come from Florissant to Saint Louis four years later, but for collegiate not pastoral work.

Diocesan Division?

Bishop Rosati sought the advice of Bishops Flaget and his coadjutor John B. David on matters of Missouri. Flaget opposed the suppression of the seminary in Perry County, and urged a division of Upper and Lower Louisiana. "Until it (the division) is made," Flaget wrote to the Vincentian superior general, "all the zeal and talents of Bishop Rosati are kept, as it were, in concealment."[14]

Often the varying personalities of Rosati and Du Bourg appeared in striking contrast. Du Bourg, a splendid orator, spoke in the grand style of a Webster or a Bossuet whether in English or in French. Rosati spoke simply; usually he gave a homily on the scripture reading of the day — as some outlines in his diary attest.

In approaching a major decision, Du Bourg always tried more than he could handle, and jumped from one project to another. Rosati, on the other hand, set realizable goals and stuck with them. While Rosati dealt in objective reality, Bishop Du Bourg took a subjective outlook. Anyone who opposed a plan of his, even on objectively valid grounds, opposed *him*. When the Creole populace rejoiced exuberantly on a major religious occasion, for instance, Du Bourg accepted their demonstration as a personal tribute to him. Rosati never took approval or disapproval of plans or programs in so personal a way.

Rome gave the two men another chance to show their varying reactions a short time later. Without consulting Du Bourg, Rome named one of the Louisiana priests, Michael Portier, vicar apostolic of the Floridas. Du Bourg twice contested this appointment. He said that he was glad to be rid of the responsibility for the territory and he thought that Portier should be sent elsewhere. The young man, in Du Bourg's estimate, was purposeless and changeable. (In spite of Du Bourg's charge that he was "changeable," incidentally, Portier was to serve faithfully as bishop for a third of a century.) In a passage filled with characteristic self-pity, Du Bourg accused Portier of having turned the people against their bishop.[15] Rosati in contrast expressed his satisfaction at Portier's appointment. He saw the position more a challenge than an honor; and he wished Portier well.[16]

This correspondence, incidentally, pointed up another contrast between Du Bourg and Rosati: the former was more a church dignitary of the old regime than a spontaneous religious leader. Rosati, in contrast, was a spiritual servant of his people.

Ordinations in 1826

In spite of the shortage of priests in the American Midwest, the Jesuit vice-superior, Charles Felix Van Quickenborne, still hesitated to present any of his seminarians for ordination. Yet, some of them, such as John Baptist Smedts, and John Elet, had finished several years of theology at the major seminary in Mechlin in their native Belgium before they entered the Jesuit order, and Peter Verhaegen had taught in the minor seminary of the same city.

A peremptory letter of Bishop Du Bourg to the Jesuit superior in Maryland, Father Francis Dzierozynski, in the summer of 1825, finally brought action.[17] Still months were to elapse before Father Van Quickenborne finally sent seminarians John Baptist Smedts and Peter Verhaegen to Perry County. Bishop Rosati ordained the former on January 29, 1826, and the latter on March 11.[18]

Father Smedts was to be pastor at St. Charles, and master of Jesuit novices at Florissant for six years — a steady, solid pioneer, hard-working but over-shadowed by many of his more conspicuous fellow Belgians. Peter Verhaegen was to be the organizer of the Missouri Jesuit Mission, the organizer of Saint Louis University, adminis-

trator of the Diocese of Saint Louis — a truly outstanding co-worker of Bishop Rosati in the region.

On the same day he ordained Verhaegen, Bishop Rosati raised to the priesthood one of his fellow Vincentians, John Bouillier.[19] Father Bouillier began mission work in the long-established French parish of Saint Joachim in Old Mines the same year. Two years later, he was to begin a brick church there.

Du Bourg's Surprise Resignation

A short time later, Bishop Du Bourg arrived at the seminary in Perry County, on his way to Europe. Rosati recorded in his diary that the bishop hoped to tour the continent for financial aid and for recruits for the seminary in Louisiana.[20] Du Bourg remained three days, then Rosati accompanied him to Ste. Genevieve. On May 3, 1826, Du Bourg reached Saint Louis. It was to be his last visit.

Du Bourg inspected the parish and the college — both under the management of Father Edmund Saulnier. As mercurial as Missouri's March winds, Saulnier wanted to work elsewhere, even on the Indian missions. His letters often reflected extreme self-pity. His French sermons were poor. He rarely tried to preach in English. The French-Irish language rift continued to split the Saint Louis congregation. Procedural arrangements hamstrung his pastoral work. He had to get routine church permissions from the Jesuit superior at Florissant, Vicar-General Van Quickenborne. But he was a tenacious young man. He alone of Du Bourg's diocesan priest recruits was to persevere in the diocese, come depressions or Mississippi floods. Some of the others, like Niel, Dusassory, and De la Croix, who became secretary of the Association for the Propagation of the Faith, were to return to Europe. Others, like Martial, were to move to other American dioceses.

Bishop Du Bourg visited Saint Louis College. He found that Saulnier did not have rapport with his faculty and was soon to lose his best teachers. Du Bourg decided to suppress the college; and informed Rosati shortly afterward that he had done so.[21] But he had not reckoned with the strange persistence of Father Saulnier who was to keep the college alive for a few more crucial years.

The next day Du Bourg preached at Mass. Then, permitting no one to accompany him, he boarded a steamboat for the East. He was never to return to Saint Louis.

Father Saulnier asked Bishop Rosati to transfer Father De Neckere to Saint Louis since he alone, among available priests, could speak English fluently. This, Bishop Rosati did on May 15, 1826. Father Saulnier viewed the coming of De Neckere as a favor to the Irish and other English-speaking elements of the population. But certain Irishmen demanded that a sermon should be in English at Mass every second Sunday, instead of exclusively at Vespers on Sunday evening.

Father Saulnier called a meeting of the Irish members of the parish before Vespers on Sunday a few weeks later. Twelve men came. The priest told them that as a favor he would have Father De Neckere preach to them every Sunday at Vespers. They thought this unsatisfactory, and asked again for a sermon at High Mass every second Sunday. Saulnier insisted that unless a higher superior were so to order him, he could not abolish a custom that had always existed in Saint Louis. He insisted that the French would leave the church if the sermon were in English —

just as the Irish did when the sermon was in French.

Some Irishmen held a meeting in the city [Saulnier wrote to Rosati] and made up a lengthy petition, signed, not by the most respectable amongst them, but mostly by men of objectionable conduct. For those, who I know practice their religion, refused to sign . . . I expect more assistance for Mr. De Neckere from non-Catholics than from the others. If the French did not pay better than the Irish, I do not know what would become of my support.[22]

Contrary to Father Saulnier's claim, a prominent Irish name or two, at least six men of French background, and a large group of Irish names destined to remain a strong part of the Catholic community down through the years, appeared among the list of sixty-five who petitioned Bishop Rosati on August 27, 1826. They respectfully reviewed developments in the parish since the agreement with Father Francois Niel in 1823. They deplored the distinction between "what is termed the French and the American part of the congregation." They admitted that the Irish-Americans did not speak French; but they insisted that "a very large majority of the French population that composes in part this congregation, does understand perfectly the English language;" and, the many guests of other denominations who came to the Cathedral also understood only English. Thus few who came to church did not understand English. They appreciated the presence of Father "Denackary" (sic) but protested the hour of the English service — a time few of the American Catholics found convenient since they resided at a distance in the country.[23]

It is interesting to note, incidentally, that the use of the English language rather than length of residence constituted "American" in the view of these people. In their own minds, they were "American"; the older inhabitants of the city were "French." Such unusual distinctions were not uncommon at the time. The German Catholics moving into the Missouri River farmlands above St. Charles, for instance, identified "German" with "Catholic" and "American" with "Protestant."

Unfortunately, at this time, the illness of De Neckere and his departure for a rest in his native Belgium, compounded the problem. Bishop Rosati wrote a cordial letter to the trustees of the Cathedral on September 1, 1826, "French and American, Creole and Irish are equally dear to us," he wrote, "because we think them equally entitled to the spiritual assistance that is in our power to afford them . . . . In the meantime, we think it our duty to exert ourselves in order to raise a national clergy who, knowing the languages spoken in the country, may be able to assist all their countrymen."[24]

On September 23, 1826, Bishop Rosati ordained three more of his fellow Vincentians, Peter Vergani, Joseph Paquin, and John Timon.[25] Vergani had belonged to the group of students at Milan who had answered the call to the American missions shortly after Du Bourg's consecration in Rome. He was to do parochial work in various frontier communities. Joseph Paquin, the first native-born Missourian to join the Congregation of the Mission, became the second son of Upper Louisiana (the first was Father Henri Pratte) to become a priest. He was to serve as president of Saint Mary's College in Perryville, and as superior of the Vincentian seminary in Saint Louis, before leaving for the Texas mission.

The third member of the ordination class was to have an eminent career. Born in Pennsylvania of Irish ancestry, John Timon had lived for a time in Kentucky before moving with his parents to Saint Louis. He had attended Saint Louis College for one term, then joined the Vincentians at Perryville. In his early work as a priest, Timon was to teach English and natural sciences at Saint Mary's in Perryville, to discharge the duties of treasurer and procurator, help in the parish, to direct the Lorettines in their neighboring convent, and at regular intervals to visit the mission stations in the lead-mining district of Missouri and the English-speaking settlements of Southwestern Illinois, such as O'Harasburg, near Prairie du Rocher.[26]

A man of marked intelligence, serious outlook, winning manners, medium height, and fine physique, Timon was to leave his mark on the history of the American Church as superior of the Vincentians, as a recruiter of outstanding missionaries for the West, and as a missionary bishop. His name will come up often in the history of the Church in Saint Louis.

A few days after the ordination ceremony, Saulnier asked Bishop Rosati to send Father Timon to Saint Louis.[27] Rosati sent him to the city for the last part of the year.

In the meantime, Bishop Du Bourg had returned to his native France. Depressed by his many great problems and still embarassed by the Inglesi affair, he had tendered his resignation to Pope Leo XII. By this time, the Roman authorities had become convinced that he had shown too much suspicion of his fellow clergymen to function effectively in America. Shortly after he landed in France, Rome accepted his resignation.

On October 5, Rosati received from Father Niel the report that Du Bourg had resigned. Papers in New Orleans, New York, Saint Louis, and Charleston also carried this information. On hearing the news, Rosati wrote to Father Baccari:

I was absolutely bewildered and could not persuade myself that it was true. The conversations . . . which I had with the Prelate before he left here and the letters which he wrote me before sailing made me expect something quite different from his resignation. Accordingly, I considered the report as absurd and a pure invention.[28]

On November 4, Rosati was in Saint Louis for the consecration of Bishop Portier. At this time, he received official notification of Du Bourg's resignation from Cardinal Di Somalia, the prefect of Propaganda. By a Pontifical Brief, dated July 14, Rome had divided the territory, and appointed Rosati administrator of the two dioceses, New Orleans and Saint Louis. Presumably, he would be bishop of New Orleans until Rome decided on a bishop for Saint Louis. The Diocese of New Orleans included the states of Louisiana and Mississippi. The new Diocese of Saint Louis included the state of Missouri, the western portion of the state of Illinois, the territories of Arkansas and Iowa, and the rest of the Louisiana Purchase to the Rocky Mountains.

Saint Louis' First Episcopal Consecration

The consecration of Bishop Portier had many interesting aspects. It was Saint Louis' and Bishop Rosati's first episcopal consecration. The consecrating bishop was only thirty-five years old, and the bishop consecrated, thirty-one. Fathers Van Quickenborne and Donatien Olivier assisted. Following the ceremony, Bishop Rosati notified the clergy of both dioceses of the resignation of Bishop Du Bourg and the new arrangements authorized by the Holy See.

Shortly after, he wrote to the pro-prefect of the Propaganda asking that he be assigned to Saint Louis rather than New Orleans. Three main reasons seemed to outweigh all others. First, he found the climate of New Orleans deadly. On his three visits there, he had experienced an attack of fever each time. In spite of pictures that suggest an ascetic physique, Rosati was corpulent. Even in good health, he could not function well in New Orleans. Second, Rosati felt he did not speak French well enough to be at his best in the Bayou Country.[29] Third, Rosati set for himself limited and attainable goals. He had sacrificed a great deal for the seminary of Saint Mary's in southeast Missouri. The Roman province of the Vincentian Fathers had made even greater sacrifices for that institution. This first center of classical and clerical education in the trans-Mississippi region was soon to receive from the Missouri legislature the right to confer A.B. and M.A. degrees — the first such grant in the state. Within six years, Saint Mary's was to have one hundred and fifty students, two-thirds of them boarders. The Roman province of the Vincentians had supplied seven priests, six Brothers, and large sums of money for the establishment of the community in America — a sacrifice offering great hope for the cause of religion. Rosati wanted to bring this work to its full fruition.

Rosati made a winter trip on horseback to Bardstown to consult Bishop Flaget and his coadjutor, Bishop David, on the question of his choice of diocese. They agreed that his arguments for Saint Louis were compelling.[30] Rosati then went to New Orleans in March, 1827, and set up an episcopal council with extensive powers in routine business. Fray Antonio served as chairman and Father Auguste Jeanjean as secretary. The other members were Fathers Benedict Richard, O.S.B., Louis L. Moni, O.S.B., and Philip Borgna, C.M. During the succeeding years Rosati was to go to Louisiana twice a year and make a visitation of all the parishes.

Shortly after his return to Saint Louis in early summer, Rosati received heartening news. Rome had seen the wisdom of his request to work in the Missouri area. Thus Rosati became the first bishop of the newly erected Diocese of Saint Louis.[31] Rome also asked that he remain for a time administrator of New Orleans. The Holy Father Leo XII and the Vincentian general, Francis Baccari, sent along substantial donations for the diocese.

Baccari had, in the meantime, sent Father Angelo Boccardo to take Rosati's place as superior of the Congregation of Mission in North America. Boccardo arrived in New Orleans with further donations amounting to two thousand dollars from the Society for the Propagation of the Faith, from the Vincentian Superior, and from other friends. As he walked down the gangplank to disembark, he accidentally dropped his traveling case into the river. No one was able to recover the money from the swift brown waters.

Utterly depressed, Boccardo decided to return to Europe on the next ship. Rosati heard of the misfortune and wrote to reassure his stricken colleague. Unfortunately, Rosati's letter arrived in New Orleans after Boccardo's boat left. On July 14, Rosati informed Cardinal Cappellari, prefect of the Sacred Congregation, of the double mishap. Nothing could be done about the loss of money. But the Cardinal might try to persuade Boccardo to come to Saint Louis.[32] Boccardo, however, never returned to America. Rosati had to continue the three-fold office of bishop of Saint Louis, administrator of New Orleans, and superior of the Congregation of the Mission.

Du Bourg's Last Days

Du Bourg, too, received a new commission: The Pope made him bishop of Montauban in France. He continued his interest in the Saint Louis diocese, directing contributions of friends to various good works such as the church,[33] the college in Saint Louis,[34] and the missions among the Indians.[35]

After seven years in Montauban, Du Bourg was to become archbishop of Besancon, a pre-Roman French city, two hundred miles southeast of Paris. The archbishop before him in that see had been a cardinal. The archbishop after him became a cardinal. Had he not died so soon, Du Bourg may well have become a cardinal of the Church. He passed away December 11, 1833, within a year of his appointment as archbishop.

In spite of all his deficiencies then, the final judgment still has to be that in relation to churchmen of his time in the United States, Du Bourg was a distinguished figure. It was easy, even for saints, to be annoyed with him. He appreciated grand concepts without visualizing details. He did not consciously close his mind to them. He just did not see them. Those who came after him had to pick up the pieces. Without Rosati to follow and organize the diocese, Du Bourg would not have accomplished much of permanent value. Yet this much must be recognized. Even though his departure had its part in the return to Europe of half a dozen priests who had come over to assist him, Du Bourg recruited many outstanding apostles who stayed. Among them, Rosati, De Andreis, Van Quickenborne, Verhaegen, DeSmet, Blanc, De Neckere, Portier, and Mother Duchesne contributed greatly to the development of the Church in the United States.

Du Bourg was initially responsible for the first Vincentian mission in America, the Vincentian seminary and college at Perryville, the Jesuit seminary at Florissant, the Saint Louis College that was to grow into Saint Louis University, the original foundations of the Religious of the Sacred Heart in the United States, and first foundation of the Sisters of Loretto in the trans-Mississippi region. These were no small achievements.

Circumstances of the time, then, brought a man fitted for an ancient institutionalized see like Lyons or Bordeaux to an expanding, unorganized frontier of the Church. It is not surprising that in so many instances he failed. What is surprising is that he accomplished so much.

PART III

Joseph Rosati: Saintly Pastor (1827-1843)

Joseph Rosati, C.M., founder of St. Mary's College and Seminary, Perryville, superior of the Congregation of the Mission in the new world, and first bishop of Saint Louis. (Photograph by Jack Belch.)

Bishop Rosati appoints Father John Baptist Smedts, S.J., pastor of St. Charles.

JOSEPH ROSATI

Congregationis Missionis

Dei et Apostolicæ *Sedis Gratia,*

EPISCOPUS S. LUDOVICI.

Rev. P. *Ioanni Bapt. Smedts Soc. Iesu Sacerdoti*

Quum ab adm. Rev. *P. Verhaegen Miss. Soc. Iesu Sup. Generali*

Nobis præsentatus fueris ad *Congregationem S. Caroli regendam*

cujus cura *Soc. Iesu* Sacerdotibus commissa est; quumque Nobis, tum præfati Superioris tui testimonio, tum aliunde de tua

scientia pietate et prudentia, quibus ad pastorale munus obeundum te idoneum judicamus, satis et abunde constet, te ejusdem *Congᵉ*

Pastorem, per præsentes ad revocationem usque valituras, constituimus, et facultates omnes ad illam regendam tibi impertimur.

Datum S. Ludovici ex Ædibus Episcopalibus, sub nostro signo et sigillo, et nostri Secretarii subscriptione

die *19* Mensis *Augusti* Anni MDCCCXXXVI

+ *Joseph Epᵘˢ S. Ludⁱ*

Chapter 7

A Missionary Bishop Lays Plans

The Nation and the Church in the Mid-Twenties

When Joseph Rosati became bishop of Saint Louis in 1827, the nation had already moved out of the "Era of Good Feeling" that followed the War of 1812. The 1820's were a time of mixed emotions. The Federalist John Quincy Adams, son of a former president, who had been an excellent secretary of state under Monroe, but was turning out less happily as the Chief Executive, occupied the White House from 1824 to 1828 as a result of a disputed election. Andrew Jackson, the hero of New Orleans, waited in the wings, firmly convinced that he had been cheated out of the presidency in the 1824 election.* Many Americans agreed with him.

John Marshall still served as chief justice of the Supreme Court. He had raised the court to a plateau of prestige and authority, asserted its powers to review laws of Congress, and emphasized the power of the central government over the individual states.

The great westward migration moved at flood tide. In the decade between 1820 and 1830, Missouri gained 109% in population. The Land Act of 1820 offered the public domain in 80-acre tracts for cash at a minimum price of $1.75 an acre. A large percentage of the people moving into Missouri came from the four states straight east of the Missouri Boot Heel: Kentucky, Tennessee, Virginia, and North Carolina. A group of Saint Louis fur traders had organized the Rocky Mountain Fur Company in 1822. In the next twelve years, until it succumbed to the competition of the American Fur Company, this firm shipped approximately half a million dollars worth of beaver packs to Saint Louis.

The population of the city at the time of its incorporation in 1823 approached four thousand.[1] Close to half of these were French. With the Catholics of other national backgrounds, Bishop Rosati's flock made up over half the residents. The United States census in 1830 would show the city's population at 4,977.[2]

At Bishop Rosati's appointment, all the lands east of the Mississippi, except Florida and Michigan Territory (later to become the states of Michigan and Wisconsin), were full fledged commonwealths of the Union. West of the Mississippi lay two states: Louisiana and Missouri, and one organized territory, Arkansas. Beyond these, a vast unorganized region stretched to the Continental Divide. Over these high plains nomadic Indian tribes roamed, among them the Sioux, the Cheyenne, and the Pawnee. To the southwest lay the vast Republic of Mexico.

The ecclesiastical map likewise, reflected America's phenomenal growth. America's first diocese, Baltimore, had included the entire United States at the consecration of Bishop John Carroll in 1789, the year Washington became president. In 1808, Baltimore became an archdiocese and four new dioceses split off from it. The Diocese of New York was coterminous with the state of New York. Boston included all of New England. The states of Delaware, New Jersey, and Pennsylvania comprised the Diocese of Philadelphia. Bardstown, the center of a large settlement of Maryland Catholics in Kentucky, became the seat of a large diocese that included Kentucky, Tennessee, and all the old Northwest Territory (an area that was eventually to comprise the five states of Ohio, Indiana, Illinois, Michigan, and Wisconsin). Two southern dioceses split off from the mother see in 1820: Charleston included North Carolina, South Carolina, and Georgia; Richmond comprised the then large and influential state of Virginia, but remained temporarily under the jurisdiction of Baltimore. The Diocese of Cincinnati, comprising the state of Ohio, split from Bardstown in 1821. The states of Florida, Alabama, and Mississippi formed a vicariate apostolic that was to become the Diocese of Mobile in 1829.

At the time of the appointment of Bishop Rosati, the Saint Louis diocese included the state of Missouri, the western half of Illinois and all American territory west of the Mississippi, and north of the state of Louisiana. This largest American diocese stretched from the Canadian border on the north, to Louisiana and the Republic of Mexico on the south, from the Continental Divide on the west to the lower Mississippi and an imaginary line running through central Illinois on the east. Bishop Rosati's territory roughly equalled in extent all other nine dioceses of the country together.

Archbishop Marechal of Baltimore had estimated the Catholic population of the various dioceses east of the Mississippi for the year 1821-1822 as follows: Baltimore 80,000, Boston 3,500, New York 24,000, Philadelphia 30,000, Charleston 3,600, Richmond 2,400, Bardstown 20,000, making a total of 163,500.[3] The Catholic population of the area that was to become the Saint Louis diocese went over 30,000 at this time.

What did the Diocese of Saint Louis look like? In terms of active Catholic communities, there were two clusters of settlements along the Mississippi, one in the vicinity of Saint Louis, the other fifty or sixty miles south. The first included the city itself, and the satellite villages of Carondelet not far to the south, Cahokia to the east of the river, Florissant to the northwest, St. Charles to the west, on the far bank of the Missouri River, and various smaller villages scattered here and there.

The "Old Settlements," sixty miles south of Saint Louis, included villages on both sides of the river. On the Illinois side stood Prairie du Rocher, Kaskaskia, a cluster of Irish and Kentucky families living at O'Harasburg, about seven miles from Prairie du Rocher, and an English

---

*In a four-way election in 1824, neither William Crawford, Andrew Jackson, Henry Clay, nor John Quincy Adams got a majority of the electoral votes. Jackson had a plurality, but when Clay threw his support to Adams, John Quincy Adams became President.

Catholic settlement (later called Hecker) eighteen miles to the north. On the Missouri side of the river stood Ste. Genevieve half-way between Prairie du Rocher and Kaskaskia. Perryville lay ten miles from the river, about twenty miles south and a little east of Ste. Genevieve. About forty miles west of Ste. Genevieve lay the mining villages of Potosi and Old Mines (both with churches) and several clusters of dwellings where the French-speaking residents gathered at the home of one of their neighbors on the occasion of a priest's visit. Twenty miles west of Perryville, in turn, another cluster of villages included Mine La Motte and Fredericktown. A few other French river-villages dotted the diocesan map, such as Prairie du

Bourg had promised this equipment to the Sisters.[4]

During the same spring, in order to insure help from the Association of the Propagation of the Faith in Lyons, Bishop Rosati asked Father Charles Cholleton, an active member of the association, to represent the interests of the Saint Louis diocese in France. Cholleton agreed to do this.[5]

Meanwhile, the Jesuits at Florissant still walked in circles under the inconsistent direction of Van Quickenborne. The Indian school had not met the expectations of Bishop Du Bourg and President Monroe, of Secretary Calhoun and Father Van Quickenborne. But it did give future missionaries initial contact with the Indians. The

The Daughters of Charity conducted the Saint Louis Hospital at Fourth and Spruce, on land donated by John Mullanphy.

Chien on the Mississippi at the mouth of the Wisconsin in the north, New Madrid near the mouth of the Ohio, and the Arkansas Post at the mouth of the Arkansas River in the south, Peoria on the Illinois, and Chouteau's Settlement (later Kansas City) at the junction of the Kansas River with the Missouri.

Strengthening the See City

Bishop Rosati did not let the vastness of the task overwhelm him. He viewed the assets of the area as well as its debts. He appreciated the generosity of his many co-workers. In order to enhance the religious spirit of the city of Saint Louis, he encouraged Mother Duchesne to come to Saint Louis, where she had originally intended to set up the convent. She was able to locate on Broadway near Hickory on May 1, 1827. This move resulted from a contract between Mother Duchesne and John Mullanphy. He leased the property to the Sisters for 999 years, and asked them to agree to take care of twenty orphans in perpetuity, for a stipend of five dollars each per year. Father Saulnier sent the desks and benches of the old Saint Louis College to the new "City House." Bishop Du

seminary continued, though the last four candidates for the priesthood had long seemed ready for ordination.

Finally in the summer of 1827, the Jesuit superior in Maryland, Father Francis Dzierozynski, made a special visit to Missouri. As a result, Bishop Rosati came to Florissant and on September 23, 1827, ordained the four remaining Jesuit seminarians: John Elet, Judochus Van Assche, Pierre Jean DeSmet, and Felix Verreydt. All were to have distinguished careers in the American West: Van Assche, a faithful and devoted pastor at Florissant; Elet, president of Saint Louis University and founder of Xavier College in Cincinnati; Verreydt, a successful home and Indian missionary; and Pierre Jean DeSmet, the best-known missionary of the American Northwest, and the most world-famous Jesuit of the nineteenth century.

Another indication of the growing maturity of the Church in Saint Louis came with the ordination of John Francis Regis Loisel in 1828. The father of the young priest had come to Saint Louis from Canada in 1793 and married Helene Chauvin.[6] Regis Loisel was related to many of the Creole families of the city. Bishop Rosati ordained him in the old brick cathedral on June 29, 1828. Father Loisel assisted Saulnier at the parish and taught at Saint Louis College during its last year under diocesan auspices. Though not a brilliant orator, he spoke simply and clearly in both French and English. He was to serve many years as pastor at Holy Family in Cahokia.

In the same month that Bishop Rosati ordained Father Loisel, he appealed to the Sisters of Charity of Emmitsburg, Maryland, through their spiritual director, Father Simon Bruté, S.S., the future bishop of Vincennes. Rosati wanted the Sisters to start a hospital in Saint Louis. He sent word that businessman John Mullanphy had offered a piece of ground with two houses, and another plot with four other houses that would bring a revenue of $600 a year. Mullanphy promised $150 for the journey of the Sisters and $350 to furnish the house. Bishop Bruté presented the petition to the Sisters' Council. After careful deliberation the council approved the plan and assigned four Sisters to the new foundation. Bishop Rosati had set down an extensive agreement for the organization of the hospital where the Sisters were to work.[7]

In spite of this detailed planning, the four Sisters of Charity arrived by stagecoach on November 5, 1828, with Bishop Rosati away and the people of Saint Louis ignorant of his plans. The newly arriving Sisters stayed with the Religious of the Sacred Heart. When the bishop returned later in the month, he signed the deed whereby John Mullanphy handed over the hospital building and the four houses as sources of revenue. The next day (November 26), the Sisters took possession of their new home in the Saint Louis Mullanphy Hospital, the first hospital west of the Mississippi.

Bishop Rosati immediately expressed his appreciation to Mother Augustine Decount, the superior in Emmitsburg. He assured her that the Sisters would be under no control other than that of the bishop of Saint Louis. He promised to allow them full rein to function conformably to their customs and rules. He had appointed as confessor of the Sisters, an assistant at the Cathedral, Father Louis Dussassoy, a nephew of Mother Madeleine Sophie Barat, and a recruit of Bishop Du Bourg. Rosati ordered the other three clergymen residing in the town to render the Sisters every assistance. He admitted that until a bishop came to New Orleans, he would not be in Saint Louis too often.[8]

A third institution under the auspices of a Catholic religious order opened in Saint Louis in 1829. Bishop Rosati had repeated Bishop Du Bourg's requests to the Jesuits to teach in Saint Louis. By 1828 it had become clear both that the diocesan priests could not continue to staff Saint Louis College and that the Indian school at Florissant was not the best approach to the Christianization of the tribes. Further, the young men who had come out as novices at the instigation of Father Nerinckx in 1823 had completed their Jesuit training and were ready for new ventures. Van Quickenborne was anxious to send some on the Indian missions, and, incidentally, to go west himself; he promoted parishes in St. Charles and in neighboring towns. At Bishop Rosati's request, he gave serious thought to the possibility of educational work in Saint Louis. In the autumn of 1828, after consultation with the bishop, Van Quickenborne announced that he would open a school in Conner's Addition (later to be the area at Ninth and Washington) the following year. During the school year 1828-29, the Jesuits would teach white boys at Florissant. In launching a drive for funds, Van Quickenborne spoke to the leading citizens of Saint Louis at the home of Major Thomas Biddle, brother of Nicholas Biddle, president of the Bank of the United States, and a son-in-law of John Mullanphy.[9] Van Quickenborne collected enough money to get the school underway by the following fall.

In the autumn of 1828, also, Bishop Rosati consecrated the new church in St. Charles. This building was the first project of Peter J. Verhaegen, S.J., a man destined to be one of the pillars of the young diocese of Saint Louis. A tall, robust man, with a full, plain face, alert eyes, and a tendency to over-weight, Verhaegen spoke and wrote fluent English. Outgoing in personality, easy of access, a popular man and a loyal friend, he had the characteristics of the frontier, enthusiasm, optimism, open-mindedness. The true organizer of the Jesuit Missouri Mission, he will appear regularly in the development of the diocese during the succeeding thirty years.

The Jesuit superior, Van Quickenborne, had planned a new stone church in St. Charles and had commissioned newly ordained Verhaegen to superintend the building in 1826. Verhaegen had preached on the needs of the parish, and received a donation from Governor John Miller. St. Charles, incidentally, was the state capitol at the time.[10] Verhaegen expressed amazement that Van Quickenborne always came up with money when needed. Some came from Belgian benefactors; the rest from Van Quickenborne's personal patrimony.[11]

Bishop Rosati consecrated the new building on October 12, 1828. Father Theodore De Theux preached in English. Father Louis Dussassoy spoke in French.[12] Bishop Rosati confirmed sixty-six persons the next day and preached to an audience of Protestants as well as Catholics.[13] Father John Baptist Smedts, S.J., the first Jesuit ordained in Missouri, became permanent pastor, succeeding Verhaegen who soon began a distinguished career as president of Saint Louis College.

The city of Saint Louis reached a landmark in February, 1829. Auguste Chouteau, Jr., the step-son of the founder of the city of Saint Louis, and for many years the senior citizen of the town, passed away. Father Saulnier had the funeral Mass at the Cathedral on February 25, with a dignity not matched, he felt, by the small donation of Auguste's relatives.[14] Chouteau had seen Saint Louis since its founding on February 15, 1764. By his death, Saint Louis had already lost its original character as a French village and would soon become a major American city.

A Provincial Council

Bishop Carroll had gathered America's twenty priests together in 1791. In 1810, the year he became archbishop, he had called a meeting of the newly consecrated members of the hierarchy who were about to assume their episcopal duties — the bishops of Bardstown, Philadelphia, New York, and Boston. They discussed at that time some plan for national uniformity. Archbishop Carroll planned to convene a first provincial council within the next two years, but the imminent outbreak of the War of 1812 prevented this. After Carroll died in 1815, his coadjutor, Leonard Neale, did not have the health and strength to work out the details for a council. His successor, Archbishop Ambrose Maréchal, refrained from calling his suffragans to Baltimore for various reasons, among them the troubled state of affairs of the various dioceses in the East.

When Archbishop James Whitfield succeeded Archbishop Marechal in 1828, he responded to the urgent appeals of some of his suffragans, especially Bishop John England of Charleston, South Carolina, and called the first provincial council at Baltimore for October, 1828. The diocese of Saint Louis did not belong to the Province of Baltimore but was directly under the Holy See.* Bishop England wanted unity of action throughout the United States and thus urged Whitfield to invite all American bishops, including Portier and Rosati.

The Charleston bishop felt a deep regard for the bishop of Saint Louis. England's authoritative biographer, Monsignor Peter Guilday, wrote: "To no one does he (England) seem to have given his confidence, except to Rosati."[15] The bishop of Saint Louis, in turn, had expressed his regard for Bishop England's far-sighted Constitution of the Church in South Carolina. "If carried into execution," Rosati had written to England, "it will secure to your flock the deposit of faith, to ecclesiastical jurisdiction respect of mission, to the clergy honor and support, and to religion at large propagation and stability. I therefore congratulate your diocese for all these blessings."[16]

As a result of England's entreaty, Archbishop Whitfield sent an invitation to Saint Louis and remarked how pleased all the bishops would be if Rosati came. The Saint Louis prelate was happy to do so. It was his first opportunity to meet most of the bishops personally. He left for Bardstown in August and journeyed to Baltimore.

During the session devoted to the instruction of youth, Rosati pushed for the translation of the catechism of Cardinal Bellarmine into English. The fathers of the council wanted a uniform textbook for the country, and assigned Rosati and England to do the translating. These two prelates also had the task of preparing the English translation of the ceremonial book. This they were to do a short time after the conclusion of the council. The assembled bishops finally asked Rosati to draft a letter to the newly elected Pope Pius VIII. In this message, Bishop Rosati described the development of the Church in America with both warmth and objectivity:

Two centuries have elapsed since in a remote and obscure Maryland a little band of Catholics guided by a few missionaries, exiled from their native land, flying from the cruel persecution inflicted upon them for adhering to the faith of their forefathers, laid the foundations of the American Church. It is scarcely 40 years since this body of faithful in the United States of America was found sufficient to demand, in the opinion of the Sovereign Pontiff, the erection of the first Episcopal See at Baltimore. Not twenty years have rolled by since the decree of the Holy Pontiff Pius VII exalted the Church of Baltimore with the dignity and

rights of a metropolitan, and like a joyful mother of children she 'has beheld in recently erected suffragan dioceses ... an off-spring in new churches which it has borne to Christ ... We see so many blessings bestowed by God on these rising Churches ... the number of the faithful increases daily ... six ecclesiastical seminaries, the hope of our Churches, have already been established ... nine colleges under ecclesiastical control, the glory of the Catholic name, have been erected in different states to train boys and young men in piety, arts, and the higher branches of science: three of these have been chartered as universities by the legislatures: thirty-three monasteries and houses of religious women of different orders and congregations, Ursulines, Visitandines, Carmelites, Sacred Heart, Sisters of Charity, Loretto, and others are everywhere established in our dioceses ... Houses of the Religious of the Order of Preachers, and of the Society of Jesus, of secular priests of the Congregation of the Mission and of St. Sulpice, from which, as centers, priests are sent out to missions; many schools where the poor of both sexes are taught gratuitously; hospitals where these examples of Christian charity were formerly unknown are now daily given by religious women to the great benefit of souls and of religion. These, Most Holy Father, are the signal benefits that God has bestowed upon us in a few years.[17]

When the council came to a close on October 18, the bishops decided to pay a joint visit to America's great Catholic layman, Charles Carroll of Carrollton, at his home, Doreghan Manor. The lone surviving signer of the Declaration of Independence, then in his 93rd year, still enjoyed the best of health. The bishops marvelled at his keen mind and retentive memory as he spoke to them of many events in his long life.

Bishop Rosati visited the Jesuits at Georgetown to appeal for more priests for the college in Saint Louis and for the Indian missions.[18] He visited Emmitsburg and prevailed upon the Sisters to open an orphanage in New Orleans. He stopped at Philadelphia, New York, and Boston to discuss with each of his new episcopal friends the state of the Church in his diocese. Everywhere he went, he observed the hospitals, the schools, and the asylums, in order to better things at home. He made a winter journey to Quebec to discuss the work of missionaries in the area of the Great Lakes where the two dioceses came together. Bishop Rosati and Archbishop Bernard Panet of Quebec worked out an amicable arrangement whereby priests from either jurisdiction could exercise powers in the northern regions of the United States bordering on Canada. Bishop Rosati granted to Bishop Provencher, then the vicar apostolic of the Canadian territory west of the Great Lakes, the power of vicar-general of Saint Louis and the extraordinary powers of the Holy See that the Saint Louis bishop possessed, thus reconfirming powers previously granted by Bishop Du Bourg.[19]

While in Canada, Bishop Rosati also paid a visit to Father LeSaulnier, a Sulpician professor at the Seminary in Montreal, a friend and confrere of Bishop Du Bourg, who had sent contributions to Bishop Rosati for missionary purposes.[20]

---

*According to the Council of Trent, a missionary bishopric was required to attach itself in practice to a neighboring province in conciliar activities.

Chapter 8

The Bishop Moves to Saint Louis

Relief From Rome

Bishop Rosati was ready to hurry back to Missouri. He had heard the good news that his Vincentian confrere, Leo De Neckere, would be bishop of New Orleans, as he himself had recommended.[1] De Neckere, the youngest of Du Bourg's recruits, had experience and maturity far beyond that of most young men of twenty-eight. As with so many other Flemish missionaries, he had learned English readily and become totally American in outlook and spirit. His only weakness was poor health. In fact, when he and Bishop Rosati started for New Orleans, illness delayed him at Ste. Genevieve. Rosati went on to the Crescent City to tell Bishops England and Portier that the bishop-elect would not reach his see in time for the planned consecration on May 16, 1830. The two would-be co-consecrators returned to their respective sees.

At this juncture Bishop Rosati welcomed to the United States his successor as superior of the Congregation of the Mission, Father John Tornatore. Rosati immediately wrote a letter of appreciation to the Vincentian superior general in Paris. He believed that now the work of the Congregation in the Middle West would take new life.[2]

Bishop-elect De Neckere arrived in New Orleans in June, 1830. On the 24th of that month, Bishop Rosati consecrated Leo De Neckere as his successor in New Orleans. Bishop Portier of Mobile came back to the Crescent City in time, but Bishop England could not return. In his place, Father Benedict Richard acted as co-consecrator. In the elevation of De Neckere, both dioceses of New Orleans and Saint Louis gained. But in losing De Neckere to the hierarchy so soon after Rosati, the Congregation of the Mission sacrificed its internal development to the interests of the growing Church in mid-America.

Bishop Rosati and Father Tornatore steamed up the Mississippi together. Rosati remained at the seminary in Perry County throughout the summer, introducing Tornatore to the intricacies of his three-fold task as master of novices, director of the seminary, and superior of the Congregation of the Mission in the United States.

In the fall, Bishop Rosati left the seminary where he had worked so whole-heartedly since 1818. Relieved at last of the administration of the diocese of New Orleans, and of the superiorship of the Congregation of the Mission, he could now turn his attention with a singleness of purpose to the administration of his see. A new era in the history of the diocese of Saint Louis now began.

"There are indeed, many things to be done," he wrote to a friend in Europe, "but little resources. A certain number of priests are still necessary to fill vacant posts, to establish new ones, and to furnish the Catholic population the means of salvation, at the same time not neglecting the Indians and the Protestants."[3]

In Saint Louis, where Bishop Rosati now fixed his residence, he had two priests with him. One of them took care of two parishes five miles apart; the other priest was so busy he could scarcely take care of the parish of Saint Louis. Every Sunday and feast day, multi-lingual Rosati preached in French in the morning at the High Mass and in English at Vespers in the afternoon. He may have spoken with an accent, but there is no evidence that he did. He heard confessions of the two religious communities of nuns. He gave retreats to the Sisters at the hospital.

Four Jesuit Fathers — three Belgians and one Irishman — taught at the Saint Louis College at Ninth and Washington; all spoke English well and assisted the bishop with sermons at the Cathedral. Two years later they were to preach in English at Mass on the first and third Sundays of every month.*

Survey of the Diocese

The organized mind of Rosati shows forth clearly in the objective report on the diocese sent to the Leopoldine Foundation in Vienna in 1830. This society had begun one year before, under the sponsorship of the Austrian Emperor, Francis I, at the request of the bishop of Cincinnati. After an initial contribution to Cincinnati of roughly $14,000, the society accepted requests from other bishops.[4] Hence Bishop Rosati sent his diocesan report.

The exact number of Catholics in the diocese has never been determined. But according to an approximate estimate there are 40,000 Catholics; 3,000 Catholics live in Saint Louis in a total population of 8,000.** More than three-fourths of the Catholics are French-speaking. The Cathedral that was started eleven or twelve years before is on the verge of collapse due to lack of money for repairs and previous poor workmanship.[5]

The Sacred Heart nuns took care of a number of orphan girls, Rosati reported, conducted an educational institution for the daughters of wealthy parents, as well as a tuition-free school. Approximately one hundred young ladies enjoyed the benefits of these institutions. The Sisters of Charity conducted the Saint Louis Mullanphy Hospital, accepting free of charge a number of poor people of both races, to the admiration of Protestants and Catholics alike.

Saint Louis had an impressive Catholic college under Jesuit administration. The Jesuits had opened the college the previous November and already had more than eighty students enrolled. Twenty boarders paid tuition. The day students paid no fees.

*Monsignor F. G. Holweck discusses the language question at the Cathedral fully in the *St. Louis Catholic Historical Review* 11, no. 1 (January 1920).
**Rosati's figures include the population of the areas adjacent to the city. Between six and seven thousand people lived within the city limits by 1830. "Sketch of St. Louis," in *The St. Louis Directory* (St. Louis: Keemle, 1840), p. v.

The seminary of the diocese was situated in Perry County, eighty miles south of Saint Louis and ten miles from the Mississippi. Founded by the Vincentians approximately twelve years before, it had proved to be beneficial for the area. The seminary numbered twenty-eight non-paying seminarians, and seventy-two paying seminarians. Four priests and nine brothers of the above congregation made up the faculty. The resident church community numbered about two hundred American families and had two churches. One church lay fifteen miles distant from the seminary. A Vincentian priest visited it every month to say Mass. The other church was in the vicinity of the seminary. The priests celebrated Mass on all Sundays and feast days.

Ste. Genevieve was a French-speaking Catholic town, on the west bank of the Mississippi, sixty miles south of Saint Louis. The parish consisted of two thousand Catholics. The care of souls was in the hands of a Vincentian priest of German descent, Father Francis Xavier Dahmen. The only other church in the vicinity was built in an area called "Little Canada," fifteen miles from Ste. Genevieve. St. Michael's, a small parish with a resident priest, near Fredericktown, had approximately two hundred Catholics of French descent.

Carondelet, ten miles south of Saint Louis, had many French families. The main American military post in the trans-Mississippi region, Jefferson Barracks, was located in this parish. A large portion of the thousand soldiers stationed there were Irish Catholics. The priest who attended the parish lived in Saint Louis because the poverty of the residents made it impossible for them to support him.

St. Ferdinand, or Florissant, twenty miles northwest of Saint Louis, had about eighty families of French ancestry. They had an attractive brick church that had not yet been paid for due to lack of funds. The Jesuits who had their novitiate two miles from the town administered this parish. The students in the school numbered fifteen. Near St. Ferdinand's Church stood a convent of Sacred Heart nuns who conducted a girls' boarding school as well as a day school. The nuns also made their novitiate at this convent.

St. Charles, not far away on the far bank of the Missouri, had one hundred families, mostly French Catholics. Two Jesuit priests and a brother staffed the parish and served the neighboring missions. They also conducted a free day school. The church was an attractive edifice made of stone that had been completely finished and blessed two years earlier. Sacred Heart nuns conducted a large day school there.

Two neighboring parishes under Jesuit care were Portage Des Sioux, a French town of forty families, with a wooden church dedicated to St. Francis, and La Dardenne, a small town with only thirteen Catholic families.

Sixty French families lived near *Cote Sans Dessein*, on the north bank of the Missouri, two miles below the mouth of the Osage, about eighty miles above St. Charles. The Jesuits visited them regularly.

A missionary priest from the seminary in Perry County visited the eighty French families at New Madrid on the lower Mississippi, twenty miles below the mouth of the Ohio. Many Catholics of French descent had scattered here and there through the Arkansas Territory. Adequate care for them had been impossible up to the time. The bishop hoped eventually to send two priests among them.

The district of the lead works in the state of Missouri, fifty miles west of Ste. Genevieve, numbered over two thousand Catholics, the majority of them of French ancestry, and the remainder Irish. The priest had his residence in the village of Old Mines. In place of an earlier wooden church, another was being built out of brick. Eight miles distant lay the village of Potosi with American and Irish inhabitants. They had an attractive stone church served by the priest from Old Mines.

The bishop of Saint Louis also shepherded Catholic settlements in the state of Illinois. The old French town of Prairie du Rocher, with forty Catholic families, had a church. Eight miles east, at O'Harasburg, a considerable number of Catholics of American and Irish background had built a church of wood.* In other English settlements such as Harrisonville and Edwardsville, some Catholic families lived.

Kaskaskia, an old French hamlet, had been the center for the Jesuit missions in Illinois. An Indian tribe of the same name, and a neighboring tribe, were almost entirely Catholic. But these had almost all disappeared with the exception of a few individuals who still professed the Catholic faith and lived in the vicinity of the hamlet on their lands, supporting themselves, not by farming, but by hunting. The number of French Catholics in Kaskaskia ran about fourteen hundred.

Up the Mississippi, at Fever River and Prairie du Chien five hundred Catholics lived, but the lack of priests prevented the bishop from sending them assistance at the time. "Sangamo" was a strip of land one hundred miles from Saint Louis in central Illinois. The fifty Catholic families here constantly welcomed new immigrants.

This was the vast diocese as Rosati saw it in 1830.[6]

The Cathedral

When Bishop Rosati turned his full energy to the upbuilding of his episcopal city, he began to lay plans for a true cathedral. The half-finished old brick building was both ugly and inadequate. Representatives of the Catholic congregation of Saint Louis, among them William Higgins, John O'Rourke, Michael O'Rourke, M. P. LeDuc, L. Menard, and James C. Lynch, met on April 4, 1830, with Bishop Rosati as chairman and M. P. LeDuc as secretary. The men discussed the building and financing of a new cathedral. They decided to lease the north half of the church block, where the old cemetery and the church stood. They planned a drive among the citizens of Saint Louis. The bishop assured them that the diocese could depend upon the Association of the Propagation of the Faith for a yearly subsidy and agreed to appeal to the Pope for help. Since the bishop himself was a native of the Kingdom of Naples, he promised to petition the Neapolitan King, Ferdinand II, for assistance. The bishop had also acquired a large section of land on the bank of the River de Peres, worth $4,000, from Bishop Du Bourg and a tract in town from a Mrs. La Caise. The bishop was willing to dispose of these to help defray cathedral costs.

When the parish leaders set up a permanent committee, they chose Wilson Primm as secretary. Louis Menard, Patrick Walsh, and John O'Rourke resigned before any substantial accomplishments. William Higgins died. Colonel Rene Paul, Hugh O'Neil, Sr., and General Bernard

---

*For a fuller treatment of this first English-speaking parish in Illinois, confer William B. Faherty, S.J., "The First English-speaking Parish in Illinois," *Mid-America* 20 (July 1938): 165-169.

Pratte filled the vacancies on the committee.

On April 23, of the same year, Bishop Rosati paid $4,000 to Pratte and the Chouteaus from the annual contribution of the Society of the Propagation of the Faith to remove most of the debt of $4,500 on the earlier church.[7] Even though Bishop Rosati was still uncertain where he might acquire the needed revenue for the cathedral, the committee considered details of construction that summer.

Bishop Rosati chose as architects Joseph Laveille and George Morton who had formed the first architectural firm in the trans-Mississippi region. They had designed the First Episcopal Church at Third and Chestnut in 1824 and the first court house two years later. They chose a design of Greek Revival style, with Doric pillars and a facade of Joliet limestone. In recompense for their efforts, they received a ninety-nine year lease on the north portion of the church block.*

The new structure would face south on Walnut. The people of Saint Louis assembled at 5:00 p.m. on Sunday evening, August 1, 1831, for the laying of the cornerstone. All the priests of the area took part. Father L. Rondot began with a sermon in French. The bishop blessed the cornerstone and placed in it a group of U.S. silver coins minted the previous year and two pieces of parchment, one relating the history of Saint Louis, the other memorializing the events of that day. After the ceremony of blessing, the people again filed into the church. Father P. J. Verhaegen, the Jesuit superior, preached in English. With his usual care, Bishop Rosati records the collection as $62.50.[8]

As the months went on, money came in driblets. After the completion of the first year's work, Rosati wrote to Bishop Du Bourg at Montauban, France:

> I have already paid about $11,000 and every Saturday it is necessary to pay the contractors from $300 to $500. Until now I have been able to meet all my debts ... we will not be able to finish the church without $18,000 more, because I figure it will cost about $30,000. But it will last for centuries.[9]

In response Bishop Du Bourg arranged a loan of $8,800 at six percent interest. Pope Gregory XVI sent $3,000. The Propagation of the Faith continued its liberal allowance, and the Leopoldine Foundation sent 10,000 florins (approximately $4,700).[10] Bishop Rosati sold the farm on the River de Peres to an advantage. Father Sibourd, the former vicar-general of New Orleans, gave the bishop $700.[11] The drive among the Catholics of the city netted about $4,106.50. Bishop Rosati was the largest contributor with a gift of $450.[12] The first true cathedral beyond the Mississippi was underway; the diocese had begun to feel a sure hand at its helm.**

In the meantime the hospital in Saint Louis had so outgrown the original building that the Sisters opened a commodious building at Fourth and Spruce Street. The new hospital immediately proved its worth during the great cholera epidemic of 1832. No qualified nurses were at hand to take charge of the hospital conducted by city authorities. The Sisters considered the possibility of dividing up into two groups. Realizing that it was impossible to do this, they offered their hospital for the afflicted. The mayor of the city gladly accepted the offer. The city sent all cholera patients to the Sisters' hospital.[13] The Sisters proved heroic in attending the plague victims; two of them succumbed to the epidemic. The priests at the cathedral regularly visited the patients. By early November the epidemic had begun to decline. The United States government also defrayed the expenses of sick and disabled boatmen who had no home in Saint Louis.

On November 14 three new Sisters arrived from Emmitsburg. Bishop Rosati gave to the Sisters a small house on Third and Walnut to be used as an orphanage for boys. Underway a few years later, it became the first Catholic orphanage for boys in the West. The Daughters of Charity also hoped to open a home for orphaned girls.

While Rosati was putting his see city on a more solid religious foundation, he did not neglect the rest of his diocese. He and Flaget met to discuss a division of the parishes of Illinois. At the time, they made a visitation of these parishes together. The regular companion of Bishop Flaget, Father Robert Abell, accompanied them. This tall, rough-hewn frontier priest shared the outlook and eloquence of his fellow Kentuckian, Abraham Lincoln.

Abell drove the closed carriage and took part in such missionary activities as hearing confessions. The bishops expected him to preach at each place they stopped. On their way to Kaskaskia they went through a driving snowstorm. As a result, they arrived hours late, cold and tired. Nonetheless, the bishops insisted that Abell give a sermon — but a short one. Rosati remarked that even another Fenelon could not keep him awake a half an hour. When the bishops and the pastor began the services, Father Abell remained in the sacristy. After the exertion of his long trip, Abell felt he deserved a drink of wine. By the time he finished his third goblet, it was time for his sermon. He spoke fluently for two hours. Rosati stayed awake for every word.

When Abell finished, the bishops hastily retired to the sacristy. Rosati threw his arms around the young priest and congratulated him on his eloquence. "You spoke as if you were inspired," Rosati said. When Abell told him the source of his inspiration, Rosati laughed heartily.[14]

---

*John Albury Bryan discussed the building of the cathedral in *Missouri's Contribution to American Architecture* (St. Louis: St. Louis Architectural Club, 1928), pp. 9-10.

**A guide book for the recitation of the divine office in the diocese for 1832 carried a list of the priests and their assignments. Father Tornatore, C.M., vicar-general of the diocese, administered the Cathedral parish with the assistance of Fathers Louis Rondot, Joseph Lutz, Matthew Condamine, and Benedict Roux. Father Francis Xavier Dahmen, C.M., was pastor of Ste. Genevieve. Father John Bouillier, C.M., served Old Mines, Potosi, and neighboring settlements. In his absence, Father Philip Borgna, C.M., attended these villages.

The remainder of the list read as follows: in the town of St. Michael's, near Old Mines, Father Francis Cellini, C.M.; in the town of St. Charles on the Missouri, Fathers John B. Smedts, S.J.,

and Felix Verreydt, S.J.; at Florissant, Fathers Theodore De Theux the superior, and Judochus Van Assche, S.J.; at the college in Saint Louis, the following Jesuits: Fathers Peter Verhaegen, Charles Van Quickenborne, Peter Walsh, John Elet, Pierre Jean DeSmet, James Van de Velde, and Jude Van Sweevelt; in the town of Kaskaskia, Father Victor Paillaisson; in the town of Cahokia, Father Peter Doutrelingue, C.M.; and at the Seminary of Saint Mary's in the Barrens, Father Donatien Olivier, Father John Odin, C.M., the president of the college, Father Paquin, vice-president of the college, John Timon, C.M., Regis Loisel, D. N. Brands, C.M., D. N. Bonnot, Angelo Mascheroni, Ennemond Dupuy, John McMahon, and John M. St. Cyr. The last priest listed is Father Edmund Saulnier in the city of Saint Louis (*Ordo Divini Officii... Diocesis Sancti Ludovici*, MDCCCXXXII [St. Louis: C. Keemle, 1831], pp. 31-32).

The "New" College

The Jesuit College that had opened on Washington Avenue in November, 1829, drew from four earlier institutions: the Saint Louis College for lay students founded by Bishop Du Bourg under the direction of Father Niel; the Vincentian-staffed seminary for candidates of the Louisiana diocese and the Vincentian order, that functioned for several years adjacent to the Saint Louis College; the St. Regis Indian school, twenty miles away at Florissant, co-sponsored by Secretary Calhoun and Bishop Du Bourg; and the Jesuit seminary there where the young Belgian Jesuits, who were destined to man the school on Washington Avenue, took the last stages of their training.

The school offered English and classical courses. The day students received their education free of charge but the boarders had to pay one hundred and twenty dollars. Protestant students had to be willing to participate in public religious exercises, but, following the earlier pattern set by Bishop Du Bourg and Father Niel, the school promised no pressure towards religious conformity.[15] The first of many Louisiana students, Peter Poursine, entered on February 27, 1830.[16]

Father Peter Verhaegen headed the institution. Father Theodore De Theux combined the duties of superintendent of domestic affairs, professor of French, and spiritual director of the students. Father John Elet served as treasurer of the college. Father Peter Walsh, a recent arrival from Maryland, filled the office of prefect of studies.

The impact of the city on the students and professors who came from elsewhere might be gauged from the remarks of Walsh on his arrival from Maryland.

This city ... contains about five thousand inhabitants of all colors and conditions .... It is a thriving place, promises fair to prosper, being the mart of all the trade west and northwest. The English language is pretty generally spoken and, of course, the French is falling into disuse. Catholics are numerous. The Cathedral, the only church, is a long, ill-constructed, unfinished pile. The bishop intends to destroy it and raise one more suitable and becoming the dignity of our religion.[17]

In the fall of 1830 the Jesuit general in Rome announced the separation of the fifteen Jesuits who made up the Missouri mission from the authority of the superior in Maryland. He appointed Father De Theux superior of the Missouri Jesuits. Father Peter Verhaegen had a freer hand in running Saint Louis College.

Father Verhaegen, Saint Louis College, and the city gained national publicity at this time as the result of a visit of the controversial author and publisher, Anne Royall. A shrewd observer, an aggressive ferret of graft, prone to violent expression of sympathy and antipathy, Mrs. Royall described the city of Saint Louis as she saw it in 1831: "It rises gradually from the river, and terminates upon a most delightful even green, which commands a magnificent prospect of Illinois and the river."[18] On this grassy terrace at the edge of town Saint Louis College stood. Mrs. Royall praised the liberality of the school,[19] and the affability and kindness of the Catholics of Saint Louis.[20]

In the fall of 1831, at the direction of the Jesuit general, faculty reinforcements arrived from Maryland. One of these men, James Van de Velde, was to have a long and distinguished career both at Saint Louis University and in the infant church of the Midwest. Like the other Belgian Jesuits, Van de Velde had heard the challenging words of Father Charles Nerinckx. Leaving the major seminary in Mechlin, he had planned to go to the Bardstown

diocese. The enthusiasm of his young Belgian comrades on the trip across the ocean in 1817 had changed his mind. He entered the Jesuit order at Georgetown College near Washington, D.C., in the fall of 1817. Ordained ten years later, he had remained at Georgetown College until October, 1831. The best businessman among the early Jesuits, he was to serve as president of Saint Louis University, superior of the Midwestern Jesuits, bishop of Chicago, and later bishop of the then more important see of Natchez.

Another Jesuit to visit Saint Louis in the fall of 1831 remained only a short time, but left a lasting mark on the Missouri Jesuit Mission and on religious activities in the area. Father Peter Kenney of the Irish province came to Saint Louis as official "Visitor" of the mission. He spent an entire winter. Father Kenney insisted that the Fathers at the college lend Bishop Rosati every possible assistance in the solemn services at the cathedral. Twice a month one of the priests should accept the bishop's invitation to preach in English. They should write for the Catholic press, continue their teaching and home missionary work — but not to overextend their efforts. Since the Salt Creek Mission in northeast Missouri lay beyond both the area of the original Jesuit agreement with Bishop Du Bourg and the normal compass of Jesuit missionary journies, Father Kenney scratched it from the list.

Kenney explored the question of tuition fees with Bishop Rosati, a discussion that was to have order-wide repercussions.[21] According to the Jesuit rule, the Jesuits could not receive tuition money for their services. Verhaegen had felt this was an impossibility in the United States. Bishop Rosati took up the matter directly with the Congregation of the Propaganda in Rome and with the Jesuit general, outlining the reasons for modifying the Jesuit rules in regard to the Saint Louis school.[22]

As a result of Bishop Rosati's request, Pope Gregory XVI outlined a new course for the Jesuits. On January 13, 1833, he granted the dispensation as being absolutely necessary under the circumstances. And he commissioned the general to determine the precise terms under which it was to be applied.[23] Thus Saint Louis College and Bishop Rosati participated in one of the most significant changes in the Jesuit way of conducting schools since the origin of the Society of Jesus.

Saint Louis College took one further step forward when it petitioned the government of Missouri for the university charter. On December 28, 1832, Missouri's fifth governor, Daniel Dunklin, signed the bill that made Saint Louis University the first university west of the Mississippi.[24]

The Visitandines

In 1832 Bishop Rosati invited the Sisters of the Visitation to his diocese to open a school comparable to the one they operated so successfully in the District of Columbia.[25] He suggested that they locate in Illinois' original capital, Kaskaskia, on the east bank of the Mississippi, almost equidistant from Ste. Genevieve to the north and Perryville to the south.

In those days of poor communications, the arrival of Mother Agnes Brent and eight companions on May 3, 1833, came as a surprise to the people in the old French village. Learning of the Sisters' coming, Bishop Rosati wanted to go to Kaskaskia immediately; but the cholera epidemic in Saint Louis prevented his departure. He sent a gift of money to help defray their immediate needs. He arranged for workmen at the seminary in Perryville to prepare permanent quarters for the Sisters.

Fortunately, the two most prominent men of Kaskaskia, merchant William Morrison and Illinois' first lieutenant governor, Pierre Menard, had come to the immediate aid of the nuns. Both of these men had prospered in the western trade. Morrison, in fact, had financed the initial American trading expedition to Santa Fe.* These men provided lodging for the Sisters; and when the Visitandines were offered more commodious quarters in the old Kaskaskia Hotel, rent-free, the two civic leaders solicited furnishings for the new convent.

The Visitandines opened their first academy of the west in this building in the fall of 1833. Four daughters of William Morrison attended classes. Pierre Menard sent his one daughter, and many granddaughters and nieces. One of the Sisters wrote, "He (Colonel Menard), likewise procured us patronage among his friends and agents in Saint Louis and the country around; but for him and the Morrison families, we could not have remained in Kaskaskia."[26]

Two years later Bishop Rosati and Mother Agnes chose a site for a permanent convent. Menard advanced the money for the purchase. But building proved a great obstacle. In those expanding days of Andrew Jackson's administration, the few skilled workmen had employment elsewhere. No materials were available. The architect who had built the convent in Georgetown came west to erect its Kaskaskia counterpart. He had to set up the first brick-kiln in the region.

During the next few years, several Visitandines were to write to Archbishop Samuel Eccleston of Baltimore deploring life in the West and asking to be allowed to go back to Georgetown. Their debts were heavy. They saw little prospect in the place. Four nuns died. Eccleston corresponded with Rosati several times on these matters.[27] Eventually new nuns came to the convent. And for a few years the school moved along well.

Second Council of Baltimore

The internal needs of the American Church caused Bishop England of Charleston, with the support of his friends, Bishop Rosati and Bishop Francis P. Kenrick, coadjutor of Philadelphia, to insist that the bishops meet in council at three year intervals as they had agreed to do. But Archbishop James Whitfield of Baltimore took the position of his predecessor Marechal, and saw no special need for a convocation at the time.

England and his friends believed that the bishops in council and not a few uninformed individuals should determine diocesan boundaries. Bishop England believed further, that dioceses should not divide states. Thus, for instance, he could not see why his friend, Bishop Rosati, should keep the Illinois settlements on the east bank of the Mississippi (Cahokia, Prairie du Rocher, and Kaskaskia), and so wrote to him on January 14, 1833. England thought these towns, along with the whole of Illinois, should go with the projected diocese of Vincennes. Father Auguste Jeanjean had tried to explain to England that Bishop Rosati had to travel through these towns on his

regular journeys from Saint Louis to the seminary at Perryville. England thought Jeanjean confused. Ignorant of western geography, the Charleston bishop could not see why anyone had to go through Illinois to get from one place in Missouri to another town in the same state. England presumed that Rosati wanted to keep these towns out of his own love for missionary work. England hoped that the bishops could explore the entire question at the council. But he assured Rosati: "I would never give you a moment's pain."[28] Actually, Jeanjean was right. The curve of the river below Saint Louis combined with the rough hill country on the Missouri side to make the road through Prairie du Rocher and Kaskaskia the shortest and easiest route from Saint Louis to Perryville.*

Mother Mary Agnes Brent founded the first Visitation Academy in the Midwest at Kaskaskia, Illinois, in 1833, and the first Visitation Academy in Saint Louis in 1844 on Sixth near Pine.

As a result of England's appeal, Archbishop Whitfield called a council for October 1833. But before he left for the East, Bishop Rosati gave the last sacraments to John Mullanphy, who died on August 29. At the council, the bishops discussed diocesan boundaries. Rosati explained his position on the east bank towns. They stood astride the direct road from Saint Louis to Perryville — thanks to a swerve of the Mississippi. For a time the towns remained in the Saint Louis jurisdiction. The new diocese of Vincennes included the eastern half of Illinois. Except in this instance, England's viewpoint that dioceses should

---

*Morrison, incidentally, failed to profit from this prosperous expedition. His men had so liked Sante Fe that they pocketed the proceeds and never returned to the Mississippi Valley.

*Incidentally, the road on the Illinois side remained the most simple and direct way from Saint Louis to Perryville even after the Federal Highway program 130 years later.

St. Ferdinand de Florissant – The oldest Church in Upper Louisiana. Built in 1821, the year Missouri entered the Union. This sketch by artist and missionary Father Nicholas Point shows the original facade, replaced during the 19th century. (Historical Photograph Collections, Washington State University Libraries, Pullman, Washington).

respect state lines prevailed totally over Rosati's concern for regional unity. This principle was often in the future to create artificial religious units.* Yet one hundred years later, the biographer of John England, Monsignor Peter Guilday, could still suggest that the Saint Louis diocesan boundary was illogical.[29]

Several bishops recommended John Timon, C.M., for the next vacant see in the United States. In order to retain Timon for the Saint Louis area, Rosati wanted Timon as his coadjutor in Saint Louis — a request that his fellow Vincentians were to misunderstand a year or two later.[30]

The council, lastly, set down methods of nominating bishops for vacant sees, and placed the Indian missions of the far West under Jesuit care.[31]

*At the time of this writing (1969), for instance, the "Old Settlements" in a forty mile radius of Ste. Genevieve lie within three different dioceses, Saint Louis, Springfield—Cape Girardeau, and Belleville (Illinois).

SHEPHERD OF THE VALLEY.

BY FRANCIS H. TAYLOR.]   ("ONE LORD, ONE FAITH, ONE BAPTISM.")   [VOLUME 1.——NUMBER 27

ST. LOUIS, MISSOURI, SATURDAY, JANUARY 12, 1833.

TERMS

☞ TWO DOLLARS PER ANNUM IN ADVANCE.

☞ Communications must be POST PAID, and addressed to the Editor.

OFFICE............On Spruce Street, Between Main and Church Streets.

SUBSTANCE OF A SERMON.

Preached in St. Patrick's Church, Pittsburgh, Sunday Nov. 11, 1832, by the Right Rev. FRANCIS PATRICK KENRICK, Coadjutor Bishop of Philadelphia.

Render therefore to Cæsar the things that are Cæsar's and to God the things that are God's.

BELOVED BRETHREN:—

Such is the conclusion of the gospel recited by the Church in the sacrifice of her altars on this day.   They

tutions, however diversified, whensoever they come not into collision with the divine doctrines of her funder, or the general interests of piety. Thus she adapts her children to every state of society, and enables them to coalesce with men of every character, uniting and cementing all hearts in all things whereby social order and happiness are promoted. Others may investigate abstract questions in regard to the excellence of particular systems of civil polity, the immediate origin of power, and the limits wherein it is circumscribed. She attends to practical lessons applicable to established order; and teaches the exercise of those virtues, which, under every form of government, are calculated to render men good and happy——Whether popular choice confer a Presidential chair, or ambition grasp a Crown, or victory brandish the sword of power, she regards the vicissitudes of human things as subordinate to divine providence, and considers every just exercise of established authority as sanctioned by Him from whom all power emanates: "for there is no power but from God: and those that are, are ordained of God." Romans 13.

been expected from the minister of a foreign establishment. In point of morality Dr. Walsh bears testimony that the clergy by no means deserve the unfavourable character usually imputed to them. The establishment of the public library under ecclesiastical care, is universally creditable to all parties."

"There are two public libraries; one at the convent of St. Bento, and the other the imperial library in the Rua Detraz de Cormo. This latter consists of 60,000 volumes, in all languages, ancient and modern, with plates, maps, charts, and manuscripts; but it is particularly distinguished for its collection of Bibles, more extensive perhaps than in any other library in the world; they fill a whole compartment."

"The books are arranged in several rooms, particularly in two grand long saloons; one intended exclusively for the use of the royal family, and the other open to the public, who have free access to all the books in every part of the library.

"I passed much time in this noble establishment; and think it inferior to nothing of the kind I have seen in Eu-

Bishop Rosati sponsored a Catholic paper in the 1830s, the SHEPHERD OF THE VALLEY. Articles appeared in English and French. It was one of the few papers that called for fair treatment of the Mormons in Missouri.

Chapter 9

A Surprising Surge of Nativism

Attacks and Answers

As if the mere necessity of providing for the spiritual needs of the Catholic people of the Upper Louisiana region was not enough to tax his best energies, Bishop Rosati had to fend off attacks from without. In the 1830's, nativistic ill-will supplanted the earlier national good feeling of the Monroe era. Certain Protestant groups led by Samuel F. B. Morse and Lyman Beecher, who had accepted the presidency of Lane Theological Seminary at Cincinnati for this specific purpose, determined to combat the allegedly anti-American influence of Catholicism in the Mississippi Valley.

The pre-eminent historian of Protestant-Catholic tensions in the United States during the pre-Civil War days, professor Ray Allen Billington, began his book *The Protestant Crusade, 1800-1860: A Study of the Origins of American Nativism,* with these words: "Hatred of Catholics and foreigners had been steadily growing in the United States for more than two centuries before it took political form with the Native American outbursts of the 1840's and the Know-Nothingism of the 1850's."[1] This turmoil, Billington insisted, could never have happened if the American people had not been so steeped in anti-papal prejudice. The American colonies had sprung from an England newly committed to the Protestant cause. The new religion had a strongly nationalistic flavor in contrast to the supra-national character of the old Church. Anti-Catholicism, therefore, had become a patriotic as well as a religious concern. A quasi-historical propaganda added to the growing anti-papal attitudes of the English colonists. Finally the long struggle with Catholic France brought nativism to a peak during and immediately after the French and Indian War.[2]

A wave of toleration temporarily swept the United States in the early years of the Republic. After the close of the Napoleonic wars, however, large-scale foreign immigration revived the anti-Catholicism of colonial days. The coming of immigrants brought about an unprecedented growth in American Catholicism. The trustee conflicts in Philadelphia in the 1820's and the strong tone of the Provincial Council of Baltimore in 1829 focused attention on this growth. In reply, the cry of "No-popery" grew shrill.

In the late 1820's and the 1830's anti-Catholic propaganda claimed that an alliance between foreigners and the Catholic Church sought the overthrow of the United States. The Pope and the despotic monarchs of Europe, such propaganda insisted, had hatched a plot to control the Mississippi Valley.[3] As part of this plan, the Pope had restored the Jesuits who by that time were "prowling about all parts of the United States in every possible disguise."[4] Anti-Catholic editors directed their wrath against two Catholic missionary societies, the Association for the Propagation of the Faith in Lyons, France, and the Leopoldine Society of Vienna. These two organizations gave help to Catholic missionary efforts in the Middle West.[5]

In this climate, new for the American Mid-west, Francis H. Taylor, a newcomer to Saint Louis and to the Catholic community, proposed to Bishop Rosati the publishing of a Catholic newspaper. A convert to the faith, Taylor had worked with the *Catholic Press* in Hartford, Connecticut, before opening a printing business in Saint Louis. Denominational journalism among Catholics was in its infancy at this time, except for Bishop England's *United States Catholic Miscellany,* already ten years old. Boston had had a Catholic paper for three years. Cincinnati Catholics started *The Telegraph* in 1831.[6] Saint Louis' first Catholic newspaper, the *Shepherd of the Valley* came out weekly beginning in July, 1832; it contained two sections, one in English, the other in French. Later it was published entirely in English except once a month when a French edition would also come out. Even before the first edition appeared, 900 individuals had subscribed.[7]

The *Shepherd of the Valley* had a strongly defensive cast, not unexpected in the light of contemporary journalism. Anti-Catholic papers of the time called Catholicism "anti-Christianism," "the workings of Satan," "idolatry," "the Roman beast;" Catholics were "vassals of Babylon the Great;" Catholic churches were "houses for the idolatrous ceremonies of Rome;" Catholics "bowed their knees to the Roman beast" and "were confirmed in the workings of Satan." The "Popish system" was not merely "a mass of anti-Christian doctrines, superstitious ceremonies and personal depravity," it went beyond that to be "the friend of mental darkness, the advocate of the worst despotic assumptions, the enemy of all civil and religious freedom . . . and the ruthless enemy of the whole family of man."[8]

The *Shepherd* helped to refute some of the calumnies directed against the Church. It carried on a running feud with the *St. Louis Tract Society.* The editors considered *Tract* No. 255 on "Romanism" especially offensive. They counted eighty-two notorious falsehoods, an average of two on each page.[9]

The opposition soon became aware of the *Shepherd of the Valley.* Further, it saw the hand of the Jesuits behind the publication. *The Christian Watchman,* a Baptist paper published in Boston, wrote:

The Jesuits are making use of every exertion to establish the Romish faith in the valley of the Mississippi and with great success. They have recently established a new paper at Saint Louis called "The Shepherd of the Valley" and circulate it with all diligence. The pastors of the Protestant flocks on the Eastern hills, must furnish us with abundance of Shepherds of the Valley, or the Jesuitical fold will soon enclose all the Sheep of the West.[10]

The Jesuits, especially Father Verhaegen, the president of Saint Louis University, contributed to the *Shepherd of the Valley.* And the Father Visitor of the Missouri Jesuit Mission, Father Peter Kenney, officially urged them to continue to do so.[11] But the articles did not carry by-lines. The writer for *The Christian Watchman* seemed to be using the term "Jesuit" in a way, common in those times, as synonymous with "Catholic."

Bishop Rosati did not place his name above any article. He did not endorse the paper in the columns. But news of diocesan activities appeared in its pages, such as Father Verhaegen's blessing the cornerstone of St. Peter's Church, under commission of the bishop; Bishop Rosati's laying of the cornerstone of the Church of St. Ferdinand's;[12] the confirmation schedule during the succeeding two months; the opening of the Visitation Academy in Kaskaskia;[13] the ordinations of Father John M. St. Cyr[14] and Father Louis Tucker;[15] the announcement that Father Auguste Jeanjean, pastor of Potosi, had been appointed bishop of New Orleans,[16] an honor he was to decline; and Bishop Rosati's departure for the Provincial Council in Baltimore.[17]

The *Shepherd* contained proportionately few local or original contributions, other than news items. It reprinted articles from other Catholic and non-Catholic journals. The editors translated articles from foreign journals. Even the obituary of Archbishop Du Bourg that covered three issues[18] originally appeared in the *Catholic Telegraph* of Cincinnati. The *Shepherd* did not make a single comment or tribute of its own to the memory of Bishop Du Bourg.

A most interesting communication in the *Shepherd* was a defense of the civil and religious rights of the Mormons, a matter that most other papers side-stepped. "Let Catholics, I say," the writer insisted, "imitate the example of . . . Carroll, and proclaim to their Protestant fellow citizens that *no man shall be molested on account of his religious opinions.*"[19]

Under the name of the Western Catholic Association, a group of Catholic laymen banded together in 1833 for "the propagation, defense and support of the Catholic religion in the Western country by all honorable and lawful means in their power."[20] The officers were M. P. LeDuc, president, Patrick Walsh, vice-president, Hugh O'Neil, treasurer, and Wilson Primm, secretary — all well known men of the city. These men set up the association primarily to support the *Shepherd of the Valley.*[21]

They acted at the time of a new threat. Elijah Lovejoy had taught in Saint Louis a few years earlier. He returned to the city from ministerial studies in the East and in November, 1833, launched violent attacks on slavery, drink, and "popery" in the *St. Louis Observer.* Most historians recognize Elijah Lovejoy's opposition to slavery. His death in defense of his printing press at Alton, Illinois, four years later, was to make him the martyr of the Abolition movement. But Lovejoy's hatred of slavery hardly surpassed his ill-will toward Catholicism. Even in an age of intense feelings and outspoken journalism, Lovejoy forgot the basic courtesies to a people who had welcomed him just six years before. His *Observer* condemned practices of the Catholic Church, warned parents against sending their young men to Catholic colleges, and called priests "oppressors and persecutors of mankind."[22] To the credit of the Catholics Lovejoy attacked with his pen, it must be mentioned that they did not react with violence as the pro-slavery men did.

Attacks on the total Catholic body would have been bad enough. Some nativists went farther and tried to split the Catholic people. An unsigned article in the *Southern Religious Telegraph,* a Presbyterian newspaper published in Richmond, Virginia, described the Catholic institutions of Missouri. The writer separated Catholics into a Jesuitical and an anti-Jesuitical party, and concluded: "The prospect is, I think, that between them, the Jesuits and anti-Jesuits, they are likely to have control of education in the state."[23]

So unfair did Bishop Rosati think this charge of hostility between himself and the Jesuits that he wrote a dignified letter, insisting that:

The greatest union has always existed between the members of the Society and myself and the secular priests of my diocese. We live on terms of truly affectionate amity, and linked together by the profession of the same faith, we actually join, as we have done since the arrival of the [Jesuit] Fathers in Missouri, our unwearied efforts for the propagation of our holy religion. If, owing to their literary pursuits and domestic occupations, incumbent on all who are entrusted with the education of large number of pupils, they cannot devote at Saint Louis, a considerable portion of their time to the duties of the sacred ministry, no sinister suspicions should arise from an impossibility of which I am perfectly aware and thoroughly convinced. I sincerely applaud and highly value their exertions for they prove to the public that proportionately to the increase of their numbers they cheerfully extend the sphere of their services which they render to me and to those under my spiritual charge.[24]

Far from being suspicious of Jesuits, Rosati wanted members as bishops of many western dioceses. He recommended Peter Kenney, the official Visitor of the American Jesuits, for the diocese of Cincinnati. And if Kenney were not available, Rosati preferred George Fenwick, the Jesuit president of Georgetown College,[25] He seconded Bishop Bruté's petition to have the Jesuit Nicholas Petit of Saint Mary's College, Kentucky, as coadjutor in Vincennes, "for he excels in piety, learning, eloquence, knowledge of the English and French languages, as also in administrative ability."[26] Rosati was also to include the name of Peter Verhaegen, at the time superior of the Missouri Jesuits, as a possibility to succeed him in Saint Louis. He was to appoint Verhaegen as administrator of the Saint Louis diocese while he traveled outside the diocese.

The Jesuit general, John Roothaan, took the position that his hands were tied by the stringent regulations of Saint Ignatius.[27] Rosati refuted this stand. He wrote:

Is it such a mighty task to keep intact the Society of Jesus that lest one or other of its members be raised to the episcopal dignity, the American churches must pine away for lack of pastors and grow old in their very youth? Are not the religious orders and societies members of the universal Church? Ought they not on occasion make a sacrifice of their private advantage for the common good of the Church? In fine, have they anything to fear from the promotion of their priests to American Churches, which have nothing to offer to the cupidity of man? Not wealth, not honors, not leisure. Not even Ignatius himself, who as long as he lived was aflame with the most ardent zeal for the salvation of souls, the glory of God and the expansion of the Church, would in the condition of things that besets us today be opposed to his followers not merely lending but even spontaneously offering themselves to meet the needs of our churches. If there were available other priests of the secular clergy fitted for a burden that is formidable even for angelic shoulders, the worthy sons of Ignatius would indeed be left in peace.[28]

Rosati was right! His own congregation, like the Sulpicians earlier, made sacrifices for the youthful Church in mid-America that held back its own progress. It was just for him to believe that the Jesuit general should have been more ready to do the same.

The Cathedral of St. Louis in 1852. The building on the right is the rectory. The building on the left housed an orphanage and then a grade school taught by Christian Brothers. (Missouri Historical Society).

Catholic Beginnings in Chicago and Kansas City

Nothing so dramatically indicates the position of Saint Louis in the mid-western Church as two simultaneous and similar events in the year 1833. Among the 150 people living at the southwest corner of Lake Michigan, in the area later to be known as Chicago, some were Catholics of French or Indian stock and a few were converts from Episcopalianism. Under the impression that they were within the bounds of Bishop Rosati's spiritual jurisdiction, these Catholics asked the bishop of Saint Louis for a resident pastor in 1833. Actually, the future area of Chicago had come under the jurisdiction of the bishop of Bardstown in 1808. The bishop of Saint Louis, however, acted as vicar-general for the western half of Illinois, and served other parts of Illinois also.

At the time, fortunately, Bishop Rosati had a capable but as yet unassigned, newly ordained missionary, John I. St. Cyr. On April 17, 1833, Rosati committed the Catholics of Chicago to his care. Rosati wrote Bishop Flaget of Bardstown of the St. Cyr appointment, and stipulated that when the limits of the diocese were fixed, he could recall St. Cyr if a need arose elsewhere.[29]

A native of the Archdiocese of Lyons, John I. St. Cyr had entered the *Grand Seminaire* in Lyons to study philosophy and theology. One of the first clerical recruits secured at this period for the diocese of Saint Louis through the agency of the Association for the Propagation of the Faith, the twenty-eight-year-old seminarian left

France for America in 1831. He finished his seminary studies at St. Mary's in Perry County and was ordained to the priesthood on April 6, 1833 — about the time the people of Chicago were writing Bishop Rosati. Twelve days later, St. Cyr set out from Saint Louis for his new field of labor in northern Illinois. One of his parishioners-to-be, Anson Taylor, had come from Chicago to serve as an escort.[30] On his arrival in Chicago, Father St. Cyr was the guest of Mark Beaubien, the proprietor of the Saugan-ash, the best-known of the town's pioneer hotels. He was to enjoy Mr. Beaubien's hospitality gratis for a year. The new pastor said his first Mass in Chicago on May 5.

A little more than a month after his arrival, on June 4, 1833, Father St. Cyr made his first report to Bishop Rosati on the religious outlook of the new field. The people of Chicago were quite ready to start collecting money for a church. Jean Baptiste Beaubien promised a site for the church. At the moment, however, Pastor St. Cyr himself hardly had money to pay the postage to send the letter to the Bishop.[31]

In September of the same year, Father St. Cyr said Mass for the Potawatomie Indians and their allies, the Chippewa, and the Ottawa. These tribes had signed a treaty with the government and were giving up the remnants of their holdings in Michigan, Indiana, and Illinois for one dollar an acre and a grant of five million acres of land on the left bank of the Missouri River. The first church in Chicago seems to have been built more through the generosity of the Catholic Indians, especially Potawatomies, than the white men. Father St. Cyr said the first Mass in the new church in October, 1833. The people of Chicago had given of their limited resources and the church was still unplastered, but they had made a start.[32] Father St. Cyr traveled extensively, visiting settlements throughout northern Illinois, such as Springfield, Peoria, and Galena. He returned to Saint Louis for the winter.

The following year Rome set up the diocese of Vincennes, which included the area of Chicago. According to the original agreement, Father St. Cyr was to return to Saint Louis at such a time. But Bishop-elect Simon Bruté asked Bishop Rosati to continue sending a priest from Saint Louis. Bruté listed four men, among whom he preferred Father St. Cyr because Chicagoans already knew and esteemed the young priest.[33] Bishop Flaget of Bardstown joined in this appeal. As a result, Bishop Rosati sent Father St. Cyr back to Chicago for another year. He was to stay for several more years, until, on April 17, 1837, Bishop Rosati assigned him to Quincy, Illinois, whence he made periodic excursions to the Catholics of the neighboring counties. Six years later, his original parish of 150 Catholic people was to become the diocese of Chicago.

At the time when Father St. Cyr was going to Chicago, his friend and fellow recruit of the Association for the Propagation of the Faith in Lyons, Father Benedict Roux, founded the first Catholic parish in Kansas City. From the time of his arrival in America, Father Roux had systematically set about learning English. He served successively at the Cathedral in Saint Louis, at the Jesuit parish in St. Charles, and in Dardenne, Missouri.

From the first, Father Roux had wanted to work among the Indian tribes. He had asked Bishop Rosati if he could establish a mission on the Missouri frontier, among the tribes. In November, 1833, the bishop sent Father Roux west — but not to the Indians. Rosati wanted him to serve the Catholic settlements in the western part of the state, not far north of Kansas City. Later Father Roux went to the settlement at the mouth of the Kaw River founded by various of the Chouteau brothers. Members of the Chouteau family were the chief agents in securing the first church in Kansas City.

Father Roux held services for the first time in Kansas City on Sexagesima Sunday, February 2, 1834, but he did not celebrate Mass for the general public until Easter.[34] He worked in the area for one year. After this period he returned to take up work in the Mississippi Valley, as pastor in Kaskaskia, and then as assistant at the Saint Louis Cathedral. After this, he apparently withdrew from the Saint Louis diocese and returned to France.

His name will endure as the first resident pastor of Kansas City. He organized the first Catholic parish, acquired the property for the first Catholic church, and left on record, in letters to his ecclesiastical superior in Saint Louis, the earliest detailed accounts of pioneer religious conditions on the Missouri frontier. For the succeeding eleven years Jesuit Fathers were to continue the work of Father Roux in Kansas City.[35]

During the years that Father St. Cyr worked in Chicago and Father Roux in the Kansas City area, Bishop Rosati sent a succession of priests to the less promising Territory of Arkansas. Three main river settlements made up the mission, the old Arkansas Post, near the junction of the Arkansas and the Mississippi, Pine Bluff, seventy miles northwest, and Little Rock, fifty miles further north, both on the right bank of the Arkansas River.

Unlike the Chicago and Kansas City areas, the Arkansas region, to become a state in 1836, did not lie athwart the path of westward expansion. Further, the Catholics there, mostly *voyageurs* and traders of French background, did not seem overanxious to have a priest permanently among them; and often wagered among themselves on how long a new priest would last in the discouraging area.

In November 1831, Bishop Rosati had sent Father Edmond Saulnier and a young Fleming, Father Peter Beauprez, to the Arkansas Post. They visited settlements along the Arkansas River, including Pine Bluff and Little Rock. Saulnier went on a successful begging tour to Louisiana, and came back with four hundred dollars and plans far beyond the amount of money he had collected or the ability of Arkansas Catholics of the time to carry them through. Both missionaries soon became discouraged. Saulnier returned to Saint Louis in 1832, and Bishop Rosati assigned him to Carondelet. Beauprez left for the diocese of New Orleans.[36]

Undaunted by this failure, Bishop Rosati sent Father Ennemond Dupuy from the seminary at Perryville to the Arkansas Post in October, 1833, the same year that St. Cyr went to Chicago and Roux to Kansas City. Dupuy worked alone in the lower Arkansas Valley for over a year. In the spring of 1835, Bishop Rosati sent as his assistant the newly ordained Father Charles Rolle, a native of the Province of Lorainne in France. Rolle died of illness during his first summer in the territory. Late the following year (1836), Father Dupuy returned to Saint Louis to seek help for Arkansas, recently admitted as the twenty-fifth state of the Union.

Four deacons of the diocese were completing studies at Perryville. Of these, Bishop Rosati chose Peter R. Donnelly for Arkansas. The bishop ordained this first Gaelic-speaking priest of the region, a quiet and reticent man in dealing with people, but quick and active physically. In a short time, Donnelly supplanted Dupuy as head of the Arkansas mission, and Dupuy followed Beauprez to the more favorable spiritual climate of Louisiana.[37] After two years, Donnelly himself found the work unpromising and asked permission to visit his native Ireland. Bishop Rosati relieved him of his duties along the Arkansas. Donnelly did not return to Ireland but accepted the pastorate at St. Peter's in Gravois Township, Saint Louis County, whence he launched many missionary journeys among Irish immigrants along the Meramec River, where he began the parish of St. Patrick's at Armagh.

Bishop Rosati was to send his last missionary team to Arkansas in 1838, two priests of the Archdiocese of Besancon in France, Fathers Joseph Richard-Bole and Augustine Paris, who had volunteered for work in the Saint Louis region. In the same year, three Loretto Sisters from Ste. Genevieve founded St. Mary's Convent School in Pine Bluff.

When Rome came to set up the diocese of Little Rock in 1843, the French priests and Loretto Sisters were to return to Missouri. The Saint Louis effort in Arkansas proved a stop-gap measure. Bishop Andrew Byrne was to begin anew with priests from Ireland.[38]

Cathedral Dedicated

Back in Saint Louis, workmen moved steadily toward the completion of the great Cathedral of the West, a structure of Greek revival architecture. The Leopoldine Foundation sent another 5,000 florins — about $2,400 —

in 1833. Rosati thanked the society and stated frankly that the people of Saint Louis could give only one-tenth of the money necessary for the completion of the structure.[39] In view of the general prosperity of the early thirties, and the individual wealth of several Saint Louis Catholic families, this percentage is surprising. The Leopoldine Foundation sent about $2,600 the following year. In response, Bishop Rosati sent a lengthy report, describing the dedication of the Cathedral and the octave of celebration that followed the ceremony.[40]

The building was one hundred and thirty-six feet in length, eighty-four feet in width, and forty feet in height. The entire facade was of polished stone. Four pillars, twenty-seven feet high and four feet in diameter sustained the portico. It was forty feet long and twelve feet deep. A Latin subscription on the frieze read: "In honor of St. Louis, and dedicated to the one and triune God in the Year of Our Lord 1834." Even in a built-up area it would have been an impressive cathedral. On the western frontier in 1834 its effect was overwhelming.

The bishop set October 26, 1834, as the dedication date, before the builders finished the spire. Rosati invited Bishops Flaget of Bardstown and Purcell of Cincinnati to participate. Rosati also suggested that they use the occasion to consecrate the bishop-elect of Vincennes, Simon Bruté. Diocesan priests came from their far-flung parishes for the ceremonies, the Vincentians from Perryville and their other mission stations, the Jesuits from Florissant and the towns beyond. The three companies of militia in Saint Louis, captained by members of other Christian denominations at the time, volunteered to participate in the ceremony. A military band from Jefferson Barracks, ten miles south of Saint Louis, came in for the occasion.

On the two days before the solemnity, the weather had been bad. A heavy rain and a strong wind led to a fear that the ceremony could not take place. But about midnight on Saturday, the storm passed over, the clouds disappeared, and Saint Louis awoke to a golden resurge of autumn. Catholics as well as non-Catholics attended the ceremony of dedication of the church. Many viewed the day as a civic rather than a strictly religious ceremony. The ceremony began at seven in the morning with two priests, one in French and one in English, alternately explaining the ceremonies. The rich ceremonial ended about three o'clock in the afternoon.

Two days later, on the occasion of the feast of the Apostles Simon and Jude, Bishop Flaget, assisted by Bishop Rosati and Bishop Purcell, consecrated Simon Bruté as bishop of Vincennes. All Saints Day, too, was a great solemnity that week. Finally, on the following Sunday, Bishop Bruté chanted a Solemn Mass and Vespers to close an extraordinary week in the history of the diocese of Saint Louis.

Saint Louisans rejoiced in the possession of a beautiful structure. They could point it out to visitors with a feeling of satisfaction. But at least one citizen demurred. Elijah Lovejoy had many misgivings about the dedication of the Catholic Cathedral. Protestants had taken part in a Catholic ceremony; they had defamed the Sabbath by playing in or listening to a band; they had united church and state by allowing military units to take part.[41] Further, he made these charges in a city marked by a spirit of cooperation between religious faiths!

On the night of April 7 of the following year (1835), a fire burned a large livery stable and the old "cathedral" that served at the time as a warehouse. Bishop Rosati records in his diary that the people of Saint Louis feared for the safety of their new Cathedral.[42] The intense heat broke some of the windows of the new building and caused other damage — not enough, however, to prevent use of the church for religious service. As a result of exposure and anxiety during the fire, Bishop Rosati became seriously ill. Eventually he regained his strength.

On September 22 of the same year, Bishop Rosati held a dinner for those who had cooperated in the building of the church.[43] It should have been a moment of triumph. And it was in this: the most memorable Catholic church of the West had been completed. But a huge cloud stood on the horizon. Three years earlier Bishop Rosati had estimated in a letter to Du Bourg that the Cathedral would cost thirty thousand dollars.[44] Actually, Rosati's carefully kept account books show that the building cost more than twice that much, $63,360.85 to be exact; while his total receipts from all sources had barely amounted to $21,000.[45]

The bishop had not been extravagant in his plans. He had ordered the reconditioning of ninety-two pews from the old church; carpenters built one hundred and eight new ones to give the building a total seating capacity of almost one thousand. Rosati gave up his dream of marble altars and stained glass windows in the face of economic necessity. He brought over the paintings from the old church. He kept business-like records of all transactions.

The bishop had underestimated the cost of the project; but he overestimated even more dramatically the willingness of the Saint Louis Catholics to contribute. While Rosati could give six hundred dollars of his limited personal estate, and Father Sibourd of New Orleans seven hundred, only four lay people gave over a hundred dollars. Bernard Pratte, Bryan Mullanphy, and Madame Le Compte each gave three hundred. Ann Biddle gave one hundred and twenty-five dollars. And later Madame Le Compte bequeathed an additional $1,100.[46] The bishop had expected pew rental to reach fifteen thousand. Instead it barely went to three thousand.

To add to his difficulties, some individuals misrepresented his dinner for the workers on the Cathedral as a banquet worthy of a Renaissance bishop. This story crossed the Atlantic to the office of the Association for the Propagation of the Faith in Lyons and seems to have reached Vienna. During 1835 and 1836, the Leopoldine Foundation sent no gifts to the Saint Louis diocese.[47]

"I am at a loss as to the means of having my letters reach the Leopoldine Institution," Rosati wrote to Bishop Blanc in August 1836. "I have written repeatedly, yet no answer has ever come . . . . It was reported in Lyons that I need no help, live in a house whose appointments are shockingly luxurious, and keep for myself all the money sent."[48]

Rosati answered these charges. "There is not a carpenter in Saint Louis whose furniture is not better than mine. I used to have a horse and buggy for my trips; three years ago I sold both of them."[49] He spoke of the frugality of his table. He had invited guests, other than priests, only on the occasion of the dinner for the Cathedral workers. He concluded: "As to sharing the help received, I can assure you that there has not been a church started, or an establishment begun, which did not receive a portion of the money contributed by the charity of the faithful of Europe."[50]

Chapter 10

Religious Institutes Develop

The Vincentians

The general assembly of the Congregation of the Mission, meeting in Paris in 1835, brought changes that seemed to threaten some hard earned successes of the Saint Louis diocese. The assembly carefully examined a report on the condition of the American mission written by Father John Odin, president of Saint Mary's College at Perryville. He had two misgivings: one, the situation of priests on remote missions; and two, certain arrangements at Saint Mary's College and Seminary.

At the time individual priests resided alone in distant and isolated parishes. Odin suggested that the missionaries live in central mission house, where three or four priests and a lay brother might lead a common life in conformity to the rules and constitution of the Congregation. Further, to insure a renewal of community spirit, Odin recommended that John Timon be made superior, or "Visitor" in Vincentian terminology, in place of theologian John Tornatore, who lacked administrative skill and fluency in English.

At Perryville, those seminarians who were not in the position to pay their own tuition taught in the lay college to defray their expenses — a system common in America at that time. It had these disadvantages: first, many seminarians were not qualified to teach; and second, many more were not interested in the work. Further, the Vincentian community was not able to provide a sufficient number of priests to keep the faculty of the college at a high standard. Thus the general assembly decided to close the college and to require the bishop of the diocese to pay a stated fee for each diocesan student preparing for the priesthood.[1]

The general assembly agreed with Father Odin's recommendations. It named Father Timon Visitor and superior of the House of Saint Mary of the Barrens, and Father Joseph Paquin assistant.[2] It ordered the suppression of the college, with the proviso that the Missouri Vincentians could reopen it in the future once conditions became more favorable. The diocesan seminary could continue on condition that the bishop would pay an annual sum for the education and lodging of each seminarian. The seminary of the community and the diocesan seminary were to be lodged in separate buildings, although they could use the same classrooms, church, and dining hall. The American superior had to keep a more realistic relationship between the number of missionaries and the missions accepted.

Bishop Rosati had anticipated some of these decisions, but he had not been consulted. The individual decisions had merit in themselves, but the total impact was overpowering. The copy of the decrees that reached him on November 7, 1835, coming so soon after the death of his good friend, Leo De Neckere, overwhelmed him. For the first time he spoke of offering his resignation to the Holy Father.[3] One month later, the cardinal prefect of Propaganda informed Rosati that the sacred congregation had not been pleased with the dispositions of the general assembly, and asked him what he proposed to do.[4]

In a lengthy letter to Jean Baptiste Nozo, the superior general of the Congregation of the Mission, Bishop Rosati expressed his willingness to accept the decision of the assembly as regards the missions. As long as the priests did not abandon the parishes, he agreed to let them live in centrally located rectories and concentrate their work in Perryville, Ste. Genevieve, Old Mines, and Cape Girardeau.

Rosati thought that the suppression of the college, however, would be a detriment both to the diocese and to the Vincentians themselves. The college was a vital adjunct to the diocese. It provided a well-instructed Catholic laity and yielded vocations that otherwise might have been lost. To suppress it would be utterly unwise. The enrollment had taken a leap upward in the meantime.

With Father Timon at the head, the seminary could look to a more prosperous future. Rosati recalled the expenditures that he and Bishop Du Bourg had made on behalf of the seminary. But he simply could not pay 600 francs for each seminarian's tuition.

Rosati next discussed another aspect of his relationship with the congregation. Some Vincentians had suggested that Rosati in reality cared little for the college. After all, at the Baltimore council, Rosati had recommended Timon for a bishopric. Rosati had an explanation of this action.

In 1835 Bishop Simon Bruté had asked for Timon as his coadjutor in Vincennes, and Bishop John Dubois, also a Sulpician, had wanted him in New York.[5] Rosati had written to the cardinal prefect of the congregation for the Propagation of the Faith in Rome at the time. He insisted that Timon was indispensable to the progress of the faith in the Saint Louis diocese. He had won back to their duties more lapsed Catholics, and received into the Church more converts than all the other priests laboring in the diocese combined.[6]

Rosati wrote to the Vincentian superior general in Paris, explaining that he had sought Timon as his coadjutor in Saint Louis precisely to keep him in the valuable missionary work he was doing.[7] This letter had its part in forestalling the full implementation of the decrees of the Vincentian assembly. Under the organizational skill of Father Timon, the college, seminary, and the entire Vincentian mission effort moved ahead with determination. Before the end of 1836, Father Odin wrote that conditions in Missouri had already improved, invalidating much of his original report.[8]

As a result, the superior general modified the former regulations and settled on these: those seminarians who did not want to teach in the college did not have to do so; the number of diocesan students supported by the college would be kept at a just proportion; a separation would be maintained between the community seminary and the college; and at least two priests and one lay brother would reside in each of the mission houses.[9]

Within two years of his appointment as Visitor, Timon put real organization into the Congregation of the Mission in America, clarifying the work of the college and seminary, and strengthening the parish centers. He made a trip to Europe in 1837, the first of four, to recruit personnel. Ultimately over one hundred men, priests, clerics, and Brothers, were to answer his challenge and cross the ocean to work on the American mission.[10] In 1838, he set up the core of a cluster of missions on the Upper Illinois River around the settlement of La Salle, organized the parish of Saint Vincent's at Cape Girardeau, and accepted three foundations for the Congregation of the Missions in Louisiana.[11]

Saint Louis University in the Mid-1830's

Saint Louis College grew rapidly during its early years. Of the original one hundred and fifty students listed in the 1829 catalog, all but three came from Saint Louis and vicinity. By January 1832, local scholars still counted about eighty percent of the registration. Then Father Van de Velde started canvassing the Louisiana parishes. During the school year 1832-33, fifty-four students came from Louisiana, while only forty-nine came from Saint Louis and eight from the surrounding area. In the following year Louisiana numbered one hundred and thirteen, Saint Louis and vicinity fifty-four, other states six, and Mexico one.[12] Pastors in the Bayou area offered continual assistance in acquainting their parishioners with the educational advantages in Saint Louis. Two agents represented the university in the New Orleans area.[13]

The university trustees held one of the most fruitful meetings in September, 1835. They passed two resolutions: one to petition the United States government through Senator Thomas Hart Benton for a grant of public land as an educational endowment; the second, to consult with certain doctors of the city about the establishment of a medical faculty.[14]

Father Verhaegen opened negotiations with Catholic doctors in the city that looked toward the formation of a medical faculty. The Saint Louis Medical Society came into existence early in 1836. At its September 17 meeting of that year, the secretary read a letter of Father Verhaegen on the proposal.[15] The doctors were pleased with the liberal proposal of Father Verhaegen. They voted to proceed with plans.

Many distinguished citizens served on the board of trustees for the medical department to be set up at Saint Louis University: Dr. B. G. Farrar, the Reverend William Greenleaf Eliot, who was to found Washington University and its affiliated institutions, philanthropist John O'Fallon, General William H. Ashley of Rocky Mountain fur trade fame, and others. The board met to select a faculty that included the noted Dr. William Beaumont, army surgeon whose studies of digestion had won him high acclaim. After these initial efforts, there was no follow-through. Six years were to elapse before the medical college actually got underway.

During that year (1836) Edmund Flagg, a widely-read travel-writer, visited Saint Louis University. He described the school in his book, *The Far West,* published in New York two years later:

In the western suburbs of the city, upon an eminence, stand the buildings of the Saint Louis University, handsome structures of brick. The institution is conducted by Jesuits, and most of the higher branches of learning are taught....The chapel of the institution is a large, airy room, hung with antique and valuable paintings . . . . The library embraces almost twelve hundred volumes, mostly in the French language.... Most of the pupils of the institution are French, and they are gathered from all quarters of the South and West; a great number of them are from Louisiana, sons of the planters.[16]

An early sketch of the university had described the site at Ninth and Washington as "in a secluded position in the western suburb of the city, airy and salubrious."[17] In the prosperous days of President Andrew Jackson, however, numerous buildings rose in the vicinity of the university. Lots in the area sold at high prices.

The trustees of the university found a new prospective campus on the ridge north of the city near the homes of Colonel John O'Fallon and other prominent citizens. It purchased the Clark estate adjoining O'Fallon's. But the panic of the following year (1837) was to halt the rapid expansion of business throughout the nation, ending the hope of a satisfactory sale of the original college property. The trustees delayed the plans to move. The temporary·delay proved permanent. The university was never to move to the north side area.

In his efforts to get a national land grant in favor of Saint Louis University, Senator Benton finally brought his bill to discussion in the Senate on June 5, 1838. Two precedents already existed for aiding private colleges and universities, even those with religious affiliations. The Senate, however, voted to table the motion — an action equivalent to rejection.[18]

The close association of the university with the flow of life in the city stands out clearly in the *Personal Recollections* of Mayor John Darby. He wrote of the many times he dined with the Fathers on the occasions of visits of such guests as Bishop Rosati, Senator Benton, and the Belgian minister to the United States.[19]

Every prominent visitor to the city stopped at the university in those early years. Senator Daniel Webster addressed the student body when he came west on a political jaunt. Bishop Simon Bruté of Vincennes visited the school in March of 1838, and Lieutenant Robert E. Lee of Jefferson Barracks, in 1839. Later visitors included General John Charles Fremont, Father Peter Paul Lafevere, soon to be bishop of Detroit, Bishop John Baptist Purcell of Cincinnati, Senator Henry Clay, and President Martin Van Buren who came to Saint Louis shortly after completing his term in the White House. The most distinguished European visitor in the early years was the English novelist Charles Dickens who spoke in neutral terms of the college even though he wrote negatively about most things in the U.S. in his book *American Notes.*[20]

Sisters of St. Joseph

A combination of circumstances worked together to bring about the first establishment of the Sisters of St. Joseph in the new world. A wealthy French woman, the Countess de la Rochejacquelin, had great admiration for Mother St. John Fontbonne, superior of the Sisters of St. Joseph. The countess had hoped to participate in the good works of the Sisters by financing new foundations in France. She was also interested in the Society for the Propagation of the Faith. At that time Father Charles

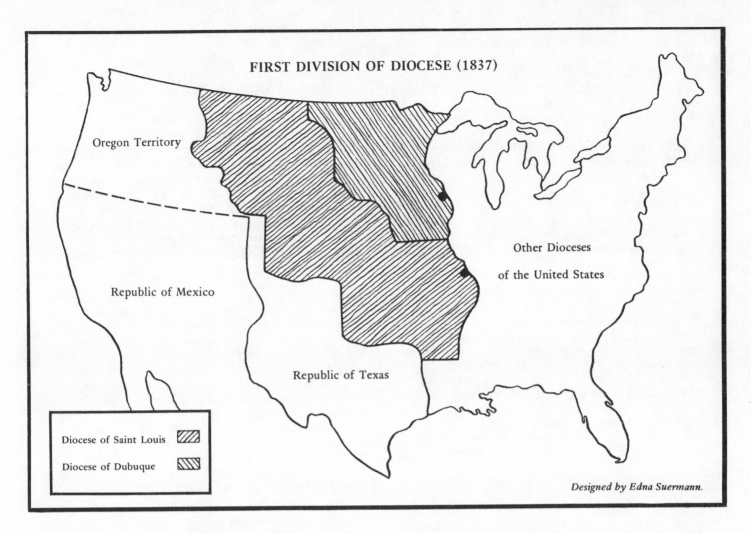

FIRST DIVISION OF DIOCESE (1837)

Oregon Territory

Republic of Mexico

Republic of Texas

Other Dioceses
of the United States

Diocese of Saint Louis

Diocese of Dubuque

Designed by Edna Suermann.

Cholleton, an active member of the society, served as Bishop Rosati's vicar in France. He represented the interests of the Saint Louis diocese to the society and served as spiritual director of the Sisters of St. Joseph.[21] The countess read about the needs of the church in the Mississippi Valley in the *Annales* of the society. She was anxious to assist in the establishment of a foundation of the Sisters of St. Joseph in the distant missions of Missouri.[22]

In the year 1835, Bishop Rosati had appealed to Father Cholleton for a small company of Sisters to undertake the direction of an institute for the deaf he hoped to set up with the aid of the United States government. The bishop planned that this institute be established according to the system of Abbe Secard, a program followed by several religious communities of women in France at the time.[23]

Only one religious community in the diocese of Lyons taught deaf children in those days — the Sisters of St. Charles. Unable to secure any of these teachers for the diocese of Saint Louis, Father Cholleton had recommended that Mother St. John Fontbonne assign several Josephites to learn the methods of the Sisters of St. Charles as a preparation for a mission to America. Mother St. John saw difficulties, but had hopes of undertaking missions in the new world. Countess de la Rochejacquelin agreed to finance the journey of the Sisters to mid-America. The countess wrote directly to Bishop Rosati expressing her desire to send six Sisters of St. Joseph to North America to work among the Indians and the American families.[24]

At this time, Father John Odin, C.M., was visiting Lyons. The Vincentian shared Father Cholleton's enthusiasm for the proposed mission and communicated the offer to Bishop Rosati in Saint Louis. Bishop Du Bourg would have approved the plans immediately. Rosati, however, had far greater concern for the practical aspects of lodging and sustenance; and so studied the matter carefully. Eventually he informed Mother St. John Fontbonne of his delight at the prospect of obtaining the Sisters for his diocese. He hoped Mother St. John would assign two sisters to work with the deaf.

Shortly afterward, Mother St. John Fontbonne announced her plan for the mission in the new world. She accepted six volunteers, among them two of her own nieces. Father Cholleton chose one of the nieces, Febronie Fontbonne, as superior of the missionary group. Father James Fontbonne, brother of Sisters Febronie and Delphine, who had volunteered earlier for the Missouri mission, became spiritual director of the group. Besides the first band of six, Sister Celestine Pommerel, and postulant Julie Fournier went to the school at Saint Etienne to take special training in deaf education. They would follow to America at a later date.

After a hurricane-touched voyage, the six Sisters reached New Orleans March 5, 1836. Bishop Rosati met them and arranged for them to stay with the Ursuline Sisters. After two weeks in New Orleans, the little party boarded the river steamboat "George Collier" in the company of Bishop Rosati and Father John Timon, C.M. They reached Saint Louis on March 25, 1836. The Sisters visited the Cathedral and then took up temporary residence at the hospital of the Sisters of Charity. Three nuns, Delphine (Fontbonne), Felicité, and Philomene were destined to go to Carondelet, a few miles south of Saint Louis. Until such a time as their residence would be ready for them, they devoted themselves to the study of English.[25]

Though Carondelet came to be the cradle of the Josephites in the United States, the Illinois-bank village of Cahokia turned out to be the scene of their first missionary labors. Directly across the river from Saint Louis, this predominantly French-Canadian village was a fairly prosperous and industrious farming community. The Cahokians, under the direction of their zealous pastor, Father Peter Doutreluigne, C.M., had readied a two-story frame house in the center of the village for the Sisters. On April 7, 1836, accompanied by Bishop Rosati and Father Fontbonne, the three pioneer teachers, Mother Febronie Fontbonne, Sister Febronie Chapellon, and Sister St. Protais Deboille, left by boat for Cahokia. On reaching the shore they found a large assembly of villagers waiting to welcome them. A few days after their arrival, the Sisters opened the school with an enrollment of thirty pupils. The friendly and appreciative villagers spoke French. The prospects seemed bright.

The swampy conditions of the area, however, impaired the health of many who lived there. Father Matthew Condamine, the successor to Father Doutreluigne, was in Cahokia only a few months when he contracted a fatal fever and died on August 8, 1836. The Sisters were so ill at the time that they could not attend his funeral. Despite these adversities, the school prospered. The Sisters had excellent rapport with the people. During the pastorate of Father Regis Loisel, the school was enlarged the following year (1837).

The bluffs of Carondelet overlooked the bottomland on the far side of the river where Cahokia stood. The people in Carondelet were not as prosperous as their neighbors in the farming community on the bottomland, as their town's nickname "Empty Pockets" long had indicated. They lived in log cabins, earned their livelihood chiefly by wood cutting, and showed little interest in either religion or education.

The Sisters of St. Joseph went there in the fall of 1836. They lived in a small cottage built three years before to house the Sisters of Charity and a group of orphans, now in a new orphanage in Saint Louis. The pastor of Our Lady of Mt. Carmel parish, Father Edmund Saulnier, formerly of the Saint Louis Cathedral, told the Sisters frankly that he was in no financial position to assist them. What little he had, he would share with them. They would have to visit the families and ask for the food they needed.

The three young Sisters had come from comfortable homes in a well-established society. They had spent most of their lives in Lyons, one of the most prosperous cities of Europe. They had hoped to labor among the Indians. Instead they settled among a listless people, not enlightened in their faith and not too much concerned.

In spite of the more healthful physical surroundings of Carondelet, this group of Josephites was not to find life as smooth as their Sisters across the river. This stemmed from two added causes, the Jansenistic outlook of Father James and Mother Delphine Fontbonne, and disputes between Father Fontbonne and Father Saulnier in matters of jurisdiction over the work of the Sisters. Father Saulnier felt that Father Fontbonne was interfering with his work as pastor, and that the convent was too small to require a spiritual director. Father Saulnier came to a just judgment that Mother Delphine "required from the Sisters more than God Himself requires from his creatures."[26]

In the meantime, Sisters Celestine Pommerel and Julie Fournier, the two trainees in deaf education, arrived in Saint Louis. In the fall of 1837 they began classes for four deaf girls. During the following summer, Bishop Rosati interested the Missouri legislature in his plans for the education of the deaf. In February, 1839, the government of Missouri granted funds for the annual tuition of those pupils who were citizens of the state and had spent six months in the school.[27] This arrangement was to last until the opening of a state school eleven years later. The education of the deaf was to remain a prime apostolate of the Sisters of St. Joseph in the Saint Louis region.

In an awkward attempt to equalize the burdens of the Sisters on both sides of the river, Father Fontbonne decided to remove from Cahokia his more popular sister, Febronie, and have her replaced by his younger sister and fellow-Jansenist, Delphine. That would have made both groups equally unhappy. His two sisters obeyed. But consternation hit the community and he withdrew the decision. Affable Mother Febronie decided that she might ease the situation by leaving America. After deliberation she decided to return to France with her devoted friend Sister Febronie Chapellon. These two early missionaries, incidentally, were never to return to America but lived and worked for almost a half a century in their native France. In 1838 severe Sister Delphine resigned as superior at Carondelet, and went to teach in Cahokia. Bishop Rosati named Mother Celestine Pommerel to succeed her.[28] By this time the community in America consisted of eight professed members and three novices. At last it seemed to be moving on a sure-footed path.

The Third Provincial Council (1837)

Thirty-six year old Archbishop Samuel Eccleston, a native of Maryland, who had succeeded Archbishop Whitfield a year after the previous council, called the Third Provincial Council of Baltimore for 1837. The hierarchy of that time consisted of Archbishop Eccleston and thirteen bishops, John England of Charleston, Joseph Rosati, C.M., of Saint Louis, Benedict Joseph Fenwick, S.J., of Boston, John Dubois, S.S., of New York, Francis P. Kenrick of Philadelphia, John Baptist Purcell of Cincinnati, Frederick Rese of Detroit, Benedict Joseph Flaget, S.S., of Bardstown, his coadjutor, Guy Ignatius Chabrat, S.S., Simon Bruté, S.S., of Vincennes, William Clancy, coadjutor to Bishop England in Charleston, John Baptist David, S.S., retired coadjutor of Bardstown, Michael Portier of Mobile, and Antoine Blanc of New Orleans. Nine of these attended the council. Bishop Dubois of New York declined to take part but sent Father Felix Varela as his representative. Bishop Rese of Detroit resigned during the council itself. Bishop Flaget was in Europe at the time. Bishops David and Portier were unable to be present.

Among the five provincial superiors and college presidents invited to participate in the deliberations was Father Peter J. Verhaegen, S.J., of Saint Louis, superior of the Missouri Jesuits. Father Regis Loisel accompanied Bishop Rosati as his consulting theologian. Bishop Bruté asked Father Peter Richard Kenrick of Philadelphia, the brother of Bishop Kenrick, to be his consulting theologian. Bishop Rosati met the younger Kenrick at this time.

The Fathers of the council took a special note of the intensity of anti-Catholic activity that had burst forth in the previous four years since the last council: the attack on the Leopoldine Society by Samuel F. B. Morse, the burning of the Ursuline Convent at Charlestown, Massachusetts, and the publication of a vicious and salacious anti-Catholic literature, particularly the *Awful Disclosures of Maria Monk,* in 1836.

The bishops issued a remarkable pastoral letter on April 22, 1837. They denounced the persecution of Catholics, called for equal justice under the law, especially from the negligent legislature of Massachusetts, and pointed out clearly that while the Catholics in the United States owed no *religious* allegiance to any state in the union or to its general government, they likewise owed no *civil* allegiance to any but the several states where Catholics resided and to the general government of the United States.

The council sent to Rome for approval the manual of the church ceremonies compiled by Bishop Rosati. It recommended the establishment of three new sees, Natchez in Mississippi, Nashville in Tennessee, and Dubuque in Iowa.[29] The diocese of Dubuque, the first of many subdivisions of the huge area that originally constituted the diocese of Saint Louis, covered the land between the Mississippi and Missouri Rivers from the state of Missouri to the Canadian border. Iowa, an organized territory for only one year at that time, lay in the path of expanding westward immigration and offered rich land for immigrants.

The newly appointed bishop of Dubuque, Father Mathias Loras, vicar-general of Mobile and president of Springhill College, visited Europe at the suggestion of Bishop Rosati to recruit personnel for his territory.[30] He hoped to send his new recruits to St. Mary's at Perryville for their final training in English and pastoral theology.[31] In late November, 1838, Bishop Loras and an outstanding French priest, Father Joseph Cretin, destined to become bishop of St. Paul, arrived in Saint Louis by steamboat from Pittsburg. Bishop Rosati greeted his new colleagues most cordially.

The onset of winter prevented further travel northward. Bishop Loras and Father Cretin assisted Bishop Rosati and the priests of the region in their ministries. The two visiting clergymen spent much of their time ministering to the people of Carondelet. Father Cretin visited the parish of Harrisonville in Illinois; and Bishop Loras gave a mission in Cahokia. The Creole populations welcomed the two French priests everywhere they went.[32]

In early spring the Dominican missionary, Father Samuel Mazzuchelli, the only priest working in the diocese of Dubuque, took the first steamboat to Saint Louis to welcome his new bishop. Disembarking at the city, he and Bishop Rosati rode out to Carondelet to see Bishop Loras.[33] It was not until April that the Dubuque-bound party was able to leave for the north. Bishop Loras agreed to care for the Catholics in the adjacent areas of Wisconsin and Illinois for a time, even though they did not belong to his diocese.

St. Philippine Duchesne taught white and Osage girls at her convent in Florissant. (John Wm. Nagel, Photograph)

St. Philippine Duchesne fulfilled a life-long wish to work with the Native Americans. Potawatomi braves welcome her to their reserve in Kansas Territory.

Chapter 11

Missions in a Melting Pot

German Catholics in City and Country

The parish of Saint Louis had long had its language problems. The English-speaking people identified themselves as "Americans." They thought of the founding families as "French." Thus the Creoles had to face a "stranger in their own land" attitude on the part of many new-comers, both Protestant and Catholic. But they did have a sense of status from having been there first, and in the case of some, from their business successes.

The new-coming Germans from Westphalia, Paderborn, and the Rhineland, had no such status. They were foreigners seeking citizenship, generally poor people beginning to work their way up the financial ladder. They spoke a foreign language and usually found that their attempts at English merely provoked laughter. They were to face a cross-fire of opposition: hostility from the non-Germans because they were German; hostility from their fellow Germans because they were Catholics. Sometimes they too tenaciously clung to Germanisms long after it was wise.

Instead of a dual language problem, Bishop Rosati now faced a triple difficulty. Fortunately, Father Joseph Anthony Lutz, a Baden-born, but French-educated and oriented priest, had come to the United States in November, 1826, at the request of Father Francois Niel. An exuberant man with a zeal not matched by physical energy, he had hopes of working on the Indian missions. He did missionize the Kansa Indians for a time. On his arrival in Saint Louis, he could not ride a horse, or speak English. But he learned to do both. In spite of the fact that he had received his education in France and was ordained for the Archdiocese of Paris, he did not really speak French well. He suffered recurrent illness, but proved himself a devoted and faithful priest.[1]

In the 1830's Father Lutz served the Cathedral parish. At first, the bishop granted the Germans the privilege of having the eight o'clock Mass every Sunday with a sermon in their native language. This hour proved difficult. As a result, in January, 1834, Bishop Rosati set aside for the use of the Germans the little building that had formerly housed the Saint Louis Academy in the days of Bishop Du Bourg and later had been a chapel for Negro Catholics. Father Lutz celebrated Mass every Sunday for the German-speaking people. He preached to them in their native tongue. At two in the afternoon he taught Catechism to the children in both German and English.

When fire destroyed this chapel in 1835, the German worshipers used the Cathedral for Mass on Sunday morning. In that same year, Father Lutz had welcomed a former classmate from Europe, the Belgian Jesuit with an unpronounceable name, Helias D'Huddeghem. Born in Ghent, Belgium, in 1796, a descendant of one of the distinguished families of the country, Father Helias — as people came to call him in Missouri — had worked for a time in Switzerland, where he learned German and held important positions. He left for the American mission in 1833 and arrived in Saint Louis in August, 1835. Even before Father Helias reported to his own community on Ninth and Washington, Father Lutz took him to the Cathedral rectory to meet Bishop Rosati. They discussed the needs of the German Catholics in the city. Bishop Rosati hoped that Father Helias could give some attention to this work. Not long afterwards the newcomer began to hold services for the northside Germans in St. Aloysius Chapel of Saint Louis University.

At the beginning of 1837, Father Joseph H. Fischer arrived to help Father Lutz, and again the southside Germans attended Sunday Mass at the Cathedral.

When Bishop Rosati received another gift from the Leopoldine Foundation in the spring of 1837 — the first since 1834 — he reported again on his diocese. His territory numbered eighteen diocesan priests, twenty Jesuits, fourteen Vincentians, and thirty-two candidates for the priesthood. The number of Catholics — German, Irish, French, American — grew steadily. He had two German priests with him at the Cathedral; eighteen other priests who spoke German worked elsewhere in the diocese.[2] Less than a year later he reported continued progress, and brought to the attention of the foundation the advantages the Midwest offered to the immigrant.[3] On July 21, 1838, he acknowledged another gift of four thousand florins that went to help defray the debt on the Cathedral. The city now had two thousand German Catholics, the bishop estimated. Three priests at the Cathedral spoke German. The Jesuits at Saint Louis and St. Charles were either German or understood the language. Parishes at Ste. Genevieve and Westphalia in Missouri and Quincy and Teutonia (later called Paderborn) in Illinois, had German pastors.[4]

Buoyed up by the fact that Bishop Rosati had sent Father August Brickwedde to Quincy as resident pastor at the request of the German population there, the Saint Louis Germans hoped to have a parish of their own. Bishop Rosati bought a piece of ground and laid plans for a church for the southside Germans. Unfortunately, the property stood on a peninsula, surrounded on the south, east, and west by arms of Chouteau Pond. Neither Father Fischer nor his lay helpers succeeded in collecting money for the new church because the site was inaccessible for the German congregation who lived south of the lake. German practicality, plus the shortage of funds following the Panic of 1837, stopped the project.[5]

While plans for parochial organization reached a standstill in the city, German Catholics in Illinois and Missouri counties moved ahead. While other bishops, such as Benedict Fenwick in Boston and, in the next decade, Mathias Loras of Dubuque, personally promoted colonization projects of their dioceses, Bishop Rosati encouraged immigration to Missouri through his letters and correspondence with the Leopoldine Association in Vienna. The region of Saint Louis had much to offer Catholic immigrants from Europe: freedom, opportunity, rich land, and the basic organization of Catholic life. Besides these positive factors, nativism in other parts of the United States drove some Catholics to the diocese. At least so Bishop Fenwick of Boston thought when he wrote to Bishop Rosati in 1837: "The persecuting spirit that prevails here is driving all our best Catholics to your Missouri."[6]

Even though the diocese did not officially sponsor immigration societies, groups of Catholics, especially northwest Germans, mutually promoted immigration. And Bishop Rosati offered the support of religious ministrations.

German Catholics from Westphalia and Hanover began to come in large numbers to Clinton County, Illinois, about forty miles east of Saint Louis, in the mid 1830's. The first two, Ferdinand Boehne and Friedrich Hemann, liked the area along Shoal Creek, especially because it resembled their native country near Osnabrück in Hanover. They decided to buy farms in that area. The two men notified fellow immigrants in Saint Louis and friends and relatives in the old country of their intention of starting a German Catholic colony on the rich prairie land. By 1837 about fifty people had joined them in the area.

In the beginning, the settlers had to go to Saint Louis to fulfill their Easter duty; but in the spring of 1837 they held a meeting to discuss the possibility of securing a German priest to make a regular visit to their colony. Ferdinand Boehne and a newcomer, Frank H. Schroeder, went to see Bishop Rosati. The bishop promised to send them Father Charles Meyer who was living in the vicinity of Belleville, just west of Clinton County. Boehne visited him and secured a promise that the priest would come on the third Sunday after Easter.

Father Meyer stayed for three days in Clinton County, conducted a mission in the houses of Boehne and Hemann, officiated at the baptism of two children and married two couples among whom was the original settler, Ferdinand Boehne. For some time after this, Father Meyer made regular monthly visits of three days. During the summer of 1837 the colonists obtained money for a church and purchased 120 acres of land. After debates on the name to be given the settlement, all finally agreed on "Germantown." The settlers then sub-divided the excess acreage that they had purchased and laid out town lots around the church section. Thus they were able to keep 80 acres for the church, rectory, and cemetery and still to pay their original investment. More settlers arrived in 1838. Unfortunately, Father Meyer received a new pastorate at Teutonia, Illinois, a town too far away to allow him to serve the needs of the residents of "Germantown."[7]

Boehne and Schroeder again went to see the bishop to ask for a resident priest. Bishop Rosati recorded in his diary during October, 1838, that sixty families in Clinton County wanted to build a church in honor of St. Boniface.[8] During the following year, Bishop Rosati appointed German-born Father Henry Fortmann the first pastor at Germantown. Fortmann had studied at Perryville, been ordained in November, 1837, and had taken care of the German congregation at Apple Creek in southeast Missouri for a while. Before the end of August, 1839, he took up residence in Germantown.

Besides his work in Clinton County, Father Fortmann occasionally visited a group of prosperous Swiss Catholics who had settled earlier in the decade in neighboring Madison County, and invited many of their countrymen to locate in the region. They had laid out the town of Highland in 1836. Gradually other Swiss, Badeners, and Bavarians joined them to build a thriving community. Father Fortmann and other traveling missionaries said Mass from time to time in private homes. He organized St. Paul's parish that eventually became the center of nine parishes within a radius of ten miles.[9]

Clinton County and the southeast corner of adjacent Madison County was to remain one of the most Catholic rural sections in the state of Illinois.

In Missouri during the same decade, extensive Catholic colonization also took place on the south bank of the Missouri River, in the area seventy to ninety miles west of Saint Louis, where the Gasconade and Osage rivers flow into the Missouri. German immigrants formed several settlements, the most important being Westphalia. These immigrants had passed through Saint Louis; while there, the Jesuits ministered to their spiritual needs. Following upon this, Jesuit missionary, Christian Hoecken, visited the Westphalians in the summer of 1835. In the autumn of 1837 Father Peter Verhaegen, superior of the Jesuit Mission of Missouri, visited Westphalia on a missionary journey. He reported to Bishop Rosati the presence of almost fifty Catholic families in the colony.[10] Many of these people surpassed the average contemporary immigrant in education and background. Father Verhaegen had long hoped to establish a Jesuit residence among them. With the approbation of Bishop Rosati, Verhaegen sent a priest and coadjutor brother to Westphalia on April 23, 1838, to set up a central mission station for many satellites eventually to develop in a wide area.

The Belgian Father Helias organized the central Missouri Mission. Since his arrival in the Missouri metropolis in August, 1835, he had taught at Saint Louis University and marshalled the German Catholics of near northside Saint Louis into what was to become Saint Joseph's parish. Central Missouri became the area of his finest apostolate.*

Practical man that he was, Father Helias decided to establish agricultural colonies in various other settlements under his charge. Before the end of 1838, one hundred families had gathered in and around New Westphalia. A friend of Father Helias, Father James Busschots, S.J., who had come with him from Havre to America, arrived in central Missouri. On October 14, 1838, Bishop Rosati made his first visit to the settlement, blessing the church, and confirming thirty-five members of the parish.[11] Many satellite missions grew up in this area which was to remain one of two strongly Catholic sections of out-state Missouri.

"Frenchtown"

The Creole settlers who clustered in "Frenchtown," an area about fifteen blocks south of the Cathedral and five or six blocks west of the river, had long wanted a church of their own. Bishop Rosati believed that such a church could relieve the congestion at the Cathedral and serve the neighborhood.

In 1836, Madame Julie Soulard, widow of Antoine

---

*A school, Helias High in Jefferson City, Missouri, today recalls his memory.

The lunette on the west wall of the Great Cathedral memorializes missionaries in three centuries: Jacques Marquette in the 17th, Peter De Smet in the 19th and the archdiocesan team in 20th century Bolivia. One hundred years before the founding of St. Louis, Father Jacques Marquette began the first mission in the area on the Illinois River. When the missionary died of typhoid fever at the age of 38, his fellow explorer, Jacques Largillier, became a religious brother and continued the mission. He moved with the tribe to the River des Peres and later to Kaskaskia. In 1840 Father Peter John De Smet answered the call of the Salish to go to their Montana home and preach the Gospel. In 1956, the Archdiocese of St. Louis began a mission in La Paz, Bolivia. (John Wm. Nagel, Photograph)

Soulard, decided to subdivide the family property, then known as "Soulard's First Addition." The property stood between Park Avenue and Lesperance Street (later to become Lafayette Avenue). In order to insure the erection of a church, Madame Soulard reserved two lots for that purpose. On September 6, 1838, Bishop Rosati accepted the plot, three hundred by one hundred and fifty feet in size.[12] At the same time he purchased an adjoining plot of the same size for four thousand five hundred dollars; and contracted with Hugh O'Neil, a local businessman, to erect ten houses that he could rent for purposes of revenue.

Bishop Rosati planned a Catholic complex to include church and seminary. The rental revenues from the ten houses would, he hoped, support twelve seminarians and three or four Vincentian Fathers who cared for the parish and taught in the seminary.[13] This new arrangement had many advantages. The bishop could care for the needs of the residents of Frenchtown. He could obviate the dif

ficulties that had come up in trying to keep the diocesan seminary in Perryville. He would have his major seminary in his see city. He seemingly had set up a means of financing the education of his seminarians.

Rosati drew up plans for the new Holy Trinity Church. In the spring, the contractor began construction. On Sunday, May 5, 1839, five thousand people assembled to witness the laying of the cornerstone. Father Timon preached a sermon in English.[14]

The Panic of 1837 had struck the nation shortly after Madame Soulard had subdivided her property. The financial crisis continued to grip the country. The expansive spirit of the days of Andrew Jackson gave way to an attitude of depression-day caution. The houses Bishop Rosati built near the proposed church remained vacant. Philip Le Duc headed Bishop Rosati's drive for funds for the church, but met with little success.

By the summer of 1839, the builders had finished only the foundation of the church. Lack of funds forced the

56

discontinuance of the building. The parish of Holy Tinity never became a reality, and "Frenchtown" had to wait until the following decade for a church of its own. Seminary plans, too, remained for a time unfulfilled.

Northeast Missouri Mission

While southeast Missouri was the scene of spiritual ministrations of many priests since the early French days, only a few Jesuits had occasionally visited northeast Missouri and the adjoining area of Illinois before the coming of Father Peter Paul Lefevere in January, 1833.

A farm boy from Roulers, Belgium, Lefevere had received his seminary education in his native town. In 1825, at the age of twenty-one, he went to the Vincentian Seminary in Paris. He became acquainted with the work of the Vincentians on the American mission and three years later decided to come to the United States. When he had completed his theological course at the Barrens, Bishop Rosati ordained him, November 20, 1831. Lefevere worked at New Madrid in southeast Missouri for over a year. Then he accepted an appointment to St. Paul's in Ralls County, about a hundred miles northwest of Saint Louis along the west bank of the Mississippi.*

In this area, later to be associated with the name of Mark Twain and his unforgettable fictional heroes, Tom Sawyer and Huck Finn, a large group of Kentucky and Maryland Catholic families had settled. Lefevere's parish included lands stretching a hundred and seventy-five miles south of the Iowa border on both sides of the Mississippi. The Black Hawk War, incidentally, had occurred just one year before (1832). Father Lefevere became one of the middle border's first circuit-riding missionaries. A man of rugged strength and courage, inured to frugality and poverty, grave and taciturn in manner, he spent most of his time on the road, especially during the terrible epidemics of cholera and influenza that hit the pioneer families so often. Lefevere reported extensively on his mission. In his 1837 report he recalled that Bishop Rosati had not recently visited that portion of the diocese.[15]

In the fall of the following year, Bishop Rosati, accompanied by the Jesuits Verhaegen and Van Quickenborne, made a visitation of northeast Missouri to bless churches, confirm the people, and assist Lefevere in his many tasks. Bishop Rosati wrote approvingly of Father Lefevere's work both in his diary and in a letter to Father Timon.[16]

In 1840 Lefevere was to enjoy a respite from his steady rounds of circuit-riding. He attended the Fourth Provincial Council of Baltimore as theologian to Bishop Simon Gabriel Bruté, S.S., of Vincennes. At this council many American prelates came to see the unusual qualities of the frontier missionary. When John Odin, C.M., turned down the position of coadjutor bishop of Detroit, the Holy See named Father Lefevere administrator of Detroit and coadjutor to Bishop Frederic Rese in 1841. Lefevere was the first diocesan priest who labored in Missouri to accept a bishopric.

Northwest Indian Missions

The year 1839 saw the happy conclusion of a series of astonishing events that had covered almost a decade. In the autumn of 1831, four Indians of Pacific Northwest tribes arrived in Saint Louis. They attended Mass in the cathedral to the amazement of many of the populace.

Two of the Indians took ill, and after receiving baptism, they died. The priests at the cathedral buried them with the full rites of the Church. In the spring, the remaining two started on their return journey with the prospect that a missionary would visit their villages within a few years. One brave died on the way. The other reached his people. In 1835, an Iroquois living among the Flatheads — "Old Ignace" the French called him — with two of his sons, came to Saint Louis. Instructed and baptized by the priests at the college, they set off for their northwest homeland. Sioux killed them on the way.

Finally, in 1839, a third expedition, led by young Ignace, and a man the French called "Left-Handed Pierre," arrived at Saint Louis after a voyage of three months. These Christian Iroquois spoke French. They went to confession and received Communion. The bishop confirmed them in the Cathedral. In late fall they departed with the good news that a missionary would soon come among them. This time the promise proved true. Father De Smet* soon left for the Pacific Northwest to begin the first Catholic Indian mission of the area. Father Nicholas Point, a French Jesuit who had been president of St. Charles College, Grand Coteau, Louisiana, joined him. Later others followed. De Smet soon gained worldwide fame as a missionary in the Northwest. The nation did not come to appreciate Point's work until the second half of the twentieth century.**

Father De Smet was not satisfied with having only priests in the Indian mission work. In early 1841, he was back in Saint Louis and appealed to Mother Duchesne, now seventy-two, to open a school among Potawatomie Indians in Kansas. She wrote to her superior Mother Gallitzin, in Louisiana. A few weeks later, De Smet presented the letter to Mother Gallitzin and five hundred dollars in gold that he had begged from the planters along the Mississippi and Catholics in New Orleans for the project. Mother Gallitzin approved the mission and assigned the individuals for it. Only at the insistence of the Jesuit superior, Father Verhaegen, did she allow seventy-two-year-old Mother Duchesne to make the difficult journey. Verhaegen had decided to visit the Sugar Creek mission in Kansas and thought it best for the Religious of the Sacred Heart to travel in his company on the steamboat.[17]

Mother Duchesne was to remain less than a year among the Indians. But this venture was a fitting crown to the life of the West's first beatified.

---

*The Mississippi River runs in a south-southeasterly direction from the Iowa border to the confluence of the Ohio. Thus northeast Missouri lies about one hundred miles west of southeast Missouri.

*For a more full account of the mission of Father De Smet, see W. L. Davis, "Peter John De Smet, the Journey of 1840," in the *Pacific Northwest Quarterly* 35 (1944): 29-43. It was not Father Davis' intention, nor is it the present author's, to explore the controversial points regarding these Indian delegations to Saint Louis. These points pertain to the history of the American Northwest rather than of the Archdiocese of Saint Louis. See also *Pacific Northwest Quarterly* 33 (1941): 167-196; 34 (1942): 123-152; 35 (1944): 121-142.

**His fame was secured by the recent publication of Joseph P. Donnelly, S.J., trans., *Wilderness Kingdom: The Journals and Paintings of Father Nicholas Point* (New York: Holt, Rinehart and Winston, 1967).

Chapter 12

The Diocese Faces the 1840's

Diocesan Synod

Back in 1827, Bishop Rosati had been able to boast of only fourteen priests, including the members of two religious communities. This small group had to care for two seminaries, a college, a boys' school, fourteen parishes and missions, and a territory almost as large as the rest of the United States. Ten years later, the bishop listed a body of diocesan and regular clergy numbering sixty-five, who administered twenty-six parishes and forty-seven missions. This was indeed an inspiring achievement in a pioneer diocese. The rapid settlement of this vast area required a speedy expansion on the part of the Church. The diocese still contained two main centers: Saint Louis and vicinity, and "The Old Settlements" — Kaskaskia, Ste. Genevieve, Perryville, and environs. Bishop Rosati had dispatched Jesuits to the Indian missions, the Dominican Samuel Mazzuchelli to whites and Indians of Iowa and Wisconsin villages, Father Benedict Roux to lay the foundation of the Church in the Kansas City area, and Father John St. Cyr to the region of the present city of Chicago. It was truly a significant development.

The bishop called his priests together for the first synod of the diocese on Sunday, April 21, 1839. The meeting opened with a solemn High Mass in honor of the Holy Ghost. Rosati addressed the people in French and English. After Pontifical Vespers in the afternoon, twenty-two of the diocesan clergy and seventeen members of religious orders answered the roll call. Seventeen priests could not attend. To prepare for the assembly, Father Verhaegen, the Jesuit superior, gave a three-day retreat to the priests and the bishop. On the opening day of the synod, Rosati promulgated the decrees of the First Provincial Council of Baltimore and then set up the statutes of the diocesan synod. He named the Very Reverend John Timon, C.M., vicar-general, and J. M. Odin, C.M., pro-vicar-general. Fathers Timon, Odin, Verhaegen, Elet, Lutz, Cellini, Fontbonne, and Loisel were episcopal consultors, and Father Lutz the bishop's secretary. Fathers Timon, Odin, Verhaegen, Elet, Tornatore, and Fontbonne became examiners of the clergy. The bishop set up statutes and procedures that were to last for a century.

The decrees of the synod of Saint Louis were few in number but important in quality. In those days before American priests universally wore the Roman collar, each diocese determined its own garb. For Saint Louis, the priests were to wear a black suit with a long coat and a black tie; the official garb in the Church at all times was the cassock. The synod laid down specific instructions with regard to the administration of the sacrament of baptism, Holy Eucharist, and matrimony. The priests were not to announce the banns in the case of mixed marriages. The synod promulgated the decree of the Council of Trent requiring the presence of the priest and two witnesses for the validity of a Catholic marriage anywhere

in the diocese. The synod prescribed four holy days of obligation, Ascension Thursday, Assumption, All Saints, and Christmas.

This synod, then, represented the complete organization of the diocese. Saint Louis no longer had the character of a missionary region in the strict sense of the term.

In the diocese at this time there were forty-seven churches with resident priests, five without priests, five chapels, and sixty mission stations. The clergy consisted of one bishop, thirty-one secular priests, twenty-two Lazarists, twenty-seven Jesuits — a grand total of eighty. The three convents of the Sacred Heart numbered forty-two Sisters. Nineteen Sisters of Charity served the orphans' home and the hospital. The four convents of the Sisters of St. Joseph housed eleven nuns, and the convent of the Visitation, nineteen. The Lorettines in Southeast Missouri and Pine Bluff, Arkansas, brought the number of nuns working in the diocese to well over one hundred. Within the city, the Cathedral was still the only church. Our Lady of Mount Carmel was in Carondelet, St. Ferdinand's in Florissant, and St. Peter's in what was then called Gravois and would soon become known as Kirkwood.*

At the same time Bishop Rosati was planning the removal of the diocesan seminary from Perry County to Saint Louis. The Vincentian seminary itself, however,

---

*The churches beyond Saint Louis County included St. Charles Boromeo in St. Charles, St. Peter's in Dardenne, St. Simon's in Louisville, St. Francis of Assisi in Portage Des Sioux, St. Joachim in Old Mines, St. Stephen's at Richwoods, St. James in Potosi, St. Michael's at Fredericktown, St. Genevieve in Ste. Genevieve, St. Anne's in French Village, St. Mary's near Perryville, St. Joseph's at Apple Creek, St. John the Baptist at New Madrid, St. Vincent's at Cape Girardeau, St. Francis De Sales at Tywappity Bottom, St. Paul's in Salt River, St. Stephen's at Indian Creek in Monroe County, St. Joseph's at New Westphalia, St. Francis Borgia in Washington County, with many mission stations from eleven centers; on the Illinois side, Holy Family in Cahokia, St. Philip's at French Village, St. Thaddeus at Silver Creek, St. Liborius at Fayetteville, St. Andrew's at Teutonia, St. Augustine at Prairie du Long (later Hecker), St. Patrick's at O'Hara's Settlement (later Ruma), Sts. Philip and James at Harrisonville, St. Thomas at Johnson's Center, St. Joseph at Prairie du Rocher, Immaculate Conception at Kaskaskia, St. Simon in Fountain Green, St. Augustine in Fulton County, and a church in Chicago. Cairo and Alton were both without churches and priest, but had regular services. St. John the Evangelist in Springfield was the center of missions spreading out from there, such as Holy Cross at La Salle, and Holy Trinity in Ottawa. Quincy had two churches, the Ascension and St. Lawrence. Arkansas had two churches: St. Denis at the Arkansas Post and St. Mary's in New Gascony. In the Indian Territory the Jesuit Fathers had established two missions: the Potawatomie Mission at Council Bluffs under Fathers De Smet, Verreydt, and Eisvogels and the Kickapoo Missions under Father Hoecken and Father Ehlen. These missionaries also attended the white settlements of Westport (Kansas City), Independence, and Liberty, Missouri, and Leavenworth, Kansas.

would continue at its former location. Bishop Rosati stuck to his plans to build some revenue producing rental homes in the Soulard Addition and to erect a seminary building there. In this way he would have sufficient priests on Sunday for services at the Cathedral and for the needs of the many Catholics in the vicinity. The Vincentian Fathers liked the plan of the bishop.[1] But the seminary was not to get underway until two years after Bishop Rosati left Saint Louis for the last time.

Outside the city of Saint Louis, Bishop Rosati was anxious to provide churches and chapels in various parts of the diocese for the burgeoning population throughout the states of Missouri, Arkansas, and western Illinois. He hoped to set up parishes as soon as possible. In most of these areas in the thirties, he could purchase land at low prices. If the circuit-riding priests could set up mission stations early enough, they could form living Catholic communities. Around these, groups of immigrants could reaffirm their relationship with the old Faith in the new world. Otherwise, in remote areas, they would gradually drift and lose themselves in the larger general Christian population.

By 1840, then, Saint Louis had a population of 16,469 — over three times as many as ten years before — and was on its way to becoming one of the major cities of the nation.[2] As a Catholic center, Saint Louis rivaled Baltimore, the primatial see of the nation. Founded as it was by Catholics, Saint Louis could still claim to be a Catholic city, both in the sense that Catholics formed the largest denomination, and that the spirit of the city reflected a distinctly Catholic outlook — in contrast, for instance, with the Calvinistic ethos of Protestant Boston.

The *Catholic Directory* for that year (1840) showed that the Diocese of Saint Louis with 73 priests led the nation in the number of clergymen. Baltimore followed with 68 and New York had 63. Saint Louis had the largest combined number of churches, chapels, and mission stations, 113. Bardstown had 110, New York 94, Philadelphia 78, and Baltimore 73. Baltimore, incidentally, had more churches than Saint Louis, but had few mission stations.

The prospects for the future were good, too. With twenty-seven clerical students, Saint Louis stood second to Baltimore. Only the Archdiocese of Baltimore and the Diocese of Saint Louis had Catholic universities. Saint Louis had twice as many female religious foundations with eleven, and followed only Baltimore and New York in the number of charitable institutions.[3]

Saint Louis diocese had a theological seminary, a college and a novitiate at the Barrens, a novitiate at Florissant, Saint Louis University, Saint Vincent's Academy for boys in Cape Girardeau, seven day schools for boys in the following localities: Saint Louis, St. Charles, Florissant, Old Mines, Westphalia, La Salle, and Cahokia, Illinois,[4] and ten academies for girls in these places: Saint Louis, Florissant, Carondelet, St. Charles, Ste. Genevieve, New Madrid, Cape Girardeau, Pine Bluff, Arkansas, and at Kaskaskia and Cahokia in Illinois.[5] By contrast, the Diocese of Boston had only three schools at this time: Mt. St. James in Worcester for boys, Ursuline Convent, and the Sisters of Charity Convent for girls. Philadelphia had two schools for girls, one in Wilmington, Delaware, the other in McSherrytown, Pennsylvania, a theological seminary in Philadelphia, and a boys' boarding school in Wilmington.[6] New York had a seminary, two academies for young ladies,[7] and six parish schools in the city, one in Albany and two in Brooklyn.[8]

In recruiting personnel for the west, Rosati had some success; but he did not have the capacity of Du Bourg in this matter nor the challenging ways John Timon and Pierre Jean De Smet were to demonstrate. In the solicitation of funds for his many projects, he had gotten help from the Pope, the Association for the Propagation of the Faith at Lyons, the Leopoldine Association in Vienna, and the general of the Vincentians; yet he had little confidence in his capacity for begging.[9]

The expansion of the diocese still depended upon financial aid from sources in Europe, especially the mission societies in Lyons and Vienna. Unfortunately, because of the amazing growth of the diocese, the rumor had arisen that the bishop of Saint Louis no longer needed assistance. These false rumors had caused the diocese to be dropped from the list of recipients of aid. Rosati began to consider ways of increasing contributions at home.[10]

But the prospects of developing resources in the region were no brighter than in Europe. The diocese was already heavily in debt, especially to the Bank of the State of Missouri. It had obtained the bulk of its loans at a rate of six percent interest with a promise to pay a stated portion of the principal each year. Following the Panic of 1837, depression still gripped the nation. The peoples of the region, whether Creoles or newcomers, still followed European church-support programs and attitudes. They had not yet begun to realize what an expanding church in a free society would require of them.

Timon and Texas

Back in 1835, Rosati had prevented the nomination of Father John Timon to the coadjutorships of both New York and Vincennes, by claiming him as his aide and logical successor in Saint Louis.[11] Now he had to act again. In 1838, through the offices of Bishop Antoine Blanc of New Orleans, a recruit of Du Bourg's who had worked in Vincennes before going to Louisiana, Rome asked Timon to undertake a reconnaisance mission to the newly independent Republic of Texas. Only belatedly did Rome remind Bishop Blanc to notify Bishop Rosati.[12] Rosati knew that the Congregation of the Mission was considering a new venture in Texas. He moved to forestall the loss of Timon, by asking Rome to appoint the Vincentian Visitor his coadjutor in Saint Louis.[13]

The Vincentian superior general in Paris accepted the Texas mission. He believed that if the Congregation of the Mission lost Timon, the American province would fall apart. After all, the loss of Rosati to the episcopacy in the mid-twenties had set the congregation back. Further, it had sacrificed Father Leo De Neckere to the greater needs of the universal church. It could not stand the loss of Timon. So the superior general thought he could save Timon for the congregation by adding the prefecture of Texas to his many duties.[14]

This left Timon with a difficult decision. He had to choose between the needs of the Republic of Texas and of his own congregation on the one hand, and the demands of the Saint Louis diocese and his close friendship for Bishop Rosati on the other. The documents came from Rome appointing him titular bishop of Vera in Tunisia and coadjutor of Saint Louis. He sent them back the next day.[15]

During the following spring, Timon received the documents appointing him to the prefecture of Texas and separating the Lone Star Republic from the spiritual juris-diction of Mexico.[16] As prefect-apostolic of Texas, and Visitor of the Vincentians, he was to choose a resident substitute for Texas and to preserve his mobility.[17] He chose John Odin as vice-prefect of Texas and appointed Joseph Paquin as head of the seminary in Perryville.[18]

On April 17, 1840, Timon visited Saint Louis and met with the bishop. He told Rosati that he was sending Odin and three Spanish recruits, Father Eudald Estany, Father Michael Calvo, and Brother Raymond Sala to Texas.[19] Rosati felt deeply the loss of Timon as his coadjutor and then his next closest co-worker, John Odin.[20]

The Bishop's Departure

Because of the financial needs of the diocese, Rosati decided to go to Europe at the conclusion of the Balti-more council in the spring of 1840.[21] No unusual con-cern attended the bishop's departure. His trip to Rome seemed routine. No one in the diocese, least of all the bishop himself, ever considered his departure as the end of his great service to the people of Saint Louis. Yet when he said goodbye to his priests on the morning of April 26, 1840, it was to be his final parting from the territory that had been the scene of his life for twenty-two years.

The Saint Louis area had many outstanding priests who could have administered the diocese in the bishop's absence. Peter Paul Lefevere was to become bishop of Detroit the following year. But he was temporarily in poor health and Rosati does not seem to have considered him. Timon was busy with his combined duties as apostolic-prefect of Texas and Vincentian Visitor. Odin had a new task in Texas and would become bishop there a year later. John Elet had finished his term as president of Saint Louis University and was now starting Xavier College in Cincinnati. Father James Van de Velde, the best businessman among the early Jesuits, had just be-come president of Saint Louis University. Later he was to be bishop of Chicago. Rosati's third choice for his co-adjutor had been the Jesuit superior, Peter Verhaegen. But one month before, Verhaegen had become vice-provincial when Rome raised the Missouri Jesuit Mission to the status of a vice-province on March 9, 1840.[22] When Rosati asked Verhaegen to assume the responsi-bilities of administrator of the diocese, the Jesuit hesi-tated because of his new duties as vice-provincial. Ver-haegen finally agreed to the bishop's request on two con-ditions: first, that the Vincentian superior administer the southern part of the diocese from his office in Perryville; and, secondly, that a layman take care of temporal af-fairs.[23] Rosati agreed to both stipulations and assigned Judge M. Le Duc to this latter task. Thereupon Verhaegen became vicar-general and superior of the Episcopal Resi-dence.[24] One day a week he went to Saint Louis Univer-sity to discharge his duties as vice-provincial of the Mis-souri Jesuits.[25]

Verhaegen was to write long letters to keep Rosati acquainted with events in the diocese;[26] and, at Rosati's request, offered suggestions on ways Rosati's European journey could better serve the diocese. He urged the bishop to seek priests who could speak English, to be more forthright in asking financial aid for the diocese, and to make an appeal for help in Belgium.[27]

Rosati left for Baltimore. He, Flaget, England, and Fenwick were the only members of the hierarchy in attendance at the Fourth Provincial Council of Baltimore in May, 1840, who had been present at the first one in 1829. The council prescribed for the entire country the regulations on mixed marriages that had been decreed in the Synod of Saint Louis. The bishops discussed the mat-ter of the transference of church property at the death of one bishop to his successor. The council commissioned Rosati to send to Rome for final approval the ritual that had been prepared for use in the province. The council also authorized two letters, one by Bishop England to the Holy Father, the other by Bishop Rosati to the arch-bishops of Cologne and Gnesen-Posen, offering them sympathy for the harsh treatment they had received from the Prussian government. In this, as in all his Latin letters, Rosati wrote with the eloquence of an early Father of the Church.

Shortly after the conclusion of the provincial council, Rosati went to Philadelphia to see Bishop Francis Patrick Kenrick. Once again he had a chance to talk with the bishop's younger brother, Father Peter Richard Kenrick. Rosati was still concerned with the need of a coadjutor. John Timon, the Vincentian superior, had already refused the appointment. Rosati felt that he had asked enough of the Jesuits in having Verhaegen, the new vice-provincial, administer the Saint Louis diocese in his absence. He now felt an inspiration to ask the Holy Father if young Father Kenrick might be his coadjutor.[28]

On June 1, 1840, Rosati sailed from New York ac-companied by Bishop Portier, Bishop Richard Miles, O.P., and Father Joseph Lutz. He visited the central headquar-ters of the Congregation of the Mission in mid-June and met the superior general, Father Nozo, who invited him to remain until the Feast of Saint Vincent De Paul. While in Paris, Rosati arranged for the departure of four or five Vincentian Fathers from Italy and six or seven Religious of the Sacred Heart. None of these new subjects were his recruits. Their superiors had already designated them for the American mission, but the fact they were to go to Saint Louis encouraged him; and in turn his presence added to their departure ceremony. Rosati then traveled with Father Nozo as far as Lyons. He was guest of the archbishop there. He visited the offices of the Society of the Propagation of the Faith; thanked the members of the society for their fine efforts in the Archdiocese of Saint Louis; and described the diocesan picture.

In Rome, Pope Gregory XVI welcomed Bishop Rosati with a warm show of personal affection. They talked in-formally for three-quarters of an hour on affairs of the church in America. Bishop Rosati presented the decrees of the Fourth Provincial Council of Baltimore and the other documents and memorials. When he had finished his business with the Holy See, Bishop Rosati visited his native town of Sora. His mother had died in 1829 but his brother Nicola, a faithful correspondent for a quarter of a century, and a great many friends and relatives, still re-sided in the little village. The return of a native son was the occasion of a tremendous demonstration. A long line of dignitaries, including the mayor of the city, met the bishop three miles from the town. A band escorted him to the cathedral where Bishop Montiere came out to wel-come him. The people of the town enjoyed a *festa* that lasted far into the night.

On November 14 Rosati again had an audience with the Holy Father. The Pope received him in the same informal manner; and again spoke highly about the Amer-ican church, reviewed the proceedings of the council, and praised the work that had been accomplished. He likewise expressed deep satisfaction at the letter of Bishop Rosati to the archbishops of Cologne and Gnesen-Posen. A short time later the Pontiff bestowed upon him the title Assistant to the Pontifical Throne.[29] Rosati had time to accept invitations for several retreats and missions. A mission that gave him deep personal pleasure was at the little town of Poggio-Nativo where he had given his first mission shortly after his ordination.

Rosati intended to return home the following spring, but the Pope had other work for him. The Holy Father wanted him to conclude the negotiations with the Haitian Republic first undertaken by Bishop John England of Charleston in 1833. Rosati hesitated because he did not want to leave his diocese for so long a time without a bishop. If the Holy See would grant him a coadjutor, he would accept the Haitian Mission. The Pope asked if he had a choice. Bishop Rosati suggested the name of the vicar-general of Philadelphia, Peter Richard Kenrick, who was in Europe at the time, and requested that the appointment be made mandatory. His second and third choices were Edward Purcell and Peter Verhaegen.[30] Kenrick accepted. Rosati assumed the burden of the apostolic delegation to Haiti.

The story of Bishop Rosati's work in Haiti lies beyond the scope of the history of the diocese he had founded, organized, and brought to a position of honor.

Rosati in Retrospect

The picture of Rosati that emerges from the many records of the time then, is that of a remarkable man. More spiritual and less flamboyant than Du Bourg, he possessed an organizing ability that Du Bourg lacked. He was as steady as the current of the Mississippi. He rarely tried too much. What he set out to do, he did. Justly sure of himself, he could deal in objective realities. He admitted honest differences of opinion, and respected, even revered, the one differing with him.

Rosati's sound ideas remained unshaken throughout the years. He appreciated education and the demands it made on the clerical teachers. He viewed bishoprics on the frontier as challenges not crowns. An orderly man, he kept diaries and copies or digests of all his letters. He taught both Odin and Timon to do the same. Rosati's reports to the Leopoldine Society on the state of his diocese showed a commander-in-chief's grasp of far-flung campaigns. He made friends in the various European associations for the support of missions and secured considerable help from them. Domestic financing of the various churches of the diocese would come only with time. Rosati borrowed money to build a cathedral. His call to Haiti and his early death at the age of fifty-four kept him from paying much of the debt. Thus he left a debt for his successor that was large, but not disproportionate to the resources of the Catholics of Saint Louis, once they forgot old-world ways.

Rosati had all the characteristics a missionary bishop should have: organization, zeal, order, discipline, dedication. He was in love with his work and a loving associate of all his co-workers. He organized the diocese. He put spirit back into despondent missionaries who would have otherwise returned to Europe. He was appreciative of everything well done. Peter K. Guilday, eminent historian of the American Church, concluded that his fellow bishops recognized Rosati as "one of the most remarkable bishops of Christendom."[31] A century later, Apostolic Delegate Archbishop Amleto Cicognani acknowledged Rosati's deep dedication to God by including him in his book of short biographies, entitled *Sanctity in America*.[32]

Rosati began the Vincentian seminary and kept it in the diocese. He built an impressive cathedral. He began a Catholic paper. He persuaded the Jesuits to man Saint Louis College, and later urged them to send men to the Indian mission country. He invited the Religious of the Sacred Heart, located in the rural areas by Bishop Du Bourg, to open a school in Saint Louis. He welcomed three sisterhoods to the diocese. The Sisters of Charity began the first permanent hospital west of the Mississippi. The Sisters of St. Joseph began their first American foundation. The Visitandines moved into the American West for the first time with the opening of a school in Kaskaskia. Rosati encouraged the Lorettines, already active in Southeast Missouri, to open a school at Pine Bluff in Arkansas in 1838. The commitment of these seven religious societies — five of women and two of men — to the Diocese of Saint Louis furthered the religious spirit of the people in a profound way.

Rosati was the only priest who had spent his early priestly years in the area to become chief shepherd. Like so many of his contemporaries in that age of heavy immigration, he was born elsewhere. But this was his home. He was an outstanding pastoral bishop.

Irish railroad workers built the railroad towards Jefferson City along the Missouri River, prompting the zealous Father John J. Hogan to seek permission from Archbishop Kenrick to leave Saint Louis for the rural missions of out-state Missouri. (Photograph by Missouri-Pacific Railroad.)

The "Western Watchman" himself! Father David Phelan was the most independent newspaper editor the Catholic Church of the Midwest ever saw. He called them "as he saw them" – no matter who disliked what he saw.

Senator Henry J. Spaunhorst served three terms in the state senate where he promoted freedom of choice in education. The only Catholic member of the constitutional convention of 1875, he worked against restrictions of the Drake Constitution enacted in the previous decade. He was president of the Central Verein from 1873 to 1891, and then honorary president for life. A native of Hanover, he came to America with his parents at the age of eight, lived on a farm west of Saint Louis. He was an early member of the Saint Vincent de Paul Society. (Photograph by the Missouri Historical Society.

PART IV

Peter Richard Kenrick:
The Lion of Saint Louis (1843-1895)

Left: Peter Kenrick, second bishop and first archbishop of Saint Louis, theologian, financier, father of the immigrant, friend of the poor – the first American bishop to celebrate a golden jubilee in the episcopacy. (Photo by Saint Louis Globe-Democrat.)

Father Servatius Altmicks, OFM, meets with the first members of the Third Order of St. Francis in St. Louis, among them John Withnell, Christ Ghio, John Byrne and Judge J. O'Neill.

Chapter 13

Kenrick as Coadjutor

Early Years

Peter Richard Kenrick, who was to be Bishop Rosati's successor, and chief shepherd of the Saint Louis Catholics for the next half-century, grew up in his native Dublin. As a young priest ordained slightly over a year, he had, in October, 1833, accepted the invitation of his brother, Francis Patrick Kenrick, the coadjutor bishop of Philadelphia, to come to the United States. The older brother had received his education at the Irish College in Rome; but, Peter Richard had studied theology at Maynooth Seminary in Ireland — a fact that was to play a part in their differing theological and political viewpoints.

Although the young priest was not yet thirty years of age and there were thirty-five other priests in the diocese of Philadelphia at the time,[1] Bishop Kenrick appointed Peter Richard rector of the seminary, vicar-general of the diocese, and editor of the diocesan weekly, *The Catholic Herald.* The bishop seemed ill-advised in giving his brother so many positions, no matter how talented the young man might have been. When Bishop Kenrick added the pastorate of St. Mary's parish to his brother's long list of duties in 1834, he found it necessary to state that he was not playing favorites. This was not to be the last time churchmen accused Bishop Kenrick of favoring his brother.

Peter Richard acted as theologian to Bishop Simon Bruté, S.S., of Vincennes at the Third Provincial Council at Baltimore in 1837. At this time his name appeared third in the list of recommendations for the see of Detroit.[2] Once again his brother, Bishop Francis Patrick Kenrick, had to justify himself. The bishop wrote to Bishop Paul Cullen of the Irish College in Rome stating that he had allowed his brother's name to appear third on the list, but that he really needed him in Philadelphia. Bishop Kenrick asked Cullen to prevent Peter Richard's appointment, should there seem to be any disposition on the part of Rome to choose him.[3]

Peter Richard was a scholarly rather than a pastoral type of man. He leaned, throughout life, towards solitude rather than to the enjoyment of company. In the summer of 1838 he went to Europe intending to join the Jesuits. Since Peter Richard's health was poor, Bishop Kenrick did not take his intentions seriously. When Peter Richard recovered his health some time later and seemed bent on applying for admission to the Society of Jesus, the bishop, hard-pressed as he was for priests, opposed his brother's joining. Quite interestingly, even though Peter Richard liked the Jesuit way of life as a personal approach to God, he never particularly cared for what he called "Jesuit politics" or for religious orders in general, especially their specific goals that did not appear to him always to jibe with the purposes of the local ecclesiastical administrators.

Kenrick remained in Europe a year and a half and returned to Philadelphia in December, 1839. He had not, however, totally given up his intention of joining a religious order. During May of the following year (1840), he attended the Fourth Provincial Council of Baltimore. The fathers of the council submitted his name along with those of John Chance, S.S., president of Saint Mary's College, Baltimore, and John Elet, S.J., president of Saint Louis University, as bishop of Natchez.[4]

Kenrick wrote several books at this time, *The New Month of Mary,* a devotional book that gained wide popularity, and *The Validity of Anglican Orders,* an analytic view of the question. The latter was to evoke two answers from Anglicans within the ensuing decade, one in the United States in 1844, the other in England in 1846.[5]

When Kenrick returned to Europe the following year, hoping this time to join the Jesuits in Rome, a new possibility came up. The Holy Father planned to send Bishop Rosati on a special mission to Haiti, and agreed to name as coadjutor of Saint Louis the priest Bishop Rosati suggested. Rosati asked for Peter Richard Kenrick. In turn, Bishop Francis Patrick Kenrick consented to give his brother leave from the diocese of Philadelphia to become coadjutor bishop of Saint Louis.

Bishop Rosati consecrated Bishop Kenrick in St. Mary's Church, Philadelphia, November 30, 1841, assisted by Bishops Francis Patrick Kenrick and Peter P. Lefevere, the new coadjutor of Detroit and former northeast Missouri missioner, whom the older Kenrick had consecrated only eight days before in Philadelphia.

Saint Louis in 1841

At this time the Diocese of Saint Louis, a huge strip of land four hundred miles wide and twelve hundred miles long, diagonaled north and west from the lower Mississippi to the Canadian border. It included the states of Arkansas, Missouri, and the western half of Illinois, and a vast unorganized territory between the Missouri River on the east and the Rocky Mountains on the west, between the Red River on the south and the Canadian border on the north. A few years later western Illinois was to become a part of the new diocese of Chicago and Arkansas to become the diocese of Little Rock.

Missouri was growing much more rapidly than Arkansas, a state only since 1836. Kansas City was becoming a depot for the growing Santa Fe trade that moved out to Bent's Fort on the Arkansas, a project of Saint Louisans Ceran St. Vrain and several of the sons of Judge Silas Bent. The Republic of Texas bordered the diocese on the southwest.

The forties and fifties were still the heyday of the Plains Indians. Men from Saint Louis went west to hunt, trap, and trade. For the moment the Cheyennes, Sioux, and other tribes were legendary great "red hunters" with whom European noblemen went out to shoot buffalo.

The population of the city of Saint Louis had doubled between 1835 and 1840, going from about eight thousand to slightly over sixteen thousand. It was to triple that figure in the next decade. The city still stretched along the river for sixty-four blocks. It went inland only eighteen blocks. In the central west end of the city, Chouteau's Pond, the dammed-up waters of Mill Creek, extended from Ninth to a point west of Eighteenth, with three large fingers moving north from the main valley. Pictures suggest a park-like atmosphere around Chouteau's Pond. But the area was soon to see the growth of factories of various kinds, and the Pond lost its idyllic aspect and became a menace to health.

In the Mississippi, directly in front of the city, three large islands stood: Arsenal Island, the largest, at the south end of town; Duncan's Island at the foot of Park and Soulard streets; and Bloody Island, site of many duels, directly across from the ferry landing at the foot of Carr Street, on the north. On the ridge along Bellefontaine Road, north of the city, many of the wealthier people, such as John O'Fallon and Major Dougherty, had built their homes. Saint Louis University had purchased the Clark estate there in 1836 in the hope of locating its permanent campus on that site. Unfortunately, the Panic of 1837 had set back these plans.

Carondelet Avenue stretched south of town, an extension of Broadway on the south as Bellefontaine Road was on the north. At the west end of the city at this time, a Carondelet Street drove straight south, and at the downstream end of the town, ran into the Carondelet Avenue, swerving southwest along the river. The east-west streets of the city had been set up perpendicular to the river. Since the river formed an arc, and most streets going away from the river were perpendicular to it, many streets at the north and south ends of town tended to converge at the west end. In contrast, Carondelet, Gravois, Chouteau, Manchester, Clayton, St. Charles, Natural Bridge, and Bellefontaine roads moved out from town as spokes from a hub.

In the vast, partially uncharted diocese, seventy-seven priests worked in thirty-four churches and chapels in Missouri and thirteen in Illinois, Arkansas, and the Indian territory.

Kenrick Comes to Saint Louis

It would have seemed wise for Bishop Rosati to have brought his coadjutor to Saint Louis and introduced him to his people and his duties. Instead, Rosati had to go directly to Haiti. Bishop Kenrick set off alone for the west. This was his first trip into the interior of America. He was not, as Rosati had been, a priest who had worked in and knew the area. He did not share the French background of the largest group of Catholics. Kenrick came as a stranger to an area expansive in attitude but still reeling under the financial impact of the Panic of 1837.

Bishop Rosati had done many things well. One of the things he hoped to do when he returned from Haiti was to pay off the huge diocesan debt. Further, he had not yet been able to organize the self-support machinery that came to characterize the American church. Father Verhaegen had been handling the routine administrative duties of the diocese, and Judge LeDuc, a layman, the financial administration.

Kenrick's entry into Saint Louis on December 28, 1841, contrasted sharply with the heralded coming of Bishop Du Bourg on the Feast of the Epiphany in 1819. The whole town had come out to meet Du Bourg. Few seemed to know of Kenrick's coming in 1841.

When Kenrick arrived in Saint Louis in 1841, only one priest met him at the riverfront. The two then walked back to the bishop's residence carrying valises. The total picture certainly would have dampened the spirits even of one who took as his motto: *Noli irritare leonen!* — "Don't goad the lion!"

Kenrick found much to depress him on his arrival in Saint Louis. In spite of the fact that English-speaking people constituted five-sixths of those who frequented the Cathedral, on his arrival no clergyman on the Cathedral staff could speak the language.[6] The huge debt of the building appalled him. "It had cost upwards of $90,000," he wrote, "a great part of which remains unpaid, or rather has been paid for by money borrowed at ten percent."[7]

The city numbered between four and five thousand German inhabitants who professed the Catholic faith, yet Kenrick could point to no "efficient German clergyman"; and suggested that Bishop Purcell of Cincinnati loan him one. Twice during the year 1842 he wrote to Purcell about the need of a German seminary in the region.[8]

During these early months in Saint Louis, Peter Richard had reassuring advice from his brother in Philadelphia. Francis Patrick was happy that his brother had reached Saint Louis safely; but sorry to learn of the discouraging features of his new task. He urged that Peter Richard not allow himself to be over-burdened by the thought of the debt. "It will not appear so great if you consider what has been done, and that almost without the aid of the faithful."[9]

Francis Patrick believed that most of the problems were simply a result of the absence of Bishop Rosati. He listed some unfortunate events: fire destroyed certain buildings; a citizen recommended by the bishop had absconded with funds; another layman had failed to turn in the collection. Francis Patrick stated that Bishop Rosati had already told him these things and expressed regret that Peter Richard had to take up the administration of the diocese in the midst of these difficulties. Francis Patrick reminded his brother: "It will be his (Rosati's) whole care to help you in any way that he can; and I, if I can do anything, will not be wanting. Have courage therefore; and, if the burden becomes very heavy, let me know of your difficulties."[10]

Kenrick Views His Problems

A month later, Kenrick wrote to Rosati, giving his solution to the problems, especially the heavy debt of over $53,000. Father Verhaegen had advised against appealing to the congregation. And so Kenrick wanted to spend all the money to come from the Leopoldine Association the following year in part payment of this immense debt and to sell whatever property the diocese did not need either for churches or other religious purposes.[11]

In a letter to Rosati later that summer, Kenrick called Saint Louis "a city of bankrupts."[12] The failures, unfortunately, had occurred among precisely those people who had heretofore been the mainstays of the Church. Judge LeDuc died. He had given much assistance to Rosati but left nothing to the Church in his will. Rosati owed him $7,000 and the LeDuc heirs demanded the money. If they pressed for payment immediately, Kenrick saw only ruin. In conclusion, Kenrick wrote, "I hope you will not forget him whom you have placed in so perilous an eminence and that you will excuse me if in any respect my desire for promoting the welfare of religion makes me appear importunate."[13]

Francis Patrick had already chided his brother for taking too harsh a line in letters to Bishop Rosati.[14] The older brother was certainly correct. Peter Richard let his few difficulties — only one, the financial problem, was a major one — play too great a part in his outlook. He could have counted the obvious blessings. He had more priests than any other diocese of the country. Catholics stretched through all areas of society from the richest to the poorest. The Church had honor and prestige in the city. Though he did not realize it, he had one of the most beautiful, if not the most beautiful Cathedral, in the United States.

His diocese boasted a fine seminary and college in Perryville and the first university chartered west of the Mississippi. It was soon, in fact, to be a true university with the inaugural of medical and law schools. The Religious of the Sacred Heart conducted schools in Saint Louis and Saint Charles, and were to begin missionary work among the Indians in Kansas. The Sisters of Charity staffed the Saint Louis Hospital. The Visitandines taught girls in Kaskaskia. The Lorettines had come from Kentucky to open a number of schools and the Sisters of St. Joseph taught in Cahokia and Carondelet. No American diocese except Baltimore matched the strength of Saint Louis at the time.

Kenrick seemed to overlook for a time the fact that in the days of the steamboat, Saint Louis was the hub of the intercontinental water network. Secondly, unlike the midcontinent sees of Natchez, Mobile, Bardstown, Vincennes, and Dubuque, Saint Louis had a commercial and industrial base that could ride out depressions and survive transportation changes.*

In spite of his misgivings, however, Kenrick put new vigor into activities. He appointed Father Lutz as his secretary, sent Father Fontbonne from the Cathedral to Carondelet, and brought George Hamilton, the best English preacher, an American of Kentucky-Maryland background, from Alton, Illinois, to the Cathedral. Father Saulnier went to the French village in Illinois, and eventually to New Madrid. A young priest, Ambrose Heim, took up residence at the English settlement in Illinois, about thirty-five miles east and a little south of Saint Louis.

Kenrick took an interest in the orphanage for girls that the Daughters of Charity planned to open. In 1842 he wrote to the spiritual director of the nuns in Emmitsburg, Maryland, and referred to a generous offer of Ann Biddle.[15] Mrs. Biddle gave her own home as temporary quarters, offered property for a permanent orphange, made a donation of three thousand dollars, and promised to support the institution for three years.[16] By May, 1843, the number of girls at the orphanage was to reach forty-five.[17]

In the spring of 1842, Kenrick visited part of his far-flung diocese, including settlements in Arkansas, soon to become the diocese of Little Rock. He knew immediately that Rome should split the region into several dioceses. He thought it a mistake, however, that the Territory of Iowa had a diocese, Dubuque, before the states of Illinois and Arkansas, and the Territory of Wisconsin.[18]

Advances at Saint Louis University

The long negotiations between the Jesuit trustees of Saint Louis University and the local physicians for the beginning of a medical school ended happily on March 28, 1842. Professor Josephus Wells Hall, M.D., gave the first lecture to the students and a large audience of the general public in a residence belonging to Dean James V. Prather, adjoining the university buildings, on the north side of Washington Avenue, between Tenth and Eleventh.

The faculty for the first year included such distinguished men as Dr. Daniel Brainard who was to found the Rush Medical Center of the University of Chicago, and Dr. Moses Linton, professor of obstetrics, gynecology, and pediatrics, who began the *Saint Louis Medical and Surgical Journal* in 1843. This journal was destined for many years to be the only medical publication in the vast region west of the Alleghenies.[19]

Even more remarkable than the outstanding quality of its faculty was an article in the constitution of the medical school explicitly calling for trustees from all the major religions of the city: Presbyterian, Unitarian, Episcopalian, Methodist, and Baptist, as well as Catholic. With a breadth of vision hardly to be equaled anywhere in the contemporary world, the Jesuit trustees approved this recommendation.

The significance of the opening of the medical department in the history of the city and the diocese stands out against the background of contemporary collegiate medicine. Only eight universities and one college in the entire country had functioning medical departments at the time. Only two of these, Transylvania University in Kentucky (later to become the University of Kentucky) and the short-lived Willoughby University in Ohio, were west of the Alleghenies. None but Saint Louis was west of the Mississippi. No Catholic university was to follow Saint Louis' example until Georgetown opened a medical department in 1851.

At the beginning of the winter term in 1844, Dr. Charles Alexander Pope replaced resigning Dr. Brainard. Two years later he was to become dean of the Saint Louis University School of Medicine, and eventually president of the American Medical Association. A contemporary witness, a Protestant clergyman, made this statement:

The medical school was eminently successful, especially after the accession to the faculty of Doctor Charles Alexander Pope, later dean of the faculty. So popular did this position become, that the medical school was referred to in common parlance as Doctor Pope's College.[20]

Thus Saint Louis University and the Diocese of Saint Louis could claim an exceptionally fine medical school, the only one at the time under Catholic auspices on the North American continent.

With an excellent medical school in operation, Saint Louis University was soon able to offer training in law. Throughout much of the nation at the time, men learned law by studying in the office of a practicing attorney. At those colleges where law was taught, a single professor usually lectured to undergraduates. There were few fully organized law schools.

---

*John Gilmary Shea, premier Catholic Church historian of the United States, put the Rosati debt in focus in *A History of the Catholic Church* (New York: John G. Shea, 1892), p. 217. He spoke of the diocesan debt incurred "in establishing institutions which placed St. Louis in a most favorable position for good."

A distinguished political figure of Kentucky, Judge Richard Aylett Buckner, wanted to teach law courses. He thought that Saint Louis, where his daughter, Marie Louise Buckner Barret, lived, would be the best place to carry out his plans. His grandsons, Richard Aylett Barret, destined to serve in the American Diplomatic Corps in Paris, and Arthur Buckner Barret, a future mayor of Saint Louis, attended Saint Louis University. Their cousin, J. Richard Barret, later to represent Saint Louis in the national congress, had just completed his undergraduate studies.

Judge Buckner corresponded with university President James Van de Velde on the project. In the *Saint Louis Republican* during July, 1843, Father Van de Velde announced that law courses would begin on the university campus in the fall.[21]

The end of the term of Father Van de Velde as president slowed negotiations a bit, but Father George Aloysius Carrell, the first American born president of Saint Louis University, resumed negotiations. Judge Buckner began law lectures at Saint Louis University that fall. The Saint Louis University School of Law got off to an auspicious start.

The year 1844 was to mark a high point in the early history of Saint Louis University. In the twelve years since it received its charter, it had advanced amazingly. The basic liberal arts program trained many outstanding young men. Physicians had opened a medical department with the full support of the young Saint Louis Medical Society. The law department under Judge Buckner's guidance gave promise of equal distinction.

The faculties numbered outstanding laymen and priests. Many American and European candidates were augmenting the already qualified Jesuit personnel. Four were outstanding: two Americans, Isidore and Florentine Boudreaux, influential spiritual directors; and two immigrants, ordained by Bishop Kenrick in 1843, Arnold Damen, noted pastor and home missioner, and Peter Arnoudt, author of a book historian John Gilmary Shea was to call "the greatest ascetical work produced in the United States."[22]

Saint Louis University had wide support from citizens of various religious denominations. The earlier emphasis on residential students from Louisiana had given way to a balance between local and out-of-state students. Saint Louis University seemed destined for a bright future.

Kenrick on Seminaries and Colleges

Bishop Rosati had determined to transfer the diocesan seminarians from Perryville to a new site in the Soulard section of near south Saint Louis. The building of the Church of the Holy Trinity had been part of this plan. As a result of the enduring depression following the Panic of 1837, the Church never got beyond foundation stages. The projected seminary did not open.

While he abandoned plans for the Church, Bishop Kenrick did move his seminarians and professors to the Soulard Addition in 1842. Fathers John Timon, James Tiernan, and Thaddeus Amat, later to be bishop of Monterey, taught six theology students and administered to the needs of the Creole population in the vicinity. Bishop Rosati remodeled one of the houses on the church property to serve as a chapel for seminarians and parishioners.[23]

In the meantime, across the Atlantic, Bishop Rosati had prevailed upon a group of Clerics of St. Viator to come from France to open a preparatory seminary in Carondelet.[24] Mrs. Ann Biddle placed a house at their disposal for two years.[25] During the school year 1842-43, *Les Clercs du Saint Viateur* appear in the *Catholic Directory* as teachers at the "Preparatory Seminary of Saint Louis."[26] But Kenrick wrote Bishop Purcell of Cincinnati at this time that the Viatorians would not have the seminary as planned.[27] Instead the minor seminarians of the diocese would go to Perryville in the fall of 1843. The Vincentians decided to devote the entire St. Mary's plant to the training of clerical students, and moved the lay college to a new site in Cape Girardeau, Missouri, about thirty-five miles to the southeast. The Viatorians appear in the *Catholic Directory* for 1844 as conducting a "Catholic Academy" in Carondelet.[28]

When Kenrick opened a major seminary in Saint Louis scarcely fifteen blocks from an existing Catholic university, he was duplicating facilities unnecessarily. But he acted on long-held attitudes not whims. He did not approve the religiously pluralistic makeup of the student bodies on Catholic-sponsored colleges. In a letter to Purcell at this time he spoke of the dangers "to which vocations and even faith itself was exposed in our nondescript Catholic-Protestant colleges."[29]

Kenrick gave his views at length on the colleges in a letter to Purcell on March 27, 1843.[30] Kenrick began with a little reference to the newly opened St. Xavier College in Cincinnati; and stated that:

Catholics appear to lose rather than gain in religion by frequenting such academies; and as for Protestants, they lose, if you will, some prejudice, but they are rarely otherwise benefited by residence in our colleges .... How supremely inconsistent of us to be speaking of the dangers arising from the mixture of different religions in the public schools, and yet in our own colleges recognize the principle we seem to condemn."[31]

Catholic Journalism

In his early years in Saint Louis, Bishop Kenrick repeatedly tried to promote a successful Catholic journal. His first effort bore the unpromising title of *The Catholic Cabinet and Chronicle of Religious Intelligence*. A layman, William J. Mullin, published the magazine. Bishop Kenrick wrote an introductory article for the first issue; he gave his approval to the magazine and thought it would promote the interests of the Catholic religion in the diocese.[32] His brother in Philadelphia spoke of Peter Richard as the "editor" of the new magazine.[33]

One of the first literary magazines published west of the Mississippi River, *The Catholic Cabinet* presented historical and critical essays, poetry, and religious news. Since an early editorial insisted that the *Cabinet* place high among its goals "to publish whatever may tend to shed light on the history of Catholicity in the West,"[34] a reader could well expect an article on the discovery of the Mississippi River.[35] The writers of articles on the history of the diocese had access to the careful records of Bishop Rosati. Most of these historical articles offered a pleasant contrast to the hostile sectarian writing so conspicuous in those nativist days.

Bishop Kenrick sent a number of copies to his brother in the hope that some Philadelphians might subscribe. Francis Patrick encouraged Peter Richard, but gave little hope of substantial sales in the East.[36] He urged his brother to continue publication. "I am quite sure," he wrote in December 1843, "if the publication can be continued for two or three years, it will have many patrons throughout the United States."[37] Francis Patrick did not prove a good prophet. The magazine lasted slightly over two years. Its last issue was No. 2 of Volume III, under date of July, 1845.[38] But it was not to be Peter Richard's last venture in journalism.

The Death of Rosati

In the early spring of 1843, Bishop Rosati left the island of Haiti to report to Rome on his mission. He presumably had done his work well, only to have the unsettled political status of the country frustrate his efforts a short time after his departure. Further, the Caribbean climate had weakened him as the Louisiana climate had done years before. He did not rally on his return to Europe, and died in Rome on September 25, 1843.

Just as Rosati had differed from his predecessor, Du Bourg, so Coadjutor Kenrick contrasted sharply with Rosati. Du Bourg had recruited outstanding individuals and brought into the Missouri area four religious societies, but left the organization of the Church in Upper Louisiana to Rosati. So Kenrick inherited relatively large diocesan debts, when Rome called Rosati to other tasks. But Rosati had organized the new diocese.

Contemporary correspondence and comment shows a boundless warmth of feeling for Bishop Rosati on the part of all who met him. This was true of popes and future popes, presidents of Caribbean republics, bishops, mayors of cities, priests of various dioceses and orders, countless nuns — a deep affection for Bishop Rosati shows through the many pages of Louise Callan's life of Philippine Duchesne, for instance — lay people of all stations and of various religious affiliations. No other Church dignitary ever matched Bishop Rosati in the esteem of the midwestern Jesuits.[39] None of this is surprising in view of the deep love Bishop Rosati had for his fellowman.

Kenrick, in contrast, seems to have had few close friends. No one, it was alleged, ever said a familiar word to him.[40] He was extra-formal in manner. There was little of "the lilt of Irish laughter" in his life. As years went on, he was to correspond extensively with many bishops besides his brother, such as William Elder of Natchez, Martin Spalding of Baltimore, and John B. Purcell of Cincinnati. Only with Purcell did Kenrick give some slight evidence of personal friendship. And only Bishop Van de Velde spoke openly of his closeness with Kenrick.[41] In later life, Kenrick's closest friend seems to have been Patrick Ryan, his coadjutor.[42] Kenrick showed deep appreciation of non-Catholics, a great concern for the poor immigrant, and extreme consideration for different nationalities. Though he tended to solitude and a fellow bishop called him "Peter the Hermit,"[43] Kenrick made himself accessible. During his early years in Saint Louis, he "saw people at all hours of the day,"[44] and spoke often from the Cathedral pulpit. He had a fine command of language, a voice of unusual warmth and faultless pronunciation, with just a memory of Dublin in it. He never thundered from the pulpit or indulged in theatrics; but spoke clearly with careful logic and an abundance of scriptural references.[45] He was to leave no quotable passages of oratory and no book of collected sermons.

An inveterate reader, he covered a wide range of fields, including geology, a subject that fascinated him. He read Hebrew, Latin, and Greek as well as French, German, and Italian. He had deep respect for his contemporary John Henry Newman. He read James Clarence Mangan, the Irish poet and several Italian authors whose names no one else in American had ever heard.[46] Kenrick deeply appreciated a love of study on the part of his priests — even though that alone would not keep his admiration, since he knew that men became priests not for study but for souls.[47]

In administering affairs of the diocese, Kenrick was a delegator. "When he gave a clergyman a position," one of his priests wrote, "he presumed that he was competent and willing to fulfill that position."[48] On one occasion the name of a certain priest came up in conversation. "He must be a very good man," Kenrick remarked. "I have heard nothing of him in ten years."[49]

Frugal by nature, Kenrick "fared no better than the poorest priest of his diocese."[50] He disliked display both in dress and in attitude. He acted with dignity, and expected to be treated in the same way. He approached the golden mean between undue familiarity and excessive reserve. Over the years, however, many who knew him only slightly considered him cold and stern. Those who were close saw his warm tenderness and affectionate nature.[51] Kenrick gave the impression of being concerned with great things, and could not be trivial. "He was absorbed in God and could not take interest in the frivolities of the world."[52]

Kenrick lived a monastic routine. At home or away, he rose at four and prayed for an hour before beginning Mass at 5:30. After prayers of thanksgiving, he ate his breakfast. Throughout the rest of the day, he followed an exact schedule of business duties. interspersed by prayer. At four every afternoon, regardless of weather, he took a walk.[53]

During his long episcopate, the Church was to advance organizationally in the city and surrounding territory. But it does not appear to have been a *direct* public force in the city. Kenrick was never to deviate from the "no politics" rule of his Maynooth upbringing. During his years, "city hall" did not have to worry "what the chancery might think." Unlike so many other prelates, he avoided public functions other than those of his sacred office. "He could not be induced to take part in public meetings, political or otherwise."[54]

Kenrick may have avoided civic and political activities. But he knew the Church's and his own rights. A later governor of Missouri, David Francis, was to quote approvingly a remark of Francis Patrick Kenrick about his brother in Saint Louis: "The archbishop of Saint Louis knows his duties well; fulfills them; knows his rights and will maintain them."[55]

Even more surprising than his avoidance of civic politics was Kenrick's avoidance of ecclesiastical politics. He never set out to build a "Kenrick party" in the western Church. The idea would never have entered his mind. He was serving God and the people of the west. His integrity burned bright. Few men matched his remarkable consistency. These qualities of course, became manifest only as the years rolled on. His very durability was to elicit in his late years the type of awe that men might have for a founding father of the Republic.

Rosati had been a great pastoral bishop; Kenrick early showed himself a gifted financier and a father of the poor; as years went on, even a momentary meeting with Kenrick made people realize they had met an extraordinary man.[56]

Chapter 14

The Lion in Spring

Expansion of Parishes

Shortly after his arrival in Saint Louis, Kenrick had called a meeting of the prominent Catholics of the city. They discussed the debt on the Cathedral, but took no action. At a second meeting, Kenrick recommended that each make a pledge to meet the needs of the Church. Only one person responded. He promised twenty-five dollars. The bishop calmly dismissed the group. He said he would dispense with their services and adopt some other means of paying the debt.

Bishop Rosati had previously leased for one hundred years the north half of the Church block. Now Bishop Kenrick found it expedient to put to new use the greater part of what remained. He built some commercial properties. In the next decade and a half he was to rent and finally to sell these properties in order to liquidate the remaining debts on the Cathedral parish. This transaction was to leave the Cathedral less than one-fourth of the original church block.[1] But, for the time, Kenrick did not easily get over his chagrin at the cost of the building. He wrote to his friend, Bishop Purcell: "This Cathedral has retarded the progress of religion in this diocese by twenty years at least."[2]

The expansion of the city had already made the need of new parishes clear. Back in 1839 Rosati had begun the erection of the Most Holy Trinity Church in Frenchtown; but it never got beyond its foundation. A second church — this one on the near north side — had been underway at Kenrick's arrival. In one of the last public acts before departing for Europe, Bishop Rosati had laid the cornerstone of St. Francis Xavier Church in conjunction with Saint Louis University at Ninth and Christy on April 12, 1840. The group supporting this new church were mostly of Irish background, with a few members of Creole families joining them. On his arrival Kenrick thought plans for this large church premature in view of the large debt on the Cathedral.[3]

Since preaching at St. Francis Xavier's was to be entirely in English, Kenrick abolished French sermons at Sunday morning Masses at the Cathedral, keeping French, for a time, only at vespers. The Jesuits opened Saint Francis Xavier's Church for services on Easter Sunday, 1843. The Sisters of Charity conducted a free school for girls in the parish and four scholastics of the Jesuit order began a school for boys in the basement of the new building. In the following year, October, 1844, the Jesuits opened a third school exclusively for boys of German background.

In the meantime, Ann Lucas Hunt gave a half-block of land on Third and Gratiot Streets, about twelve blocks south of the Cathedral, for Our Lady of Victories Church. Bishop Kenrick bought the other half from her brother, J. H. Lucas. On Sunday, June 25, 1843, Bishop Anthony Blanc of New Orleans laid the cornerstone of the new church. Bishop Kenrick summoned Father Fischer from his parish in the country to be administrator of the new church. So popular was he with his people that they still called Our Lady of Victories "Father Fischer's Church" even after he had retired from the pastorate.

Coadjutor Bishop Kenrick laid the foundation stone of St. Patrick's Church on Sixth and Biddle, about twelve blocks north and three blocks west of the Cathedral, on October 17, 1843. Mrs. Ann Biddle contributed the lot. Her mother, Mrs. John Mullanphy, gave a thousand dollars to the erection of the church.[4] Once again, support was not widespread and the bishop incurred considerable debt in bringing the church to its completion.[5]

In the same year (1843) that Kenrick promoted new churches in Saint Louis, he also pressed for new dioceses in the West at the Fifth Provincial Council of Baltimore. As a result, Andrew Byrne became bishop of Little Rock, William Quarter bishop of Chicago, and John Henni bish-

Anne Lucas Hunt, daughter of Judge J. B. Lucas, and wife of Captain Theodore Hunt, U.S.N., donated many pieces of property to Catholic institutions: at Tenth and St. Charles for the St. Francis Xavier parish school for girls; at Third and Gratiot for Our Lady Victories Church; at 17th and Chestnut for the Convent of the Good Shepherd; and in Normandy for the church that bears the name of her patron, St. Ann. She wrote extensively on early Saint Louis and left a record of early times in her Memoirs. (Photograph by the Missouri Historical Society.)

op of Milwaukee. Two religious superiors from the Missouri area, John Timon, C.M., and Peter Verhaegen, S.J., attended the meeting. The assembled fathers spent much of their time in routine church administration; but they did praise the Rocky Mountain Jesuit Indian Mission, and the American efforts in Liberia.

On March 17, 1844, Bishop Kenrick laid the cornerstone of a second southside church, St. Vincent's, situated in Soulard's addition, near the unfinished Holy Trinity Church that it supplanted. Since the occasion was St. Patrick's Day, various organizations, such as the Hibernian Society, the Catholic Temperance Society, and the Young Catholic Friends, joined in the celebration. When Bishop

The following year Mrs. Biddle gave a piece of property adjoining the St. Joseph lot, worth six thousand dollars, and three thousand dollars in cash for a new orphans' home conducted by the Daughters of Charity.[8] The nuns themselves raised three thousand more dollars from the general public, and Bishop Kenrick borrowed the remaining four thousand.[9]

Up to Sunday, May 25, 1845, the Cathedral had been the parish church of the entire city. In a pastoral to the people on that day, Bishop Kenrick announced the division of the city into four parishes: the Cathedral, St. Francis Xavier, St. Patrick's, and St. Vincent's. The two German-speaking congregations, Our Lady of Victories on

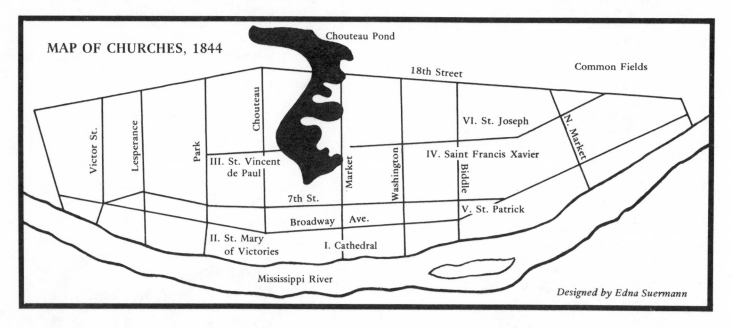

MAP OF CHURCHES, 1844

Chouteau Pond

Common Fields

18th Street

Victor St.

Lesperance

Park

Chouteau

III. St. Vincent de Paul

Market

Washington

Biddle

VI. St. Joseph

IV. Saint Francis Xavier

N. Market

7th St.

Broadway Ave.

V. St. Patrick

II. St. Mary of Victories

I. Cathedral

Mississippi River

Designed by Edna Suermann

Kenrick consecrated St. Vincent's one year and a half later, on November 16, 1845, he had the assistance of two men who were soon to join him in the episcopate. The Jesuit vice-provincial James Van de Velde was to become bishop of Chicago three years later and the Vincentian Thaddeus Amat bishop of Monterey, California, in 1853. Father Francis Cellini, C.M., sang the Solemn High Mass.

The German Catholics on the near north side around Saint Louis University had gradually formed a community that attended Mass at the Chapel of St. Aloysius. They needed a church. Mrs. Ann Biddle donated a lot, one hundred fifty feet by one hundred feet on Eleventh Avenue and the street that bore the family name, in what was then the northwest corner of the city. Again a great concourse of people, including the Hibernians, came for the cornerstone laying of St. Joseph's Church on April 14, 1844.

A month later Kenrick wrote to Timon in a much more sanguine mood about the financial situation. He had cleared up all the money owed at ten percent, but there remained about sixteen thousand dollars at eight percent. "The only debts of Bishop Rosati that remain unpaid," he stated "are those to Madame Biddle, Reverend M. DeAngeli, Madame Soulard, and about seven hundred dollars which I can at any time pay by giving a note to the person for Bishop Rosati."[6] Kenrick wanted Timon to negotiate with Father DeAngeli; he believed he could work out satisfactory terms with Mrs. Soulard and Mrs. Biddle.[7]

the southeast side of the city and St. Joseph's on the northwest, were not parishes in the technical sense. They were subsidiary churches, Our Lady of Victories for the German-speaking Catholics within the Cathedral parish, and St. Joseph's for those in St. Patrick and St. Francis Xavier parishes. Only the German Catholic people could fulfill their obligations in these subsidiary churches. Saint Louis County had five churches at this time: St. Ferdinand's in Florissant; St. Peter's in Manchester Township; St. Martin's in Central Township; Mt. Carmel in Carondelet; and Assumption Parish in Meramec Township.[10]

Within a few years after Kenrick's arrival in Saint Louis, the bishop's attitude toward his diocese had changed dramatically. In a report to the Leopoldine Society in Vienna on December 10, 1844, he spoke enthusiastically of the great extent of the Saint Louis diocese, of the new churches under construction — with a quite natural attention to progress among German-speaking Catholics — of the schools and colleges, of the minor seminary at Perryville, and the major seminary recently begun near the episcopal residence in Saint Louis. He called the Cathedral "a very beautiful building,"[11] and gave a fine tribute to his adopted city: "As no city of the United States enjoys greater opportunities for the practice of the Catholic religion, so there is none that expresses Catholic life and Catholic character better than Saint Louis."[12] This was no idle boast. Catholics enjoyed more prestige and freedom to develop in the Missouri metropolis than in most cities in the world at the time.

Educational Progress

Catholic education, disproportionately strong in Saint Louis already, took another step forward in 1844. The establishment of the Chicago diocese the year before had separated the Visitation Sisters in Kaskaskia from the jurisdiction of Bishop Kenrick. The Saint Louis prelate asked that some Sisters continue to work in his diocese. As a result, in the spring of 1844, Mother Agnes Brent and six Sisters left the Illinois village for Saint Louis. They opened a school for girls on Sixth near Pine.

Shortly after this, Bishop Kenrick planned to visit Kaskaskia in the company of the new Chicago bishop, William Quarter, and two men destined to be bishops before the end of the decade, John Timon, C.M., and James M. De Saint-Palais. By the time the four clergymen reached the old Illinois capital, a great flood had inundated the Visitation Convent and school. The remaining Sisters and their students had to take refuge in the Pierre Menard Home, on a terrace east of the Kaskaskia River.* On June 26, 1844, a steamer picked them up and brought this second group of Sisters to Saint Louis. Mrs. Ann Biddle offered the newcomers her own house on Fifth Street, that had been serving as the girls' orphanage, for a convent and school. She reserved for herself only one room of the capacious building. Two years later, in July, 1846, the two communities of the Visitandines reunited under Mother Agnes' direction in a convent on Ninth Street offered them by the bishop.

The same flood drove the Sisters of St. Joseph from Cahokia across the river to Carondelet. They were to return to the Illinois village three years later. But further floods and unhealthy conditions in the lowland area eventually forced their permanent withdrawal. The congregation began several schools in Saint Louis proper.

Under the direction of Father Augustus Paris, three Sisters opened a school for Catholic Negro girls in a brick building at Third and Poplar on February 5, 1845. Soon the enrollment reached one hundred.[13] Most of the youngsters were daughters of free Negroes.** A few were slave-children whose masters wanted them to learn to read and write. The curriculum included the "three R's," French, sewing, and catechism lessons from Father Benedict Roux twice a week. Father Paris showed continued interest by regular visits to the school, and took a personal concern in the improvement of "his children."[14]

In spite of a strong Missouri prejudice against the education of Negroes — lest they might be able to read Abolitionist literature — the Sisters started out courageously. Their work offered great promise. Further, on Sundays, the Sisters taught religion to slave children.

In late 1845 Bishop Edward Barron came west. This Irish-born priest had worked in Philadelphia and then, at the recommendation of Francis Patrick Kenrick, had become vicar apostolic of the American Negro Colony of Liberia in West Africa. Death had depleted the ranks of European priests working with him in the Liberian mission. As a result, the Holy See decided to transfer the vicariate to the hands of an order especially trained for mission work in those latitudes. Thereupon, Bishop Barron resigned and returned to the States.

Peter Richard Kenrick wanted Barron to be the new bishop of Vincennes; but Francis Patrick Kenrick did not approve of this recommendation. He wanted Barron to remain in Missouri and occasionally, at Peter Richard Kenrick's request, to exercise episcopal functions.[15] Bishop Barron confirmed at parishes in Southeast[16] and Northeast Missouri[17] during the summer of 1846.

Among the institutions of the city that Bishop Barron visited in the company of Bishop Kenrick was the school for Negro girls at Third and Poplar, to close shortly afterward, under pressure of civil authorities. A year later (1847), incidentally, the Missouri legislature was to outlaw the teaching of Negroes even in the basic subjects of reading and writing.[18]

Bishop Barron received a substantial money gift for his support from the bishop of Philadelphia in a second letter shortly after. Francis Patrick also wrote that the newly converted polemicist, Orestes A. Brownson, wanted the bishop of Saint Louis to write an occasional article for his review.[19] Peter Richard presumably did write at least one article, in the judgment of the editor of the Kenrick-Frenaye correspondence,* who carefully checked the style and presentation. The article dealt with Christian ethics and appeared in the April, 1846, edition of *Brownson's Review.*[20] If the article were Peter Richard's, he must have written it immediately upon receiving his brother's request.

In the meantime, the Sisters of St. Joseph undertook two more ventures in Saint Louis. At the request of Father Thaddeus Amat, C.M., pastor of the recently opened St. Vincent de Paul's Church, three Sisters opened a parish school on Seventh Street in November, 1845. In the summer of the following year, Bishop Kenrick asked the Sisters to take charge of a boys' orphanage on Third and Walnut, formerly staffed by the Daughters of Charity. Four Sisters began this project, destined to have a far longer history than the recently ended effort at education of Negro girls.[21]

New Paper, Pastoral Support, New Parish

The Catholic Cabinet, the second Catholic newspaper of Saint Louis, concluded its career of twenty-seven months in the summer of 1845. In November of the same year, a third newspaper, the *Catholic News-Letter,* made its appearance. The publisher, W. J. Mullin, had previously published the *Cabinet.* An unidentified "Association of Gentlemen" edited the new weekly.[22]

These unidentified gentlemen were Kenrick and some of his priests. A study of the style of writing suggests that a chief contributor was Father John O'Hanlon, a priest of the diocese at the time, who later returned to Ireland and

---

*Sister Josephine Barber, V.H.M., a postulant at the time of the Visitandines' arrival in Kaskaskia, left a graphic memorial of these pioneering years: *History of the Foundation in Kaskaskia,* unpublished manuscript in the Archives of the Visitation Academy, Saint Louis County, Missouri. Perhaps because of the unfortunate circumstances surrounding the Visitandines' unexpected arrival in Kaskaskia, this document does not reflect the warm regard for Bishop Rosati so evident in other contemporary documents.

**By 1860 half of the Negroes in Saint Louis were to be free.

*An Augustinian scholar at Villanova University selected for publication a group of letters in the Cathedral Archives of Philadelphia, written between 1830 and 1862. The writers were Bishop Francis Patrick Kenrick and a layman, Marc Anthony Frenaye. Hence the title of the book, *The Kenrick-Frenaye Correspondence* (Philadelphia, 1920). One hundred and ninety-eight of these letters of Francis Patrick went to his brother in Saint Louis.

published two books, *Life and Scenery in Missouri* and *Irish Saints and Shrines.* The *Catholic News-Letter* carried a regular column of religious news, a series of letters from Father Pierre Jean DeSmet on mission activities in the Canadian Rockies, historical articles of a religious ("The Divinity of Christ") or secular ("The Storming of Stony Point") character, and articles on Mexico, sympathetic in nature, in spite of American hostility toward that country.[23] The *News-Letter* discounted the possibility of war with Mexico;[24] but correctly showed worry about the impending failure of the potato, the staple crop of Ireland.[25] The paper carried on through its second volume under the title of the *St. Louis News Letter,* but by that time the editor had to announce that patronage did not warrant continuance.[26]

In his pastoral letter of September 14, 1846, Bishop Kenrick set down procedures for the support of the church in a free society. He wanted every parish priest, or priest in a district not yet formally constituting a parish, to take a census of all the Catholic families in his area. Next, the pastor was to appoint two men each year to solicit contributions from these families of not less than three dollars each. This was to be over and above the weekly collections, pew-rents, and special donations at the time of baptisms and marriages. Where the parishioners could not collect two hundred and fifty dollars annually for the support of a pastor, the priest did not have to reside permanently in the area. Kenrick authorized every clergyman, who had the charge of several congregations, to recognize the diversity of support in apportioning his time. And lastly, Kenrick required of each pastor one-twentieth of the money collected for episcopal expenses.[27] The bishop was to modify the last provision a few years later. Only those parishes whose annual income went over five hundred dollars had to contribute to the support of the bishop, and then only a thirtieth of their revenue.[28]

Kenrick, lastly, recognized the new direction of the city's growth. All the early churches had been within twelve blocks of the river, as the city stretched lengthwise along it. Soon Saint Louis was to begin a new push straight west. In 1847 Bishop Kenrick commissioned Father Patrick O'Brien, assistant at the Cathedral, to organize a new congregation in the west end. Father O'Brien chose a site at Sixteenth and Chestnut for a church that he placed under the patronage of St. John the Apostle.

Caring for the vast diocese alone would have taxed the energies of a lesser man. But Kenrick had the drive and zeal to concern himself with the Church in the entire country. He took an important part in the Sixth Provincial Council of Baltimore in 1846. He gave the memorial sermon at the Mass of Requiem for the deceased prelates, including his revered predecessor, Bishop Rosati, who had passed away since the last council. Kenrick prepared the formal letters of the council to the Holy Father, Gregory XVI. The council chose the Immaculate Conception as the patronal feast of the United States.[29]

The Coming of Melcher

Kenrick had taken the first doctor of divinity of the diocese, Father Joseph Melcher, as his theologian to the council. This distinguished man, destined to be bishop of Green Bay, had an interesting part to play in the development of Catholicism in Saint Louis. The last recruit of Bishop Rosati, Joseph Melcher was born in Vienna and

reared in Modena, one of the little Italian principalities under the influence of Austria at the time. His father had a position at the court of the Duke of Modena. The young man spoke both German and Italian. In 1830, at the age of twenty-three, he became a priest and pursued his degree of doctor of divinity. For twelve years he worked as court chaplain with the incidental duty of caring for the German Catholics of Modena. Then he felt a call to the foreign missions. Fortunately for Saint Louis, he ran into Bishop Rosati who enlisted his services.

Even though Bishop Kenrick had spoken of the great need of German-speaking priests in Saint Louis, he sent the newly arrived doctor of divinity to the Arkansas Post. When Little Rock became a diocese in 1843, Kenrick recalled Melcher to a cluster of villages along the Meramec River, about thirty miles south of Saint Louis. Three years later, Kenrick invited him to attend the Sixth Provincial Council.

On returning from Baltimore, Kenrick appointed Father Melcher vicar-general for the German-speaking Catholics and sent him back to Europe for the purpose of securing priests for the rapidly increasing German settlements of the diocese.[30] This was the first of three journeys Melcher was to take for this purpose. Eventually, he recruited four priests and twelve theological students, seven of whom eventually worked in the diocese. Melcher's second recruiting trip was to result in the arrival of two men destined for long prominence in the German Catholic community of Saint Louis, Henry Muehlsiepen and Francis Goller.

On his return from his first trip to Europe, Father Melcher took charge of Our Lady of Victories Church in place of Father Fischer, who stayed on as assistant and carried on the routine parochial duties while Father Melcher busied himself with his duties as vicar-general. At this time also Father Melcher turned down the bishopric of Quincy in Illinois.

In the fall of 1846 Peter Richard was host to his brother, Francis Patrick, who came west for a vacation. The Philadelphia prelate spent a week in Saint Louis and also visited Cincinnati, Louisville, Bardstown, and Vincennes. Francis Patrick wanted to see his brother, to promote his own theological works, and to urge his brother to put out a revised edition of the book on Anglican Orders. This work Peter Richard began shortly after Francis Patrick's visit.[31]

Saint Vincent de Paul Society

Saint Louis, the premier city of the mid-continent, pioneered in one of the great lay movements of the nineteenth century, the Saint Vincent de Paul Society. Impelled by the spirit and goals of the great French saint of charity, a young Frenchman of an ancient Christian-Jewish family, Frederic Ozanam, began a new society of educated laymen in 1833. These men pledged themselves to personal works of charity as a manifestation and an enlargement of their own faith and as an evidence of the divine origin and perennial vitality of the Church. By 1840 the total membership of the organization had gone over one thousand, with conferences in many French cities, and one beyond France's borders, in Rome.[32] Conferences sprang up during the succeeding few years in Brussels, Constantinople, London, and Dublin.[33]

Saint Louis folklore dramatically but unhistorically credits the foundation of the first American conference to

This mosaic in the great Cathedral of Saint Louis shows Frederick Ozanam, founder of the St. Vincent de Paul Society, and three of the four principal personalities of the first unit in the Western Hemisphere: John Timon, C.M., who brought the idea to Saint Louis and later became bishop of Buffalo; Bryan Mullanphy, secretary, who became mayor of Saint Louis; and Dr. Moses Linton, president, who was one of the most versatile of all Saint Louis Catholic laymen. No likeness of Father Ambrose Heim, the first spiritual director, is available. (Photograph by Robert Arteaga.)

a chance meeting in Paris of young Bryan Mullanphy, son of John Mullanphy of Saint Louis, and Frederic Ozanam, the founder of the Saint Vincent de Paul Society. Historical records offer no evidence of such a meeting. Bryan Mullanphy was, indeed, an important man in the first conference. But historian, Daniel T. McColgan, sees evidence that points to Father John Timon, the Vincentian superior, as the man who brought information of the society to Saint Louis.[34] No doubt Timon spoke to Bishop Kenrick and to a number of prominent laymen of the city about the work in France. On November 20, 1845, a group of Catholic laymen of the Cathedral parish met together to hear about the program of Frederic Ozanam. A committee, composed of Dr. Thomas Anderson, John Everhart, Dr. Moses Linton, and Judge Bryan Mullanphy, called on Bishop Kenrick. The bishop approved the

plans.[35] As a result the group set up the first American conference with Dr. Moses Linton as president, Judge Bryan Mullanphy as vice-president, and Father Ambrose Heim as spiritual director. These three began the initial St. Vincent de Paul Society in the United States. Contemporary records give the title "Founder" to the deeply loved Father Heim.[36]

Father Heim, a native of the diocese of Nancy in Alsace, had come to Saint Louis in 1832, and received his seminary training in Perryville. Bishop Rosati ordained him on July 23, 1837. Heim served for a while in outstate Missouri and Illinois and then in the city at Our Lady of Victories. He encouraged his people to save and set up a bank for them. This work for the poor of Saint Louis brought Father Heim to the attention of Bishop Kenrick, who reassigned him to the Cathedral.

Dr. Moses L. Linton, a Kentuckian by birth, and a convert to the faith, had moved to Missouri to teach in St. Louis University's Medical School. He edited the first medical and surgical journal of the West, authored several books of medicine, engaged on occasion in religious controversy, and later was to distinguish himself as a member of Missouri's constitutional convention at the end of the Civil War.

Judge Bryan Mullanphy, the only son of John Mullanphy, was to serve as mayor of Saint Louis in 1847, and to leave a large sum of money as an aid for immigrants arriving in Saint Louis. As the wealthiest member of the initial group, it should not surprise anyone that early members of the society recalled his generosity to the poor.[37]

The conference was soon to prove its worth in the cholera epidemic that hit the city.

Anticipating the founding of the local St. Vincent de Paul Society by a few years, a group of Catholic ladies under the leadership of Miss Angela Hughes had begun the Catholic Orphan's Association of Saint Louis in 1841. Gradually men joined their efforts. In 1849, the year of incorporation, the board of directors included John B. Sarpy, Edward Walsh, Thomas O'Flaherty, and Amadee Vallee. They supported the two diocesan orphan asyla.[38]

About the same time, Father John Higginbotham of the new Saint Michael's congregation on the north side started the Catholic Total Abstinence and Benevolent Society. He called the first meeting on August 15, 1848. In a few years membership reached one thousand. Originally established strictly as a temperance society, the organization gradually had to widen its fraternal benefits.[39] In the mid-fifties, a new benevolent group, the Shamrock Society, was to lure away many young Irish-Americans. Eventually both organizations succumbed to dissension arising from the Civil War.

Chapter 15

The Midwest's First Archdiocese

Manifest Destiny for the Archdiocese

The early development of the Archdiocese of Saint Louis came during a momentous period of American history. The mid-forties saw the growth of the notion of "manifest destiny." Under this theory, Providence had decided that the nation should stretch from the Atlantic to the Pacific. Texas had become independent from Mexico in 1836. West of Texas, the entire Southwest remained part of the Republic of Mexico. The land of Oregon beyond the Rockies, where Father DeSmet and his associates worked, had long been in dispute between the United States and Britain. Soon the two nations were to recognize as American territory the land below the forty-ninth parallel, the areas eventually to become the states of Oregon and Washington.

In 1846 the Mexican War broke out. Troops moved southwest from Jefferson Barracks near Saint Louis. Soon the entire Southwest, including Texas and California, was part of the American Union. Into these western lands poured countless frontiersmen. They moved out of Saint Louis up the Missouri by steamboat to Independence near Kansas City and then overland along two trails, one to Oregon, the other to Santa Fe. The discovery of gold in California would soon add a further impetus to the trek west. Steamboats plied the Mississippi in great numbers. This was, indeed, the heydey of steamboat travel.

Saint Louis became the first ecclesiastical province in the mid-continent on July 20, 1847. Baltimore had been the first in the entire nation. Rome had set up a province in the Oregon Territory one year before, in 1846, but Oregon was not as yet a state of the Union.

At the Baltimore council in 1846 the bishops had talked about creating a province in the west because of the travel difficulties in getting back to Baltimore for provincial councils. Many thought that New Orleans, an older see than Saint Louis, should have the preference. Easterners showed more concern for the Atlantic seaboard and believed that New York should have preceded Saint Louis. It was generally believed that Francis Patrick had used his considerable influence with Bishop Cullen in Rome to promote his brother's see. Francis Patrick disclaimed having exerted any *pressure* towards that goal. He did admit, however, that he mentioned Saint Louis to Cardinal Franzoni when that cardinal asked him what city in the West ought to be raised.[1]

Peter Richard did not receive the pallium, the woolen vestment that symbolized his office. Further, Rome did not appoint any suffragan bishops. Kenrick could partially blame himself for this. He had suggested in 1846 that the next council determine the suffragan bishops.

During the summer that he became archbishop, Kenrick made a long tour through the Ozarks and then up the Missouri River as far as Kansas City, visiting, preaching, and confirming, as he went. This trip was typical of others he took through his diocese. Since he carefully described it in a letter to the office of the Propagation, a lengthy discussion of it will serve to illuminate the story of the archdiocese at the time.[2]

Father Melcher was in Europe on a recruiting tour; so Kenrick took Father Francis Rutkowski as his companion. He traveled southwest from the city, visiting Gravois (later Kirkwood), Manchester, Pacific, Union (where he found only one Catholic), and Gallagher Mills. Usually the archbishop preached on a street corner. Some Protestant people came out of curiosity; others because of the novelty of the situation; still others to find out what Catholics felt. When Kenrick preached at Steeleville, where there were no Catholics, several ministers came to listen to him. One man said that he had walked eight miles to hear the Saint Louis prelate.

Kenrick went as far as Meramec* Spring, near Saint James, about a hundred miles southwest of the city. Then he turned east towards the lead mining region. Now in French-speaking territory, he ventured a few words in that language to the children. He visited Old Mines, Potasi, Fredericktown, and Caledonia. He moved on to Ste. Genevieve, where he explained to the children the nature of confession as far as his "poor knowledge of French would permit."[3]

He took a steamboat back to Saint Louis, then went up the Missouri River through the "Little Dixie" counties to Kansas City. He visited the west Missouri towns in reverse order, beginning at Independence, and coming back through Lexington, Marshall, Booneville, and Columbia. The entire trip south and west took two and a half months.

Attitudes of the Archbishop

Archbishop Kenrick was autocratic in outlook. "A bishop should not reason with his flock," he was to write, "but authoritatively direct them."[4] At the same time, he strongly opposed over centralization in the church. He could not understand why the bishops of the United States had to request a permission every five years that the Irish bishops presumed without reference to Rome. Kenrick believed that the Vatican made too many decisions without benefit of facts. One such was the assumption that after five years parishes would so flourish in the midwest that they no longer needed help from foreign lands.[5] He believed that Americans could better handle their own problems. Consistent with this belief, he opposed the setting up of a college for American semi-

---

*The official title is still "Maramec." For a while many referred to the region along the river as "Merrimack." For the sake of simplicity, this book will always employ Meramec, the more accepted spelling of the word in Missouri.

narians either at Louvain or at Rome. When such a college did open in Rome later on, however, he was to send a contribution to its development.[6]

He encouraged the development of subsidiary national churches. These helped the immigrant make a transition from the old world to the new without losing his identification with the church. The newcomer found sympathy, understanding, and an explanation of his religion in a language he could understand. As transitional devices, these parishes performed great service to the cause of religion.

Kenrick did not favor the approach of the French curés to the issues facing American congregations of the Midwest. They seemed too little concerned with parochial organization. This proved true even of priests with German names who grew up in the French tradition, such as Joseph Anthony Lutz and Joseph Fischer. A small exodus of priests of the old regime took place in 1847. Even though Kenrick had made Lutz vicar-general for the Germans — to whom he had in fact paid little attention — Lutz transferred to the diocese of New York in the summer of 1845. Fischer returned to his native Lorraine. Francis J. Renaud, along with two other priests of Du Bourg's old Archdiocese of Besancon, Fathers Joseph Richard Bole and August S. Paris had come to the diocese in the fall of 1838.[7] Renaud returned to France at this time.[8] Father Paris was to serve as pastor of the Cathedral from 1844 to 1857, and then left Saint Louis.

As a graduate of Maynooth, a seminary with a strong "no politics" tradition, Kenrick never meddled even indirectly in the political activities of city, state, or nation. He had no special line of communication with city hall, recognized no political dignitaries in the congregation on occasions when he gave sermons in their presence, and refrained for long periods from reading newspapers to avoid entangling himself in political controversy.

As a young priest, Kenrick had wanted to join a religious order. Yet he had grave misgivings about the relations of religious institutes and the dioceses where they worked. In the late forties, the local Jesuits came under his criticism. Saint Louis University planned a boarding facility on the college farm in north Saint Louis, a piece of property near the O'Fallon estate (later O'Fallon Park). President Verhaegen had originally purchased the property in 1836 with a view to locating the entire university there. But by 1849 the Jesuits planned a dual campus. The day college would remain at Ninth and Washington. The new building would be for boarders only. Father John Elet, Jesuit vice-provincial, presumed he could authorize the new building under existing permissions. Kenrick saw it as a new establishment that required distinct episcopal approval.

This circumstance gave Kenrick occasion to express his full views on religious orders. In a letter to Bishop Purcell, he wrote:

I do think and hope that the time is not far distant when the religious orders will be placed in immediate subjection to the bishops and those privileges and exceptions be removed which make men who have vowed obedience the born antagonists of those whom the Holy Ghost has placed to govern the Church of God.[9]

In writing to the editor of the *Freeman's Journal* the following year, Kenrick complained of the corporate spirit of the Jesuit order:

The *esprit de corps* had unfortunately attained more than due proportion in the working of the system and has caused men otherwise respectable to assume a position with respect to the ordinaries and secular clergy which is anything but promotive of harmonious and united cooperation.[10]

The Jesuit superior, John Elet, grew aware of Kenrick's outlook. In a letter to the general of the order in Rome, Elet quoted Kenrick as saying about the Jesuits: "You constitute a band apart; you sow discord in the diocese."[11] Elet could not resist contrasting Kenrick's attitude with that of his predecessors. He wrote: "Kenrick will take from us what Du Bourg and Rosati begged us to accept."[12] Pierre Jean De Smet complained that Kenrick even found fault with the Men's Sodality at the College Church — "the best thing ever done in Saint Louis."[13]

At the request of De Smet, Bishop James Van de Velde of Chicago wrote an amazingly frank letter to his friend Peter Richard Kenrick. Van de Velde said that the Jesuits felt Kenrick's coldness towards them, and added with amazing frankness that others might call the archbishop a tryant, but the Jesuits would never do so.[14]

Kenrick's dislike of Jesuit "policy" did not turn him against individual Jesuits. Kenrick wanted several as bishops. At one time, he sought Van de Velde for his coadjutor. Later on he was to recommend Jesuits Miege for Kansas, De Smet for Nebraska, and Patschowski for Southern Illinois. On another occasion, he listed Jesuit pastor Arnold Damen as his third choice for coadjutor of Saint Louis.[15] Other midwestern bishops, however, understood that the general of the Jesuits, with the Pope's approval, was refusing to allow any of his men to be bishops.[16] The matter of Jesuit bishops became a grave concern for the Jesuit general; and only served to confirm Kenrick in his opinion that the Jesuits put the good of their order above that of the local church.

In writing style, Peter Richard and his brother sounded like their early contemporaries, the English writers, Thackery and Dickens. Almost no suggestion of humor appeared in the writings of either brother. Francis Patrick occasionally asked Peter Richard to show a kindness to someone moving west. But little warmth of personal friendliness and hardly a personal touch showed up in the letters between the two. Francis Patrick never used his brother's first name, but always addressed him as "the Bishop of Drasa," or as "my very dear brother, the Bishop of Saint Louis." Peter Richard was almost equally formal. Later on, when Archbishop Martin Spalding talked of writing a life of Francis Patrick, Peter Richard claimed that he really knew little about his brother, who had left for the seminary when he, the younger brother, was only nine years old.[17]

On a rare occasion, Kenrick might refer to a continental-born priest who had been in the United States longer than he as a "foreigner." He did this with Peter Verhaegen, at the time Bishop John Hughes included the Jesuit superior on a list of possible coadjutors for New York.[18] On the whole, however, Kenrick tended to see the middle west as a melting point. He did not identify Irish and American, or Irish and Catholic, as so many Irish clergymen of his time did. He wanted priests who could speak the language of the people among whom they worked. He allowed immigrants to go to those churches where they could hear their native tongue. He urged Rome to appoint bishops who spoke German in those areas where German-Americans were numerous, such as parts of Wisconsin and Illinois.

At a time when many indulged in nationalistic prejudices, Kenrick remained silently impartial.

Nativism in the Forties

Open anti-Catholicism in the United States in the *early* thirties had consisted in erratic outbursts of a radical fringe of the Protestant populace. Efforts against Catholics in the *late* thirties had taken the form of a crusade to "save the West from the Pope." Conflicts over the use of the Bible and biased textbooks in the public schools of New York City in the early forties brought more moderate Protestant groups into the fray.

A Protestant Reformation Society entered the anti-Catholic crusade with a less sensational lecturing program that "attracted large audiences even in such centers of sober Christianity as Harvard and Princeton Universities."[19]

At Princeton, interest was so great among the students of the Theological School that they named a "Committee on the Romish Church, Public Morals and Infidelity," to which was committed the task of diffusing knowledge of popery not only among the students but also among the townspeople.[20]

Small local societies sprang up in many cities and towns to defend the nation against Catholicism.

Riots broke out in Philadelphia in 1844. A mob burned St. Michael's and St. Augustine's Catholic churches. Francis Patrick Kenrick had urged his people to a conciliatory position,[21] only to find that two grand juries blamed the Catholics for the destruction of Catholic churches by the Protestant rioters.[22] Bishop John Hughes kept outward calm in New York by calling on his people to use force if necessary in defense of the Catholic churches of the city.[23]

The Philadelphia riot triggered trouble in many places of the country, among them Saint Louis. A mob attacked the Saint Louis University School of Medicine, destroying the scientific equipment. A force of Catholic citizens gathered to defend the other buildings of the university clustered around Saint Francis Xavier Church. For the moment, the mob subsided.[24]

While his brother in Philadelphia had taken a conciliatory tone in the face of threats, and John Hughes of New York a more effective belligerent attitude, the Lion of Saint Louis kept silent. He extended his "no politics" rule into the realm of violent "political" expression.

As the nativists became more insistent in their anti-Catholic outburst during the ensuing years, the medical professors requested the trustees of Saint Louis University in 1848 to allow the Medical College to separate from the parent institution. Fortunately at that time the school enjoyed the services of its best president since Verhaegen. As long as the strong hand of popular and friendly John Baptist Druyts (1847-1854) guided the school, the nativists were able to inflict no permanent damage on its educational efforts. Druyts called a meeting of the university trustees on October 15, 1848. The trustees believed that separation would prove harmful to the Medical School and to the entire university. They thought it unwise to yield to the groundless prejudices. In fact they even suggested that they might seek other physicians to conduct the Medical School if the current staff insisted on disaffiliating.[25] The trustees considered a similar but informal proposal at their January 24, 1849, meeting. They stood by the decision of the previous year.[26]

For the moment, the storm passed. The following year, Colonel John O'Fallon, father-in-law of Dean Charles Alexander Pope of the medical school, erected a handsome and capacious bank-style building to house the medical department at Seventh and Myrtle (later Clark Avenue). This site about ten blocks from the main campus, seemed relatively safe from attacks should nativists again move against Saint Louis University or the College Church.

The "Year of Revolutions" and Saint Louis

The year 1848 saw two events in Europe that dramatically affected the history of Saint Louis and the development of the Church in the Missouri metropolis. First, a potato blight in Ireland in the late forties turned the surge of Irish immigration to America into a true flood. Great numbers came to Saint Louis, expecially the old Irish neighborhood around Saint Patrick's Church on the near-north side.

Secondly, revolutions swept the continent of Europe. As part of the revolutionary unrest, many doctrinnaire liberal Germans wanted to unify their country under the leadership of the Prussian king. The Austrian emperor thwarted this, aided by the threat of Russian assistance and the hesitancies of the Prussian king. A great number of these North Germans, called Forty-eighters, came to Saint Louis. They brought with them a desire for national unity that was to make them strong adherents of the Union in the coming American Civil War; but they also brought an anti-clerical, an anti-Catholic attitude that was quite out of place in the free American life of Saint Louis, and definitely affected the mood of German Catholicism in the city.

The German Catholics faced hostility from two sides: from their Irish or French fellow Catholics because they were German; from their fellow Germans, the Forty-eighters, because they were Catholic. The bitter writings of some of these free-thinking Germans against their Catholic fellow countrymen astounds the twentieth century reader. There is little wonder then that for a time the Saint Louis Catholics of German background assumed a defensive posture. They built their own schools, kept their own language, and started their own mutual benefit associations such as the "Saint Louis Society." Alone in a strange world, they withdrew into a citadel of German Catholicism in the heart of the American Midwest. Assimilation would come later and in gradual steps.

The prefect of the Congregation of the Propagation of the Faith had urged that a knowledge of the language used by the faithful in each diocese should be a consideration in the choice of bishops. Kenrick appointed successive vicars-general for the German-speaking Catholics.

Other continental exiles besides the Forty-eighters came to Saint Louis as a result of the troubles of that year. Among these were a group of middle European Jesuits who belonged to the South German or Swiss Province. Some of these men were priests; most of them were seminarians. Exiled from Switzerland, many came to Saint Louis and completed their studies either at the seminary at Florissant or at Saint Louis University. Most of these men returned to Europe when calm prevailed again; but a significant group, including John Baptist Miege, who became vicar apostolic of the territory of Kansas, Peter Spicher, Joseph Patschowski, and others, stayed to work in parishes and schools in Saint Louis and other dioceses of the Midwest.

The revolutions of 1848, finally, gave the two Kenrick brothers another chance to show their diverging views on the question of the relation of Church and state. Rome was the scene of one of the many disturbances of the time. This revolt disturbed the arrangement whereby the Pope ruled a strip of land across central Italy called the Papal States. These states of the Church were, indeed, an anachronism, a structure that had lived beyond its time; yet it was difficult for those concerned to see a reasonable alternative. No one offered such an alternative. Revolutionists overthrew the Roman civil government set up by the Pope. Shortly thereafter the French troops of Napoleon III restored a semblance of the previous arrangement.

True to his Roman education, Francis Patrick Kenrick wrote a pastoral deploring the Italian action against the Papal States. Peter Richard, on the other hand, gave a much more practical pastoral. He insisted that the Saint Louis faithful knew the distinction between the spiritual position of the papacy and his temporal power as sovereign of the Papal States.[27]

Seminary in Carondelet

Archbishop Kenrick transferred the diocesan seminary from the Soulard addition to Carondelet in 1848, and put it under the direction of diocesan priests. The Vincentian Fathers had so widely expanded their missionary activity that they could no longer staff the seminary. Father James Duggan, ordained a year earlier, taught rhetoric and acted as director of the seminary until Father Anthony O'Reagan, rector of St. Jarlath's Seminary in Tuam, Ireland, and a classmate of Archbishop Kenrick at Maynooth, arrived in 1849. O'Reagan taught moral theology and sacred Scripture. Father George Ortlieb taught dogmatic theology. Father Patrick Fleming taught logic. For the next ten years, the archbishop drove a buggy twice a week to Carondelet and taught classes in English literature, rhetoric, and composition. Frequently he asked Father John O'Hanlon to accompany him, as that priest recalled in his book, *Life and Scenery in Missouri*.[28] O'Hanlon taught a while at the school, but later returned to Ireland.

The directorship of the little Theology Seminary at Carondelet proved to be a sure-fire path to Church advancement. Father Duggan became bishop of Chicago, as did his successor Father O'Reagan. Father Patrick Feehan, the third president, became bishop of Nashville and first archbishop of Chicago; and Father John Hennessey, his successor, ultimately became the first archbishop of Dubuque.

In his pastoral letter of February, 1849, Archbishop Kenrick informed the people of Saint Louis of the new theological seminary. "Under the direction of three competent professors," he wrote, "eight young men are engaged in the study of philosophy and theology."[29] The building could hold no more. Further, he had to transfer to Carondelet a number of those who had completed their preparatory studies at Perryville. Thus, he had to call on the generosity of the people to meet the needs of the expanding Church.[30]

Financial needs always plagued the seminary, now that the European missionary societies no longer sent aid. The archbishop brought up the question of seminary maintenance at the Archdiocesan Synod of August, 1850.[31] During the fall term of that year, twenty-four students enrolled in the seminary.

By the end of the following year, Archbishop Kenrick thought seriously of closing the institution. The seminary continued for a few years longer. The priests assigned there assisted in various religious functions at the St. Joseph Sisters' Convent nearby.

New Sisterhoods

When Father Melcher was in Europe recruiting missionaries for mid-America, he talked to the Ursuline Sisters* at the convent at Odenburg, a town about thirty-seven miles from Vienna. He found that Mother Magdalene Stehlin, superior of the convent, had a great interest in the American mission. On his return to Saint Louis in 1847, Father Melcher spoke to Archbishop Kenrick about the possibility of securing Ursuline Sisters. As a result, Father Melcher wrote to Mother Magdalene to come as soon as possible. While traveling through Bavaria, Mother Magdalene stayed with the Ursulines at Landshut, Bavaria, and promoted interest in the American Midwest among that group of Ursuline Sisters. One postulant joined the Austrian Sisters and others promised to follow as soon as they could secure the necessary permissions.

Vicar-general Melcher welcomed the first group of Austrian Ursulines to Saint Louis on September 25, 1848, and arranged for them to stay at the Visitation Convent where they lived for a month. They moved to a small house on Fifth Street and opened a school there on November 2. In the following May, six Bavarian Sisters arrived in Saint Louis, bringing with them almost one thousand dollars in donations to advance their work. King Ludwig I of Bavaria added four thousand dollars for their project. The *Ludwigs-Verein* at Munich was to send an average of six hundred dollars a year for the next seventeen years. These gifts were characteristic of the generosity of the King of Bavaria and the association of Munich. Contractor Francis Saler erected a convent for the Ursulines southwest of the Cathedral. They opened an academy and later boarding facilities.

The archbishop sought and gained limited changes in the rule of this cloistered order so that they might function more effectively in parochial schools. By 1855 this first American effort of the German-speaking Ursulines had grown sufficiently to allow them to begin a new establishment in the state of New York. A few years later they opened a convent in Alton, Illinois.

The cholera epidemic year of 1849 saw the arrival of another group of sisters, the Order of the Good Shepherd. Back in seventeenth century France, St. John Eudes, a native of Normandy, had become interested in work for the rehabilitation of delinquent young women, and sought dedicated women for such work. Almost two hundred years went by before the various groups who worked in this apostolate joined together in the Sisters of the Good Shepherd under the direction of Sister Euphrasia at Angers, France. Just four years later, Bishop Flaget of Bardstown, Kentucky, had come to Angers and prevailed upon the Sisters to open a convent in his diocese. This they did, near Louisville, Kentucky.

In January, 1849, three Sisters of the Louisville community set out for Saint Louis to start a convent there. An interesting feature of this group was its multi-national background. The religious institutes coming to Saint Louis before had been predominantly French, American, or as

---

*The Ursuline Nuns in colonial New Orleans had been the first religious order of women who worked within the present limits of the United States.

in the case of the Ursulines, South German. The Mercy Sisters, to come a short time later, were of Irish ancestry. The Sisters of the Good Shepherd, like lay immigrants to the American mid-west at the time, came from various nations.

In the meantime, Father Francis Cellini, C.M., one of the earliest priests in the Louisiana mission, a practicing physician, and later vicar-general of the Archdiocese of Saint Louis, bequeathed a large home to Archbishop Kenrick. The property was a gift of Mrs. Mary Smith, a native of Louisiana and a benefactress of the Church there, who had later moved to Missouri. Father Cellini had thought the property might be used as a residence for retired missionary priests; but at the particular time, 1849, Archbishop Kenrick had no such priests. All were in good health and busy around the diocese; so he turned the Smith home over to the work of the Good Shepherd Sisters at their arrival on January 24.

In his pastoral of February 2, 1849, the archbishop explained the program of the Sisters of the Good Shepherd and recommended the work to the encouragement and support of the people of Saint Louis.[32] While the Smith home was in the process of rehabilitation, the Sisters needed a residence for themselves. Archbishop Kenrick acquired one by purchasing an adjoining property for $1400. In the meantime, Mrs. Anne Lucas Hunt became interested in the work of the Sisters and donated a piece of ground in the suburbs of the city, later to be the block bounded by Sixteenth, Seventeenth, Pine, and Chestnut streets, near St. John's Church. Ten years later, the Saint Louis house of the Sisters of the Good Shepherd became a provincial center; and from it, convents spread to a great number of the cities of the south and west.

Shortly after the coming of these sisters, Kenrick went to Baltimore for the Seventh Provincial Council. In May 1849 the assembled bishops petitioned Rome for three additional archbishoprics: New Orleans, New York, and Cincinnati, and for a solemn declaration of the dogma of the Immaculate Conception. The council formalized the organization of the Province of Saint Louis by declaring the sees of Dubuque, Chicago, Milwaukee, and Nashville as suffragans. The first three, Chicago, Dubuque, and Milwaukee formed a regional unity with the diocese of Saint Louis, consisting of a compact, contiguous area of four states: Illinois, Missouri, Iowa, and Wisconsin and Indian Territories to the north and west. Nashville, on the contrary, more naturally belonged to either of two provinces set up the following year, New Orleans or Cincinnati. A casual glance at a map would show that the addition of Tennessee made the Saint Louis province a geographical monstrosity.

1849: Year of Disasters

In that same year, 1849, the entire Midwest suffered a general tragedy, and the city of Saint Louis a local calamity. Cholera epidemics had hit Saint Louis in 1832 and 1833. These paled in contrast with the terrible visitation of 1849. In a way, the city could blame itself. Through the negligence of officials, unsanitary conditions prevailed. Most of the alleys were unpaved and filthy. The 70,000 inhabitants crowded together in an imperfectly drained area, interspersed with sink holes and stagnant waters. The city hardly had a sewer. Most of the new streets were unpaved. Chouteau Pond, once a park-like lagoon, now seemed more like a cesspool.

On December 28, 1848, a steamboat had reached Saint Louis with thirty cholera victims among passengers and crew. At first the deaths were few. Thirty-six people died in January, twenty-one in February, but in March the number rose to seventy-eight, and in April to 126.

At this time the Cathedral parish included only one-sixth of the territory of the city. Yet the daily interments registered in the mortuary records of the Cathedral during the height of the epidemic regularly ran from thirty to thirty-five. Archbishop Kenrick visited the hospital every day.

The Saint Louis Hospital of the Sisters of Charity, on the corner of Spruce and Fourth Street received 2,705 patients during the year. Almost half of these were victims of cholera; 510 died of the disease and 820 were cured. Two Sisters of Charity, three Sisters of Saint Joseph, one Visitandine, and six Religious of the Sacred Heart died in the epidemic, most of them victims of charity.[33] The epidemic eventually took away seven percent of the population, moving indiscriminately through every area and social level of the city.

In the midst of this cholera epidemic, another tragedy struck. It killed only three persons, but destroyed ten million dollars worth of income-producing property. About 9:00 p.m. on the night of May 7, 1849, fire swept the steamboat *White Cloud* at the foot of Cherry Street on the northern edge of the city. According to the custom of the times, rivermen pushed the boat into midstream in the hope that the current would take it safely away from other boats. Instead, the wind swept from the Illinois shore and kept the boat near the Missouri bank as the current pulled it down stream. Eventually the burning *White Cloud* set fire to thirty-three boats in all. At Locust Street the blaze jumped the levee. It moved up a block to First Street. As it crossed Market, it had reached Second, the church block. The volunteer fire brigades were soon out, but the fire at the riverfront cut off their source of water supply. Captain Thomas Targee of the Missouri Valley Fire Brigade decided to blow up a number of buildings to thwart the spread of the flames. This maneuver helped to save the Cathedral, but resulted in the accidental death of the heroic Captain Targee. The fire finally came under control.

To care for youngsters orphaned by the cholera, clergy and laity of the German-speaking parishes set up the German St. Vincent's Orphans Society. Under the presidency of Valentine Reis, the Society was to open a home for orphaned boys and girls on the near north side.[34]

Chapter 16

The Expansive Fifties

The Christian Brothers

When historians look back to the year 1849 in Saint Louis Catholic history, another event stands out as having more enduring effect than the two disasters: the coming of one of the religious congregations most closely associated with the development of education in the archdiocese. As has been seen earlier, three Brothers of the Christian Schools, founded by St. John Baptist de La Salle, had come from France with Bishop Du Bourg and opened an Academy for Boys in Ste. Genevieve in 1819. The remoteness of the frontier and the lack of community life had brought this early effort to a termination.

In 1849, at the invitation of Archbishop Kenrick, three more Brothers came to Saint Louis from Baltimore where the Christian Brothers had set up their first permanent American establishment. They moved into the Rider Mansion at the corner of Eighth and Cerre Street, on the near south side, not far from St. Vincent De Paul's Church.

The first task of the Christian Brothers in Saint Louis was the care of the Cathedral School. With the addition of nine more members a few months later, the Christian Brothers were able to enlarge their scope of activities. They built an addition onto the building on Cerre Street and opened a college in 1852. Brother Patrick (John Patrick Murphy) directed it for eight years. In 1855, the school sought a charter from the state legislature. Archbishop Kenrick gave the college a big push. He urged his priests to send their young parishioners to the Brothers for their education, especially those who gave indications of a vocation to the priesthood.[1]

To further the pre-seminary training, Brother Patrick secured permission from the superior general at the general chapter of 1854, to inaugurate the necessary courses, particularly Latin. Other American colleges of the Christian Brothers adopted the same plan, and trained many gifted, saintly priests.[2]

A single effort did not exhaust the zeal of the Christian Brothers in Saint Louis. They were to establish a branch academy on the north side at Seventh and Cass in 1869 and to call it St. Patrick's. Over the ensuing years, they were to undertake parochial schools at the following parishes: St. Francis Xavier's (1850-54), St. Patrick's (1851-53), St. Mary and Joseph (1858-88), St. John's (1862-92), St. Lawrence O'Toole's (1863-99), Sts. Peter and Paul (1866-1870), Annunciation (1868-1893), St. Bridget's (1868-1911), St. Michael's (1870-72), and St. Malachy's (1872-77).[3] Most of these were English-speaking parishes of predominantly Irish background.

With these establishments, the Christian Brothers merited the distinction of being the founders of the parochial school system in the Saint Louis Irish community. By 1870 fifty-seven Christian Brothers were to work in the Saint Louis area. They had set up a novitiate in Carondelet with thirty aspirants.

Kenrick the Banker

With the rising tide of immigration, many poor people in Saint Louis found great difficulty in getting money at reasonable rates of interest for their needs. Further, many of the immigrants, especially those who did not know the language of the country as yet, felt a greater security in leaving their accumulated savings in the hands of a representative of the Church.

While still at Our Lady of Victories, in the early forties, Father Ambrose Heim, Spiritual Director of the St. Vincent de Paul Society, had encouraged his people to save. They began to deposit their savings in his safekeeping. Gradually more and more parishioners put their money in Father Heim's little bank. Bishop Kenrick learned of Father Heim's activities. He transferred the priest to the Cathedral in 1846 and made him his secretary. The "little bank" of Father Heim became the "large bank" of Bishop Kenrick in 1850. In that year the balance rose from $588.69 on February 1, to $19,509.03 on December 31. The names of Patrick Ryder, Owen Timon, Francis Saler, and other substantial businessmen appear among the depositers.[4]

When people heard that the bishop of Saint Louis was willing to accept any amounts on deposit and promised a fair rate of interest, money flowed in from all sides. The bishop set apart a small room in his residence for the banking enterprise. In the course of time, he found it necessary to set up an office. At first, Father Heim handled details but later the bishop hired a layman to assist. After the premature death of Father Heim, Kenrick personally ran the bank, with the assistance at various times of Patrick Ryder, F. Deneny, and Owen Timon.[5] Kenrick kept careful accounts of all transactions, as he had done of the liquidation of the cathedral debts, the building and rental of commercial properties in the church block, and donations to the archdiocese.[6]

A casual glance at the list of depositors in the early years shows the wide range of national origins: Bernard Schlangen, Joseph Strelciki, Arnold Van Hock, Lambert Vervoorst, Bernard Vitkar, Bartolomeo Bernero, and Michael Brennan.[7] In one particular month, the archbishop noted deposits ranging all the way from Luke Kennedy's $9.00[8] to Thomas McHale's $2,099.41.[9] Occasionally he would write a personal item. Under McHale's two thousand plus, for instance, are the words: "Do not pay his wife more than $100 at any time."[10] In contrast, under John Riordan's $500, Kenrick noted: "Pay his wife when she brings the receipt. Her name is Catherine Riordan."[11] Below Patrick Gibbons' deposit of $200 is the notation: "The last place he worked he was not paid."[12] Subadini Ficonio deposited $604.86 with the provision that in case he died, the money should go to his children.[13] As the years went on, Irish surnames came to predominate among the depositors.[14] Further, many individuals of various national origins accumulated considerable savings.[15]

One of America's first "businessman bishops," Kenrick guided his bank along sound paths, unlike his friend Purcell in Cincinnati, who met disaster in a similar venture. The "Bishop's Bank" of Saint Louis provided loans on easy terms to the struggling parishes, such as Saint Patrick's, and for the expansion or renovation of such religious communities as the House of the Good Shepherd.[16] Kenrick's bank proved so sound that when the Panic of 1857 came, the archbishop was able to loan the city a large sum for public works.[17]

Some might wonder if the Church should have involved itself so intimately in purely financial operations. In a frontier and immigrant society, the Church frequently found it necessary to promote directly the social and economic betterment of its people. In a later day, parish credit unions offered such personal services as Bishop Kenrick rendered. But in 1850 the credit union movement had not yet gotten underway. As to the financing of an expanding church, other distinguished prelates were to adopt his methods decades later, as if they were innovations.

The Developing Archdiocese

The original city had been a small rectangle, four blocks from the river, and almost twenty blocks north and south. This generally rectangular pattern of development was to remain constant as the city grew. In the 1830's the boundaries had been Seventh Street on the west, and a few blocks farther north and south of the original limits. By 1841, Eighteenth Street formed the western boundary. The north and south limits extended in such a way that the city, while no longer a perfect rectangle, still was twice as long as it was wide.

Several important streets radiated from the original town site near the river as spokes from a wheel; so religious development spread from the Cathedral on the waterfront. The Cathedral parish had been coterminus with the early city. In the mid-1840's, three other parishes and two German-speaking congregations took care of worshippers in the newly-enlarged boundaries of 1841. By this time Archbishop Kenrick had come to see a tremendous future for the city of Saint Louis. He wrote to Archbishop Cullen in Rome: "The new archdiocese of Saint Louis is likely to become of considerable importance . . . . Saint Louis will probably be the largest inland city in America and may one day be the seat of the Federal government."[18]

Two years later, in an analysis of his diocese for the office of the Propagation, Peter Richard wrote in the same vein: "Saint Louis will in all likelihood become the central city of the United States."[19] The population had been only six thousand in 1830, and sixteen thousand in 1840, but by 1850 it approached 80,000 — almost five times what it had been ten years before.[20] German and Irish immigrants came in great numbers, making the foreign-born residents outnumber the native-born.

Kenrick still had considerable difficulty in supplying his own basic needs. By 1850 Catholics had pledged only a thousand francs for the seminary when twenty thousand francs were needed.[21] That same year he had required from each church one-thirtieth of its gross income for his expenses, but most churches were exempt from this because their annual income was less than five hundred dol-

lars. Only three or four churches gave anything at all. He revealed to his friend, Purcell, that his income for the year 1851-52 reached only four hundred and fifty-one dollars and ninety-four cents.[22] But Kenrick was, in fact, moving rapidly towards archdiocesan solvency by this time.

In 1850, the year of the Second Diocesan Synod, Saint Louis had ten churches, all within eighteen blocks of the river, the western limits of the city since 1841. St. Patrick's had the largest number of parishioners with 5,000, the Cathedral was second with 4,450, St. Joseph third with 4,000, and St. Francis Xavier fourth with 3,000. St. John's served the new west end north of Mill Creek. St. Vincent's, St. Mary's, and Sts. Peter and Paul were on the south side; and Holy Trinity and St. Michael's on the north side.[23]

With the drainage of Chouteau Pond by the end of 1853, and the subsequent vigorous western growth of the population, Saint Louis moved its southern boundary from Wyoming Street to Keokuk Street, its northern boundary from Deck to East Grand, and its western boundary from 18th Street to a new western limit just beyond Grand Avenue on the fourth terrace* west of the river. A second line of religious advance kept pace with the city. A group of churches sprang up not too far on either side of Jefferson Avenue, such as St. Bridget's in 1854, Sts. Lawrence O'Toole's, Liborius', and Malachy's in 1855. St. Boniface opened in Carondelet a short time later. The Archbishop's Bank financed these churches in part.

With the setting up of the Indian Territory to the west as a Vicariate Apostolic under Jean B. Miege in 1850, the archdiocesan boundaries became identical with those of the state of Missouri. Outside of Saint Louis, the archdiocese had thirty-six churches with resident pastors. By far the largest of these out-state parishes, St. Mary's in Perry County had thirty-five hundred parishioners. Sts. Mary and Joseph in Carondelet had two thousand; St. Joseph in Westphalia (Osage County) had nineteen hundred and twenty parishioners, St. Ferdinand's in Florissant had seventeen hundred and twenty, St. Peter in Dardenne (St. Charles County) had fourteen hundred and eighty. Ste. Genevieve had nine hundred and the neighboring German parish of St. Joseph at Zell had one thousand and eighty-five.[24]

Of the forty-three pastors in the archdiocese at the time, thirty-three were members of the diocesan clergy, while only ten of religious orders — an evidence of the tremendous growth of the diocesan clergy in the ten years of Archbishop Kenrick's presence. Most of the rural parishes served from one to six mission stations, depending upon the nature of the region and the number of clergy involved. The Jesuits at St. Francis Borgia's Church in Washington, for instance, served seven mission stations on both sides of the Missouri River. St. Mary's in Perry County remained the center of an extensive regional missionizing by the Vincentian Fathers.

---

*Laclede chose the location for Saint Louis precisely because it rose in terraces back from the river. Third Street formed the first terrace. As the city grew, Eighteenth Street ran along the second terrace, Ewing, just west of Jefferson along the third, and Grand Avenue along the fourth. In the past, geographers occasionally omitted the Third Street Terrace from enumeration and called the Eighteenth Street Terrace the first. Thus Grand would be the third in this enumeration.

The heavy Catholic areas of the archdiocese were three: Saint Louis and environs, the "Old Settlements" of southeast Missouri, such as Ste. Genevieve and Perryville, and a cluster of towns chiefly in Osage County on the south bank of the Missouri, about eighty miles west of Saint Louis. The rural counties were to remain stable; a tremendous growth was to come in the see city.

By this time, a noteworthy Catholic colonization project had gotten underway at Millwood in northeast Missouri. A group of Marylanders, under the leadership of Dr. Hilary B. Mudd and Judge Henry T. Mudd, had moved to the area in the early forties. The site was equidistant from Saint Louis to the southeast, the German settlements of Father Helias below the Missouri River to the southwest, and St. Paul's Parish in Ralls County to the northwest, where Father Lefevere had worked before he became bishop of Detroit. The two Mudds furnished money, land, and moral support towards the establishment of the Church in this area.

Father Daniel Lyne came to this parish in January 1850. A talented orator, Lyne set about building the community and caring for the welfare of his Irish countrymen. He was one of two delegates who represented Missouri at the Buffalo colonization convention in 1856 and, through efforts at that meeting, induced hundreds of Irish to come to Missouri and particularly to Millwood so that it became known as an Irish settlement rather than, as it originally was, a settlement of Marylanders.[25]

Father Lyne addressed a meeting of the colonization society established in Saint Louis a few months after the Buffalo meeting. Practical in his approach to the problem of colonization, he believed that it was better to get good prairie land, even if the initial cost was higher rather than the forest lands that took so much time to get into cultivation.

The flourishing parish of St. Alphonsus in Millwood never became a significant part of the midwestern church; but, like a similar Maryland-Irish parish, O'Harasburg in Randolph County, Illinois, it was a transitional step between Ireland or Maryland and modern urban Catholic life.

A comparative study of the activities of religious orders and congregations in the archdiocese at mid-century shows Saint Louis well ahead of most other dioceses. The Vincentians had a seminary and college in the Saint Louis archdiocese, the Jesuits a Seminary and a university, the Christian Brothers a college. The Religious of the Sacred Heart taught in several schools; the Sisters of Charity conducted a hospital and several academies; the Sisters of St. Joseph taught schools of various kinds, including one for the deaf and the academy in Carondelet, to be chartered in 1853; the Lorettines taught in southeast Missouri, and now at the convent in Florissant; the Ursulines had a school in the city; the Sisters of the Good Shepherd worked for the rehabilitation of disturbed young women, and the Visitation Sisters had moved their Academy from Kaskaskia. In all, seven religious orders of women (and three of men) worked in the diocese. Some of them had been there for over thirty years.[26]

By way of contrast, the Archdiocese of New Orleans, older than Saint Louis, had only five religious institutes.[27] New York, the most rapidly growing city in the nation, also had five;[28] Boston, two;[29] Chicago, eventually to challenge Saint Louis as the Catholic center of the Midwest, two;[30] Baltimore, the first archdiocese of the country, had the same number as Saint Louis, ten. Only

Father John B. Bannon, Pastor and Builder of St. John's Church and Chaplain of the Missouri State Guard, served with Price's Army during the Civil War. He did not return to St. Louis after the conflict, but spent his last half-century in giving home missions and doing pastoral work in Ireland.

Philadelphia, with eleven, surpassed Saint Louis.[31]

These figures point to the amazing religious strength of the Archdiocese of Saint Louis.

Time of Controversy

The 1850's were years of religious controversy. On the national scene, men like convert-writer Orestes Brownson and Archbishop John Hughes answered the critics of the Catholic Church with blistering counterattacks. In Saint Louis, another convert writer, Robert A. Bakewell, joined in the fight.

Archbishop Kenrick had offered Bakewell the editorship of a new paper that bore an old name, *The Shepherd of the Valley*. A Scot by birth, Bakewell had studied for the Presbyterian ministry. After his conversion, he edited a Catholic paper in Pittsburg. Coming to Saint Louis, he put out the first edition of the new paper in October 1850. It had little resemblance to the old *Shepherd*; but was similar to the *St. Louis News Letter* that had ceased publication two years before. It carried articles, reviews, digests, biographies of prominent people, news of Catholic events, and lectures of such dignitaries as Archbishop Hughes.[32] Broadminded in editorial policies, Bakewell even reprinted an article from the *Commonwealth* that was highly critical of Catholics for supporting the Fugitive Slave Law and opposing anti-clericals, Giuseppe Mazzini and Lajos Kossuth, men who had fought for freedom in their native lands.[33]

In November, 1851, Bakewell wrote an editorial on the subject of religious liberty that inflamed public opinion in wide circles. It eventually made its way into Protestant and Catholic literature on the subject.[34] Bakewell predicted an ultimate Catholic numerical superiority in the United States. He looked on the practical toleration of his day as the result of circumstances rather than of principles. If any group, he insisted — Mormon, Presbyterian, Catholic, or what have you — gained "a decided superiority, it (toleration) is at an end . . . in the sense . . . that a

Christian people will not consider the ridicule of Christianity, the denial of its fundamental truths, of the immortality of the soul and of the existence of God, the overthrow of all religion and morality, matters beneath their notice and condemnation . . ."[35]

The delicate distinction Bakewell made jibed with Catholic thinking in the days of Pius IX; but aroused justifiable fears among non-Catholics. The controversy that ensued raged well into the following year.[36] This doctrine was distasteful to Americans at all times. It was especially bitter in those days because of the Know-Nothings.

Bakewell continued his editorship until the demise of the paper on June 11, 1854.[37] A group bought *The Shepherd* and turned it into a Know-Nothing organ, under the title the *True Shepherd of the Valley and St. Louis Know-Nothing*, thus causing great confusion for some time.[38]

The American Party, or "Know-Nothings" — as they called themselves — were to prove the most formidable expression of political nativism in America. They galvanized the forces that had bred hostility to foreigners and Catholics for fifty years. They did not intend, originally, to enter politics as a distinct party, but merely to support nativist candidates of the existing parties. Gradually they moved into direct politics. Scarcely heard of generally until 1854, they enjoyed amazing success in many states of the south and east for two years. They then disappeared as rapidly as they had come upon the scene. Unfortunately, in that short time, they did lasting damage in many places — among them, Saint Louis.

This phenomenal growth resulted from several factors besides anti-Catholic and anti-foreign prejudices: the glamour attached to being a member of a secret society; the overwhelming defeat of the Whig Party in the election of 1852 that left its members no place to go; and the dissatisfaction of some northern Democrats with the pro-slavery aspects of the Pierce administration. The Know-Nothings gained adherents from the dissatisfied of both parties.

Even though Saint Louis had French, German, English, and second generation Irish Catholics, the Know-Nothings gradually began to identify Saint Louis Catholicism with the newly immigrating Irish who lived for the most part in St. Patrick's parish not far from Saint Louis University. The newly arriving Irish, in turn, tended to identify Catholicism with their own outlook and nationality. They protested, for instance, when Archbishop Kenrick sent to St. Patrick's parish an outstanding young priest of American origin, Father Charles Ziegler, a native of Ste. Genevieve who spoke English with a southeast Missouri twang. As might be expected, Archbishop Kenrick neither appreciated nor acted on this complaint.

The off-year election of 1854 saw the most serious election riots in Saint Louis history. When several Irish Americans were denied the vote on August 7, 1854, an argument arose. In the scuffle that ensued, one of the disinfranchised Irishmen stabbed a boy. A riot broke out. Mobs attacked Irish homes and stores along Second between Market and Cherry Streets in downtown Saint Louis. Soon the violence spread into various parts of the city.

Members of the mob threatened to destroy Catholic churches in the city. Word went out that they were about to attack Saint Louis University. Fortunately, a counter rumor alleged that a great force of armed men waited at the college to meet their attack. Moving rapidly, Mayor John Howe called for eight platoons of volunteer soldiers to assist the usual police force. The mob raged throughout the city that night.

The rioters approached the university a second time. The president, Father John Baptist Druyts, calmly walked back and forth in front of the College Church reading his Psalms. A mob destroyed two restaurants in the vicinity but did not dare approach the college itself. They suspected that thousands of armed men lay in ambush.

The mayor decided to forestall the fear being generated by incendiary members of the mob. He sent several prominent Protestants to inspect the college premises. They found no evidence of defensive activity. The mayor immediately announced the fact by newspapers and printed bulletins. The more sensible inhabitants, already surfeited with violence, supported the mayor's efforts to suppress further disorder. The common sense and good will of the citizens of Saint Louis prevailed.[39]

But once again the medical properties had been in jeopardy, even though they now stood ten blocks from the main campus. A short time later, the majority of the medical faculty voted to separate from the university and function under a distinct charter. These were broadminded, exceptional men, in no way associated with the intolerance that faced the Catholics at the time. They presented their request to young John Verdin, the new president of the university in place of Father Druyts who, in the meantime, had risen to be regional superior of the Missouri Jesuits. The new president called together the university trustees to discuss the compelling arguments of the medical faculty. This time the administration acceded to the proposed separation.

No unfriendly feeling marked either side. In fact, on June 18, 1855, the university conferred the degree of master of arts on Dr. Moses Linton and Dr. Charles Alexander Pope. Dr. Linton and Missouri legislator J. Richard Barret, a Presbyterian, spoke at the university's Washington Day celebration in 1856. Barret alluded to the difficulties the community faced and rejected the unsound presumption "that either Protestantism or the country needed the 'Know-Nothings' for its protection."[40]

In spite of the efforts of such outstanding citizens, and others like Mayor John Darby, the whirlwind of prejudice stirred by the Know-Nothings compelled the withdrawal of the faculty of medicine from a mutually profitable association. It tended to make many Catholics wonder whether an ecumenic spirit really was not premature in American life. The university had leaned over backwards in cooperation with civic leaders of various faiths. But responsible Saint Louis Protestants had no way of controlling their more extreme brethren. Saint Louis University had been from its start a community enterprise with a wide basis of support. Anti-Catholic spokesmen failed to recognize the true spirit of Saint Louis and especially the wide tolerant service the university offered to the community from its earliest days. Know-Nothingism drove Saint Louis University back within its own walls. It emerged only fitfully during the ensuing years.

It was extremely unfortunate both for the Medical College and for Saint Louis University that they could not preserve unity for three years more. By that time the more sound groups that had made common cause with the Know-Nothings joined the newly-forming Republican Party. Nativism as an obvious external force went momentarily in disrepute. But the change had come too late.

The cooperative spirit of the entire Saint Louis community had received a severe shock. This was especially noticeable among citizens of Irish background. Before the Know-Nothing period, for instance, Protestant and Catholic Irish had worked together for the improvement of conditions in Ireland through such organizations as the Erin Benevolent Association. After the Know-Nothing identification of the word "Irish" with the recent potato famine refugees, many old-line Protestant Irish families gradually coalesced with the wider Anglo-American Protestant community.

Councils, Plenary and Provincial

Francis Patrick Kenrick enjoyed Roman ecclesiastical politicking and tried to influence as many episcopal appointments as he could — frequently in favor of his fellow Irish. Peter Richard, on the other hand, rarely recommended names for sees beyond his own metropolitan area. Further, he saw a danger in recommending candidates only of American or Irish background. In a letter to Purcell,[41] he mentioned that Rosati had wished for a division of the state of Illinois. Kenrick thought that the southern part of the state should have a bishop who would speak German and French as well as English. "I believe the exclusive promotion of Irish or American subjects will not have a favorable influence, either on the discipline of the Church or the reputation for impartiality in our selection which is so necessary for them to have weight, especially with the German population which in the southern part of Illinois constitutes the principal portion of Catholics."[42]

Kenrick wanted a coadjutor for Saint Louis. He seems to have had the idea that the coadjutor would constantly visit the outlying areas while he himself cared for business in the city. He suggested as a candidate James Van de Velde, the Jesuit bishop of Chicago, eminently acceptable to clergy and people alike. Francis Patrick, now in 1852 archbishop of Baltimore, did not approve this choice,[43] even though he had approved Van de Velde for Chicago four years before.[44]

The new archbishop of Baltimore presided over the First Plenary Council of Baltimore in May, 1852. The nation now had six archbishops: Francis Patrick Kenrick himself, his brother Peter Richard, F. N. Blanchet of Oregon, Antoine Blanc of New Orleans, John J. Hughes of New York, and John B. Purcell of Cincinnati. Twenty-four bishops came from the rest of the country, including Joseph S. Alemany, O.P., bishop of Monterey in America's newest state, California. This plenary council witnessed a multitude of readjustments in diocesan boundaries, the creation of ten new dioceses, and the elevation of San Francisco to the rank of archbishopric.

In spite of a temporary lull as a result of the Compromise of 1850, the question of slavery still clouded the country. While his brother, Francis Patrick, had held that slavery as it existed in the South at the time was not evil in itself,[45] Peter Richard had not gone on record in the matter. The Plenary Council said nothing on slavery, even though many people expected this largest and greatest of all American Catholic assemblies to take a stand on the question.[46]

Perhaps historians can justify the silence of the bishops as the lesser of two evils in view of the relatively weak position of the Church, the intensity of feeling at the time, the alliance of Abolitionist and anti-Catholic, the close tie-in of the slave question with that of states'

rights, and the lack of an immediate alternative. But it could hardly be called, as Peter Guilday does, in *A History of the Councils of Baltimore*, "the outstanding proof of the wisdom of our prelates."[47]

Archbishop Kenrick called the First Provincial Council of Saint Louis for October, 1855. Bishops Mathias Loras of Dubuque, Richard Miles, O.P., of Nashville, John M. Henni of Milwaukee, Anthony O'Regan of Chicago, and Joseph Cretin of the newest diocese, Saint Paul, assembled on October 19 at the Cathedral of Saint Louis. The bishops resolved that they should propose candidates for vacancies within the province; that every bishop should establish and support a preparatory seminary, and that the province have one theological seminary. The Fathers insisted that the decrees of the Plenary Council as well as those of the seven provincial councils of Baltimore would be the ecclesiastical law of the Saint Louis Province.

The bishops asked Rome to set up a number of new dioceses. John Baptist Miege, a native of Savoy, a province between France and Italy, had already become vicar apostolic of the Indian territory west of the Missouri River. The new bishop of Saint Paul, Joseph Cretin, disapproved the division between his and Miege's jurisdiction. He felt that the boundaries gave all the white people in Indian territory to Miege and left the Indians — Chippewa, Winnebago, and Sioux — under Saint Paul.[48]

The bishops asked Rome to divide Miege's territory, with Miege in charge of the southern section (Kansas), and De Smet as vicar apostolic of the northern part (Nebraska). They proposed several names, including Father Joseph Patschowski, Jesuit pastor of St. Joseph's Church in Saint Louis, for the see of Quincy that Bishop O'Regan of Chicago still administered.[49]

In the wake of the council, Rome moved the see of Quincy downriver to Alton, thirty miles north of Saint Louis, and chose Father Henry D. Juncker, a native of Lorraine ordained for the Cincinnati diocese, as first bishop. It rejected the suggestion that Prairie du Chien, Wisconsin, become the center of a diocese. It approved Archbishop Kenrick's request that Father James Duggan be auxiliary of Saint Louis.[50] The Irish-born rector of the Seminary in Carondelet had doubled as vicar-general since 1854. Consecrated at the Saint Louis Cathedral on May 3, 1857, along with Bishop Timothy Smyth, O.C.S.O., coadjutor of Dubuque, Duggan remained auxiliary of Saint Louis less than a year. In 1858, at the age of thirty-three, he became apostolic administrator of Chicago.

The Second Provincial Council, meeting in Saint Louis on September 5, 1858, spent most of its time on technical affairs of canon law, and carefully avoided the momentous question gripping the nation, the slave issue. The participants were more interesting than their accomplishments. The colorful Bishop John Baptist Lamy crossed the plains from Santa Fe to attend. Dubuque's new bishop, Abbot Timothy Smyth, O.C.S.O., had founded the Trappist Abbey of New Melleray, Iowa. Old Father Edmund Saulnier, the last of Du Bourg's pioneer recruits, served as notary.

A year later, Kenrick consecrated another Trappist and two Dominicans as bishops for the province in ceremonies at the Saint Louis Cathedral. On May 8, 1859, he consecrated James Whelan, O.P., as coadjutor of Nashville, and James M. M. O'Gorman, O.C.S.O., as vicar apostolic of Nebraska. Two months later, on July 24, he consecrated Thomas Grace, O.P., the successor to Bishop Cretin of Saint Paul.

Chapter 17

Continued Growth

The First Bohemians in Saint Louis

The city of Saint Louis, the center of midwestern Catholicism at mid-century, grew to be the focal point of Catholicism for the Bohemian immigrant. The first Bohemian church in the United States, and one of the first anywhere in the world outside of Bohemia, St. John Nepomuk's, opened on the near southside in 1854.[1] It set the pattern of organization and parish dynamics for hundreds of subsequent Bohemian communities in the nation. It taught the immigrant how to adjust to an entirely new religious environment. It bound him closely to the old Church.

The ancient Kingdom of Bohemia, a Slavic country in Central Europe, surrounded on three sides by German principalities, had been a part of the Holy Roman Empire in the Middle Ages. In the early fifteenth century, a Bohemian theologian, John Hus, had recommended church reforms similar to those advocated in contemporary England by John Wyclif. The Church excommunicated Hus; and, in spite of a promise of safe-conduct from the Emperor, Hus suffered death at the stake. This led to civil war, and a legacy of mistrust during succeeding centuries. Throughout modern history, Bohemia remained a part of the Hapsburg Empire. In the middle of the nineteenth century, however, many Bohemians hoped for a better political framework within or without the Hapsburg community of nations.

Since the Church in the Hapsburg domains closely cooperated with the government, hostility to the Hapsburgs frequently brought hostility and dissatisfaction with the Church. The Prussians to the north, anti-Hapsburg in politics and free-thinkers in religious outlook, frequently influenced the Bohemians in an anti-Church attitude. These religio-political conflicts drove many individuals from the Church.

During the 1850's and '60's a great number of Bohemians landed at New Orleans and came to the Midwest, especially to Saint Louis, Cincinnati, Chicago, and later on to many farm communities in Nebraska. The Saint Louis Bohemian Catholic community became the center of Catholic activities for these people.

Since many of the Bohemians who came to Saint Louis spoke German, they attended Mass for a time at the Church of Sts. Peter and Paul. In 1854 they began a small frame church on the corner of Soulard and Rosati streets, the original St. John Nepomuk's.

The first priest, Father Henry Lipovsky, an officer in the Austrian army before his seminary days, proved too aristocratic in manner and outlook for democratic life in the new world. He found it necessary to return to Europe. His successor fared little better; and in the middle 1860's the church was to close — but only temporarily.

"Mercies" and "Notre Dames"

Two Jesuit pastors on the near north side gave the initial invitations to two groups of nuns who began their Saint Louis apostolates in the late fifties. The pastor at the College Church, Father Arnold Damen saw need for an apostolate of visiting the sick and the poor, and catechizing those in need of instruction. With his usual systematic approach, Father Damen planned for the coming of Sisters for this work. He discussed the Saint Louis needs with the Sisters of Mercy at St. Catherine's Convent in New York. Archbishop Kenrick approved the plans and sent an official invitation to Mother Agnes O'Connor.

While the Sisters of the Good Shepherd had to come from Louisville by steamboat just a few years before, the Mercy Sisters from New York were able to make much of the journey by rail. Six Sisters arrived in Saint Louis in the company of Father Patrick J. Ryan on June 27, 1856. They made their first visitation of the sick-poor in the neighborhood on the Feast of the Visitation of Our Lady, July 2. On July 16 they made their initial visit to the city jail. In August they opened St. Patrick's parish free school.

Living in near destitution in their convent at Tenth and Morgan Street, the Sisters had to take in sewing and laundry to support themselves. They appealed to Archbishop Kenrick for assistance. With the archbishop leading the way, and a number of Catholic families supporting them, the Sisters were able to set up a much more commodious building — the St. Joseph's Convent of Mercy at 22nd and Morgan Street, and to devote their time directly to their inner-city mission activities.

In 1858, the pastor at St. Joseph's Church, Father Joseph Patschowski, S.J., brought the School Sisters of Notre Dame to Saint Louis to conduct the parish schools in place of the Sisters of Charity, whose many other duties required their services elsewhere. The School Sisters of Notre Dame had come from their motherhouse in Munich, Bavaria, to open an institute in Baltimore in 1847, at the request of Redemptorist missionaries. Three years later, they set up a center for a western province in Milwaukee.

In the fall of 1859, Father Francis Goller of Sts. Peter and Paul parish obtained three Sisters to teach the three hundred pupils in his parochial school. Father Stephen Schweihoff of St. Liborius Church on the north side, not far from St. Joseph's, also obtained Sisters for his parish school. A month later three other Sisters began parochial education in the town of Washington in Franklin County not far west of Saint Louis.

In a few years, the Notre Dames, along with lay teachers, taught four hundred pupils at St. Mary's parish school, one thousand pupils at Sts. Peter and Paul's parochial school, one thousand at St. Joseph's school, four hundred at St. Liborius school, and about the same number at Holy Trinity. St. John Nepomuk's school had two hundred pupils. The total number of pupils under the direction of the School Sisters of Notre Dame and their lay associates in the German and Bohemian schools went over three thousand — two-thirds of the children in parochial schools in the city. The Notre Dames were to do for parochial education in the German parishes of Saint Louis what the Christian Brothers did in the Irish parishes.

Father Goller of Sts. Peter and Paul's tried for a time to organize a religious brotherhood of German-Americans to teach in the parochial schools. This organization, however, did not attain permanence.

The Thornton Bequest

The elder Archbishop Kenrick, Francis Patrick, indulged in a rare pleasantry in his letter of January 25, 1858. In a reference to Peter Richard's development of the immigrant bank, Francis Patrick addressed his message "to his brother, now grown wealthy, from the Archbishop of Baltimore, poor and lowly."[2]

The "now wealthy" brother grew even more "wealthy" later in the same year. A Saint Louis bachelor businessman, John Thornton, willed ten thousand each to five nephews and nieces and a similar amount to Archbishop Kenrick. The remainder of Thornton's estate was to go to the charitable works of the Archdiocese of Saint Louis. Archbishop Kenrick, Edward Walsh, and Joseph John Withnell were executors of the will.

The final settlement in March, 1861, showed that the amount for the archdiocese went over half a million — $579,440.06.[3] In 1862 Archbishop Kenrick synopsized the distribution of the Thornton request for charitable and religious purposes under four headings: convent expenses of charitable institutions, $96,688; expenses of buildings and other permanent improvements in such institutions, $127,192; convent expenses of institutions for the promotion of religion, $29,461; liquidation of church debts, $325,470. This money totaled $578,811. This included much of the Thornton bequest and seventeen thousand dollars from other sources.

Religious institutions that shared Thornton moneys included St. Anne's Asylum, House of the Guardian Angel, LaSalle Institute, St. Louis Hospital, St. Vincent's Hospital, the House of St. Philomena, the Convent of the Good Shepherd, and St. Bridget's Asylum. The churches sharing in the generous gift were St. Mary's, St. Michael's, Holy Trinity, St. John Nepomuk, St. Boniface, St. Mary's in Carondelet, St. Bridget's, the Annunciation, the Assumption, St. Malachy's, St. Patrick's, Sts. Peter and Paul, Immaculate Conception, St. Lawrence O'Toole, and St. John's.[4] Kenrick also designated certain moneys to go to the seminary, to the missions of the archdiocese, and to a new Catholic paper, the *Western Banner*. The archbishop ear-marked three thousand dollars for its development.[5]

Kenrick made one provision for distribution of the Thornton three hundred and fifty thousand dollars to parishes. "If the assets of the undersigned," he wrote, "suffice to meet the immense indebtedness, then the foregoing distribution is to be considered as permanent."[6] If this did not come about, then the archbishop could call on the parishes to supply the amount up to their indebtedness. In that eventuality, the money to each parish would have the status of an interest-free loan. Within the decade the parishes were to remit two-thirds of the total. Annunciation and Immaculate Conception led the way

with a full return plus interest.[7] Thus in one of its most expansive periods, the Church in Saint Louis had a tremendous push from the generosity of a single donor.

Surprisingly little is known about John Thornton, the most generous benefactor of the Saint Louis archdiocese in its long history. Records of the time indicate that he owned a livery stable. Analysis of his will shows also that he had invested wisely in real estate in the Saint Louis and Dubuque areas.[8] And in those days such investments oftentimes brought surprising capital gains. They did so in Thornton's case.

Strangely, the archdiocese reared no memorial to his name; in fact, it forgot him.

Laymen's Societies

One of the best known pastors of the Middle West, the Dutch Jesuit, Arnold Damen* began the Gentleman's Sodality at St. Francis Xavier's (College) Church. This organization stemmed from a tradition almost as old as the Jesuit order itself, but without parallel in the United States at the time. As an extension of their individual apostolate, many Jesuits had gathered about them a group of laymen who promised to follow the Ignatian way to God. The sodality brought the spirit of St. Ignatius to lay people in the same way the Third Orders brought the outlooks of St. Francis and St. Dominic to countless people. At its start in 1848, the Gentleman's Sodality had drawn its members from the alumni of Saint Louis University. Gradually, it enlarged its base, drawing alumni and non-alumni from the entire city. By 1856, it had three hundred active members.[9]

Members of the sodality were among those who supported the Catholic Institute of Saint Louis, an organization for the promotion of lectures by prominent members of the Church. The institute sponsored two series of lectures by controversialist, Orestes Brownson. Archbishop Kenrick felt Brownson took too hard a line in the first lecture.[10] He preferred a more irenic approach for Saint Louis even in those Know-Nothing days. The institute also invited Dr. Levi S. Ives, in the late fall of 1858. The first Protestant bishop ever to become a Catholic, Dr. Ives found it difficult to obtain a position commensurate with his outstanding talents.** He held minor educational posts around New York and became chairman of the local conference of the Society of St. Vincent de Paul. In his Saint Louis lecture at the Mercantile Library Hall, Dr. Ives spoke on the work of the society, and urged that the Catholics of Saint Louis form more parish conferences. He gave a similar message to the Cathedral parish conference of the society. Father Patrick J. Ryan, local director, proposed the formation of a unit in every parish in the city. The response was enthusiastic.[11]

Shortly after Ives' address and Ryan's recommendation, St. Joseph's and St. Francis Xavier's churches set up

---

*Even though he was well known in Saint Louis, and Archbishop Kenrick listed him among candidates for the coadjutorship (PRK to Purcell, Oct. 17, 1855, LUND), Father Damen gained even greater fame in Chicago, where a thoroughfare bears his name. Joseph P. Conroy, S.J., wrote his life (Joseph P. Conroy, S.J., *Arnold Damen, A Chapter in the Making of Chicago* [New York: Benzegar Bros., 1930]).

**Archbishop Francis Patrick Kenrick urged that Dr. Ives receive minor orders and that Rome make him vicar apostolic of North Carolina, the state he had served earlier as Episcopal bishop (FPK to PRK, Jan. 29, 1853, in *KFL*, p. 351).

Vincentian conferences. St. Lawrence O'Toole's parish, not far west of St. Joseph's, had its own charitable society. Eventually it affiliated with the international society. Most of the city parishes started conferences; and by March, 1860, Saint Louis had thirteen units.[12] The members saw the need of coordinating the work on a city-wide scale. As a result, they set up a general directive agency with Dr. Timothy L. Papin its president.

By this time the roster of members included many of the best known Irish-American, Anglo-American, and German-American names of the city. Among the Irish were O'Fallon, Walsh, Maguire, Dillon, Ryder, O'Neill, Byrne, and Fitzsimons. The Anglo-American membership included Hugh Ewing and Joseph Elder. Three members of the German-American communities were to have prominent places in the future development of Catholicism in Saint Louis and the Middle West: Francis Saler, John Amend, and H. J. Spaunhorst.[13]

Matching the generosity of the men, women of the city began the first American unit of the Ladies of Charity, an organization founded by St. Vincent de Paul in Paris in the seventeenth century. Under the chairmanship of Mrs. Catherine Harkins, the ladies met at St. Vincent de Paul's Church on December 8, 1857, to lay plans for aiding the poor. The local ladies of charity never gained the public attention that the men's society did; but this initial American affiliate saw units start in other cities. It continued quietly at its work through the years, ultimately numbering over a thousand active members.[14]

Irish Catholic Colonization in Outstate Missouri

During the middle 1850's newly ordained John J. Hogan worked in the city but dreamed of Catholic communities in the country. As assistant pastor at several parishes in Saint Louis during the years 1854 and 1855, he had observed a disproportionate number of Irish girls at Mass. Their brothers, unfortunately, could not find jobs in the city. As a result, the young men worked on the railroads and moved south and west with the advancing rails. The separation of Catholic young men and women caused the zealous young priest grave misgivings.

Even the Gasconade River disaster on the opening day excursion of the Pacific Railroad from Saint Louis to Jefferson City did not slow rail progress for any length of time. That event occurred, incidentally, on November 1, 1855. A wooden trestle over the tributary of the Missouri River collapsed, injuring one hundred, and pitching thirty-four prominent citizens, among them Henri Chouteau and Thomas O'Flaherty, to their deaths. The city mourned the loss of its sons. But soon engineers repaired the bridge, the railroad moved west, and Irish workers went with them. Father Hogan felt that his vocation lay with these men.

After repeated requests to Archbishop Kenrick, Father Hogan received permission in June, 1857, to go into south Missouri to seek land for his projected Catholic settlements. Father Hogan knew that the soil in north Missouri was more fertile but the prices forbade the project he had in mind. Reluctantly, he decided on south Missouri.

Father Hogan had been in the Ozark country before. As a young priest he had spent the winter of 1852-53 at Old Mines, near Potosi in Washington County, about forty miles west of Ste. Genevieve. He had taught a catechism class of about forty Negroes every day for several months, in preparation of First Communion. Hogan wrote:

> The Negro Catholics of that congregation, and they were many, were devoted to the Church. The young men and young women, though not able to read or write, being debarred from such knowledge by statute, had nevertheless learned by heart the *Gloria* and *Credo* of the Mass, and several Psalms and Hymns which they took delight in singing.... Their masters did not engage in the business of buying and selling slaves, hiring them out for payment, or separating wife from husband or parents from children.... The black and white families went to the same church together. They lived in friendship and in neighborship, mutually aiding and depending on each other. The same priest ministered to their spiritual wants. The same family physician attended them in their ailments. They lived for each other, died near each other, and were buried near each other.[15]

Hogan made two trips deep into the Missouri Ozarks: one with Father James Fox of Old Mines in 1857; a second early in 1858 with Father William Walsh of Jefferson City, "ever a loving friend of the immigrant."[16] Walsh took the greatest possible interest in every effort to move Irish Catholics out of railroad shanties and back alleys to the open prairies.

Through the kindness of Father Fox, Father Hogan got land in the Ozarks about twenty miles north of the Arkansas border. By the spring of 1859, forty families had already settled in the vicinity. Many more families were on the way. Some of the Protestant people of the neighborhood told Father Hogan that their ancestors had originally been Irish-Catholics who had drifted from the faith through lack of contact with the Church. Some of these, Father Hogan brought back to the practice of Catholicism. By 1860 the railroads were moving deeper into Missouri. More immigrants came. Father Hogan selected four places where he would say Mass once a month and a dozen less important ones where he promised to come every three months. Around these, Catholics tended to congregate. They built churches in the larger centers. Unfortunately, the Civil War burst on the nation the following year. Guerilla bands from both sides, bushwackers, and plain renegades swept across the area. The settlements of Father Hogan never recovered from the devastation of the war.[17]

The undaunted young priest did not go down, however, with the destruction of his colonizing ventures. He was to become the first bishop of the second diocese set up in Missouri; and, in this position, he gave strong support to another colonization project that Father James Power had begun in northwest Missouri at the same time as Hogan had started his work in the Ozarks.

A native of Waterford, Ireland, Father James Power became a priest in Philadelphia in 1845. He planned a colonization project in Nodaway County in northwest Missouri for sixty Irish immigrant families. All came west from Philadelphia. But most stayed in St. Joseph, Missouri, where Father Power had his parish. Only fourteen took up land in the colonization project at Conception, Missouri. On June 9, 1860, Father Power dedicated a chapel there.

The zealous priest visited his colony twice a year, even during the war years when he worked in Illinois. During the ensuing decade, he made several efforts to bring a religious order to Conception to give strength to that island of Catholicism; but he did not succeed during Archbishop Kenrick's tenure. When John Hogan became bishop of Northwest Missouri, the Benedictines were to accept his invitation to open Conception Abbey.[18]

Chapter 18

Civil War Divides an Archdiocese

Missouri and the Impending Crisis

A peninsula of slavery, Missouri stretched north into a sea of free states: Illinois on the eastern border, Iowa on the northern, and Kansas, admitted in 1861, on its western boundry. Slavery, however, was on the decline in Missouri. In 1830 slaves had made up 17.8 percent of the state population. By 1860 they formed only 9.8.[1] Most of the slaves were cooks, household servants, or general farmhands. Slavery was not extensive in the Catholic rural sections of Missouri, the area around Ste. Genevieve and Perryville in southeast Missouri, the German farm communities in St. Charles, Franklin, Gasconade, Osage and Cole Counties along the Missouri, west of Saint Louis. Half of the 3,297 colored people in Saint Louis were free by 1860. The total population had doubled in the previous ten years and reached 160,773, so that slaves numbered less than one for each fifty persons in the city.[2]

The political strength of the Missouri slaveholders lay less in the "Boot Heel," the cotton lands of Southeast Missouri, than in "Little Dixie." This crescent of counties stretched south along the Mississippi River from the Iowa border almost to Saint Louis, then swung west along the Missouri toward Kansas City. Out-state Missourians of Anglo-American background had come for the most part from the northern tier of the southern states, Kentucky, Tennessee, Virginia, and North Carolina. This group probably reached three out of every four American-born white citizens in the out-state area. It had great influence politically, especially since it included Governor Clairborne F. Jackson, a secessionist. Jackson felt that the destiny of the slaveholding states was to stand together.

While the American-born newcomers to the state, often southern sympathizers, scattered throughout Missouri, fifty-seven percent of the German immigrants and sixty-six percent of the Irish immigrants settled in Saint Louis. Almost all the Germans and a heavy percentage of the Irish opposed secession.

The economics of Saint Louis and the state argued strongly against leaving the Union. The railroad gave Saint Louis direct access with Chicago and the Great Lakes in 1853 and with Cincinnati and the Atlantic seaboard in 1857. Within five years the state's trade turned from the Mississippi to the trunkline railroads. The "river" city had become a rail center by 1860. Many local businessmen hoped for a transcontinental railroad through Saint Louis, still the central city in the Midwest. These businessmen saw that secession would destroy this possibility. They knew that their future prosperity would grow out of commercial relations with the eastern markets.

The older wealthy families of Saint Louis had ties of sentimentality with the South. They had looked to the river trade. They had not yet readjusted their sentiments to meet their pocketbooks; while as a matter of plain economic fact, their interest lay no longer with the river, but with the railroads.

Some wealthy slave owners gradually came to see the folly of secession. They began to realize that, in an effort to save slave property — then only about nine percent of the wealth of Missouri — they would expose all property to destruction. Few Missourians really wanted secession in the way some of the states of the Deep South did. They had little feeling for an independent southern confederacy. Missouri was one of two states that voted for Douglas, the moderate Democrat candidate in 1860.

A great number of Missourians might have best been described as "neutralists." They disliked both the all-out abolitionists and the fire-eating secessionists. They loved the Union and did not want to see it dissolve. They did not want bloodshed between their brothers of the North and the South. They feared that extremists were taking over on both sides. Most of those who came to advocate secession did so only after the states of the Deep South had already left the Union. Many "neutralists" of the state turned south in retaliation for the capture of the state militia encampments, at Camp Jackson in Saint Louis in May, 1861, by federal troops. Quite interestingly these "neutralists" had not felt similar outrage when Confederates fired on the flag of the United States at Fort Sumter a month before.

Kenrick — Incredibly Neutral

Archbishop Kenrick presided over a divided flock. Personally, he was a moderate states' rights man in political views, just as he was a strong decentralist in ecclesiastical administration. It seems that he had a personal slave himself, working in his household at various times, but he expressed no views on the issue of slavery. True to his "no politics" attitude, traditional to Maynooth men, Kenrick determined that the Church would not involve itself in the forthcoming conflict between the North and the South.

Before hostilities began, Kenrick refused to allow his priests to assist either side. On December 26, 1860, he had issued a circular to the clergy of the diocese directing them to say additional prayers for peace and advised them to "inculcate the necessity of cherishing feelings of mutual charity and forebearance and avoiding all causes of unnecessary excitement among the laity."[3]

At that time, only South Carolina had seceded from the Union. But tension was growing. On January 8, 1861, Brigadier General Daniel M. Frost, a prominent Catholic officer in Missouri, the head of the state militia, a northerner by birth, but a neutralist by conviction, issued a secret command aimed at preventing the U.S. Arsenal from falling into the hands of a mob. The mob in the mind of Frost would be the German radicals, the Forty-Eighters whose homes completely surrounded the area of the arsenal. According to this order of General Frost, all

Tribute to friend and foe! The combined Missouri monument on the battlefield of Vicksburg poignantly recalls the horror of a war that sent brother gunning for brother. (Photograph by Brad Emerson.)

militia units were to assemble at the sound of the pealing of the church bells in the city at five minute intervals. Kenrick was absent at the time when Frost sought permission. Upon his return, the archbishop countermanded the order and strictly prohibited the use of the bells for any such purpose.

In February, the Gulf states followed South Carolina out of the Union. In April, the South fired on the nation's flag at Fort Sumter. In May, General Frost summoned the annual encampment of the state militia in Lindell Grove, on the third ridge at the west end of the city.

General Nathaniel Lyon, U.S.A. commander at the arsenal, along with such Union leaders as Frank Blair, presumed that Frost had chosen the site to awe Saint Louis while the state legislature in Jefferson City voted to secede. Using as a pretext the fact that Governor Clairborne Jackson had sent to Camp Jackson some supplies captured at the federal arsenal in Baton Rouge, Lyon mustered thousands of German unionists into the federal service on May 10, 1861, surrounded Camp Jackson, and overwhelmed the state militia. Completely outnumbered, Frost surrendered. Unfortunately, on their way back to

the arsenal, some of Lyon's men panicked and fired into the crowd. Twenty-six civilians met their death. Lyon gained the sobriquet "Butcher" Lyon. Many neutralists, including General Frost, began to look towards active participation in the Confederate service.

Three days later, on May 13, 1861, Archbishop Kenrick issued a pastoral urging moderation and a return to common sense:

Remember that any aggression by individuals or bodies not recognized by the laws, from which the loss of life may follow, is an act of murder, of which everyone engaged in such aggression is guilty, no matter how great and galling the provocation may have been....A firm reliance on the superintending care of Providence, a humble submission to His will, which has permitted the present trial to befall us, doubtless for our correction, and to remind us of the dependence on Him, and a generous sacrifice of every feeling incompatible with that spirit of brotherhood with which all men, and especially the inhabitants of the same city, should be animated, are dispositions which will be more efficacious in restoring public tranquility and maintaining order than the promptings of vindictiveness which will surely increase and aggravate evils.[4]

When war broke out, not long afterwards, it split Kenrick's flock as few flocks were split.

Frank Blair tried to have Father Pierre Jean De Smet, a strong Unionist, as chaplain at the arsenal, since a large number of Catholics belonged to the regiments there.[5] Many citizens took this move on Blair's part as an attempt to recruit a number of St. Louis Irish for the Union army. Kenrick nullified Blair's plan and insisted that the Jesuit superior refuse authorization to Father De Smet to accept the chaplaincy.[6]

While the poor Irish of Saint Louis generally were pro-Union, neighborhood rivalries with the Germans had caused many of them to join the Minutemen, a pro-Southern military group that formed even before the secession of South Carolina. General Frost drew them into the state militia. Interestingly, those on the Confederate side who wanted to enlist Irish help, constantly referred to the Germans as "The Dutch." They tried to capitalize on the Irish hostility to William of Orange and his Dutchmen who had joined the English in beating the Irish and the French at the Battle of the Boyne several hundred years before. It did not turn out to be a totally successful ploy.

In many northern cities bishops authorized the flying of the Stars and Stripes from the Cathedral or other church spires. Kenrick turned down such a request in Saint Louis. Secretary of State Seward heard of this and made an effort through Archbishop Hughes of New York to have the archbishop of Saint Louis removed by the Roman authorities to another see.[7] Kenrick did not preach during the first two years of the war; a rumor persisted that he did not even read a newspaper during this time. This allegation is not improbable. Kenrick avoided newspapers for long periods during his life.

The war might rage around him. Kenrick concerned himself with spiritual things. The *Calendarium*, or list of feasts celebrated in the United States, was meager. In 1862 the archbishop published a new calendar for the ecclesiastical province that eventually spread through twenty dioceses of the "Greater Interior."[8]

While Kenrick maintained his silence on the civil conflict, other bishops spoke out clearly in word and action. Bishop Martin Spalding of Louisville, for instance, issued an outspoken pastoral that reflected a states' rights point of view and questioned the justice of the attempt to suppress the southern states. Archbishop John Hughes of New York was willing to go to Europe to gain sympathy for the cause of the Union, although he refused an official mission as ambassador. Bishop Michael Domenec, C.M., of Pittsburgh used his influence to prevent his native land, Spain, from recognizing the Confederacy. Bishop John Fitzpatrick of Boston influenced Belgium in the cause of the North. In the Deep South, Bishop Patrick Lynch of Charleston accepted an invitation of the Confederate president to visit European countries in behalf of the Confederacy. He carried a letter of Jefferson Davis to the Holy Father. After Appomatox, he was to have some difficulty in obtaining permission from the federal authorities to return to his diocese.

Divided Priests and People

Some of Kenrick's priests, too, found his aloof neutrality impossible of imitation. Father John O'Sullivan, pastor of St. Malachy's, an ardent secessionist, came in conflict with military authorities. The archbishop permitted his removal from the parish but recommended him to Bishop Juncker of Alton. He became pastor of the parish of the Annunciation in Springfield, Illinois.[9]

Father John Bannon, young pastor of St. John's Evangelist Church, a Dubliner by birth and a volunteer for the Archdiocese of Saint Louis, did not remain long after the solemn dedication of his church on November 4, 1860. He had served as chaplain for the Missouri militia under General Frost's command. Later when General Sterling Price, former governor of Missouri, began recruiting volunteers for the Confederacy, many of Father Bannon's parishioners enlisted. Without any formality of leave-taking, and presumably without the archbishop's permission, Father Bannon left the parish and joined Price's army in January, 1862.[10] Kenrick's close associates insist that he left Bannon's letter of withdrawal unopened. After serving as chaplain for several years with the army of the West, Bannon went to Ireland as special envoy of the Confederate government, presumably to slow down immigration of potential soldiers to the north. Bannon remained in his native land.[11]

The Jesuit vice-provincial, William Stack Murphy, an immigrant from Ireland, and French by education and outlook, saw the conflict in the light of Irish experience, as a just struggle for "home rule." The attack on Camp Jackson was an unauthorized effort of free-thinking "Dutch" rabble against the authority of the state of Missouri.[12]

Father De Smet, in contrast, felt deep outrage at the firing on Fort Sumter. He had just returned from Europe on the day news of the surrender reached New York. He predicted a long and bloody war. He saw the national conflict as arising over the *theoretical* question of slavery in the territories of the West where *practically* the institution could not function.[13] Through his close friendship with the Secretary of War, Edward Stanton, and other government officials, De Smet saved clergymen of Missouri from the necessity of bearing arms in the conflict.

Father Frederick Garesche, a professor at Saint Louis University, militantly advocated the southern cause, even though one of his brothers was a colonel in the Union army. Since his fire-eating sermons disturbed the peace of St. Francis Xavier parish, this bearded prophet moved to the missions of Texas for the duration.[14] Father Edward Keller, a Bavarian by birth, but a resident of Saint Louis during his early years, took a neutral view. He believed the federal government could not suppress the states; but expressed no personal preference.[15]

Laymen were divided too. Many of the older wealthy French and Irish families had had economic ties through river trade with the South. Some of them were slaveholders. Many more leaned toward the South in sympathy, an attitude that the alliance of Abolitionist and anti-Catholic accentuated. Thus General Frost served in the Confederate Army of the trans-Mississippi for two years. General Gabriel Rene Paul, on the other hand, fought for the Union until blinded at Gettysburg.

Dr. Moses Linton, noted physician, controversialist, editor and professor at Saint Louis College of Medicine, faced the moral issue squarely. He simply did not see how any good man could condone slavery; and thought that all Catholics should support the Union.[16] At the end of the war, Dr. Linton was to work in vain to keep control of the Missouri government from revenge-minded radical Republicans.

Archbishop Kenrick appointed Father Patrick J. Ryan chaplain of Confederate prisoners at the Gratiot Street prison. This zealous priest succeeded in baptizing about six hundred prisoners during the course of his work. The government offered Father Ryan a chaplaincy at the Federal Hospital in Saint Louis. He declined the honor but continued without remuneration the work assigned him by the archbishop, the work of administering to the Confederate prisoners.[17] After the war, he was to become archbishop of a northern see. Father Patrick Feehan, soon to become bishop of a southern capital, served the spiritual needs of the northern wounded. The Sisters of Mercy visited the prisoners at the Gratiot Street prison, and four Daughters of Charity, under the leadership of Sister Othelia Marshall, D.C., a trained nurse, cared for the sick and wounded there and in the prison hospital in Alton, Illinois, where they were to remain during the last year of the war.

The Church and War-Time Missouri Politics

In October, 1861, the pro-Union convention of Missouri had prescribed an oath of loyalty to the Provisional Government to be taken before December 17, 1861. Clairborne Jackson, the secessionist-minded governor, had fled to Texas in the meantime. In June, 1862, a provision outlined three forms of test oaths: one for all voters; the second for all candidates for civil office; and the third for all jurymen, attorneys, teachers, and clergymen. Some apparatus of the police state appeared here and there in Saint Louis and throughout Missouri.

Kenrick refused to take the oath; nor would he authorize the diocesan clergy to do so. He left the religious orders free to declare their allegiance to the Provisional Government if they thought it necessary to do so.

The person taking the oath had to promise to support, protect, and defend the state and federal constitutions, and to swear that since December 17, 1861, he had not taken up arms against the United States, or against the Provisional Government of Missouri, and that he would not do so. He also had to agree that neither directly nor indirectly would he "give aid and comfort to the enemies thereof."[18]

Apparently the state made no serious effort to enforce this ordinance. But it augured ill for days ahead. A retroactive law — a type of legislation totally forbidden by the Constitution — it anticipated an infamous enactment to come shortly after the conclusion of the War. Technicalities so clouded the entire question that many Missourians forgot the basic moral issue of the time.

In one of his last important letters to his brother, Peter Richard wrote on August 22, 1862: "I have decided to stay out of these troubles as much as possible for the sake of the law so that with God's help, I shall be useful up to the end."[19]

The following summer, on July 8, 1863, a few days after the battle of Gettysburg, the older brother, Archbishop Francis Patrick Kenrick, died in Baltimore. Because of the difficulties of war travel, Peter Richard could not get back in time for the funeral. He did reach Baltimore later on that summer.

In spite of the War in the West, Archbishop Kenrick carried on a correspondence with Bishop William Henry Elder of Natchez. Once the Mississippi was opened with the fall of Vicksburg in 1863 this correspondence grew. On September 2, 1864, for instance, Bishop Elder asked Kenrick what he should do if the South would draft clergymen.[20]

As the War drew to its inevitable close in the spring of 1865, Kenrick faced a second important decision in regard to the troubles of the nation. His first decision had been one of absolute "hands off" — a decision based upon his principle of "no politics." The next decision was based entirely on the principle of religious liberty.

Even before the War had ceased, the Union faction in Missouri had split into two groups, the conservatives or "Clay-banks," and the radicals, or "Charcoals." On July 1, 1863, the conservative leaders had succeeded in securing the adoption of an ordinance providing for a gradual emancipation of the slaves so that by July 4, 1870, every man in Missouri would be free. The radicals, however, had refused to accept this measure as final. They continued to agitate for immediate emancipation. They took over the state in the election of 1864, won a vote on a new constitutional convention, and had three-fourths of the sixty-six delegates to that convention.

The constitutional convention met in the hall of the Mercantile Library in Saint Louis on January 6, 1865, to consider amendments deemed necessary for the emancipation of the slaves, for restricting the elective franchise to loyal citizens, and other amendments "essential to the public good." On January 11, they voted the immediate and unconditional emancipation of all slaves in Missouri. They decided not to amend the old constitution but to draft a new one.

Under the leadership of Charles Drake, a Saint Louis lawyer, the radicals adopted a new constitution on April 1, 1865, called by its friends "The Drake Constitution." Its opponents, such as the distinguished physician, editor, and controversialist, Dr. Moses Linton, called it the "Draconian Code." Failing to calm the radicals by reason, the versatile Linton tried to laugh his opponents into moderation. His humor makes marvelous reading;* but it was ineffective in stemming the extremists in control of the convention. Drake and his followers embodied in the constitution an iron-clad test oath. Every voter, officeholder, attorney, and clergyman had to take an oath that he had not aided the South in any of eighty-six different ways. In short, if a person had even so much as sympathized with the Confederacy, he was legally incapable of performing his clerical function in Missouri.

Following the example of Archbishop Kenrick, no priest took the oath; but all continued their priestly functions. The law moved against two clergymen, the pre-war colonizer, John J. Hogan, then pastor of Chillicothe in northwest Missouri, and small impetuous, twenty-five-year-old Father John Cummings of Louisiana, in Pike County, along the Mississippi above Saint Louis. A grand jury indicted Father Hogan. Ashamed to present the summons in person, the sheriff sent Drury McMillen, a choir member at the church, to arrest the pastor. Drury felt equally cheap and asked Father Hogan to ride down one street, while he took another. Instead, Father Hogan dressed in cassock, surplice, stole, and biretta, refused the deputy's offer of his horse, and, carrying a large Bible, walked down the street alongside the mounted deputy. Father Hogan signed his bond; then left the next day to say Mass at the town of Cameron. So strong did feelings rise against the authorities that the Catholics held a protest meeting at the neighboring town of Brookfield. This was the first such protest against the Drake oath in the entire state.[21]

---

*The work of Dr. Linton in the convention is the subject of a splendid article in the *Missouri Historical Review* 59, no. 3 (April 1965): 293-301. The writer is William E. Parrish.

Over in Pike County, Father John Cummings went to jail. Judge Fagg of the circuit court at Bowling Green found him guilty. Cummings refused to pay the fine, would not allow his friends to pay it, and took the alternative of imprisonment for six months. He even refused to accept bail pending an appeal to the Missouri Supreme Court. In October, 1865, the state supreme court sitting in Saint Louis and composed of three justices who had just received their position as a result of the ordinance ousting their predecessors, voted unanimously to uphold the decision of the circuit court.[22] Cummings took his case to the United States Supreme Court.

The case transcended the imprisonment of one clergyman to become a landmark in the reaffirmation of religious liberty. Top lawyers in the nation defended Cummings: David Dudley Field of New York, brother of Supreme Court Justice Stephen J. Field, and of Cyrus W. Field, who the previous year had laid the first Atlantic cable; and Montgomery Blair, postmaster general in Lincoln's first term, who took up the case at the request of his brother, Major General Frank Blair, leader of the moderate Unionists in Missouri. The appeal dragged on through the next year. Finally a decision came in January 14, 1867. The United States Supreme Court reversed the judgment of the Missouri court on the grounds that the oath was retroactive and presumed a person guilty by legislative act rather than by judicial procedure, and thus contravened the constitution. Quite interestingly, in spite of these weighty considerations, the decision was only five to four.

The archdiocese suffered in another, and indirect way, from the Drake oath. Mrs. Mary L. Lamarque of Old Mines in Washington County, about forty miles west of Ste. Genevieve, included in her will a bequest of $20,000 to the archbishop of Saint Louis for the education of priests for the archdiocese. Louis Bolduc and other heirs of the deceased lady contested the will under the provisions of the Drake Constitution. The archbishop took the stand and admitted without hesitation that he received the money not as an individual citizen but only in his capacity as archbishop of Saint Louis. The court instructed the jury to set aside this provision of the will. An appeal to the Missouri Supreme Court in March, 1870, affirmed the decision of the trial judge in these words: "Legacy to Peter Richard Kenrick is void and of no effect, in violation of Section 13, Article 1, of the Constitution of the State of Missouri."[23] Father Hogan was to refer to this incident many years later in his good-humored way: "A horse-thief or the keeper of a bawdy house was competent to be legatee, but not Peter Richard Kenrick, Archbishop of Saint Louis. May the good Lord keep our State and our courts from the infamy of another such decision."[24]

Civil War Aftermath

The Civil War brought dramatic changes to the city of Saint Louis and to the Church in Saint Louis. The Missouri metropolis was to remain the fourth city in the nation in population for many years to come. But its dominant position in the heart of mid-America had ended with the Civil War and the period immediately after it.

The colorful steamboat race between the "Natchez and the Robert E. Lee" from New Orleans to Saint Louis in early July, 1867, looked to an era that really had gone. Steamboating still had its glamour but the day of the railroad had arrived; and Chicago was becoming the hub of the transcontinental systems. When railroad men sank the golden spike near Ogden, Utah, in 1869, uniting the Pacific and the Atlantic, the railroad went through Chicago, not Saint Louis. The main north and south railroad between New Orleans and the Great Lakes, already built before the Civil War, had been going through the Illinois prairie seventy miles east of Saint Louis. Saint Louis was a rail center, but definitely a secondary rail center of the Midwest.

Many civic leaders of the ante-bellum period had economic ties to the river trade, and psychological bonds with the South. A significant percentage of these had been Catholics. Now a new leadership came in, northern in viewpoint, and economically bound to the rising industrial interests of the eastern seaboard. Only a minority of this new leadership was Catholic.

A similar change occurred in the intellectual community. Saint Louis University had long held a unique position in frontier education. But in the late forties, its promising law school had closed, and the Know-Nothing movement had forced a withdrawal of the medical department in the fifties. Reduced to the status of an arts college, it slowly withdrew behind its walls at Ninth and Washington, as the business section of the city engulfed it.

As Saint Louis University pulled back into the cloister, young non-denominational Washington University gradually moved into a central position in higher education. It had conferred its first college degree in 1863; in 1867 it began a course in law; and was to organize schools of engineering and architecture in 1870. Washington University won the support of the rising power structure of the region.

A further indication of the intellectual trends of the times would come with the development of the so-called "Saint Louis Movement" in philosophy, literature, religion, and psychology. Stated as simply as possible, this movement held that the outlook on life advocated by German philosopher George Wilhelm Hegel (1770-1831) offered a means to the realization of an ideal democratic society. Its membership included such distinguished personages of the region as Lieutenant Governor Henry C. Brockmeier and educator William Torrey Harris, who was later to become United States commissioner of education. The "Saint Louis Movement" hardly touched the Catholic community.

Chapter 19

Lion Rampant

The Second Plenary Council of Baltimore

Even before the Civil War had ground to its inevitable close, Archbishop Martin John Spalding, successor to Francis Patrick Kenrick as archbishop of Baltimore, hoped to call a plenary council shortly after the close of hostilities. Rome wanted the American bishops to gather in council. Spalding decided to invite a Roman theologian to represent the Holy Father. When the Lion of Saint Louis heard this, he wrote to Spalding in January, 1865, condemning the intention of inviting a foreigner.[1]

The War ended in the spring of 1865. In the fall, Archbishop Kenrick consecrated one of his priests, Father Patrick Feehan, as the new bishop of Nashville, Tennessee. Feehan had earlier served as rector of the Saint Louis Seminary in Carondelet, done pastoral work in the city, and ministered to the religious needs of Union troops. During the embattled days of the War, he had wisely declined the nomination to Nashville; but with the restoration of peace, he accepted the call. He was to distinguish himself by personally administering to the sick in repeated epidemics of cholera, and to give support and a name to the Catholic Knights of America, the first Catholic fraternal insurance association in the country — a society that was to spread rapidly in the Saint Louis archdiocese during the succeeding thirty years. Eventually Bishop Feehan was to become the first archbishop of Chicago.

During the May following his consecration of Feehan, Kenrick again wrote to Spalding in preparation for the coming council. He discussed various ways of selecting bishops. He believed the priests should share in the election of their bishops, as they did in Ireland at the time. Kenrick suggested other alternatives, and insisted: "in any case, the method used at Rome . . . is wrong."[2]

In a third letter to Spalding a week later, Kenrick deplored the necessity for episcopal immersion in temporal administration. He discussed contemporary methods of transferring ecclesiastical property, concluding that the worst of all was the plan offered by the Sacred Congregation in Rome. Finally, he alluded to his own economic difficulties arising from the dislocations of the Civil War.[3]

As the economy of the nation recovered its equilibrium, incidentally, Kenrick was able to put archdiocesan economic affairs in good order during the ensuing years. The main factor was this: the parishes that had received grants under the Thornton bequest returned either half or all of the original to the central archdiocesan fund — according to their ability to pay, as Kenrick had originally stipulated.[4]

The avowed purpose of the projected Second Plenary Council of Baltimore was to allow the bishops, in the midst of grave dissension in the country, to present a pattern of unity, to prepare for a new era in the nation, to establish a uniform discipline, and to care for the spiritual needs of the Negroes.[5]

Feeling for a council was not unanimous. Some felt that discussions would be too unpleasant in view of the tensions between the sections. After all, even the bishops had reflected the part of the country where they governed — north, south, or border. The overwhelming majority, however, wanted a council and insisted that it concern itself with strictly religious matters. Rome made Archbishop Spalding apostolic delegate to the council with plenary authority to guide the legislation necessary for the uniformity of discipline, the growth of diocesan organization, and the increase of faith among clergy and people.

In the previous twenty years the Church had come a long way both organizationally and psychologically. The American Church had jumped from one province, Baltimore, set up in 1808, to seven: Oregon (1846), Saint Louis (1847), Cincinnati (1850), New York (1850), New Orleans (1850) and San Francisco (1853). The number of suffragan bishops was forty. Twelve years before, the nativist movement moved toward its most virulent period with the surge of the Know-Nothings. By 1866 the Church had assumed a place of acceptance in American society, thanks in part to the loyalty of Catholics to their respective areas of the country, and to the work of Sisters as nurses on the battlefield.

Before he left for Baltimore, Kenrick had the joy of consecrating another of his outstanding priests, John Hennessey, pastor of St. Joseph, Missouri, also a former rector of the seminary in Carondelet, as bishop of Dubuque, Iowa, on September 30, 1866. Like Feehan, Hennessey was to become an archbishop.

When Kenrick left for the Second Plenary Council of Baltimore a few days later, he took a strong team with him: Vicar-General Patrick Ryan, soon to be coadjutor in Saint Louis; theologian Joseph Melcher who had refused Kenrick's nomination as bishop of Quincy, but was later to become bishop of Green Bay; and the archiepiscopal secretary, Missouri-born Father Charles Ziegler, who continued to be one of Saint Louis' outstanding pastors for many years.

Church historian James Hennessey called the Baltimore Council of 1866 an "American Syllabus" because, in the spirit of Pius IX's "Syllabus of Errors" of 1864, it spent much of its time in condemnations. "The unique contribution of the council of 1866, and its most significant departure from past practice," Hennessey wrote, "lay in the doctrinal statements which it made."[6] Had Kenrick had his way, this would not have been so.

When Archbishop Spalding handed out a printed scheme containing the matters for discussion, Archbishop Kenrick and Bishop Peter Paul Lefevere, administrator of Detroit, wanted to drop the entire negative section on "Inroads of Error," in favor of positive pastoral matters. Kenrick also opposed Spalding's haste in pressing for adoption of decrees. Ultimately, he protested this procedure to Rome; thus helping to delay the approbation of the decrees for two years. Kenrick also demanded that the prelates send the traditional cablegram to Pope Pius IX in English rather than French or Latin.[7]

An advocate of collegiality in a day of Roman centralization, Kenrick gave his opinion shortly after: "We as bishops are vested by the Holy Spirit with the right to decide how to rule the Church of God and are not bound just to follow the instructions sent out from the Holy See."[8]

The bishops heatedly discussed the status of the newly freed Negro, especially the proposal to name a national director for the Negro apostolate. Bishop John Verot of Savannah wanted special aid for the Negro. Bishop John McGill of Richmond opposed this recommendation. Kenrick thought a new decree on the Negro would imply that the bishops had been remiss.[9] Kenrick believed that the priests and bishops had done all they could. Archbishop John Odin of New Orleans agreed with him on this; but differed with Kenrick by opposing the opening of churches exclusively for Negroes.[10]

On the question of Negro Catholics, incidentally, Kenrick was to follow out these two notions he expressed at the Baltimore council: first, that the bishops had done as much as they could; therefore, he gave no new impetus to the ministry among the black Catholics in Saint Louis, who for the most part were descendants of slaves of French families; secondly, he looked upon separate churches for Negroes in the same way he looked upon distinct churches for national groups — as places of privilege and security; though as a matter of fact in this instance no language barrier existed and the second generation would not find a home in the wider white Catholic community.

During several decades, Negro Catholics had gathered for Mass on Sunday in one of the galleries of St. Francis Xavier Church. Over the years a number of individual Jesuits attended to their spiritual welfare. In the days immediately after the Civil War, Catholic Negroes living in the city could still come there on most Sundays without reasonable inconvenience. The Jesuits laid plans for a church for Negroes on the corner of Seventeenth and Christy. Consistent with his attitude at the council of Baltimore, Kenrick was to set down stringent regulations for the ministry of this parish. He required the Jesuit provincial to assure him in writing that the pastors would devote the Church exclusively to blacks and administer no sacraments to the whites.[11]

Kenrick's participation in the Second Council of Baltimore had been at times erratic, but always arresting. His sermon on "The Apostolic Ministry" at the final session on October 21 raised many eyebrows and comments. Carrying his "no politics" rule to an extreme, Kenrick did not so much as acknowledge the presence of President Andrew Johnson, his secretary, Colonel Robert Johnson, and the mayor of Washington, Mr. Richard Wallach.[12] Yet this presidential attendance, no matter what its political connotation, reflected a new public acceptance of American Catholicism.

John Lancaster Spalding appraised the impact of the council on the nation in a passage of classical dignity:

> The country had just come forth from a most terrible crisis in which many ancient landmarks had been effaced and the very ship of state had been wrenched from its moorings. House had been divided against house and brother's hand had been raised against brother. The sects had been torn asunder and still lay in disorder and confusion, helping to widen the abyss which had threatened to engulf the nation's life. Half the country was waste and desolate; the people crushed, bowed beneath the double weight of the memory of the past, which could no more return, and with the thought of a future which seemed hopeless. On the other side, there was weariness and exhaustion which follow a supreme effort, and the longing for peace and happiness after so much bloodshed and misery. All were ready to applaud any power that had been able to live through that frightful struggle unhurt and unharmed; and when the Catholic Church walked forth before the eyes of the nation, clothed in the panoply of undiminished strength and of unbroken unity, thousands who but a while ago would have witnessed this manifestation of a power with jealous concern now hailed it with light as a harbinger of good omen.[13]

Church historian Peter Guilday called the council "the most important ecclesiastical assembly ever witnessed in the United States up to that year.[14] The Irish Cardinal Cullen sent word of congratulations to Spalding. Cullen believed the work of the council could "not fail to be of the greatest value to the Church of America and, indeed, to every other church."[15]

An analysis of the fourteen decrees of the council, however, does not show any particular American genius or freshness. They dealt chiefly with the internal structure of the Church and seemed to aim at producing conformity between the various dioceses in a European pattern.

The pastoral issued by the bishops at the close of the council gave evidence of the limited vision of the council in these words:

> We have taken advantage of the opportunity of the assembling of so large a number of bishops from every part of our vast country, to enact such decrees as will tend to promote uniformity of discipline and practice among us, and to do away with such imperfect observance of the rites and approved ceremonies for the church as may have been made necessary by the circumstances of past times but which no length of prescription can ever consecrate and thus to give to services of our religion that beauty and dignity which belongs to them and for which we shall all be so zealous.[16]

The spirit of John Carroll no longer seemed evident in episcopal councils.

David Phelan: The "Western Watchman"

No Catholic newspaper or journal of the time matched the "Western Watchman" of Father David Phelan in verve and flamboyance. A Nova Scotian by birth, David Phelan had moved with his parents to Saint Louis at the age of twelve in 1853. After his ordination during the Civil War, Archbishop Kenrick sent him to northeast Missouri. He became pastor of Edina, near Kirksville, a place not heard from before he went there, nor after he left. The Sisters of Loretto began a convent school in Edina. Because of outbursts of bigotry against them, however, the Lorettines planned to leave for more acceptable surroundings. To forestall this, Father Phelan bought the equipment of two small papers then published in Edina. He began the *Missouri Watchman*, later the *Western Watchman*, in 1865, to support the Sisters and defend the Church. Father Phelan soon came to excel in a type of personal militant journalism, rarely known in the American church at that time or any time.

Three years later Archbishop Kenrick brought him into the Saint Louis area. In 1878 he became pastor of the Church of Our Lady of Mount Carmel, in Baden, then a suburb north of the city. He was to remain pastor at Mount Carmel for over forty years. He was a good preacher, a pleasant, witty companion, a hard working and beloved pastor, a fair German scholar, a translator of three French works on theology, and the author of two books. Characteristically, he gave his sermons after Mass.

Anyone who wished to leave could do so. He spoke straight-forwardly, bluntly at times. He pulled no punches. He wrote the same way.

When he first came to Saint Louis, the city had no other Catholic paper. He resumed his publishing and for a time enjoyed a monopoly. His brother, Michael Phelan, helped secure the physical equipment for setting up the *Watchman*. For many years Michael continued to handle the business while Father Phelan built up the circulation by his editorial fireworks.

Phelan loved controversy. He feared no foe, whether bishop or bigot. He opposed American interference in the political strife between the Pope and the Italian government — a position Archbishop Kenrick, but not many other American bishops, took. Phelan supported the Ancient Order of Hibernians when Kenrick had misgivings about the organization. He defended priests and laymen alike, such as Father Edward McGlynn of New York, advocate of social reformer Henry George, against what he held to be the uncanonical arbitrariness of some American bishops.[17]

Yet he was arbitrary and one-sided himself. During the spring and summer of 1886, for instance, when the Knights of Labor engaged in a major dispute with the southwestern railroads, Phelan generally ignored this question that immediately involved so many of his readers; and devoted most of his attention to Home Rule for Ireland.[18] He strongly opposed the determination of the Third Plenary Council of Baltimore to promote parochial schools. He spoke openly on Archbishop Ireland's side in the school controversy and the question of the "Americanization of the Church." He was to win nation-wide attention by his checkmating nativism in Saint Louis. Perhaps no priest in American history survived so many major condemnations from higher churchmen — including his own archbishops.

A commentator described his approach to journalism:

Father Phelan never wrote a dull line. Every question he took up, he lifted out of the commonplace. He raised it to the dignity of an issue. He stimulated interest in the discussion of it . . . . He pinned his faith to the vigorous offensive . . . he did his fighting in the enemy trenches . . . he not only routed the enemy but he routed him ignominiously. His antagonist never made a strategic retreat. He simply ran away and he ran as hard as he could . . . . Father Phelan's coming meant a new era in Catholic journalism. His daring, his wit, his versatility, his pungency, his resourcefulness, confounded opposition . . . . Father Phelan was not only a wit, he was a humorist and he often expressed himself after the manner of Swift, of Defoe . . . . He dearly loved intellectual horseplay. His best friends were its constant victims.[19]

Phelan summed up his own work in this way:

In 1867 I was called to Saint Louis and brought the *Watchman* hither. At that time there was no Catholic paper published in this city and for many years I had the field all to myself; but there was little interest in Catholic questions then and people did not feel the necessity or utility of a Catholic paper. Gradually a spirit of Catholic enterprise took possession of our people and I eventually got a good hearing. The first trouble I got into was over the action of some bishops in excommunicating the Ancient Order of Hibernians. I spared no man, however high in the Church who abused his power to oppress a body of good, honest Irish Catholics whose only fault was standing up for their clergy always and everywhere. Catholics forget just how many bishops denounced the paper at that time . . . the next trouble I encountered was over the educational clauses of the Third Council of Baltimore. I said they were silly and impracticable. . . . .

Contrary to the general impression, I am not at all a contentious individual. I have been in conflict nearly all my journalistic life but I have always had for antagonists, silly bishops and stupid editors who insisted on making our people more Catholic than the Holy Father and more orthodox than the Church . . . . My style, if it can be dignified with the name, is epigrammatic; often sharp and bitter. But I have never said an unkind thing of any man who showed a particle of that modesty which would characterize the utterances of a man who speaks for the great Catholic Church.[20]

"He was feared by many," Monsignor Rothensteiner wrote, "yet loved by more, partly because he was a tower of strength for the present, partly because he had bravely stood his place at a time when it was dangerous to do so."[21] He would appear prominently as the archdiocese moved on through the years.

Father Phelan succeeded with his Catholic weekly in Saint Louis. Others followed. One was the *Church Progress and Catholic World*, as calm and dispassionate as the *Western Watchman* was provocative. Conde Pallen, later managing editor of the *Catholic Encyclopedia,* edited it for a time. Pallen, like Phelan, was to merit inclusion in that encyclopedia of significant Americans, *The Dictionary of American Biography*.* During the late seventies, a prominent Catholic layman, B. M. Chambers, gave great effort and much money in an attempt to turn the *St. Louis Times* into a Catholic daily.[22] His efforts came to naught; but the mere fact that he tried speaks much for the maturity and Catholicity of the city.

Archdiocesan Expansion After the Civil War

At the close of the Civil War, the vigorous growth of the city that had marked the pre-war period came again in full force. By 1870, Saint Louis was to be the fourth city in the nation in population after New York, Philadelphia, and Brooklyn, and to be one of the larger cities in the world — relative positions that it would never again assume in later decades. It was the largest city of the nation beyond the eastern seaboard, with a population of 310,864 — almost double its size of ten years before.[23]

With the heavy concentration of business establishments and the congestion in the area around the Cathedral at Third and Walnut, Archbishop Kenrick moved his residence and the center of archiepiscopal operations to Saint John's Church at Sixteenth and Chestnut. This more convenient residential-area church became his pro-cathedral while he planned a new one for a site six blocks farther west. The consecration of Bishop Feehan in 1865 proved to be the last significant religious event at the "old cathedral" for many years to come. Now hidden amid the tall buildings of downtown Saint Louis, the lovely Cathedral of Bishop Rosati went temporarily into obscurity.

Several of the parishes that began at this time had distinctive histories of their own. The Church of the Holy Angels at Fourteenth and LaSalle Street, just northeast of Lafayette Park, looked backward rather than forward. At the time of its inaugural in 1866 on land donated by John Dillon, the congregation numbered old and distinguished Catholic families like the Delaneys, Barrys, Papins, Boislinieres, Primms, and Dillons. Archbishop Kenrick laid the foundation of the big structure of Gothic design on July 9, 1866. Neither Father Michael Willoughby, the first pastor, nor the second, Father Francis M. Kielty, believed in the parochial school system. This conviction helped to bring the parish to an early decline.

---

*Those two excellent sketches appear in *Dictionary of American Biography* 14:17; 520-521. R. J. Purcell's sketch of Phelan is especially noteworthy.

Midway through Father Kielty's long pastorate, the majority of the old families took flight westward.

On the north side of the Mill Creek Valley, the new parishes anticipated the westward trend. Four parishes began a vigorous growth on North Grand Avenue during the post-war years. One of them grew out of the congre-

Theresa's and five blocks north of Lindell. Here they opened a residence in 1868, and began St. Alphonsus' Church. The Jesuits, too, looked to the commanding ridge that stretched along Grand Avenue. They purchased property at Grand and Lindell, across from the site of old Camp Jackson, in 1867. They hoped to move the univer-

German immigrant homes clustered around old St. Joseph's Church at Eleventh and Biddle on the near-northside, the only Baroque Church in the area. An authenticated miracle occurred here in the middle of the nineteenth century. The "Friends of St. Joseph" have restored the Shrine. (Sketch by Roscoe Misselhorn: used with permission of the Misselhorn Art Foundation of Sparta, Ill.

gation that gathered each Sunday in north Saint Louis in the chapel of St. Thomas the Apostle on the Jesuit college farm. The trustees of Saint Louis University had purchased this property in the mid thirties to move the college from the downtown site at Ninth and Washington. Circumstances prevented the removal of the school. The Jesuits used the college farm at various times as a seminary and as a summer camp for students and faculty members. As the years went on, the university sold sections of the property. Subdividers brought in residents. These newcomers attended Mass at the chapel on the college farm. The Jesuit fathers turned over the chapel to the archdiocese in 1865, and the parish of the Holy Name began in the general area of North Grand and Florissant.

In the same year, at Grand and North Market, about fifteen blocks south of the Holy Name site, Father Francis P. Gallagher organized St. Theresa's parish and began a new church. Grand Avenue, the main thoroughfare north and south at the west limits of the city at the time, also beckoned two men's religious communities. The Redemptorist Fathers, who had staffed the old cathedral for several years (1866-68), hoped for a residence and church of their own. They selected a site on the east side of Grand at Finney, about eight blocks south of St.

sity and the College Church from their downtown sites at Ninth and Washington. Some years were to elapse, however, before either of these projects got underway.

The pioneer German churches of St. Mary's, Sts. Peter and Paul, and St. Joseph spawned three new churches in the five year period after the Civil War: St. Nicholas began in November, 1865; St. Francis de Sales, destined to supersede Sts. Peter and Paul as the foremost German Catholic parish of the city, in 1867; and St. Agatha's on Ninth and Utah in 1871.

The post-war period also saw the development of central Catholic cemeteries for the north and south sections of the city. Saint Louis' first Catholic cemetery had adjoined the original church in the northern half of the church block at Third and Market. Later it moved to Seventh and St. Charles, near the downtown site of Saint Louis University, and still later, to the vicinity of Seventeenth and Franklin. Several parishes in the city and country, such as St. Vincent's and, later on, St. Monica's in Creve Couer, had cemeteries of their own. In 1849 a new Catholic burial ground, the Rock Springs Cemetery, opened at Sarah and Bates in the Mill Creek Valley west of the city limits.

Two years after the close of the Civil War, Archbishop

Kenrick set up the Calvary Cemetery Association to direct the development of the cemetery on the old Clay farm between Florissant Avenue and Broadway, northwest of the city. The pre-bellum mansion on the estate had been Kenrick's favorite residence for a time, and later housed the Carmelite Sisters for a short period. This new Catholic cemetery of Saint Louis adjoined the well-known Bellefontaine Cemetery, the burial place of many prominent Saint Louisans of other religious denominations. Three years later, Catholics on the south side developed Sts. Peter and Paul Cemetery on Gravois Avenue. Calvary and Sts. Peter and Paul supplanted the many earlier Catholic cemeteries of the city.

The immediate post-bellum period also proved a time for the expansion of old organizations and the development of new ones. Among the Irish Catholics, the United Sons of Erin Benevolent Society led the way in 1866. The Ancient Order of Hibernians had gotten underway in New York, but did not reach Saint Louis until 1870. It grew rapidly thereafter, in spite of opposition from some bishops of the country. It found a strong champion in Saint Louis editor Father David Phelan. In 1870 also, Father Matthew's Total Abstinence Society, made up of men of Irish lineage, began a Saint Louis unit. The Fenian Brotherhood, a secret society with revolutionary leanings, had a few members in the city; but it found a strong foe in Archbishop Kenrick, who, on one occasion, forbade public ceremonies in connection with the funeral of a Fenian.[24]

German-American Catholics in Saint Louis had formed a benevolent union in 1850 and had given leadership to the national *Central-Verein* during the Civil War years. In 1868 men of Sts. Peter and Paul parish formed the St. Paul's mutual-aid society. It developed in many German-language parishes in the city and throughout the archdiocese.

The German Catholics of the city had held an impressive torchlight procession on the 25th anniversary of Archbishop Kenrick's episcopal consecration, November 30, 1866. The "Old Lion" did not approve this type of demonstration. He believed that torchlight processions properly belonged to the political scene. But he had allowed this one because the people had already gone to great expense in preparation.[25]

When Kenrick returned from a visit to Rome with Vicar-General Ryan in the spring of 1868, a procession three miles long welcomed his return. During that same summer, he consecrated two more of his outstanding priests as bishops: Father Joseph Melcher as bishop of Green Bay, on July 12, 1868; and Father John Hogan, outstate Missouri missionary, as the bishop of St. Joseph in northwest Missouri, on September 12. When Kenrick had presented Hogan's name to the bishops at the Baltimore council two years before, one of the eastern prelates had remarked that the bishops did not know who Hogan was. "I do," Kenrick answered.[26]

The new diocese of St. Joseph fragmented the state of Missouri for the first time. This scarcely viable religious unit had only seven parishes with resident pastors at the time.[27] It included all of northwest Missouri, a parallelogram of land with the Iowa border on the north, the Chariton River on the east, and the Missouri River, that turns sharply east at Kansas City, on the west and south. It was not the first nor was it to be the last ridiculous arrangement of ecclesiastical territory in the mid-continent.

As to Saint Louis itself, Kenrick wanted a coadjutor. He recommended these priests: Patrick Ryan, vicar-general of the archdiocese; Edward M. Hennessy, C.M., rector of St. Mary's Seminary in Perryville; and Charles Ziegler, secretary of the archdiocese and newly appointed pastor of Saint Malachy's Church in Saint Louis.[28] Since the archbishops of New Orleans and San Francisco had made similar petitions at that time, Cardinal Barnabo of the Propaganda responded that the council would provide an opportunity to take up the matter of coadjutors.[29]

The First Vatican Council

This first ecumenic council since the sixteenth century proved a watershed in the life of the Church; it was equally a turning point in the career of Archbishop Kenrick. Many events of the council did not greatly affect the progress of the Archdiocese of Saint Louis. But they affected the Saint Louis archbishop intimately, and the remaining twenty-five years he was to live and work in Saint Louis showed their effects. Therefore, a discussion of Kenrick's part in Vatican I is in place.*

Kenrick was one of the most powerful American prelates at the council. He "spoke Latin with most admirable ease and excellence," in the opinion of Bishop, later Cardinal James Gibbons.[30] Kenrick had long been concerned with the prerogatives of the bishops and had opposed over-centralization in Rome on theological and practical grounds. He disliked the Roman tendency to involve theological questions with political considerations such as the continued existence of the Papal States, soon to go down before the rising tide of Italian unification.

Many bishops, especially those from countries with heavy Protestant populations, thought a declaration on the infallibility of the Pope inopportune at the time. They believed it would cause misunderstanding and hinder Catholic-Protestant relationships. Further it was not one of the leading topics on the original agenda, but gradually came to the forefront only under the personal impetus of Pope Pius IX.

Kenrick was more than an "inopportunist." He simply opposed the doctrine in the way the majority party advanced it. Thus, once again he came into opposition to Archbishop Martin Spalding, as he had done at the Plenary Council of Baltimore four years before. Spalding had earlier questioned the advisability of defining infallibility — though he did hold it as Church doctrine. As the opening of the Vatican Council approached, Spalding changed his position and supported the definition. He attributed his reversal to a visit to Europe where he came to see at first hand how alive and dangerous certain separatist ideas were.[31] Opponents of Spalding felt he had gone over to the pro-definition party because of memberships in two conciliar commissions.

A group of American bishops, led by Kenrick and Purcell, objected to the presumption of Spalding to speak in the name of the American bishops, when such diversity of opinion on the question at issue existed among them. In a courteous letter to Spalding, Kenrick concentrated on a single issue: Spalding's use of a quotation from the

---

*For a more detailed discussion of the part American bishops played in the council, confer James Hennessey, *The First Council of the Vatican: the American Experience* (New York: Herder & Herder, 1963).

writings of the elder Kenrick in support of the infallibilist position. Peter Richard admitted his brother had deep devotion to the Holy See; but insisted that Francis Patrick had taught that the consent of the bishops was needed to make a pontifical decree infallible.[32]

At the opening sessions of the council, several bishops, Kenrick among them, requested a delay in the proceedings to give a greater chance for the diocesan bishops, as opposed to the curial officials, to have representation on the various committees. The controlling group cavalierly dismissed this request.[33] When Pope Pius IX insisted that he had the exclusive right of proposing matters for consideration at the council, Kenrick joined twenty-five prelates of Germany, Austria, and Hungary in sending a dignified, firm, but unavailing protest against this limitation of the rights of the bishops.[34]

When the council got underway, Kenrick asked to speak on the question of infallibility. He had the assurance that he would be free to do so. As archbishop for twenty-three years of the fourth largest city in the western hemisphere, one of the most important Catholic centers in the English-speaking world, and the twelfth largest city in the world with an archbishop at the council,[35] he should have had his chance to express himself. The council moderator narrowly limited the debate. As a result, Kenrick arranged for the printing of his projected statement on infallibility in Naples, beyond the boundaries of the Papal States. He presented a copy to all the prelates after the debate was over, but before the vote.

The address of the Saint Louis prelate — widely called "Kenrick's *Concio,*" the Latin word for address — had the form of a speech, even though it was in print. Ponderous rather than persuasive, long-winded rather than to the point, personal rather than objective in the early part, especially where Kenrick directed his remarks critically at Cardinal Manning or approvingly at Archbishop MacHale of Ireland, the long document contained powerful ideas.[36] Early in his message, Kenrick spoke of "collegiality" in a way hardly heard of again until Vatican II.

> The bishops, taken universally, have an universal jurisdiction [he said], not in that sense exactly that the universal jurisdiction is made up of the sum of the local jurisdictions; but that the bishops universally, whether dispersed and separated from each other, or united in General Council, constitute the Apostolic College.[37]

Kenrick discussed for a time the primacy of the Pope, then turned to the question of infallibility. He insisted that the opinion that the Roman Pontiff was infallible, when he spoke alone, without the concurrence of the bishops, lacked the certainty for a defined dogma; and even if it were certain enough, it was not expedient for the Vatican Council to so define. In his view, neither Scripture nor tradition made the doctrine crystal clear; Christ's commission to Saint Peter proved nothing beyond the primacy; Church tradition seemed to require the consent of the churches in any dogma. Papal infallibility, further, would lead to endless misunderstandings because of the difficulty of making a distinction between the Pope as a non-infallible private teacher and as "an infallible doctor teaching *ex cathedra.*" Instead of proclaiming the Pope infallible, Kenrick insisted, the Church should convoke more frequent general councils; the lack of councils since the sixteenth century had provoked many evils. Kenrick believed in the infallibility of the Church. But that infallibility belonged to a general council presided over by the Pope. He felt, further, that a declaration of

papal infallibility would augment a trend towards over-centralization already strangling the administrative procedures of an expanding church, would denigrate the individual position and collegial status of the bishops, and psychologically have a detrimental effect on the Church in the world.[38]

Kenrick had no human or personal motives for opposing the definition. His close friend Patrick Ryan stated:

> On the contrary, all the human motives were the other way. When the question was being discussed, some utilitarian man came to him and said: "You have sent three names before Propaganda to the Pope, that one of them might be selected as your coadjutor to aid you in the discharge of your duties in your old age. The authorities fear that these men sympathize with you, and that they may be, if not heterodox, at least cold in their allegiance to the Holy See, if you persevere in your arguments. You are, therefore, injuring yourself and you are injuring your friends in the position you are taking." How little they knew him. He would have sacrificed himself and every friend upon earth to what he believed were the interests of God and the Church of the living God.[39]

Kenrick joined the fifty-five prelates who signed a letter to the Pope telling him that they would absent themselves from the final session, rather than have to follow their consciences and vote against the definition.[40]

Don Cuthbert Butler, English historian of the council, said of Kenrick: "He was perhaps the stiffest opponent of the definition."[41] James Hennessey, historian of the American contribution to the council, had this to say:

> The First Vatican Council transported the great majority of the bishops of the United States into a world that was wholly new to them. . . . It was inevitable that they should at first seem to be inexperienced, perhaps naive. . . . When the council was over, that attitude had changed to some extent. Men of the stamp of Kenrick and Verot and Amat were not easily forgotten, even if they were not yet fully understood or appreciated.[42]

Kenrick's stand brought on him the suspicion of Rome. But the vantage of time would confirm the wisdom of the statement made at his death twenty-five years later:

> In 1870 the American episcopacy did not cut a very conspicuous figure in the Councils of the Church. Archbishop Kenrick opened the eyes of the Catholic world to the existence of a great Church in these United States. He set her ahead on the road of progress a whole generation.[43]

Council Aftermath

Kenrick was one of the few opponents of the definition to remain in Rome during the late sessions. Many North European prelates left as the danger of war between France and Prussia grew. The French soldiers who protected papal territory returned to defend their country; Italian troops marched into Rome. The council did not officially close. It simply ceased to meet. Kenrick visited Spain and other places in Europe during the fall of 1870.

A rumor spread that Rome had set up a commission of archbishops to examine Kenrick's writings. A distinguished Sulpician, Father Henri Icard, heard that the Saint Louis prelate would have to accept in writing the definitions of the council and disavow certain propositions in his secular statements.[44] Bishop William McCloskey of Louisville spoke of these "disagreeable rumors" in a letter to the influential Irish Benedictine, Father — later Titular Abbot — Bernard Smith in Rome.[45] An Italian cardinal, Luigi Bilio, noted in his diary in October, 1870, that a commission of cardinals passed a resolution demanding of Kenrick a public retraction of his errors, with a threat of condemnation if he failed to do so.[46]

Kenrick returned to Saint Louis in late 1870. On January 2, Vicar-General Patrick Ryan formally welcomed him in a gathering at St. John's Church. Kenrick responded:

> ... Up until the very period of the assembling of that Council, I held as a theological opinion what that Council has declared to be an article of Christian faith; and yet I was opposed, most strongly, to the definition. I knew that the misconceptions of its real character would be an obstacle in the way of the diffusion of Catholic truth ... I was not convinced of the conclusiveness of the arguments by which it was sustained, or of its compatibility with certain well ascertained facts of ecclesiastical history which rose up strongly before my mind. The motive of my submission is simply and singly the authority of the Catholic Church.[47]

Kenrick had always believed in the infallibility of a general council; and this general council declared that the Pope exercised infallibility under certain circumstances. Thus, he could honestly accept what he had ardently fought. A week later he so assured Cardinal Barnabo, head of the Propaganda: "I indicated in a public meeting that I adhere to what was done in the fourth session of the Vatican Council."[48]

In the meantime, another Italian Cardinal, Filippo de Angelis, one of a self-appointed committee to promote the declaration of infallibility,[49] had written to Bishop Hogan of Kansas City, directing him to inform the Saint Louis archbishop that the Sacred Congregation of the Index had condemned the *Concio*. This strangely-routed message, dated October 15, 1870, did not reach Kenrick until March 28, 1871.[50] It confirmed the rumors that the post-conciliar commission was acting in the case.

In a letter to the eminent English Catholic historian, Lord Acton, dated March 29, 1871, the day after he finally received the letter from Cardinal de Angelis, Kenrick stated that the papal commission had unanimously condemned his *Concio*, but through personal considerations had not included it on the Index. Kenrick answered De Angelis immediately stating that he had already written Cardinal Barnabo on the matter. But he had misgivings about Rome's reaction.

> I have reason to think that my answer will not be satisfactory, as the Pope said to the Rector of the American College, when he announced to him my submission: "Still he must retract those pamphlets published at Naples." This I shall not do no matter what the consequences may be.[51]

Father Phelan was to write:

> His submission to the Vatican decree might not have cost other natures much; to Archbishop Kenrick it was like personal annihilation; but he made it; not perhaps with all the grace and theatrical eclat we would desire; but he made it truly and honestly.[52]

In spite of the urging of Archbishop Joseph S. Alemanny of San Francisco, of one of his own suffragan bishops, and of Cardinal Barnabo himself, the "Old Lion" refused to write a pastoral letter to the people of Saint Louis on the council. Further, he did not act on Cardinal Barnabo's suggestion that he send a personal letter to the Pope. He did not sign a statement of sympathy to the Pope on the occasion of the Italian occupation of the Papal States; but he did not prevent his vicar-generals from signing it.[53]

Kenrick was consistent with his life-long principle of "no politics" in not commenting on the Italian seizure of the Papal States. He had always differentiated between the position of the Pope as spiritual head of the Catholic people, and as temporal head of the Papal States. Eventually the entire Catholic world would come to see what Kenrick saw: that the papal principality, as then consti-

Patrick J. Ryan, "all but archbishop" of Saint Louis (1872-1884), the outstanding priest of the Saint Louis archdiocese, who became archbishop of Philadelphia.

tuted, was an anachronism and a hindrance to religious progress.

Kenrick's *next* action seemed sheer bull-headedness. Even though the Saint Louis Catholics, as so many other American groups of the time, held processions whenever occasion offered, Kenrick believed that parades belonged exclusively to civic celebrations. During the summer of 1871, the Catholic societies of the city planned a huge parade to honor the silver anniversary of Pius IX's pontificate. Kenrick refused persmission. Only at the request of Vicar-General Patrick Ryan did Kenrick give reluctant consent for the parade. As the four-mile-long procession wound through the generally illumined city, the archbishop did not witness it. He was out of town at the time.[54]

Even the most friendly critic can fault Kenrick here. This was not a matter of personalities, but of position. The people of Saint Louis were honoring their Holy Father. The local shepherd should have been with his flock. Vicar-General Ryan had to explain to Rome his personal position in this matter. "Had I acted in open opposition to the Archbishop," the vicar-general wrote, "*I might have lost my influence with him* [italics are Ryan's own] and that influence has always been used for the restoration of cordial feelings with Rome."[55]

Rumors began shortly, and were to persist through the years that Rome silenced Kenrick because of his staunch opposition to the declaration of infallibility. No absolute evidence exists either to affirm or deny this. At the time of Kenrick's death, Father Constantine Smith, his theologian at the council, flatly denied that Rome had silenced the Saint Louis archbishop.[56] Father Phelan held the same view.

> This talk of Rome's remorseless pursuit of Archbishop Kenrick for the part he took in the Vatican Council [Phelan was to write in 1896] is the veriest nonsense; Archbishop McCloskey was anti-infallibilist, and he was afterward raised to the cardinalate; Bishop Fitzgerald voted non-placet on the final vote and he was afterward offered the Archbishopric of Cincinnati ... whatever punishment Archbishop Kenrick received for his part in the Vatican Council was self-inflicted.[57]

Chapter 20

Patrick J. Ryan: All But Archbishop

Rome's Choice of Ryan

One good thing came out of the Vatican Council for Archbishop Kenrick. He had wanted a coadjutor. His first choice was his vicar-general and closest friend, Father Patrick Ryan. Kenrick had ordained Ryan on September 8, 1853, and employed him in a variety of ministries, including that of chaplain of the Confederate prisoners detained in Saint Louis during the war, and theologian and official preacher at the Second Plenary Council in Baltimore in 1866. At the invitation of Pope Pius IX, Ryan had given the English sermons in Rome during the Lent of 1868. When Kenrick left for the Vatican Council, he put Ryan in charge of the archdiocese. Kenrick's theologian, Father Constantine Smith, believed that Kenrick talked to the Propaganda about the appointment of Ryan as his coadjutor.[1]

Ryan knew that Kenrick was ill and needed help in the archdiocese. Further Ryan knew that he was the "Old Lion's" first choice. He would have gladly accepted the position of auxiliary to Kenrick; and on the latter's death, have moved to a smaller western diocese. But he did not feel that, under the circumstances, he measured up to the responsibilities of coadjutor.[2] Ryan always showed an excessive deference and awe in the presence of the great archbishop of the West.

In spite of his misgivings, however, Ryan remained Rome's choice. The Office of the Propaganda notified Kenrick on January 29, 1872,[3] of Ryan's appointment as titular bishop of Tricomia and coadjutor of Saint Louis with the right of succession. Assisted by two former priests of the diocese, Bishops Melcher of Green Bay and Feehan of Nashville, Archbishop Kenrick consecrated Bishop Ryan on April 14, 1872.

A month later, on May 20, 1872, Kenrick wrote a complete financial report of his thirty-one years in Saint Louis. He described his procedures in paying the cathedral debt, the disposition of money from the Thornton estate, the purchase of a piece of property on the southwest corner of Twenty Second and Chestnut for a new cathedral, and the annual *cathedraticum*, the money from the parishes for the support of the archbishop. In the previous years he had contributed all of this to St. John's Church, where he resided. He concluded with the statement that "his successor will have no debt or encumbrance to discharge."[4] With this testament, he retired from day-to-day administration of the archdiocese, but he did make his presence felt on occasion.

Bishop Ryan handled routine business well. In case of doubt or a matter of larger moment, he would always say, "I'll speak to the Archbishop about it." Some priests felt that Ryan should have acted on his own. But his personal regard for the archbishop and his conviction that Kenrick's patient manner of acting was the best, would have prevented this.

In the same year (1872), Father Ignatius Panken, S.J., accepted the pastorate of the city-wide Negro parish begun a few years earlier. During Christmas week of that year he conducted a fair in the Vinegar Hill Hall at Fourteenth and Gay Streets. This hall had formerly been a Baptist and later a Presbyterian church. With the proceeds of the fair, Panken was able to buy the hall and equip it for divine worship.

Ten thousand Catholics of Saint Louis joined in the procession on May 18, 1873, when Coadjutor Patrick Ryan dedicated the refurbished building as Saint Elizabeth's Church. For the moment, the prospects for Negro Catholics looked hopeful.

Father Panken immediately tried to clarify principles and procedures for this city-wide parish. He asked his superior, Father Joseph Zealand, to find out what should be done if white people presented themselves for Holy Communion, since the archbishop had forbade the conferring of the sacraments on whites. Some days later, Zealand returned the letter with this notation: "The answers to the questions proposed were: let Communion be refused. No further explanation is needed. As the Archbishop has expressed his mind on the subject in a manner that cannot be mistaken, it would be improper to consult him about it again."[5]

This decision had long-range repercussions. As time went on, it tended to segregate Negroes in one parish, even though Negroes lived here and there beyond the central city. Carondelet, for instance, had its own Negro section, now a part of the city, but about fifty blocks from St. Elizabeth's Church. Gradually segregationist attitudes excluded Negroes from other churches in the various neighborhoods where they lived. The "separate but equal" status became more separated and less equal. No one made an effort, for instance, to bring qualified Negro Catholics into Catholic schools on the academic or college level. The new Negro immigrants from the South gained little contact with the Church. White Catholics generally neglected their Negro brothers.

Rome ignored Saint Louis in a dramatic way in that same year (1873). The Office of the Propaganda planned to raise Milwaukee, a suffragan see of Saint Louis, to the rank of an archdiocese. Rome took up the matter with the archbishops of Baltimore, New York, and Cincinnati, without notifying Kenrick. James Roosevelt Bayley, the new archbishop of Baltimore, urged Kenrick to protest this improper procedure either through him or directly with Rome.[6] It seemed that if Kenrick ignored Rome, Rome would in turn disregard Kenrick.

During 1873, also, Kenrick recalled one of his outstanding priests, Christian Wapelhorst, from his post as professor of the Salesianum, an inter-diocesan seminary in Columbus, Ohio, to be chancellor of the archdiocese. As a young priest, Father Wapelhorst had done parochial work in St. Charles for seven years (1857-64). Then when Saint Louis began to send many seminarians to St. Francis Seminary in

Milwaukee, Father Wapelhorst began a professorial career.[7] Wapelhorst remained chancellor only one year; then Kenrick allowed him to accept the post of rector of the Salesianum.[8]

In 1874, Archbishop Kenrick named a Hollander, Father Henry Van der Sanden, pastor of St. Peter's parish in Kirkwood, chancellor of the archdiocese. A burly, gruff man with a flowing red beard, the "Great Chancellor"[9] — as many of his fellow priests came to call him — spoke and read French, German, Flemish, and English. He had a penchant for historical research, a great interest in the Church in the Mississippi Valley, and took part in setting up the first Catholic Historical Society of the West in 1878.

On November 8, 1878, members of the "Sodality of Priests of the Archdiocese of Saint Louis" met at St. Teresa's Church. Father Charles Ziegler presided and Father James J. McCabe acted as secretary. On the motion of Father David Phelan, seconded by Father James Henry, the priests decided to set up a Church history society. They elected Chancellor Van der Sanden president, Father Henry vice-president, Father W. H. Brantner treasurer, and Father McCabe recording secretary. Father Ziegler served as corresponding secretary for the English-speaking and Father H. Leygraff for the German-speaking members.[10]

The new society held quarterly meetings in St. John's library hall. At one of these, for instance, on May 6, 1879, Father David Phelan spoke on "The Hierarchial Succession in the Present Diocese of Saint Louis."[11] The society did not fully meet the expectation of its founders but President Van der Sanden set about guarding, preserving, and collecting materials connected with the history of the archdiocese.

The "Great Chancellor" left the archdiocese indebted to him by his careful preservation of the Rosati papers. He sought to increase the collection by adding most of the official documents issued during the long period of his chancellorship. After a vacation trip to his native Holland, Van der Sanden went to Rome. While there he copied many letters and other documents that had reference to the early history of the diocese of Saint Louis.

Later on, Van der Sanden was to move the chancery from St. Mary's Church to the old cathedral and became chaplain of the Alexian Brothers Hospital. He took all the papers with him to his rooms at the hospital. There he daily and carefully pored over them, extracting with infinite patience the data concerning every priest and every parish in the diocese. Van der Sanden often spoke in a general way of writing the early history of the diocese, but otherwise he sat on these documents "like a dragon on a hidden treasure," preserving them for future generations.[12]

The Great Religious Controversy

Coadjutor Bishop Patrick Ryan spoke on the subject "What Catholics Do *Not* Believe" to an overflow crowd at the Mercantile Library Hall on the evening of December 16, 1877. In a conciliatory and jovial opening, the bishop told the story of the man who learned "the truth" about the Democratic Party from a Republican. Ryan recommended that people hear a Democrat on the Democrats, and a Catholic on what Catholics do and do not believe.

The next morning the *St. Louis Globe-Democrat* devoted five columns to the speech. An accompanying editorial gave these reasons for the lecture: "The aiding of the St. John's School Fund" and a request of "the Reverend Dr. Snyder and several other Protestant clergymen."[13]

The following day the flamboyant editor of the *Globe-Democrat*, Joseph B. McCullagh, called the attention of his readers to the bishop's speech and arranged for the Reverend S. H. Sonneshein, a Jewish Rabbi, to reply to Ryan in the same hall. McCullagh hoped that the Protestant divines would contribute their views to the "important controversy" inaugurated by the Catholic bishop. He assured them that the *Globe-Democrat*, as the organ of all creeds and denominations, would welcome the fullest and freest discussion, and do its duty, "as a religious daily newspaper," by publishing both sides.[14]

In his story of the *St. Louis Globe-Democrat*, historian Jim Allee Hart credits McCullagh with thus having started the "great religious controversy" that was to run more than three months. McCullagh sent his reporters through the city. By Christmas the *Globe-Democrat* had published interviews with over thirty clergymen.[15]

The following Sunday issue of the *Globe-Democrat* gave a whole page of responses, twenty-eight in all. "They all admire the Bishop's ability as a rhetorician," an editorial writer stated, "but they do not admire his utterances as a teacher of pure Christianity." The editorial quoted Reverend Doctor S. H. Sonneshein, who would deliver an answering lecture: "I believe it to be the best rhetorical as well as scientific effort that has ever been produced by a modern Catholic priest to apologize for, and to correct the many prevailing errors in regard to the Catholic Church."[16]

The Reverend John Snyder, pastor of the Church of the Messiah denied the *Globe-Democrat's* statement that he had asked the bishop to speak, but he knew about the lecture and had complimentary tickets. He, too, admitted that, "as a piece of rhetoric, it was striking." Among the Negro pastors, Pastor R. H. Smith of the Wesley Methodist Chapel had read the lecture, considered it a very strong one, and agreed with Bishop Ryan on many points.[17]

The vast majority of the twenty-eight ministers who commented, including Bishop Thomas Bowman of the Methodist Church, spoke favorably of the positive presentation of Bishop Ryan. Only three demurred. Reverend John A. Wilson, pastor of United Presbyterian, called the speech "a mess of Jesuit casuistry." In a similar vein, the Reverend Doctor Green of the Barnard Street Baptist Church, called it "a piece of Jesuitical ingenuity, admirably calculated to deceive the public mind." Only the German-speaking preachers refused to take part. The Reverend E. Roos of the Evangelical Lutheran, paid no attention to Catholics and admitted frankly that "they could have no possible effect on him."[18]

In many pulpits of the city that day, ministers noted Bishop Ryan's discourse. Among them, Reverend William C. Falconer of North Presbyterian Church devoted his whole sermon to an analysis of Ryan's statement. The *Globe-Democrat* carried his entire message the next day.[19] In a letter to the editor, R. A. Holland of the Episcopalian Church admitted how persuasive Ryan's arguments were. He made no attempt to analyze the coadjutor's statements; but, delving into the recent history of the Catholic Church for several controversial quotations, he quoted Archbishop Kenrick against papal infallibility and Pope Pius IX, who was, incidentally, on his deathbed at the time, against religious freedom. Holland described the earlier age of suppression and persecution when both Catholics and Protestants acted intolerantly against each other. The Protestants had reformed, he said, but the Catholics continued "without freedom of conscience."[20]

In the same issue, Bishop Ryan had a letter that told of the projected publication of his lecture at the request of several important citizens such as Pierre Chouteau, Major H. S. Turner, and General William T. Sherman, the Civil War general, whose wife and family were Catholics. On Christmas Day the *Globe-Democrat* carried another interview with Bishop Ryan. In this he clarified certain misquotations of his lecture that had come up in the discussion.[21]

Two days after Christmas the *Globe-Democrat* pointed out that Bishop Ryan's lecture was not the only subject of religious controversy at the time, but that many clergymen were engaging in a controversy on the duration of hell.[22]

In the wake of the interest stirred by Bishop Ryan's lecture, a group of nine prominent pastors of English-speaking Catholic churches of the city and a host of prominent laymen, announced a forthcoming address by Francis Dillon Eagan, a well-known lecturer. *Globe-Democrat* reporters interviewed Father Phelan, the editor of the *Western Watchman*, and a Jesuit Father at Saint Louis University who was the first participant to remain anonymous. Phelan approved the bishop's speech and spoke positively throughout his interview. The Jesuit thought the Bishop tried to do too much in one speech, but spent most of his time criticizing the bishop's critics.[23]

The following day, Dr. R. A. Holland answered the Jesuit by quoting an "infallible Pope" (Benedict XIV) as calling Jesuits "disobedient, contumacious, crafty and reprobate men."[24] By this time religious interest was so high that the *Globe-Democrat* devoted five columns to a lecture by the Reverend P. B. Morgan of St. John's Episcopal Church, even though he did not allude to Ryan and this was the sixth lecture in a series he had given.[25]

The *Globe-Democrat* announced a printed edition of Bishop Ryan's lecture on December 30, and gave the introduction in full.[26]

On the last day of the year, the paper carried a four column reply of Dr. Sonnesehein to bishop Ryan. On January 3, its readers heard from outstate areas. Reverend Hughey, a Methodist elder in Alton, Illinois, and Father C. F. O'Leary of Mexico, Missouri, wrote letters to the editor. Father O'Leary wrote an orderly letter, but tended to the caustic and personal.[27] The following day Father O'Leary wrote again, this time in a poetic vein. He pictured the Church as a city on a rock, serene amid confusion. O'Leary defended Ryan and attacked several of the bishop's critics, especially Dr. Holland and Dr. Falconer.[28] The following day Dr. Falconer replied to Father O'Leary, calling "the new Catholic voice" that of "not only a theologian but a poet — an artist in fact."[29]

Under the headline "The Great Controversy Now Raging in the Religious Circles of Saint Louis," the *Globe-Democrat* brought the opinions of two Catholic bishops, Patrick Ryan of Saint Louis, and Peter J. Baltes of Alton, Illinois, and twelve priests including James McCaffrey, William Walsh, and James Henry. Among the Unitarians, the Reverend William G. Eliot declined to "take part in this, as he had hitherto done in every other religious controversy."[30]

On the following day the pastor of the Episcopal Church of the Good Shepherd, who signed himself H. D. J. throughout the controversy — the J. stood for Jordine, the readers were to learn later from the responses of his adversaries — had a most interesting viewpoint in his letter. He spoke of the Episcopalian Church as the true "Catholic church of the United States" and the church of Bishop Ryan as "an intrusion of the Roman schism."[31]

On January 6, the *Globe-Democrat* spoke of a fight between the Pawnees and the Cheyennes in the Texas Panhandle.[32] Two days later, it headlined an article, "Father O'Leary on the Warpath" against the Reverend Dr. Falconer. O'Leary's letter, over a column long, discussed Protestantism philosophically and theologically, and quoted Martin Luther extensively.[33] The following day the paper carried five and a half columns of Dr. J. G. Reaser's speech in answer to Bishop Ryan at the Mercantile Library Hall. In this conciliatory address, Reaser admitted truth in the Catholic Church and sanctity among its members. He showed acquaintance with Augustine and Bellarmine and presented a positive treatment of Protestantism.[34]

In response, Father O'Leary wrote sharply: "Reaserism is the latest form of Protestantism."[35] O'Leary's fifth letter appeared the next day. It was belligerent, caustic, short.[36] But his dignified sixth letter, on the third successive day, challenged Protestantism as a "logical denial of the Incarnation... of reason... of faith... of the Church." It was "in opposition to the plan of salvation and redemption... an inversion of the order of knowledge.... Philosophically, theologically and historically," O'Leary charged, "Protestantism is not a church."[37]

The controversy and the circulation of the *Globe-Democrat* grew. In his seventh letter, Father O'Leary gave a clever, witty, and learned discussion of British history and an indictment of Anglicanism from quotations of British historians.[38] For the moment, O'Leary was the Catholic champion, while Bishop Ryan remained calmly on the sidelines. In general, O'Leary showed himself a versatile and able penman. He could write learnedly and objectively, calling on history, theology, and philosophy; or he could write caustically and subjectively — sometimes to the point and sometimes off the point.

Towards the end of the month, Bishop Baltes of Alton, Father A. J. Sauer of Carrollton, Illinois, Father M. Walsh of Catawissa, Missouri, Father Martin Harts, S.J., and Father Charles Coppens, S.J., both of Saint Louis University, appeared more regularly;[39] and in February, Brother Barbas of Christian Brothers College joined in the discussion.[40] The Protestant champions continued to be Dr. Holland, Dr. Falconer, and Dr. Hughey, who quoted Kenrick extensively against infallibility.[41] Quite interestingly, the Protestant devines often referred to Archbishop Kenrick, but the Catholic protagonists never mentioned the "Old Lion's" name in the controversy.

On February 8, 1878, Pope Pius IX passed away peacefully; and for a day or two the controversy did not wax so vigorously. Usually the *Globe-Democrat* omitted any letters or discussion on Sunday and would begin the Monday edition with "The Great Controversy" on the first page. This lasted during most of January and February.

Everyone had a chance to air his views. Interest in religious discussion, if not in religion itself, gripped the people for a time. No great Christian accord came as a result, but at the same time the two Christian bodies came to know more about the beliefs of each other; and continued the Saint Louis tradition of tolerance.

Bishop Ryan had enhanced his high reputation as a speaker and a man of deep charity. Several Protestant ministers spoke and wrote excellently, such as W. C. Falconer, J. T. Reaser, and R. A. Holland. Bishop Baltes of Alton came to the attention of people within the core of the metropolitan area, and young Father O'Leary out in Mexico, Missouri, made his name known. The *Globe-*

Democrat gained many subscribers, and, for a long while, kept the title "The Great Religious Daily" that McCullagh gave it during the lively and vocal winter of 1877-78.[42]

Ryan, Rome, Routines

During the twelve years Ryan was to serve as coadjutor of the archdiocese, he was in no position to move ahead on his own, to give new directions or introduce fresh policies in the archdiocese. He did dedicate the following English-speaking parishes in the city: St. Columcille's, Mount Carmel, St. Kevin's (later to become the Church of the Immaculate Conception), St. Cronan's, St. Rose's, Visitation, and St. Thomas. But he could not move the archdiocese forward in any dramatic way. Often, routine matters, such as the setting up of new parishes, dragged on endlessly, with the archbishop growing more aloof.[43]

Communications with Rome broke down, too. In one particular instance, Bishop Ryan spoke of the delicacy of "my position in regard to the Sacred Congregation and our Archbishop." Kenrick had agreed to write to the cardinal prefect; then presumed Ryan was doing so. The bishop could only offer his apologies.[44]

Rome, on its part, answered the needs of the province tardily. As early as the Second Baltimore Council (1866), Kenrick had recommended the elevation of Chicago to an archbishopric. In 1879, thirteen years later, Ryan renewed the archbishop's request. He stressed the vast importance of the city — just then passing Saint Louis in population and already the center of the mid-continental rail networks. Chicago was larger and had more churches than Baltimore, New Orleans, San Francisco, Milwaukee, and Oregon City — all metropolitan sees, but had no archbishop. Ryan also suggested bishops for Kansas City and Council Bluffs, and hoped Rome would not postpone these decisions.[45]

Early the following year, Ryan passed on to Rome Bishop John Hennessey of Dubuque's recommendation of Reverend Roger Ryan, his chancellor, as bishop of Council Bluffs, Iowa. Coadjutor Ryan said that Kenrick had already written in the same vein, and complained that Rome left American sees vacant for so long. He instanced the currently empty sees of Chicago and Columbus. He was happy that Rome had named Bishop William Elder of Natchez as coadjutor of Cincinnati.[46]

Rome did name Kansas City a diocese in 1880 with Bishop John Hogan of St. Joseph, Missouri, as the first incumbent. It selected Davenport in eastern Iowa, rather than Council Bluffs on the western boundary of the state, as a new see and named Father John McMullen, administrator of the diocese of Chicago, as first bishop. When McMullen died two years later, Bishop Ryan urged as his successor Father Philip Brady, zealous pastor of Annunciation Church in Saint Louis, and instructor in religion at City House, the Academy of the Religious of the Sacred Heart.[47] Brady, however, was not destined to succeed McMullen as Bishop of Davenport; he was to succeed Patrick Ryan as vicar-general of Saint Louis.

The German-American Catholics

Archbishop Kenrick had granted only subsidiary not full parochial status to all the foreign-language churches. This procedure had advantages for the recent arrival. He could attend a church of his own language, recognize the customs, and feel a sense of belonging in the face of the ridicule and rebuffs he sometimes met in the English-speaking world of business. It was a helpful device for a period of transition. Unfortunately, Archbishop Kenrick continued such arrangements long after they had served most of their purposes.

He had appointed two vicars-general: Father Patrick Ryan, now his coadjutor, as vicar for the English-speaking parishes; and Father Joseph Melcher as vicar for the German-speaking congregations. When Joseph Melcher went to Green Bay as bishop in 1868, the approachable, zealous, dependable, but unspectacular Father Henry Muehlsiepen succeeded him.

A native of the Archdiocese of Cologne, Muehlsiepen had heard the challenge of Father Melcher to work in the Saint Louis archdiocese. Coming to the United States, he had finished his theology course in Carondelet under Fathers Patrick Feehan and John Hennessey, both destined to be bishops. Kenrick had ordained him on December 8, 1857, and sent him to St. Mary's Church. In 1866 Muehlsiepen became the first editor of *Pastoral Blatt*, a magazine for the clergy, sponsored by Archbishop Michael Heiss of Milwaukee and supported strongly by the priests of Saint Louis.

Father Muehlsiepen furthered the development of these new German-speaking parishes in Saint Louis during the ensuing years: Perpetual Help, St. Augustine's, St. Bernard's, and Holy Ghost; and he gave encouragement to other non-English speaking national congregations. In order that he might be less incumbered by routine pastoral duties and free to travel more extensively throughout the archdiocese, he brought Father William Faerber, an excellent writer and a man of broad cultural interests, from the rural missions near Washington, Missouri, to assist him at St. Mary's. Early in 1873, Faerber was to become editor of *Pastoral Blatt*. He was to give the magazine a deeper interest in the ecclesiastico-political questions of the time, and to work closely with the newly-forming Catholic publishing house, B. Herder and Co.

Extensive organization has always been a significant feature of German life. In this, the Saint Louis German Catholics followed national traditions. Before the Civil War they had set up many benevolent societies, such as the St. Vincent's Orphanage Society. They had sent representatives east to the first convention of the *Central Verein* in 1855. Saint Louis had welcomed the fifth convention of this national body. At that meeting, Saint Louis delegate John Amend became president. He remained in office throughout the Civil War and on into 1868. In its early years the headquarters of the *Central Verein* had changed with the residence of the officers. Eventually, Saint Louis became its permanent home. In 1873, another prominent Catholic of Saint Louis, State Senator Henry Spaunhorst, like Amend, an early member of the St. Vincent de Paul Society, became president, and was to serve for almost twenty years.

Since 1868, the *Central Verein* had worked closely with the German Catholic immigrant societies. In 1871, under the leadership of a Swiss-German importer, Peter Paul Cahensly, also a member of the Saint Vincent de Paul Society, Catholics in Germany began a new immigrant-serving league, the *St. Raphaelsverein*. Originally entirely German and suspect by the new German Imperial Government, the *St. Raphaelsverein* gradually became more European in outlook. At first, the *Central Verein* worked closely with it; but in 1877, the German-

American group formally disassociated itself from immigrant work.

Six years later, Peter Paul Cahensly decided to travel to the United States for the two-fold purpose of seeing the immigrant's plight, and of restoring working agreements with the *Central Verein* and its member societies. Cahensly traveled incognito to view the unsatisfactory steerage conditions first-hand. Carrying a letter of introduction from Cardinal Simeone, Cahensly visited Archbishop Michael Corrigan in New York and spoke about the needs of the immigrant. He then toured the middle west. He called Saint Louis "the headquarters of Catholic Germanism."[48] Returning to New York, he worked out with Archbishop Corrigan plans for an American branch of the *St. Raphaelsverein*. Unfortunately, he had not sought extensive episcopal support, nor a wider national base for the American branch of his society. This was to prove hurtful in years ahead.

In line with Cahensly's tribute to Catholics in the Missouri metropolis, if German-American Catholics anywhere in the nation began a beneficial organization, they could count on the support of their Saint Louis compatriots. Priests and lay people of the diocese, for instance, played a part in the founding of the American *Cecilians Verein*, in 1873, an organization that pioneered in the reform of Church music.

These associations stepped up their activities with the heavy immigration of Catholics, especially from the Northwest German Province of Paderborn, after the unification of Germany in 1870-1871. Chancellor Otto Von Bismarck began the *Kulturkampf* — a drive to force all Germans into a rigid, nationalistic pattern, Prussian and Protestant in spirit. This policy drove many Catholics from the new German empire. Such a great proportion of the post-1870 German immigrants to Saint Louis were Catholics that they more than counter-balanced the anti-clerical immigrants of the '50's. Members of the Saint Louis Catholic community, as a result, had almost no ties with Bismarck's empire. Either their ancestors had left Germany before the Kaiser's empire came to be; or they came as expelees from that empire. And so, while they remained culturally united, their tie was to German traditions and the Catholic religion rather than to the German empire. In the succeeding generation, interestingly, a secular liberal of non-Germanic background would have been more inclined to sympathy for the Prussian empire than the Saint Louis Catholic of German background.

The intellectual leadership in the German community had long lay with the liberal non-Catholics. This changed with the conversion of Dr. Edward Pruess. He had been a prominent Lutheran theologian. He had written vigorously and intelligently against certain trends in the contemporary Church. On becoming a Catholic, he edited *Amerika*, a German-language daily paper for many years.

Other Foreign-Language Groups

Neighbors of the Germans in central Europe, and closely associated for a thousand years with the German community in the Old World, the Bohemian immigrants to Saint Louis found a temporary home in the German church of Sts. Peter and Paul. From here they began to set up a Catholic community of their own, St. John Nepomuk's. The pre-Civil War Bohemian priests had abandoned their flocks and returned to Europe.

Shortly after the Civil War, Father Joseph Hessoun, a Bohemian-born priest ordained for the diocese of Saint Louis, had come to St. John Nepomuk's Church. The religious life of the Bohemian Catholics in Saint Louis and throughout the nation gradually centered around this zealous, gifted, kindly priest. He was a perceptive man with keen judgment and a real sense of the needs of the time, a true father of his people. He made the Church the center of the immigrant's spiritual, cultural, and social life. He advocated gradual but steady assimiliation of American life.

Father Hessoun's first building venture aimed at adequate school space. He thought of his school not only as a place for instruction, but also as a meeting hall for societies and sodalities. He opened a parish library. With the school ready by 1869, Father Hessoun then set to work on a new church. All Saint Louis Catholic groups paraded at the dedication of this Gothic structure in November, 1870.

During the last quarter of the century, Bohemian immigrants went in greater proportion to other cities and to towns in Nebraska. But by that time, Saint Louis, with only 1500 Bohemians, had already established leadership in the Czech community. (Chicago, incidentally, had almost twelve thousand Bohemian residents by the same time.) Since many of these new Bohemian settlers had no priests, churches, or spiritual guidance, Father Hessoun inaugurated several activities to help them. He undertook missionary work to establish nuclei for other Bohemian parishes. He began the publication of *Hlas* (The Voice), to unite the Bohemian-Americans under the banner of Catholicism, to guide them spiritually, especially those lacking priests and churches, and to defend the Catholic cause against the free-thinking elements among the Bohemian immigrants. Father Hessoun also tried to consolidate the Catholic ranks and to advance the faith by founding the Catholic Central Union, an insurance and fraternal society, in 1877. This union helped to Americanize the Bohemian people while keeping them loyal to the Catholic faith.

At the time the Bohemians were settling on the South side near Sts. Peter and Paul's Church, a group of Italian Catholics came to the district of St. Patrick's parish on the near North side. The first attempt to give the Saint Louis colony of Italians a semblance of unity was the establishment of a fraternal society in 1866. The Italians also hoped to have a church and a school of their own. In this latter project they had the sympathetic ear of the vicar-general, Father Muehlsiepen. This kindly man took great interest in the struggles of the different immigrant peoples and endeavored to aid them in every way possible. His first effort to help them resulted in the opening of St. Bonaventure's Church at Sixth and Spruce in 1871. The location, unfortunately, was too far from the homes of any considerable number of Italian people in the downtown area.

Just as Saint Louis Germans and Bohemians pioneered in forming organizations among the Americans of their respective national backgrounds, so the *Societa d'Unione Fratellanza Italiana*, was one of the first Italian fraternal organizations in the country. The founding of this society in the fall of 1866 exerted a most enriching influence upon the Italian colony in Saint Louis. The *Fratellanza* promoted humanitarian enterprises, especially among impoverished people in the Italian homeland. Within four years of its founding, it supported a movement to organize a national federation of Italian benevolent societies.

Even though its purpose was social, it aided in the founding of St. Bonaventure's parish. It began the celebration of Columbus Day with a parade and a civic ceremony. This eventually consisted of ceremonies at the statue of Columbus, near the east end of Tower Grove Park.

Over the years, many Italians found employment in the clay pits on Fairmount Heights in the southwest section of the expanded city. Gradually these workers built homes in that area, eventually to become nationally famous as "The Hill." It was to remain for a long time the solidly Italian section of Saint Louis, and deserve careful discussion after the turn of the century.

While the Italians, Germans, and Bohemians of Saint Louis took a leading part in the organizations of their respective nationalities throughout the nation, the Saint Louis Poles did not exert such wide influence. One major reason was the relatively small number of Polish immigrants in Saint Louis — disproportionately small in contrast to such cities as Milwaukee and Chicago. Settling in the vicinity of St. Patrick's and St. Joseph's Churches, the Poles decided to organize a parish of their own. Fortunately, several Franciscan Fathers who had come to Saint Louis were of Polish background. These priests offered the first Masses for the Polish congregation in the basement of St. Patrick's school. In the meantime, work began on St. Stanislaus Church on Twentieth Street near Cass. Bishop Ryan consecrated the new church on November 12, 1882.

Father Urban Stanowski took charge of the parish in 1886. He organized building and loan societies to help his people acquire homes near the new church. As the Poles swarmed into the neighborhood, what formerly had been an "Irish Channel" became a "Polish Corridor." Father Stanowski was to continue as pastor of St. Stanislaus for forty years.

Another group of Slavic people, the Croatians, moved in small numbers to an area along Second Street between Market and Arsenal after 1880. They began to organize parochial life only after the turn of the century. Their story belongs in a later chapter.

Older Religious Communities Move West

As the city expanded west and new parishes grew in the area, religious institutes began to look for new locations in the western part of the city. The Sisters of Loretto had worked in southeast Missouri since the days of Bishop Rosati. In 1846 they had begun a convent school at Florissant in place of the one previously under the guidance of the Religious of the Sacred Heart. In 1862 the Lorettines had come to Saint Louis to open St. Mary's Academy. In 1874 they opened Loretto Academy on property at Pine and Jefferson donated by Mrs. Anne Lucas Hunt. They taught in a growing number of parish schools.

Three years after St. Alphonsus "Rock" Church opened on North Grand Avenue, in 1872, the Redemptorist Fathers announced the setting up of a new province for western America with the parochial residence as the provincial headquarters.

The Religious of the Sacred Heart, one of the three pioneer congregations in the Saint Louis region, planned to separate their boarding and day schools. In 1872 they moved the residential facilities to a gentle ridge overlooking the Mississippi River in the old French community of Carondelet, now a part of the city. Twenty-one years

later, they were to abandon their old City House, and set up a new one on Taylor Avenue, a few blocks north of Lindell.

Under the direction of Brother James (Hugh Carney), the Christian Brothers moved their flourishing college from the former Rider mansion at Eighth and Cerre Streets to a campus of thirty acres on Kingshighway at Easton, in the northwest part of the recently expanded city. When classes began on the new campus in 1882, Christian Brothers College offered the only boarding facilities for Catholic young men in the area, since Saint Louis University had discontinued its boarding department the previous year.[49] In this new location, the Christian Brothers continued their excellent pre-seminary courses, wherein so many future priests and bishops came to excel in the use of Latin.

Coadjutor Patrick Ryan joined with a group of distinguished laymen of the city a few months later in an appeal for help for the new college. Ryan spoke of the school as "so widely and so favorably known." It had "identified itself with the best interests of Saint Louis." The list of co-signers included such outstanding names as Matthias Backer, B. Gratz Brown, Samuel Cupples, A. N. DeMenil, R. Graham Frost, Louis Fusz, Charles Green, Henry F. Harrington, H. J. Spaunhorst, and Julius Walsh.[50]

The Visitation Sisters likewise moved their convent and academy from the downtown site that they had held since 1858 to a new location on Cabanne on the far west end in the year 1887.

Even though Saint Louis University had purchased property along the west side of Grand Avenue between Lindell and Pine in 1867, twenty-two years elapsed before the Jesuit Fathers moved to the new site. Two factors delayed the move: the difficulty of selling the downtown property, and the unwillingness of the archbishop to give the Jesuits a territorial parish in an area already subdivided among other parishes. Finally the archbishop designated a parish for the new St. Francis Xavier College Church, drawing a map in his own hand and taking parts of other parishes and putting it into the new Jesuit parish. No evidence exists that he officially notified the other pastors that they had lost portions of their territory.[51]

An estimated fifty thousand people gathered for the procession from the old site of St. Francis Xavier Church at Ninth and Washington to the projected new location on Grand and Lindell, on Trinity Sunday, June 8, 1884. Thirteen thousand men of almost every parish and Catholic society of the city marched in the parade. Bishops Joseph Dwenger of Fort Wayne and William Gross of Savannah spoke at the cornerstone laying. Father Phelan devoted the entire first page of the *Western Watchman* to the event. He called it: "A gathering such as has been seldom seen in this country."[52]

Some years later, Phelan and other priests were to have misgivings about this move. They criticized the Jesuits and Redemptorists for leaving poor areas in the heart of town for the wealthy west end. On one occasion Archbishop Feehan of Chicago refused to grant a religious order permission to move its parochial effort out of the inner-city. Father Phelan used this action of Chicago's archbishop to call attention to Kenrick's failure to do the same in regard to two religious orders in Saint Louis, who "settled on Grand Avenue within a few blocks of each other."[53]

At a meeting of the St. Vincent de Paul Society at the same time, a priest rose and criticized the pastors of two rich parishes on Grand who abandoned the poor in the downtown districts. He urged the laymen of these parishes to go to the poor, even if they lived beyond their parish limits, and "thus relieve somewhat a very dark page in the ecclesiastical history of Saint Louis."[54] The priests received this remark with applause; and the representatives of the orders with embarrassment. Phelan concluded: "It will not be the last time they will hear it. Priests, too, have no sympathy for their fellow priests if they are not friends of the poor."[55]

While other congregations were moving out of the central city, the Sisters of St. Joseph were moving in. Their academy already was in the suburb of Carondelet, on the road to Jefferson Barracks; they taught at St. John's, the parish that included the future Bishops Patrick Ryan and John Joseph Hennessey among its pastors, and was then the residence of Archbishop Kenrick. Under the guidance of Mother Agatha Guthrie, the Sisters of St. Joseph taught at these centrally located parish schools: St. Patrick's and St. Nicholas' in 1873, St. Francis Xavier (still on Ninth and Christy at the time) in 1875, and St. Michael's in 1876.

The Sisters of St. Joseph had moved their novitiate away from the convent school overlooking the river at Carondelet to an inland site five miles to the south, called Nazareth, in 1872. Father John M. I. St. Cyr, the pioneer missionary of Chicago, who had been the chaplain at Carondelet, accepted an assignment to the new retreat. A simple, patient, and devoted man, he continued his work of spiritual instruction of the novices even after he became blind in 1876. He died shortly before his fiftieth anniversary as a priest. Bishop Ryan preached his funeral sermon. By the time of his death, the Sisters had already moved the novitiate back to Carondelet.

By the year 1877, further, Rome gave final approval to the Constitutions of the Sisters of St. Joseph of Carondelet, completing the separation from the French foundation, adapting the life to the New World, and setting up an American generalate. This event culminated twenty years of effort on the part of many, including Mother St. John Facemaz and Archbishop Kenrick, who originally appointed her to head the congregation.

New Religious Communities

The Archdiocese of Saint Louis always had a large number of religious orders and congregations. Some of these, such as the Vincentians, the Religious of the Sacred Heart, and the Sisters of St. Joseph, began their first American ventures in the archdiocese. Others, such as the Jesuits, Visitandines, and the Lorettines opened their second American foundations in the area. Saint Louis became the provincial headquarters of many religious institutes, such as the Redemptorists and School Sisters of Notre Dame.

The development of new religious orders and congregations after the Civil War matched that of pre-bellum days. One branch of the Franciscan Fathers, the Recollects, had worked in the Illinois country during the colonial days. Father Bernard de Limpach, Saint Louis' pioneer pastor, had belonged to another branch of the Franciscans, the Capuchins. Fittingly, the sons of St. Francis returned to the middle west to open two friaries in Illinois in the 1850's. In 1862 Father Servace Altmicks came to Saint

Louis to organize a parish in the area between the city limits and Carondelet. The following year, he set up the friary on an eminence dominating that part of the city. In 1869, Bishop John Hogan dedicated a new church to St. Anthony of Padua adjoining the friary.

A few years later, Chancellor Otto von Bismarck of the new German empire began his campaign to strait-jacket the German people along rigid Prussian Protestant lines. Catholics by the hundreds of thousands fled to the New World to escape this so-called *Kulturkampf*. Several hundred Franciscans came to the American Midwest, and opened many new parishes and missions. Under the direction of Father Vincent and Father Maritius, an independent province of the Sacred Heart grew up, with headquarters at St. Anthony's in Saint Louis, and Father Vincent as provincial. Besides assisting at such parishes as Holy Trinity and St. Liborious, the Franciscans served for many years as chaplains at a number of civic and religious institutions, including the Convent of the Sacred Heart that moved to Meramec and Nebraska, three blocks from St. Anthony's Friary, in 1872.[56] At first the superior of the Franciscan Friary was also pastor of St. Anthony's parish. Some years later, however, the offices became distinct; and a former chancellor of the archdiocese and rector of the Salesianum, Christian Wapelhorst, now Father Innocent, O.F.M., became pastor. Already well known beyond the middle west, his *Compendium Sacrae Liturgiae* remained a guide for rubrics in church worship.

From Germany, too, another group of men religious, the Alexian Brothers, came to the Midwest in 1866. Dedicated to the care of the sick, the Alexian Brothers hoped to open a hospital in Saint Louis. Brothers Paulus and Alexius arrived in Saint Louis in September, 1869. They purchased an old mansion and a five-acre tract of land, overlooking the Mississippi at Osage and Broadway, midway between downtown Saint Louis and Carondelet. Five years later, Coadjutor Bishop Ryan consecrated a new hospital on the same southside site.

The last of the men's orders to begin work in the archdiocese during Kenrick's long regime, the Passionist Fathers, had, as their chief apostolates, missions for the laity and retreats for the clergy. They first settled in the diocese of Pittsburg, where their work came to the attention of the Saint Louis archbishop. Passionist Fathers conducted missions in Saint Louis during the winter of 1883-1884. As a result of interest stirred by this visit, the Passionist Fathers began a retreat on Page Avenue in late 1884. Five years later, they moved to a new site in Normandy, and assumed control of the parish church of St. Ann. The monastery at Normandy served as a seminary for candidates for the congregation, a place of retreat, and the center of religious activities that included the chaplaincies at various institutions in the region.

Bismarck's *Kulturkampf* also drove several sisterhoods to Saint Louis. But the oldest sisterhood in the United States came West because of the continued brotherly interest of the archbishop of Baltimore, Francis Patrick Kenrick, in the archdiocese of Saint Louis.

The Carmelite order had set up its first American foundation in out-state Maryland the year after the ratification of the American Constitution (1790). Seventy years later, shortly before his death, Archbishop Kenrick of Baltimore had proposed to the prioress of the Carmelites that his brother Peter Richard would gladly welcome the members of her order to Saint Louis. After negotiations, several nuns started west in September, 1862.

Archbishop Kenrick offered the Sisters his own country residence, the old Clay Mansion, at the edge of Calvary Cemetery. He served as their confessor for three years. These Sisters carried on a life of prayer rather than a public apostolate. By the middle of the 1870's, the convent was moving along fairly well. In that year the Saint Louis community could send four Sisters to set up a new monastery of the order in New Orleans. In 1878, the local Carmel moved to a new location at the corner of Eighteenth and Victor streets in the city.

Archbishop Kenrick also invited the Little Sisters of the Poor from their motherhouse in Brittany, France. Six Sisters arrived in Saint Louis on May 1, 1868, to begin their charitable work in Saint Louis.

Shortly after, the Sisters of St. Mary of the Third Order of St. Francis, dedicated to the task of nursing the sick in hospitals and the sick poor in their homes, left Bismarck's Germany and came to Saint Louis at the invitation of Vicar-General Muehlsiepen. They received the hospitality of the Ursuline convent for the first three weeks of their stay. Then they rented the upper part of a tenement just opposite St. Mary's Church. Father William Faerber of St. Mary's directed their spiritual life and was to continue in this task for the next forty years.

The Sisters did excellent work in the smallpox epidemic that broke out shortly after their arrival, and in the cholera epidemic of 1873. They bought property for a motherhouse at Arsenal and Arkansas in 1876 and began St. Mary's Infirmary at Fifteenth and Papin, just south of the Union Station area. In 1878 an epidemic of yellow fever broke out in the southern states. Thirteen Sisters of St. Mary's offered their services. Five succumbed to the disease as martyrs of charity. The remaining eight contracted the disease, but recovered and returned to Saint Louis in November of the same year.

The Sisters continued their work in private homes and when another epidemic of smallpox hit Saint Louis in 1883, the Health Commissioner requested the Sisters to undertake the nursing of the smallpox patients at the Quarantine Hospital. This they did for two years, taking care of more than fourteen hundred patients. After this, the city authorities called on the Sisters regularly to cooperate in the general care of health. The Sisters of St. Mary's conducted the Missouri Pacific Railroad Hospital from 1884 to 1889 and took care of the railroad hospital in Sedalia. They opened a hospital in St. Charles, Missouri, in 1885 and a new St. Mary's Infirmary on Papin Street in 1887.

Another group of Franciscan Sisters came at the same time from the Province of Paderborn in northwestern Germany, at the invitation of Father Ernest A. Schindel, the pastor of St. Boniface's Church in Carondelet. He hoped to provide a hospital for the sick poor of the parish. Three sisters arrived in Carondelet in December, 1872, and opened the St. Boniface Hospital the following year. Two years later a second company of eight nuns arrived; in December of the same year, five sisters lost their lives in the wreck of the ill-fated steamer *Deutschland*. Cardinal Manning gave a memorable sermon at the memorial service for the Sisters in England. English poet, Gerard Manley Hopkins, wrote one of his more noteworthy poems to commemorate the event.

The Franciscan Sisters opened several parish schools in out-state Missouri and a second hospital in Cape Girardeau. Gradually the Saint Louis foundation of the community became the center of a province. The Sisters eventually set up a motherhouse adjoining the newly erected St. Anthony Hospital at Grand and Chippewa in 1900.

Under the stimulus of Father Ignatius Panken's work at St. Elizabeth, the Oblate Sisters of Province, a congregation of Negro Sisters, came to Saint Louis in 1880. They taught fifty Negro children in the school and a few years later planned an orphan asylum at the Taylor Mansion on Page Avenue.

The Sisters of the Most Precious Blood came to southern Illinois in the year 1870. They set up convents at Belle Prairie, later Piopolis, at Effingham, and at Edwardsville, not far from Saint Louis. They built a motherhouse at Springfield. A disagreement, however, arose with Bishop Peter J. Baltes of Alton, the successor of Bishop Henry Juncker who had invited the Sisters to the diocese. The superior, Sister Augusta, refused the bishop's condition that all the property must be held as diocesan property. She got in touch with Vicar-General Muehlsiepen in Saint Louis. As a result, twenty-one Sisters came to Saint Louis. They accepted the school of St. Agatha's parish in the city and two out-state schools. They planned a motherhouse at O'Fallon not far from St. Charles. By this time Bismarck's *Kulturkampf* had restricted the activities of nuns in Germany. The entire congregation looked to the New World. Forty-nine Sisters set out for the United States on August 26, 1873. They arrived in New York the following month. The Catholics of O'Fallon gladly welcomed them.

In 1875, however, a group of Sisters, who had remained in Illinois under the direction of Mother Clementine, accepted Bishop Baltes' conditions. They set up their own motherhouse at Ruma, the new name of the pioneer Maryland-Irish settlement of O'Harasburg. Thus, two distinct sisterhoods of the Precious Blood grew up within the radius of fifty miles of Saint Louis. Both were to do memorable work in the archdiocese.

A New Archbishop — for Philadelphia

Bishop Ryan represented Kenrick at the Rome meeting of archbishops of the United States in the late fall of 1883 in preparation for the Third Plenary Council to be held the following spring.[57] While Ryan was in Rome, Pope Leo XIII conferred on him the title "Archbishop of Salamis." The new archbishop returned to Saint Louis, and during the first half of 1884, carried on his usual duties. On May 22, 1884, he ordained fifteen seminarians, including John Rothensteiner, destined to become archdiocesan historian. Two weeks later, Pope Leo XIII named Ryan archbishop of Philadelphia.[58]

The *Western Watchman* predicted that Ryan's appointment to Philadelphia would be a blessing to the whole country.[59] His voice was to ring clearly for liberality and moderation in the councils of the American hierarchy. But the country's gain proved a severe loss to the archdiocese of Saint Louis.

A contemporary newspaper writer stated:

It would have been exceptionally good for the Archdiocese of Saint Louis, and caused Kenricks's name to be held in higher historical veneration had he resigned and let his dear friend, his one close friend, Archbishop Ryan, take over in Saint Louis. Unfortunately that did not occur. Archbishop Ryan took his great skill, his devotion, his flair for oratory to Philadelphia where he continued his distinguished career.[60]

He showed his interest in the immigrant, in the Negro, in social work, and, preeminently, in education.

When Ryan became coadjutor back in 1872 it would

have been psychologically impossible for Kenrick to have resigned. The Vatican Council was too close. It would have appeared that he was bowing to the centralizing forces of the Roman curia, forces he had fought all his life in the name of subsidiarity and collegiality. He honestly, and in many instances, correctly, felt that these forces were strangling the operation of an expanding Church, then becoming in fact as well as in theory, a world-wide organization.

By 1884, however, Vatican I was far behind; and Kenrick definitely approached the sunset of his life. He was seventy-eight. Neither the archdiocese nor the "Old Lion" himself had much to gain from his continuance in office. Had Ryan, already fifty-three years old, and with over thirty years service in Saint Louis, gone in as archbishop at this time, he would have given the Church a new infusion of leadership for the ensuing decades. Instead, Ryan went east, and Kenrick resumed command. Historians can only agree with the newspaper statement of the time that Kenrick's name would have gone down in greater veneration had he resigned. They also see the validity in the tribute that until the rise of Cardinal Gibbons, Kenrick was "the greatest American ecclesiastic of his time."[61]

Kenrick had expressed many ideas on the choice of bishops. He does not seem to have had any conviction about the need or means of retiring them. Patrick Ryan, a man whom historian Joseph Durkin was to call "the outstanding ecclesiastical orator of his time," left for Philadelphia.[62] The *Western Watchman* correctly judged: "Archbishop Ryan would have worn a mitre ten years sooner than he did if Archbishop Kenrick could have consented to part with him."[63] Ryan never received an honor that he did not deserve; and under any other bishop, he would have advanced more rapidly.

Archbishop Ryan's last act in Saint Louis showed his consummate skill as a diplomat. "During his (Kenrick's) long episcopate," Ryan was to say, "there was but one appeal from his decision, on occasion of the only one great scandal that occurred in all that time."[64] Two years before, unwise actions of the pastor of Holy Name Church at the northwestern end of the city, led to charges against him. The priest ignored the entire proceedings, including the summons before the ecclesiastical court. Kenrick removed him from his pastorate in April, 1882.[65]

The priests of the city believed their colleague innocent, however, and asked for his reinstatement. The priest went to Rome to plead his case. The matter dragged on for two years. Finally Rome overruled the Saint Louis decision and ordered the archbishop to restore the accused priest to his parish. This, Kenrick refused to do.[66] Once again, the old proverb among the Catholics of Missouri held true: "What the Archbishop has said is irrevocable."[67]

In the impasse, Ryan pointed out to the Roman authorities that the priest in the dispute had appealed for dismissal from his religious congregation, but had not cleared all details; for that reason he had no legal right to the pastorate in the archdiocese of Saint Louis; though, of course, he had a right to his good name. In the end, Rome vindicated the honor of the priest; and, at the same time, allowed Kenrick's appointee, Father Thomas Bonacum, to remain as pastor.[68]

Friends of the removed pastor had repeatedly expressed their confidence in his innocence during the time of his troubles. On June 10, 1884, they held a festival to celebrate his vindication by the Roman authorities.[69]

That was about all the joy any Saint Louis priests felt that summer. With Ryan's departure imminent, Archbishop Kenrick suffered a serious attack of illness. Unfortunately, he insisted on getting up and saying Mass the following morning with sad consequences.[70] Father Constantine Smith, who had served as consultant of Kenrick at the Vatican Council, expressed his personal fears for the Saint Louis Church and said that Ryan's departure, "cast a gloom over the declining year's of Kenrick."[71] Father Phelan agreed. "Seldom has any event so stirred Saint Louis society to its deepest depths as the departure of Archbishop Ryan." Phelan described a "feeling of regret so deep and profound, shared by Protestant and Catholic alike."[72]

Saint Louis was sad. But Philadelphia rejoiced, and so did other cities in between. Groups of clergy and laity met Archbishop Ryan's train at Indianapolis, Columbus, Pittsburgh, and Altoona. When the train reached Harrisburg, a "special" from Philadelphia met it for the final triumphal leg of the trip. A huge demonstration marked the new archbishop's arrival in his see city, causing an eyewitness to remark: "Nothing like it has ever been known in the history of the Church in America, or in any other country."[73]

On Ryan's departure from Saint Louis, a strong current of public hope centered on a former priest of the archdiocese, Bishop John Hennessey of Dubuque.[74] But Rome did not act. In late August, Kenrick named Father Philip Brady, pastor of Annunciation Church, vicar-general of the English-speaking parishes. "It is well understood that this appointment is but a preliminary to his assumption of the office of bishop," Father Phelan wrote. The bishops of the province had twice recommended him for the episcopal office. Archbishop Ryan had pressed for Brady's elevation while in Rome earlier in the year. Phelan could not speak for the priests of the archdiocese, but he believed they would eventually see the selection as fortunate. He described Brady in this way: "Not a man of exceptional talents or scholarship; but . . . a most laborious and successful priest . . . (who) never sought the office."[75] Physically, Phelan described him as "small of stature . . . and of ample proportions."[76] The new vicar-general lacked Ryan's great gifts of mind and personality, and the prestige of the episcopacy.

Chapter 21

Kenrick Resumes Control

Cradle of Bishops

The appointment of Coadjutor Archbishop Patrick Ryan to Philadelphia offers a convenient occasion to survey a significant aspect of the Saint Louis Church. Often during the long episcopate of Peter Richard Kenrick, diocesan or regular clergymen working in the Saint Louis archdiocese left to assume the position of bishop either in the Midwest or beyond. In all, seventeen priests who worked in Kenrick's jurisdiction, nine of the diocese, five Vincentians, and three Jesuits, became bishops during Kenrick's time. Some of these men, besides Archbishop Ryan, have appeared often in these pages: Vicar-General Joseph Melcher, who became bishop of Green Bay in 1868; Father John Odin, C.M., vicar apostolic of Texas, and later archbishop of New Orleans; the Vincentian Visitor Father John Timon, bishop of Buffalo; and Father James J. Van de Velde, S.J., president of Saint Louis University, superior of the midwestern Jesuits, and later bishop of Chicago. Anthony O'Reagan and James Duggan,* rectors of the seminary in Carondelet, and Thadeus Amat, C.M., rector of the seminary in Saint Louis, appeared briefly in earlier pages. The first two became bishops of Chicago; and the third served in Monterey and later in the combined sees of Monterey and Los Angeles.

Patrick Augustine Feehan did pastoral work in the archdiocese, served as hospital chaplain for federal soldiers, became bishop of Nashville shortly after the Civil War, and later the first archbishop of Chicago. Jean Baptiste Miege, S.J., professor of theology at St. Stanislaus Seminary at Florissant, served as vicar apostolic of the Indian territory to the west of the Missouri River. Father John J. Hogan, who had started Catholic colonies in the Ozarks before the Civil War, became bishop of St. Joseph, Missouri, in 1868. He left an interesting memorial of his work in a book *On the Mission in Missouri*. His appointment, incidentally, marked the first division of ecclesiastical territory within the state of Missouri. In 1880, he accepted an appointment to the newly created bishopric of Kansas City.

George A. Carrell, S.J., a native of Philadelphia, served as president of Saint Louis University and rector of St. Francis Xavier Church during the days of Kenrick's coadjutorship in Saint Louis. Later he moved to Cincinnati, and in 1853 became the bishop of the neighboring diocese of Covington, Kentucky. Vincentian Michael Domenec, a native of Spain, spent his early priestly years in the missions near Perryville, and as a member of the faculty of St. Vincent College in Cape Girardeau, Missouri. Later he served in Pennsylvania. In 1860 he became bishop of Pittsburgh. At the Vatican Council, he made his presence

felt with strong opposition to the declaration of papal infallibility, and with occasional pertinent but perhaps injudicious remarks on the Church in Italy. The last of the Vincentian bishops to work in Missouri during Kenrick's time, Stephen M. V. Ryan, a native of Canada, took part of his education at Perryville, and, after serving for a number of years as professor and rector of St. Vincent's College in Cape Girardeau, became Visitor of the Congregation of the Mission in the United States. He served in this post eleven years; then became bishop of Buffalo in 1868.

A third rector of the seminary in Carondelet to rise to the episcopacy, John Hennessey, became bishop of Dubuque in 1866, and its first archbishop in 1893. Another John Hennessey worked as pastor in Saint Louis for a number of years; he was to become bishop of Wichita in 1889. The last priest of the diocese during Kenrick's time to become bishop, Thomas Bonacum, was to attend the Third Plenary Congregation Council of Baltimore as theologian for Archbishop Kenrick in 1884. The prelates of that council named him as first bishop of the proposed diocese of Belleville. Instead the Sacred Congregation of the Propaganda appointed him to a newly erected see of Lincoln in Nebraska in 1887.

All of these *diocesan* priests to become bishops came from Ireland except Joseph Melcher, who was from Vienna. The members of religious orders represented, however, a far more varied pattern of national origin: Carrell and Timon were born in the United States, Ryan in Canada, Van de Velde in Belgium, Odin in France, Miege in the Italo-French Province of Savoy near the Swiss border, and Amat and Domenec in Spain. Few dioceses could challenge Saint Louis' position as cradle of bishops.

The Subsidiary German Parishes

No sooner had Kenrick come back from "retirement" at the appointment of his Coadjutor Patrick Ryan as archbishop of Philadelphia, than the question of the foreign-language parishes came to the fore. When the old archbishop had first come to Saint Louis in the early forties, he had set up German churches as subsidiary to English-speaking parishes. The priests in charge of the German churches did not enjoy the juridical status of "pastors" but had full pastoral rights in regard to their own people. Kenrick had based this arrangement on the legislation of the Council of Trent that did not allow a division of authority within a given territory.

During the succeeding forty years, other peoples, the Bohemians, Italians, Poles, and Negroes, worshiped under similar arrangements. In some cases, the national congregations grew larger and more active than juridical parishes. Eventually most Catholics thought the subsidiary churches were true parishes.

*A mental and physical breakdown forced Bishop Duggan to resign his see in 1869. He was the only one of Kenrick's nominees who did not match the onerous duties facing him.

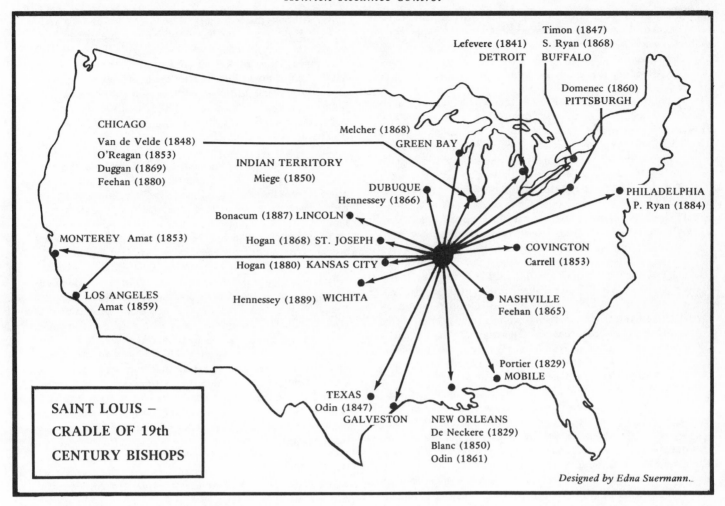

Timon (1847)
Lefevere (1841)   S. Ryan (1868)
DETROIT   BUFFALO

Domenec (1860)
PITTSBURGH

CHICAGO
Van de Velde (1848)
O'Reagan (1853)
Duggan (1869)
Feehan (1880)

Melcher (1868)
GREEN BAY

INDIAN TERRITORY
Miege (1850)

DUBUQUE
Hennessey (1866)

PHILADELPHIA
P. Ryan (1884)

Bonacum (1887) LINCOLN

MONTEREY Amat (1853)

Hogan (1868) ST. JOSEPH

COVINGTON
Carrell (1853)

Hogan (1880) KANSAS CITY

LOS ANGELES
Amat (1859)

Hennessey (1889) WICHITA

NASHVILLE
Feehan (1865)

Portier (1829)
MOBILE

TEXAS
Odin (1847)
GALVESTON   NEW ORLEANS
De Neckere (1829)
Blanc (1850)
Odin (1861)

SAINT LOUIS –
CRADLE OF 19th
CENTURY BISHOPS

Designed by Edna Suermann.

The technical question of the rights of foreign-speaking congregations and their pastors did not in itself appear too difficult to solve. But the underlying ideological conflict touched raw religious and cultural nerve centers.

A sane and balanced review-essay by the mild-mannered historian John Gilmary Shea in the July, 1883, issue of the *American Catholic Quarterly Review* proved to be the firing on Fort Sumter that triggered the civil war between German and Irish Catholic leaders in the United States. He spoke of the "descendants of the original Catholic body" as "timid and not self-asserting." When Irish immigrants came in great numbers Shea wrote:

[The native-born Catholics] found themselves put aside by the newcomers and looked upon with a kind of suspicion for not entering into feelings which, from their American birth and education they could not share, and which really had no relation to Catholic doctrine, practice, or thought. They (the native-born Catholics) found themselves regarded by their Protestant fellow-countrymen, on the other hand, as belonging to a foreign and un-American Church.

Converts found this especially galling, Shea stated and listed a number of individuals who "went to Canada or to Europe to find more harmonious surroundings."[1]

When German immigration grew, another foreign element isolated the old-line Catholic, "unless he acquired the language and identified himself with the hopes and desires of Germans. Even now, one finds in German Catholic papers the most contemptuous allusions to American and Irish Catholics."[2]

"To foster these national feelings unduly is a great mistake," Shea insisted. "They breed animosity; and as the rising generation will be American in feelings, they must look upon this as their country, and if their religion is a matter of nationality, it will expire with it."[3] To conclude this part of his essay, he wrote of the dioceses west of the Mississippi River: "There are thousands of miles where no American-born bishop has ever been seen."[4] Shea deliberately chose a section where there were only two German-born bishops, Fink of Kansas and Junger of Nesqually, Washington,* French like Lamy and Salpointe, Canadians like the two Blanchets, one of whom had died one month before the article appeared, Spaniards like Alemanny, Swiss like Marty, and Irish like Kenrick and Ireland. The issue of Shea's article was national-identification, not German-national-identification.

While the Irish had always considered themselves one hundred percent Americans and generally overlooked Shea's valid criticism of their attitudes, the German-Americans answered in force. Father William Faerber of Saint Louis, editor of *Pastoral Blatt*, gave the first retort in November, 1883, and Father Innocent Wapelhorst, O.F.M., followed in April of the next year (1884). These two articles shortly came out in English translations. Faerber's pamphlet bore the name *The Future of Foreign-Born Catholics*, and Wapelhorst's *Whither Are We Drifting*.[5] Father Faerber ridiculed the notion that German-American Catholics would prefer Prussia or

---

*The old Northwest (east of the Mississippi) had six German-born bishops at this time. See Joseph B. Code, *Dictionary of the American Hierarchy* (New York: Longmans, Green and Co., 1940), p. 480.

Bismarckism to the freest Republic in the world; but he opposed forcible Americanization.* Father Wapelhorst amassed statistics that suggested high numerical losses in the American Church. Both writers associated the succursal church situation in Saint Louis with the Shea article.[6]

In the summer of 1884, Father Phelan published an article entitled "A German Bishop for St. Louis." "Lay and clerical orders," he wrote, "are not a little agitated just now over rumors of combinations, conferences, and caucuses among the Germans of this diocese, looking to the appointment of a German bishop to take the place made vacant by the transfer of Bishop Ryan."[7] Where the new bishop had first seen light of day did not bother Phelan. He simply wanted a man who spoke flawless English and knew and loved American institutions.[8]

The priests of German-American background did not ask for a bishop of their nationality. But in the name of eighty-two members of the diocesan and religious clergy of Saint Louis, Father Muehlsiepen queried Cardinal Simeone of the Propaganda, on the subsidiary status of their congregations and their own lack of pastoral prerogatives. They feared that the approaching Third Plenary Council of Baltimore would sanction, extend, and make permanent this unfortunate situation, and asked equal and independent rights in their pastoral offices.[9]

At first glance, this direct appeal to Rome might seem to have disdained local authorities; but Archbishop Kenrick had not changed in forty years, and the Pope had reserved to the office of the Propaganda in Rome the drawing up of the agenda for the coming Third Plenary Council of Baltimore.

Father Faerber was in Rome during the summer of 1884 and pushed the petition at the Propaganda. Muehlsiepen wrote personally to assure the Propaganda that the request implied no dissatisfaction with Kenrick, who had always provided for the needs of all national groups making up the Saint Louis archdiocese. Cardinal Simeone referred the matter to the American archbishops. When Faerber notified Muehlsiepen of this action by Rome, the vicar-general sent Archbishop Gibbons a copy of the petition and a covering letter insisting that the signers made no accusations against Kenrick.[10] Gibbons regretted that the priests of Saint Louis had taken such a step.[11] Archbishop Ryan, newly arrived in Philadelphia, held that no diocese in the country treated the Germans better than the Saint Louis archdiocese; but he wisely felt that the coming council should define the rights of priests of foreign-language flocks, and had so expressed himself to Rome, as similar complaints had come in from other places. He believed that action by the council might forestall future misunderstandings.[12]

In his capacity as apostolic delegate to the forthcoming council, Gibbons wrote Simeone, protesting the public discussion of the issue in the German-American press:

It would have been enough to bring this matter to the notice of the Sacred Congregation of the Propaganda by letter, as it was afterward done, or to reserve it to the notice of the Fathers of the Third Plenary Council of Baltimore .... Insofar as I am able I will see to it that ... the just desires of the Germans and other nationalities in this matter be justified.[13]

When the Third Plenary Council met in Baltimore in

---

* For a thorough and balanced analysis of the entire controversy, see Colman J. Barry, O.S.B., *The Catholic Church and German Americans* (Milwaukee: The Bruce Publishing Company, 1953).

1884, Gibbons placed the matter in the hands of a well chosen committee, composed of three archbishops: locally-born John Williams of Boston, Patrick Feehan of Chicago, a native of Ireland who had been a priest of the Saint Louis diocese, and Michael Heiss of Milwaukee, who as a young priest had engaged in pastoral work in Bavaria before coming to the United States in 1842. Unfortunately, and contrary to Gibbons' promise, the council took no action on the Saint Louis petition.

In later years when some German-Catholics publicly questioned this lack of action, Cardinal Gibbons did not hesitate to answer that Archbishop Heiss and the other bishops of German background had remained silent on the subject throughout all the executive and public sessions.[14]

The council called for the establishment of a school in every parish and set penalties on parents who did not send their children to parochial schools. This quite naturally brought joy to the Saint Louis Germans who had long supported religious schooling. It brought pain to Father David Phelan who denounced this provision of the council. Phelan supported the position of John Ireland who became bishop of St. Paul that year and was to try to bring Catholic education within the orbit of the public school system. Ireland believed that too many parochial schools, employing, as they did, a foreign language, most often German, removed Catholics from the mainstream of American life. Ireland was often to make extreme remarks; his opponents likewise reacted too strongly on many occasions.

At the close of the Third Plenary Council, Kenrick, as the patriarch of the American prelates, thanked Archbishop Gibbons in the name of his conferees for a benign judiciousness.[15]

Back in the Episcopal Carriage

The archbishop tried to resume a full schedule of episcopal visitations as he approached his eightieth birthday. He visited every part of the archdiocese, an area 150 miles east and west, and three hundred miles from north to south — slightly larger than his native Ireland. He did all the work required in these official trips, including the confirming of six thousand children each year.[16] Such a schedule would have taxed the strength of a man half his age.

Kenrick's log for late spring, 1886, for instance, shows a steady round of parish visits and a surprising warmth of good fellowship. On Sunday, May 30, he confirmed at St. Vincent's, St. Thomas', and St. Elizabeth's.[17] The following Sunday he confirmed at Holy Angels' and St. Teresa's.[18] On Wednesday, he went out to Florissant to confirm twenty at the Sacred Heart Church and fifty at St. Ferdinand's. While there, he visited the Loretto Academy and the Jesuit Novitiate. At St. Stanislaus Seminary, a novice said to him: "Your Grace, if you were forty years younger, we would invite you to stay."

With a smile, Kenrick replied, "If I were forty years younger, I *would* stay."[19]

The following week, the archbishop visited the home for the aged and the poor. An old man said to him: "I've been in Saint Louis for twenty years, and I have never spoken to you before."

Kenrick answered, "I have been here forty years and never before had the pleasure of talking to you."[20]

Pope Leo XIII chose Archbishop Kenrick as his representative to confer the cardinalatial biretta on James Cardinal Gibbons of Baltimore. "The selection of Kenrick to invest Gibbons is eminently proper," the *Catholic Standard* of Philadelphia stated on this occasion.[21] The editorial writer singled out the conspicuous geographical separation of the sees of the two men; and their difference in ages. Kenrick was the oldest; and Gibbons almost the youngest archbishop in the country.

Kenrick went to Baltimore for the ceremony on June 30, 1886. In late summer he vacationed in the White Mountains of New Hampshire and then visited Canada.[22]

While Kenrick was out of town, Archbishop Germano Straniero, a representative of Pope Leo, visited the city. "Archbishop Kenrick is a saintly, a holy man," Straniero said in a press interview, "and I would like to see him a cardinal. But this is only my view. I do not think his Holiness intends to give more than one cardinal to the United States."[23]

During much of the late spring and early summer, the effort of Prime Minister William E. Gladstone to win home rule for Ireland gripped the attention of Irishmen everywhere. And almost every Irish-American had more than his share of words to offer on the subject. Kenrick alone kept silent.[24] But, if he avoided political questions, he was planning to talk in the council of the archbishops during the coming fall on several social questions.

Such a strenuous year as 1886 would have taken a toll even on a much younger man. It was evident that Kenrick could not keep such a pace. Vicars Muehlsiepen and Brady had to carry on with the steady growth of the city that saw six new urban churches: St. Henry's, St. Leo's, St. Engelbert's, Holy Rosary, St. Agnes', and St. Aloysius', in the seven years between 1885 and 1892.

And besides all these things, there were the Knights of Labor, and their advocate Father Cornelius O'Leary.

Father Henry Muehlsiepen, — vicar-general for the German-speaking parishes of the archdiocese during the last part of the 19th century.

General Daniel M. Frost, veteran of the Mexican War, commander of the state militia at Camp Jackson, May, 1861, his grandson, Joseph G. Frost, and his son, R. Graham Frost, representative from Missouri in the 46th Congress, who successfully defended the indicted railroad workers at the request of Father O'Leary, and headed the delegation of laymen who welcomed Archbishop Kain.

Chapter 22

Catholics in Controversy

Cornelius O'Leary and the Knights of Labor*

Writing in the days before the Great Depression of 1929, archdiocesan historian Monsignor John Rothensteiner could dismiss the strong support that DeSoto (Missouri) pastor, Cornelius O'Leary gave the striking railroad workers forty years before with this simple statement: "During the railroad strike of 1886, his (O'Leary's) imprudence in speech brought the threat of early removal of the (Missouri-Pacific) machine shop from DeSoto. This led to his transfer to Webster Groves in October, 1886."[1] A later priest historian, Henry J. Browne, placed Father O'Leary in a niche among the few priest-heroes in the cause of social justice at the time.[2]

The story of the thirty-six-year-old Irish-born pastor and the Knights of Labor adds light to the social history of the archdiocese; it shows what happens when a learned young priest, an authority on canon law, a vigorous writer and a colorful orator, runs afoul of his ecclesiastical superior; it presents the "Old Lion" in a situation where cherished principles militated against each other; and moved the two men into the center of one of the most heated ecclesiastical controversies of the time.

The Noble Order of the Knights of Labor, America's first great labor union, began in 1869 as a secret, fraternal organization to encompass all workers, skilled and unskilled, black and white, native-born and foreign. Secrecy would shield the workers from the "black lists" of employers and the indiscretions of individual members. The fraternal ritual corresponded to the spirit of the times. While the specialized craft unions, by way of contrast, concentrated exclusively on gains for the skilled workers in wages and working conditions, the more visionary Knights of Labor tried to rally all workers into one large union that would give working class solidarity; they saw a destiny for labor to lead the country into a wide range of social reforms.

The outstanding leader of the Knights of Labor, Terrence V. Powderly, a skilled worker himself, became "Grand Master Workman" or chief officer of the Union in 1878. Elected Mayor of Scranton on the labor ticket the same year, this mild, diplomatic, sensitive Catholic layman tried to please the general public as well as labor. By 1886, the Order claimed seven hundred thousand men under his direction.

Though Powderly was a devout Catholic, his program did not please Archbishop Elzear Taschereau of Quebec, who had condemned the Knights in a message to Roman authorities. In a response, dated August 27, 1883, the Holy Office reprobated the Knights of Labor as a prohibited society. Archbishop John Joseph Lynch of To-

ronto, on the other hand, took a much more favorable view of the Knights and expressed concern for the mistreated workers in many places on both sides of the border.[3] Archbishop James Gibbons, to be named a cardinal that same summer (1886) along with Archbishop Taschereau, supported a street car strike in Baltimore, and urged his fellow bishops to follow a benevolent policy toward the laboring man.[4]

Out west, in the meantime, railroad workers struck against the Jay Gould system. A first strike had occurred in the previous March (1885) when several thousand workmen of the Missouri-Pacific in the states of Missouri, Texas, and Kansas demanded a restoration of wages. The wage cut without warning or justification at a time when company earnings had remained high outraged the general public, already hostile to Jay Gould. The governors of Missouri and Kansas moved to end the strike. The rail officials had the good sense to yield.

In March, 1886, a greater strike began. Nine thousand shopmen struck. They not only quit work, but set out to stop all freight traffic in a five-state area by removing small but essential mechanisms from the engines. The workers had few here-and-now demands. Their main concern was union recognition. Thus the strike became a power struggle.

Father Cornelius O'Leary, pastor since 1881 of St. Rose of Lima's Church in DeSoto, Missouri, where the Missouri-Pacific Railroad had one of its largest shops, was away when the strike broke out on March 6. Many of the strikers were among the best members of his parish. They had just built a new stone church and paid two-thirds of the debt on it, through their own contributions and proceeds from a series of public lectures Father O'Leary gave. When O'Leary returned from New York and found the strike in progress, he did not take sides immediately. He studied the situation. He found wages inadequate at best and employment spasmodic for many men during much of the year. The company hired strike-breakers, many of whom O'Leary believed to be "fit for the penitentiary." He saw each little disturbance arising from the strike magnified beyond proportion; while in the previous year ten murders had occurred in the vicinity with "no stir about it."[5] On the last day of March, Father O'Leary addressed a public meeting of all citizens on the strike.

Rumors spread through DeSoto that the Missouri-Pacific would move its shops,[6] and that former employees would get their jobs back only "as individuals." They, presumably, would have to give up membership in the Knights.[7] General distress marked the plight of the strikers and their families. No credit was available.

O'Leary organized a committee of five for relief work among the poor families. He prevailed upon lawyer Richard Graham Frost, a former member of Congress, and a scion of several distinguished Saint Louis families, to defend indicted railroad workers. "Through his (Frost's) influence," O'Leary wrote, "the Company and the Court

*For a detailed study of the matter, confer William B. Faherty, "The Clergyman and Labor Progress: Cornelius O'Leary and the Knights of Labor," *Labor History* 2, no. 2 (Spring 1970): 175-189.

(practically one and the same) seemed to relax their rigor by letting them off very easily."[8]

The strike had forced business to a standstill. Shortage of coal closed factories. Food no longer reached the family table. The general public began to reassess the struggle. Then in early April violence broke out.[9] People did not ask who committed the violence. Both sides did its share. But the public blamed all trouble on the strike walk-out. And they wanted it to end. Thus, with the aid of the public authorities, the railroad company was able to crush the strike. The Knights met a decisive defeat.

With the strike already doomed to failure, the House of Representatives sent a committee to investigate labor troubles "in the Southwest." Three men made up the committee: Andrew J. Curtin, Civil War-time governor of Pennsylvania; John W. Stewart, one-term governor of Vermont; and James N. Burnes, a former judge and president of the Missouri Valley Railroad. They began hearings on April 20. While no other Catholic clergyman spoke in their behalf, Father O'Leary testified on May 12.[10]

O'Leary explained his concern for the working man; described how company policies goaded the men to violence; stated his belief that some corporations wielded a power that overshadowed state and federal authorities; gave evidence of gross inequities in pay scales; condemned the use of gunmen as strike-breakers; and denounced the "black list."[11]

Throughout his testimony, O'Leary never took a neutral posture, but defended the Knights of Labor in all their actions and policies. At times he spoke excessively. Yet a careful perusal of the entire report leads the objective observer to the conclusion that O'Leary acquitted himself well, at times brilliantly, and performed a significant service to the public and the cause of justice.

O'Leary got little support from his fellow churchmen in Saint Louis. Even Father Phelan, ordinarily a defender of the underdog, did not like the leadership of the Knights[12] and opposed them for excessive demands.[13]

Rumors made the rounds that the Missouri-Pacific would move its shops. Loyal union men could find no work in DeSoto; many people moved away, business declined, and property values dropped dramatically.[14] The *Records* of Father O'Leary's church stated that the strike dispersed the congregation, crippled the resources of the parish, and almost ruined the town.[15] Ill feeling and discouragement gripped DeSoto.

During the summer, a representative of Pope Leo XIII, Monsignor Germano Straniero, visited Saint Louis on a tour of the United States.[16] Straniero had no official capacity, except to bring to Archbishop James Gibbons of Baltimore the symbols of his new dignity as cardinal. The remainder of his tour was simply "sight-seeing." But O'Leary took the opportunity of talking to him about the Knights of Labor. He presented the Italian prelate with documents explaining the nature and work of the order.[17] On the gangplank before re-embarking for Europe a few months later, Straniero gave an interview favorable to the Knights. He said that membership in the Knights of Labor was compatible with good Catholicism and claimed few American bishops were really hostile to it.[18] The story made the rounds of the press and elicited from O'Leary an admission that he had met with the Italian prelate.[19]

Back in DeSoto, feelings on the part of some residents turned against Father O'Leary. Grand Master Powderly wrote:

I have heard that the Missouri-Pacific Company has offered to build a church in DeSoto if you are removed; is that true? If it is, I will bend every energy of mine to the building of a church for Father O'Leary and keep him just where he is. At any rate you should have a church and if you will consent to it I will start the ball a rolling that will put one up for you. Let me know your wishes. . . .[20]

In his large free-flowing script, O'Leary thanked Powderly for his generous offer of help for a new church. He had already built a fine stone church. He admitted that he was perhaps over-zealous in that his parishioners were "tenants at will, so to speak." The church still had a debt of four thousand dollars and the parish could not even pay the interest. He appreciated Powderly's offer of help, but could not consent to it. He felt it might establish a bad precedent.[21]

O'Leary had heard the rumor that the railroad officials offered to pay the debt if he were removed; and a contrary rumor among Catholics that he would *not* be removed precisely because the debt existed. The railroad officials had encouraged a petition for his removal, O'Leary stated, discharged a friend of his simply because of the friendship, threatened to move the shops on his account, and turned many citizens against him.[22]

While Father O'Leary was speaking out in defense of the Knights, many churchmen discussed the matter privately among themselves. In Philadelphia, the new archbishop, Patrick Ryan, for instance, supported the Knights on the basis of a principle of action he learned from Kenrick: to distinguish between Catholic societies with religious purposes, and societies of Catholics with secular goals; and in regard to the latter: "To let them alone unless anything really objectionable should develop itself, and then condemn them if the obnoxious features were not removed."[23] "The matter becomes of very grave importance," Ryan wrote, "in view of the great labor *contra* capital movement in the country. The Knights of Labor are in some places almost exclusively Catholic."[24]

Archbishop Kenrick, presumably, would support the Knights. Rome had condemned them in French Canada; and Kenrick usually opposed the overcentralizing tendencies of the Roman Curia. But he had misgivings about the boycott and the tampering with the rolling stock.[25] Most surprisingly, he visited French Canada for two weeks in late summer as a guest of Cardinal Taschereau.[26] Father David Phelan took the occasion of Kenrick's visit to criticize Taschereau's stand on labor issues; and predicted that the American bishops would not follow the Canadian cardinal's lead on the Knights.[27]

As far as the bulk of archbishops was concerned, Phelan was correct; but not in regard to Kenrick, nor to the archbishop of the Southwest, John Baptist Salpointe of Santa Fe. After Kenrick's return from Canada, Salpointe visited the Saint Louis prelate on the way east. Many blamed Salpointe's stand on his talk with Kenrick.[28] In the meantime, Kenrick had another crucial interview — this one a two-hour meeting with rail executive H. M. Hoxie. Father O'Leary, incidentally, blamed Kenrick's negative stand on this meeting.[29]

With Kenrick and Salpointe in opposition to the Knights, and several other archbishops preferring to let Rome decide the matter, Cardinal Gibbons could not win unanimous approval of the order at the fall archiepiscopal conference. Rome would have to decide the issue.

O'Leary's work in DeSoto, however, soon ended. Kenrick appointed him to a newly forming parish in a suburb of Saint Louis, called Webster (later Webster Groves).

O'Leary believed that three factors caused his transfer: his criticism of Kenrick's conferring with railroad executive, H. M. Hoxie, his support of the Knights, and his testifying before the Curtin Committee.[30] O'Leary's successor at the parish in DeSoto, Father Joseph Connolly, later vicar-general of the archdiocese of Saint Louis, wrote in the parish history:

> In March, 1886, the strike on the railroad and in the shops, known as the "Southwestern Strike of '86" occurred . . . forcing, as a result of the part taken in siding with the Knights of Labor, and utterances in public and private, the departure of Father O'Leary in November 1886.[31]

In the letter to Powderly of January 23, O'Leary spoke of his friendliness for Father Edward McGlynn who had run into trouble with Archbishop Michael Corrigan of New York because of his support of Henry George's social theories and political campaign in New York. A few months later, the *New York Sun* featured an article that compared O'Leary's story with that of Father McGlynn in the East.[32]

As an expression of his appreciation to O'Leary for the debts he had incurred in assisting the striking railroad men, Powderly sent him a check for four hundred dollars as a start in paying the debt, and asked him to become a regular contributor to the *Journal of United Labor.*[33] Two months later Father O'Leary and Powderly met in Philadelphia. Not long afterward Powderly asked the priest to serve as intermediary in carrying a letter of gratitude from the Knights to Cardinal Gibbons. Powderly thanked Gibbons, and praised O'Leary in this letter.

> No one, [the Grand Master Workman wrote] rendered the cause of law and order more effectual service at that time than Father O'Leary who proved himself indeed to be the true priest of the people . . . I thank Father O'Leary more than any living man for the termination of the strike before violence was resorted to.[34]

Powderly also asked Cardinal Gibbons to use his influence in behalf of the priest.[35] No evidence exists that Cardinal Gibbons attempted to intercede with Kenrick in behalf of O'Leary. Perhaps he felt that if Pope Pius IX had not budged Kenrick on another issue, he had little hope in this. But Gibbons did plead the cause of the Knights of Labor in Rome during 1887; and though he won only grudging approval, he was able to meet with Powderly and win from him agreement to Rome's few conditions. So that by the time the report of Rome's approval came out, it proved a prestigious victory for the cardinal and the Knights.[36]

Father O'Leary took a leave of absence and visited his native Ireland. There he "avowed that he was a socialist and rebel at heart, as was every Irishman."[37]

After his return to Saint Louis, he wrote to Powderly in June, 1888: "My friends here have corrected their errors and I forgive them."[38] He was to serve spasmodically as assistant pastor at various parishes during the nineties. After the turn of the century, the newly appointed Archbishop John J. Glennon commissioned him to develop a suburban parish, Notre Dame, in Wellston, Missouri. This work consumed his remaining years. He took no further part in domestic struggles for social justice, though he did continue to plead the cause of Ireland. Quite interestingly, O'Leary died as a result of injuries received when a tornado struck the railroad station in Mineral Point, Missouri, where he and a number of priests waited for a Missouri-Pacific train.

Historian John Rothensteiner described O'Leary's manner and outlook:

> It is regrettable that the peculiarities of his temperament, his lack of prudence, his gift, if it be, of quick caustic retort, and above all, his habit of universal criticism should have accompanied him all through life, and made him many enemies and detractors . . . . No one was immune from his censorship . . . . Yet there was no malice or envy in his makeup. . . . He saw many things that he thought needed correction and, as he never shirked a duty, he was often in contention, and rarely yielded his position.[39]

The historian can only say that had Father O'Leary possessed more "prudence" he probably would have remained throughout his life a proper and highly respected upper-middle class pastor; but as a matter of simple fact, he did not have the "prudence" that counsels silence in a crisis, or the aloofness of total objectivity. Instead, he supported the Knights of Labor at a time when few men stood with them; when the cardinal archbishop of Quebec had already outlawed them; and his own Archbishop Peter Richard Kenrick voted to condemn them.

Years later, Terence Powderly called in question the lack of involvement of most clergymen during the struggles of the Knights. In his memoirs, *The Pathway I Trod*, Powderly listed the names of several bishops and many priests who supported the Knights *after* Cardinal Gibbons returned from Rome with an approval of the order in 1887. Before that, Powderly mentioned the name of only one Catholic pastor who stood up publicly for justice for the Knights of Labor, Father Cornelius O'Leary of Missouri. This is Powderly's tribute: "No man in or out of the organization did greater service to the men than Father O'Leary."[40]

This was no little achievement.

Americanizers Versus Conservatives

Growth brings controversy, and the American Church was growing. In the latter quarter of the nineteenth century, Catholics debated, besides membership in the Knights of Labor, the theories of Henry George, the place of the parochial schools, the foundation of the Catholic University of America, participation of Catholics in interfaith gatherings and secret societies, the best ways to promote temperance, and the nationality question. From these controversies stemmed the alleged heresy of "Americanism."

All of these issues reflected a central question: How was the Church to adjust to the American environment? Catholics tended to divide into two camps, the Americanizers and the conservatives. The most prominent of the Americanizers were Archbishop Ireland of St. Paul, Bishop John J. Keane, president of the Catholic University of America at the height of the turmoil, and Monsignor Denis J. O'Connell, rector of the American college in Rome. Although a moderate by temperament, Cardinal Gibbons generally supported these men. Archbishop Michael A. Corrigan of New York and Bishop Bernard J. McQuaid of Rochester led the conservatives. Most of the German-American clergy, especially in the mid-continent, allied themselves firmly with the conservative camp.

This controversy involved all Catholic Americans; it affected in a special way the German-speaking clergy and laity in Saint Louis as well as in Milwaukee and Cincinnati — the three ecclesiastical provinces in the country not Irish-dominated.[41]

The Americanizers held that Catholicism and the institutions of the United States were admirably suited to each other. The prospects of the Church were brighter in the open society of the United States than in the tradition-bound states of Europe. They called for flexibility and adjustment. They criticized the tendency to view American civilization as too materialistic or basically incompatible with the beliefs or inherited values of Catholics. They opposed the use of foreign languages and the continuance of cultural traditions not in accord with American practice. They wanted speedy assimilation.

The conservatives pointed to the indisputable Protestantism and the periodic nativism of Americans. They stressed, in opposition, a preservation of Old World traditions that bulwarked the faith of the immigrant. They supported parochial schools and strictly Catholic organizations. The German-American Catholics especially liked the conservative attitude. For them Catholicism tied in with language and culture. They believed that the maintenance of the cultural heritage supported the immigrant's faith. They saw assimilation as inevitable, of course, but they believed it was a slow and natural process — far too slow for Archbishop Ireland.

While the general discussion between the Americanizers and the conservatives had American prelates of Irish background leading both sides (Ireland-Keane vs. McQuaid-Corrigan), in the specific nationality question the German-Americans played a leading role. The issue became essentially a quarrel between Germans and Irish. For one thing, German Catholics resented being lectured on "Americanism" by those who were as much immigrants as themselves.

In his excellent book, *The Conservative Reformers*, Professor Philip Gleason pinpoints these questions:

Were the Irish-Catholics really closer to true Americanism, as they seemed to think, simply because they spoke English? Did the Germans have to drop their language to become real Americans? If they did, would their faith survive? Would their culture survive? Did Americanization require the disappearance of the German-Catholics as a group?[42]

"In their resistance to the Germans," another Church historian of the period, Gerald Fogarty wrote, "the Americanizers often magnified and sometimes falsified their [the German-Americans'] proposals as if they were measures in a conspiracy to preserve German colonies in America."[43] "Some, like O'Connell, even passed themselves off as native-born Americans,"[44] while they questioned the disposition of native-born Americans of German ancestry, such as Bishop Joseph G. Dwenger, C.P.P.S., of Fort Wayne, Indiana.[45]

In Saint Louis, the controversy had broken out sharply in 1884 over the question of national parishes. David Phelan attacked the German-American position in the *Western Watchman*. William Faerber defended his fellows in the monthly theological magazine for the clergy, *Pastoral Blatt*.[46]

In 1886 Father Peter M. Abbelen, vicar-general of the Milwaukee archdiocese, carried a petition to Rome requesting a clarification of the status of German national parishes and discussing in general the relationship of Irish Catholics and German Catholics in the United States. Abbelen had his archbishop's approval and had notified Cardinal Gibbons of his mission. Nonetheless many bishops of Irish-American background reacted unfavorably to this petition. They saw it as a criticism of their way of handling domestic problems, and as an effort to gain special privileges for one national group.

Rome granted three of Abbelen's requests but deferred an answer on the last six: there might be parishes for different nationalities within a given territory; in general,

children should remain in their parents' parish until they reached their majority; and rectors of national parishes might gain the status of "irremovable pastors" in accordance with the Third Plenary Council.[47] The involved Roman procedures led to a mistranslation of the second answer. As a result of this error, Bishop Richard Gilmour of Cleveland unjustly reprimanded Father Faerber of Saint Louis. Gilmour had to retract his remarks in this instance; but he retaliated with a severe attack on Abbelen and the *Pastoral Blatt*.[48]

The entire Abbelen affair stirred up rather than calmed the Irish-German controversy. The Americanizers spoke more sharply; the German-Americans, in turn, became even more sensitive to the status of their parishes and to other infringements of their "rights."

Sixty-five German-speaking priests from various dioceses gathered in Chicago for the first meeting of the newly forming German-American Priests' Society in February, 1887. Under the chairmanship of Vicar-General Henry Muehlsiepen of Saint Louis, the conferees planned a huge meeting of German-Americans to be held the following September in Chicago at the time of the *Central Verein* Congress. The entire meeting was to follow the model of the public demonstrations of faith, called *Katholikentage*, then common in the German states. Father Francis Goller agreed to take charge of a central committee to collect a golden jubilee gift for the Holy Father, Leo XIII.[49]

An unidentified New York pastor of German background remarked that the upcoming meeting would promote the advance of German-American priests to the episcopacy and retard the advancement of Irish-Americans.[50] This intemperate statement brought denials and denunciations. The atmosphere grew so clouded that many despaired of concrete results of the projected *Katholikentage*.

In spite of this, and an unfortunately worded attack on the Knights of Labor by a St. Paul delegate at the opening meeting of the *Central Verein*, the first German-American Catholic General Assembly met in Chicago on September 9, 1887. Leo XIII sent his blessing; and on the following day, the first assembly of the German-American Priests' Society opened. The priests elected Henry Muehlsiepen president, and William Faerber first secretary. The conferees expressed devotion to the Pope, the parochial school system, and the Catholic press; and furthered the immigrant home in New York, to bear the name of the Holy Father. Father Muehlsiepen reported on the progress of the collection for "Leo House"; and announced a big drive for the autumn months. The vicar-general himself collected forty-five thousand dollars.[51] Father Goller also promoted the project across the country.[52]

The second meeting of the priests' society the following year accepted a resolution for mutual cooperation with other groups. Father Goller had insisted that the members should build a strong German-American organization first. But the more liberal approach passed. Unfortunately, the intransigence of some of the German-American priests, and the lack of sympathetic understanding on the part of the opposing non-Germans, especially Archbishop Ireland of St. Paul, prevented union in annual public manifestations of Catholic faith and purpose.[53]

The German-Americans were barely holding their lines against the attacks of the Americanizers. In 1891, a severe blow shattered their position. Seven countries, including Canada, sent representatives to a Lucerne (Switzerland) meeting of the various St. Raphael Societies for the help of immigrants. United States, unfortunately, had no representatives present. In a statement called the Lucerne Memorial, the delegates made eight major recommendations for dealing with Catholic immigrants to the United States. The memorial asked for separate churches and schools for each nationality, and priests who spoke the respective languages; and thought it desirable to have representatives of each national group in the episcopacy. They asked the Holy See to sponsor mission seminaries to train priests for work among immigrants in the United States, as Bishop Giovanni Scalabrini of Piacenza was doing for Italian immigrants; and to encourage the formation of St. Raphael societies in all Catholic countries of Europe whence the immigrants came.

In itself the document seemed harmless; but reports of it that came to the United States proved disastrous for the German-Americans. A series of cablegrams attributed the memorial to the German nationals alone, omitting the other six nationalities that took part. These cables misquoted the moving spirit behind the memorial, the zealous German layman, Peter Paul Cahensly, and accused him of having consulted Hurd von Schloezer, the Prussian minister to the Holy See, on the document. The wording of these cables, incidentally, developed in the minds of "the Americanist Agent to the Vatican," Monsignor Denis O'Connell, and Monsignor Eugene Boeglin, a Vatican correspondent.[54] Finally the reports accused Cahensly of asking the Pope to appoint bishops of various national ancestry because "the Irish bishops in the United States only nominate Irish priests, who do not know the languages spoken by the immigrants."[55] Cahensly's membership in the Prussian parliament brought the wholly unjustified allegation of political inspiration and pan-Germanism.

Americanist agents in Rome had brought about the misrepresentation of the memorial; the Americanizers in the United States immediately opened fire on it. Bishop John Kain of Wheeling urged Cardinal Gibbons to prepare a counter-memorial in anticipation of the annual meeting of the American archbishops.[56] In an interview, Archbishop Ireland accused Cahensly of trying to harness the Church in America into the service of German immigrants; he blamed the German-language editors for promoting separatism for personal advantage; and accused Cahensly of singular malice in his attempt to picture the American Church as Irish-oriented.[57] In a second interview, Ireland pointed out the similarity in wording of the Lucerne document and the Abbelen memorial that "the German priests of St. Louis, founders of the *Verein* (the German Clerical Society) sent to Rome in 1886."[58] In a letter to Cardinal Gibbons, Ireland condemned what he called the "Lucerne conspiracy" and viewed the memorial as "an effort . . . to dethrone us and to foreignize our country in the name of religion."[59]

In Saint Louis, the *Western Watchman* made a similar charge that the memorial had its origin in the German-American Priests' Society.[60] In answer, Father William Faerber, secretary of the German-American Priests' Society, issued a formal statement in the *Church Progress* disclaiming any direct or indirect connection with the Lucerne Memorial.[61] Cahensly published a refutation of Phelan's charges in the Saint Louis *Westliche Post*. He denied that the memorial had originated in Saint Louis or that the Center Party in Germany had sponsored it. Unless Phelan repudiated his charges, Cahensly thought it

mandatory that he accuse Phelan of slander and untruth.[62]

During the same month, unfortunately, Cahensly made a most imprudent remark in an Associated Press interview. He said: "It is a well-known fact that the Irish in America try to obtain all the bishoprics possible for themselves."[63] Even though actualities seemed to confirm the charge, the reaction was bitter. The legitimate claims of the various national groups in national parishes disappeared in the wake of this European intrusion.

As Archbishop Kenrick's fiftieth episcopal jubilee approached in 1891, Father Francis Goller hit upon the idea of having a noted German historian, Paul Maria Baumgarten, at the time a clerical student in Rome, bring to Archbishop Kenrick the greetings of Pope Leo. At the same time Baumgarten, who considered himself an agent for the Catholics in Germany, could tour the United States and get a first-hand view of the German-American Catholics. Unfortunately, Baumgarten talked too much. One of his "friends" relayed the plans to Monsignor O'Connell, who cabled the information through the Associated Press in a controversial context. As a result, on the day Baumgarten arrived in New York, a New York *Herald* story announced that he had come to implement Cahenslyism.[64]

Archbishop Ireland blamed all the troubles on "the clique of foreign-minded and short-sighted Catholics of Saint Louis." He made it clear that he had in mind the writers for *Church Progress*, edited by the outstanding Catholic layman journalist, Conde Pallen.[65] A protege of the St. Paul prelate, Father John Conway, wrote in the *Review of Reviews* that same year: "The priest promoters of foreignism belong chiefly to the Archdiocese of St. Louis and Milwaukee. St. Louis is even more aggressively foreign than Milwaukee."[66] Conway singled out as "tireless workers in the cause of foreignism Very Reverend H. Muehlsiepen, Vicar-General of St. Louis," and "Reverend W. Faerber of St. Louis, Mo."[67] and called the entire effort "a conspiracy against this country."[68]

Both sides went to extremes. The Americanist forces deliberately misrepresented their opponents. They projected this basically domestic Church struggle into the wider arena of American life to win public and political support for their viewpoint.

The Catholic leaders of the St. Raphael Society, on their part, did not view the United States as a nation with its own characteristic ethos. Amid the intense nationalisms of contemporary Europe, they simply thought of it as a place where Germans, Irish, Bohemians, Italians, Poles, and others currently resided. Ultimately, it would become a "nation." And Rome took an ambivalent official view in this matter: it still treated the United States as a mission country.

The American Catholics of German ancestry found themselves in the jaws of a vice. Their dedication to the cause of a German-American Catholicism seemed to be dangerous and divisive both to the Catholic Church and to the American national community. The backlash to the Lucerne Memorial identified them with the Bismarck empire that had expelled many of them, and threw them on the defensive psychologically. Thus they moved into the last years of the nineteenth century embittered by the controversy, profoundly disheartened and with dwindling self-confidence.[69]

In Saint Louis, further, the German-speaking priests still labored in an uncertain pastoral status.

Chapter 23

The Saint Louis Lion in Winter

Catholic Negroes Advance Briefly

Saint Louis Negro laymen and their white pastor took part in the five Negro Catholic congresses held in successive years beginning in 1889. These initially successful meetings gave great promise of rapid advance of Catholicism among Negroes, and of participation by Negroes in a wide variety of Catholic organizations. The architect of the movement, the energetic and ambitious Daniel Rudd of Cincinnati, a devout Catholic, whose parents had been slaves in Kentucky, owned and edited the *American Catholic Tribune*, the only successful newspaper printed for and by Negro Catholics in the nineteenth century.

Father Augustus Tolton, a native of northeast Missouri, and the only full-blooded Negro priest in the United States, celebrated Mass at St. Augustine's Church in Washington to open the congress on New Year's Day, 1899. Cardinal Gibbons delivered the sermon. The delegates elected Daniel Rudd president, and Lincoln G. Valle, editor of the Saint Louis *Advance*, as first vice-president. Father Ignatius Panken of St. Elizabeth's Parish in Saint Louis spoke at one of the meetings. President Grover Cleveland received the delegates at the White House.[1]

In the most interesting address of the session, Father Tolton told of his boyhood in slavery in northeast Missouri, of his family's escape to Illinois after the death of his father during the Civil War, of his education by the Franciscan Fathers in Quincy, and of his ordination at the Basilica of St. John Lateran in Rome on Holy Saturday, 1886.[2]

This first Catholic congress excited the interest, surprise, and admiration of the Catholic press. Editors saw in it the most remarkable manifestation of racial progress this country had yet seen.[3]

The congress authorized President Rudd to confer with the *Central Verein* on the possibility of holding a general Catholic congress; and thus assured the Negro a place in the first national gathering of Catholic laymen ever held in America. Many white Catholic lay leaders had already been discussing such a meeting. A committee of organization met in the spring, under the leadership of William J. Onahan of Chicago, secretary of the Irish Catholic Colonization Society, Senator Henry Spaunhorst of Saint Louis, head of the *Central Verein*, and Daniel A. Rudd, president of the first Negro Congress. This Catholic congress met on November 11 and 12, 1889. It included a resolution for an improvement of the status of the Negro, and brought Archbishop John Ireland of Saint Paul forward as the great champion of the cause of the Negro among the hierarchy.[4]

Buoyed up by such tokens of good will, the second Negro Catholic Congress met in Cincinnati July 8 - 10, 1890. Once again, a Saint Louisan, Donald McLeod, occupied the position of first vice-president. At the third congress in Philadelphia, January 5 - 7, 1892, no Saint Louisan served in an official capacity, but the still active Lincoln Valle made a practical proposal. The conferees wanted to set up a permanent organization to coordinate the activities of the 150 to 200 Negro Catholic societies in the country. Valle suggested that this have the form of a building and loan association.

Valle also took an active part in the fourth Negro Catholic Congress held in Chicago in conjunction with the World's Fair or Columbian Exposition in 1893. By that time, however, he had left Saint Louis for Chicago. Valle also served on the board of directors of the newly created St. Peter Claver's Catholic Union that began at the Chicago congress. The fifth and last congress took place in Baltimore, Maryland, in October, 1894.

The precise causes of the end of the Catholic Negro Congress movement at this time do not appear in the documents. Catholic churchmen viewed with unease the growth of lay leadership in the late 1880's and early 1890's. The Negro movement seemed a part of this. The Negro delegates themselves displayed a growing militancy; in turn, the clergy reacted to the independence and outspokenness of the Negro delegates. Lastly, the unconcern of some and the racial bias of others played a part. The 1890's, too, were years of growing tension and conflict within the Church in America; and Archbishop Ireland, the Negro's staunchest supporter, soon found himself on the defensive in some of the controversies of the time.

Many of the delegates themselves came to think of the congress movement as futile. They attended in less and less numbers. Some dissension between northern and southern delegates showed itself, especially in the matter of the exposing of discrimination within the Church. The southern delegates strongly opposed open divulging of this aspect of Church life. Northerners felt the truth would free them.

The mood of the country, lastly, was to change dramatically. The decision of the Supreme Court in the case of Plessy vs. Ferguson, (1896) with its specious "separate but equal" doctrine, served to harden and extend that pattern of segregation that the Church so vehemently denounced at the Negro congresses.

The movement did have many pluses, however: the community experienced a sense of identity, a feeling of pride and accomplishment; the educated Negro won a measure of acceptance, an unpatronizing welcome into such organizations as the Catholic Young Men's National Union, the Catholic Press Association, and the Irish Catholic Benevolent Union; and the press showed a genuine concern for the Negro.

Kenrick's Jubilee

As the time approached for Kenrick's fiftieth anniversary as a bishop, the first such occasion in the history of the American Church, Archbishop Patrick Ryan of Philadelphia suggested to Cardinal Gibbons that he ask Rome to make Kenrick a cardinal.[5] Gibbons did not specifically suggest the "red hat," but instead asked Rome for a significant token of recognition for Kenrick's fifty years in the west. "In honoring Kenrick," the Baltimore cardinal stated, "the Pope would be honoring the American Church and the entire nation."[6] Many felt with Ryan that this enlightened and liberal Pontiff who had made Newman a cardinal could have bestowed the "red hat" on the "Lion of Saint Louis," and given him a post of honor for his declining years. Instead Pope Leo sent a portrait of himself as his jubilee gift.

Sixty bishops and archbishops came to Saint Louis for the anniversary on December 1, 1891 — a remarkable percentage of the reigning bishops. Before his sermon at the jubilee Mass, Archbishop Ryan of Philadelphia read the letter of Bishop Rosati introducing Peter Richard Kenrick to the people of Saint Louis fifty years before. Cardinal Gibbons celebrated the Solemn Pontifical Mass. Six hundred guests went to the Lindell Hotel for the banquet. Vicar-General Brady paid tribute to Archbishop Kenrick. The archbishop responded briefly and graciously.

In an eloquent address, Father Francis Goller, pastor of Sts. Peter and Paul's Church, the intellectual leader of the German-American priests of the archdiocese, and a strong advocate of parochial schools, praised Kenrick for his treatment of the immigrants who came into the greater interior of America. Goller spoke of the United States as "the most prosperous, the most enlightened, and the most powerful empire in the world." He recalled the contributions of immigrants to this greatness and their loyalty on many battlefields. "They may still retain a fond regard for the land of their birth ... but far dearer to them than the memories of childhood is the strong and beautiful bride, Columbia, who taught them to walk erect on God's earth in the proud consciousness of manhood."[7]

Goller then distinguished the notion of "country" from that of "nationality." America was a country; but not yet a nation. Rather it was a nation in formation, with a grander destiny ahead than England or any European nation. A century later, an ideal American character would come to be an amalgam of the best qualities of many European nations.

Goller insisted that:

Archbishop Kenrick discovered in Catholic immigration, not a danger to the republic, but a priceless acquisition ... our noble prelate welcomed all the children of the Church, unconcerned about their disparity in language and manner. For he based his hopes of a bright future upon the unifying bond of faith. ... He was firm in exacting what was just, yet ever ready to grant freedom of action in all matters not defined by Divine or human law.[8]

Goller's just and highly restrained presentation did not sit well with everyone in the audience. A call arose for Archbishop Ireland. Later on in the proceedings, members of assembly prolonged a second call, until the archbishop of St. Paul rose briefly at his place. He called for religious loyalty to the Holy See and political loyalty to the nation.

That evening the last great torchlight parade in the history of Saint Louis saw twenty thousand men, eight abreast with banners afloat and bands playing, march for two hours by the new home of Archbishop Kenrick at 3810 Lindell, a gift of laymen for the occasion. Governor David Francis of Missouri and Mayor Edward Noonan of Saint Louis rode in the parade. Archbishop Kenrick and Archbishop Ryan stood at the window of the residence until the last of the marchers were past.

The unbelievable outpouring of respect reflected the admiration of the venerable prelate and the local pride in the strength of the "Old Lion," as well as the amazing organization of the parishes of Saint Louis and the liking of the people of the nineties for a parade.

Many parishes and schools had their own celebration of the occasion. At St. Bridget's Church, Bishop John Hogan of Kansas City spoke. While Archbishop Ryan had praised the characteristics and personality of the jubilarian to his vast audience at the cathedral, Bishop Hogan concentrated on the development of the Church during Kenrick's fifty years. He pointed out that no other bishop in the contemporary English-speaking world had served for fifty years. In, that half century, Chicago had six bishops; Charleston, New Orleans, and Baltimore five each; and New York, Philadelphia, and Detroit four.

In this golden period of fifty years [Hogan went on] the See of Saint Louis has begotten more sees than any we read about in authentic history ... Little Rock was made a see in 1843; Santa Fe and St. Paul in 1850; Leavenworth in 1851; Alton and Omaha in 1857; Green Bay, LaCrosse, St. Joseph and Denver in 1868; Kansas City in 1880; Wichita, Cheyenne, Concordia and Lincoln in 1887.[9]

Of the territory once served by the diocese, Rome had raised Milwaukee, Santa Fe, Chicago, and St. Paul to the status of metropolitan sees. "Five archbishoprics and twenty bishoprics in less than fifty years!" Hogan exclaimed.[10]

While in Saint Louis, the bishops held a meeting. They discussed and condemned the Cahensly Memorial.[11] Cardinal Gibbons invited Archbishop Ireland to explain in detail the plan for cooperation between parochial and public school authorities in the Minnesota towns of Faribault and Stillwater. Ireland stated that the local schools boards leased the parochial school buildings in these two towns from nine to three and hired the Sisters to teach the secular subjects during those hours. The Sisters taught religion in non-tax supported times. Ireland hoped by this method to get the best advantages of public and parochial education for the children of the two towns.

The full story of the "School Controversy" transcends the development of the Saint Louis archdiocese. The reactions of two individuals deserve mention. Ireland's strongest supporter in the hierarchy in this instance, proved to be Bishop John Kain of Wheeling. In a letter to the cardinal prefect of the Propaganda, Giovanni Simeoni, Kain accused the Jesuits of starting a campaign against the archbishop of St. Paul, and of allying themselves with the Germans who resented Ireland's opposition to their anti-American spirit.[12] The archbishop of St. Paul thought the letter so strong that if it did not convince Rome, he considered his cause hopeless.[13]

Kain was to write in support of John Ireland even more strongly two months later: "The fight now is one of vital importance and the Germans and their allies should not be allowed to have things their own way."[14]

Ireland's strongest supporter in the Saint Louis community, Father David Phelan, did not totally approve the secular system of education; but thought it best for a pluralistic society. He deplored denominational education because, in so many cases, it meant inferior education in a foreign language. His views on this matter gained national attention.[15]

A month later Cardinal Gibbons intervened in a domestic affair of the archdiocese of Saint Louis. Father Faerber of St. Mary's of Victories had protested to the

Propaganda in Rome that Kenrick would not allow him to build a new church. The Propaganda notified Gibbons who made an investigation. The cardinal came to the conclusion that the neighboring St. Vincent's Church adequately cared for the needs of the people; and he accused Father Faerber and Vicar-General Muehlsiepen of disturbing the peace of the archdiocese.[16]

Cardinal Gibbons had acted as if Saint Louis had no archbishop, or as if he were incapacitated. But Kenrick still lived and had been working on one last goal — the establishment of a permanent seminary. The Jesuits at Saint Louis University had opened a school of philosophy for its own seminarians in 1889 and planned a theology seminary for the immediate future. When Jesuit Provincial Rudolph J. Meyer discussed the matter of the proposed seminary with Archbishop Kenrick, the archbishop must have given some indication that he intended to use the facilities of Saint Louis University's School of Philosophy for some part of the training of his seminarians; at least so Father Meyer wrote in his last entry in the *Provincial Records*.[17]

Jesuit historian, Father Thomas Hughes, later to gain prominence as the author of *The Jesuits in Federal and Colonial North America*, must have been aware of this consideration of Kenrick. He spoke of the planned seminary at Saint Louis University as becoming a "Louvain of the Midwest."[18] Nothing came, however, of these hopes for a university-based theological center of regional stature.

Instead, in December, 1892, the Vincentian Fathers began an archdiocesan seminary in the old convent of the Visitation at Nineteenth and Cass. At last, the project Kenrick intermittently tried to accomplish had come to be. Ultimately it was to gain nation-wide recognition and to bear his name proudly.

The Lion Seeks a Successor

The archbishops of the United States were to hold their annual meeting on November 17, 1892, in New York City. Kenrick sent Vicar-General Philip Brady as his representative. Father Brady presented a letter of Archbishop Kenrick to the assembled archbishops. In it, the archbishop asked for Father Brady as his coadjutor.

In an answer three days later, Cardinal Gibbons reminded Kenrick that he had not consulted his suffragans; nor had he appointed diocesan consultors as the Third Plenary Council of Baltimore had insisted. In short, he had tried to use the outmoded system that the Third Plenary Council of Baltimore had replaced.[19]

In the meantime, the priests of the archdiocese had taken their own initiative in submitting a list of three names to Cardinal Gibbons and the assembled archbishops. Fathers James and Michael McCabe of Sacred Heart Parish had been classmates of Bishop John Kain of Wheeling, West Virginia, in the ordination class of 1866 at the seminary of St. Mary's in Baltimore. These two men canvassed the priests of the city in the interests of their classmate.[20] Under the secretaryship of Father Ziegler of St. Malachy's Church, the priests sent a letter to Cardinal Gibbons requesting the appointment of a coadjutor with the right of succession, in view of Archbishop Kenrick's declining strength.

In accord with the decrees of the Third Plenary Council of Baltimore (1884) the pastors submitted the names of Bishops John Kain of Wheeling, John Lancaster Spalding of Peoria, and Edward Fitzgerald of Little Rock.[21] The signers of the petition included four rural pastors and all the important pastors of Saint Louis except Jeremiah Harty of St. Leo's, a future archbishop, and Joseph A. Connolly of St. Teresa's, soon to be Kenrick's appointee as vicar-general of the archdiocese. Both refused to sign. The outstanding pastors of foreign language churches, Fathers Goller, Faerber, and Hessoun, joined with Fathers McCabe, Foley, and other Irish-American pastors in submitting the list of three names. The editor of the *Western Watchman*, David Phelan, signed the document and expressed great pleasure in the unanimity of the priests of both German and Irish background in supporting the request.[22]

On the very day the archbishops met in New York, November 17, 1892, Father Ziegler notified all the pastors of the archdiocese of the action the group in Saint Louis had taken. He explained the necessity for haste in transmitting the letter to Cardinal Gibbons. Fathers James McCabe, James McCaffrey, and J. T. Foley co-signed the letter.[23]

Four days before the suffragan bishops of the Saint Louis province were to meet, Cardinal Gibbons wrote Bishop Richard Scannel of Omaha. He suggested the name of Bishop Kain — as the priests of Saint Louis had done.[24] The suffragans recommended Kain as their *second* choice. They placed John Lancaster Spalding first and Francis S. Chatard of Indianapolis third.[25]

When news reached Kain of his possible shift to Saint Louis, he wrote Gibbons of his apprehensions.[26] Nonetheless, Cardinal Gibbons advised Rome that Spalding did not want the office. The Saint Louis priests had not asked for Chatard. Therefore it should be John Kain.[27]

A sad aftermath came in late winter. Vicar-General Philip Brady bore up bravely under his disappointment at the archbishops' reaction in New York. He could even have accepted the ignoring of him by his fellow priests, since they had recommended only men already bishops of dioceses. But when the matter went to Rome, the pastors of Saint Louis had to speak openly about his qualifications.[28] They did not think he was sufficiently endowed for the position. Already weakened by strenuous work and frugal living, Vicar-General Brady died at St. John's parochial residence on March 5, 1893, though only forty-six years of age. Visibly shaken, Archbishop Patrick Ryan came west to preach the sermon at the funeral of his friend and successor.

Archbishops John J. Kain and Peter Richard Kenrick stood far apart in life. Their bodies lay close together in the priests' plot in Calvary Cemetery. (Eldon Arteaga Photo)

Christian Brothers taught at ten grade schools, two academies, and a college in St. Louis. Here Brother Alnoth (left) Father Gaudentius, P.P. and Brother Augustine, sit with fourth graders while the third graders with "burr cuts" sit on the ground.

PART V

John J. Kain:
"Journeyman" Between Giants (1895-1903)

Archbishop John J. Kain, first American-born archbishop of St. Louis, met no welcome from his predecessor, and alienated popular priests who supported his coming from Wheeling, West Virginia.

This issue of the SUNDAY WATCHMAN featured the career of Father Theobald Matthew, Apostle of Temperance. More often, the editor, Father David Phelan, defended Catholics against unjust attacks.

Chapter 24

In the Shadow of the Lion

Kain the Man

The Most Reverend John J. Kain, first American-born bishop of Saint Louis was born in Martinsburg, Virginia, May 31, 1841. At the northern edge of the Shenandoah Valley, about ten miles south of the Potomac River, and sixty miles northwest of Washington, this region became the center of national attention with the ill-starred John Brown's raid on the arsenal at Harper's Ferry, twenty miles form Martinsburg in 1859. By this time young Kain had completed two years at the Sulpician College of St. Charles in Ellicot City, a suburb of Baltimore. One of his classmates bore the identical-sounding, but differently spelled name of John J. Keane. Keane, destined to become the first rector of Catholic University, and archbishop in Dubuque, graduated *summa cum laude*, the future Saint Louis Kain *maxima cum laude*.[1] Two classmates were Saint Louisans, the brothers James and Michael McCabe, later to be pastors of prominent Saint Louis churches.

Graduating from St. Charles College in 1862, the future archbishop of Saint Louis entered St. Mary's Seminary at Baltimore where he pursued his course during the entire length of the war. Archbishop Martin Spalding of Baltimore ordained him a year after Appomatox, on July 2, 1866. His first assignment brought him back to his home ground, now part of the new state of West Virginia.

From his pastorate at St. Peter's Church in Harper's Ferry, he missionized a rural area that north-bound Confederate armies had repeatedly traversed: Lee's in 1862, when he crossed the Potomac and met McClellan's forces at Antietam twelve miles away; Lee's again in 1863, when the Confederate commander moved towards Gettysburg; and Jubal Early's, when Lee sent him on a diversionary raid through the Shenandoah Valley in 1864. Even more important than the devastating military campaigns was the fact that Catholicism had never really been vigorous in the area at any time.

Young Father Kain had not been too strong during his seminary days; but the years on the mission trail in the hill country built up his strength and health. A handsome man, eventually his strength matched his fine frame. Personally frugal, he displayed fair financial ability in building and paying for mission churches in poor areas. He prepared his sermons well and spoke to as many people as possible on the message of the gospel. He never developed any notable oratorical skill, but spoke plainly and directly all his life, with no conscious effort at literary development. Though simple in tastes, he never gained the common touch in dealing with people. He craved warm regard, but his brusque manner offended people.

Bishop of Wheeling

On July 7, 1874, Bishop Richard V. Whelan of Wheeling died. Bishop James Gibbons of Richmond, one of the

suffragans of and soon to be successor to Archbishop James R. Bayley of Baltimore, recommended the thirty-four-year-old country pastor, John J. Kain, as his second choice for the vacant see of Wheeling.[2] When Rome selected Kain for the diocese of Wheeling, the new prelate expressed the hope that "he would be able to consult with Bishop Gibbons 'first of all.' "[3] Gibbons was one of Kain's co-consecrators.

A slight tension soon disturbed the friendship of the two bishops. Without consulting Gibbons, Kain appealed to Rome less than eight months later to have the boundaries of Wheeling made co-terminus with the state of West Virginia. This would have given Richmond more territory but fewer Catholics.

In a letter to the archbishop of Baltimore, Gibbons expressed just irritation. He pointed out that the center of the area in question, Martinsburg, stood ninety-six miles closer to Richmond than to Wheeling; the previous bishop of Wheeling had not questioned the boundaries; and state lines, he insisted, had never previously been a matter of consideration in determining diocesan boundaries.[4] Kain had acted in a "rather untactful way," as John Tracy Ellis, the biographer of Cardinal Gibbons, rightly stated.[5] But Martinsburg was Kain's home town and he wanted it in his jurisdiction; the state of West Virginia came into existence during the war; the question of boundaries had to wait a more calm time; and Gibbons simply erred in his statement that the Church had not regarded state lines in setting up diocesan boundaries. At the Second Provincial Council of Baltimore in 1833, Bishop John England of Charleston had taken this view for granted. A few months later, Kain wrote to Gibbons about asking Rome to "transfer to Richmond that part of Virginia which is now in this diocese."[6]

Rome did not act on the matter. Gibbons readily forgave Kain's breach of protocol. "In the years ahead," Monsignor Ellis wrote, "the two men were even closer friends, and when Gibbons became Archbishop of Baltimore he found no more prompt cooperator in all the business of the Church than he did in John J. Kain."[7] Kain felt close enough to the archbishop to give him a brotherly warning against accepting too many fatiguing lectures. He thought Gibbons looked "worn and overtaxed"; and jokingly reminded him "of the expense of burying Archbishops."[8] In 1880, Gibbons recommended Kain as coadjutor to Archbishop Joseph S. Alemany of San Francisco.[9]

In administering his own diocese, Kain found the Catholic communities in the mining camps, railroad settlements, and mountain villages so poor that he had to seek funds for support outside his areas. Institutionally, Wheeling stood quite low among American dioceses.

At the Third Plenary Council of Baltimore, Bishop Kain served on the Committee on the Catechism; and took part in the discussions on the care of poor immigrants, on procedures in clerical trials, on the distasteful practice in some places of collecting "seat money" on entrance to Sunday Mass, on the promotion of dances as money-raising ventures, and kindred topics.[10] In spite of this, Monsignor Peter Guilday, historian of the Councils of Baltimore, does not mention Kain's name in his discussion of the Third Plenary Council.[11]

Bishop Bernard McQuaid of Rochester regarded Kain as a supporter of the claims of Baltimore, the first American see, over New York, the largest American city and the see of a cardinal, for leadership in the American Church. McQuaid did not like the composition of the Commission on Indian and Negro Missions: James Gibbons, John Kain, and Alfred Curtis, who became Bishop of Wilmington shortly after the Third Plenary Council. All three were from the same general area of the country – the Potomac borderlands, and had received their training at St. Mary's Seminary in Baltimore.[12]

In following out the directive of the plenary council, Gibbons called a meeting with Kain and Curtis in October, 1886, to set down regulations for support of the Indian missions.[13] As chairman of the commission, Gibbons informed all American bishops to take up a collection for the missions on the first Sunday of Lent and established procedures for the management and disbursal of this fund.

When Gibbons became a cardinal the following year (1887), he used the occasion of a public address in Rome to praise the harmonious relations of Church and State in the United States.[14] Up to that time, American Catholics faced a cross-fire of criticism: their Protestant neighbors in the United States questioned their Americanism because they were Catholic; their co-religionists in Europe questioned their Catholicism because they were American. Bishop Kain expressed a common opinion in his congratulations to the new cardinal: Gibbons' praise of American institutions in this context did much to dissipate prejudice against the Church in the United States.[15]

Bishop Kain publicly backed Cardinal Gibbons in his support of the Knights of Labor. Further, he took a unique step forward in the interest of the beleaguered workers by making an anonymous contribution to the fund for striking miners in 1888.[16] A month later Kain joined Gibbons in opposing the condemnation of the theories of Henry George with words of far-sighted wisdom. He expressed his fear that the few bishops who wanted to condemn George were "actuated too much by local consideration." Kain felt ". . . they are narrowing their views on this subject to the horizon of their own immediate surroundings, instead of extending them so as to embrace the best interest of the entire Church of America for the future as well as the present."[17]

While American bishops heatedly discussed secret societies, an unidentified colleague of Bishop Kain sent to Cardinal Simeone, the prefect of the Propaganda, a copy of the *Colorado Catholic* for October 18, 1890. The issue quoted Bishop Kain to the effect that while the Masons of Latin countries were enemies of Christianity, those in English-speaking countries were essentially Christian. As harmless as these words seem today, Simeone regarded the matter as of grave consequence at the time; and asked Gibbons to investigate.[18] The cardinal studied the matter; and reported back to Rome that Kain repudiated the words attributed to him. Gibbons added his own comment that the bishop of Wheeling never compromised Catholic doctrine or interests.[19]

In a letter to a fellow prelate a year later (May, 1892),

Bishop Kain spoke of the bronchial trouble that had begun back in 1880. He had to discontinue the Lenten lectures that he liked to give and his people liked to hear. His doctor had warned him to take care lest he would not be in good health until fall. "My normal condition now is hoarseness," he wrote. "At times, I feel right discouraged."[20] But he was happy about Archbishop John Ireland's successful mission in Rome.[21]

Kain conducted Church affairs as he would have conducted a business. "He had early acquired habits of industry, assiduity and economy that clung to him through life," David Phelan wrote. "He was saving almost to the point of parsimony, but he had his purse ever open to the calls of the orphans and the outcasts of the city's streets. He left $130,000 behind him in Wheeling when he came to Saint Louis to continue the works of charity he had begun."[22]

Such, then, was the story of the man who would leap from Appalachia to the fourth city in the nation, from a minor diocese to one of the mightiest spiritually and institutionally in the western hemisphere. He had supported the Faribault and Stillwater school plans, and now was moving to a center of Catholic education. He had backed Archbishop Ireland against the German-Americans; and now he packed his suitcases for a predominantly German-American city.

And if these obstacles were not enough, the Lion of Saint Louis still lived; and had not asked him to come!

Kain Comes West

By July, 1893, even Chancellor Van der Sanden thought that John Kain was coadjutor of Saint Louis. Kain answered Van der Sanden's letter with the information that a letter had come from Rome for his interim successor in Wheeling, but that Rome had not yet officially notified him of his new position in Saint Louis. Perhaps Kenrick had pigeon-holed the document, Kain wrote in his distinctive but not too easy-to-read script.[23]

The chancellor visited the Old Lion at the episcopal residence on 3810 Lindell. Kenrick had received no documents from Rome. But Van der Sanden found Kenrick well disposed to receive Kain, contrary to any rumors.[24] Kain, thereupon, paid a flying visit to Archbishop Kenrick in early August, 1893, and announced that he would take up permanent residence in Saint Louis the following month.[25]

Twenty-two Saint Louis priests went to Wheeling to accompany the new coadjutor to the West. The people of Wheeling gave Kain a torchlight procession, a resounding farewell,[26] and a money gift, surprisingly large for so small a diocese.[27] On his arrival the *Western Watchman* carried his picture,[28] and welcomed him to Saint Louis with these words:

Archbishop Kain is now among us . . . He comes a stranger to our clergy and people but it can scarcely be said that any bishop is a stranger who comes in the name of the Holy Father. Archbishop Kain is a man of mature years and has had a quarter of a century's experience . . . He comes to us with the best recommendation any man could bring, the regret and blessings of the people he leaves behind.[29]

Archbishop Ryan and Vicar-General Brady had resided in their own homes or rectories. They paid weekly visits to the archbishop on business of the diocese. The seminary prepared rooms for Kain and expected to house him. Instead the coadjutor moved into Kenrick's residence at 3810 Lindell. He proved to be an unwelcomed guest.

Shortly after arriving in Saint Louis, Coadjutor Kain went to Chicago with Fathers M. J. McCabe and J. G. Foley to attend the banquet of the St. Mary's Alumni Association of Baltimore,[30] the Catholic Congress, and the reception for Cardinal Gibbons and Archbishop Satolli, first apostolic delegate in residence in this country. "After Cardinal Gibbons and Monsignor Satolli," the *Western Watchman* remarked, "the prelate who attracted the most general attention was the new Archbishop of Saint Louis."[31]

In the meantime, back in River City, the Old Lion was again rampant. While Coadjutor Kain was in Chicago, Kenrick named the pastor of St. Theresa's Church, Father J. J. Connolly, vicar-general of the archdiocese in place of the late Philip Brady.[32] An editorial writer gave the opinion that Connolly should have paid no attention to Kenrick's appointment as Father Harty had done in a similar instance a few years before. Kain ignored Connolly,[33] but for the moment, Kenrick had checkmated his would-be coadjutor.

The affair confused and disedified the people. To add bitterness, public discussion in the newspapers was sharp. One priest spoke of Kenrick's traditional aloofness from his priests; and the resultant unconcern of the priests for the Old Lion.[34] Another spoke of Kenrick's senility, and stated: "If Archbishop Kain came here with only the powers of an ordinary coadjutor, he did an unwise thing. . . . He may very soon be pervaded with the desire to follow the refrain of the old anti-bellum song, 'Carry Me Back to Old Virginny.' "[35]*

A layman spoke of the scandal in all the bickering and maneuvering that had gone on since Kenrick's jubilee.[36] He criticized the priests for having tried to set up their own rulers. And concluded: "There is in some of the criticisms of the Archbishop absolute brutality."[37]

Kenrick Seminary had opened classes for forty-two students on September 14; on September 21, Coadjutor Kain made his first public appearance in Saint Louis at the dedication of the new seminary. Several bishops and two hundred priests attended dinner after the ceremony.[38]

Coadjutor Kain heard that Rome had sent faculties making him apostolic administrator; but these had not yet come; naturally he was worried. Archbishop Ryan had spoken to his old friend Kenrick about sharing powers with the coadjutor; and arranged for the two to dine together;[39] but Kain had little confidence in Ryan's intervention. "The truth is," Kain wrote to Cardinal Gibbons, "Archbishop R. is too timid — perhaps I might put it — too reverential."[40]

On his part, Archbishop Ryan advised Gibbons to do nothing for the moment.[41] Matters grew worse during the fall. Kenrick's health steadily declined. In December (1893), Kain asked Gibbons to intercede in his behalf.[42] Now Gibbons moved decisively. He urged Miecislaus Cardinal Ledochowski, successor to Cardinal Simeone as prefect of the Propaganda in Rome, to grant Kain more power. Kenrick no longer had the strength to administer the diocese, Gibbons insisted, but obstinately held tight control.[43]

Even before Gibbons had written, Rome had acted. By a decree of December 14, 1893, signed by Cardinal Ledochowski, prefect of the Congregation, Rome made Kain coadjutor of Saint Louis and titular archbishop of Oxyrhynchia. When Kain received this decree, he notified Gibbons of the fact.[44] At the same time Ledochowski asked Gibbons to induce Kenrick to cede the administration into the hands of his coadjutor.[45] Kain now had a little more power, but he was not yet in full command. He was still in the embarrassing position of writing to Chancellor Van der Sanden for his six months' salary of a thousand dollars. And he had to write his letters on the old archiepiscopal letterhead.[46]

Two decades before, Kain had begun his career in Wheeling by provoking his neighbor, Bishop James Gibbons of Richmond, soon to become the world-famous Cardinal Gibbons of Baltimore. Now in 1894, before he had secured his position in Saint Louis, he tangled with one of the toughest in-fighters in the Church of God, the "Western Watchman" himself, Father David Phelan. In a letter of February 17, 1894, Coadjutor Kain called Phelan's attention to Decrees number 230 and 231 of the Third Baltimore Council. He ordered Phelan to desist from "scandalous criticism of the Sacred Hierarchy and their administration," or face censures.[47] Kain ordered Chancellor Van der Sanden to deliver the letter in person and to keep the matter strictly confidential.[48]

Phelan retorted that the new archbishop had been born in a slave state; and that it would take some time for the people of Saint Louis to teach him how free men lived.[49]

A month later, Coadjutor Kain sent a circular for all the priests of the archdiocese to read from the pulpit. The coadjutor denounced Phelan's paper as "unfit to be introduced into our Catholic families . . . subversive of ecclesiastical discipline and even dangerous to the faith of our Catholic people."[50] "The Reverend Editor," Kain went on, "defiantly denies our authority in the premises."[51] The coadjutor wrote an apology for Phelan to sign. In it, the editor "publicly disavowed any utterance derogatory of the person or sacred office of any Bishop . . . and recalled any reflection on the administrator of this diocese." Phelan changed a few words and signed his name.[52]

Before the end of April Kain removed the censure, "inasmuch as the Reverend David S. Phelan, editor and proprietor of the *Western Watchman* had fully complied with our injunctions and has, in a manner creditable to himself as a priest and the responsible manager of a Catholic newspaper, published the apology and retractation which we felt it our duty to require."[53]

This incident served to turn the attention of the archdiocese to the man who four months later was to gain national notoriety by "submarining" the most formidable group of nativists since the Know-Nothings of pre-Civil War days.

The Western Watchman Smokes Out the APA

During the early nineties, a new surge of Nativism spread through the Midwest. The causes were many. At its base lay the hereditary prejudice that had prevailed in much of English-speaking society since the days of Queen Elizabeth. In the 1890's other factors contributed to ill-feeling: conflict over the use of funds for students in schools under religious auspices; dissatisfaction with the two older parties and the subsequent rise of a third party, the Populists; and the economic depression that began in the summer of 1893. Further, certain actions of Catholics

---

*Perhaps this remark had an extra edge for Coadjutor Kain. During his seminary days his classmates called him "Old Virginny," and John J. Keane "My Maryland." (Shea, *The Two Kenricks*, p. 398.)

caused alarm among Protestants. Several Irish-American politicians engaged in questionable party schemes in various cities. The Catholic sponsorship of parades, especially during 1892, the occasion of the 400th anniversary of Columbus' voyage of discovery, seemed to many Protestants a sign of "military preparation." The arrival of the papal delegate, Monsignor Satolli, further aroused the Protestants.[54]

Externally the American Protective Association — as the new Protestant organization called itself — had political motives and political purposes. Many of its members were mainly bent on winning public office. But the association had hidden purposes. These were all too evident in the oath its members took. Washington Gladden, the contemporary social observer, summarized the APA oath in these terms: "I will do all the hurt I can to Roman Catholics unless it involves hurting myself."[55]

Predominantly a midwestern organization, totalling at its peak in the mid-nineties about a million members, the APA grew strong in central Illinois, southern Iowa, eastern Kansas, and northern Missouri.[56] It dominated Kansas City and Louisville, and grew strong in Saint Louis.

The APA used the printing press, the lecture platform, and political arena. The Nativists brought out all the time-tested weapons, such as *Maria Monk's Awful Disclosures*, talks by ex-priests, and bogus documents of various kinds. A counterfeit encyclical of the Pope called for the wholesale slaughter of Protestants "on or about the feast of St. Ignatius in the year of Our Lord 1893."[57] As a result of all this agitation, many APA members gained political positions, Catholics lost jobs, certain Protestants renewed their ancestral fear of Catholicism, and strangely, the Republican Party suffered.

In some ways, the whole movement eventually boomeranged in favor of the Catholics. Many Catholics became more alert to their rights and privileges; and many American citizens of other denominations found the APA attacks so distasteful that they came out in support of the Catholics. These included Jewish editors, Protestant ministers, state legislators, public officials, and Negro journalists. Negro Protestants almost universally refused to participate with their co-religionists in the attacks on the Catholic Church. The Catholic members of the Democratic party drove APA-ism out of its ranks. In some cities Catholics demonstrated against anti-Catholic lecturers and engaged in counter-movement in various ways. The chief weapon, however, was the press and the open forum.

The rise of the APA in Saint Louis gave occasion for a similar rise to national fame of editor Father David Phelan. Some of Phelan's friends found that several APA secretaries were willing to provide them with copies of the rosters for a slight fee. In this way, Father Phelan gained access to all but one list of memberships.[58] That one came into the hands of a group of young men from Holy Name Parish when the secretary dropped it as he fled their threats.[59] During August and September, 1894, Father Phelan listed the occupations of the Nativists.[60] The Carondelet Council No. 9 contained such interesting names as Murphy and Marquette. Phelan could not refrain from publishing the roster of that council again the following week.[61]

Some neutral observers shouted: "Foul," but Phelan did not desist. Others charged that Phelan's friends had burglarized the APA offices. Phelan responded: "In every case these burglaries were committed from the inside."[62] To the claim that his "minions" had terrorized the APA, Phelan answered: "The *Watchman* has no minions but greenbacks."[63]

The APA could not stand the light and the heat. In a short time Phelan had brought an end to the effectiveness of the Saint Louis affiliates of the American Protective Association.

The tornado of 1896 chose its targets capriciously: it leveled St. Francis de Sales Church but left the school intact.

Chapter 25

Kain Becomes Archbishop

Kain Acts

When Kenrick survived the next winter, Kain reached a point for drastic action in May, 1895. The coadjutor felt that unless he gained clear legal title to archdiocesan property, Kenrick's relatives might attempt to claim certain items. Kain consulted lawyers. They advised him to go to court while Kenrick lived; and, if possible, to go as archbishop. In letter of May 3, 1895, Kain asked Rome to make him archbishop, but to say nothing of the property question.[1]

Cardinal Ledochowski notified Kain on May 25, 1895, that by the decree of December 15, 1893, Rome had intended to give him all faculties previously held by Kenrick.[2] This would, in fact, have made Kain administrator-archbishop. Slightly over two weeks later Ledochowski sent the decree naming Archbishop Peter Richard Kenrick titular of Marcianapolis.[3]

Kain instituted court proceedings on July 27, 1895, to establish his right to administer the business and properties of the Saint Louis archdiocese.[4] Kain arrayed a group of prominent priests and laymen in his name "versus Peter R. Kenrick." Kain's lawyers could get no assurance from Kenrick's doctors that the "Old Lion's" health was as bad as some claimed. The lawyers, in fact, feared that Kenrick might have carried the day in court.[5]

But Kenrick ignored the matter.

Kain had won, but at great cost. His action against the aging "Lion" provoked much criticism. He had had to take action for the good of the archdiocese; yet any action would have been unpopular, while inaction might have been disastrous. Kenrick had built up an immigrants' bank that could loan a huge sum to the city in time of crisis; he had accepted large gifts for the expansion of the diocese; he had administered vast holdings; he regarded the Church property as his own; but, at the same time, he took it for granted that the Church of God owned him; he had given his life for it totally. Everything he cared for belonged to it.[6] Kenrick had left no money to friends or relatives — even his cousins Lucy and Lizzie Eustace who had come from Ireland in the 1870's to take charge of the archiepiscopal household.[7]

During the next few years, cousins of Archbishop Kenrick were to question Kain about this; some suggested that the new archbishop had taken advantage of Kenrick's declining faculties. The new archbishop of Saint Louis tried to settle these matters with a token grant of two hundred dollars each to relatives who spoke of specific needs, such as the education of a son or mounting hospital bills. One or two of the relatives did not even spell the Old Lion's name correctly. In one instance, Archbishop Kain asked Canon John O'Hanlon, who had served in the Saint Louis archdiocese at mid-century, then returned to Dublin, to act as intermediary with Lucy Eustace Gormley and her family in Ireland. These efforts of the archbishop merely served to uncover more relatives during the ensuing years.[8]

Kain still had no home. He took breakfast and handled official calls at the archiepiscopal residence, then left for the day, accepting the hospitality of one pastor after another. Archbishop Kenrick's permissiveness and his delegation of authority to his vicar-general on the one hand, and the freer spirit that came down from frontier times, had allowed the pastors of the archdiocese to exercise a great deal of initiative and self-reliance. It was almost inevitable that Archbishop Kain would have to rule with a little more surveillance of all diocesan activities. Unfortunately, he was not able to do this with sufficient tact.

Problems — Parochial and Personal

He had governed a diocese with thirty-five priests — thirty-one diocesan and four Capuchin — four ecclesiastical students, sixty-four churches, four sisterhoods, and a Catholic population estimated at a mere twenty thousand.[9] In Saint Louis he had under his charge 227 diocesan priests and 127 priests of various religious communities. One hundred and sixty-five churches had resident priests. There were sixty-nine mission churches, a total of 234 church buildings and twenty-six mission stations in the archdiocese. Priests said Mass at fifty-four chapels connected with religious houses. The seminary had seventy-two ecclesiastical students; each of five religious orders conducted a seminary of its own with the total of 265. Of the 165 parishes, 135 had parochial schools with an attendance of 28,527. In place of his former small diocese, Kain now had control of a giant with an estimated Catholic population of two hundred thousand.[10]

The seminary collection on Christmas Day, 1895, gives an indication of the relative generosity of the parishes at the time. These were the top eight: 1. St. Teresa's, $466.60; 2. St. Bridget's, $375.00; 3. St. Alphonsus, $333.85; 4. St. Francis Xavier's, $300.12; 5. St. Vincent's, $238.90; 6. Sts. Peter and Paul, $215.00; 7. St. Malachy's, $200.00; and 8. St. Kevin's, $190.00.[11]

During these years, both Kain and Kenrick suffered from an unfortunate system that provided no graceful and automatic method of retirement. The fame of Kenrick outlived the unpleasantness of these late years. Kain never got over the unhappy legacy.

Archbishop Kain had a tendency to nervousness and impatience that showed up often in church functions. Many stories long made the rounds among the older residents of Saint Louis. One brought him into misunderstanding with the priest probably most responsible for his coming to Saint Louis. Kain's classmate, James McCabe, had a rich voice, played the organ well, and directed the Priests' Choir at all clerical funerals. On Archbishop Kain's first visit to Sacred Heart parish, Father McCabe lead his parish choir in a beautiful and long rendition of a favorite hymn. The archbishop fumed for a few minutes

Father David Phelan, editor of the WESTERN and SUNDAY WATCHMAN, gathers his flock at Our Lady of Mount Carmel Church in Baden for the annual parish picnic. He was the most outspoken Catholic editor of all time.

on the altar, then interrupted the hymn with the words: "That's enough!"[12]

David Phelan wrote:

Archbishop Kain was not a man to surround himself with a coterie of friends. He had no favorites in the diocese. The men he advanced were those who seldom darkened his door, and were as indifferent to his friendship as he was to theirs. He did not understand that the honor of the sanctuary should follow personal regard. *The men who did most for him were the men who received least from him.*[13]

Kain's actions repeatedly verified Phelan's statement.

It is to be regretted, [Monsignor Rothensteiner wrote] that the Archbishop, who really wanted to be a father and friend to his priests, should, through a wrong interpretation of this spirit, have been brought into open collision with some of his best and some of his ablest priests.[14]

Another of these was Father Charles Ziegler, the pious and gentle man who had hosted the priests' meeting that had asked for Kain. Less than a year after Kain became archbishop of Saint Louis, the archdiocese prepared for the visit of the apostolic delegate, the newly created Cardinal Francisco Satolli. Satolli was expected to bring the archiepiscopal pallium to Saint Louis. Kain desired to make the occasion a memorable one. In a meeting of his priests at the seminary on February 7, 1896, he requested the assembly to hold a banquet for his visiting Eminence. Father Ziegler, pastor of St. Malachy's and former secretary of Kenrick, rose and asked the archbishop whether or not he wanted his priests to offend against the spirit of Lent by attending a banquet.

Caught off guard and a bit irritated, Archbishop Kain made a few slighting remarks about the "Old Lion," who lay dying at the time.

In response, Father Ziegler exclaimed, "I hope the pallium celebration will be a great success, but the reception to the Cardinal a great fiasco."

In this heated moment the assembled priests voted on whether or not to hold the banquet. Forty-three voted with the archbishop, thirty-seven with Father Ziegler.

Someone close to the gentle priest heard him say: "If Cardinal Satolli comes now, we should not hold a banquet, but a black fast."[15]

The Passing of the Lion

Archbishop Peter Richard Kenrick died the next month, on March 4, 1896. Men of the St. Vincent de Paul Society formed a guard of honor at his bier. A stream of people passed through the Cathedral for seven days. The outpouring of respect caused a local newspaperman to write: "The people revered him as much as the Sovereign Pontiff."[16]

Seven archbishops with a cardinal at their head, thirty bishops and three hundred priests attended the funeral. Cardinal Gibbons presided at the Solemn Requiem in the Cathedral. Archbishop Kain knelt in the sanctuary, along with Archbishops Patrick Ryan of Philadelphia, Patrick Feehan of Chicago, John Ireland of St. Paul, William Elder of Cincinnati, and Frederick Katzer of Milwaukee. In the funeral sermon, Archbishop Patrick Ryan, deeply affectionate by nature, showed his warm regard for his father and mentor. Commentators presumed that it would be the last time the eloquent Archbishop Ryan spoke in the city where he had devoted thirty years of loyal service.[17]

The church bells of the city had rung out for fifteen minutes at the beginning of the Requiem Mass. Again, at ten they pealed for a quarter of an hour. As the funeral procession moved slowly up Walnut to Twelfth, over to Pine, then west to Grand, and north toward Calvary

Cemetery, churches on the route tolled their bells in final tribute.[18]

A man to match the mighty Mississippi, Peter Richard Kenrick had served the Church in the West during a significant half-century. He had come to Saint Louis shortly after the election of General William Harrison as ninth president of the United States. He was still archbishop of Saint Louis after the general's grandson, the twenty third president, Benjamin Harrison, had finished his term. Kenrick had gone to Saint Louis in the days of Clay, Webster, and Calhoun. He passed through the era of Abraham Lincoln into the term of Grover Cleveland. He saw the United States move from a frontier nation to the threshold of imperial power. His years stretched from those of pioneer bishops Flaget and Loras to the new age of Ireland and Gibbons.

He had inherited a vast territory, a diocese with more priests than any in the country, with religious institutions solidly established, congregations and orders flourishing, a beautiful cathedral, a great percentage of Catholic people; but with heavy debts and a flock not yet trained to support the shepherds or the sheep-fold.

The city had been the hub of western development in that heyday of western expansion. A constant growth through immigration marked the entire fifty years that he was in the city. Schools and parishes expanded, while the diocese itself grew smaller, as one after another new western diocese took birth. A diocese that had been almost half a nation became a little more than half of one state; but as it lessened in size, it grew in strength. While no longer the metropolis of the Midwest, Saint Louis was still fourth city of the nation, and the largest city in the trans-Mississippi region. It would so remain for several decades to come.

If one might pinpoint significant aspects of Saint Louis Catholicism that owed themselves to Peter Richard Kenrick it would be his early concern for the diversity of immigrants and his willingness to let the diocese grow. He allowed the various nationalities to retain their language, their characteristics, their national customs, their neighborhood security, until such time as they could more orderly move into wider English-speaking society. He set up a separate but scarcely equal parish for Negro Catholics. He promoted a bank that helped the immigrant in many ways. He approved the first St. Vincent de Paul conference in the nation. He did not initiate many movements, but allowed freedom for growth. He welcomed many religious congregations to the diocese. He refused admission to only one; but that one was to come in later.

The diocese would have moved forward in the same way, for the most part, had Rosati's earlier choices, John Timon or Peter Verhaegen, become bishop in the early 40's. Timon and Verhaegen may have been closer to the people because of their previous ministries in the region and their more outgoing personalities. Both would have taken a more forthright stand on the Civil War issue, since they were staunch Unionists; and Timon would have done more for the Negroes. Had Archbishop Ryan succeeded to the see of Saint Louis when Kenrick reached the age of seventy-five, he would have given stronger impetus to religious education, settled the national parish controversy, and forestalled the unhappy incidents of Kenrick's late years. Great orator that he was, Ryan would have given more personal direction to the spiritual development of the people of Saint Louis.

But few doubt that Kenrick was a greater individual. His very longevity and durability made him a formidable figure. His courage at Vatican Council gained him a reputation as "the greatest churchman of the Americas."[19] In a changing world, he was as consistent as the Ozark Mountains. His influence on the people of Saint Louis was indirect. "The morality of the people," a Saint Louis newspaper stated, "received a tonic from his holy and devoted presence that has had appreciable affect on the manners and motives of our people."[20] His influence on his priests was more direct.

The imprint of his religious character has long been noticeable in the clergy he reared up around him. Anywhere in the United States that you saw a clergyman trained under the eye of Peter Richard Kenrick, you might know him from the unconscious reflection of the great churchman's manner.[21]

Most Reverend Peter Richard Kenrick ... [Archbishop Ryan said at the time] will survive in the ecclesiastical history of America as in many respects the greatest of her bishops. In profound and varied learning, in marked individuality and fortitude of character and in enlightened and tender piety, and withal in practical judgment and financial ability and foresight — in each of these qualities he was the equal of any one of them; while in their unusual combination he stood alone.[22]

One need not like what he did at all times; but one has to stand in awe that the man rarely showed weakness. He abhorred ecclesiastical politics. He stood above secular politics. He brought honor to Saint Louis and to the American hierarchy. The Church of God would not see another like him for a long time.

Chapter 26

In "Tornado Alley"

Kain Assumes Command

Cardinal Satolli came to Saint Louis a month after Kenrick died. Archbishop Kain welcomed him. Father David Phelan preached the sermon at the Solemn High Mass on Thursday, April 9. The high point of the apostolic delegate's visit turned out to be his gracious visit to Kenrick's grave. This action seemed to heal many wounds – but not all.

A month later, on May 10, 1896, Cardinal Gibbons returned to the old Cathedral. In the presence of twenty-five archbishops and bishops he celebrated Pontifical High Mass and placed the pallium on the shoulders of Archbishop Kain. After the ceremony, to the surprise of many, a delegation of laymen including R. C. Kerens, Julius Schotten, Louis Fusz, and State Senator H. J. Spaunhorst, and headed by Congressman Richard Graham Frost, scion of several distinguished laymen of the city, welcomed the new archbishop in the name of the people of the archdiocese.[1]

The archbishop replied graciously to Congressman Frost; but commented on the absence of many priests of the archdiocese – even though three hundred priests were in attendance. "Their very absence," Kain remarked, "is a testimony to that firm devotion to duty." Kain also took the occasion of the crowded conditions in and near the Cathedral to recall Kenrick's wish for a new cathedral.[2]

Father Edward Fenlon, founder and pastor of Visitation Parish, in the new west end of the city, toasted the archbishop and clergy of Saint Louis at the banquet at Kenrick Seminary, following the investiture. He rose to the defense of the priests of the area with the words: "The priesthood of this diocese, diocesan as well as regular, is not surpassed in this country."[3] He singled out, but did not mention by name, the archbishops of Philadelphia (Ryan), Chicago (Feehan), Dubuque (John Hennessey), the bishops of Wichita (John J. Hennessey), and Lincoln (Bonacum), and the late bishop of Green Bay (Melcher).

In the same month of May a disastrous tornado roared through the southside of Saint Louis. On its deadly way it destroyed a number of religious buildings, including St. Francis de Sales and St. John Nepomuk's churches. The total archdiocesan property loss reached a half-million dollars.

The Third Archdiocesan Synod

In September of that memorable year (1896), Archbishop Kain summoned a diocesan synod – the third in Saint Louis' history, and the first since 1850. In preparation for the synod, he had written to the Sacred Congregation of the Holy Office on the powers of plenary or provincial councils. He asked, first, if bishops in such councils had legislative power. To this Rome answered affirmatively. And, second, if the decrees of such councils, after approval by the Holy See, had validity only when incorporated into the statutes of the respective diocese. To this second question Rome gave a resounding no. Validity did not require such incorporation.

Buoyed up by this response from Rome, Kain introduced the legislation of the Third Baltimore Council of 1884, especially the requirement that Phelan fought so hard against, namely that each pastor establish a parochial school near his church within two years. Kain set up a school commission for the purpose of unifying the educational methods of the schools and introducing a uniform series of textbooks, thus establishing the parochial school system of the archdiocese.

Archbishop Kain granted to the German, Polish, and Bohemian parishes all rights and privileges of English-speaking parishes and defined the situation of a person with continental background who wished to affiliate with the English-speaking parish in his neighborhood. The synod enjoined every pastor to celebrate the Forty Hours adoration annually, recommended the erection of the Sodality of the Blessed Virgin, the Association of the Holy Family, and a Conference of St. Vincent de Paul for the poor in all parishes. The synod also declared that newspaper attacks by Catholic writers, lay or cleric, on ecclesiastical persons, especially on bishops in regard to the government and administration of their dioceses, were scandalous acts worthy of severest censure. Archbishop Kain insisted on systematic annual reports from all the parishes. The synod forbade the celebration of mixed marriages in private homes – a decision that brought many complaints in the succeeding years.

The synod also decided to submit for Rome's approval a richer calendar of Church feasts that accorded more with the liturgical customs of other countries. The Congregation of Rites was to approve this proposal the following spring.[4]

The synod confirmed Father Henry Muehlsiepen, now a Monsignor, as vicar-general – though it was clear his powers would be less than before, since Archbishop Kain would take a more active part in routine church affairs; and also confirmed Father Henry Van der Sanden as chancellor of the archdiocese.

Thus Kain resolved the two pressing problems of the late Kenrick years: the implementation of the decrees of the Third Baltimore Council and the rights and duties of the foreign-speaking congregations. Unfortunately, the archbishop pulled a tactical error in choosing the archdiocesan consultors. He rejected the two who received the most votes from their fellows – Monsignor William Walsh and Father Francis Goller. The archbishop explained that he intended to name these two "irremovable rectors," and that the six consultors and the fifteen irremovable rectors would then form an electoral assembly of twenty-one. This explanation satisfied few.

As pastor of Sts. Peter and Paul, the premiere parish of south Saint Louis, Father Goller has regularly appeared in these pages as a champion of parochial schools and spiritual guide of various religious congregations. He was at that time hoping to invite the Society of Mary to his parish. Monsignor Walsh, too, was a colorful and formidable personality. He had done colonization work in central Missouri before the Civil War. In 1862 Kenrick had called him to St. Bridget's on Jefferson Avenue. He gained a reputation as a friend of the poor and an enemy of dance halls. He spoke against them from the pulpit almost every Sunday. He built so spacious a rectory that people dubbed it "Father Walsh's Hotel." Archbishop Kain had already recommended him along with Father Muehlsiepen for the title and the purple of the Roman Monsignori — a dignity the new archbishop had just introduced into the archdiocese.[5] The rejection of these two outstanding priests badly hurt Kain.

The *Church Progress* for September 12 carried a criticism of this action of the archbishop. A query in the *American Ecclesiastical Review* pursued the matter further. The writer wondered if the exclusion of Monsignor Walsh was "based on positive law or only on special agreement of the clergy." The editor of the *Review* responded that it was not based on general or positive laws. The archbishop could do what he wanted. But the exclusion did not bind his successor.[6]

Father John M. May, secretary of the synod, immediately sent a long letter explaining the reasons for the archbishop's action. This proved another tactical error. The answer to the first communique stood on the ground of what a prelate could rightly do. The second analyzed what he ought to do. The editors answered Father May:

We should be quite in accord with the view expressed, if it could be established that the aim of securing a large electoral voting capacity is of greater importance to the Diocese than that of securing Consultors who represent the spirit and voice of the clergy. The office of Consultors is supposed to carry with it very weighty responsibilities and proportionate influence.... They are supposed, therefore, to be selected from the clergy of first rank in point of piety, zeal, learning, practical experience and ecclesiastical observance. The names proposed by the clergy for such an office, must, we suppose, largely indicate the possession of these qualities....[7]

This controversy clouded the picture, but did not prevent the third synod from becoming a landmark in the development of the archdiocese. The synod gave strong support to parochial education. It set down principles for the operation of the national parishes and the gradual assimilation of the immigrants. For twenty years more, public opinion in Saint Louis looked favorably on the cultural plurality of its varied peoples.[8] Archbishop Kain wisely read the spirit of the times.

Interestingly, Father Phelan carried the story of the synod on the *last* page of his paper. Father Walsh's monsignorship formed his front-page story.[9]

Kain issued a pastoral letter a month after the synod. Printed in English and in German, this message discussed Holy Mass, hearing the word of God, Christian burial, the sacraments, and Christian education. It set down regulations governing mixed marriages as outlined at the synod. It listed forbidden societies: the Masons, the Odd Fellows, the Knights of Pythias, and the Sons of Temperance. It prohibited Saturday night dances under church auspices, but tolerated fairs and picnics. It forbade sacred concerts in churches because of the danger of irreverence and levity — a sin generations of clerics condemned in a people who did not know what the word meant.[10]

The pastoral outlined the plans for the new cathedral.[11] The archdiocese had begun solicitation of funds for the site, but the tornado of the previous summer had stopped this. The archbishop himself was to use his own

Dr. Hynek Dostal, editor of *The Voice*, led Bohemian laymen during many years in the late 19th and early 20th centuries and worked for self-government in his native land.

personal estate, a ten thousand dollar departure gift from the priests and people of Wheeling, to purchase a lot near the cathedral site, and he designated this property by will to the cathedral board as his personal contribution to the great project.[12]

The message discussed the orphanage for boys, opened a few years earlier on Grand at Itaska, through the generosity of Mrs. Eliza Patterson. The girls of St. Mary's Orphanage that stood for fifty years on Tenth and Biddle, the gift of Ann Mullanphy Biddle, had thereupon moved to the boys' former quarters at Fifteenth and Clark, where they were to stay for four years until an anonymous benefactor provided a new home at Emerson and Harney on the north side. Orphan children, incidentally, seemed to be the only group who could penetrate the archbishop's gruff exterior; and he, in turn, never was more at home with any other company.[13]

In the fall following the synod, the decree against mixed marriages in private homes brought fire from some prominent members of Saint Louis society. Before this attack died down, preparations for a church wedding that involved two well-known Catholic families brought further voices into the brouhaha. A news feature in the Saint Louis *Star* for November 13, 1896, began: "These are the days when some of the prettiest mouths in Saint Louis are saying some of the awfullest things about His Grace, Archbishop John J. Kain."[14]

The writer told the entire story in the form of a play. The three principal characters were Archbishop Kain, groom-to-be Howard Benoist, a member of an old Saint Louis family, and his prospective bride, Agnes Foy, daughter of Peter Foy, a prominent Saint Louis businessman and nationally known Catholic lay leader, who had served as president of the Missouri Historical Society. The request of the families that Archbishop Patrick Ryan have the wedding brought this alleged retort from Archbishop Kain: "I suppose there is nobody in Saint Louis good enough to marry Miss Foy."

Miss Foy offered an alternative suggestion. She wanted Father Daniel McErlane, assistant priest and popular confessor at the Saint Francis Xavier parish. Father McErlane, incidentally, was gaining great fame as chaplain of the city jail at the time. The archbishop insisted that canon law required the pastor, Father Henry Bronsgeest, to conduct the ceremony. Miss Foy then asked if the organist might play the Wedding March from *Lohengrin*.

"That's a pagan piece of music," retorted the Archbishop.

The newspaper writer concluded his playlet with the remark that the Benoists and the Foys "had everything they didn't want and nothing they did."[15]

Shortly after the Foy affair, Archbishop Kain had to set the record straight in a matter of wider ecclesiastical concern. At the annual meeting of the American archbishops, he served as secretary and as chairman of the Committee for the Revision of the Catechism. The archbishops discussed, among other topics, support of the Catholic University of America in Washington. As a result of this discussion, the acting president of the university, P. J. Garrigan, sent a Christmas appeal for funds to the Catholics of America. In this letter, Garrigan suggested that the archbishops had authorized such an appeal. As secretary of the archbishops' conference, Kain wrote a blunt response to Garrigan in early January. Kain denied

that the archbishops had voted for this collection; and enclosed a copy of the minutes of their meeting to prove this.[16]

Parochial Growth

Archbishop Kenrick had occasionally given thought to a new site for the Saint Louis Cathedral, but had taken no steps to accomplish this project after securing a corner piece of property twenty-five years before. Archbishop Kain took action. He announced the site of the new cathedral as the northwest corner of Lindell and Newstead. He put the organization of the new parish in the hands of Father James McCaffrey, who had served at old St. Patrick's for over a third of a century.

Planning the new cathedral was not the only parish development during the Kain years. Franciscan Fathers took over direction of St. Francis Borgia Church in Washington, Missouri, and its satellite rural parishes, formerly in the charge of the Jesuits. Nineteen new parishes grew up in the city: ten for English-speaking people, three for Italians, two for Germans, and one each for Bohemian, Slavic, and Syro-Maronite congregations. The decline in the percentage of growth of new German parishes indicates two factors: first, the assimilation of second generation Germans into the English-speaking Catholic community; and secondly, the shrinkage of immigration from Germany after the end of the *Kulturkampf*.

Immigration to America in the twenty years before

Father Joseph Hessoun, shown here (left) with his first-graders, made St. John Nepomuk's, the first Bohemian parish in the United States, the center of a wide cultural and religious program that influenced Bohemian immigrants throughout the nation.

World War I (1894-1914) came heavily from the empires of Austria-Hungary and Russia. These newer immigrants, for the most part Catholics, did not come to Saint Louis in as great a proportion as they went to Chicago, New York, Pittsburgh, Detroit, and other industrial cities of the north and east. Saint Louis expansion came from internal growth and influx from surrounding rural areas that had large numbers of Catholics.

The new parishes, besides the Cathedral, were St. Matthew's at Sarah and Kennerly, St. Mark's on Page and Academy, St. Edward's on Clara and Maffit, Holy Innocents near Arsenal and Kingshighway, St. Barbara's at Minerva and Hamilton — the one west end church with a predominantly German background congregation — Our Lady of Good Counsel on the near north side, St. Michael's in Shrewsbury, just beyond the southwestern limits of the city, St. Ann's at Whittier and Page, Holy Family, just south of Tower Grove Park, St. Margaret's in the area east of Shaw's Garden, and Notre Dame de Lourdes in Wellston, a western suburb of the city.

The time of Archbishop Kain also saw a number of churches develop in the out-state part of the diocese. Among these, the most significant were the parishes of the Assumption at New Haven, in Franklin County, adjoining Saint Louis County on the west; St. Joseph parish of White Church, Howell County, in south central Missouri near the Arkansas border; the Church of St. Theodore in Flint Hill in St. Charles County; the Church of the Immaculate Conception in Augusta, St. Charles County, and the parish of the Immaculate Conception at Desloge in the lead mining district of St. Francois County.

The final years of the century witnessed the last rapid extension of the Catholic Knights of America, founded by John McLoughlin in Nashville in 1877, during Bishop Feehan's episcopacy. This soundly established fraternal insurance society set up thirty-four branches with 2,819 members in Saint Louis, and forty-one branches out-state with 876 members.

In the meantime, the Knights of Columbus, begun in New Haven, Connecticut, in 1882, with a slightly larger scope, spread throughout the nation. In 1899, members were to set up a Saint Louis Council. This slowed perceptively the growth of the earlier organization,[17] and gradually overshadowed it. The Catholic Knights of America, however, were to carry on, and ultimately to set up their headquarters in Saint Louis.

Recalcitrant Tuohy

A man of many storms, Archbishop Kain moved into another tornado in 1897. He removed Father J. T. Tuohy, "a good man, but a poor financier,"[18] according to the Saint Louis *Star*, from the pastorate of St. Patrick's. But Tuohy refused to move. Further, 1,200 men signed a petition to the archbishop asking an amicable settlement of what gained the name "the Tuohy affair."[19] Not to be outdone by the men, a thousand ladies petitioned the new apostolic delegate Sebastian Cardinal Martinelli in favor of Tuohy. So did six hundred Italian residents of the near-north side.[20]

In a feature article, the *Post-Dispatch* pointed out that Archbishop Ireland was a warm friend of Tuohy, "and has on more than one occasion taken issue with Archbishop Kain; that Archbishop Kain would brook no interference";[21] and concluded with the observation that must

have come to many minds: "The people feel that if he (Tuohy) was at fault in the management of St. Paul's Church, his former pastorate, he should have been disciplined before he was appointed pastor of St. Patrick's."[22]

While assistant at St. Bridget's for seven years (1882-1889), Tuohy had worked on the staff of the *Church Progress*. He wrote well, and published a short history of the archdiocese.[23] He had resigned his editorial duties in 1889 to take a position at the Catholic University in Washington.[24]

In 1892, Tuohy became the pastor of a newly forming parish, St. Paul the Apostle, later to be St. Ann's, in the area just west of St. Alphonsus (Rock) Church. Archbishop Kain had complained to Tuohy in December 1894 about the extended visit to St. Paul's rectory of a certain Father Fitzgerald.[25] Other complaints followed. In a letter of February 20, 1896, Tuohy gave a long account of his troubles at St. Paul's, mainly financial but some personal. He spoke of "the regular Niagara of unauthorized, unkind, inimical newspaper rumor of the past eighteen months."[26] Tuohy filled his letter with self-pity, subservience, piosity, and criticism of his "inoffensive but disappointing" assistant.[27] This letter should have given Kain adequate warning. Perhaps he thought Tuohy could do less harm in an old area such as St. Patrick's than in a developing parish like St. Paul's. The archbishop transferred Tuohy to the "quasi-parish" of St. Patrick's.[28] Seven months later, the Tuohy tornado struck.

A headline in the *Post-Dispatch* for May 2, 1897, stated: "Pastor of St. Patrick's is Defiant!"[29] The *Post-Dispatch* followed with a purported interview with Tuohy in its issue of July 14. Tuohy immediately disclaimed responsibility for the words in the interview.[30]

At this juncture, Archbishop Kain began an extended trip of Europe in the company of his seminary classmate in Baltimore, Father James McCabe. He appointed Vicar-General Muehlsiepen as administrator of the archdiocese in his absence, and left for the British Isles on July 31. He instructed Monsignor Muehlsiepen to place Father Robert Hayes, many times assistant, as pastor at St. Patrick's. But Father Tuohy would not vacate the rectory.

Archbishop Kain reached Italy on October 1; while back in Saint Louis, the siege of St. Patrick's continued. During his trip Kain regularly alluded to the Tuohy affairs in his correspondence. Attempts to appear casual did not cover his worry. He paid an official visit to Pope Leo XIII on November 22. On the following day, back in the trenches, Muehlsiepen and Tannrath made a public statement of charges against Tuohy. All were financial. He had been negligent in his financial account, lacked business qualifications and had failed to pay his debts. He had not kept the spiritual records of the parish with any notable dependability. Early stories spoke of criminal charges; but the archdiocesan authorities wisely refrained from these at the advice of lawyers.[31]

Kain returned to an archdiocese that still saw Tuohy in the St. Patrick's citadel. Early the following year, Sebastian Cardinal Martinelli, the apostolic delegate, looked into the matter.[32] The local newspapers gave it extensive coverage. On St. Patrick's Day, 1898, the *Globe-Democrat* predicted that the Tuohy case would become of national, even international importance.[33] Father Tuohy did not presume to exercise his priestly functions, but fought to hold possession of the pastoral residence. The case was to come up before Justice Thomas J. Hennessey. Tuohy preferred a Protestant judge, to the great relief of Hennessey.[34]

Archbishop Kain took the witness stand against Father Tuohy before Justice Richard B. Haughton on April 13, 1898. The defendant did not appear on his own behalf. The judge gave him twenty days to vacate the premises.[35]

By this time Tuohy had alienated many of his former supporters, including Father Phelan; some parishioners accused him of serious misconduct; but others sought to keep him as pastor.[36] Kain wanted Tuohy to become assistant pastor in Edina, where Father Phelan had begun his career. Tuohy did not budge. He appealed to the apostolic delegate. In late summer, Martinelli wrote to Kain that he had suggested to Tuohy an amicable non-public settlement.[37]

Three days later Kain wrote a strong answer to Martinelli:

In dealing with Rev. Tuohy [Kain never used first names in his correspondence] you are dealing with a first-class trickster....At the outset of my controversy with him I charged him with incompetency to administer a parish; but developments convince me ... that he lacks honor, conscience — aye, and I fear, he lacks faith....It is hard to know what to do with a priest so devoid of even natural virtues.[38]

Martinelli still wanted an amicable settlement.[39] Kain wanted Tuohy to go to a monastery and do penance.[40] Tuohy took indefinite leave.*

Archbishop Kain had won an inevitable triumph; but it was a Pyrrhic victory.

Last Echo of the Americanist Controversies

The Tuohy struggle should have satisfied even the most indefatigable fighter. But Archbishop Kain had one more fray to enter. The man he attacked this time was a far more secure adversary than J. T. Tuohy.

The long controversy between the Americanists and the conservatives had come to a crisis shortly after the 1897 publication of a French edition of the life of Father Isaac Hecker, founder of the Paulist Fathers. The introduction to this book brought forth a flood of acclaiming and critical articles in Europe. In America the chief voice of the anti-Americanists was the *Review*, edited by Arthur Preuss in Saint Louis.[41]

The extensive controversy in Europe prompted Pope Leo XIII to act. In spite of the protests of Cardinal Gibbons and Archbishop Ireland, the Holy Father issued an encyclical letter, *Testem Benevolentiae*, on January 22, 1899. In it, he condemned a number of heretical views that the French lumped together with many sound ideas under the term "Americanism." Of the fourteen American archbishops, three kept silent, four thanked the Holy Father for his interest, four — Kain and Cardinal Gibbons among them — denied that the enumerated heresies existed in this country, and two — Corrigan of New York and Katzer of Milwaukee — thanked the Holy Father for checking the growth of heresy.[42]

Arthur Preuss took a position with the last two prelates. He reprinted articles that saw the encyclical as a justified and paternal warning to the Catholics of the United States.[43] At the same time, quite distinctly, he quoted the words of a French priest, Abbe M. Charbonnel, in an alleged interview with Cardinal Gibbons. Charbonnel had said that Gibbons spoke critically of

Roman administration as "complex and inert," and capable of moving "forward only by intrigue." Preuss concluded: "We confidently expect His Eminence of Baltimore to give the lie to M. Charbonnel. The scandalous utterances attributed to him by the French priest cannot possibly be genuine."[44]

Five days later, Kain wrote to Preuss. Instead of attacking the major issue — the question of the alleged prevalence of heretical opinions among American Catholics — he confined his words to the Charbonnel article. "A newspaper which like the *Review*," he wrote, "poses as an exponent of Catholic thought and defender of the Church, should refrain from publishing articles reflecting on the Sacred hierarchy."[45] Preuss published the archbishop's letter without comment.[46]

In a letter to a professor at St. Mary's Seminary in Baltimore a few days later, Kain enclosed a copy of the *Review* containing his letter. He seemed to think that he had defended the honor of the cardinal in an effective manner. "I can almost imagine His Eminence, on reading my *mild* protest, say: 'Age is mellowing Abp. Kain.'"[47]

Really, [Kain went on] I was not displeased at the few comments of Preuss, for I feared he might be ugly. There would be no use in my using extreme measures with a man, who, year after year, receives from Cardinal Satolli such high commendation for his services to religion. In fact, Conde Pallen, Ed. of the *Church Progress*, is just as bitter as Preuss, and the concluding sentences of my letter were meant as much for that paper as for the *Review*.[48]

Catholics in Creative Literature

Toward the end of the 19th century, Saint Louis boasted many nationally known names in Catholic journalism. Among them, David Phelan, Conde Pallen, Arthur Preuss, and William Faerber have already come up in this narrative. At the same time three local-born Catholic writers gained international prominence in the field of creative literature: one in juvenile fiction, another in short stories and the novel, the third in essays, literary criticism, and creative editing. The first two spent some time in other parts of the country and located their stories there. The third never strayed far from Grand and Olive. All three gained fame during their lifetimes. One was to suffer eclipse before she died because of one work that anticipated trends in American writing, but then to develop a great following long after her death. The editors of the *Dictionary of American Biography* were to include biographies of all three of them.[49]

Francis J. Finn, the son of a Saint Louis alderman who once ran for the post of mayor, began studies for the priesthood at the Jesuit seminary in Florissant. He had to interrupt his course because of ill health and went to teach at St. Mary's High School in Kansas. From his experiences there, he began to write stories of American Catholic boarding school life. Eventually he published twenty-seven books. Fifteen went into French editions, eighteen into Flemish, six into German, four into Italian, Polish, and Bohemian, and several into Hungarian, Spanish, and Portuguese. Thirteen came out in braille editions. In 1911 the *American Catholic Who's Who* was to single him out "the foremost writer of fiction for young people."[50]

Saint Louis was the locale of at least some sections of Finn's books, such as his most popular story, *Tom Playfair*. But he himself was to have little identification with the city after completing his studies at Saint Louis Uni-

---

*Father Tuohy returned to the archdiocese in 1905 and served the rural parish of Jonesburg until his death in 1919 (*Catholic Directory*, 1905, p. 948; 1906, p. 920; 1919, p. 1140; 1920, p. 1008).

versity and his ordination at Saint Francis Xavier Church. He spent many of his late years as pastor of a church in Cincinnati.

The second prominent Saint Louis writer was Kate O'Flaherty Chopin, the daughter of Saint Louis businessman Thomas O'Flaherty, who died in the Gasconade Bridge disaster of 1858, and of Eliza Faris. After attending the Sacred Heart Convent, Kate married Oscar Chopin in June, 1870, and moved to Louisiana. Here she became acquainted with Creole and Cajun folklore.

After the death of her husband in 1882, she returned to Saint Louis. She began writing short stories that won gradually increasing acclaim. Her book of stories, *Bayou Folk*, published in 1894, won favorable reviews in a variety of newspapers and magazines including the *Boston Beacon*, the *New York Times*, the *Atlantic Monthly*, and *The Nation*.[51] "No more exquisite work," the *Cambridge History of American Literature* was to state "may be found in the whole range of the local colour school...."[52]

When Kate Chopin neared the height of her popularity at the end of the century, her novel *Awakening* brought mixed reviews from the critics and ostracism from Saint Louis society. Her frank treatment of an adulterous relationship proved a bit premature for American readers. Mrs. Chopin died in 1904, before the trend was to turn back in her favor. Ultimately, interest in her work was to wax. She came to hold a significant place in American letters, as the following quotation from the *Cambridge*

History of American Literature was to attest: "Such stories as *Desiree's Baby* ... and *Madame Celestin's Divorce* ... are among the few unquestioned masterpieces of American short story art."[53]

At the time of Mrs. Chopin's death, William Marion Reedy, the third of the significant Catholic literary figures of Saint Louis at the turn of the century, was to call her "a true literary genius."[54] Reedy grew up in the old Irish neighborhood on the near northside of Saint Louis and attended Christian Brothers College and Saint Louis University. The son of a police captain, he became a reporter for the *Missouri Republican*, a freelance writer and later editor of a weekly magazine, *The Mirror*. This amazingly sophisticated essayist had a remarkable sense of humor, a penchant for disturbing the sensibilities of Saint Louis society women by word and contrived situation, and an extremely wide range of interests. He never feared to take an unusual position on any social or cultural issue. Ultimately *Reedy's Mirror* — as he later called it — was to become known throughout the English-speaking world.

Reedy added to an acute evaluation of established writers an amazing eye for prospective talent. He was to publish the first of Edgar Lee Masters' poems that eventually formed the *Spoon River Anthology*. He published the poetry of Edna St. Vincent Millay, Vachel Lindsay, and Carl Sandburg before these writers had gained wide recognition. Just as with Mrs. Chopin, so with William Marion Reedy, critics of the 1960's were to "re-discover" his genius, and to publish two biographies of him.

The funeral of Father Joseph Schroeder who was pastor of Holy Trinity (June, 1907). The priests are Fathers George Hildner (left) and Joseph Siebert. The pall-bearers include prominent northside businessmen Chris Muckerman, Fred Krey, and E. Hanebrink.

Chapter 27

Kain's Late Years

Educational Ventures

A religious society of men destined to have a distinguished record of service in the archdiocese came to Saint Louis in 1897. Father William Chaminade had founded the Society of Mary in Bordeaux, France, in 1817, shortly after the turbulent Napoleonic days. The society included priests and lay members, and dedicated itself to the education of youth. It laid strong stress on the development of sodalities of Our Lady.

In 1849, one year before the death of Father Chaminade, the society had begun its first American activity in Dayton. In the middle nineties, Father Francis Goller sought members of this society to teach the boys at St. Peter and Paul's parish school. In August, 1897, three Marianists, under the direction of Brother Albert Kaiser, began to teach one hundred and eleven boys of the top grades, and twenty-three boys in the first year high.[1] Thus the original Marianist activity corresponded to a present-day junior high school. It was the start of a vigorous and productive apostolate.

While the Society of Mary began to expand in the archdiocese, Christian Brothers faced curtailment of their program. In the near half-century that the Christian Brothers had taught in Saint Louis, they had more than fulfilled Archbishop Kenrick's confidence in their skill at educating future clergymen. They had taught a surprising number of the locally-trained diocesan clergy, including the late Father Philip Brady, vicar-general for the English-speaking parishes, and Father Jeremiah Harty, pastor of St. Leo's, soon to be archbishop of Manila in the Philippines.[*2]

In his semi-official report on higher education in the state of Missouri at the end of the century, Professor Marshall S. Snow of Washington University commented on this aspect of Christian Brothers' College:

> That the courses were of high grade even in the early period of the college is evident from the fact that a large number of students who were aspiring to the ecclesiastical profession were in attendance during those years. On graduating at the college such students were usually credited by the diocesan authorities with two years' work in the philosophical courses pursued in Catholic Theological Seminaries.[3]

> For fifty years the College of the Christian Brothers had been an important factor in the upbuilding of the fame that belongs to Saint Louis as an educational center ... it may confidently be asserted that no other institution of its kind has done more to encourage the higher standards of collegiate worth than this institution.[4]

In spite of this excellent record, the general chapter of the Christian Brothers in Paris decided in 1897 to discontinue the teaching of Latin in all schools. This decision followed the tradition of the Brothers. The Saint Louis

request of Brother Patrick back in 1854 had admitted an exception; and other American schools had followed the Saint Louis example. Now the general chapter was going back to traditional practice.

Many American prelates, including Cardinal Gibbons, opposed this decision. Archbishop Kain of Saint Louis expressed double chagrin. He depended on the Christian Brothers College to give his seminarians their preparatory training. He severely criticized the attempt of the French to dictate a policy for this country that the American hierarchy strongly disapproved. Kain hoped Gibbons would speak directly on the matter when the French representatives arrived.[5] At the meeting of the bishops in the following autumn, Kain pushed the matter. The bishops unanimously authorized Gibbons to name an American bishop to petition Rome in person in favor of the fifty-five-year-old practice in the United States.

Rome refused the petition of the American hierarchy. Even though it favored the study of the classics, the Holy See felt it necessary to uphold the perfect observance of the rule of religious orders and so supported the ruling of the general chapter.[6] This decision proved a blow to the work of the Christian Brothers in the Saint Louis archdiocese. It limited their collegiate educational program to commercial courses; and eventually forced their work to the secondary level exclusively.

In June, 1898, the state of Missouri granted a charter to Kenrick Seminary under the official title of the Saint Louis Roman Catholic Theological Seminary. Father Edward Shea, pastor of St. Kevin's (later Immaculate Conception) parish was president of the seminary corporation, Monsignor Muehlsiepen secretary, and Father Ziegler treasurer. Monsignor Walsh and Fathers Faerber, Fenlon, and May served on the board.[7] In those days of proliferating seminaries, the School of Theology of Saint Louis University got under way in a new building on West Pine, a half-block west of Grand in 1899. The archdiocese also opened a preparatory department at Kenrick Seminary on Cass Avenue in 1900. The students lived at home and commuted daily to the school. Archbishop Kain encouraged the pastors to show a watchful care over their spiritual development.[8]

At the opening of the forty-first general assembly of the state of Missouri in 1901, Representative E. J. Simmons of Shelby County introduced a compulsory public education bill that would have drastically affected private and parochial education in the State of Missouri. Among other provisions, House Bill No. 210 stated that: "Every parent, guardian, or other person having control over any child between eight and fourteen years of age, shall be required to send such child to a public school in the district, city, or village in which he resides. . . ."[9] The bill also required the parents of deaf children to send such children to the deaf school in Fulton for six months each year. It put all private colleges with preparatory departments under the control of the board of education.[10]

---

*The reader can find a total list of 173 priests who attended Brothers' schools in Saint Louis between 1849 and 1925 in Hubert Gerard, F.S.C., *Mississippi Vista*, pp. 118-119.

Catholics reacted strongly. The *Amerika* Press printed and distributed copies of House Bill No. 210 so that all Catholics could read the proposal.[11] Representative W. P. Lightholder of the sixth district of Missouri, an alumnus of Saint Louis University, assured Father William Banks Rogers, the president of the school, that he would speak against what he called the "odious measure" at a forthcoming hearing.[12]

Archbishop Kain called a mass meeting of representatives of all city parishes for early February. Three hundred delegates attended the protest at St. Bridget's Church. Judge Daniel Dillon presided and William P. Dwyer served as secretary. Various speakers presumed diverse intentions in the mind of the supporters of the law, but agreed on its potential ill effects. The assembled representatives of the various parishes authorized a committee, composed of Paul Bakewell, F. C. Townsend, W. H. O'Brien, John L. Duffy, and J. L. Hornsby, to draw up resolutions of protest.[13]

Principal H. W. Prentis of Hodgen School asked to speak. To the surprise of most in the audience who thought he supported the measure, Prentis opposed the bill. He said that the legislators had not consulted the teachers' association before drawing up the proposal. He favored a compulsory education law that would get children out of the factories and into the classrooms, but wanted parents to have a say in the choice of schools.[14]

As a result of such protests, the Missouri legislature amended the bill in the way Prentis had sought, namely, compulsory education with parental choice of public or private schooling. Prentis served on the legislative committee of the State Teachers' Association that pushed the amended bill. In April, the assembly passed the bill. But it still did not meet the requirements of Governor Alexander Dockery. He vetoed it.[15]

The interest in general educational questions that the "Second Founder" of Saint Louis University, William Banks Rogers, evidenced in his correspondence with Representative Lightholder in this matter carried over into a wide field of educational expansion. He had come to Saint Louis in 1900 as president after serving for two years in a similar capacity at Marquette University in Milwaukee.

Rogers did many things for Saint Louis University and for Catholic education in Saint Louis. One of his first goals was to bring about greater rapport between those priests engaged in the parochial and those in the educational apostolate. At the beginning of each school year he wrote a letter to all the pastors asking their cooperation. On all major university celebrations, and whenever any important religious ceremony took place in the College Church, Rogers invited all the local clergy. He took every occasion to visit the pastors personally and discuss the common Catholic cause.

When Rogers set up the academic department as a distinct entity in 1901, he extended the Doyle Scholarship Fund to all parishes of the city. Previously, these scholarships, a legacy of businessman John Doyle, had been available only for members of the St. Francis Xavier parish. The academic department, now called Saint Louis University High School, occupied the same building as the university at Grand and Pine, but enjoyed its own internal administration and received a distinct identification.

Within the university itself, Father Rogers set out to re-open a medical school. The earlier Saint Louis University School of Medicine, the first university-affiliated medical school west of the Mississippi, had separated from the University during the Know-Nothing troubles. In 1902, Father Rogers began negotiations to bring the combined Marion Sims and Beaumont Medical Schools on Grand and Caroline, not far south of Mill Creek Valley, into an association with the university. This project had the backing of many outstanding citizens of the city who agreed to serve on the university's board of trustees.

Saint Louis University had opened a school of philosophy in 1889. In 1899 it had begun a school of theology. Now, in 1903, with the inaugural of a school of medicine, it resumed true university status.

A New Day for Italo-Americans

The history of Italo-Americans in Saint Louis during the first three decades of the nineteenth century was to revolve around the dynamic and devoted Father Cesare Spigardi. After ordination at the age of twenty-five, this native of northern Italy worked in his own neighborhood and at an industrial parish where he directed the St. Vincent de Paul Society, organized pilgrimages, and counseled young people.

After nine years, Spigardi joined the Society of St. Raphael for work among the immigrants, left his parish, his diocese, and his native land. The Society of St. Raphael, founded by Bishop G. B. Scalabrini of Piacenza, later developed into the Congregation of the Missionaries of St. Charles Borromeo. The first group of "Scalabrini," as the Italians called them, had come to the United States in 1888. Spigardi arrived in 1894. He labored on the east coast until 1897 and then went west to Kansas City.

In the meantime in Saint Louis, since the closing of St. Bonaventure's Church in 1883, no one had attempted to organize the Saint Louis Italians into a distinctive parish. Priests of the diocese who had studied in Europe and were familiar with Italian, such as Fathers Fredrick Holweck and John Long, assisted the Italian immigrants at various times. In the last decade of the century, for instance, Father Long had successive assignments at St. Augustine's Parish, at St. John's, and lastly at St. Patrick's. In each of these, a good number of Italians resided. When Father Long broached the subject of a distinct Italian parish to Archbishop Kain, the archbishop casually remarked, the Italians attend "somewhere, everywhere, and no where."[16]

Father Long heard about the work of the Scalabrini Fathers in Kansas City and wrote the pastor of Holy Rosary Church. As a result, Father Spigardi came to St. Patrick's Church and offered a mission for the Italians living within and without the parish boundaries. The *Western Watchman* noted this manifestation of the faith of the Italians: "The Church was crowded to the doors every night and much good was accomplished."[17]

Father Spigardi began to look around for a temporary place of worship for the Italian people. He rented a former Baptist Church on 19th and Morgan Street for seventy-five dollars a month. The second floor hall formed the church, the first floor provided living quarters for Father Spigardi, his sisters who served as his housekeepers, and his brother Luigi, who served as sexton. Archbishop Kain blessed the church on February 11, 1900, and placed it under the invocation of Our Lady Help of Christians.

Father Spigardi next began a drive for funds to build or purchase a permanent church. To this end he planned his first bazaar, a means that he used throughout his life to promote his parishes and his projects. Father Phelan praised the work of Father Spigardi and his congregation.[18] The proceeds from the fair were good; the development of an *esprit d'corps* among the people proved even more pronounced. Father Spigardi hired Professor Michaelangelo Gilsinn, formerly of St. Francis Xavier Church, to organize a choir, built up parish sodalities and societies, urged his people to participate in the St. Patrick's Day parade, and had a number of processions during the course of the year. In the one on the Feast of the Immaculate Conception, three thousand pilgrims marched a distance of three and a half miles, passing seven other Catholic churches on route.[19]

By this time, Father Spigardi realized that the Italo-Americans needed a more commodious and convenient church. Fortunately, many Protestant congregations had already moved west of Grand and their older plants were available for purchase.[20] One of these, St. John's Methodist Episcopal Church, South, on the corner of Locust and Ewing seemed to offer what Father Spigardi needed. He secured the church and two halls adjoining it in the latter part of the year 1902 for $25,000. He spent a few more thousand in adapting and renovating the church. Father Spigardi left Our Lady Help of Christians on 19th and Morgan Street and moved to the new St. Charles Borromeo on November 2, 1902. Bishop John Hennessey of Wichita sang the Pontifical High Mass. Bishop Glennon of Kansas City gave the sermon and Archbishop John Kain of Saint Louis congratulated Father Spigardi and the assembled congregation on their great advance.[21]

The Italo-Americans, already well organized fraternally, now had a rallying point for their religious identification, and a pastor worthy of their warmth and generosity. Father Spigardi was a true priest of the people, at home in the basement apartments of the poor and the conspicuous dwellings of the wealthy. He had great rapport with all, especially children, and fine organizational ability. He often caused businessmen to worry when he undertook needed projects with more confidence in God than money in the bank. Usually someone came to his help.

Last Days

The intermittent brouhahas that had marked Kain's years in the Mississippi Valley gradually took their toll on the archbishop's health. He took lengthy trips and extended leaves. During the summer of 1899, for instance, he spent July in Atlantic City, and August in Deer Park, Maryland.[22] The following summer he was to spend in Europe.

But before he left in late April, Kain announced that Bishop George Montgomery of Los Angeles, a Kentucky-born graduate of St. Mary's in Baltimore, would make a series of special appeals during May and June for the Catholic Indian schools.[23] Chancellor Van der Sanden had already listed two months of confirmations on Bishop Montgomery's schedule. Montgomery would also lay the cornerstone of the new St. Teresa's Church on Pentecost Sunday; and would ordain the new priests of the diocese on June 9 at Kenrick Seminary, Jesuit seminarians on June 27, and Franciscan friars on June 30.[24]

On his European trek, Kain had as companions Fathers David Phelan and John Tracy who had come to Saint Louis as his secretary after eighteen years in Appalachia. In a private conference with Pope Leo XIII, Kain seemed to have shown more interest in the wider affairs of the Church in America rather than the particular concerns of his own archdiocese. In speaking of the meeting, he stressed that he had recommended his seminary classmate, John J. Keane, for the archbishopric of Dubuque, the choice, Kain asserted, of all the bishops of the province and of the archbishops of the entire nation. Kain had not yet left Ireland in late August, when he wrote: "Someone sent Father Tracy a clipping from the *P.D.*, announcing that Father Harty was to be auxiliary bishop of Saint Louis. This was news to me, but queer things are sometimes done at Rome."[25]

During the following February (1901), because of the widespread prevalence of the grippe, Archbishop Kain exempted his people from the Lenten fast.[26] In May, Kain showed his concern for the Catholics of Florida, by calling the attention of the pastors to the needs of the Church in Jacksonville, where fire destroyed most of the church property.[27]

The archdiocese hosted the national Eucharistic Congress in September, 1901. The program announced the coming of His Eminence Sebastian Cardinal Martinelli for the opening Pontifical Mass.[28] Instead, Archbishop William Elder of Cincinnati officiated at the fall opening ceremonies of St. Francis Xavier Church. In an ecumenic tone, Father P. McClean of Milford, Connecticut, spoke on "The Eucharist and our Separated Brethren."[29] Bishop John J. Glennon, auxiliary of Kansas City, gave an eloquent address. As a near neighbor, Glennon often accepted invitations to assist in Saint Louis during the succeeding months.

Archbishop Kain invited Cardinal Martinelli to visit Saint Louis the following year before leaving the United States for a new post in Rome. The local chairman of arrangements, Father Phelan, notified the priests that the retiring apostolic delegate would visit the city on Pentecost Sunday.[30] Once again, Martinelli was not able to come.

During the same month, Archbishop Kain granted jurisdiction over Saint Louis members of the Maronite Rite to the Church of St. Anthony the Hermit. All Maronites were, if at all possible, to attend Divine Service in that church and to bring their children there for baptism. Only the pastor of St. Anthony the Hermit or a priest delegated by him or by the archbishop himself could validly witness the marriage of Maronites.[31]

In September, Kain called a Fourth Diocesan Synod to meet at Kenrick Seminary. Two hundred and nine priests attended. The synod reconfirmed previous conciliar decrees with a few modifications. It dropped the statute of the third synod forbidding mixed marriages in private houses because of loud complaints about its severity. The fourth synod repeated the insistence of the third on attendance at parochial schools, and invoked stringent penalties on parents who did not conform. The synod named a school commission that consisted of Fathers Edward Fenlon, Henry Hukestein, and Urban Stanowski.

Kain Seeks an Auxiliary

As Kain's health steadily declined, he authorized two men to notify Cardinal Gibbons in October, 1902, of his need of an auxiliary. Father Tannrath wrote on October 4 at the command of the archbishop who could not hold a pen in his right hand because of an arm ailment; and sent a clipping from a local paper, the *Republic*, that reported

Kain's illness.[32] Four days later, with the archbishop's consent, his physician, Doctor John P. Boyson, wrote to Gibbons in a similar vein.[33] The Baltimore prelate immediately urged Rome to appoint an auxiliary bishop for Saint Louis.[34]

On his part, Kain put in requests, too. He wanted Father Joseph A. Connolly of St. Teresa's parish to assist him. When this request did not bring action, he asked for Father Jeremiah Harty of St. Leo's Parish, who was to become archbishop of Manila a year later. Again, Rome took no action. Early the next year, on January 6, 1903, Kain called a meeting of his consultors and irremovable rectors for the purpose of requesting a coadjutor. The assembled representatives of the archdiocese chose three names: Bishop Edward J. Dunne of Dallas, Coadjutor Bishop John J. Glennon of Kansas City, and Bishop Sebastian Messmer of Green Bay. The bishops of the province listed Glennon first, Dunne second, and John J. Hennessey of Wichita in third place.

Out in Kansas City, in the meantime, Bishop Glennon was not unaware of these proceedings. When Bishop Denis O'Connell accepted the appointment as rector of the Catholic University of America, Glennon congratulated him. He used this occasion to acquaint the influential prelate with the prospects in Missouri. Glennon contrasted the recommendations of the bishops of the province and the priests of Saint Louis. Behind the name of Bishop Messmer he had placed three exclamation marks.[35]

The bishops of the province and the archbishops of the United States passed on the nominations. Archbishop Patrick Riordan of San Francisco believed strongly that neither Dunne nor Hennessey was the man for Saint Louis.[36] Cardinal Gibbons warmly approved the choice of Glennon with only conventional approval of the other two candidates.[37]

On April 27, 1903, in one of his last decisions regarding the American Church, Pope Leo XIII named forty year old Bishop John Joseph Glennon coadjutor of Saint Louis with the right of succession.

Final Appraisal

Like Du Bourg before him, Kain came amid public jubilation. He left with a tear in his eye. The task had been too much for him. To fill the "Old Lion's" shoes would have taxed the capacities of almost any bishop of the time.

Kenrick had not asked for Kain; and did not make him welcome. In the early years, with Kenrick still alive, coadjutor Kain had to do many unpopular things, such as going into court to establish his right to carry on business matters of the archdiocese. And on his own part, instead of building up the support of the men who had petitioned for his coming, such as Fathers McCabe, Ziegler, and Phelan, Kain turned on these men. When the priests wanted Monsignor Walsh and Father Goller as consultors, he spurned these choices on such flimsy grounds that the *American Catholic Ecclesiastical Review* publicly called his action unwise.

In spite of this, Kain did accomplish several important things. He settled the question of the national language churches that had hung on so long. He gave full support to the parochial school system, even though some of his priests, such as Father Phelan, strongly opposed this move. He chose the site for the new cathedral.

His deficiencies did not come from ill will; but from lack of capacity for the far-ranging aspects of the archiepiscopate of Saint Louis. Probably the best characterization came later on, when the *Western Watchman* called him, "zealous, capable, well-meaning and rather severe."[38]

Even without a clear-cut plan of advance, the clergy and people of Saint Louis continued steadily on their way. The religious life of the parishes remained on its high plane. Earlier generations had set a pattern of parochial life that continued. The proportionate growth of the city declined in contrast to that of Chicago, Detroit, Cleveland, and other cities of the Midwest. Relatively few immigrants found their way to the River City. Most of the residents of the city were children or even grandchildren of residents. Saint Louis had once been the bustling gateway to the frontier; it now had begun to settle into calm middle age.

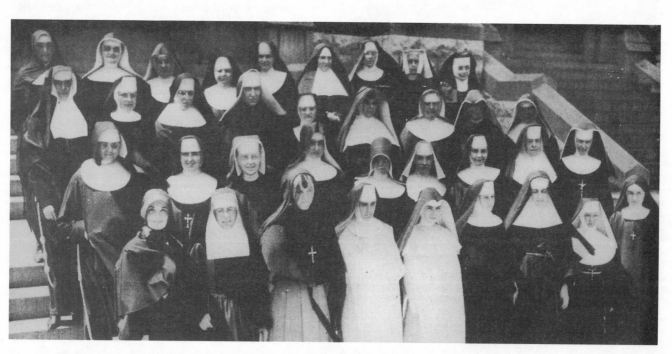

Dedicated women of seventy-two congregations served God in the archdiocese. Representatives of 36 sisterhoods appear in this photo.

PART VI

John J. Glennon: Eloquent Builder (1903-1946)

The apostolic delegate, Archbishop Diomede Falconio, O.F.M., blesses the cornerstone of the Great Cathedral on Lindell, assisted by Monsignors Connolly, Goller, and Hoog. Archbishop Glennon and architect George Barnett are in the left foreground; Father Dunne and his boy's band stand in the rear, surrounded by many prominent parishioners of the Cathedral parish.

Chapter 28

The West Awakens

Glennon's Early Years

John Joseph Glennon was born June 14, 1862, in the parish of Kinnegad in County Meath, Ireland, about fifty miles west and a little north of Dublin. His father, Matthew Glennon, had worked for a time in the United States before the Civil War, then returned to Ireland and married Katherine Rafferty. The future archbishop received his primary schooling in his home town; he later commuted by train to St. Mary's Seminary in Mullingar, and finally went to All Hallow's College in Dublin.

In 1882, Bishop John Hogan of Kansas City visited All Hallow's to recruit seminarians for his newly erected diocese. John Glennon volunteered. Not yet canonically old enough to be ordained, he came to America and assisted at the Kansas City Cathedral. Bishop Hogan urged Glennon to study German at this time so that he might be of greater assistance to the people of the diocese.

Ordained on December 20, 1884, Glennon became assistant at St. Patrick's parish of Kansas City. Shortly afterward, Pastor James Dunn took a vacation trip to the west coast, and Glennon acted as administrator of the parish. When Dunn returned, he expressed his disapproval of some changes the young priest had made. As a result, Bishop Hogan granted Glennon a leave of absence to visit his family in Ireland, and take some studies in Europe. Intelligent, but little inclined to the exacting aspects of scholarship, Glennon did not undertake a systematic study program. He arrived in Bonn, Germany, too late for the fall term. By the end of the year, he still had not accomplished much, but outlined a plan of studies for the following year.[1]

Bishop Hogan recalled him to Kansas City to serve as his secretary and assistant at the Cathedral. Later Glennon filled the post of rector of the Cathedral and concentrated his attention on parish activities. In 1892 he became vicar-general of the diocese, administrator in 1894, and coadjutor bishop in 1896. Archbishop John Kain consecrated him on June 29, 1896, with the assistance of Bishops Maurice Burke of St. Joseph, and John J. Hennessey of Wichita. Glennon remained as coadjutor for seven years.

Few men have come to office with more to recommend them than John Joseph Glennon on his arrival in Saint Louis. Tall, handsome in an almost boyish way, clever, personable, with a fine sense of humor, he carried himself with the grace of Cardinal Gibbons, and spoke with the eloquence of William Jennings Bryan. He came to a city reawakened by the challenge of the coming anniversary of the Louisiana Purchase; to an archdiocese calling for new directions as it moved into a new century.

Shortly after receiving the notification of his new position, Glennon sent a letter of thanks to Monsignor Dennis O'Connell, for "the great interest" the monsignor had taken in Glennon's appointment to Saint Louis. As rector of the North American College in Rome between 1885

and 1895,* and a vicar of the Church of Santa Maria in Transtevere for the following eight years (1895-1903), O'Connell had acted as unofficial "Americanist" agent at the Vatican, working in behalf of Archbishops John Ireland, John Keane, and their friends — in this last instance, John Glennon. Now he was accepting a new position himself, that of rector of the Catholic University in the national capital. Glennon pledged O'Connell full cooperation. "Need I add," he wrote, "that I also want to commit myself to the unequivocal support of the University — that I am at your service in all you undertake in its behalf."[2] Glennon ended his letter by inviting O'Connell to visit Saint Louis.

The Catholic University of America in Washington was not the only institution of higher learning that demanded Glennon's interest. Saint Louis University had taken a new birth with the new century. It had opened a school of theology in 1899. In 1900, Father William Banks Rogers, its finest president in sixty years, had taken office. He began negotiations for a medical department. He soon invited distinguished citizens to serve on an advisory board, among them Richard D. Kerens, Daniel C. Nugent, David Walker, Festus Wade, John Scullin, Julius Walsh, and August Schlafly.

Two months after Glennon came to Saint Louis as coadjutor bishop, he visited Saint Louis University. In his greetings, he challenged the school to move farther ahead by opening a law school: "The Trinity which constituted a perfect university," he remarked, "embraced philosophy, the study of the human soul, medicine, the study of the human frame, and law, the study of the relations of men."[3]

Six months after his appointment as coadjutor, Glennon went east to take part in the golden sacerdotal jubilee of the greatest priest of the Saint Louis archdiocese, her former coadjutor, and now archbishop of Philadelphia, the silver-voiced Patrick Ryan. In the course of the banquet after the church solemnities, Bishop Glennon paid tribute to Archbishop Ryan and his mentor in Saint Louis, Archbishop Kenrick: "By the rolling waters of the Mississippi the Lion of the West lies sleeping, and if the waters could speak as they flow, their every wavelet would echo the greatness of his name. For there is not a stream tributary to that mighty river that does not reflect the golden cross of Saint Louis."[4] Glennon again proved a master of hidden meanings — as he was to do so often in the future. His hearers caught his message that the great see of the West, as well as "the Lion of the West," lay sleeping.

A month later the West awoke. Glennon succeeded John Kain who died October 3, 1903.

---

*Monsignor William O'Connell of Massachusetts succeeded him. William O'Connell was to become cardinal archbishop of Boston.

First Acts as Archbishop

In his first official act, the new archbishop designated Fathers Joseph A. Connolly of St. Teresa's parish and Otto J. S. Hoog of St. Peter's Church, Jefferson City, as his vicars-general in place of the late Monsignor Muehlsiepen who had served the archdiocese so long and so well. Glennon confirmed Henry Van der Sanden as chancellor of the archdiocese.

Among the programs of welcome for the new archbishop, top social billing went to the reception at the St. Louis Women's Club on May 5, 1904. Eighteen ladies whose French ancestors built the first church of Saint Louis under the prodding of the Spanish governor — or arrived a few years later — greeted Archbishop Glennon and the ever-popular Archbishop Patrick Ryan of Philadelphia. Mrs. Armand Peugnet, a descendant of five Creole families — the Labadie, the Chouteau, the Gratiot, the Sarpy, and the Cabanne — led an all-star cast that included Mesdames Bates, Benoist, Faris, Lee, Lindsay, Lucas, Morrison, and Walsh, and Miss Maffitt.[5] Such gentlemen as Pierre Chouteau, John Harney, and Theophile Papin added further historical perspective.[6]

At the first meeting of the American archbishops with Glennon in attendance, Cardinal Gibbons had presented a statement of Gerolamo Cardinal Gotti, prefect of the Propaganda, on the humiliating status of Catholic Negroes in various dioceses. Investigation and discussion disclosed that the Church was doing little for the Negroes. As a result Gibbons appointed a committee consisting of Archbishops Ryan, Ireland, and Glennon, to study the status of the Negro Catholics.[7] A year later, Archbishop Ryan, the spokesman of the committee, recommended the establishment of a permanent bishops' committee of northern and southern prelates, and a bureau for the Negro apostolate with a priest in charge.[8] Glennon did not serve on this permanent committee.

In his initial years as archbishop, Glennon governed the eastern half of the state of Missouri, an area stretching one hundred and fifty miles west of the Mississippi from the Iowa border on the north, to Arkansas on the south. Two hundred and seventy-four diocesan and two hundred and nine regular clergymen worked in seventy-one parishes in the city, and one hundred and twenty-six beyond the city limits, and in seminaries, colleges, hospitals, orphanages, and other institutions.

As in the early days of the diocese, there were three centers of Catholicism: the city itself and its immediate suburbs; certain counties immediately to the west along the Missouri — St. Charles on the north bank, and Franklin, Gasconade, and Osage on the south bank; and the old settlements of Ste. Genevieve and Perry counties, slightly more than fifty miles below Saint Louis on the west bank of the Mississippi. The remainder of the eastern half of Missouri had an occasional isolated Catholic town, such as Old Mines in the south and Millwood in the north, entirely surrounded by a predominantly Protestant region. The remainder of the province of Saint Louis consisted of two dioceses in Missouri — Kansas City in the west and southwest, and St. Joseph in the northwest corner; and Leavenworth, Concordia, and Wichita in the state of Kansas.

On Glennon's arrival, geographical Saint Louis had the shape of two crescents facing each other, their points meeting at the north and south. The arching Mississippi River formed the crescent on the east. An agreement between state and city in 1876 had set up the other crescent. The southwest boundary roughly followed the River des Peres from its junction with the Mississippi almost to Manchester Avenue. On the west, by the time of Glennon's arrival on the scene, the boundary followed McCausland and Skinker Avenues at the west end of Forest Park; and, on the northwest, stretched along a line a few blocks beyond Goodfellow Avenue.

The city continued its push west, as it had done since the draining of Chouteau's Pond before the Civil War. The built-up area extended to Kingshighway. Beyond this, housing was full immediately north and south of Forest Park, and along Florissant and Natural Bridge avenues on the north side, and along Arsenal, Watson, and Gravois avenues on the south side. Between these built-up sections, truck-farms continued to flourish.

Housing in the county followed the main highways that spoked out from the city: Broadway to the north, Florissant, Natural Bridge, St. Charles, Page, Olive Street Road, Delmar, Clayton, Manchester, Big Bend, Watson, Gravois, Lemay Ferry, and the other end of Broadway to the south. Businessmen who lived far from the center of the city commuted by such trains as the Frisco and Missouri-Pacific or any of the numerous street cars to their work downtown.

The city itself had changed dramatically in the national picture over the years. Sixty years before, when Peter Richard Kenrick had arrived, Saint Louis, the center of the inter-continental network of waterways, was about to become the principal city of the Midwest. In the view of her leading citizens, she was destined to stay on top. One had only to look at the map of the midwestern rivers to realize that a beneficent Providence had designated prominence for Saint Louis — or so they thought.

When the railroads began to push across the open prairies, a few Saint Louis "boosters," such as businessmen John O'Fallon and James Lucas, and Senator Thomas Hart Benton, had tried to rally a sufficient number of citizens to the need of prompt action to make Saint Louis the hub of the future transcontinental rail system. In spite of their best efforts, however, the city, emotionally as well as geographically, continued to look to its river and the river trade. Added to this, the Civil War, with its guerilla struggles and the divided allegiances in Missouri, set Saint Louis back in favor of youthful, aggressive Chicago.

Before the Civil War, the commercial leadership of the city had tied itself to the river and the South; many of these leaders were Catholics. After the War, however, the new leadership that looked to the railroads and the northeast was predominantly Protestant. By the time Archbishop Kain came to Saint Louis, Chicago had become the hub of the transcontinental rail system, the principal city of the mid-continent and one of the great cities of the world. Saint Louis had slowed down dramatically in the last half of the nineteenth century and at Archbishop Glennon's arrival, Saint Louis had definitely settled in second place in the Midwest.

With the coming of the Louisiana Purchase Exhibition, the World's Fair of 1904, however, new vitality made itself felt in Saint Louis. Catholic leaders of old families and new families came to the fore and restored the balance between Catholic and Protestant community leadership. Saint Louis University, under the direction of Father William Banks Rogers, surged forward, as it had not in the forty years since the war. The youthful, vigorous, alert new archbishop matched the revitalized spirit of the city. Saint Louis would never be top city in the Midwest again, but in those early years of Archbishop Glennon's term it gave promise of reasserting itself in a dramatic way.

World's Fair Activities

Saint Louis prepared for the centennial of the Louisiana Purchase. The Ministerial Alliance of Saint Louis wanted a religious congress such as the one held at the Chicago World's Fair in the previous decade, 1892. A delegation of ministers approached Glennon. He chose not to participate. When it was certain the Church would not take part in a general religious congress, several laymen, including Professor James Edwards of Notre Dame, tried to promote one. Again Archbishop Glennon refused his support.

The World's Fair board of directors wanted some ex-

hibits of religious character and sent a committee, headed by Walter Stevens, a Saint Louis newspaperman, to Rome to obtain certain art objects. The Vatican gladly shipped a number of such treasures to Saint Louis. Mr. Stevens also asked the Holy Father to send a representative to the Fair. He suggested Cardinal Satolli. Communications between Rome and Saint Louis momentarily broke down. Archbishop Glennon stated that he knew nothing at all about the invitation until after the cardinal had consented to come.[9] But he prepared for the visit.

The Catholics of Saint Louis had a grand reception in honor of the Italian prelate. Archbishop Glennon spoke words of warm welcome as did Monsignor Denis O'Connell, Judge O'Neill Ryan, and civic leader Fredrick W. Lehman.

On the occasion of the World's Fair, numerous groups held educational conventions in Saint Louis. Catholic edu-

Governor David R. Francis, director-general of the World's Fair (right, front), welcomes Cardinal Satolli (on his right), the representative of Pope Pius X, accompanied by Archbishop Glennon and Bishop Denis O'Connell (left, front).

This view of buildings at the World's Fair of 1904 looks west from the Palace of Education where thirty Catholic Colleges had exhibits. George D. Barnett, who designed the Palace of Liberal Arts, was chief architect of the Great Cathedral of St. Louis a few years later.

cators of three groups — the Association of Catholic Colleges and Universities of the United States, the Conference of Diocesan Representatives of Catholic Parish Schools, and the Educational Conference of Seminary Faculties — decided to hold their first joint meeting in Saint Louis. Monsignor Denis O'Connell, president of the Catholic University of America, directed the program. Archbishop John J. Glennon of Saint Louis appointed a local committee of leading Catholic educators to host the meeting. Father Banks Rogers offered the facilities of Saint Louis University — meeting rooms, residence halls, dining room, and chapel.

Archbishop Glennon opened the conference at Saint Louis University with an address on two needs of Catholic education: greater lay cooperation and better public relations. He did not confine his participation to formal appearances on the program, but joined spontaneously in the discussion as did Father Rogers. One day the conferees discussed the growing secularization of so many American universities.

"The Catholic College," Archbishop Glennon insisted, "has remained a Catholic College. The others have changed; consequently, they are popular, because they appeal to the secular world." The archbishop gave, as his solution to the problem, the adoption of "the clothes of

secularism," while retaining the religious commitment. "By maintaining the full faith within the institution, but before the world remaining largely secular . . . by mixing with the world and by having a man for every position the world may need." He called for greater concern for public relations. "We would rather concentrate our energies in the classroom, in the meditation room, in the chapel," he insisted, "and so people do not come to us. . . . The one who parades his claim is the one who will secure patronage."[10]

Father James A. Burns, C.S.C., reported on the meetings of the Joint Committee on High Schools, set up by the Catholic Educational Association at a meeting the previous October. He gave statistics on the small number of Catholic high schools in relation to the number of Catholic colleges. He discussed the gap between existing high schools and the parochial schools; the lack of proper relationship with the Catholic colleges; the terminal nature of most high schools; and the tendency to start high schools by adding a few more years to the existing parochial grade schools. Father Burns called for inter-parish high schools, under the authority of the bishop, financed by the parishes, and staffed by communities of teaching religious.[11]

In this discussion, Archbishop Glennon agreed with the

report of the committee. He pointed out the importance of episcopal leadership, and the difficulties of inter-parish cooperation:

> Unless the bishop takes the lead, the priests would hardly come together of their own *proprio motu* and build a high school. . . . I am a little afraid when you get eight or ten parishes converging . . . they might discuss parochial friction rather than the high school. Still I think . . . the parish priests are coming to think of it as a common cause, and little jealousies must be laid away for the purpose of upbuilding the great work of Catholic education.[12]

This educational meeting in Saint Louis took a step of historical significance. The three groups — the Association of Catholic Colleges and Universities of the United States, the Conference of Diocesan Representatives of Catholic Parochial Schools, and the Educational Conference of Seminary Faculties — combined at this meeting to form the National Catholic Educational Association. But many years were to elapse before Saint Louis took action to open inter-parochial high schools.

Glennon and the Catholic University

Archbishop Glennon kept his early promise to Monsignor Denis O'Connell, the rector of the Catholic University in Washington. He supported a proposal of Milwaukee's Archbishop Sebastian Messmer to win for the Catholic University wider support of Catholics of German-American background. Messmer wanted an American educator of German ancestry as vice-rector of the University to counter-balance the earlier "Eastern Irish" emphasis of the school.[13] Glennon encouraged O'Connell to support the plan of faculty member (later university president) Father Thomas J. Shahan and erect a great basilica on the university campus.[14]

In 1906 Glennon accepted an invitation to serve as a trustee of the university. He soon began to advocate an elaborate proposal for a long-range endowment by Catholic societies of the nation, such as the Knights of Columbus and the Ancient Order of Hibernians. He suggested that such groups raise one half million dollars, or a burse of five thousand dollars for each of the nearly one hundred dioceses in the country for current expenses. Then the annual diocesan collection of the people could go into building up the permanent endowment of the university.[15] As a result, the Hibernians set up a number of scholarships; and, after some delay, the Knights gave strong support to the university.[16]

When Pope Pius X condemned Modernism in September, 1907, the trustees of the university set up a committee to inspect theology books in the library. Glennon served on this committee, along with archbishops John Ireland and John Farley of New York, Bishop Matthew Harkins of Providence, and the Rector Denis O'Connell.[17]

A few months later, the same group — O'Connell was now a bishop also — formed a committee to examine the curriculum, finances, and attendance of the students.[18]

Most of the work of the committee goes beyond the scope of the history of the Archdiocese of Saint Louis. One recommendation has interest in view of the fact that Glennon urged the opening of a law school at Saint Louis University. The committee recommended the discontinuance of the already existing School of Law at the Catholic University.[19]

Glennon was to serve as a trustee of the university for many years and to support every effort of the chancellor, Cardinal Gibbons, in its behalf.[20]

Apostolic Missionary Band

At the turn of the century, most religious orders and congregations had a team of home-missionaries, not tied to any parish, seminary, or college, who gave missions, novenas, and Forty Hours and helped pastors in various other parochial work. Such priests usually had special training, experience, and ecclesiastical prerogatives for the good of souls.

Early in Archbishop Glennon's years in Saint Louis, an archdiocesan Apostolic Missionary Band began under the direction of Father William E. Randall, pastor of Assumption Church. This devout priest was to win the title "saintly" from two historians. John Rothensteiner called him, "a saintly martyr of fervor."[21] Constance Smith said: "He is remembered as a saintly priest and a generous friend of the poor."[22] Since the founding of St. Agnes Church in 1891 at the edge of the Assumption parish, the old parish had few families, and the pastor few duties. To prepare himself for his new task, the forty-five-year-old priest went to the Paulist Mission House in Washington, D.C., during the year 1904-1905.[23] In 1906, his young assistant, later to be vicar-general of the archdiocese, Father Patrick P. Crane, took a similar year of training.[24]

The Apostolic Missionary Band was under way by 1907, with a three-man team of Randall, Crane, and James Moore, a priest on temporary leave from the Springfield (Massachusetts) diocese. Father Joseph P. Fitzkamm resided with Randall and Crane at Assumption, but spent his time in parochial duties.[25] Father John Peschges of the diocese of Winona (Minnesota) was to join the team in 1908,[26] Joseph Siebert of the Saint Louis archdiocese, the following year,[27] and another Saint Louis priest, Albert Gass, S.T.D., in 1913.[28]

In spite of declining health, Father Randall was to remain head of the band even though he did less and less active mission work. At his death October 9, 1916,[29] Father Gass was to succeed him as pastor,[30] and Joseph C. Hoelting as missionary.[31]

These men served the archdiocese well. They gave of their energy and time to neglected areas, both in the city and in remote rural areas, such as Ham's Prairie and Portland in Callaway County.[32] The financial records of the Apostolic Missionary Band attest the generosity and frugality of the members.[33]

Chapter 29

Builder, Colonizer, Orator

The Cathedral Builder

Almost from his arrival in Saint Louis, Glennon gave thought to a new cathedral. The once impressive old cathedral near the river lay submerged by old buildings in a crowded, rapidly deteriorating industrial and commercial area. Archbishop Kain had already selected a site on Lindell Boulevard at the northwest corner of Newstead. Glennon inspected other possible locations; then settled on the Kain corner. On the first Sunday of February, 1905, the archbishop began his sermon with the words of Solomon: "I propose to build a temple to the name of the Lord My God." The archbishop reviewed Kenrick's attitude towards the building of a new cathedral, and Kain's plans and subsequent purchase of the property.[1]

The archbishop called together a number of outstanding laymen to constitute a cathedral board: among these were John Lee, Festus Wade, John Scullin, Richard Kerens, William McBride, Louis Fusz, Philip Scanlan, Howard Benoist, Daniel Nugent, August Schlafly, W. J. Kinsella, and John Leahy.

On the morning of May 14, 1905, the hierarchy of America, led by Cardinal Gibbons, gathered in Saint Louis for the conferring of the pallium on the new archbishop. Archbishop John Ireland of St. Paul spoke with his usual fire. He called for a new cathedral in Saint Louis; he almost demanded that the archbishop move forward and build it. At the banquet given for the visiting dignitaries that same evening, the priests of Saint Louis presented the archbishop with a personal gift of $60,000. (They were later to raise it to $71,000.) In the course of the reception, Ambassador R. C. Kerens announced that thirty-two lay members of the Church of Saint Louis had subscribed the sum of $260,000. Two of the donors had contributed $25,000 each. The archbishop recalled that his predecessors had gathered another quarter of a million. The total then reached $600,000. A few months before, when he had spoken of a million dollars, the sum had seemed impossible. Now with $600,000 already in, the other $400,000 seemed merely a matter of time.

The archbishop wanted the cathedral to have the largest seating capacity of any church in the nation. He excluded the Classic, Gothic, and Renaissance styles, presumably because Americans had already built so many churches in these styles. He invited a number of famous architects of the United States and Europe to submit sketches. During the summer (1905), he visited his home in Ireland and various cathedrals of western Europe. He returned in September with the announcement that the new building would combine Romanesque, Byzantine, and Renaissance features.

During the Fifth Diocesan Synod at Kenrick Seminary in October, 1905, he spoke in a general way about the new cathedral, but divulged none of the plans regarding the building. He named various diocesan boards and announced the elevation of Father Francis Goller to the dignity of a Roman prelate. During the following year, 1906, plans continued for the new cathedral. Finally a special committee appointed for the purpose selected a design of architects Barnett, Haynes and Barnett of Saint Louis. That combined a Byzantine interior with a Romanesque exterior.

The archbishop broke ground for the huge building, to seat between four and five thousand people, on May 1, 1907, in a simple ceremony witnessed by Archbishop James Harty of Manila, on a home visit at the time, Fathers Gilfillan and Tannrath, architect George Barnett, and general contractor Jerome Casey.

In early summer, the archbishop presided at the Sixth Diocesan Synod at Kenrick Seminary. He discussed the encyclical of Pope Pius X, *Pascendi Gregis*, on modernism, and other papal decrees.

In response to the request of the Fathers of the synodal board, Glennon issued a pastoral letter on August 25, 1908, challenging all the people of Saint Louis, to give their share for the cathedral. The archbishop hoped for a half-million dollars from the people of the diocese — an average of two dollars each from every man, woman, and child. He announced at the same time that Sunday, October 18, 1908, would be the day for the cornerstone laying.

A rainy fall day saw the grandest religious demonstration ever held in mid-America, as forty thousand men marched from a mid-town site to Lindell and Newstead. The apostolic delegate, Archbishop Diomede Falconio, O.F.M., five archbishops of the United States and Australia, and bishops from all over the nation, took part in the ceremony. The archbishop blessed the cornerstone in a brilliantly staged ceremony at twilight. The apostolic delegate brought the special blessing of Pope Pius X.

Three weeks later, the Holy Father terminated the missionary status of the Church in the United States and removed the archdiocese from the rule of the Sacred Congregation of the Propaganda. The laying of the cornerstone of the new Saint Louis Cathedral marked a fresh day in the history of the Church in the West.

Outstate Colonizer

Like his mentor, Bishop Joseph Hogan of Kansas City, Archbishop Glennon had a high regard for the life on the land. Even though the American Church was predominantly urban and especially so in the state of Missouri, Archbishop Glennon still viewed rural colonization in a semi-romantic way and thought of it as a major social enterprise. Some wondered when he eventually came to see that the future of the Church willy-nilly belonged to the city.

In May, 1910, the Saint Louis archbishop sponsored an organizational meeting of the Catholic Colonization Society of the Church Extension Society of the United States. This society grew out of earlier efforts of Belgian

The new cathedral underway. The Cathedral Chapel that served temporarily as the parish church is at the rear right.

and Dutch priests to establish a society to aid their own immigrants. The new meeting broadened the base of earlier efforts, set up a central bureau under the direction of the American archbishops, and diocesan bureaus under each bishop. Glennon was episcopal moderator, and Father Julius E. DeVos, a Chicago pastor, president. The hierarchies of Belgium and Holland promised Glennon strong support in an effort to secure chaplains from Europe. In cooperation with land companies, the colonization society sought sites in Florida, Arkansas, Mississippi, Missouri, Wisconsin, and Minnesota as homes for immigrants.

Glennon believed that of the seven hundred thousand immigrants each year, three-fourths were farmers from the south and east of Europe who should be directed to colonies on the land rather than to large metropolitan and industrial centers. Both Glennon and DeVos recognized that their work had to begin in Europe and sought the help of Peter Paul Cahensly. To the German Catholic lay leader, these plans seemed to vindicate his words of many years before. From this time until his death, Cahensly worked with the Catholic colonization society and through his publications directed immigrants to settle in the society's western land projects. Cahensly visited the United States in 1910 for the first time in twenty-seven years, and received enthusiastic receptions in Buffalo, Pittsburgh, Chicago, Saint Louis, Washington, Baltimore, Philadelphia, and New York. He spoke of Saint Louis as the most important center of German-American Catholic life.[2] Unfortunately, this colonization effort came a half-century too late. World War I was to break out soon after and to bring an end to heavy immigration.

In his own archdiocese, Archbishop Glennon promoted several projects, such as one at a place named for him, Glennonville, in southeast Missouri. In that colony, a re-

markable man, Father Frederick F. Peters, had an opportunity to show the tremendous strength that lay in him. The land was wooded and swampy; but in spite of great obstacles, the priest and his strong pioneer flock survived in that southeast Missouri wilderness.* Another colony under the direction of Father Vincent Tesselaar, O.S.M., grew up nearby at a place called Wilhelmena.

Colonization historian Father Donald Molitor wrote:

> Archbishop Glennon should not be unduly criticized for failing to see what the embryonic twentieth century held in store. He most certainly can be criticized for not having a more realistic approach to the problem of colonization. In spite of the fact that the concept was in opposition to the trends of the times, it might still have served a useful purpose.... Unfortunately, the Archbishop had the romantic nineteenth century notion that to give a man a new start all that was necessary was to stake him to cheap land; it was up to him from then on. This proved the death of his scheme.[3]

A colony of Italian immigrants sponsored by the Frisco Railroad, showed the viability of a well-planned rural community. A group of vine growers from Italy had settled in south central Missouri near Rolla, around the turn of the century. Archbishop Glennon sent Father Ottavio Leone to guide them spiritually in 1906, and encouraged a few other newcomers to settle there.[4] Father Leone built a small church dedicated to St. Anthony. This colony had better land. Many of its people developed a number of vineyards unusual for that part of Missouri. Eventually this colony took the name Rosati. It was an example of what others might have done in other places at earlier times.

Premier Orator

Even before John Glennon came to Saint Louis, men recognized him as an orator of great promise. He had the voice, poise, looks, and intelligence; and soon succeeded Patrick Ryan, whose funeral sermon he gave in 1911, as the topmost preacher of the American hierarchy. He spoke with fluency anywhere and anytime, from country parish to the cathedral, from local meetings to national political conventions. He was equally good with prepared addresses and extemporaneous remarks.

John Glennon preached at almost every important occasion in the American Church during his first ten years as archbishop, such as the dedication of the cathedral in

---

*Father Donald Molitor of the Archdiocese of Saint Louis made a thorough and excellent study of this colonization enterprise. On reading it one can only wish that the colonization society had purchased better land for Father Peters and his people. See Donald Molitor, "The History of Glennonville and Adjacent Catholic Colonization Ventures in Southeast Missouri: A Study in Changing Rural-Urban Patterns, 1905-1947 (Saint Louis University thesis, 1965).

Richmond, the conferring of the pallium on the archbishop of New Orleans, the golden priestly jubilee of Cardinal Gibbons, the consecration of St. Patrick's Cathedral in New York, the dedication of the Cathedral of Denver, the centennial of the Bardstown diocese, the seventy-fifth anniversary of the establishment of Chicago as a diocese, the diamond jubilee of the diocese of Galveston, and the funeral of the cardinal of Baltimore.

He gave monthly sermons in the cathedral, usually on topics suggested by the scripture reading of the Sunday. He regularly alluded to events of the day or to conditions of the time. When he spoke to confirmation classes or at parish anniversaries of immigrant groups, he showed his acquaintance with the religious customs and traditions of the respective countries.

As a matter of record, and of convenience for the press, he prepared advance copies of all his important addresses. But often his most quotable and felicitous phrases were spontaneous inserts that never appeared in the prepared and published test. "Thus it often happened," a *Post-Dispatch* feature pointed out, "that his discourses were fuller and better than the published versions of them."[5] His most stirring remarks, in fact, rarely appear in any of his published messages.

In his early years, his speeches showed a freshness of thought and expression that reflected his wide reading. His style had the grace and flow of Cardinal Newman; his manner was dignified rather than impassioned. He delved into history often; but he did not come up with new historical insights; rather he added grace of expression to well-known ideas.

Glennon's speeches had a poetic quality that came through vividly in this passage from a sermon on the spirituality of his fellow countrymen:

That mystic light — it comes from the wild sea that washes the Irish coasts; from the heather that covers its hills; from the moaning winds that crowd its woods; from the woods themselves with their silent life and mystic gloom; from the open meadows and the summer night; from out of the scenery and association and life that becomes a part of the Irish character, there comes that strange yearning, that great desire, that unwillingness to be part of the commonplace, that restlessness, energy and fire, which as a dissolvent set here in American life makes crass materialism impossible and sets across the face of our land a rainbow of light and hope which in color, form and setting takes from the earth its fascination and tells us of the better things and the brighter land.[6]

Glennon showed interest in the main public questions of the day during his first years in Saint Louis — prohibition, peace, woman suffrage, socialism. In 1909 he proposed a Catholic labor union with a labor association in each parish.[7] At the end of World War I, when the bishops of America issued their first joint statement on social reform, he called for a fair wage and wanted workers to be shareholders or profitsharers.[8] He regularly attacked socialism. In his September sermon in 1916, for instance, he stated: "All our recent legislation makes more and more for the assertion of state control."[9] In response, Frank and Kate O'Hare, the editors of the *National Ripsaw*, a socialist paper, put out in Saint Louis, condemned him for constantly berating socialism.

Glennon opposed woman suffrage in addresses in 1909, 1911, 1913, and 1917. In 1918 he refused to sign a petition drawn up by the Saint Louis Chamber of Commerce. After woman suffrage became a law, he reluctantly came to accept it.

Glennon regularly was to speak out against plays, movies, and dances. One of his first condemnations brought him in opposition to the antagonist of so many earlier bishops, Father David Phelan. Early in 1914, the editor of the *Western Watchman* had endorsed the tango, a newly introduced Spanish-American dance step. Phelan pointed out that many clergymen of various denominations had reprobated the waltz some time before, and lived to see how silly their action was. They should not make the same mistake with the tango, he advised with a good deal of humor. Archbishop Glennon, nonetheless, in a front page story in the *Globe-Democrat* condemned Phelan and the tango.[10]

In the years before the adoption of the eighteenth amendment, Archbishop Glennon spoke frequently on behalf of temperance. He recommended it for all and enjoined total abstinence on the young; he held, however, that it was "better to take the man from the drink than to take the drink from the man." He doubted the value of prohibitory laws. When the nation passed the eighteenth amendment, he was to remark: "The Constitution has been weakened by the adoption of the Eighteenth Amendment; for the prohibition law limits rights where the rest of the Constitution grants rights."[11]

In his early years as archbishop, Glennon often engaged in sharp debate with Protestant leaders. He had a controversy with Dr. William Bitting of the Second Baptist Church. The *Globe-Democrat* commented on Glennon's subdued and subtle sarcasm.[12] On the four hundredth anniversary of Luther's break with the church, Glennon strongly denounced the Augustinian friar. Later on, Glennon took a more conciliatory posture. While he never gave strong support to interdenominational religious discussions, he joined leaders of other denominations in civic and community ventures. He served, for instance, on the original board of the Rosalie Tilles non-sectarian charity fund, along with Rabbi Leon Harrison, Judge Henry S. Priest, Louis P. Aloe, and Breckinridge Jones.[13]

Glennon did not have the passionate attachment to certain causes within the Church, such as Archbishop Ireland had for the American spirit or for interracial justice. Such an attachment might have given to Glennon's eloquence an enduring intensity. He battled *against* movies, socialism, prohibition, rather than *for* any of the great causes he might have championed.

His listeners came for edification and entertainment; they rarely met a shock to their spiritual sloth or imperviousness. Like the speeches of his later contemporary, President Franklin Delano Roosevelt, Archbishop Glennon's words accomplished their immediate goals, but did not come to live in any collection of great speeches. A contrast with another and later Irish-American orator might place Glennon's style in even clearer perspective. He shared with President John Fitzgerald Kennedy a ready wit and an appealing and lofty presence. Cardinal Glennon spoke more smoothly than John Fitzgerald Kennedy did in his early speeches; but Glennon never matched President Kennedy's knack of quotable expression. This stemmed in part from the fact that Glennon's words had their beauty in poetic expression; while Kennedy's strength lay in the pertinence of the ideas and the importance of the cause.

Chapter 30

Archdiocesan Development

Territorial Retrenchment

The Catholic Encyclopedia

Since the days of Archbishop Kain, many people had discussed the possibility of adding the whole of northeast Missouri to the small diocese of St. Joseph. No large cities lay in this area, and few Catholic centers. Here and there, amid the larger Protestant population, stood Catholic communities such as Indian Creek, Palmyra, Monroe City, Millwood, the Irish-Maryland settlement developed by the Mudds and Father Lyne, Bishop LeFevre's mission of St. Paul's on Salt River, and St. Patrick's in the northeastern county of the state. Two larger settlements had substantial Catholic congregations, Moberly in Randolph County and Hannibal on the Mississippi, where Father Michael McLaughlin, "one of the first priests of the diocese, a ripe scholar, a superior preacher and a model ecclesiastic"[1] — to quote Father Phelan — had guided the people from 1884 to 1903.

When news spread that all north Missouri might go to the jurisdiction of St. Joseph, priests and people in the area of Moberly protested the proposal. Rome reconsidered, and left nine counties in the wedge between the lower Missouri and the Mississippi River with the archdiocese of Saint Louis. The south boundary of the St. Joseph diocese, then, became the Missouri River in the western part of the state and a line from the Missouri just above Booneville to the Mississippi just below Hannibal. Quite interestingly, Moberly, the area of greatest protest, did not win its fight. It became part of the St. Joseph diocese.

This addition almost doubled the number of priests and churches in Bishop Maurice F. Burke's jurisdiction. It gave eighteen more parishes, seventeen more missions, a third more people and a third more territory. Even with this addition, the diocese of St. Joseph had only thirty-five thousand Catholic people in an area of 18,206 square miles, a region larger than Belgium or Holland. The change came on June 16, 1911. Saint Louis Chancellor J. J. Tannrath stated the alternatives facing the priests of the shifting counties: they could give up their parishes and remain with the Archdiocese of Saint Louis; or they could retain their parishes and serve the newly enlarged diocese of St. Joseph.

Among the priests to resign a northeast Missouri pastorate, Father Christopher Byrne became pastor of Holy Name Parish on North Grand near the Water Tower. From this vantage he promoted the Holy Name Society among Irish-background parishes. This confraternity had begun in the Middle Ages under the impetus of the Dominican Fathers, and flourished in Dominican parishes throughout the world. In 1896, Pope Leo XIII had authorized its spread to other parishes. Father Byrne succeeded in establishing an Archdiocesan Union of Holy Name Societies before he accepted Pope Benedict XV's call to be bishop of Galveston, Texas, in 1918.

Scholars of the archdiocese played a part in the publication of the *Catholic Encyclopedia*, the major publishing endeavor of American Catholics in the early decades of the century. The project began in January, 1905, with Conde Benoist Pallen of Saint Louis as managing editor. Pallen had been editor of the *Church Progress* in Saint Louis from 1887 to 1897. Eventually he wrote eleven books and revised articles on Catholic subjects for the *Encyclopedia Americana* and the new *International Encyclopedia*. Besides serving as managing editor of the entire operation during the eight years, 1905-1913, Pallen wrote three individual articles, and served as president of the Encylopedia Press, the corporation that published the *Catholic Encyclopedia*.[2]

Father Frederick G. Holweck, rector of St. Francis de Sales Church, consultor of the archdiocese, and author of several books, wrote fifty articles on prerogatives and feasts of the Blessed Virgin Mary.[3] Father William H. Fanning, professor of canon law and ecclesiastical history and dean of the Saint Louis University School of Divinity of 1899 to 1913, wrote almost a hundred articles, mostly on technical aspects of canon law. He also contributed the sketch of missionary Pierre Jean DeSmet and a superb article on "Women in English-speaking Countries."[4]

Reverend Charles L. Souvay, C.M., D.D., French-born professor of Holy Scripture and Hebrew at Kenrick Seminary, had previously written two French works on *Inspiration* (1902) and the *Psalms* (1903). An anti-clerical French government in the early part of the century enacted laws that sent members of religious orders into exile. As so often in our history, from the first French exile, Bishop DuBourg, so in this case Saint Louis became the beneficiary of persecution of the Church in Europe. Father Souvay was one of the most valuable additions to the Saint Louis Catholic community. After his first two books in French, he had hesitated to write because of the papal condemnation of a large group of theories bound together under the name of "Modernism." The *Catholic Encyclopedia* gave him an opportunity to write once again in Saint Louis. He contributed over seventy articles on biblical terms and personalities.[5]

A scion of one of the old French West Indies families, Father Edward Garesche, S.J., who was to become editor of the *Queen's Work* magazine in 1913, and eventually to publish three books, contributed five biographies to the *Catholic Encyclopedia*.[6]

The work began in January, 1905, and reached completion in 1914. As with many multi-authored works, the articles were of uneven quality; some were excellent, some average, some poor. The editors had to publish a list of emendations and additions shortly after the appearance; but with these, the work stood as a more-than-satisfactory addition to the knowledge of Church practice and history. In view of the suppression of Catholic universities in so many countries, along with the tensions and the excessive reactions of some to Pope Pius X's condemnation of modernism, and with the immature state of Catholic intellectual and collegiate development in the United States, the *Catholic Encyclopedia* proved surprisingly successful.

Homes for the Homeless

An astute observer of the local scene once remarked that historians would look back on the Archdiocese of Saint Louis in the first half of this century and be amazed at the breadth of development that Cardinal Glennon allowed. The archdiocese was too big, too many-sided to expect his initiative at every turn. Further, such action would have required a sixty-four hour day of the archbishop. As a direct result of Archbishop Glennon's climate of permissiveness, many Catholic activities, projects, and movements took root in the area.

Two of the most notable social welfare projects in the Midwest stemmed from the distinctive personalities of their founders, Fathers Peter Dunne and Timothy Dempsey. Orphaned on a Kansas farm at the age of nine, Peter Dunne worked his way in a print shop while his younger brothers and sisters went to orphan homes. Given more to work then to study, he had little formal schooling; but when he applied for admission to clerical studies for the archdiocese, Archbishop Kain had wisely accepted him. Archbishop Glennon ordained Dunne shortly after coming to Saint Louis and named him assistant pastor of St. Rose's Church. Here he laid plans to do something for orphan boys, especially those who sold newspapers or shined shoes.

Slightly less than three years after his ordination, Dunne began his Newsboys Home at 1013 Selby Street. Unfortunately the neighbors tended to blame all difficulties, usual or unusual, on Father Dunne's youngsters. He found a new place at 2737 Locust. Here he moved his thirty-five boys on May 4, 1906. Archbishop Glennon freed him from parochial duties to manage the Newsboys Home. Father Dunne began a drive for permanent quarters. Finally on November 10, 1907, Archbishop Glennon dedicated "Father Dunne's Newsboys Home" at Washington and Garrison Avenue. His work proved successful and ultimately Father Dunne became nationally famous, especially when the story of his work became the basis of the film "Fighting Father Dunne."

A far more colorful personality, expansive Father Tim Dempsey had become pastor of St. Patrick's Church in 1898. One of the four original city parishes in the 1840's, the area had deteriorated rapidly by the turn of the century. The young pastor had opportunity to see the baneful effects of the saloons and the cheap lodging houses on the thousands of men who drifted in and out of the city. He conceived the idea of an inexpensive dormitory where men could get lodging for the night, wholesome meals, and a bath.

After long thought and planning, Father "Tim" finally opened his "hotel" with sixty-eight rooms and 207 beds. Archbishop Glennon blessed the building on May 5, 1908, amid an assembly of distinguished visitors including Mayor Rolla Wells. In 1908, Father Dempsey welcomed almost eight thousand guests. The number soon went up to ten thousand where it remained for many years.

In addition to his hotel for working men, Father Tim later started a hotel for working girls, the St. Patrick's Day Nursery and Emergency Home, and a home for convalescents. He bought a lot in Calvary Cemetery as an "Exiles' Rest" for his deceased "boys." As the years went on, Father Tim became a Saint Louis institution and the arbitrator of many labor disputes and even of gang warfare in the post-World War period. Ultimately Father Harold McAuliffe, S.J., wrote his life story, entitled *Father Tim* (Milwaukee: Bruce Publishing Co., 1944).

Archdiocesan High Schools

During the nineteenth century many parish schools had existed in the archdiocese. Members of religious orders taught most of the classes. The religious superiors and individual pastors ran their schools according to their own personal lights, with little formal preparation for educational administration.

Archbishop Kain had insisted on carrying out the decree of the Third Plenary Council of Baltimore that called for a parochial school in every parish. He also appointed a school commission with the task of bringing the parochial schools into a system by coordinating the course of studies, choosing books, and setting up examinations. But the commission never became that efficient.

Archbishop Glennon had strong views on Catholic education. He believed that educators could not divorce religious training from secular training. "Take subjects like history, philosophy, and even sciences," he insisted, "you have either to walk with God through these, or exclude Him. To exclude Him would be not properly to interpret history, science, nor indeed human life itself."[7] Schools that concentrated on secular subjects and trained the mind without training the heart, ended up with a half-formed man.[8] He thought moral training impossible without religious training.[9]

Glennon had great concern for education in citizenship; and he believed that the religious school best provided good citizens for the country. "I hold that religious education leads to a purer patriotism, a more representative government, and a happier people, than any other; for it joins together in its citizenship the two-fold patriotism for God and country, for our altars and our homes."[10] A Christian education, he believed, gave vigor to the state, to the government, and to society for two reasons: it led the student to his basic purpose in life; it sustained the moral standards among the people.

Unlike many of his contemporaries who felt that the privilege of opening schools should satisfy, Glennon asked for a fair share of tax monies for the education of all children. He suggested a direct subsidy to teachers of non-religious subjects in all schools. This, he suggested, would forestall the charge so often made that aid to religious schools would violate the traditionally separate spheres of Church and state.[11] (Quite interestingly, this idea propounded by Glennon was to gain currency a half century later.)

He strongly supported the accepted practice among Catholic educators of separate schools for boys and girls. "It will be found that the normal life of the boy is different from that of the girl," he stated. "There are certain sanctities about life that cannot be disregarded. . . . Speaking of high schools, I am opposed to coeducation. It may be more economic . . . but as a system it runs counter to Christian 'tradition, to the data of experience and pscyho-morality."[12] He wanted men to teach boys and women to teach girls, whenever possible.[13] Archbishop Glennon presented these ideas in addresses at commencement exercises, in speeches to the Catholic Educational Association, and in informal gatherings. He had special interest in high school education because he saw the adolescent years as critical, a time when the youngsters needed greater guidance of the church.[14] Further, since the archdiocese had well developed grade schools and a flourishing university, he urged the foundation of archdiocesan high schools to form a link in the entire system.[15]

In 1910, with the approval of his priests, Archbishop Glennon named the pastor of St. Mary's Church, Father Aloysius V. Garthoeffner, superintendent of schools for the archdiocese. Father Garthoeffner had been a teacher most of his life, even as a student in college and in the seminary. Further he was an energetic man and enthusiastic for the betterment of the Catholic schools. At the Sixth Synod of Saint Louis the same year, the archbishop named him, along with vicars-general Hoog and Connolly, to a committee for the development of high schools.

In his preliminary study of the school situation, Father Garthoeffner found that more than twenty-two thousand children attended seventy Catholic schools. Attendance was high in the first six grades, but low in the last two. In many cases seventh and eighth graders attended public schools to prepare more directly for entrance into the free public high schools. Garthoeffner estimated that one thousand of the 6,352 *public* high school pupils were Catholic.[16] Some parishes, such as Sts. Peter and Paul, and St. Leo's, maintained parish high schools. Religious orders and congregations had long conducted academies, permanent parts of the educational scene. The Jesuit Fathers had just begun two new academies, Loyola Hall at Compton and Eads (near Lafayette), and Gonzaga Hall at 1437 North Eleventh.

During the course of the ensuing year, Father Garthoeffner laid plans for four archdiocesan high schools to bear the names of Bishops Rosati, Kain, Ryan, and Kenrick. During the summer of 1911 he announced the opening of three — not four — schools: one for boys under the direction of the Society of Mary at Sts. Peter and Paul, where even then a parochial high school was in operation; and two for girls, one at St. Teresa's on the north side taught by the Sisters of St. Joseph, and a second at St. Frances de Sales on the south side taught by the Sisters of Notre Dame.

In order to support the new high schools, the archdiocese set up the Catholic High School Association on November 15, 1911. The association had three classes of members: founders contributed a thousand dollars or more, life members gave five hundred, annual members

Prominent priests of the archdiocese, including Monsignor Cesare Spigardi, gather around Apostolic Delegate Archbishop John Bonzano and Archbishop John Glennon on the steps of Kenrick Seminary on the occasion of the consecration of the seminary.

gave six dollars a year. The archbishop, as ex officio president of the association, contributed $2,200 during the first two years, one half the total donated by the clergy.[17] The major contributors to the cause of Catholic high school education were the three religious congregations who taught in the schools. They did not receive pay for the first ten years.[18] Financial outlay during the first year did not go high for this and two other reasons. Enrollment included only one year of high school. Friends donated equipment.[19]

Once Father Garthoeffner had the plans underway, he received letters of encouragement from such distinguished Catholic educators as Monsignor Thomas J. Shahan, president of the Catholic University of America, Monsignor M. A. Hehir, president of Duquesne University and Father Francis Howard, secretary-general of the Catholic Educational Association. Locally, however, support was not universal. The *Post-Dispatch* claimed that many priests would not openly oppose the school program because of the archbishop's sponsorship, but that "much of the discussion has been of adverse character."[20] Since only a few priests promoted the project, Father Garthoeffner, himself, feared that some would look upon it simply as a hobby of the chief promoters.[21]

Most opposition stemmed from these arguments: 1. the existing debts of the parishes; 2. the threat of a division in parish loyalties; 3. the charge that the initiators of the program had acted high-handedly; 4. a belief on the part of some that a great need for trade schools existed;[22] and 5. a strange fear on the part of others, such as the *Western Watchman*, that free schools smacked of socialism.[23] Many individual families had long paid tuition to send their children to one of the Catholic academies of the city, and felt no immediate tie to the archdiocesan high schools. In spite of these misgivings, 125 ninth-graders enrolled in the three high school centers on September 5, 1911. They came from thirty-six different parishes. The first school year closed on June 14, 1912 — the archbishop's fiftieth birthday. Had the school authorities purposely chosen the day because it was his birthday, Archbishop Glennon stated, it could not have been more pleasing to him.[24] Before the end of June 196 eighth-graders from forty-five parishes sought admission for the second school year.

The Kain and Rosati centers for girls could not house all the girls. As a result, the Catholic High School Board leased the massive three-story Saint Vincent Seminary centrally located at Grand and Lucas, formerly an academy and convent of the Daughters of Charity. The new school, to bear the names Rosati-Kain, would combine students from two centers, and faculty members from both the Notre Dames and the Josephites. A year later, in 1913, the boys' school, called Kenrick High School, found a new location at Leffingwell and Locust.

Vincentians at Kenrick

At the same time as the archbishop was building his cathedral and planning his high schools, he looked to the opening of a new seminary in the county. In 1907 he purchased the Barnes estate, a tract of land comprising 228 acres on the southwest corner of Price and Ladue roads. By 1912 he had changed his mind about the location, and sold the entire tract to the new Saint Louis Country Club.[25] Thereupon he purchased Drummond farm and some adjoining property on the east side of Laclede Station Road, just beyond the southwest city limits, south of the village of Shrewsbury.

The archbishop broke ground on April 21, 1913, and laid the cornerstone on Thanksgiving Day of the same year. He announced that the priests of the archdiocese had given one-sixth of the six hundred thousand dollars needed for the new institution. He anticipated another one hundred thousand from the forthcoming Christmas collection in the parishes. He was floating a four hundred thousand dollar bond issue; and had complete confidence in the people of Saint Louis who had already contributed one million seven hundred thousand dollars for the building of the new cathedral.[26]

One hundred and sixty students began their studies at the new Kenrick Seminary on September 14, 1915. Very Reverend Michael S. Ryan, C.M., a Roman-trained dogmatic theologian and a close friend of the Saint Louis archbishop, held the post of rector — a title he was to carry for two decades. The most distinguished faculty member, Father Charles Souvay, C.M., had received a doctorate in Sacred Scripture in Rome in 1912, and had already contributed more than seventy articles for the *Catholic Encyclopedia*. He was to become editor of the St. Louis *Catholic Historical Review*, to write extensively on the history of the DuBourg days in Saint Louis, and to end his career as superior general of the Congregation of the Mission.

Among other faculty members of prominence over the years were canon lawyer and counselor of bishops, Joseph Donovan, C.M., and Dogma Professor Francis V. Corcoran, C.M., a founder of Kappa Gamma Pi, the national honor society of Catholic women's college graduates,[27] and later president of DePaul University.

Within a year of the opening of Kenrick Seminary, the apostolic delegate, His Excellency John Bonzano, came from Washington to officiate at the services of dedication on April 27, 1916. On that very night, a group of alumni of the old Kenrick formed the Kenrick Seminary Alumni Association to cement and strengthen the friendship of seminary days.

Kenrick Seminary was soon training men from over twenty dioceses in Missouri, Illinois, Kansas, Nebraska, and other states. One alumnus of the old Kenrick downtown had already received the call to the episcopacy, Most Reverend Joseph Lynch of Dallas, in 1911. Most Reverend Jules Jeanmard was to follow in 1918. Eventually the new Kenrick was to line its corridors with portraits of episcopal alumni.*

The Vincentian Fathers of the seminary faculty also taught at Loretto (later Webster) College for women that opened in neighboring Webster Groves on October 15, 1916. Mother Edith Loughran, S.L., was first president, and Sister Vitalis Forshee, S.L., the first dean of studies. Father Joseph P. Donovan, C.M., served as chaplain. The school granted its first degrees on June 4, 1919, to Miss Florence Waddock and Sister Ann Frances McArdle, S.L.[28] Interestingly, Sister Ann Frances was also one of the first two women to win her master's degree from Saint Louis University.[29]

---

*Kenrick's living episcopal alumni at the time of this writing include John Cardinal Cody, Archbishops Leo Byrne, Paul Schulte, Daniel E. Sheehan, and Ignatius Strecker; and Bishops William W. Baum, Charles A. Buswell, Mark K. Carroll, Augustine Danglmayr, Francis J. Dunn, Thomas J. Drury, Glennon P. Flavin, Marion F. Forst, John B. Franz, George J. Gottwald, George A. Hammes, Charles H. Helmsing, Charles R. Koester, Michael P. McAuliffe, Joseph A. McNicholas, Andrew Schierhoff, Paul F. Tanner, and Albert R. Zuroweste.

Chapter 31

Last Look at Nationalities

The Social Encyclicals and the Central Verein

German-American Catholics of Saint Louis had taken an active part in the work of the *Central Verein* from its very beginning in 1855 as a national federation of parish mutual aid societies. Gradually it had assumed the role of spokesman for the German-American Catholics on a broad range of social issues. It became the organizational vehicle whereby the German Catholics could participate as a group in the life of the American Church and the American society on a national level.

In spite of the great defeats the German-American Catholics had suffered in various controversies of the late nineteenth century, the *Central Verein* moved strongly into the area of social reform at the start of the twentieth century. In 1901 it pledged itself to champion the principles laid down by Leo XIII in his encyclical on labor and spelled out its stand in a twelve-point program of social action.[1]

In 1908 the *Central Verein* set up a special office for such social reform activities. It published the bilingual *Central-Blatt and Social Justice*, the first Catholic magazine in the United States to make social problems and reform its primary interest. The *Central Verein* worked energetically to stimulate social reform activities on the part of its member societies. Within a few years it became the most socially conscious of American Catholic organizations, and Frederick P. Kenkel, its able director, had won a leading position among Catholic social theorists.

In his book, *The Conservative Reformers: German-American Catholics and the Social Order* (Notre Dame: University of Notre Dame Press, 1968), historian Philip Gleason brought out the paradox that such dedication to progressive reform should exist in a group that had been consistently conservative on all issues just a few years earlier. The members of the *Central Verein* had opposed those tendencies referred to as "Liberal Catholicism" in America. Further it was not a new society taking its start at the turn of the century under the impetus of Pope Leo's encyclical, primarily for social reform purposes. It had already existed for close to a half century when suddenly it turned its attention to social reform. Its members were not primarily reform-minded intellectuals but typical joiners of benevolent societies and insurance fraternals. Professor Gleason believed that these developments came "as a response to a critical phase in a process of assimilation of the German-American Catholics at the turn of the century."[2]

A first factor influencing these German-American Catholics was the national quest for social justice of the time. Dramatized by President Theodore Roosevelt, and promoted by the journalistic exposure of social ills called muckraking, progressivism greatly influenced states and cities. Secondly, socialism had been strong among German-Americans, both intellectuals and working men; and so German-American Catholics were aware of the Marxist

menace. To offset the inroads of socialism, German Catholic laboring men organized workers' societies on the parish level in Saint Louis, and also Dubuque and Buffalo. Thirdly, the example of "Social Catholicism" in Germany provided a stimulus and interest in the social question. German-Americans had closely followed the work of the social reforming Bishop Wilhelm Von Ketteler; and read of the annual Catholic congresses in the "Old Country."

Fourthly, in an effort to Americanize the church, some Americanizers of the 1890's had seemed to suggest that this country had no social question. To some members of the *Central Verein*, this fatuous optimism that saw America as ideal in everything betrayed complete insensibility to the social question. The German Catholics believed that the generality of "liberals" were misguided in their enthusiasm for American institutions, too complacent, and too satisfied with the status quo. The Americanizers had indeed glossed over defects of American life and were insufficiently critical of the blemishes on the American scene. With other Catholics indifferent to the need of social reform, the German-Americans took great pride in their entry into the work.

Lastly, the struggle for social reform served an organizational need of the *Central Verein*. It gave the association a purpose that could spur its members and promote cooperation with other societies. It brought within itself a number of state federations of German Catholic societies. It demanded a place within the newly formed American Federation of Catholic Societies as the national representative of the German Catholics. Thus the organization gained internal strength, bulwarked its position within the German Catholic community, and established a place for itself and all the Germans in the total American community.

The *Central Verein*, lastly, had skillful leaders. The most important nationally, and most directly connected with Saint Louis, Frederick P. Kenkel, shaped the *Central Verein's* outlook and ran the bureau for over forty years. A highly intelligent and cultivated man, Kenkel was a good administrator and dedicated worker. He had studied in Germany in the same school of economic and social thought as did those men who were to draw up background material for Pope Pius XI's famous social order encyclical *Quadragesimo Anno* of 1931. Thus Kenkel came to be writing in the vein of the papal letter long before other people in America were familiar with its principles. His concerns, however, were not primarily economic or political; rather they were aesthetic, moral, and religious. "His interest in the social reform question," Professor Gleason writes, "was grounded in a profound personal experience of spiritual alienation from the modern world. Like the early German romantics, he was tremendously attracted by the Middle Ages — a society that was a true organic community."[3]

Kenkel edited the first Catholic journal in the country to make the discussion of social problems its primary con-

Frederick Kenkel meets with Charles Korz, president of the Central Verein, *and an unidentified member of the committee on local arrangements at Richmond, Indiana, before a meeting of the national association.*

cern, set up a press service, and promoted social education through pamphlets and study courses. In 1914 he recommended the setting up of a women's branch of the *Central Verein.* The ladies accepted his challenge and formed the Catholic Women's Union two years later. Rose Rohman of Saint Louis was to stand high among its national officers. Kenkel also started a young people's section to insure continuance of the movement.

In 1920 Kenkel resigned as editor-in-chief of the daily newspaper *Amerika* to devote his full energies to the work of the *Central Verein.* During the 1920's when the reform spirit was to slacken in the United States, the *Central Verein* promoted cooperatives, a rural life program, a liturgical revival that had its fulcrum at St. John's Abbey in Minnesota, and an extensive parish credit union development, with the first charter in Missouri going to St. Andrew's Parish Credit Union in Lemay.

From his desk in Saint Louis then, Frederick Kenkel influenced German Catholics throughout the nation; and they, in turn, continued to look upon Saint Louis as a center of reforming social thought. In *A History of the Catholic Church in the United States*, published some years after Kenkel's death, historian Thomas T. McAvoy, C.S.C., singled him out as "an ideal Catholic lay leader, exemplary in personal life, able to express his thoughts clearly in good English, and learned in the social problems of the day."[4]

Father Spigardi Carries On

Shortly after Father Spigardi opened the central Church of St. Charles Borromeo, he began to look to two distinct groups of Italian residents in Saint Louis. In the downtown section of the city, on North Tenth, he opened Our Lady Help of Christians, in some way a continuation of the earlier parish and in some way an entirely new concentration of people in the neighborhood.

Many other Italian immigrants had found employment in the clay pits on Fairmount Heights, west of Kingshighway and south of the Mill Creek valley, in the southwestern section of the city. Gradually these workers built homes in the area. When St. Aloysius Gonzaga parish opened just to the west, the multilingual pastor, Father F. G. Holweck, set aside a basement chapel for the Italian families and preached to them in their native tongue. In

1903 Father Spigardi erected a one-story frame church on the corner of Cooper and Wilson and dedicated it to St. Ambrose. He sent his assistant, Father Luciano Carotti to guide the congregation.

In 1904 Father Spigardi served on a committee of five priests to prepare for the visit of the representative of the Holy Father to the World's Fair, His Eminence, Francisco Cardinal Satolli, former apostolic delegate to the United States, and at the time archbishop of Frascati in Italy.[5] The entire congregation of St. Charles Borromeo joined in the welcoming reception.

During the Christmas season in 1905, James C. Ghio, one of the prominent Italians of Saint Louis, donated $7,500 to pay off the entire debt of St. Charles Borromeo Church. Mr. Ghio had already received the silver cross "Pro Ecclesia et Pontifice." Now the Holy Father named him a Knight Commander of the Order of St. Gregory the Great, one of the seventy who bore this title in the entire world at the time.[6]

The press played a large part in preserving the national consciousness and the sense of unity among the Italians of Saint Louis. A former editor from Calabria in southern Italy, Luigi Carnovale, established two papers, the *Gazetta Illustrata* and *Il Pensiero* in the first decade of the century. After him, Giovanni Cattone successfully edited *Il Pensiero* until his death during World War I.

In 1912 Father Spigardi set up a free parochial school for the children of Our Lady of Christians. As a rule, the Italian immigrant did not understand the school situation in the United States. He saw no need of a parochial school and trusted in the public schools to give his children the necessary intellectual and moral training. This may have been acceptable in a country like Italy where public schools functioned in a Catholic environment. Father Spigardi had to acquaint his people with the realities of the American situation at the time. To teach in his new school, he secured a recently founded Italian sisterhood, the Missionary Zelatrices of the Sacred Heart. He had met them while giving a mission at the Church of St. Michael in New Haven, Connecticut. At St. Ambrose, too, Father Carotti had begun a parochial school even before 1907, when St. Ambrose became a full-fledged canonical parish. Ultimately the Sisters of Loretto took charge of this school.

Father Spigardi plunged ahead with his school program, trusting in the providence of the Heavenly Father. The bills began to pile up. He resorted to his tried expedient, a carnival. He planned a mammoth one for Saturday, November 22-23, 1913, at the Coliseum in downtown Saint Louis. Many civic groups participated. It turned out to be a notable success.[7]

In the years ahead, Father Spigardi was to send another of his assistants, Father Giulio Giovannini, to serve as administrator at St. Ambrose, and to dedicate a handsome church of Lombard-Romanesque style on June 13, 1926; and to see the completion of an orphanage for Italo-American children in October four years later. He was to die shortly after its opening and before the dedication ceremonies.

A historian of the Catholic Italians of Saint Louis, Walter Galus, C.R., could rightly say, "After the study of local Italian ecclesiastical history, the outstanding fact still remains clearer than ever that the history of the Italian parishes and associated institutions has been largely the history of the life and labors of Father Cesare Spigardi. He was the inspiration of them all."[8]

Smaller Congregations

During the last ten years before World War I, great numbers of Slavic immigrants came to the industrial cities of the north and east, especially those of the Great Lakes region, such as Cleveland, Detroit, Chicago, Milwaukee, and Pittsburg, as they had been doing since 1880. The only part of the Saint Louis metropolitan area that saw a great influx of these industrious people from the empires of Russia and Austria-Hungary proved to be the Madison County industrial complex across the river in Illinois. Few came directly to Saint Louis.

Saint Louis Catholicism retained its predominantly Irish-German cast; and when heavy Irish-German immigration to the United States had ceased after 1880, heavy overseas immigration to Saint Louis ceased. New arrivals to Saint Louis were American-born from the neighboring towns of Missouri and Illinois.

Still several small Slavic communities grew up in Saint Louis, besides the Bohemians and Poles already mentioned. The Bohemians of St. John Nepomuk Parish had long exerted a national leadership among their fellow nationals throughout the Midwest. In the early years of Archbishop Glennon, the people of St. John Nepomuk's, under the guidance of Father Charles Bleha, began a drive to open an orphanage in Fenton in memory of the great Bohemian-American leader, Monsignor Joseph Hessoun.

Dr. Hynek Dostal, promoter of Czech independence, and friend of Thomas Masaryk, soon to be the first president of Czechoslovakia, edited the Bohemian newspaper *Hlas*, begun the previous century by Monsignor Hessoun. An outstanding orator and linguist, Dr. Dostal expanded publishing activities to include books of an educational and cultural nature. His wife, Anna, edited the newspaper *Ceska Dena*, for Bohemian women.[9]

The Saint Louis Poles had begun their first church, St. Stanislaus, on the near north side, back in the 1880's. In the early years of the twentieth century they opened three new parishes: St. Casimir's in north Saint Louis, St. Hedwig's on the far south side, and Our Lady of Czectochowa, named for the great Polish shrine of the Blessed Mother, on the near south side. The Poles at no time constituted a significant percentage of Saint Louis Catholics. Nor did they play a leading part in the wider life of the American-Polish community. But they did remain an amazingly staunch segment of the Catholic body.

Among the smaller Slavic groups, the Croatians and their neighbors, the Slovenes, had retained their strong Catholicism in the otherwise Greek Orthodox Balkan peninsula of southeastern Europe. For over two hundred years before World War I, the Croats had belonged to the Austrian Empire, whose armies had freed them from Turkish rule. After World War I, they were to join the Serbians in the south Slav country of Yugoslavia.

A small group of Croats had settled on Second Street, between Market and Arsenal in the early 1880's. They worked as manual laborers, or opened grocery stores, meat markets, or taverns. In 1902 Croatian laymen organized the St. Joseph Croatian Roman Catholic Church Society, and purchased a Jewish synagogue at Eleventh and Chouteau for use as a church. By the end of 1904, eighty-two families worshiped there. Father Oskar Suster offered Mass for a time in the old Slavonic rite.[10]

During the long pastorate of Father Joseph Kompare (1909-1925), the religious life of the Saint Louis Croatians flourished. He succeeded in getting the Precious Blood nuns to teach in St. Joseph's Grammar School. Before this, it had only a precarious existence.

After 1909, the Croatian community split on ideological grounds. One group remained close to the old customs and devoted to the Church. Another group sought rapid "Americanization." They moved away from their Croatian identity and from the Catholic church.

By the end of World War I, five thousand Croats were to live in Saint Louis. Almost half of these resided in the neighborhood where they had originally settled. The rest had scattered, some of them moving to the vicinity of Calvary Cemetery for stone work. No new "Little Croatia" grew up, comparable to "The Hill" for the Italians. By the mid-thirties, six thousand Croats lived in the Saint Louis area. Intermarriage with older American groups tended to break up the national and spiritual ties that had been so strong at the outset.

Another Slavic people, the Slovaks, lived next to the Bohemians in the old Austrian empire. After World War I they were to form with the Bohemians (the Czechs) and other nationalities the independent state of Czechoslovakia. The Slovaks rivalled the Poles in intense loyalty to the Catholic faith. A few came to Saint Louis and purchased a Baptist assembly at Twelfth and Park, in the late years of Archbishop Kain. They opened Holy Trinity Church. During the first few years, they had no pastor of their own nationality. Bohemian and Polish priests took care of their spiritual needs. In 1910 the Franciscan Sisters began a parish school.

Two other East European peoples established parishes in Saint Louis: the Ruthenians and the Lithuanians. The Ruthenians, who belonged to the Slavonic Rite, worshipped together in a chapel of St. John Nepomuk's Church. In 1908, they bought the old Episcopal church of St. John at Dolman and Hickory Streets, three blocks west and one block north of Holy Trinity. They chose the name, St. Mary's Assumption, for their parish. When in 1913 the Holy See established the Ruthenian Greek Catholic diocese with the Right Reverend Stephen Soter Ortinski as first bishop, all the Ruthenian parishes in the United States — including St. Mary's Assumption — came under his jurisdiction. During World War I, under the leadership of Father Michael Vitkus, the Liths were to purchase and remodel a Protestant church on Armstrong and Park, nine blocks west of Holy Trinity and adjacent to Lafayette Park. They named the church after St. Joseph.

Saint Louis numbered one group of near Eastern Catholics. The Lebanese who had lived in the territory not far from the Holy Land, and belonged to the Maronite Rite, had organized their first church in October, 1898, under the direction of Father George Emanuel. The congregation, numbering about fifty families, met for divine service in a stone building on Broadway and Poplar Street which was named St. Anthony the Abbot. They moved a few years later to St. Ange Avenue and Hickory Street. In 1914 the Maronite Catholics of Saint Louis set up another parish, St. Raymond's, on Ninth and LaSalle Street just south of the Saint Louis business district. The Maronites never made up a large part of the Saint Louis Catholic community; but they did contribute to the rich and distinct Catholic life of the city.

The city had a fairly constant Mexican population of more than three thousand. No Mexican colony as such existed; but Mexican-Americans dwelt in two main areas east of Grand Boulevard: on the south side between

Victor Street and Carondelet; on the north side, between St. Louis Avenue and Baden. They did not have a neighborhood identification, but began several clubs as focal points.[11] Father William F. Mullaly, pastor of Annunciation Church on South Sixth, organized a choral society and promoted athletic teams among them.[12]

In general, these and earlier nationality-based congregations provided a center of identification and a means of gradual assimilation to American life. They were a major factor in helping the immigrant become American without ceasing to be a Catholic.

The Saint Louis Negroes: A Story of Neglect

The amazing growth of the Catholic Church in Saint Louis was an exclusively white growth. The vast majority of Negroes moving into the city of Saint Louis in the twentieth century were Protestants. The Church seemed unconcerned about them religiously or socially. The Catholic Negroes were, for the most part, descendants of slaves of Creole families who had grown up in an atmosphere of Catholic ceremonial. Their parish remained city-wide and segregated; they formed a small minority both among their fellow Catholics and among their fellow Negroes.

During the years of Kain and the early years of his successor, John Glennon, Father Michael Speich, S.J., served as pastor of St. Elizabeth's Church. The choir, under the direction of Lorenzo Harris, gained prominence in musical circles. Parochial societies of various kinds developed. The parish remained solvent.

Father John McGuire, the next pastor, began to look for a new church site. As the wealthier white families moved west to the vicinity of Forest Park, the old Walsh mansion at 2731 Pine Street served as a club for some years. The club managers had enlarged the residence. The plant would afford ample room for chapel, school, and community center. Fortunately Father McGuire was able to secure this property. As was customary in those days before World War I, most of the Catholic societies of the city turned out for the procession on the day of the opening of the new St. Elizabeth's. Mayor Henry Kiel and Archbishop John Glennon addressed a large assemblage.

The Oblate Sisters remained behind in the old neighborhood, conducting lessons in sewing and cooking, teaching Catechism, and showing concern for the social welfare of their people. But the Sisters of the Blessed Sacrament, founded by Mother Catherine Drexel to work among the Indians and Negro people, opened a mission in 1914 on Pine Street adjacent to St. Elizabeth's Church. In 1916 the Sisters began a two-room school in the rectory enrolling 125 children.

At the same time, Saint Louis took a major step *backward* in black-white relations. During the early years of the century, as part of the progressive movement in the nation, Saint Louisans had sought various reforms to make government more democratic. Thus they urged the adoption of the initiative whereby the citizens at large could introduce and vote on issues. The Saint Louis City Charter of 1914 included this feature.

In the previous four years, *officials* in several border and southern cities, led by Baltimore, had passed laws requiring residential segregation of blacks and whites. In 1916, Saint Louis became the first city in the country where *the people* initiated and voted directly into law such mandatory segregation. The neighborhood improvement groups at the edge of the main Negro community provided most of the local impetus for the law. The Church did not take an effective stand on the issue.[13]

The opponents of the restrictive measure, however, won a temporary injunction in April, 1916, from Judge D. P. Dyer, restraining the city from operating under the new segregation ordinance, pending the decision of the United States Supreme Court in a similar case in Louisville. On November 5, 1917, the Supreme Court decided unanimously that the Louisville law was unconstitutional. Judge Dyer made the Saint Louis injunction permanent.[14]

But the court decisions proved ineffective in stopping residential segregation. The citizens of Saint Louis had spoken. Private restrictive covenants took the place of the rejected law. Compulsory segregation became a fact, even though the courts had rejected its legal support.[15]

A few years later, Archbishop Pietro Fumasoni-Biondi, the apostolic delegate to the United States, asked Archbishop Glennon what the archdiocese was doing for its colored population. In Glennon's long report of all the things that had been done — relatively little in contrast to the vast activity among whites — two currents stood out clearly. The archbishop believed that the colored people expected and demanded equal rights in the churches and wished to eliminate the colored line altogether. "Unfortunately," Archbishop Glennon wrote, "this is impractical for the present at least in a city such as Saint Louis which is by sentiment and tradition a southern city, and where consequently putting in operation the demands of the colored Catholics would lead to much disturbance."[16] Glennon secondly insisted that the colored people thought only of their rights and forgot their duties of supporting the church and schools that had been sustained by members of the white race.[17]

Glennon would live by this viewpoint until his death many years later; and so he missed one of the greatest opportunities of his lifetime. He could have challenged the position of his flock. As a great Catholic leader, he should have prepared the way for a change of viewpoint. Yet no sentence in any pastoral, speech, or communication pointed out to white Catholics what Christ-like living required of them in this area.

The Archdiocese and World War I

The outbreak of World War I offered Archbishop Glennon an opportunity to show his broadmindedness and great skill as a diplomat. He was against the war; and so spoke in an address to the young ladies' sodalities of the archdiocese at the Cathedral on May 30, 1915.[18] But members of his flock felt bonds of sympathy with almost everyone of the belligerents.

Many of the early families of Saint Louis had ties with their French homeland; but these were so ancient that they had few known relatives among the French participants in the war. Still a feeling of sympathy for France and even more for ravished Belgium spread through the city. The recently immigrating Italians still had strong ties to their native land. While the German Catholics had no love for the Kaiser's empire or his military machine, they did have ties of cultural loyalty to the fatherland.

In an article "Pan-Germanism and American Catholicism," in the *Catholic Historical Review*, Edward Cuddy looked at the entire nation, and had a few remarks about Saint Louisans. He found that Frederick Kenkel purposely pursued a policy of neutrality in order to further the religious influence of the *Central Verein.* Kenkel wrote shortly after the outbreak of the war: "It is not the province of a strictly Catholic paper to be partisan."[19] In evaluating Catholic papers of the nation, Cuddy found the Saint Louis-edited *Church Progress* and the *Fortnightly Review* "neutral but with muted sympathy for Germany," and he listed *Die Amerika* among seven pro-German Catholic papers in the nation.[20] *Die Amerika* began to speak strongly against the United States munitions trade in the spring of 1915.[21]

The Irish in Ireland gave their usual disproportionate number of men to the British service. At the same time, Britain did not reciprocate with justice to Ireland. The Easter Rebellion broke out in 1916. Many Irish-Americans felt the outrage of Britain's refusal to be fair. In Saint Louis, Father Tim Dempsey spoke in a surprisingly pro-Kaiser tone.[22]

The partition of Poland in the late eighteenth century had divided the Poles among three different empires, the Russian, the Austrian, and the German; and so the concern of the Saint Louis Poles lay towards independence and political freedom for their relatives across the sea. The Slavic people from the Austrian empire had divided loyalties: some hoped for freedom for their national groups outside the empire; and some wanted a better status within the empire. They did, however, have a certain affection for the grandfatherly emperor, Franz Joseph, as the great number of Saint Louis boys who bore the name Francis Joseph indicated. When the old emperor died, Archbishop Glennon had a Requiem Mass for the repose of his soul, on December 2, 1916, in the presence of priests and people representing six different language groups: German, Hungarian, Bohemian, Slovak, Croatian, and Ruthenian. The Austro-Hungarian consul, John Schwegel, sent out invitations to Catholics of various national backgrounds.[23]

On Palm Sunday, 1917, sensing the imminent American declaration of war, the archbishop expressed his strong conviction that Holy Week was not an appropriate time to send brother against brother. Nonetheless, when President Wilson did deliver his message to Congress on Good Friday, 1917, Archbishop Glennon joined with seven other archbishops of the country in a statement of Catholic loyalty and patriotism. In his sermon the first Sunday of May he called for victory without abuse of our enemies. Glennon saw the growing national hostilities as unnecessary for victory and detrimental to lasting peace.

When Pope Benedict XV submitted his proposal for peace to the United States and the Allies, Archbishop Glennon pointed out that this was not a religious document binding them in conscience but a move for civilization's sake with great moral force and suasion. In the midst of the anti-German frenzy that saw Saint Louisans

change the name of several streets and temporarily, even of several meat dishes, Archbishop Glennon continued to allow priests and people to use the German language in various churches. He saw no need to push the German language out immediately by edict. "I have the unquestionable right to suppress disloyalty or heresy in whatever language it is voiced," the Archbishop said, "but no complaint of disloyalty or heresy in any Saint Louis church has come to me."[24]

In June, 1918, at the solemn military high Mass held on the grounds of the orphanage of the Sisters of St. Joseph in south Saint Louis, the archbishop again took occasion to emphasize the point to the many thousands present:

> We are not fighting for Anglo-Saxon supremacy. We are fighting for the supremacy of justice and right.... Neither is this a war of languages. Language is but a vehicle of thought; and is cursed or blessed by the thinker whose servant it is. Sentiments of disloyalty may find their place in any language and equally so, sentiments of loyalty and fidelity.[25]

A month after the United States entered the war, a group of Catholic ladies, among whom Mrs. Theo Benoist had a prominent place, founded the Catholic Women's League to assist Catholic soldiers at Jefferson Barracks. They began programs of social service for the Catholic soldiers similar to those started in Cincinnati. Eventually twenty thousand Saint Louis women participated. This valuable organization wisely decided to continue after the war and engaged in social service activities.[26] Another group of women, mostly from the south side, formed the Cheer Club in 1917 to aid soldiers in ways similar to the Catholic Women's League. After the war the ladies continued their work by affiliating with the Guardian of Angel Settlement House on 1029 Marion and engaging in home visiting and other charitable activities. Mrs. A. A. Cervantes served as perennial president of this association.[27]

At the conclusion of the war, the archbishop continued his broadminded work for peace and justice. He encouraged the charity of the people of Saint Louis to the suffering children of both sides, especially the children of Belgium and Austria. Further, the archbishop welcomed to the city distinguished citizens of the Allies and the central powers such as King Albert and Cardinal Mercier of Belgium, Marshal Foch of France, and Cardinal Faulhaber of Germany.

Glennon spoke in favor of a good League of Nations in Louisville, Kentucky, in early 1919.[28] On the fifth anniversary of the Armistice, November 11, 1923, the *Post-Dispatch* held a symposium on peace. Archbishop Glennon joined Belgian Cardinal Mercier, the Slavic scholar and patriot Thomas G. Masaryk, the British secretary of foreign affairs, Lord Curzon, former American secretary of state Robert Lansing, and the president emeritus of Harvard, Charles Elliott. Archbishop Glennon spoke more hopefully than the rest of the panel.[29]

Cardinal Mercier of Belgium visits Kenrick Seminary, October 25, 1919. Seated at his right is Bishop Thomas Lillis of Kansas City, Missouri. In the second row (left to right) are Monsignor Tannrath, Fathers Souvay, Corcoran, Barr, and Conroy, an unidentified layman who travelled with the Belgian prelate, and Monsignor Charles Van Tourenhout.

Chapter 32

Organizations Galore

The Saint Louis Catholic Historical Society

Priests of the archdiocese had begun a church history society in the late 1870's. As an association it did not endure. But individual members, especially Chancellor Van der Sanden, carried on valuable historical work, especially in preserving the records of the early years of the Church in the area. Historical interest continued high in German-background societies, especially the *Central Verein*. It issued a brief history of the church in Saint Louis as a souvenir of its sixty-second general congregation convention in 1917.[1] Archbishop Glennon praised the preservation of church documents in his letter to the *Central Verein* at that time.

The archbishop had also suggested the foundation of a historical society on February 7, 1917. He singled out fourteen priests as charter members, but he also wanted lay members. The organization began with the archbishop as president, Monsignor J. A. Connolly as vice-president, Father John Rothensteiner as secretary, and Fathers Frederick G. Holweck and Charles L. Souvay, C.M., as librarians and archivists. The first big project was a commemoration of the centennial of the arrival of Bishop Du Bourg in Saint Louis. This, they held at the old cathedral June 6, 1918.

The Saint Louis Catholic Historical Society served many purposes. It provided mutual encouragement for the able historians then in Saint Louis. It assigned Fathers J. Rothensteiner and F. G. Holweck to examine the contents of Father Van der Sanden's tin cases and to sort out what was of value. As these two men went through box after box, they stood amazed at the treasure they found, especially the Rosati papers. Even more amazing was the fact that Father Van der Sanden had used none of these valuable documents, except in a limited correspondence with church historian John Gilmary Shea, and in a few translations he made for a local newspaper.

The society chose a five-member committee on publication — one layman, Edward Brown, and four priests, Fathers Rothensteiner, Holweck, Souvay, and Gilbert Garraghan, S.J., of Saint Louis University. They contributed to various historical reviews and began the *Saint Louis Catholic Historical Review* in December, 1918, with Father Souvay as editor-in-chief. The review published much valuable source material, such as selections from Rosati's *Diary* and the correspondence of Bishop Du Bourg.

Besides the editor, the three most consistent contributors were Fathers Holweck, Rothensteiner, and Garraghan.

Father Holweck wrote about pioneer priests of the archdiocese, such as Regis Loisel, Edmund Saulnier, and Joseph Lutz. Father Rothensteiner covered a variety of historical themes. Jesuit Garraghan concentrated on the beginnings of his order's work in Saint Louis and on the Indian frontier.

The list of contributors included Edward Brown, the one lay member of the board, who wrote on Alexander McNair, first governor of Missouri; Bishop Patrick McGovern of Wyoming on the history of the diocese of Cheyenne; and Ida M. Schaaf on Pere Henri Pratte, Missouri's first native-born priest. Sister Monica edited "A Diary of the Sisters of St. Joseph," on their journey from Saint

Monsignor John Rothensteiner carried to conclusion the monumental two-volume history of the Archdiocese of Saint Louis.

Louis to Tuscon, Arizona, in 1870.[2] The magazine carried two commemorative speeches of Archbishop Glennon: "The Dawn of Missouri History," on explorers DeSoto and Marquette, given at the old cathedral, October 9, 1921, the centennial of Missouri's statehood; and an eloquent tribute to the Jesuits, especially to missionary Pierre Jean De Smet, on the occasion of the hundredth anniversary of their coming to Missouri (1923). The fifth volume of the *St. Louis Catholic Historical Review* (1923) proved to be the last.

This fine enterprise ended for the time, but it promoted a climate of interest that culminated in the publication of a two-volume history of the archdiocese before the end of the decade. Four members of the society had the background and interest for this task. Father Souvay possessed in an eminent degree all the qualities of the true historian, but had so many priestly and professional duties along with his literary work that he was not able to undertake the task.[3] Eventually, the Congregation of the Mission called him back to Paris to be its superior general.

Jesuit Garraghan had already written books on church beginnings in Chicago and Kansas City and on the parish of St. Ferdinand in Florissant. In the early twenties he had to undertake, at his superior's request, the history of his own order in the middle west. Versatile Father Holweck, a facile writer in German and a formal writer in

English, was busy at this time with his two projects: *The Biographical Dictionary of the Saints*, and *The Calendarium Liturgicum Festorum Dei Et Dei Matris*. The layman on the committee, Mr. Brown, a writer of ability but not a professional historian, served the society as business manager. Father Rothensteiner alone had both the ability and the time. His extensive two volume work was to come out in 1928, a vast storehouse of information collected over the years and given in usable form.

Laymen's Retreat League

A group of Catholic laymen had been accustomed to go to the Jesuit novitiate at Florissant and later to Kenrick Seminary for annual spiritual retreats. During World War I they began to meet regularly in Sodality Hall on the Saint Louis University campus to discuss their spiritual progress. In a meeting shortly after the close of the War, they decided to erect a permanent retreat center.[4]

In 1921 Father James Monaghan, S.J., came to Saint Louis University to direct the retreat movement. During the fall he found an excellent site for a rural retreat — a southern mansion called "White House," overlooking the Mississippi River on the bluffs about ten miles south of the city limits. Many of the retreat league men were university alumni or members of the Gentlemen's Sodality of St. Francis Xavier Church. As a result, Saint Louis University, intimately concerned with the progress of the movement, purchased the "White House" property in February, 1922, under a financial guarantee from the Laymen's Retreat League, and financed the building of a retreat center on White House property. Until pledges would come to cover the cost, the Saint Louis University advanced one hundred thousand dollars interest free.[5] Ultimately Saint Louis University furthered the development by paying the interest of a loan of one hundred and fifty thousand dollars.[6] Dayton Mudd of Saint Louis gave money for a beautiful chapel.

Father Monaghan and his assistants followed closely the Spiritual Exercises of St. Ignatius. He insisted on careful regimen of silence and meditation beginning on Thursday night, and ending on Monday morning, in time for the men to drive back to the city to work. Gradually units of retreat league men formed in the various parishes of the city. The archbishop encouraged his priests to make their retreat at the same time as the men of their parishes, or at least to go to White House for the closing ceremonies on Sunday evening. White House soon gained recognition among outstanding retreat houses of the nation.

Ten years later women's groups were to follow the example of the men with formalized retreat centers and associations. A group of women who had been making retreats at Sacred Heart Convent in St. Charles formed a women's retreat league and set up a retreat center on Partridge between Page and Olive in University City.[7] In August, 1928, the Missionary Sisters of the Servants of the Holy Ghost opened the Little Flower Retreat House for women at Eighth and Victor,[8] and the Cenacle began on Natural Bridge in April, 1931.[9]

Two organizations of Catholic women looked to proper accommodations for young women who came to the city to obtain work. The Queen's Daughters had begun back in the last century as a sewing club under the leadership of Miss Mary Hoxsey. Approved by Pope Leo XIII for worldwide adoption in 1894, the Queen's Daughters

Association spread to other cities. It opened a residence for employed young women on Lindell just west of Spring Avenue.[10] The Catholic Women's Association undertook a similar work in the cathedral parish.[11] The Council of Catholic Women began its Saint Louis work in the early 1920's and sponsored a Catholic School Health Bureau, the first in the United States, in 1927. It provided medical check-ups and health guidance for children in parochial schools.[12]

Sodality Center

An action of the Missouri Jesuit provincial, Father Alexander Burrowes, in the autumn of 1913, made Saint Louis the American promotional center for sodalities of Our Lady. The sodality movement had begun shortly after the foundation of the Jesuit order in the sixteenth century. During two centuries it influenced laymen associated with the Jesuits in their ministry to follow the way of life inculcated by St. Ignatius Loyola, the Jesuit founder.

At the end of the eighteenth century, the Holy Father made the sodality movement a wider church movement and authorized the admission of women as members. Under this impetus, many diocesan priests and members of other religious orders, especially the newly-found Society of Mary under the direction of Father William Chaminade, devoted much attention to the promotion of sodalities. In the early part of the twentieth century many existed independently in various parts of the country with almost no mutual help or interchange.

Editor and sodality promoter, Father Daniel A. Lord, S.J., is in a characteristic pose, surrounded by young people.

In the autumn of 1913, the Jesuit general, Father Francis Xavier Wernz, as ex officio head of the primary sodality in Rome, directed the Missouri provincial, Father Alexander Burrowes, to arrange for the publishing of an American sodality magazine. Complying with this directive, Father Burrowes chose young Father Edward Garesche, a contributor to the *Catholic Encyclopedia*, as director of the projected publication. Father Garesche immediately began a two-part survey. He explored the actual conditions of the sodalities of the Blessed Virgin in the United States and he studied the possibility of a successful magazine to promote sodalities. When prospects appeared encouraging, he began a new publication, the *Queen's Work*, and obtained office space at Saint Louis University. Catholics did not publish too many magazines in those days. As a result Father Garesche began the magazine as a journal of interest for all Catholic readers. Among early contributors he invited such noted writers as Cardinal Mercier, the Belgian philosopher, Cardinal Gasquet, the English historian, Sister Madeleva, poet and educator, Joyce Kilmer, author of "Trees" and war hero, and Father Francis Finn, internationally popular author of books for boys.

The personnel of the sodality center changed as rapidly during the early years as did the format of the magazine. Finally in the summer of 1925, the Missouri Jesuit provincial assigned newly ordained Father Daniel Lord to the staff of the *Queen's Work*. Under his impetus the staff set about studying the role of the magazine and the status of the sodality in the light of American realities. The survey proved that the sodalities flourished in some areas and lagged in others, just as the religious patterns of the entire country varied. Father Lord set out to build up an organizing team of priests and lay people, put out study guides and outlines to assist in the development of active sodalities, held conventions and ultimately summer schools of Catholic Action to promote the work, and developed a national diocesan sodality directors' conference. Father Lord found in the expanding American Catholic high school system a splendid opportunity for promoting religious life of the students through the sodality.[13]

The National Catholic Rural Life Conference

In November, 1923, the archdiocese hosted the first meeting of another national association, the National Catholic Rural Life Conference. Among the leaders in the calling of this convention, Father Edwin O'Hara, Minnesota-born priest of the Oregon City (later Portland) diocese, headed the Rural Life Bureau of the National Catholic Welfare Conference. Father O'Hara was to gain prominence later on as archdiocesan superintendent of schools in Portland at the time of the famous Oregon school case, to become bishop of Great Falls, Montana, in 1930, and later bishop and titular archbishop of Kansas City in Missouri.

One of the main reasons O'Hara chose Saint Louis as the meeting place was the presence of the *Central Verein* in the city.[14] O'Hara asked Frederick Kenkel to represent the Rural Life Bureau in making local arrangement for the conference.[15] Kenkel agreed to do this, with August Brockland as his chief assistant.[16] Archbishop Glennon sent several suggestions for the meeting.[17]

The officers of the *Central Verein* arranged to have the meetings at the Melbourne Hotel on Grand and Lindell. They circularized their entire mailing list, sending notices of the conference to the many rural pastors who had taken part in other *Verein* activities.

Among the eighty rural-minded pioneers who convened for this Saint Louis convention, the most influential in the archdiocese, if not at the time, certainly later on, was Father George Hildner, pastor of a Mississippi River bottom community of Claryville in Perry County in southeast Missouri. Although born in a small town in Clinton County, Illinois, Father Hildner had grown up in St. Anthony's parish in Saint Louis. As a young assistant after his ordination in 1905, he had organized inter-parochial baseball leagues in the city and worked with youth for ten years until his appointment in Claryville.

When Hildner received his rural assignment, he had immersed himself in the issues and problems of his people. He admitted he knew nothing about agriculture, and so subscribed to farm magazines, read books, visited farmers, looked, and listened. After one year he took a strong part in the organization of a farmers' cooperative and promoted the naming of the first county agricultural agent in southeast Missouri. He believed in demonstration farming to help his people in better breeding of stock and scientific management of their farms. He especially encouraged his people to improve their livestock. In 1922 a Mississippi flood caused considerable damage in the area. Hildner launched a one-man campaign to get a better system of levees for the area. Ultimately he was to succeed in this. The levee in the area of Claryville stands as a monument to the hard-driving country pastor.[18] The city boy turned country pastor thus had eight years of practical experience in rural parish work behind him when Catholic rural leaders met in Saint Louis in 1923 and formed the National Catholic Rural Life Conference. They promptly elected Father Hildner treasurer of the association, a tribute both to his capacity for promoting the rural life movement and for his financial organization and promotion.

The newly-formed conference set up an office in St. Paul, with Father James H. Burns as director. Composed largely of clergy at the outset, the conference issued a "Manifesto on Rural Life," and published a regular magazine to acquaint its members with rural progress. It was not a "back-to-the-farm" or a colonization movement. Rather, it tried to guide the thinking of men and women who were on the farm and wanted to stay there. It did not try to teach agriculture, but to enlighten the farmers on the value of organization, the need of cooperative programs and the use of available rural services. It stressed particularly the social values of the family-type farm.

Saint Louis was to remain an important but not a central archdiocese in the program of the National Catholic Rural Life Conference. The city, in fact, had so committed itself to an urban outlook that many priests thought of a rural pastorate as a temporary appointment until such a time as an urban parish opened up for them.

This was not true, however, with Father George Hildner. His name was to come up again in the history of the archdiocese.

Franciscan Tertiaries

Another important organization, this one ancient and worldwide, the Third Order of Saint Francis, held its third provincial convention in Saint Louis, October 7-10 of that same year (1923). Archbishop Glennon, Monsignor Charles Gilmartin of East Saint Louis, and August Brookland of the *Central Verein* addressed the delegates at the first evening session. Father Charles Van Tourenhout of Ste. Genevieve gave one of the most stirring talks during the two days' deliberations with an appeal for tertiary priests' fraternities.[19] This meeting intensified local interest in the third order.

The Third Order Secular, an organization of lay people who pledged to pattern their lives according to the spirit of St. Francis, had long existed in Saint Louis. Even before the Franciscans had opened St. Anthony's Friary between Saint Louis and Carondelet during the Civil War, many individual Catholics had come under their spiritual direction during the time of their assistance at St. Liborius and Holy Trinity Churches on the north side. When Father Servatius Altmicks founded the initial Third Order Fraternity in Saint Louis in 1863, he had fifty Franciscan tertiaries as a nucleus.[20]

The Franciscans took over St. Francis Borgia Parish in Washington, Missouri, and its adjoining mission stations, in the early 1890's. The second Franciscan pastor, Father Anthony Moll, established a Third Order Fraternity in 1898.[21] This became a focus for the movement in a long-standing Catholic region of outstate Missouri.

While not a center of the regional tertiary movement, the archdiocese did have its part in gradual development. The Herder Book Company of Saint Louis printed and distributed Father Vincent Schrempp's prayerbook, *The Tertiaries' Companion* in 1915. Joseph L. D. McCarthy was among the first four lay consultors of the third order at the First Provincial Convention in Teutopolis, Illinois, in 1917. Father F. G. Holweck of Saint Louis spoke at the Second Provincial Convention in Indianapolis in 1920.[22] Saint Louis tertiaries also had their part in the first *national* congress of the third order in Chicago in 1921. From this meeting, a national secretary resided. From this office in Chicago, the leaders of the movement sent out promotional, devotional, and service material to their constituent groups.

Saint Louis was to hold a more significant place in the third order development after 1932. In that year, Father Maximus Poppy, central secretary since 1928, moved the offices to Saint Louis whence he carried on an extensive promotional campaign.

Chapter 33

Internal Expansion in the Twenties

New High Schools in the Post-War Era

The educational work of the Christian Brothers in the Archdiocese of Saint Louis had taken a destructive blow with the decision of their European superiors to discontinue the teaching of Latin. This action played havoc with their college on Kingshighway and North Market and with the total pre-seminary training program that the Brothers had handled so effectively. On top of this catastrophe, a fire on October 5, 1916, had left the college in total destruction. The Brothers suffered a financial loss unequaled at the time in the history of the archdiocese.

Christian Brothers College had long been a landmark of Saint Louis. Now it might not be able to carry on. In an appeal to the parishioners of the city on October 6, 1916, the archbishop had rallied the people in support of "an institution whose discontinuance would create a great void in the field of education."[1]

But America had entered the war shortly thereafter, and projects, such as a new Christian Brothers College, had to wait. At the end of the war the Brothers found an appropriate piece of property on the north side of Clayton Road, four blocks beyond the southwest corner of Forest Park. Fifty-five students began their education at the new Christian Brothers College on September 12, 1922. Even though the Brothers retained the traditional name of the school, they concentrated on the high school department. Over the years they built a reputation for excellence in education, athletics, military, and community service.

Of the many fine teachers and administrators among the Christian Brothers in Saint Louis, a *Globe-Democrat* feature writer singled out Brother Elzear for special acclaim. Baptized John Joseph Kelly shortly after his birth

in Newfoundland, Brother Elzear had come to Saint Louis in 1871. He taught in the Gateway City for thirty five years, and twice served as president of Christian Brothers College.[2]

During the early 1920's, also, the Jesuit Fathers closed their three small high schools, Gonzaga on North Fourteenth, Loyola at Compton and Eads, and Saint Louis University High School, on Grand and Pine. They concentrated their efforts in one large building on Oakland Avenue across from the southeast corner of Forest Park. Mrs. George Backer gave the money for the school in honor of her late husband.

At the same time, Archbishop Glennon sought better facilities for the two archdiocesan high schools, Kenrick and Rosati-Kain. On the occasion of Glennon's twenty-fifth anniversary as bishop (1921), Monsignor John J. Tannrath, chancellor of the archdiocese, presented to the archbishop a gift of a quarter of a million dollars from the priests and people of the city, and a matching donation of Mrs. William Cullen McBride and her daughters. The archbishop selected a site opposite the old Christian Brothers College property, at that time Sherman Park, on North Kingshighway. On January 6, 1925, the five hundred students of old Kenrick High moved to the new William Cullen McBride Memorial High School, under the direction of the Marianist Fathers and Brothers.

The archdiocese opened Rosati-Kain High School for girls on Lindell and Newstead opposite the Cathedral. This school pioneered in the area with a dual congregation faculty. The School Sisters of Notre Dame and the Sisters of Saint Joseph — the two congregations staffing the most grade schools in the area — formed the faculty of the new archdiocesan girls' high. These two congregations also had academies of their own, Notre Dame and St. Joseph's, and taught at two parish highs: the SSND's at Rock High and the Josephites at St. Anthony's High School for girls.

Father Paul Ritchie, archdiocesan superintendent of high schools, served as principal of Rosati-Kain. His two predecessors in the office of superintendent, Fathers Aloysius Garthoeffner and Patrick Dooley, had died prematurely. The former had organized the schools, served for seven years, then died in 1917 at the age of forty-four. The latter had written two pamphlets in 1918 to create a more favorable climate for secondary education: "The Social Value of our Catholic High Schools," and "The Diocesan High Schools of Saint Louis."[3] He died in 1919, at the age of fifty, after only two years as superintendent of high schools.

Archbishop Glennon had then assigned Father Ritchie to the task. Ritchie had a degree in theology from the

A devastating fire destroyed Christian Brothers College, at Kingshighway and Easton, and brought death to seven firemen, two Brothers, and a watchman on the morning of October 5, 1916.

Catholic University of America, but no specific training in educational administration. Further, when the archbishop named him superintendent of schools, Ritchie could have taken the pastorate at St. Lawrence O'Toole's, or an assistantship at any of several parishes. Veteran priests of the archdiocese advised him to accept the pastorate. Unless he were pastor, they insisted, he would not have the status to do his educational work. At their advice, he accepted the pastoral position. Yet it divided his energies and interests.[4]

His career pointed out the dilemmas facing the priest-educator in those days, and the need of more direct preparation and of a more clear-cut status for the superintendent.

Ritchie's years were times of continued educational expansion. Some older congregations had schools in the city, but also planned academies in the county. The Lorettines taught at Loretto Academy on Lafayette and opened Nerinx Hall in Webster Groves; the Religious of the Sacred Heart at City House and, shortly afterward, at Villa Duchesne in the west county. The Ursulines had opened an academy in Kirkwood; the Visitandines were satisfied for a time with their location on Cabanne in west Saint Louis.

The Sisters of the Precious Blood of O'Fallon taught at St. Elizabeth's in central south Saint Louis; the Dominicans at St. Mark's on Page; the Incarnate Word Sisters at their academy in Normandy. The Sisters of Charity·of the BVM were later to begin Xavier High in St. Francis Xavier parish.

Few archdioceses of the size of Saint Louis had such an extensive high school program. At each of these schools, individual teachers taught excellently, influencing generations of students, without gaining public acclaim. Their names appear in the histories of their respective institutions. A mere listing of their names would add little to this historical narrative. Even more, many distinguished individual Religious influenced their own congregations internally, without directly affecting the development of the archdiocese. They deservedly have recognition in the histories of their own congregations.

Premature Cardinalatial Predictions

Many newspapers, but no popes, had selected Glennon for the cardinalate during the first fifteen years he spent in Saint Louis. Even Cardinal Gibbons mentioned the possibility in public and in private. On the morning Archbishop Glennon received the pallium in May, 1905, the *Globe-Democrat* carried a news item on the rumor that the Pope would name new cardinals. Perhaps one would be an American. The bishops of the United States had recently met. Among other topics they discussed was a satisfactory nominee. Before this, American prelates visiting Rome had suggested "a great number of names."[5]

That evening, in praising the new archbishop of Saint Louis, Cardinal Gibbons of Baltimore spoke of taking part in the election of Pope Pius X. In case another pope were to be elected during his lifetime, the Baltimore prelate said that he would like to have another vote cast with his — that of Archbishop Glennon of Saint Louis.[6]

Other papers followed the *Globe-Democrat's* example, without a nudge from Cardinal Gibbons: the *Saint Louis Post-Dispatch* on April 6, 1905,[7] the *Baltimore Sun*, on August 8, 1909,[8] the Saint Louis *Republic* on August 21, 1917,[9] and the New York *Times* just before Christmas in 1918.[10] In a glowing letter to Glennon* on July 12, 1920, Cardinal Gibbons suggested in a roundabout way that he thought Glennon would get the red hat.[11]

During the years that newspaper writers picked Glennon for the cardinalate, Pope Pius X chose Archbishops John M. Farley of New York and William O'Connell of Boston (1911), and Pope Benedict XV named Archbishop Denis Dougherty of Philadelphia (1921).

In 1924 three arguments prompted the rumors that Glennon would get the "Red Hat." First, the significance of the Archdiocese of Saint Louis in the development of the Church in the West; second, its inherent strength as a center of Catholicism; and thirdly, the outstanding qualities of the Saint Louis archbishop himself. For almost two decades his fellow American churchmen had considered him the outstanding pulpit orator of the American hierachy — a signal honor evidenced again when he accepted the invitation to give the funeral sermon of Cardinal Gibbons in 1921. Glennon had promoted or allowed to develop many progressive church movements — colonization, secondary school education, the laymen's retreat, the sodality of Our Lady, the Central Bureau's program of social reform. He had built an impressive cathedral and a new theological seminary.

Equally sound arguments supported the contention that the Holy Father Pius XI would name more Americans than any of his predecessors had done. As a result of World War I, the United States occupied a far more significant place in world affairs, and especially in the European consciousness. Secondly, the Church in the United States had long grown to maturity. Thirdly, many European countries remained prostrate as a result of the war, while the United States enjoyed relative prosperity. And lastly, Roman functionaries in charge of the papal election of 1922 had made no effort to adjust the ancient procedures to present realities. They had proceeded with the voting before the American Cardinal William O'Connell could arrive. The Boston archbishop was hurrying from Naples to Rome when he found out that his colleagues in the college of cardinals had gone ahead without him. He went on to Rome and protested what he considered a deliberate slight to the Church in America. Rome adjusted procedures for the future, and seemed more sensitive to the United States.

In 1924 His Holiness Pope Pius XI chose two new American Cardinals, Archbishops Patrick Hayes of New York and George Mundelein of Chicago, and some obscure prelates from inconsequential Italian cities. Pius XI ignored the River City, and did not name another American cardinal during the remaining fifteen years of his pontificate.

Health Care and Nurses' Training

The practice of charity had been a major consideration in the opening of the Catholic hospitals in Saint Louis and in their program during the early years. Most of the foundations had depended in their initial stages on door

---

*On the death of Archbishop James Quigley of Chicago in 1915, the bishops had recommended Archbishop Glennon in second place, behind John P. Carroll, Dubuque-born Bishop of Helena, Montana (*Bonzano to Gibbons*, Washington, Aug. 18, 1915, BCA 112F). Rome followed neither the recommendations of the bishops of the province, nor those of the priests of Chicago, and chose Bishop George Mundelein, the auxiliary of Brooklyn, as new archbishop of Chicago.

to door begging for alms, medicine, food, and supplies for patients and the basic necessities for the Sisters on the staff. The Catholic hospitals had participated actively in the care of patients at the time of all major disasters of the city, cholera epidemics, fires, tornados, and during the various wars that the country waged.

At one time or another various hospitals under Catholic auspices cooperated with local, state, or national governmental agencies. The Daughters of Charity Hospital had served for a while as the Saint Louis City Hospital. Again, in 1856, when fire destroyed the city hospital, the Sisters' hospital functioned as the civic institution. The Sisters of Saint Mary responded to the appeal of the City Health Commissioner in 1886 to take care of diphtheria patients at the Quarantine Hospital. In November of 1904 Saint Vincent's Hospital accepted patients from Indian territory under contract with the government. Two years later the secretary of interior asked permission to send Alaskan Indians to Saint Vincent's. In 1925 when Saint Louis County had to withdraw its citizens from the overcrowded Saint Louis City Hospital, Saint Mary's Hospital and Mount Saint Rose received patients from the county. The Catholic hospitals often made special arrangements with industrial firms such as the Terminal Railroad Company, the Wabash Railroad, and the Laclede Gas Company.[12]

During the Glennon years, three thrusts predominated in hospital history: a westward movement in location that paralleled parochial and school development; a growth of nursing education; and a growing cooperation between hospitals and the Saint Louis University School of Medicine that had opened in 1903.

The Mercy Sisters had opened the first hospital under the patronage of St. John of God at Twenty Second and Morgan in 1871; they moved to Twenty Third and Locust in 1890; and again in 1912 they moved further west, to Euclid at Parkview, just east and north of Forest Park, an area that was to see the development of the Washington University Medical Center.

In addition to Saint Mary's Infirmary at 1536 Papin, just south of Union Station, the Sisters of St. Mary's had opened Mt. St. Rose Sanitarium, the first tubercular hospital in the Midwest, in 1902. In the early 1920's, they began St. Mary's Hospital on Clayton Road at Bellevue, just west of the city limits. Behind it, they located their motherhouse and novitiate.

The Daughters of Charity of St. Vincent de Paul had staffed several health care institutions. In the late Kenrick years, they had moved the Saint Louis Mullanphy Hospital to 3225 Montgomery (1874), bought property for St. Ann's Maternity and Rest Home and Hospital on Page just west of Union (1888), and transferred St. Vincent's Sanitarium for Mental Health patients from Ninth and Marion to Normandy (1895). In 1930, they opened De Paul Hospital on North Kingshighway to supplant the Mullanphy Hospital.

As hospital care became more organized, schools of nursing began to develop in Catholic hospitals. In turn, hospitals provided the clinical facilities necessary for nursing education. Thus, the two services, care of the sick and the education of the nurse, complemented each other.

Miss Charlotte Tracy had organized the first Catholic school of nursing at Mullanphy Hospital in 1894 with six students. The course lasted two years; the hours were long. By 1900 directors had lengthened the course to three years and the time on duty to twelve hours. The

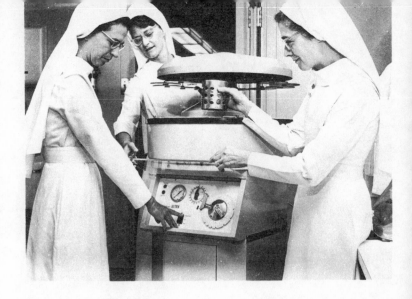

This intricate hospital device keeps three Sisters of Mercy occupied: (from left) Sisters Marjorie Marie, Mary Roch, and Mary Corde at St. John's. (Photograph by St. Louis Review.)

students moved out of the wards to their own living quarters. The first students were mature women. But by 1912 girls of eighteen could begin training, providing they had a grade school diploma.

Saint John's Hospital School of Nursing began officially in 1905. Previous to that time, the nurse-training had been exclusively for Sisters. At first the nursing candidates served apprenticeships in the wards under the supervision of the Sister Superior or doctors. In 1907, Miss Margaret Lafferty, R.N., began to direct the program of the new school. She combined theoretical instruction and practical apprenticeship.

Nurses' training under the direction of the Sisters of St. Mary remained exclusively for members of the congregation from its formalization in 1907 to its amalgamation with other schools of nursing and Saint Louis University's School of Medicine in 1928.

In 1928, also, the Alexian Brothers were to open the first training school in the country exclusively for male nurses. And in 1933, the Sisters of St. Mary's were to begin the first school in the archdiocese for the training of Negro candidates for the nursing profession.*

Higher Education in the Archdiocese

To provide opportunities for nun-teachers to pursue advanced degrees in the period immediately after World War I, Saint Louis University offered extension programs on Saturday afternoons at three convents in the city, Maryville College, Visitation Convent, and St. Elizabeth's Academy. The university granted its first degrees to nuns on February 2, 1920. A few years later it changed the program from extension services at various convents to programs for nuns on the campus itself, and became coeducational in its School of Education. It formalized its graduate programs into a full functioning graduate school in 1925.

In 1924 the officials of various local Catholic institutions of higher learning, such as Webster, Fontbonne, and

---

*For a more thorough picture of the development of health care in the archdiocese, see Ann K. Webster, R.C.S.J., *The Impact of Catholic Hospitals in Saint Louis* (Saint Louis University, 1968).

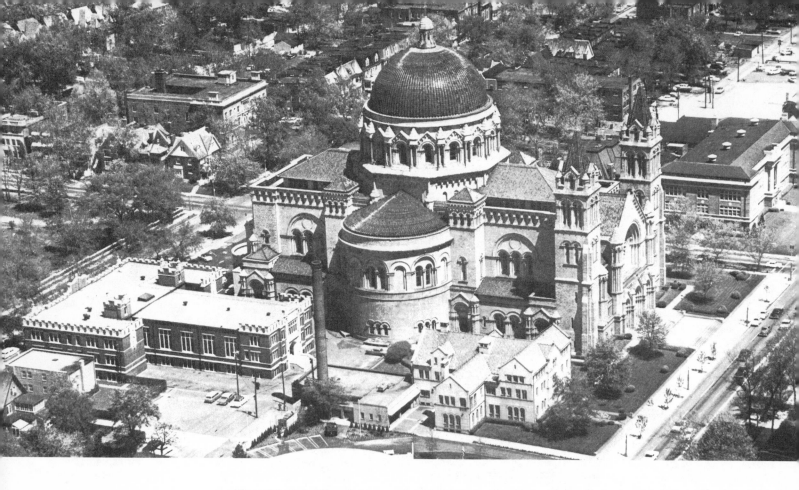

The new cathedral, with Rosati-Kain High School in the background (right).

Maryville colleges, began a program of mutual help as "corporate colleges" of Saint Louis University. Each school in the agreement retained its financial independence and considerable educational autonomy. Faculty members and students of participating schools gained the privileges of their counterparts on the Grand and Pine campus. Two representatives of each institution formed the board of the "corporate colleges."

The Reverend V. F. Corcoran, C.M., of Kenrick Seminary and Webster College, served as first president of the board, Brother Joseph Miller, S.M., as vice-president, and Father Alphonse Schwitalla, S.J., of the Saint Louis University School of Medicine as secretary. Father Samuel Horine, S.J., dean of the College of Arts and Sciences at Saint Louis University, served as regent of the corporate colleges.

Archbishop Glennon approved the plan in a letter to Father Schwitalla in early October, 1925,[13] but does not seem to have approved the participation of Kenrick Seminary in the project. Schwitalla negotiated with the North Central Association of Colleges and Secondary Schools to win approval of the new arrangements. A committee of that body, under the chairmanship of Professor E. C. Elliott of Purdue University, came to Saint Louis on October 17, 1925, and set up guide lines for the operation of the program.[14]

By 1929, the corporate college plan embraced Maryhurst Normal, St. Mary's Junior College, Notre Dame Junior College, Maryville College of the Sacred Heart, Webster College, Fontbonne College, and Saint Louis University. The program augured well for the future. It pointed the way to more extensive cooperation at a time when Catholic institutions in other parts of the country tended towards separatism and reduplication of facilities.

Later Saint Louis college-level educators, unfortunately, did not take further steps towards unity. They were to let the system disintegrate just before a national trend towards unity and cooperation began to appear.

Saint Louis was to become the center of another national Catholic organization with the 1928 election of Dean Alphonse Schwitalla, as president of the Catholic Hospital Association of the United States and Canada. In order to carry out his duties as president, Dean Schwitalla moved the offices to Saint Louis. He edited the magazine *Hospital Progress*. M. Raymond Kneifl accepted the newly created post of executive secretary. This layman had been familiar with the work of the association almost since its beginning in 1915.

Father Schwitalla was one of the first Catholic educators to take active part in the work of the North Central Association of Colleges and Secondary Schools; and was the first priest to become president of that organization. As dean, Schwitalla brought the Saint Louis School of Medicine to a high place in the nation; and on the local level he brought about greater coordination of the medical school with the hospitals under the direction of the Sisters of Saint Mary's of the Third Order of Saint Francis. The medical school had long worked in cooperation with St. John's, St. Anthony's, and the Alexian Brothers Hospitals. In 1928, Saint Louis University organized a distinct School of Nursing by unifying the already existing St. John's Hospital School of Nursing and providing for the admission of lay students to St. Mary's and Alexian Brothers' nurses' training programs.

Another advance in local higher education was to come after the Great Depression of 1929 made men conscious, as no papal encyclical had done, of the need of concern for social welfare. A year later, Father Joseph C. Husslein

164

founded the School of Sociology at Saint Louis University. Later to gain the title School of Social Service, it trained many priests and lay people connected with the Catholic Charities offices in Saint Louis and other midwestern dioceses.

A "Sunburst of Spiritual Exaltation"

Saint Louis prepared for its hundredth anniversary as a diocese in 1926. The highlight of the year would be the consecration of the Cathedral on June 29, the thirtieth anniversary of Archbishop Glennon's own episcopal consecration. Five cardinals from five different countries accepted invitations to take part — more high church dignitaries than had ever before come to Saint Louis. (A wag commented that the baseball Cardinals had to take second place in the news for a time, and reacted by winning their first World Series later that year.)

In anticipation of the centennial, a two-hundred page, tabloid-size memorial volume had already appeared in 1924. A prefatory message called it "a record of the accomplishments of the Catholic Church on the road to its present 'exalted eminence.' "[15] The publication contained a thorough account of the Church in Saint Louis until 1834, by Monsignor Frederick G. W. Holweck, a less detailed history of later years by Constance Smith, and unsigned accounts of the development of orders and institutions of the archdiocese. The editors devoted half the pages to biographical sketches (over 300) of distinguished families, such as the Backer, Fusz, Hartenbach, Hellrung, Winkleman, and Schneiderhahn families. Most were of German-American background, but the Charlevilles, Kutis, Cafferates, and Finans also appeared.

The *Sunday Watchman* prepared a special centennial number in 1926,[16] dedicated especially to Saint Louis University. The issue listed the names of one thousand living alumni of the classes between 1910 and 1925. It included an unsigned history of the archdiocese, a digest of Father Souvay's pamphlet on the cathedrals of the city,[17] a reprint of the article on Saint Louis University from the 1924 memorial volume,[18] and an account of the development of the corporate college program.

In a truly ecumenic spirit, both of these memorial volumes carried an account of the career of Colonel Nicholas Bell, a Saint Louisan of Scotch-Irish background, a member of various Masonic Lodges, and a public servant who had participated in such civic enterprises as the formation of Forest Park, and had beaten Joseph Pultizer for the State Legislature in 1872. The editors assured the readers that no history of Saint Louis would be complete without reference to that stirring citizen and eminent patriot.[19]

Writing in 1928, Monsignor Rothensteiner recalled the many scenes of religious grandeur that had marked the history of Catholicism in Saint Louis. The climax of them all came in the last week of June 1926. He called it: "one grand sunburst of spiritual exaltation."[20] Timing was excellent. Chicago had just hosted the first International Eucharistic Congress ever held in the United States. The papal legate to that congress, John Cardinal Bonzano, carried the commission from Pope Pius XI to preside over the Saint Louis ceremonies. He came to Saint Louis, as did "the severe and majestic" Michael Cardinal Faulhaber of Germany, less tall but "serene" Patrick Cardinal Hayes of New York, and — to quote Monsignor Rothensteiner again — "the lovable Cardinal-Archbishop of Armagh, Primate of all Ireland, Patrick O'Donnell, the most popular

figure of all the high visitors."[21] Cardinal Dubois of Paris had agreed to celebrate the Pontifical Mass on the second day, but could not come.[22] An estimated 50,000 people greeted the arriving dignitaries on Monday evening.

Pope Pius XI had sent Cardinal Bonzano to consecrate the Cathedral, but the latter graciously delegated this honor to Saint Louis' own archbishop. Early on June 29, Glennon consecrated the High Altar while the four suffragan bishops, Thomas Lillis of Kansas City, Francis Tief of Concordia (Kansas), August Schwertner of Wichita, and Francis Gilfillan of St. Joseph, former pastor of the Saint Louis Cathedral, consecrated the four side altars simultaneously.

At ten o'clock ushers opened the doors of the newly consecrated temple and a multitude swarmed into every non-reserved pew and the immense galleries. Fifty-nine archbishops and bishops, a thousand priests, and countless members of religious orders then marched into the church, followed by the four cardinals and Saint Louis' own Archbishop John J. Glennon. Monsignor J. J. Tannrath, pastor of the Cathedral, walked up to the pulpit. He read in Latin and in English the greetings of Pope Pius XI. Archbishop Glennon welcomed the papal legate. Cardinal Bonzano responded graciously, then sang the Pontifical Mass. Cardinal Hayes of New York preached.

That evening thousands of children from the parochial schools of the city and men of all Catholic societies lined Lindell Boulevard as the prelates moved between them to the Cathedral for the procession of the Blessed Sacrament. Cardinal O'Donnell was celebrant. Over one hundred thousand spectators crowded the sidewalks as the priests and prelates moved out of the Cathedral and up Lindell. The cardinal of Ireland blessed the bowed worshippers on the lawn of the archbishop's home, and then on the grounds of the Sacred Heart Convent on Taylor at Maryland. Finally the hymn "Holy God, We Praise Thy Name," rang through the June night. With that, Catholic Saint Louis' greatest day was over. Even had the cardinal of Paris arrived for the special centennial observance of the diocese the next day, those festivities would have been anti-climatic.

Cradle of Religious Institutes

From the earliest days when Bishop Du Bourg brought to the West the Congregation of the Mission, the Christian Brothers, and the Religious of the Sacred Heart, Saint Louis had been a center of religious institutes. A few years later, Du Bourg invited Belgian Jesuits from Maryland and the Sisters of Loretto from Kentucky. His successor, Bishop Rosati, welcomed to the diocese the Daughters of Charity of St. Vincent de Paul, the Sisters of St. Joseph, and the Visitandines. All these groups eventually flourished and received a growing number of candidates from the Saint Louis area. Other religious groups followed their example and located in the region. This development of so many religious institutes added immeasurably to the religious outlook of the people of the city among whom the tradition of commitment to religious service grew steadily.

The achievements of the orders and the activities of their outstanding members who affected the development of the archdiocese have regularly come up in these pages. The middle of Archbishop Glennon's years might provide a convenient time to reappraise this grand development and its total impact on the archdiocese.

From the coming of Bishop Du Bourg, the Congregation of the Mission had its novitiate and seminary at Perryville. Later it set up its provincial headquarters next to St. Vincent's Church in Saint Louis. It continued in parochial and mission work in the Perryville area and in Saint Louis, and continued as a central force in the archdiocese when it staffed Kenrick Seminary.

Du Bourg had brought three French Christian Brothers to the area. The dispersal of the three men to various mission areas unfortunately prevented the growth of community spirit. This initial effort came to naught. At mid-century, however, other Brothers came at the invitation of Archbishop Kenrick. They developed an outstanding college, taught in many parochial schools in the city, and fostered vocations to the diocesan priesthood. A Roman decision to exclude the teaching of classics drastically curtailed the pre-seminary work of the Brothers and the effectiveness of the collegiate program at Christian Brothers College. It forced them to concentrate on the academic level, where they continued their excellent reputation. In the meantime, they set up a center for the training of their own men at Glencoe, Missouri.

The Religious of the Sacred Heart taught at an Academy in St. Charles, at City House, Barat Hall, and Maryville College in Saint Louis, and, in the fall of 1929 were to open a second academy, Villa Duchesne, in Saint Louis County. A short time later, the Religious of the Sacred Heart were to launch Barat Catholic Action Center adjacent to Maryville College. The first program provided special late afternoon adult education classes for women. A second program offered small, informal, non-credit courses to girls who did not go to high school.[23]

At the invitation of Bishop Du Bourg in 1823, the Jesuits had come to Florissant in northwest Saint Louis county to staff a combined Indian school and Jesuit seminary. A few years later, Bishop Rosati invited them to man Saint Louis College. They discontinued their Indian school, but kept the seminary and St. Ferdinand's parish in Florissant and St. Charles' parish in St. Charles. By the mid-1920's they still conducted those three institutions. They also taught at Saint Louis University, where they had their provincial headquarters, and at Saint Louis University High School, served as pastors at St. Francis Xavier (College) Church and St. Elizabeth's Church for the Colored, and directed White House Retreat, and the Sodality Service Center at Queen's Work on West Pine.

Archbishop Glennon was at his ingenious best in his one hundredth anniversary tribute to the Jesuits in Missouri in 1923. "Great have been the accomplishments of the Jesuit Fathers of this Province, vast their energies, mighty their exploits, grand their institutions, learned their men, and mighty the spiritual empire they have builded."[24]

The first American congregation to locate in the diocese, the Sisters of Loretto, had come from Kentucky to Southeast Missouri in 1823. They taught for a while at Florissant and then came to the metropolitan area. By 1925 they staffed eighteen grade schools in the vicinity, an Academy on Lafayette Avenue, and Webster College in Webster Groves, Missouri, and planned Nerincx Hall, an academy nearby. They kept their novitiate at the original site in Kentucky.

The Daughters of Charity of St. Vincent de Paul had answered Bishop Rosati's call to the West to staff Saint Louis' first hospital. They expanded their apostolate to a wide variety of health care, educational, and social welfare activities; and opened a motherhouse and religious training center at Marillac in Normandy, in suburban Saint Louis.

The Sisters of St. Joseph had arrived in the days of Rosati primarily to teach deaf children. They set up their motherhouse in Carondelet and took the name "Sisters of St. Joseph of Carondelet." They taught at St. Joseph's Academy, St. Anthony's and Rosati-Kain High schools, Fontbonne College, St. Joseph Institute for the Deaf, and in thirty-four grade schools in Saint Louis and Saint Louis County. They also taught at Valle High in Ste. Genevieve.

The Visitandines had opened their first western convent at Kaskaskia in the days of Bishop Rosati. In the early 1840's, a contingent began an academy in Saint Louis. Floods and decline of population forced the rest out of Kaskaskia. Eventually the Visitation Sisters opened a convent and academy in west central Saint Louis north of Forest Park. The presence on the campus at the end of the decade of two fourth-generation pupils, Mary Louise Tindell and Emilie Cabanne Jenkins, focused community attention on the long traditions of the school in the area.[25]

Many congregations that came into the archdiocese in the days of Archbishop Kenrick appreciated the central location and moderate climate of Saint Louis and established regional headquarters here. The Redemptorist Fathers undertook parochial work in the city, with headquarters at St. Alphonsus (Rock) Church, began missionary work in the entire region, built seminaries in Kirkwood and DeSoto, and eventually launched the significant publishing program of Liguori Press.

In the middle of the last century, the Franciscan Friars set up a parish and priory at St. Anthony of Padua in South Saint Louis. The Passionist Fathers began parochial, missionary, and retreat activity in the archdiocese and set up their seminary at Normandy, Missouri.

The Marianists had begun their Saint Louis apostolate in the late nineteenth century by staffing the boys' school at Sts. Peter and Paul parish. As their program on instruction expanded, the superior of the Society of Mary decided to set up a second or western province with headquarters in the Saint Louis area. Thus, in 1908, the Brothers established Villa St. Joseph, a novitiate and postulate at Ferguson, Missouri. Two years later they moved into a new school called Chaminade College on Denny Road (later Lindbergh Blvd.) in suburban Saint Louis. This school was to be a combined boys' boarding school and training school for candidates for the Brothers. Eventually the Marianist developed their seminary program at Maryhurst Normal, a few miles south of Chaminade on Denny Road in Kirkwood. During the early twenties, the Marianists staffed McBride High School for boys; and were to take charge of South Side Catholic in the next decade.

The Alexian Brothers conducted a hospital on South Broadway; the Missionary Brothers of St. Francis opened a novitiate and provincial house at Eureka and were to open St. Joseph Hill Home for senior men in 1931.[26]

Many sisterhoods had come in during the time of Archbishop Kenrick to add religious vitality to an expanding archdiocese. The Ursuline nuns had their convent and academy in Kirkwood, taught one school in the city, eighteen in the county, and an academy in Arcadia in the Ozarks, and set up their novitiate near Herculaneum, south of the city. The Sisters of the Good Shepherd had a convent and a home for the rehabilitation of young women on Gravois west of Grand. The Carmelite nuns

A large class of postulants at St. Joseph's Novitiate in Carondelet. (Photograph by St. Louis Review.*)*

moved from their old convent on 18th and Victor to a new monastery in Clayton. The Sisters of Mercy who prepared to celebrate the 100th anniversary of their founding and the 75th anniversary of service to Saint Louis[27] conducted McAuley Hall, a home for businesswomen on Newstead at Taylor, staffed St. John's Hospital on Euclid, and taught in three schools in the country. They, too, had had their motherhouse and novitiate in Saint Louis County.

The School Sisters of Notre Dame set up their novitiate and training center along the Mississippi near Jefferson Barracks; they taught in eighteen grade schools in the city and the same number in the county, and at Rosati-Kain, Rock High, St. Frances de Sales, and Notre Dame Academy. Thus, along with the Josephites, they had the largest number of schools in the area at the time of Archbishop Glennon's twenty-fifth jubilee in the city (1928).

The Sisters of St. Mary's established their novitiate behind St. Mary's Hospital in Clayton, just west of the city limits; and were to staff Desloge Hospital, across from the SLU Medical School; they continued St. Mary's Infirmary, soon to be a Negro hospital, Mt. St. Rose Sanitarium, a hospital in St. Charles, and a hospital in Jefferson City, but did no school work other than the teaching of nursing. The Franciscan Sisters set up their provincial motherhouse and novitiate adjacent to St. Anthony's Hospital on Grand and Chippewa in Saint Louis, and staffed a hospital in Cape Girardeau, Missouri. The Sisters of the Precious Blood, with their motherhouse

in O'Fallon, Missouri, taught in St. Elizabeth's Academy and at several grade schools in Saint Louis. The Polish Franciscan Sisters opened a convent in South Saint Louis and their novitiate, Villa Joseph, in Ferguson. The Sister Servants of the Holy Ghost of Perpetual Adoration, popularly known as the "Pink Sisters," opened a convent near O'Fallon Park in North Saint Louis on land donated by Papal Countess Theresa Kulage* who also built the chapel for the Sisters.[28]

One congregation of religious men began its first residence in the archdiocese during Glennon's early years. Because of the restrictions of travel during World War I, Canadian and American Resurrectionist seminarians could no longer go to Rome to complete their studies. In September, 1918, they took residence at St. John Cantius House of Studies, adjacent to the Saint Louis University Schools of Philosophy and Theology. What began as an emergency measure proved to be a permanent arrangement. The Resurrectionists assisted in parochial work in the archdiocese and, later on, were to staff a parish in North Saint Louis County.

Other men's religious congregations worked in Saint Louis, but did not set up national or regional headquarters there. By 1930 the Society of the Divine Word had an inner-city parish, the Oblates of Mary Immaculate a rural parish, and the Servites three scattered parishes. The Missionaries of the Holy Family had set up a mission house; and the Precious Blood Fathers served as chaplains at the Alexian Brothers' Hospital.

Three orders of nuns staffed academies and taught on the grade level: the Sparkhill (New York) Dominicans, the Incarnate Words, and the "BVM's"; the Sisters of the Blessed Sacrament, the Zelatrices, and the Sisters of the Sacred Heart taught on the grade level. The Little Sisters of the Poor had homes for the aged on the north and south sides of town. The Helpers of the Holy Souls staffed a social service center at 4800 Washington. The Carmelite Sisters of the Divine Heart opened St. Joseph's Home. The Oblate Sisters, the Sisters of Christian Charity, and the Sisters of the Holy Cross conducted orphanages.

This listing of institutional development is impressive. But when one contrasts the great growth with that of other American cities of similar size, the record becomes even more significant. Cleveland for instance, was to move ahead of Saint Louis in the 1930 census. Yet it could boast only nine male religious institutes with 135 religious priests, while Saint Louis had sixteen men's orders with 313 priest members.[29] Cincinnati, an older diocese than Saint Louis had only half as many Catholics and half as many Catholic schools.[30] Detroit, an older city than Saint Louis, and destined to outrank it in the 1930 census, had nineteen congregations of religious women, while Saint Louis numbered twenty-seven.[31]

*For several years Theresa Kulage was the only American woman entitled to wear the insignia of a countess of the Holy Sepulchre — an honor bestowed by Pope Pius XI for her generosity to the poor. She was to leave most of her two million dollar fortune to four Catholic organizations (*Globe-Democrat*, May 15, 1932).

Chapter 34

Parochial Activities

Parish Progress

Except in the central west on both sides of Forest Park, the development of the city beyond Kingshighway went out in spokes along streetcar lines or railroads. Thus, for instance, the Tower Grove car on Arsenal provided service for Holy Family, Holy Innocents, St. Aloysius, and Epiphany parishes. The Southampton car joined St. Mary Magdalene parish on Kingshighway with the central city; and the Gravois streetcar, going to the city limits, provided access to the city for people in Our Lady of Sorrows and St. George's, just across the county line.

Between Gravois and Arsenal, west of Kingshighway, however, almost no residential development took place during the first two decades of Archbishop Glennon's term in Saint Louis. The late twenties and early thirties, however, saw the opening of such subdivisions as St. Louis Hills, and the growth of three flourishing parishes, St. Gabriel's, St. Joan of Arc's, and St. Raphael's, in an area that twenty years before had been farm land. A more extensive bus system gradually supplanted the streetcars, and few businessmen commuted by railroad to down-town Saint Louis any longer. Almost the entire city became a built-up area. With the growth of automotive transportation, too, the sections between towns in the county began to fill. A tremendous growth of county parishes took place in the thirties and early forties.

Most parishes of the city grew up in a similar way, with few differences, such as the type of organizations, that often stemmed from the national origin of the ancestors of the people or priests of the parish. Thus, Irish parishes like St. James, Holy Rosary, and St. Matthew's developed in much the same way; and German ancestry parishes such as St. Stephen's, St. Cecelia's, and Resurrection followed a similar pattern, only slightly different from their Irish counterparts. Further, in each of them, outstanding priests and lay people helped to build a strong religious life in their areas. The story of these parishes, their people, and their priests, has come out in parish jubilee booklets on the occasion of anniversaries of pastors or parishes. A mere recital of routine events of parish after parish, or a listing of the priests who served so devotedly, would not serve the purpose of this book. The reader will have to turn to parish histories for these accounts.

An historian and teacher of modern languages, Sister Grace Marie, S.S.N.D., analyzed these jubilee brochures from the standpoint of their historical content.[1] Usually they gave much initial space to pictures of the Holy Father, the archbishop and the side altars of the church. But often they provided valuable historical data, pictures of early pastors, and the religious vocations from the parish. Anna D. Cook, for instance, gave a fine description of the lay and clerical founders of St. Rose's parish.[2] Sister Grace Marie thought Bernard Tempe's story of St. Boniface parish[3] the best historical sketch.[4] She found three booklets outstanding for simplicity, completeness, and attractiveness: *The Holy Family's Golden Jubilee* booklet, the *St. Barbara's Golden Jubilee* booklet, and the *St. Michael the Archangel's Centennial* edition.[5]

In those days before mimeographed parish weekly bulletins, some of the churches of the city put out their own parish magazines. St. Lawrence O'Toole's parish, for instance, published a journal during the early years of World War I.[6] During the war, the new cathedral parish began the monthly *Oriflame*, St. Mark's published *The Angelus*, and Holy Trinity *The Messenger*. Many other parishes followed their example.

Occasionally, writers attempted detailed histories of specific parishes. Father Peter Wigger, for instance, wrote on Holy Cross Parish In 1934, Father Paul C. Schulte, pastor of the old cathedral who, three years later, was to become bishop of Leavenworth in Kansas, published the centennial history of the old cathedral parish in book length form, called *The Catholic Heritage of St. Louis*. Father Charles Souvay, C.M., wrote *The Cathedrals of St. Louis*, an historical sketch of all three churches that had served for a time as the cathedral — the early church of Bishop Du Bourg, the downtown cathedral of Bishop Rosati, and the Lindell Boulevard cathedral of Cardinal Glennon. Later on, Father Elmer Behrmann and Gregory Franzwa were to tell again the timeless story of the old cathedral at the waterfront.

Shortly before the old cathedral celebrated its one hundredth anniversary, three other old parishes celebrated significant jubilees. In April, 1928, St. Vincent's had its ninetieth year celebration.[7] In the fall of the same year twenty-five priests, sons of St. Bridget's parish, returned, for the diamond jubilee celebration during Thanksgiving week.[8] Two years later, St. Lawrence O'Toole celebrated its diamond jubilee. This once all-Irish parish now boasted that it had children of fourteen different nationalities in its school.[9]

Since its beginning around the time of World War I, the boy scout movement had spread rapidly in the Saint Louis area. Until the late twenties, however, this development did not widely affect Catholic parish life. As a result, the Knights of Columbus promoted the movement among Catholics by enlisting prospective youth leaders for training programs in scouting. Eventually, troops began in many parishes of the city and county. Troop 98 of St. Roch's parish, under the leadership of Dr. Forrest Staley, quickly reached a high standard of achievement. In its early years, Troop Maplewood 5, at Immaculate Conception parish, included five scouts who later became priests in the city and the state.

Newspaper Features of Local Catholic Interest

At regular intervals during the late 1920's and early 1930's the *Globe-Democrat Sunday Magazine* featured accounts of Catholic priests, people, and societies. Generally these sketches of priests told the basic work the men did. A writer used the occasion of Father Charles L. Van Tourenhout's learning of Spanish for an extensive tribute to his forty-year career in Ste. Genevieve. Born in Saint Louis of Flemish parentage, this outstanding priest received most of his education at Louvain. He spoke Flemish, English, German, French, Italian, and Latin. He became pastor of Ste. Genevieve in 1901 and identified himself with the hopes and future of that oldest of Missouri communities.[10]

As Father J. J. McGlynn prepared for his fiftieth jubilee, the feature writer pointed out that he had spent all but three days in St. Rose's parish in the half century.[11] Father John Rothensteiner, the author of the history of the archdiocese, had given away five thousand books of his personal library to schools and churches in the city.[12] Father John J. Butler expanded the work of Catholic charities.[13]

Father Daniel J. Lavery, pastor of Holy Rosary, had gone back to Ireland twenty times since he came to the United State forty-five years before.[14] Father John Senson had no families in St. John's parish, since the city had encroached upon what had been, at its inaugural eighty years before, a residential west end parish.[15] Father James Coffey, pastor of St. Leo's, engaged in an interesting inter-city parochial ministry,[16] and Father James Johnson took over the work of Father Timothy Dempsey.

At regular intervals the writers featured the hobbies of such priests as Father Mecislaus A. Szamotuloski, a painter,[17] Father Joseph A. Siebert, a builder,[18] Father F. J. Schlattmann, an ornithologist,[19] Father Patrick Bradley, a master mechanic,[20] and Monsignor Martin Brennan, an astronomer.[21]

An occasional feature dealt with religious women. Mother Annunciation recalled the hardships of the founding of the School of the Immaculate Heart on Natural Bridge in 1883.[22] Mother Amadeus of the Ursuline convent in Kirkwood had mastered the ancient art of illuminating books.[23]

Many parishes sponsored dramatic clubs in the 20's and 30's as a means of bringing young people together and giving them a creative outlet. Among them were the Perpetual Help Dramatic Club[24] and the twenty-five-year-old St. Andrew's parish dramatic club.[25] In 1930 the St. Luke's Dramatic Society won first place in the parish division of the Saint Louis Dramatic League tournament.[26]

The years of Archbishop Glennon were also golden years of parish choirs. The Anthony Choristers, for instance, founded by Aloys Rohde in 1909, numbered eighty-seven men and boys.[27] George T. Devereaux directed a fifty-six-voice choir at St. Francis Xavier Church during the mid-30's.[28] Many parish churches, too, had organists of note. The *Globe-Democrat* featured Professor Carl Adams, organist at St. Boniface Church in Saint Louis for thirty-three years. Professor Adams had begun his career in 1866. He composed Masses including a requiem sung on the occasion of the death of Pope Pius IX. He was still at the organ four popes later, in the reign of Pope Pius XI.[29]

The *Globe-Democrat*, also, carried features on two of the prominent sewing guilds of city parishes. At St. Roch's parish, sixty members met every Monday to sew for the city's poor.[30] The sewing mothers of St. Francis De Sales had been busy during a quarter of a century.[31]

During the 1930's the archdiocese purchased the property adjoining the Kenrick Seminary property on the east and opened Resurrection Cemetery, a successor to Sts. Peter and Paul on Gravois Avenue. In the meantime, the county had widened the once meandering and unpaved Watson Road into a four-lane concrete highway providing easy access from the south and the southwest sections of the city to the new cemetery and beyond.

Ten members of the St. Luke's Dramatic Society prepare to welcome their fellow members to the annual excursion on the Mississippi. From left, front: Evelyn Reeves, Jean Nolte, Constance Lucas, Bonnie Cummings, and Virginia Cummiskey. Second row: Francis Reeves, Edward Flannelly, Peter McCarty, Walter Armbruster, and James McAlevy. (Photograph by Saint Louis Globe-Democrat.)

New Names in the Negro Apostolate

Much of the history of the Negro Catholics in Saint Louis during the late 20's and early 30's revolved around the name of tough-fibred William Markoe, S.J. During his seminary years at Florissant (Missouri), Markoe had helped organize catechetical work for poor Negroes who lived along the banks of the Missouri and at Anglum, a village not far from the seminary. He enlisted the help of other seminarians. Priests said Mass at private homes in the first few years. Then the zeal of the seminarians prompted the seminary itself to undertake the opening of two small chapels, one across from St. Charles, and the other at Anglum, the forerunner of St. Peter Claver's Church of a later date. Markoe published a life of St. Peter Claver entitled, *The Slave of the Negroes* (Chicago: Loyola Press, 1919) and an occasional article on race relations in *America* magazine.

By the time Markoe returned to Saint Louis University to study theology in 1923, World War I and its aftermath had brought large groups of Negro people into the crowded flats lining the streets just east of Grand. Markoe encouraged fellow seminarians to work among these people. He wrote to Mother Catherine Drexel urging the Sisters of the Blessed Sacrament to come to St. Nicholas parish in Saint Louis where he and other seminarians taught catechism. The Sisters came in 1924. The following year the Fathers of the Divine Word took over St.

Nicholas. After a short transitional period, St. Nicholas became a predominantly Negro congregation.

At his ordination in 1926 at St. Francis Xavier Church, Father Markoe wanted to invite Negro friends to his ordination. The rector of Saint Louis University refused this request; but the provincial superior over-rode him. This initial refusal indicates how "Jim Crow" attitudes had frozen in the generation after the Plessy vs. Ferguson decision of the United States Supreme Court.[32]

No Catholic high school or college in the area accepted Negroes. Neither did the Catholic hospitals. Even Negro nuns could not go to the dental clinic at Saint Louis University. Further, Church authorities made no concerted effort to change this un-Christian attitude among whites of the city. As the Negroes moved steadily west, the few remaining white families steadfastly refused to admit Negroes to one parish after another. Pastors looked upon the changing racial patterns as disastrous. They did not admit all of God's children — if these children were black.

Such seemed to be the spirit of most Catholics when William Markoe became pastor of St. Elizabeth's Church in the summer of 1927. Except for a short period when he did organizational work among Negroes in various cities, he was to hold this position until 1941. Besides working with his own parishioners, Markoe preached in many of the churches of the city on behalf of the Negro apostolate. He found a specially generous reception at St. Pius V's Church, at St. Margaret's, and at the St. Alphonsus Liguori (Rock) Church.[33] On his visits to white Catholic parishes, Father Markoe often asked Ellsworth Evans, a devout Catholic Negro and principal of one of the public elementary schools in the city, to go with him, and talk to the assembled people. Markoe presumed quite rightly that the vast majority of the audience had never before talked to an educated colored person.

In the fall of 1927, in anticipation of the continual westward movement of Negroes, St. Elizabeth's parish purchased a new church and school site at Cook and Taylor Avenues, one block west and about ten blocks north of the new cathedral. This action caused consternation in Visitation parish wherein the property lay.

In March, 1928, Father Markoe, assisted by his brother, Father John Markoe, a former army officer, nationally known athlete, and one of the most physically impressive priests of his time, edited the first volume of the *St. Elizabeth's Chronicle*. This initial issue carried stories, poems, sermonettes, and features on prominent Negroes in history. John La Farge contributed to this opening number. Eventually he became a national leader in the interracial apostolate and editor of *America* magazine.

Two young ladies of the parish, Barbara Hudlin and Virginia Givens, both destined to become Sisters of Providence later on, directed St. Elizabeth's first musical comedy called "Lala." Produced at the Odeon Theater on Grand Avenue, the St. Elizabeth's musicals became annual affairs with the wide support of the white Catholic community.

In September, 1929, William Markoe attended the first national convention of the Federated Colored Catholics of the United States in Baltimore. At this meeting, the St. Elizabeth's parish *Chronicle* came to be the official organ

Father John Markoe, S.J., pastor of St. Elizabeth's Church, talks to children of the parish.

of the federation. Markoe remained editor and continued to publish the magazine in Saint Louis.[34] During 1930 the *Chronicle* reported 225 adult baptisms in the parish, with classes of from two to three hundred people at six catechetical centers.[35] The following year Markoe became a member of the board of directors of the Saint Louis Urban League. Besides serving as pastor of St. Elizabeth's, promoting the welfare of Negroes throughout the city, and fostering the cause of Catholicism among the Negores, Markoe visited many cities in the country to confer with Negro Catholic leaders.

The people of St. Elizabeth's parish planned and hosted the seventh annual convention of the Federated Colored Catholics of the United States on September 5, 6, and 7, 1931. Markoe gave a welcoming address in the Saint Louis University gymnasium where the conference held its meetings. Nearly a thousand colored Catholics came from almost every state in the Union. More than forty priests engaged in the black apostolate attended the convention, and a Negro priest celebrated Mass at the College Church before an overflow crowd. Archbishop Glennon gave a short message of greeting.

At the evening session on September 6, after a brief welcome from President Robert S. Johnston, S.J., of Saint Louis University, Father Stephen L. Theobald, St. Paul pastor, and one of the three Negro priests in America, gave the most challenging talk of the entire convention. This protege and imitator of the fighting archbishop of St. Paul, John Ireland, attacked the color line in Saint Louis Catholic institutions. His prediction that it would not be many years before Saint Louis University would give diplomas to Negro graduates brought a thundering ovation.[36]

As an aftermath of the meeting, Saint Louis University continued to show its interest in improving interracial relations by inviting the Federated Colored Catholics to present an interracial hour once a week over its radio station WEW on Sunday afternoon. Markoe organized two significant groups: a discussion club of blacks and whites in the professions; and a fundraising group called the "White Friends of Colored Catholics."

In 1932 the Federation of Colored Catholics widened its scope and membership to become the National Catholic Federation for the Promotion of Better Race Relations. In November, 1932, the *Chronicle*, the official organ of the federation, became the *Interracial Review*.[37] Early the following year, Markoe published an article by Roy Wilkins, a young Negro destined for a long career of leadership in the interracial field.[38]

In 1933, Markoe became chairman of the Industrial Committee of the Saint Louis Urban League, and in this capacity, at the request of the mayor, he successfully helped to arbitrate several strikes involving Negroes. During these years, Markoe spent much of his time as editor of the *Interracial Review* and organizer for the interracial federation. Finally the Catholic Interracial Council in New York, under the spiritual direction of Father John La Farge, took over full management of the *Interracial Review*. Markoe edited his last issue in September, 1934.[39] A new and enlarged editorial board selected layman George Hunton as editor. Now Saint Louis no longer served as editorial and publication offices.

Markoe returned to full time work as pastor of St. Elizabeth's. Among other activities, he reorganized the parish sodalities. When Father Daniel Lord began the Summer Schools of Catholic Action at Webster and Font-bonne Colleges, St. Elizabeth's parish immediately sent delegates to these meetings, integrated as they were from the outset. Further, when Father Lord began musical revues that became annual events of Saint Louis cultured life, St. Elizabeth's always put on one of the feature acts of the show.

In a way, it might be said that Father Markoe worked all his life to liquidate his own position as pastor. More and more he realized that the concept of a distinct Negro parish was both anachronistic and un-Christian. Negro Catholics should have received a welcome in any parish. According to the law of the Church, they should have worshipped in the parish where they lived. Quite often, of course, these mere arbitrary territorial alignments did not build on or result in a natural community; but that was the way the Church authorities had wanted it. The idea of "separate but equal" — a "Jim Crow" type of Church arrangement — might correspond to the transitional exigencies of American life. It denied basic Christian and American beliefs. It would have to end some day.

By this time, nearly one hundred thousand Negroes lived in Saint Louis, about ten percent of the entire population. Thus Saint Louis had the twelfth largest black population of any city in the nation. The white population was close to fifty percent Catholic, but the Negro Catholics counted less than six thousand.

The general increase and rapid individual growth of Catholic institutions has been remarkable indeed [sociologist John T. White wrote], but apparently there has been little thought of the Negro. Neither does he possess a Catholic college of his own or a suitable high school, nor is he permitted to attend those operated for white students.[40]

In spite of the large number of seminaries, motherhouses, convents, and schools of the city in 1934, few looked to the inner-city Negro apostolate. White found only these Religious — the Oblate Sisters of Providence, the Sisters of the Blessed Sacrament, the Sisters of Saint Mary, the Sisters of Notre Dame, the Helpers of the Holy Souls, five Jesuit priests, and priest of the Society of the Divine Word — working in the interest of the six thousand Negro Catholics and the ninety thousand blacks of other Christian faiths.

The Sisters of St. Mary of the Third Order of St. Francis, who had been in hospital work in Saint Louis since the 1870's, took a dramatic step forward in 1934. They opened the former all-white hospital, St. Mary's Infirmary, south of the Union Station in Saint Louis, as the first Catholic Negro Hospital of the area.

During the late thirties also, groups of Negro laymen occasionally gathered for retreats at the St. Elizabeth's parish hall or in the new school. In 1940 Charles F. Vatterott, Jr., a member of the Laymen's Retreat League, the father of a large family, and an innovator in the real estate business, built an 18-room retreat house for the use of Negro Catholics in South Kinlock Park, where Father Otto Moorman, S.J., former Indian missioner, had organized a Negro parish during Depression days.

A third influential institution, the St. Joseph Catholic High School for Negroes, opened in the year 1937, under the direction of Sister Anna Joseph, C.S.J., and later Sister Ann Adelaide, C.S.J. This interesting and influential school deserves a special section in itself.

Lack of space had forced the closing of St. Elizabeth's parish school a few years earlier; and in 1939 the parish secured the former building of St. Joseph Institute for the Deaf on Garrison and Franklin Avenue. The Sisters of the Blessed Sacrament opened the parish school here in 1939.

The Saint Louis officers of the Legion of Mary, and their founder and spiritual director, Rev. Joseph Donovan, C.M. (fifth from right, front), welcome legionnaire envoys from Ireland, Mary Duffy (right, front) and John Murray (left, front) at the first meeting of the regional senatus.

At the Sacred Heart Center on Garfield Avenue, Helpers of the Holy Souls cared for two hundred children, teaching them catechism, music, dramatics, and sponsoring a girl scout troop. The mission in Kinlock had grown into a parish plant. St. Peter's parish in Kirkwood provided a center for Negroes called St. Martin De Porres Mission. By 1940, diocesan priests and members of four men's orders, Divine Word Fathers, Redemptorists, Vincentians, and Jesuits, as well as members of seven different women's religious communities, worked among the Negroes in Saint Louis.

At the time the United States entered World War II, the Negro apostolate in Saint Louis had reached a point of reappraisal. The Jesuit superiors of the Missouri Province assigned Father Markoe to other activities out of the city. New leadership would have to step in for new times.

Legion of Mary

In the summer of 1930, Father Joseph P. Donovan, C.M., of the faculty of Kenrick Seminary, went to Paris for the General Chapter of the Congregation of the Mission. While there, he heard of a new organization, the Legion of Mary. It had begun in France the previous year according to a plan developed less than ten years before in Dublin, Ireland. Donovan immediately became interested.

Strangely he had not heard of the association during a visit to Ireland a short time before. He returned to Dublin to find out about the legion. He attended a meeting on Friday, August 22, 1930. He met the spiritual director and the founders, including unpretentious but capable Frank Duff.[41]

Donovan heard the purposes of the legion: the spiritual advancement of its members, and the general intensification of Catholic life. The legion gave great place to the initiative and the dependability of its members in the carrying out of a variety of highly personalized apostolic tasks. It employed a Roman nomenclature. The local branch bore the name *praesidium*, from the Roman term for garrison or detachment on active duty. Several *praesidia* formed a *curia*. A *senatus* guided legion activities in each region. Each member recited a daily *catena*, or chain of prayers, with Our Lady's *Magnificat* as the core.

When Donovan returned to the States, he began to talk and write about the Legion of Mary. An account in the *Register* came to the attention of N. Schall in Raton, a rail division point in northeast New Mexico, just south of the Colorado border. As a result, Catholic men of Raton formed the first *praesidium* in the United States in November, 1931.[42]

In the spring of the following year, Donovan, a regular contributor on moral and canon law questions for the *American Ecclesiastical Review*, wrote an article in the magazine on the legion entitled, "Is This the long-looked for Church Society?" He told of his learning about the legion in France and of his visit to the Dublin *praesidium*. He described its workings. While he left the conclusion to the reader, it was clear Donovan warmly approved the organization.[43]

Two months later, he started the first *praesidium* for women in Saint Louis at DePaul Hospital.[44] Saint Louis also had the first *curia* of the legion in America. An historian of the movement, Cecily Halleck, attributed the spread of the legion in the United States to "an American Vincentian Father."[45] The founder of the legion, Frank Duff himself, explicitly credited the growth of the movement to the energy and writings of Father Joseph P. Donovan.[46] Soon the legion covered the nation — thanks to Father Donovan's conviction that it was truly "the long-looked-for society."

Chapter 35

Advances Despite the Depression

Publishing

Saint Louis had long been a center of Catholic publishing. Father David Phelan of the *Western Watchman* had kept shepherds and flocks of the mid-continent on their intellectual tiptoes for fifty years. He died September 21, 1915, shortly before the golden jubilee edition of his paper.

Arthur Preuss began the *Review* in 1894, and continued this thoughtful journal under the title *Fortnightly Review* well into the twentieth century. Father Edward Garesche and later Father Daniel Lord published the sodality promotional magazine, *The Queen's Work*; the Saint Louis Catholic *Herald*, a weekly paper, rolled off the presses for the first time in 1921. The Vincentian Fathers sponsored *The Vincentian*, a family magazine. B. Herder Book Co. early moved into the publication of theological books.

In the foreign language press, Edward Preuss, his son Arthur, and Frederick Kenkel published the daily paper *Amerika*. Monsignor Holweck edited a magazine for priests, the *Pastoral-Blatt*. Both ran until the mid-twenties. Dr. Hynek Dostal edited *Hlas*, the Bohemian paper, and published books in the Bohemian language. Dr. Cesare Avigni edited the Italian paper, *Il Pensiero*.

The outstanding Catholic historians of the city combined to publish the *Saint Louis Catholic Historical Review* for five years. Professors at Saint Louis University began three journals in the 1920's: the *Historical Bulletin*, the *Classical Bulletin*, and the *Modern Schoolman* for philosophers.

In the early 1930's Father Joseph Husslein, dean of the School of Social Service at Saint Louis University, planned and edited a series of Catholic books in conjunction with Bruce Publishing Company in Milwaukee. He saw this Science and Culture Series as "a great cooperative movement, with a clearly outlined purpose, a university in print."[1] It was one of the first well-planned efforts at developing the hitherto little touched Catholic market.

The reception of the first book, James J. Daly's *Cheerful Ascetic*, augured well for the success of the entire series. Among the authors were such distinguished foreigners as Hilaire Belloc, Christopher Hollis, Martin D'Arcy, and Donald Attwater. Local writers included educators Francis Crowley, Raymond Corrigan, Bakewell Morrison, William J. McGucken, and Inez Specking.

Shortly after the series got under way, the Cardinal Hayes Literature Committee of New York praised it for having "enriched present-day Catholic literature with works of unexcelled eminence in their respective fields."[2] The *American Year Book* for 1932 wrote: "The Science and Culture Series, edited by J. Husslein, already embraces a goodly number of scholarly books well produced technically."[3]

Father Husslein showed his personal interest in the great social questions of the day with his analysis of Leo XIII's encyclical *Rerum Novarum*, entitled *The Christian Social Manifesto*, and his two volume work, *Social Wellsprings*, that contained the main encyclical letters of Pope Leo XIII and Pope Pius XI.

Within fifteen years Father Husslein could report the publication of 167 books, with the following fields leading the rest: biography with thirty-five titles, social science with sixteen, literature with fifteen, and spirituality, apologetics, psychology, religion, and history with twelve each.[4]

The best-seller in the Science and Culture Series proved to be the *New Testament*, by Father James Kleist of Saint Louis University and Father Joseph Lilly, C.M., of Kenrick Seminary. The most influential books of the series were Father Gerald Ellard's *Christian Life and Worship*, that foreshadowed liturgical changes that were to come in with the Second Vatican Council, and Father Husslein's own *Christian Social Manifesto*. Theodore Maynard's two books, *Queen Elizabeth* and *Henry the Eighth*, received the highest plaudits of the secular press.[5]

In a tribute to Father Husslein in the spring of 1944, publisher William C. Bruce was to state: "In a real sense the Science and Culture Series has been in extension of the service of Saint Louis University to liberal education and to the improvement of Catholic culture in America."[6]

William Holub, president of the Catholic Press Association, remarked:

The average Catholic's interpretation of the purpose of a university is essentially different from that which was prevalent several decades ago; the contribution of Catholic letters to the treasury of the world's great literature is being recognized today; social service is being stressed in the United States as a study important to cultural and economic progress. These accomplishments are traceable, in various degrees to the activities of Father Husslein.[7]

By the time the series reached its twentieth year, many general publishers had moved into the well-developed Catholic market. At the retirement of Father Husslein, the Science and Culture Series came to an end. It had done its work well.

Congresses and Consecrations

The entire Catholic world looked to Dublin in 1932 for the Eucharistic Congress on the 1500th anniversary of St. Patrick's arrival in Ireland. Saint Louis had a special reason for joy. At the center of the stage in Phoenix Park stood two men with golden voices: John McCormack, who sang *Panis Angelicus*; and John Glennon who gave one of his most memorable addresses in tribute to his native land.

The flow and imagery of Newman marked the archbishop's speech. But as with so many other of his speeches, people remembered most keenly a spontaneous section that does not appear in the official versions. At the high point of his prepared address, Archbishop

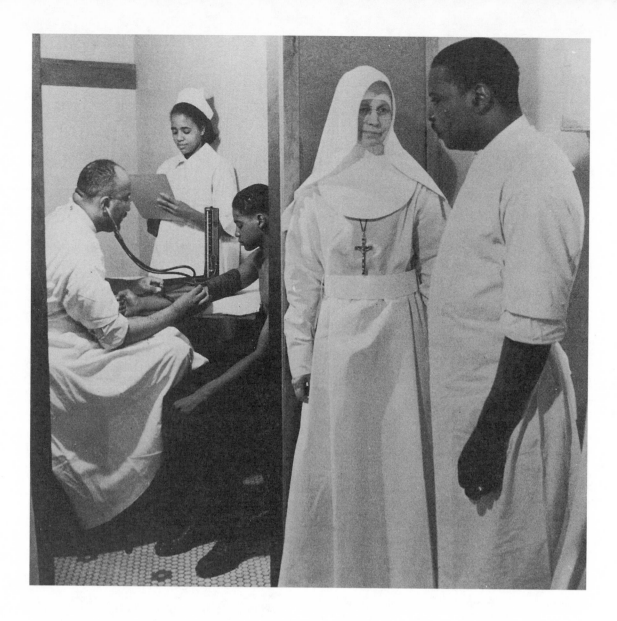

The Sisters of St. Marys welcomed black patients to their hospital on Papin St. in 1933. Sister Clementia Osthoff confers with Dr. F.D. Thurman, while they wait for Dr. L.B. Howell to conclude tests with a patient.

Glennon stopped, looked at the Cardinals of Italy, and said, "Italy has her works of art." Turning to the French representatives, he smiled benignly and said: "France has her great Cathedrals." He looked at the delegates from England with pity in his eyes, and said: "England has her —." He paused, looked from one side of the audience to the other and then with a smile of condescension, turned back to the English: "England has her regrets." And then with a ring of triumph he concluded: "But Ireland has the faith."[8]

The Irish had just concluded two great struggles: a domestic one for political independence; and a foreign one to supply her millions of exiles with religious guidance as they moved throughout the English-speaking world. She had succeeded in gaining political independence; but lacked financial aid for investment and economic development. She had sent priests, sisters, and brothers to America and the British Commonwealth of nations. A new day of Irish endeavor was at hand.

Glennon gave no guidance for that new day. He did not point out that the end of British colonialism in the south of Ireland might herald an end of colonialism in many continents of the world; he did not give guidance for the Irish missionaries as they moved from a program of following their countrymen to all corners of the world, to a new apostolate that had an interracial character; he did not point out the theological ferment heralding the end of the Counter-Reformation in northern Europe and challenge Irish religious leadership to move with this irresistible tide. He contented himself to recall the glorious Irish past of the sixth, seventh, and eighth centuries.

It was, nonetheless, a day of triumph for the Irish and for Archbishop Glennon. Many observers in Ireland and America felt that as a deserved tribute to Ireland, the United States, and to the Rome of the West, the Pope should have named Glennon a cardinal at this time.

Saint Louis did not get a cardinal, but Archbishop Glennon got his first auxiliary bishop, Christian H. Winkelmann, in September, 1933. Bishop Winkelmann was also the first Saint Louis-born auxiliary bishop of the archdiocese, and the first Saint Louisan Archbishop Glennon ordained a priest and then consecrated bishop. He continued as pastor of Saint Francis de Sales Church. In September, 1937, Archbishop Glennon consecrated another of his priests, Father Paul C. Schulte, pastor of the old cathedral, and a native of Fredericktown, Missouri, as bishop of Leavenworth, Kansas. When Bishop Winkelmann also went to Kansas, Archbishop Glennon was to consecrate the chancellor of the archdiocese, Monsignor George J. Donnelly, as auxiliary of Saint Louis, on March 19, 1940. Bishop Donnelly served as pastor of St. Pius V Church; and Monsignor John P. Cody succeeded him as chancellor of the archdiocese.

Hellriegel and the Liturgy

Even though the work of Monsignor Martin Hellriegel and several of his associates made the archdiocese a pioneer in the liturgical movement, Archbishop Glennon's position remained unclear. He did write an encouraging letter to Father Hellriegel in October, 1926. "Your work is not an innovation. It is a restoration. And especially am I pleased to see your endeavor to more closely associate, indeed, incorporate the Catholic laity in the liturgy."[9] Glennon saw the basic issue as it should be: a matter of worship, not a matter of ritual and form.

After some years in O'Fallon, Missouri, as chaplain of the Sisters of the Precious Blood, Father Hellriegel moved to Holy Cross parish in the distant north Saint Louis community of Baden near the city waterworks. He developed a spirit of worship that foreshadowed much of the later liturgical development. He regularly wrote articles on the movement for *Worship* and other liturgical journals.[10]

As a part of the program of the Summer Schools of Catholic Action, Father Gerald Ellard, S.J., professor of liturgical theology in Saint Louis University's School of Theology, then located in St. Marys, Kansas, wrote Archbishop Glennon about the Dialogue Mass. The archbishop's answer was negative. "It is my candid opinion that these new forms to increase devotion during the Holy Sacrifice of the Mass often tend to distract those who assist at the Holy Sacrifice."[11]

Shortly after this, Monsignor Hellriegel asked an opinion on the offertory procession that he had introduced in his church. Rome answered in the negative. Archbishop Glennon told Hellriegel to slow down in his use of "customs which had been in vogue in the old country."[12] Later the same year, Hellriegel received a six page reply from Father Joseph Donovan, C.M., the professor of canon law at Kenrick Seminary, that was generally unsympathetic to the whole movement for liturgical renewal.[13]

In spite of ambigious leadership, many young people of the archdiocese came to a greater interest in participation of the liturgy, especially if they attended the Summer Schools of Catholic Action, or parish schools taught by the Sisters of the Precious Blood, who had come under the guidance of Monsignor Hellriegel during his years at O'Fallon.

St. Joseph's High for Negroes

A dramatic step forward for Negro Catholics came with the opening of St. Joseph's High School in 1937. Catholic high schools for white boys and girls flourished everywhere in the city. The newest was Southside Catholic for boys at Grand and Delor.* But the Catholic Negroes had no chance for a Catholic high school education.

A white woman, Mrs. James Mowrey, decided to take the matter into her own hands. She found a number of qualified Negro Catholic boys in the eighth grade and had them go to McBride High School to register. When they did not gain admission, Mrs. Mowrey called Father Alfred

---

Left: The Catholic Rural Life Conference holds a farewell dinner at the Coronado Hotel for Bishop Christian Winkelmann as he prepares to leave for Wichita in early 1940.

*The Christian Brothers began Southside Catholic in 1931 in six "portable schools" and a section of St. Joseph's Orphanage at 4701 S. Grand in 1931; the Brothers of Mary took over in 1933; in 1935, the archdiocese built a new orphanage and turned the old building over to high school purposes.

G. Thomson, superintendent of diocesan high schools. She complained that the Brother in charge of McBride had turned away a group of qualified boys. Without being aware of the racial aspect of the question, Father Thomson assured Mrs. Mowrey that the boys should go to McBride. She was to tell the Brother in charge of entrance that the superintendent had so decided. As a result of this incident, the archdiocese decided to make some provision in the fall of 1937.

Two Sisters of St. Joseph began a small high school for Negro students at Father Dunne's Newsboys' Home. The quarters were totally inadequate, conditions hopeless, and the two sisters hardly lasted out the first term. The following year, the Josephites chose the capable Sister Anna Joseph to be director of the school. She had already served in administrative capacities in Marquette, Michigan, and in Indianapolis. With the support of Sister Tarcisia, the local superior at Rosati-Kain where the sisters resided, Sister Anna Joseph and her associates were able to find better quarters for the school in a home at 3954 West Belle. The faculty had the regular assistance of two outstanding teachers not directly connected with the school itself: Father Donald Corrigan, C.SS.R., professor of Latin and mathematics at St. Joseph College in Kirkwood, the preparatory seminary for the Redemptorist Fathers, who came every Thursday as a volunteer spiritual father, counselor, and instructor in religion; and Miss Ruth Garizio, director of music at Ursuline Academy in Kirkwood and a graduate of Webster College, who volunteered to direct the music activities at St. Joseph. Further, Patrick Molloy, then a seminarian of the archdiocese, volunteered to coach the athletic teams; and benefactor Mark Eagleton provided gowns for the chorale and uniforms for the football team. By the third year, five sisters were teaching sixty-seven pupils.

Sister Anna Joseph sought affiliation and accreditation from the state university at Columbia. Missouri University proved most cooperative, sending Doctor Lauren A. Van Dyke to the school six times during the course of the year. He observed, questioned, offered advice, and ultimately recommended accreditation; and so during the school year 1940-41, St. Joseph's became the first accredited four-year high school for Negroes in the state of Missouri.

The dwelling on West Belle did not prove adequate for the needs of the school and the teachers began to look towards the eight unused class rooms in nearby St. Ann's parish on Page at Whittier. Sister Anna Joseph appealed to Archbishop Glennon who turned down her request with a resounding no. Chancellor John Cody of the archdiocese urged the sisters not to give up hope. In a few months the archbishop reappraised the situation. St. Joseph High School for Negroes opened in St. Ann's School on Page in 1941. It was then in its fifth year, and the enrollment had reached eighty-five students.[14]

St. Joseph's played a dramatic part in opening integrated activities between schools. After his ordination to the priesthood, Patrick J. Molloy remained counselor and coach of the boys at St. Joseph. He appealed to the Brothers at McBride to begin competition between the St. Joseph and McBride athletes. Later on he sought similar contests with Saint Louis University High School and the Christian Brothers.[15] Father Molloy urged the participating schools to prepare their teams for the competition with the colored boys through a program of explanation and prayer. It might be well be recall at this time that within the boundaries of Missouri there was no integrated athletic activity of any kind except some totally unorganized sandlot ball.

Father Patrick Molloy and the first graduating class at St. Joseph's High School.

By 1943 the Catholic League formally invited St. Joseph to enter into competition. Membership in the Missouri High School Athletic Association was necessary to accept this invitation. St. Joseph's School made its application without mentioning that the students were Negro. The officers of the Missouri High School Athletic Association, presumably unaware that they were approving integrated athletics, granted the request. St. Joseph's made a creditable showing in all sports.

As a result, little St. Joseph's entered the first Negro basketball, baseball, football, and track teams in integrated high school competition. It became the first Negro team to gain membership in the Missouri State High School Athletic Association, the first Negro basketball team to compete in a state tournament with 550 other teams, all white, the first Negro team to be entered in a Missouri State High School track meet, and the first Negro High School to be a member of the High School League. This story over the years, showing a little gain here, a slight retreat before a larger gain there, had, of course, its poignant elements. Many prospective athletes met only heartbreak; but some of the stories also had their element of humor, especially the performance of Oliver Wendell Holmes of St. Joseph High School in the mile and half-mile events at the Saint Louis district track meet. The local officials of the Missouri State High School Athletic Association had consented only reluctantly and at the last minute to let the little Negro High School team enter. St. Joseph had earlier entered the basketball tournament, lost out in the first round, and moved back into oblivion. Oliver Wendell Holmes was to see that this did not occur again. He had little time to train. He wore his basketball suit for lack of anything better. He had little coaching, and no idea at all that he had to pace himself to keep his energy for the full four laps. But he had promised to finish the race. He sprinted the first lap. Suprisingly, he carried on through the next three laps and galloped in forty yards ahead of his nearest competitor, to set a track record for his class in this event.

The Missouri State High School Athletic Association found some reason to keep him out of the state meet. But this performance did bring offers of scholarships from half a dozen universities, including one from Xavier University in New Orleans that he accepted.[16]

Athletics pointed the way for other integrated activities. During the principalship of Sister Ann Adelaide, C.S.J., at St. Joseph's, the faculty sponsors in charge of the Catholic Interscholastic Speech League wanted to carry on similar experiments. They invited St. Joseph High School to prepare representatives to take part in the tournament. The priest in charge of speech at Saint Louis University High School volunteered to train the St. Joseph boys even when they were to compete with his own team. The boys and girls of the Catholic High Schools of Saint Louis graciously received the St. Joseph's youngsters in all such activities.[17]

Press and Radio

As national promoter of the Sodalities of Our Lady, Father Daniel Lord came to realize the need for further religious guidance for adult Catholics. He began publication of twenty-four-page pamphlets available at only ten cents a copy. His most popular titles, such as "Has Life Any Meaning?" and "Confession is a Joy," were to sell

Sister Mary Joseph, S.L., of Webster College, founder of the Gallery of Living Authors, did her part to further Catholic letters by giving recognition to writers during their lifetimes.

steadily through three decades. Ultimately he became the greatest Catholic pamphleteer of his time and his sales of these small booklets went over twenty-five million copies.

Gradually, with sodality promotional materials such as Father Roger Lyon's *Semester Outlines*, and Father Aloysius Heeg's catechisms, the Queen's Work Press developed into a large business, and moved from West Pine to the Dickman Building on South Grand. Father Lord gathered other assistants. Among them, Father Edward Dowling did conspicuous work through such organizations as Alcoholics Anonymous, the Cana Conference Movement, and "Recovery Incorporated" for nervous people. He became one of the most deeply revered priests of his generation and the only priest listed in the book *Top Leadership, U.S.A.*[18] Miss Dorothy Willmann worked in parish sodality promotion and other Catholic activities that won for her the *Pro Ecclesia et Pontifice* medal from Pope Pius XII.

The position of Saint Louis as a Catholic pamphlet center received further impetus with the development of the Liguori Press under the direction of the Redemptorist Fathers. This press did not specialize in one organizational activity, such as the Queen's Work did with the sodality, but offered services to parishes of the nation, especially with Sunday bulletins. It reached its greatest prominence in succeeding decades.

Father Lord also counselled Sister Mary Joseph, S.L., of Webster College, when she planned the "Gallery of Living Catholic Authors." She saw the gallery as a stimulus to aspiring young writers, a treasure house of books by outstanding Catholic writers in the English language, and a coordinating body and focal point for the Catholic writer everywhere.

Once underway, the gallery included many notables

Scouting in Catholic parishes took a great step forward in the late 1920s when the Knights of Columbus challenged its members to train as scoutmasters. Paul Venneman began Kirkwood Troop 4 at St. Peter's Parish. His son-in-law, Deacon Joe Sulze, followed in his footsteps with the troop, now 323. Here Deacon Sulze explains the use of cooking equipment.

among its members, such as Gilbert Keith Chesterton, Hilaire Belloc, Sigrid Undset, Carlton J. H. Hayes, and Sister Madeleva. Over the years most of the distinguished writers in English of Catholic background became members of the gallery, among them Maria Montessori, Helen C. White, Evelyn Waugh, Maisie Ward, F. J. Sheed, Giovanni Papini, Paul Horgan, and Alfred Noyes. At the tenth anniversary symposium in New York the speakers were Jacques Maritain, Padraic Colum, Katherine Burton, Sigrid Undset, and Peter Guilday.[19]

The local Knights of Columbus, under the guidance of Father Lester Fallon, C.M., began a local and then a national advertising program to clarify Catholic truths for the American public. In a variety of magazine and newspapers, the Knights placed adroitly written columns of five or six hundred words on Catholic teachings and attitudes. These uniformly excellent statements from the pen of Charles Kelly drew a fine response.

As the archdiocese approached the forties, it still did not have an official newspaper. Instead of building on an existing local paper such as the *Catholic Herald*, Archbishop Glennon decided to join the *Register* chain of newspapers, published in Denver under the editorship of Monsignor Matthew Smith, and circulating through many dioceses chiefly in states of the high plains. A national section went to all participating dioceses and to individual subscribers throughout the country.

Archbishop Glennon notified the pastors in a letter of December 27, 1940.[20] The pastors, in turn, read the letter to their parishioners on the following Sunday. The first issue, dated January 3, 1941, went to twenty-five thousand subscribers.[21] The archbishop set three chief purposes for the paper: "defending the faith" when attacked or misunderstood; "preaching loyalty to the country's government and institutions"; and making "better known the splendid body of Catholic literature available."[22]

Father Harry Stitz combined two new duties, that of editor of the *Register* and pastor of St. Mary's of Vic-

tories in downtown Saint Louis. Miss Celestine Brady was the first employee in the offices of the paper in the second floor of the rectory at 744 S. Third Street.

Mayor Bernard Dickman wrote Editor Father Harry Stitz the following month and joined the archbishop in hoping that the *Register* would soon be in every home.[23] In accord with the wishes of His Grace and His Honor the circulation rose steadily. At the beginning of 1943, the archbishop was to ask each pastor to send a complete roster of parishes for placement on the mailing list of the *Register*, and to accept responsibility for the charge.[24] Further, he was to authorize an exchange of pulpits whereby eighty-seven priests spoke on the Catholic press in other parishes than their own.[25] By the end of the year (1943), the circulation was to approach sixty-eight thousand.[26] The *Register* sponsored a weekly news feature over Radio station WEW, with John Lappin as commentator.[27]

Station WEW, one of the nation's pioneer radio stations, carried a day's dedication program since its inaugural in the early 1920's. Jesuit seminarians at Saint Louis University presented prayers and a spiritual message. At the outbreak of World War II, Father Eugene P. Murphy, S.J., came to work regularly with these scholastics. Out of their mutual efforts grew the Sacred Heart Program. Father Murphy offered recordings of the program to other stations the next year. Charles E. Harrison of Technisonic Laboratories prepared the records. Father Hugh Harkins, S.J., recited the prayers. Jesuits on the faculty of Saint Louis University joined Father Murphy in giving the talks. Three stations accepted: one in Denver, the second in Cincinnati, and the third in Pittsfield, Massachusetts. They presented the program as a public service on a non-commercial basis. As time went on the speakers came to include priests of the archdiocese and other archdioceses of the nation. Gradually, the program spread throughout the nation, to Canada, and overseas on the Armed Forces Network.

Chapter 36

World War II and After

Social Problems of the Forties

Archbishop Glennon approached his eightieth year. He had been in Saint Louis so long that the name Glennon had already become a common boy's name. He annually invited the young men who bore his name to a reception, usually held on the Feast of the Holy Name, early in January. On December 20, 1941, in fact, he ordained one of them, Glennon Patrick Flavin, to the priesthood.[1]

New problems were coming up to face the people of Saint Louis and the nation. Perhaps these problems would not have been too much for Archbishop Glennon in his early years with the enthusiasm and buoyancy that he brought to Saint Louis back in 1904 at the age of 42. But this was 1942. Depression had reluctantly given way before war production. The questions of labor reform convulsed the entire nation and especially industrial cities like Saint Louis. Archbishop Glennon had little guidance to give.

As America approached World War II, the even more stirring problem of race relations came to the forefront. With the development of war industries, the Negro population of Saint Louis increased. The Negro neighborhoods pushed west in an area from one to ten blocks north of Lindell Boulevard. St. Bridget's and St. Malachy's, near St. Elizabeth's east of Grand, had been predominantly Negro neighborhoods for some time. The area of St. Alphonsus Rock Church on Grand now had a predominantly Negro population. Farther west, St. Ann's and Visitation were bi-racial neighborhoods. New times and conditions demanded fresh outlooks and approaches.

In 1943 Father Patrick Molloy, assistant pastor at Visitation Church, coach and religion teacher at St. Joseph's High School, along with Fathers Charles Reinalt, S.V.D., and Donald Corrigan, C.SS.R., organized the Saint Louis Clergy Conference on Negro welfare. Father Molloy served as first president. The conference included several priests destined for distinguished careers in the diocese; such as Fathers A. E. Westhoff and John H. Smith, and the Jesuit Augustine Bork, who was to give his life a few years later in an attempt to rescue one of his Negro parishioners from drowning.

The archdiocese did not take an official stand on the conference at the time; but the following year, Chancellor John Cody accepted an invitation to attend a meeting. He asked the members not to construe his attendance as anything official; but expressed his desire to discuss with the priests the issues facing Negro Catholics and pledged his help in any way that he was able to give it.[2]

One of the first activities of this group was in conjunction with an attempt to have an outstanding Negro graduate of St. Joseph's High School admitted to Webster College in suburban Saint Louis. The Sisters of Loretto and the lay teachers at the school approved the step. President George F. Donovan of Webster College got in touch with the assistant attorney general of the state, William C.

Blair, to make sure that the Missouri statutes did not prohibit integrated education. Blair answered that state prohibitions presumably affected public schools only.[3]

The Webster College authorities brought the matter to the attention of Mother General Edwarda who was in Saint Louis at the time. On July 3, 1943, she sought the counsel of Archbishop Glennon, since he was not integrating the Catholic schools in the archdiocese at the time.

The "Council Minutes" of the Sisters of Loretto for July 11, 1943, gave this information:

> Mother General (Mother Edwarda) asked Archbishop Glennon's advice about accepting Negro students at Webster College. He said he would not approve or disapprove, that it was right in theory but difficult to follow in practice. He emphasized the fact that he did not want to be quoted. "You cannot quote me for I am the Shepherd." The Archbishop said that it was contrary to the laws of the State of Missouri for Negroes to be accepted in the same schools as white children, i.e., in public schools. . . . He said overzealous people were doing the cause more harm than good at this point.[4]

The file of correspondence of the time further elucidates the archbishop's position:

> His Excellency said that as Shepherd of the Flock he could not make any distinction of race, but must give equal rights to all. However, telling us that he was not to be quoted, he said that the time was not opportune, because Catholics had not been sufficiently instructed that the Negro was entitled to equal rights in education as well as in other fields. By careful instruction, he said that parents and pupils could be prepared to receive the Negro into the schools and hopefully no prejudice would be such that would make the colored pupils unhappy.[5]

Back in Saint Louis, nineteen diocesan and regular priests of the Clergy Conference wrote to Archbishop Glennon in the interests of the Negro applicant who sought admission to Webster College. They pointed out the difficulties Negro Catholics had in pursuit of a Catholic college education; and the resultant ill effects on the Negro population of the policy in the archdiocese. They instanced "the reported rejection" of a Catholic colored boy from Saint Louis University the previous year.[6] There is no copy of a reply from the archbishop.

On September 7, President Donovan of Webster College wrote to Mother Edwarda on the matter. He enclosed many pertinent documents, including a letter of recommendation from the applicant's high school principal at St. Joseph's, Sister Anna Joseph, C.S.J. Most important, he stated:

> The Most Reverend Archbishop declared that he would have no objection to the registration of such a student at Webster College provided the Sisters of Loretto (comprising the Mother General, the other members of the General Council, and the Sister Superior of the College), the College President, and the students were in favor of the policy.[7]

The officials of the Sisters of Loretto received no word directly from the archbishop indicating that he had changed his mind. No such letter, or any signed statement of Archbishop Glennon on the matter, appears in the Archdiocesan Archives, the files of the Clergy Conference, or the Archives of the Sisters of Loretto.

As a result, the Council of the Sisters of Loretto found it necessary to postpone the acceptance of the Negro applicant for the ensuing school year.[8] When the Clergy Conference wrote to the archbishop on the matter, he stated:

> As I advised you when you called, I agree with you in principle, but I added that the attainment of that principle was difficult, especially in the form in which it was proposed by you and your associates.[9]

The archbishop then went on to give his general view. He believed that integration should start in the grades, then move up to the high schools, and ultimately the colleges and universities.[10]

At this point, columnist Ted LeBerthon wrote an open letter to Reverend Mother Edwarda, superior general, Sisters of Loretto, that appeared on the front page of the news section of the *Pittsburgh Courier* Saturday, February 5, 1944.[11] This hard-hitting article pilloried Mother Edwarda in line after line. Yet most of the readers who knew the inside story felt that he had chosen the wrong target.

Integration at Saint Louis University

The same issue of the *Pittsburgh Courier* carried an article on Saint Louis University. Its president Father Patrick Holloran had, in the meantime, under pressure of successive Jesuit provincials, Father Peter A. Brooks and Father Joseph P. Zuercher, and with the urging of the zealous parish priest, Father John Markoe, S.J., queried prominent Catholic men of the city of Saint Louis about the admission of Negroes. His prediction that the number of qualified Negro applicants would not reach twenty in twenty years showed how little he knew about the actual situation either in Saint Louis or in the nation.

This issue of the *Pittsburgh Courier* reached the desk of Father Claude Heithaus, S.J., director of publications and of publicity at Saint Louis University. Father Heithaus had not previously engaged in interracial activity. He was by training a classical archeologist who had spent many years in the Holy Land and other areas of the Near East and obtained his doctorate from the University of London.

Stimulated by the discussion in the *Pittsburgh Courier*, he decided to devote his forthcoming Friday morning student sermon to the question of integration at Saint Louis University. In the tense atmosphere, Heithaus avoided oratorical fireworks. He delivered his carefully prepared text in clear tones and with a minimum of emotion — a speech that deserved to go down in the annals of the great speeches of America. On the following day, February 12, the *Saint Louis Post-Dispatch* carried a cartoon of Abraham Lincoln by Daniel Fitzpatrick with the caption "Dedicated to the Unfinished Task."[12] An adjoining editorial praised Father Heithaus for bringing forward the moral issue.

Letters of praise came to Heithaus from Eric Johnson, president of the Chamber of Commerce of the United States,[13] Mrs. W. Stuart Symington, daughter of a United States senator and wife of a prominent business executive, who was soon to be a senator of the United States himself,[14] and writers, Sister Madeleva, James Gillis, C.S.P., Jack Alexander, Daniel A. Lord, S.J., John La Farge, S.J.,[15] and other distinguished citizens.

The members of the Catholic Clergy Conference on Negro Welfare in Saint Louis unanimously instructed their chairman, Father Patrick Molloy, to write a letter of congratulations to Father Heithaus. "It is their considered opinion, based upon their close contact with the Negro parishioners," Father Molloy wrote, "that the sermon which you preached at the students' Mass in the College Church has had a profound effect for good on the Negro population of Saint Louis."[16]

Neither Archbishop Glennon nor Father Holloran, president of the University, however, shared the general enthusiasm for Heithaus's remarks.[17] Nonetheless, a flurry of meetings, letters, decisions and counter-decisions, rumors and denials swept Saint Louis University during the next few weeks. Finally an appeal to the highest Jesuit superior of the time in the United States, the Very Rev. Zacheus P. Maher, brought an intervention urging Saint Louis to act. In the summer session of 1944 Saint Louis University admitted Negroes on a permanent basis. Thus, it became the first University in a slave state (the Catholic University was in a slave district, the District of Columbia) to admit Negroes.

Writer James Rorty, analyzing the racial integration question thirteen years later in *Ave Maria* magazine, had this to say:

> It was as if the entire city and state had been waiting for this action. It touched off a chain reaction involving public and private institutions alike, affecting all faiths and reverberating throughout the nation.[18]

One of the first reverberations in Saint Louis occurred at St. Bernadette's School. The St. Elizabeth's property at Cook and Taylor, purchased with a view to starting a grade school some years before, had stood vacant through the thirties. By this time the vast majority of Negro parents who would have sent their children to St. Elizabeth's School no longer lived in the area east of Grand. They lived much farther west, in the area of Cook and Taylor as a matter of fact. Taxes had come due on the property; and the archdiocese had taken over. In early 1942 Maryknoll Sisters had opened St. Bernadette's Diocesan School. Father John Smith, assistant at Visitation parish, headed the school and directed the Sacred Heart Center. He moved all activities into the Visitation parish building. St. Bernadette's soon became overcrowded; and, at the same time, the Visitation School diminished in enrollment as many whites moved out of the parish. Father Smith moved St. Bernadette's School into unoccupied classrooms at Visitation. As a result, the building now had two schools: the Sisters of Loretto taught the white students of Visitation School on the south side of the building; and the Maryknoll Sisters taught the Negro students in the north side classrooms. Father Molloy headed the free lunch program. He integrated this program and also the recreation in the school yard.

Since St. Bernadette's had no seventh and eight grade, the directors of the school planned to integrate the last two grades at the beginning of 1946. The Negro children had previously gone elsewhere for these grades, either to a public school or to the St. Clement's School in conjunction with the St. Alphonsus Rock School some blocks east. Two Negro children entered the integrated seventh and eighth grades of Visitation School. Only one white family protested. Next, the directors of the school gave the Negro children a choice of either Visitation or St. Bernadette's for the first to the sixth grades. Archbishop Glennon confirmed at Visitation Church in the spring of 1945 and expressed satisfaction at what Father Smith had done. Except for this elementary approval, the archbishop's words at the confirmation reflected a 1905 mentality in a 1945 world.

At that same time, the archbishop was conducting a drive for new high schools. He met divided council from the priests in the Negro apostolate. Many insisted that there should be no interracial indication in the publicity; but that people should take it for granted that all Catholic high schoolers would benefit. The archbishop did this. A Negro mother superior severely criticized him for omitting explicit provision for the Negroes; and at least one white pastor of a Negro parish urged his people to give no money since the publicity made no provision for a Negro school.

This divergence typified the efforts of Catholics working among Negroes with no real leadership from "the Chancery." In spite of repeated efforts to select a common front toward a single goal, individuals in the Negro apostolate wanted varying procedures. A white pastor of a Negro church at this time looked upon integration exclusively as a competitive situation; and he opposed it on the plea that his people were not yet ready "to compete with the whites." Priests differed, too, on the question of a Catholic Interracial Council. One group of priests believed that they should move to the front and discuss Catholic attitudes in the light of interracial justice. The other held that the formation of such councils focused attention on problems that otherwise might not become publicly known; the attendant publicity, they believed, created more problems than the council could solve.

The coming of top leadership with vision and courage in this area proved to be closer than men thought.

High School Drive

The problems facing St. Joseph's High School were not the only concerns of Catholic high school administrators at the time. Even though in 1942 the archdiocese had opened a new school at Emerson and Thekla, called Northside Catholic, a co-institutional school with boys taught by the Brothers of Mary and girls taught by the Daughters of Charity, the area needed many more new schools. In September, 1944, the archdiocesan high schools had to refuse 628 applicants for lack of space. As a result, the archbishop called a meeting for September 20, 1944, in the Cathedral School auditorium.

Thus, his last great effort in the city was, like his first effort, a building promotion. The archbishop invited every pastor and two members of every parish to the meeting. Five hundred laymen and priests discussed plans for the building of three or four schools at the conclusion of the war.[19] John P. Cody accepted the chairmanship of the drive. The laymen pledged a million dollars in the name of the people of the archdiocese as a gift for the diamond sacerdotal jubilee of Archbishop Glennon in December. The archbishop himself promised a second million out of funds accumulated over the years from bequests and the generosity of priests and people of the archdiocese.[20]

During October, Monsignor Cody's office detailed plans for the coming drive. It would take place in November and coincide with the sixth war loan drive to begin on Armistice Day November 11. The committee suggested that the Catholics of the city each purchase an extra war bond to give to the high school drive; thus they would be fulfilling a double duty to Church and state.

The archbishop sent a letter to the people of the city on October 16, giving school statistics of the previous year: 3,493 children had graduated from the Catholic elementary schools. Of these only 989 had entered the inter-parochial high schools. If half of the graduates had entered the private Catholic high schools of the city, at least 45% of the grade school graduates attended public high schools. Confident that the priests and people would do all they could to make the campaign a success, the archbishop asked them to subscribe generously to make these schools possible in the immediate post-war period.[21] To commemorate "Catholic High School Sunday," October 29, the archbishop issued a pastoral message restating the above ideas and spoke over KMOX for fifteen minutes on the theme: "The Cross and the Flag."[22]

Seven hundred people attended the meeting the following night, October 30. The drive would last from November 1 to November 18. The central committee announced plans for six new schools, and told of the purchase of two sites — one at Newstead and Bessie avenues in North Saint Louis, the other on Olive Street Road in University City; ultimately these two pieces of property became the locales of De Andreis and Mercy High. The *Register* carried a map that showed the location of the five existing schools and the proposed location of the new ones.[23]

Once the drive was under way, each weekly issue of the *Register* brought announcements and progress of the campaign. By December 8, Monsignor Cody's committee announced that contributions had passed the 80% mark. As often as possible, the committee tied in announcements about the drive with matters pertaining to the war. It brought up the possibility of job opportunity for veterans in the building of these schools after the conflict. The last report came in the *Register* on December 15. Twenty-five parishes had oversubscribed their quotas; the drive carried to within 10% of its goal, with fifty parishes still to send in their final reports.[24]

Plans continued the succeeding year (1945) as the war came to its inevitable close in Europe and in Asia. The year after that (1946) would have been the year of the big push toward the building of the new schools. By that time Archbishop Glennon was not to be around to see the completion of them.

While the archdiocese pushed its high school program, Father Patrick J. Holloran, S.J., moved Saint Louis University forward to meet the anticipated influx of returning veterans. With the strong support of convert businessman, Oliver J. Parks, Holloran challenged a group of prominent Catholics, especially members of the Laymen's Retreat League, to promote the expansion of facilities for the post-war student enrollment. Parks himself gave to the university the air college at Cahokia, Illinois, that bore his name — a school that had trained one out of ten American flyers during World War II.

Within a few months of the close of hostilities in the Pacific, the student enrollment rose to new heights. Thanks to the generosity of its friends, the university was able to accommodate the influx. The school also inaugurated a big-time basketball program that culminated a few years later with a national championship led by All-American "Easy Ed" McAuley.

Triumph of Glennon's Last Days

In a dramatic universalisation of the college of cardinals on Christmas Eve, 1945, Pope Pius XII announced thirty-two new members, with at least one representative of nineteen different countries and of all five continents. Three became international figures: Cardinals Agajanian of Armenia, Mindszenty of Hungary, and Spellman of the United States. Of the eleven from the western hemisphere, three others besides Spellman were Americans. John J. Glennon of Saint Louis was among them.

A word-of-mouth report quoted Cardinal-elect Glennon as saying: "They forgot me, when they should have remembered me; they remembered me, when they should have forgotten me." He may well have said that. He was then eighty-three years of age, and had been bishop for forty-nine years and nine months.

His February visit to Ireland on the way to Rome for the consistory proved a triumphal tour. Front pages in the Dublin papers featured his picture, his long career, his many speeches in Ireland previously, his country-boy-to-the-center-of-Christendom triumphal progress.

Saint Louis planned a grand reception for the first cardinal of the trans-Mississippi West. Sad news from Dublin, however, delayed the plans. On his way back from Rome, Cardinal Glennon took ill at the home of the president of the Irish Republic. His close friend, Monsignor John Cody, stayed at his side, and cared for the business of the Church, even though his own mother lay dying in Saint Louis.[25]

Cardinal Glennon died of bronchitis on March 9, 1946, six days before he would have celebrated his fiftieth jubilee as a bishop. Instead of a triumphal reception, Saint Louis planned a funeral such as it had accorded Archbishop Kenrick and General Sherman back in the nineties, and Monsignor Tim Dempsey and World War II Ace Wendell Pruit in more recent years. The archdiocesan con-

sultors named Bishop George Donnelly administrator of the vacant see.[26]

In the many eulogies of the time, two themes stood out: Glennon's building and his oratory.* During his early years in Saint Louis, Glennon had inherited the mantle of Archbishop Patrick Ryan of Philadelphia as the premier orator of the hierarchy. He gave the main address at almost every significant ecclesiastical occasion during these years. He talked regularly from the cathedral pulpit. When radio came into use, he spoke over various networks. Eventually Monsignor — later Bishop Fulton J. Sheen — succeeded him as the prince of episcopal orators.

Institutional growth certainly predominated in Glennon's episcopacy. Besides the Cathedral and the major and minor seminaries, his long term saw the erection of new hospitals — St. John's, St. Mary's, De Paul, St. Anthony, Desloge, and others — the diocesan high schools for boys and girls, and many high schools and academies under the supervision of various religious orders and congregations. During his forty-three years in Saint Louis, sixteen new parishes opened in the city and twenty-three in the suburbs. Seventeen parishes in the city and adjacent suburbs built new churches at this time.

During these years Glennon ordained over 4,700 priests — an average of almost one hundred a year during the all-but-fifty years he was a bishop. He confirmed an estimated 225,000 people.[27] He succeeded in creating a strong bond of unity between priests and people. He was well informed on matters of the archdiocese and of the city. He listened to others, but kept his own counsel. His otherwise broad sympathy did not extend to priests who had not lived up to their calling. He did not challenge them to redeem themselves; he sent them to remote areas, and left them there.

In spite of this magnificent building record, many observers felt that the greater significance of his leadership appeared in a short tribute in the *Social Justice Review*:

*Archdiocesan historian Peter Rahill was to single out these areas years later in his sketch of Cardinal Glennon in the *New Catholic Encyclopedia*.

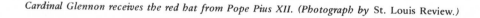

Cardinal Glennon receives the red hat from Pope Pius XII. (Photograph by St. Louis Review.)

The Irish had given Cardinal Glennon a "thousand welcomes" on his way to Rome a few days before. Now they crowd along O'Connell Street as priests and soldiers escort his remains in funeral procession.

Archbishop Glennon's was never a centralized power.... He directed and counseled, but did not drive with the aid of a curb. It is for this reason there exist in Saint Louis so many charities and cultural endeavors....[28]

Glennon continued the broad development that Kenrick had allowed. Thus he deserved acclaim for allowing clergy and laity to exercise initative in many areas. Glennon was episcopal spiritual director of the Central Bureau that promoted social action not only in Saint Louis but throughout the nation, especially in the German-background parishes. The Queen's Work office took the lead in promoting the national sodality movement and developed the Summer Schools of Catholic Action. The St. Elizabeth's Chronicle grew into the *Interracial Review*. The Liguori, Vincentian, and Queen's Work presses made Saint Louis one of the Catholic pamphlet publishing centers of the nation. The Laymen's Retreat League gained primacy of reputation in the country. The Knights of Columbus advertising program increased understanding of the Church.

Dramatic changes had taken place in the world and in the nation during the forty years that Cardinal Glennon served in Saint Louis. Two World Wars swept away empires. Inventions annihilated distances. Population almost doubled. The nation became predominantly urban instead of rural. Saint Louis had been the fourth largest city in the nation, the second largest beyond the Appalachians, and the largest west of the Mississippi. The oldest archdiocese of the area and the most significant as a result of the long years of Archbishop Kenrick, Saint Louis held, at Glennon's arrival, a position of prominence in the West that Baltimore, the primatial see of the nation, occupied in the East.

The statesman-like Cardinal Gibbons still led the American Church; and it had not seemed improbable at the time that the handsome, youthful, eloquent, new arch-

bishop of Saint Louis might succeed him as the preeminent prelate of the nation. This, however, was not to be. After Gibbons death, the apostolic delegate assumed many of the functions that Gibbons had performed for years before America had such a functionary. Among American churchmen, Archbishop William O'Connell of Boston was the only cardinal. An astute personage with a knowledge of Roman procedures gained during his years as rector of the North American college in the Eternal City, O'Connell was powerful; but he lacked Gibbons' nation-wide influence.

As Chicago grew to be the major city of the Midwest, it assumed the position of church leadership beyond the Appalachians that had formerly belonged to the Archdiocese of Saint Louis. When Mundelein became the first cardinal of the American Midwest in March, 1924, the preeminent position of the archbishop of Saint Louis went into eclipse. Baltimore suffered a similar decline in the East after the death of Cardinal Gibbons. The larger cities of New York, Philadelphia, and Boston had a succession of cardinals. Baltimore waited a half century for another of its archbishops to gain that honor.

Glennon came into the hierarchy at a time when James Cardinal Gibbons and Archbishop John Ireland held the center of attention. The official biographer of Gibbons, historian John Tracy Ellis, spoke of Gibbons as "a great soul . . . a remarkable person"; and commented on "the radiance of his spirit."[29] Monsignor James H. Moynihan looked carefully at the genius and grandeur of soul of Archbishop Ireland, as well as at his equally strong foibles and failings. Moynihan concluded his book with the judgment that Ireland was "one of the greatest bishops of the Church."[30]

When a biographer comes to write a definitive life of Cardinal Glennon, he will see a tremendous potential in the handsome young archbishop who came to Saint Louis in 1903. He will see positive achievements in the monumental buildings Glennon left behind; he will see a broad tolerance that allowed a freedom to develop; but he will also see throughout the archdiocese the growth of an unchristian attitude toward the Negro that Glennon did little to correct. He will find a bitterness toward Glennon among many interracial apostles; and hear from others the palliating words that Glennon was a man of his time, not a man who looked to the future.

Even if the historian admits, as he must, the breadth of development that Cardinal Glennon allowed, he will still not find a total liberality as eminent as that of the great cardinal of Baltimore. Even more noticeably, he will not find in John Glennon the passionate concern for the cause of justice that burned in the soul of John Ireland.

Whatever the biographer will finally conclude as to Glennon the man, Glennon's episcopacy shone brightly for twenty years. The last twenty were less brilliant, but still impressive. The cardinal's hat was a fitting close to a distinguished career.

Guests of honor at the presentation of the Vercelli medal to Rudolph Hoogstraet, outstanding member of the Holy Name Society. From the left: Rev. Arthur Hoogstraet, S.J., Rev. Thomas Lloyd, archdiocesan spiritual director of the Holy Name Society, Hoogstraet, Archbishop Ritter, Donald Gunn, Bishop John P. Cody, Rev. Harry C. Graham, O.P., national director of the Holy Name Society, and Judge Edward Ruddy, president of the archdiocesan Union.

Resurrection Church, one of the modern churches built during Cardinal Ritter's time, was designed by Joseph P. Murphy and Associates. (Photograph by Hedrich-Blessing.)

PART VII

Joseph Elmer Ritter:
Organizer, Integrator, Ecumenist (1946-1967)

Archbishop Amleto Giovanni Cocognani, apostolic delegate to the United States, installs Archbishop Joseph Elmer Ritter as archbishop of Saint Louis. With the prelates is (left) Auxiliary Bishop George Donnelly of Saint Louis, soon to become bishop of Leavenworth, Kansas, and (right) Most Rev. Paul C. Schulte, former pastor of the old cathedral and then bishop of Leavenworth, who was to succeed Archbishop Ritter in Indianapolis two days later. (Photograph by St. Louis Review.)

Chapter 37

Ritter to Saint Louis

Ritter's Early Years

At the death of every other bishop of Saint Louis, a successor had been on hand. Rosati directed the seminary at Perryville when Du Bourg left the United States to return to France. Coadjutor Kenrick resided in Saint Louis when Rosati died in Rome. Archbishop Kain was administrating the archdiocese at the death of the "Old Lion." Coadjutor Glennon had come from Kansas City before Kain died. But at the time of Glennon's death, Saint Louis had no coadjutor.

Auxiliary George Donnelly acted as administrator during the four months while rumors of the Pope's choice flew around the city. Four or five names predominated: those of Archbishop Robert Lucey of San Antonio, and bishops Edwin O'Hara of Kansas City, Michael Ready of Columbus, Christian Winkleman of Wichita, Aloysius Muench of Fargo, and Paul Schulte of Leavenworth. Bishop Schulte became an archbishop that same summer, in place of the man who was to come to Saint Louis: Archbishop Joseph Elmer Ritter of Indianapolis.

A few years later, feature writers of the *Saint Louis Globe-Democrat* were to recall the reaction to the news of the papal choice in late July, 1946. " 'I never heard of him,' said a man whose job it was to know everything about everybody," Martin Duggan wrote. "And he was right. Few in Saint Louis had ever heard of Joseph Elmer Ritter. Not once had his name been mentioned in the speculation over the successor to Cardinal Glennon."[1] Justin Faherty pointed out:

Saint Louis newspapers had to send reporters to Indianapolis to get his story. There was virtually nothing under the name: "Ritter, Joseph E.," in the file. The rolls of the North American College in Rome and the famed seminaries here and abroad were studied. The name was not found. Who was this man Ritter? What was his special background? What was his special field?[2]

One of six children of Nicholas and Bertha Ritter, Joseph Elmer had been born on July 20, 1892, in the town of New Albany, Indiana, on the Ohio River across from Louisville, Kentucky. He attended St. Mary's parochial school, and took his preparatory, collegiate, and theological studies at St. Meinrad's Seminary in southern Indiana, not too far from his home town.

Bishop Joseph Chartrand of Indianapolis ordained him on Memorial Day, May 30, 1917. His first assignment sent him to St. Patrick's Church in Indianapolis. Six months later Bishop Chartrand transferred him to the Cathedral of Sts. Peter and Paul as assistant priest. In 1925, at the

*Part VII of this book deals with events close to the time of writing. Many of the principals still live; some remain active in archdiocesan affairs. The ultimate effect of some policies and programs is not yet evident. The author wishes to insist, then, that the vantage of time and the declassification of other documents may at some time in the future place some of these more recent events in a new light. He states events as they happened. He points out that many evaluations may be only tentative.

age of 32, Ritter became rector of the Cathedral. He served quietly and effectively. Bishop Chartrand appointed him a diocesan consultor and member of the Council on Administration and Finance. He took part in a drive to raise funds for the construction of the Cathedral High School. He became vicar-general of the diocese and vice-president of the *Indiana Catholic and Record*, the official diocesan newspaper.

In March, 1933, Joseph Elmer Ritter became auxiliary bishop of Indianapolis and titular bishop of Hippus. Bishop Chartrand survived the consecration by only eight months. Forty-two-year-old Joseph Elmer Ritter, the youngest member of the American hierarchy at the time, became bishop of Indianapolis on March 24, 1934.

Depression still gripped the country, but in the next ten years Bishop Ritter was able to reduce the diocesan debt by more than three million dollars and to complete the construction of the Cathedral begun thirty years before. In putting the diocese on a firm financial basis, he had the assistance of an advisory board that included prominent businessmen of Indiana. Recognizing that Catholics were a minority in the state, Ritter worked closely with non-Catholic agencies and groups in various public welfare and social programs. He reorganized the diocesan Catholic Charities Bureau, sponsored conferences on industrial problems, launched the Catholic Youth Organization and organized the Archdiocesan Council of Catholic Women. He also promoted home missions, rural life activities, and the Negro apostolate in the diocese. He integrated the parochial schools of Indianapolis in the late thirties — a step that caused little comment at the time. He served with Patrick Cardinal Hayes on a three-bishop committee for the reorganization of the National Office of the Propagation of the Faith.

Ritter showed himself a warm human being, easy of access, interested in the individual no matter what his station in life. He did not have the color of personality or flair for the anecdote that made good copy for the press. He proved a straight-forward, unassuming man with the ability to organize and to delegate. "Personally, Joseph E. Ritter is a man of simple, natural dignity," the *Globe-Democrat* stated. "He is completely without pretense. He enjoys gardening, baseball, and friendly chats immensely during his periods of relaxation."[3]

In 1944, Pope Pius XII raised the see of Indianapolis to the rank of archdiocese. On December 11 of that year, Archbishop Amleto Cicognani, apostolic delegate to the United States, installed Ritter as the first archbishop of Indianapolis and head of the new ecclesiastical province of Indiana. A local Negro paper heralded the appointment with these words: "For many years Archbishop Ritter has been recognized throughout Indiana and other states as a champion of Negro rights, especially in education."[4] Archbishop Ritter received the pallium of his archiepiscopal office on March 31, 1946, after the conclusion of World War II. Many presumed that the fifty-four-year-old archbishop would remain the rest of his life in his native state.

Ritter Arrives

When Pope Pius XII appointed Joseph Elmer Ritter archbishop of Saint Louis, on July 20, 1946, the new metropolitan faced obstacles far more difficult psychologically than any of his precessors had faced — except John Kain. Ritter succeeded a deeply revered archbishop. Even those who sharply felt Glennon's neglect of the Negro apostolate had to admit the almost universal respect for the dead cardinal. Since Cardinal Glennon had not prepared for the inevitable change, the new archbishop would eventually have to move an unprepared clergy and laity on the path to interracial betterment.

Ritter, further, was the first archbishop of Saint Louis of German-American ancestry. This should have endeared him to the large group of Catholics of German-American background. This fact, however, was not to prove a source of rapport on two counts. First, he was archbishop of *all* the people, and did not wish to associate himself with any distinct group in the city. Secondly, unlike such revered bishops as Glennon and Winkleman, both tall and stately men, the new archbishop did not have the impressive physical presence so dear to the mind of German Catholics.

The contrast between the new and the old archbishop was striking. Glennon had been surprisingly tall. Archbishop Ritter was a man of moderate height. An impressive personage, Glennon had worn his purple with pride. Ritter, moderate of stature and of modest deportment, had no apparent relish for display. Glennon had great oratorical gifts. Ritter spoke simply, sincerely, and to the point.

On the positive side, the new archbishop brought to the city an administrative and organizational skill, a mind that could see the essential issues, a doggedness in pursuit of his goals, and a deep personal piety — all evidenced in his previous position.

Shortly before he left Indianapolis for Saint Louis, Archbishop Ritter mailed his first pastoral letter. Dated September 13, 1946, it pleaded for support of the missions. Saint Louis had long sent many missionaries of various orders and congregations to foreign lands. Those at home had contributed generously to mission support. While the letter of the new archbishop seemed routine in itself, it heralded a more central concern of the archdiocesan authorities for the overseas missions.

Archbishop Ritter arrived in Saint Louis in October, 1946. At the time, three young members of his new flock, who were destined for long-time prominence in the city, Stanley Musial, Albert Schoendienst, and Joseph Garagiola, were doing their best to beat the Boston Red Sox in the World Series. The newly-arriving Saint Louis Cardinal rooter jokingly apologized for coming to the city at such a busy time.

Recalling the event fifteen years later, a *Globe-Democrat* writer remarked: "Saint Louis has not had another World Series since, though any betting man would have given odds at the time that the Cardinals would have another pennant before the Cathedral had another Cardinal."[5]

On the day after Archbishop Ritter's arrival, October 8, 1946, Amleto Cicognani, the apostolic delegate, installed him in his new position. Acting administrator of the archdiocese, Auxiliary Bishop George Donnelly accepted a call to the bishopric of Leavenworth in Kansas a month later.

The New Archbishop Makes His Decisions

A careful perusal of Archbishop Ritter's record in Indianapolis would have suggested that his initial efforts in Saint Louis would look to a tighter administrative organization for the archdiocese, a development of archdiocesan councils according to the patterns worked out at the National Catholic Welfare Conference in Washington, and racial integration in the parishes.

When the new prelate made his first public appearance at a meeting of the Catholic Clergy Conference held at Visitation School in the city, many came to realize that integration might take precedence on the archdiocesan agenda. The priests engaged in the interracial apostolate were so happy to see the archbishop that they proudly boasted of many things they had done. Unfortunately, to one coming in from the outside and looking at these limited advances objectively, they appeared meager indeed for such a tremendous archdiocese as Saint Louis. Archbishop Ritter wanted to know if that was all they had done.[6]

During the ensuing months, the archbishop studied the picture of Catholic education carefully. He noted that only four hundred among the fifty-eight thousand pupils in parochial schools were Negroes. He saw that facilities at St. Joseph's colored high school on Page were inadequate. Some pastors were adamant about parochial prerogatives, and yet refused to allow Negro Catholic residents to participate in church activities. Within a year of his arrival in the city, Archbishop Ritter instructed all the pastors throughout the archdiocese to end segregation in the schools at the opening of the 1947 school term.

A small group of Catholics held opposition meetings and distributed pamphlets outside of churches. Later they appealed to the apostolic delegate in Washington for a reversal of the integration decision. Archbishop Cicognani rebuffed them sharply. Finally, lawyers advised them to take action in the civil courts aimed at preventing the admission of Negroes to the parish schools. Most Missourians at the time, incidentally, believed that integration would violate state laws. When Archbishop Ritter learned of this contemplated action, he was on a confirmation tour in Southeast Missouri. He phoned the chancery and dictated a letter to the Catholics of the archdiocese for the following Sunday, September 21, 1947. In calm but uncompromising language, Archbishop Ritter warned the dissident Catholics that if they continued such measures they would incur automatic excommunication for impeding an archbishop in the exercise of his pastoral office by an appeal to secular authorities. As a result, the group disbanded. The leader of this anti-integration group, incidentally, came to support racial integration both in schools and other areas of community life a few years later.

In the midst of the agitation, close to five hundred letters poured into the chancery office. Four hundred and one approved Archbishop Ritter's step. Seventy-one dissented. Thirty-two people from the archbishop's native Indiana unanimously approved the action. Forty-four letters came from Illinois, with forty-two approving. Fifteen of sixteen from Pennsylvania approved and forty-seven of forty-eight from California. In general, the letters from the big centers of population, such as New York, California, Illinois, and Pennsylvania were predominantly favorable. Of the seventy-one against, forty-nine came from Missouri itself. Of the sixty-six favorable letters from Missouri, most came from the colored neighborhoods of Saint Louis. The out-of-town approvers were for the most part educators, clergymen of various denominations, and other professional men. Most dissenting letters were handwritten, without official or business stationery with printed headings. In general, the opposing men did not sign their names. But the women did sign their names. One letter came from the Mothers Club of a Catholic high school in the city. With a large number of signatures, this dignified and courteous letter offered alternatives to the archbishop's proposal.

Many of the male dissenters were ungracious. One telegram from a Saint Louis man suggested that in view of the archbishop's great concern for the souls of Africans, he should ask the Pope to send him to Africa to exercise his zeal. This man dedicated his telegram to the priests of his parish and signed his name. One unsigned letter from Bloomington, Delaware, had an element of unexpected humor. "Dear Nero," it began. "You didn't excommunicate Hitler, but now you are excommunicating your own people."[7]

Racial apostles rejoiced at the archbishop's action. Forward-looking citizens all over the country applauded the step. But many priests and laymen privately expressed their antagonism to the action of the archbishop. Some centered their complaints on the fact that the archbishop "moved to the county while he integrated the city." The location of his new residence in Ladue, then the most prestigious suburb, was, as a matter of fact, ill-advised. But, in general, the vast majority of Catholics of the city took the integration matter in stride. They had received little pastoral direction over the years on what they should think, but the whole trend of the nation and the world was moving in the direction Archbishop Ritter pointed; and the people accepted this. Little trouble marked the inaugural of integration in any of the schools.

Religious and secular publications throughout the country hailed the archbishop's action. A year later, the Council against Intolerance in America was to give him the Thomas Jefferson Award, and the Congress of Industrial Organizations honored him. Yet the archbishop did not look upon himself as a crusader for social justice. A *Sign* magazine interviewer stated:

He made the decision, as a matter of simple justice and of obedience to Catholic social teaching, with no desire to thrust himself forward as a champion of interracial harmony. He believed in such harmony, of course, but not in the manner of a crusader.[8]

A feeling sprang up among Catholics of the city that the Vatican had sent Archbishop Ritter to Saint Louis with instructions to end segregation. "There were no orders or even suggestions from the Holy See," Ritter insisted in another interview. On arriving in Saint Louis he found a letter in the late cardinal's files directing a few pastors to admit Negroes to their schools. He felt a direct and immediate method preferable to this slow and tenuous procedure.[9] The public schools of Saint Louis, incidentally, did not follow the example of the parochial schools until the Warren Decision several years later.

Long-Range Development

Archbishop Glennon had appointed many archdiocesan officials, such as a superintendent of schools. But usually the old archbishop tended to keep major decisions in his own hands. In his late years, in fact, his rule was generally personal. Priests and people went to him for minor matters that subordinates should have handled. This followed Church policy in those days, when one had to go to Rome for a simple permission to receive Communion when unable to fast because of health reasons.

Archbishop Ritter gradually set up organizational procedures for the archdiocese, in place of the casual rule appropriate to an earlier time. He recognized that the Saint Louis archdiocese was "in the best sense of the term big business."[10] He authorized an audit of archdiocesan operations and wanted to publicize the results so that the people would know the archdiocese used their contributions wisely.[11] He delegated real powers to his department heads, such as the superintendent of schools and the director of Catholic charities, and gave them powers formerly reserved to local pastors. He consulted regularly with a selected group of laymen, experts in various fields of human activity, such as education and communications.

Shortly after coming to Saint Louis, Archbishop Ritter started a critical self-evaluation of Catholic charities. He brought in a professional consultant service to look over the forty-six member agencies and institutions. The archdiocese opened Our Lady of Grace Child Care Center in 1947. The William G. Brennan Memorial Center for the Blind extended needed service in its area. Archbishop Ritter supported the United Fund approach to charitable services throughout the metropolitan area.

In the matter of high school expansion, Ritter carried out Glennon's plans, with one major change. He did not have Glennon's aversion to co-education on the high school level. In the next few years, the archdiocese opened Mercy High in University City, De Andreis on the north side, and Bishop Du Bourg near Francis Park in southwest Saint Louis.

The archdiocese wanted to make Catholic high school education available to as many as possible, regardless of ability to pay. Archbishop Ritter sent many young priests into the educational apostolate. He gave many of them time to pursue advanced degrees for this purpose. Sometimes, perhaps unadvisedly, he sent priests into this work without reference to their apostolic inclinations. In general, however, he was to enlarge the area of the apostolate for the diocesan priests in various fields beyond the traditional pastoral concerns.

The archbishop and his consultors gave serious attention to erecting a fitting memorial to the memory of the late Cardinal Glennon. Finally in August, 1949, he announced plans to build a children's hospital near the Saint Louis University Medical School. The Sisters of St. Mary of the Third Order of St. Francis would staff it. The archbishop set a high goal and challenged the people of Saint Louis to build this memorial to their late shepherd. Catholic and non-Catholic alike responded in a most generous way and went far above the amount asked for at the inauguration of the drive.

The archdiocese had its own information bureau, with an experienced newspaperman, Jacob N. Fueglein as head, and began a radio and television apostolate under the direction of Francis Matthews. This office sponsored several panel and discussion type shows. One of these, "Quiz-a-Catholic" combined regular panelists and local or out-of-town guests, such as Patricia Morrison, Municipal Opera star of "Kiss Me, Kate."[12]

In his first few years Archbishop Ritter established only one new parish, St. Bernadette's, in the area of Jefferson Barracks, no longer an active military post. But from 1950 on, Saint Louis City and County saw an average of three new parishes each year during his episcopacy. Within ten years, he had opened twenty-nine new parishes and eleven new missions. Scores of other parishes undertook the building of new churches or schools.[13] At least three new churches merited national attention architecturally: Resurrection in Saint Louis, St. Peter's in Kirkwood, and St. Ann's in Normandy.

The *Globe-Democrat* stated:

> The archbishop is devoted to progressive art, a feeling that is shown expression in architecture and art in new buildings throughout the archdiocese. . . . "Religion would seem to have died two hundred years ago," he says, "if we cannot keep the material surroundings of our spiritual life in step with the trend of the times. We must face realism. How can we do that if we surround ourselves with art and architecture that is sugary sweet?"
>
> As one of the Catholic Church's leading champions of progressive art in religion, the Archbishop frequently finds himself at odds with members of his flock. But he holds fast to his beliefs there as in other matters.[14]

Late in 1947, the national director of the Holy Name Society, Very Reverend Harry C. Graham, O.P., announced that the second annual Vercelli Medal would go to Saint Louisan, Rudoph W. Hoogstraet of St. Gabriel's parish. Hoogstraet had served as president of the Holy Name Society for twelve years, 1931-1943. During this time, he led a vigorous and successful drive for good literature.[15] At the presentation dinner on January 4, 1948, Attorney Donald Gunn, later to be president of the board of aldermen and juvenile judge, introduced Archbishop Ritter, Bishop Cody, Father Graham, Judge Edward M. Ruddy, past Holy Name Society president (1944-1946), and other dignitaries.

A year later the Archdiocesan Union of Holy Name Societies worked closely with Archbishop Ritter on his plans for lay organizations. The archbishop leaned toward the setting up of an entirely new structure under the banner of the National Council of Catholic Men in Washington. Judge David McMullan, successor to Donald Gunn as president, and Father Joseph Anler, spiritual adviser of the archdiocesan union, felt that the new structure should build on the existing grass-roots development of sodalities, the Central Union, the Rural Life Conferences, the Holy Name Societies, and other organizations. With this wise decision, Judge McMullan served as the first president of the Archdiocesan Council of Catholic Men in 1949.[16]

Archbishop Ritter reorganized the Archdiocesan Council of Catholic Women that had been in existence since 1923. The Council of Catholic Youth soon numbered eighteen thousand youngsters in its various cultural, social, physical, or religious programs.[17]

The Saint Louis councils worked closely with the central offices at the National Catholic Welfare Council office in Washington. Quite often the bureaucrats in charge of these national offices did not respect the grass-roots development in each diocese, but tried to strait-jacket the form of organization from the top down. Archbishop Ritter followed this pattern in some instances, but more often made a reasonable effort to build the archdiocesan superstructure on the many e   ˷rganizations of the city.

Within ten years of *f*   *'˷* arrival in Saint Louis, the three archdi   affiliated organizations. Catholics had a˷ .   widely in community enterprises, as members ˵˶ _ cal parties, service clubs, labor unions, or other associations. Now they participated more directly as members of Catholic organizations in civic affairs such as slum clearance and zoning arrangements.[18] The Archdiocesan Council of Catholic Women took active interest in legislative matters on state and national levels.[19]

Individual Saint Louis Catholics, such as Judge McMullan, NCCM president in 1957-1958, held high posts in constituent organizations of the national councils. The operation was so rigidly structured, however, that the lay officials never worked in an autonomous atmosphere. They did not serve as responsible lay people working in the interests of lay Catholics or of the Church itself. They simply carried out the policies of the clerical governing committees. Thus the councils were not able to give to the American Church or to the Saint Louis archdiocese the opportunity for lay decision-making that American life warranted.

Co-Workers and Brother Bishops

The first of a number of outstanding priests of the archdiocese to become bishops during the Ritter years, the Most Reverend Mark K. Carroll, pastor of St. Margaret's Church, director of the Propagation of the Faith, and rector of the Cathedral Latin School, became bishop of Wichita on February 19, 1947. Archbishop Ritter consecrated him on April 23 of that year and he went to Kansas on May 6.

In the same month of May, Pope Pius XII named Chancellor John Patrick Cody titular bishop of Appolonia and auxiliary of Saint Louis. The Pope chose Father August F. Wildermuth, S.J., a native of Saint Louis, and a missionary in India, as Bishop of Patna, India, in July. A year later (May, 1948) the Holy Father selected another Saint Louis priest, Monsignor Leo J. Steck, archdiocesan director of the C.C.D. and of the Catholic Rural Life Conference, as auxiliary bishop of Salt Lake City.

On September 21, 1948, Archbishop Ritter consecrated Father David Hickey, S.J., a native of Saint Louis, as the first bishop of Belize, British Honduras. Previously Belize had been a vicariate apostolic. Bishop Hickey was to serve for almost twenty years as a missionary bishop and then to return to parochial work in Saint Louis.[20]

On March 17, 1949, the Holy Father appointed Most Reverend Charles H. Helmsing, the archbishop's secretary and director of the Propagation of the Faith, auxiliary bishop of Saint Louis. On April 19, Archbishop Ritter consecrated him, with Bishops John Cody and Leo J. Steck as co-consecrators. Not since the days of Archbishop Kenrick had so many priests of the diocese received calls to the episcopacy in such a short space of time. Unfortunately, one of them, Bishop Steck, died the following year (1950) at the age of fifty-two.

Monsignor William M. Drumm, J.C.D., succeeded Bishop Cody as chancellor in 1950. A less front-center man than his predecessor, Monsignor Drumm was to serve in this capacity inconspicuously but most effectively for over two decades. In a justified tribute to him many years later, Monsignor Daniel Moore wrote:

> His position calls for and demands a broad spectrum of abilities and the priests and lay people who have occasion to deal with him will tell you that he is seldom, if ever, found wanting. He is the unsung, as well as the unofficial information center of the archdiocese.[21]

Chapter 38

Domestic Development

Archdiocesan Expansion Fund

As suburbs and new housing developments mushroomed north, south, and west with an immediate demand for churches and schools, the archbishop and his advisers prepared for the future. In 1954 the archdiocese inaugurated an annual capital funds drive to meet the building needs of a growing region. The people responded generously. A *Register* writer described the resulting operation:

The revolving fund allows a new parish, without so much as a brick to its name, and no hope of a bank loan, to get as much as $400,000 for building purposes, just for a signature on the papers. The Archdiocesan Expansion Fund makes the loans to new parishes at rates which apparently do little more than cover the service cost.[1]

As parochial expansion in the immediate Saint Louis area continued at a rate of three new parishes a year, sub-dividers came to work more closely with parochial authorities. The inner-city changed. And with these changes, the archdiocese closed some churches, such as St. Lawrence O'Toole's on the near north side, and St. Malachy's in the Mill Creek Renewal Development that saw the demolition of all housing from Eighteenth Street to Grand Avenue in a stretch four blocks north of the Mill Creek Valley. Even more important, the archdiocese restored three beautiful churches, the old cathedral at the waterfront, St. John's near Union Station, and Holy Trinity. This latter edifice, long hidden and almost forgotten on North Fourteenth, now held an impressive and commanding site, as the federal highway program pushed a major through-way a few blocks in front of it.

High school expansion continued, too. The archdiocese built a new building for the former South Side Catholic, now called St. Mary's High School, and by 1961 had opened sixteen new schools, such as Rosary, Providence, Duchesne, St. Pius X, and Hildner. New private high schools opened and older schools sought new sites. Visitation and St. Joseph's moved west.

The generosity of the Catholics of Saint Louis continued high. During the decade beginning in 1954, the archdiocese invested over seventy-two millions in acquiring sites, remodeling, construction, and repairs.[2] Many Catholics jokingly complained about the archbishop's real estate skills. But they knew he used the money well and contributed generously through the years.

Though local jokes had Archbishop Ritter's heavenly record filed under "real estate agent," the *Globe-Democrat* insisted:

There is more to Archbishop Ritter than just building and integrating. Archbishop Ritter is a Church-man. It would be hard to visualize the man aside from the church. He sees himself as a shepherd, looking out for the safety of the souls Christ and His Vicar on Earth have entrusted to his care. That is his whole job. Everything else is just something extra added to his responsibilities.[3]

Long after the other achievements of Archbishop Rit-

ter may have disappeared from man's memory, the mosaics of the Saint Louis Cathedral will still exist to recall the artistic skills of men and women of the mid-twentieth century. The depression years of the early thirties had brought a halt to the adornment of the walls and domes of the cathedral. Some of the finest mosaics in the country were already in their places, but some empty spaces remained.

Archbishop Ritter wanted a sacristy added to the building according to a consistent pattern, an improved lighting system and further advance in the development of the mosaic art. In 1956, under the general direction of architect George J. Maguolo and the guidance of parish administrator, Monsignor Thomas Durkin, Paul and Arno Heuduck of the Ravenna Mosaic Company resumed the great work. Ultimately an acre of some of the finest mosaics in the world covered the Cathedral. The south dome, the dome of local history, had special interest in that it recalled the great events and personalities of Saint Louis' Catholic past.

When the artists had finished their work, critics rated the mosaics in the great arches, in the spherical triangles that connected the arches and the supporting structure, and in the vestibule — the mosaics of the life of Saint Louis IX — among the finest in the world. No church in the western hemisphere could match the Saint Louis Cathedral in the quality and the quantity of mosaic art.

"Hi Neighbor!" Policy

The archdiocese began a Catholic Information Center at 1129 Locust in July 1953. Reverend Daniel Moore directed the center, and had the assistance of a staff of volunteers. During the winter months, he scheduled regular religious lectures. As many as five hundred people sometimes visited this center during the day, to seek information, or to attend Mass in the chapel dedicated to Pope St. Pius X shortly after his canonization.

Since so many churches stood a few blocks from the periphery of the central business section of the city — Broadway to Twelfth, and Market to Delmar — few had given much thought to the lack of a chapel in this area. The old cathedral was a few blocks east, St. Joseph's and St. Patrick's a few blocks north, St. John's a few blocks west, St. Mary's and St. Vincent's a few blocks south. But since the moving of St. Francis Xavier's Church from Ninth and Washington in the 1880's, those working in the mid-city did not have easy access to a chapel for short visits or noon-day Mass. Many now visited the chapel at the Information Center.

The archdiocese undertook a religious census and information program on October 31, 1954. Thirty-two thousand laymen called on 346,000 homes to determine the number of Catholics in the archdiocese and to invite interested persons to learn about the Catholic faith. Other dioceses had held similar programs with notable success.

Father Paul Ryan, S.M., presents Archbishop Ritter to the students of Saint Mary's High, preparatory to the blessing of the statue of Our Lady on the school grounds. (Photograph by St. Louis Review.)

The Saint Louis archdiocese set as goals the spreading of the faith among the religiously uncommitted, and the recalling of lapsed Catholics. In two years the program attracted close to five thousand persons to inquiry forums set up in many parochial centers. It brought over two thousand new adult Christians into Church membership and recalled hundreds of lapsed Catholics.[4]

The archdiocese was to take part in another form of "Good Neighbor" endeavor several years later. Archbishop Ritter had always believed in cooperation on a social reform level with other religious groups. He believed that a common front would help the cause of religion in general. An opportunity came when the small city of Creve Coeur in Saint Louis County tried to block the building of Temple Israel. The archdiocese entered the suit in support of the Temple Israel congregation, as did the Metropolitan Church Federation.

In an interview, Monsignor James R. Hartnett, executive secretary of the Archdiocesan Building Commission, explained the official position of the archdiocese. First, it wanted to speak in behalf of the Jewish congregation; and second, it wanted to insure the right of churches and private schools to select sites without fear that small municipal boards would zone them out.[5]

In rendering his decision against the Creve Coeur ordinance, and in favor of the congregation of Temple Israel, Judge Raymond E. LaDriere commended the church groups for entering the suit.[6]

As a further instance of his broad benevolence, Archbishop Ritter attended the dedication of Temple Israel.

Continuing Mission Interest

Interest in the missions made Saint Louis a diocese long before it might otherwise have attained that rank. Bishop Du Bourg gave as a reason for locating there rather than in New Orleans the prospect of being nearer Indian country. The Congregation of the Mission, the Religious of the Sacred Heart, and the Jesuit Order had mission incentives in their initial coming to the West. Pierre Jean De Smet and his companions left for the northwest missions from Saint Louis. Bishops Timon, Odin, and Miege went from Missouri to missions in the plains states. When the frontier missions gave way to more routine

parish life, zealous Saint Louisans began to go to new mission fields abroad, in Latin America, in Africa, in the Far East — depending on the particular mission operation of their respective orders. Zealous lay people formed mission-support societies in the interests of a friend or relative in the mission field.

Archbishop Ritter attempted to enlarge concern and support of the foreign missions by projecting a parish mission promoters plan. By means of door-to-door visitation, lay promoters asked their fellow Catholics to say prayers for the missions and contribute an annual membership fee for mission support.

In 1953, the archdiocese planned an unprecedented World Mission Exposition at Kiel Auditorium. Three hundred mission-sending societies accepted Archbishop Ritter's invitation to prepare a booth with tangible evidence of their work for Christ in five continents. Two hundred and sixty-five thousand people witnessed the exposition. Many came to realize for the first time the universality of the Church and its mission aims, procedures, and progress.

Two thousand lay committee members began an enduring program of prayer and sacrifice for the missions. These Daily World Missionaires promised to pray three times each day for the missions, to make a daily sacrifice, and to give a donation resulting from that sacrifice. Bishop Fulton J. Sheen, national director of the Society for the Propagation of the Faith, soon called the daily World Missionaires "the most modern, complete and up-to-date approach to mission aid that has ever been developed."[7] Well could he do this. Mission support in the archdiocese more than doubled in a few years, and soon surpassed that of most dioceses in the entire world.

Religious orders centered in the archdiocese opened new fields of missionary endeavor: Redemptorists went to Brazil; Daughters of Charity and Josephites to Japan; Jesuits and Notre Dames to Honduras; Maryknoll priests and Sisters to Asia, Africa, and Latin America. Three mission congregations opened their first residences in the archdiocese: the Mill Hill Fathers, the Society of Catholic Medical Missionaries, and the Franciscan Missionaries of America. Archbishop Ritter blessed the new La Salette Minor Seminary on South Broadway and the Novitiate of the Maryknoll Sisters near Valley Park.

The Saint Louis prelate planned an even more dramatic

missionary effort. Long before Latin America became an overriding concern of the North American Church, he looked south of the border. What he saw was not always encouraging. He noticed the lack of priests, nuns, and religious workers, the widespread illiteracy, unemployment, utter poverty, and the leftist response to these problems.

In the mid-fifties, Archbishop Ritter appealed to the priests of the archdiocese for volunteers to undertake direct mission work in Bolivia. He selected three of the many who responded: Fathers Andrew Schierhoff, Andrew Kennedy, and David Rattermann. After special training, they went to the diocese of La Paz in 1956. There they founded and staffed a mission supported by the contributions of the people of Saint Louis. Under this impetus, the Sisters of St. Mary and the Lorettines undertook Bolivian missions.

The following year, the archbishop himself decided to visit La Paz and see at first hand the needs of the area and to encourage personally the Saint Louis missionaries there.

The first papal volunteers from the Saint Louis area, accountant Francis T. Clarke and Mary Jane Krekeler, were to leave for Bolivia in the summer of 1961. A veteran of World War II, with a master's degree in business administration, Clarke had worked with Blue Cross for many years, and hoped to set up credit unions in Bolivia. Miss Krekeler, a graduate of Fontbonne, who had worked in the Social Security Office in Saint Louis, planned to teach in La Paz. Both volunteers had been members of the Legion of Mary.[8]

Within a decade, the archdiocese was to set up two parishes in Bolivia: one in La Paz, with four priests, and one in Viacha with three missionaries, and a parish in Arica, Chile. Eventually, Monsignor Andrew Kennedy was to serve as secretary of the conference of the Bolivan hierarchy, and Father Schierhoff to become auxiliary bishop of La Paz. On Archbishop Ritter's second visit to Bolivia, the highest officials of that nation were to confer on him Bolivia's premier decoration, the Grand Cross of the Condor of the Andes.[9]

Gerrymandered Missouri

In January 1954, the Holy Father had appointed Saint Louis Auxiliary John Cody coadjutor to the bishop of St. Joseph, with the right of succession, and in May of that same year, had named Monsignor Leo C. Byrne, executive secretary of the Archdiocesan Catholic Charities, auxiliary of Saint Louis.

Two years later (1956), Rome changed the diocesan boundaries in the province of Saint Louis, coterminus with the state of Missouri since 1952. The new map abolished the scarcely viable diocese of St. Joseph that stretched across the northern counties of the state; but set up the equally improbable diocese of Cape Girardeau-Springfield. The northern boundary of this diocese, about seventy-five miles from the Arkansas border, followed county lines from the southernmost part of Perry County on the east to the Kansas line on the west. No rail, air, or state highway connected the two diocesan centers. Saint Louis Auxiliary Charles Helmsing, director of the Society for the Propagation of the Faith, and of the Catholic Rural Life Conference, became the first bishop of this gerrymandered diocese.

A new diocese of Kansas City-St. Joseph stretched for two hundred miles along the Kansas border and went

Father Joseph Blattner of Christ the King parish, La Paz, talks to a group of Bolivian women in the marketplace. (Photograph by St. Louis Review.)

instate for fifty to sixty miles. It combined parts of the former dioceses whose names it jointly bore. The Pope named the former St. Joseph Coadjutor John Cody bishop of this diocese in July 1956. All northeast and central Missouri formed the newly-created diocese of Jefferson City with Father John Marling, provincial of the Precious Blood Fathers, becoming its first bishop.

The Archdiocese of Saint Louis included Saint Louis City and County, and the adjoining St. Charles, Lincoln, Warren, Franklin, Washington, Jefferson, St. Francois, Ste. Genevieve, and Perry Counties — almost all the heavily Catholic parts of the state of Missouri. "Reduced in size from 27,092 square miles to 5,968 square miles," the *Register* stated, "it [the archdiocese] still retains 428,000 of its former 475,000."[10] These statistics dramatically point up the urban character of the Missouri church.

When Bishop Helmsing began his new task in south Missouri, Archbishop Ritter allowed a number of priests who wanted to work with him in the rural areas to do so. One of these, Father Marion Frost, pastor of St. Mary's Cathedral in Cape Girardeau, was to serve as vicar-general of south Missouri until 1960 when he became bishop of Dodge City, Kansas.

Saint Louis' Memorial to Pope Pius XII

In the late 1940's, two historians at Saint Louis University, Fathers Lowrie J. Daly and Joseph P. Donnelly, who also served as director of libraries, had discussed the possibility of microfilming some materials in the Vatican Library in Rome to make them available to scholars in mid-America Daly got in touch with his former classmate at Saint Louis University, Father James Naughton, then secretary of the Jesuit order in Rome.

Following Naughton's advice in November, 1950, Saint Louis University asked the prefect of the Vatican Library, Very Reverend Anselmo Albaredo, O.S.B., for permission to undertake the microfilming. The school based its request on three grounds: its central location in the New World, its extensive program of graduate studies, and the anticipated benefits to American scholars.

Scarcely a month later, on December 15, 1950, Prefect Albaredo had secured Pope Pius XII's approval. His Holiness granted the permission and made Saint Louis University the sole repository of the microfilm manuscript treasures. Father Daly and Father Donnelly drew up lists of the manuscripts for microfilming in 1951 and continued the program during the ensuing years.

Saint Louisan Luke E. Hart, supreme advocate, and later grand knight of the Knights of Columbus, enthusiastically explained the proposal of the Saint Louis University to his fellow knights. They agreed to support the project financially and to establish a permanent depository for the collection. In gratitude for the organizations' financing of the three-hundred-and-fifty-thousand-dollar microfilm project, the university agreed to name the manuscript collection "The Knights of Columbus Vatican Film Library."

In the middle fifties, the university planned a memorial library to Pope Pius XII, to house the microfilm and the rest of the university collections. Father Paul C. Reinert, S.J., president, planned a two-fold campaign — a local one and a national one. The national program was only partially successful. The local program proved much more successful, thanks to civic leaders of all faiths. Archbishop Ritter sought the support of American bishops for this memorial to the sovereign Pontiff and alerted the entire Catholic body of Saint Louis to the project. The archbishop presided at the ground breaking ceremonies on June 3, 1957, and within two and a half years on November 22, 1959, the university dedicated its library. The apostolic delegate to the United States, Archbishop Aegidio Vagnozzi, represented Pope John XXIII, the successor of Pius XII. The Most Reverend Anselmo Albaredo, prefect of the Vatican Library, was to preside at the inaugural of the microfilm section.

This library development signaled the beginning of a great expansion for Saint Louis University. Archbishop Ritter encouraged this program and took a far more immediate interest in the growth of Saint Louis University than any of his predecessors since Bishop Rosati.

Under the enduring leadership of Reverend Paul C. Reinert, S.J., Saint Louis University won the support of wider and wider segments of the Saint Louis business community in its efforts to expand educational opportunity in the area.

A New Archdiocesan Paper

"In harmony with the recent progressive program of our great city of Saint Louis," Archbishop Ritter wrote early in 1957, "we are ready to announce that another forward step has been taken — a new Catholic paper.... The first issue of the Saint Louis *Review* is a souvenir marking another milestone in the dynamic movement of Saint Louis."[11]

The archbishop had announced six months before that the archdiocese would leave the *Register* chain and publish an independent paper in February of the following year. Reverend Jasper Chiodini, S.T.D., pastor of St. Dominic Savio's Church and managing editor of the paper since 1953, would continue in charge. Father Daniel Moore, director of the Catholic Information Center in downtown Saint Louis, would be associate editor, and Father John W. Miller, Ph.D., would continue to serve as business manager. The editorial offices would remain in the former Festus J. Wade residence at 4532 Lindell, where they had been since 1945. The Nordmann Printing Company of Saint Louis would print the newspaper.[12]

Many people in the city had long expected such a change. The national section of the *Register* reflected a beleaguered minority mentality understandable in an area that had seen the burning crosses of Ku Klux Klan days but was foreign to the more ecumenic ethos of Saint Louis.

The *Register* had served its purpose in Saint Louis. The local subscriptions had passed the one hundred thousand mark by the time of the archbishop's decision to change. Only four Catholic papers, the *Chicago New World*, the *Milwaukee Herald Citizen*, the *Brooklyn Tablet*, and the *Michigan Catholic*, surpassed its 103,817 circulation in mid-1956. It had the largest circulation of any weekly in Missouri, and the fourth largest circulation of any paper in the state, behind only the *Saint Louis Post-Dispatch*, the *Saint Louis Globe-Democrat* and the *Kansas City Star*.[13]

In its last years the Saint Louis *Register* had joined with the Archdiocesan Council of Catholic Men to produce a Sunday morning TV show on KMOX-TV (Channel 4) entitled "The Great Crusade."[14] The Catholic Press Association had given it two awards in 1954: one for the best news story, and the other on the best example of teaching Christian doctrine.[15] In March, 1956, the National Council of Christians and Jews had given the editors a citation for an editorial entitled "For Gentiles Only."[16]

In the first issue of the new *Review*, the editors expressed their concern for "leading their readers to God." They pledged "courage to express the teachings of the church unwaveringly,... resolute adherence to its principles... firmness in defending truth and right... scrupulous exactness in respecting the dignity of all fellowmen... and sincere scholarship in the presentation of news."[17]

The *Review* also went to the newly created Springfield-Cape Girardeau diocese for a time. The initial issue of the paper carried Bishop Charles Helmsing's first pastoral to his new flock.[18] An early edition of the Saint Louis *Register* in 1941 had featured the ordination of Father Glennon Flavin and his classmates.[19] Four months after its first issue, the new *Review* hailed his consecration as auxiliary bishop of Saint Louis.[20]

During the summer of 1957, Father Daniel Moore moved up to the post of editor in place of Father Jasper Chiodini, who now devoted full energies to his thriving parish of St. Dominic Savio in suburban southwest Saint Louis.[21]

The *Review* took the occasion of the consecration at the Cathedral of a Saint Louis-born missionary, David F. Hickey, S.J., as bishop of Belize, British Honduras, to discuss mission support from Saint Louis. Although the archdiocese ranked only sixteenth in population, it ranked fourth in total mission contributions — behind Chicago, Brooklyn, and New York, and third, proportionately to population, behind the small dioceses of Wilmington, Delaware, and Winona, Minnesota.[22] A month later, Monsignor Fulton J. Sheen gave the First Annual World-mission award to Oliver L. Parks of Saint Louis, founder of the World Missionaires and of Parks Air College, in a ceremony at the Shoreham Hotel in Washington.[23]

The *Review* featured another prominent member of the laity that summer, Mrs. Edwin Eigel, six-year president of Kappa Gamma Pi, the honor society of Catholic college alumnae. The mother of seven children, Mrs. Eigel had been active in the United Fund and the Community Chest and was program chairman for the Family, Children

Bishop Sheen presents a plaque to Oliver L. Parks, proclaiming him "Mission Layman of 1957," as Father Glennon Flavin prepares to add his congratulations. (Photograph by Reni.)

Senator Stuart Symington, and Congressmen Frank Karsten, Thomas Curtis, and Clarence Cannon gather around the Missouri table with Editor Dan Moore at the Catholic Press Convention in 1960, that awarded the St. Louis Review a scroll for "General Excellence." (Photograph by Chase, Ltd.)

and Old Age division of the Social Planning Council. At its national convention in Detroit, Kappa Gamma Pi had honored her with its "Valiant Woman" designation.[24] A few years later, the National Council of Catholic Men honored another Saint Louisan, Professor Thomas P. Neill of Saint Louis University, Knight of St. Gregory, Daily World Missionaire, and *Review* columnist, with its biennial award for "intellectual leadership."[25]

The *Review* won a succession of awards from the Catholic Press Association. In 1958 it carried the best editorial,[26] and the following year the best campaign in the public interest, a series on obscene literature.[27] In 1960, the Catholic Press Association awarded it the "General Excellence" scroll for the following reasons:

First, wise screening of news from all fronts. . . . Second, proper emphasis and grouping of stories. . . . Third, helping readers understand a complex news development (the Puerto Rican election) with comprehensive coverage of news and views on the matter. . . . Four, good editorial and book review sections.[28]

The editorial section at the time contained columns by such national writers as F. J. Sheed, Monsignor George Higgins, Donald McDonald, and Monsignor Fulton J. Sheen, and local columnists Fathers John Maguire, and Kenneth L. Paluczak, and the husband-wife team of Martin and Mae Duggan, and a well-chosen reprint from another publication under the title "Matter of Moment." Over the next few years, the *Review* added Father John Thomas' "Family Clinic," Father Conway's "Question Box," and Brother George Wead's incisive analyses of current films.[29]

Further Interracial Advance

In telling the story "How Saint Louis Broke the Race Barrier," in *Ave Maria* magazine, writer James Rorty singled out among white laymen Charles F. Vatterott, Jr., president of the Catholic Interracial Council. "He is probably the only realtor in America," Rorty wrote, "who has used his own resources to provide decent homes, at cost, or less, to Negro families — preferably large Negro families."[30]

During the 1940's, Vatterott had opened Mary Ridge, in suburban Saint Louis, a Caucasian community of one hundred homes, with special financial arrangements for large families. In the early 1950's, he followed a similar formula with a Negro community named for Martin de Porres. He made no attempt to force integration in either area; but he worked for integration in neighborhood facilities, such as the golf course.[31]

At the same time, the Queen's Work Publishing House pioneered in a policy of interracial hiring on more than a token basis. While many other firms limited blacks to custodial and minor clerical positions, the National Sodality headquarters advanced individuals to supervisory capacities and set a pattern for other firms.[32]

Archbishop Ritter's interest in interracial justice carried on after his initial effort at school integration. In the health field, he planned the Cardinal Glennon Memorial Hospital as a place where children of all races and reli-

gions could receive proper treatment; and called for an integrated medical, nursing, and technical staff.[33]

When the Catholic Hospital Association held its Fortieth Annual Convention in Saint Louis in 1955, Ritter called for an end to discrimination in all Catholic hospitals. He told the conference on May 16:

> If any teaching of Christ is spelled out for us, it is this teaching in regard to love of neighbor. Catholic hospitals, along with the whole Church, have a more serious obligation to carry out courageously the teaching of Christ and the Church and to put aside in their policies and practice, if they exist, any and all discrimination because of race, color, or religion. If all will courageously set themselves to the task, no matter from what source opposition may come, our hospitals will not only be doing a service to humanity in these critical times, but to religion, thereby honoring the name of Christ in all sections of the country.[34]

In 1958 Ritter supported a bill before the Saint Louis board of aldermen to prohibit discrimination against Negroes in city business establishments. All civic officials, he said at the time, had a responsibility before God in justice as in charity, to recognize the dignity of all men without discrimination.

The slow steady advance towards racial justice in Saint Louis, however, was not exclusively the work of a few individuals. Many men and women had their part, both individually and institutionally. The Catholic Interracial Council continued its work through the years, giving considerable attention, in conjunction with the Urban League, to the area of employment opportunities.

Monsignor Cornelius Flavin welcomes members of the St. Joseph High School Alumni Association, their families, and former teachers at a reunion at Visitation School.

Chapter 39

Personalities and Progress

Father "Dismas" Clark and Doctor Tom Dooley

In the first half of the twentieth century, the archdiocese had been the scene of social projects sponsored by two colorful individuals, Father Tim Dempsey and Father Peter Dunne. So two Saint Louis men of the fifties promoted highly individualized projects, one in Saint Louis, the other in Southeast Asia.

While at White House Retreat before World War II, Father Charles Clark, S.J., had accepted a suggestion of Judge David McMullan to interest himself in the spiritual care of convicts. During his years as chaplain in the military service, Father Clark continued this interest at several disciplinary barracks. After the war, between retreats and missions, he pursued the prisoner apostolate.

To identify with his work, he took the alias of the Good Thief, Dismas, as his middle name. He worked to have a special Mass in honor of St. Dismas in mid-October. Father Clark came to believe that many convicts were really gamblers at heart who, somewhere in their mid-thirties, finally came to see that the odds were too high and wanted to start anew. Many of these could be paroled if they had a job and a place to live. In consultation with others, Father Clark conceived the idea of a halfway house whither such parolees could come for a time. Father Clark and his staff would help them get jobs and make the transition to life outside the walls. He wanted the parolees to help one another.

With the assistance of Morris Shenker, Saint Louis lawyer, the Jesuit provincial, Father Joseph P. Fisher, several local and national labor leaders, and others, he began the Father Dismas Clark Foundation and set up a halfway house in the Old Jefferson School at Tenth and Cole. A movie, the *Hoodlum Priest*, selected a few dramatic experiences from his work with convicts. The Ambassador Theatre in downtown Saint Louis hosted the premiere. A banquet followed at the Khorrasan Room of the Chase-Park Plaza. When Father Clark died suddenly a few years later, Father Frederick Zimmerman, S.J., pastor of St. Matthew's Church and an associate of Father Clark in various earlier activities, directed Dismas House.

During these same years, a native of Saint Louis, an alumnus of Saint Louis University High, the University of Notre Dame, and Saint Louis University School of Medicine, Dr. Thomas Dooley, gained world-wide fame for his work with refugees from Communism in Southeast Asia. After his term as naval doctor, Dooley returned to the area and continued his health care programs. As promoter and propagandist of the needs of the area, he enlisted a team of workers; and through three bestselling books brought the problems and possibilities to the entire world.

He died prematurely. His funeral at the Saint Louis Cathedral, his native parish, attracted world-wide attention. Saint Louis' newest auxiliary, Bishop George Gottwald, quoted the poet Robert Frost in his widely acclaimed sermon. The words "Promises to Keep" became the title of a subsequent life of Dr. Dooley.

The "Levee Priest" Becomes "Monsignor Conservationist"

During the long years since he had taken part in the founding of the National Catholic Rural Life Conference in 1923, Father George Hildner at Claryville in southeast Missouri had continued to provide leadership in many sectors of farm improvement. He had served as Levee Board chairman, "Good Road" representative, Soil Conservation Association official, Civil Defense chairman, and organizer and pioneer member of various cooperatives and farm organizations.

In the midst of the drought and depression, Archbishop Glennon had sent him in 1934 to Villa Ridge in Franklin County, forty miles west of Saint Louis, a short distance south of the Missouri River. The energetic pastor moved to the Church of St. John's Gildehaus — named for Deidrich Gildehaus who had given thirty-three acres for the support of the pastor a century before. Father Hildner had found no town or highway, but only a church on top of a barren hill. His parish consisted of rolling, eroded, worn-out wheat farms, and a flock of staunch, industrious, devout but impoverished farmers. They had a rich spiritual tradition and a faith in God, but a sense of frustration from trying to stave off foreclosure for another year, and occasionally a stubborn tendency not to try the new. Hildner's first task was to establish a government soil conservation demonstration area in the county. Since the county had to pay part of the cost and was short of funds, and the populace disliked the notion of government intervention in any form, Father Hildner had a touch-and-go struggle. Finally after a lengthy ses-

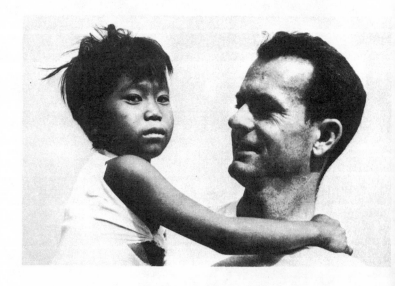

Dr. Thomas Dooley and one of his many patients. (Photograph by St. Louis Review.)

Rev. Donald F. Miller, C.SS.R., pamphleteer, editor, and organizer of the Liguori Press.

included twenty-four communities with twenty-two parishes and three missions.

During these rich years, Monsignor Hildner spoke at rural life seminars throughout the country, and won the master conservationist award of the State Conservation Commission at the state fair in Sedalia. Later he won national conservation awards. The National Catholic Rural Life Conference named him the outstanding rural life clergyman in America at its National Convention in Lafayette, Louisiana, in 1947.[2] In 1964, the Holy Father was to confer on him the dignity of pronotary apostolic, the highest rank the Church can bestow on a priest.

While other rural life pioneer priests, such as Fathers Edwin O'Hara of Oregon and William Mulloy of North Dakota, moved into ecclesiastical administration as bishops, and Father Luigi Ligutti into a position of international leadership in farm affairs, Monsignor Hildner remained in Franklin County giving guidance and support in every phase of rural activities. In his farm leadership, he moved against the tide of the time and thus had less lasting influence than he might have had at another time or in another region. Work such as he did, for instance, would have had far wider effect in a less industrialized archdiocese, such as Kansas City (Kansas) or Dubuque (Iowa). It may well be that Monsignor Hildner's influence in the eventual development of the Meramec Basin may prove to be his most lastingly influential work in outstate Missouri. Whatever that final verdict may be, he did serve his people where he found them, as he found them, with a tremendous concern for total human development. He richly deserved the awards the Church and the nation conferred upon him.

Liguorian Giant

The position Jesuit Daniel A. Lord occupied in Catholic pamphlet publishing in the thirties and early forties, Redemptorist Donald F. Miller took over in the ensuing twenty years. Both began careers as teachers, Father Lord as a teacher of English at Saint Louis University, Father Miller as a seminary professor of philosophy. Both developed publishing houses and edited magazines as well as took the lead in popular pamphlets for Catholic readers.

Donald F. Miller became editor of the *Liguorian* magazine when he was thirty-one years old in 1934. He was to remain as editor until 1956. In 1947 he founded the Liguori Publishing House. His writings covered two general areas: social order and religious counseling. He discussed racial questions when few magazines had time for them. He expounded the papal viewpoints on labor questions. He supported the C.I.O. political action committee at a time when many people resented what they thought was an intrusion of union leaders in politics. He wrote about the living wage when few men heard of it. "Wages," he said, "are not a question of markets but of morals."[3] Many of his articles on social questions or on counseling of husbands and wives appeared in his "Side Glances" feature that regularly appeared in the *Liguorian*. A conservative estimate puts his output in the magazine as over two thousand articles in forty years.

At the same time as he was writing this material, he held time-consuming administrative positions, preached, and lectured regularly before various audiences, and maintained a large personal correspondence. Many of his articles he enlarged later into pamphlets. Several became phenomenal best-sellers. A booklet entitled *Rules for*

sion, he won the local officials over to his proposal. Further, he insisted that the area was more fit for dairying than for grain farming. He ran up against strong obstacles in the stubborn wills of his people and their neighbors. Through lectures, movies, and the development of a complete dairy school, he got his people to switch. On one occasion during a drought, he contracted for fifteen thousand dollars worth of alfalfa in Kansas and organized a truck caravan to bring it back to Missouri.

Once his people had switched to dairying, they had greater need of electricity than before. The power companies weren't interested in providing service. They claimed the area would not pay. Father Hildner set out to prove that it would. With his urging, the companies built their lines out into this "unprofitable area" and picked up thirty-five extra farm customers on the way.

From his first years in rural areas, Father Hildner had been concerned to keep his young people on the land. Most of the farms in the Villa Ridge region had never changed hands since the original settlers from Germany got land over a century before. The old folks clung to them. But there was little hope for the young before Father Hildner began his program. "You hold people by holding the soil," he explained simply. He made it possible for the young people who wanted to stay to make a living on the home place. Soon modern dwellings blossomed on farm after farm.

He battled the army engineers in their initial plan for several high dams in the Meramec Basin south of his parish. He believed that this plan served the interests of the barge lines on the Mississippi River rather than the needs of the people of the area. A few years later the engineers came up with a plan designed primarily for soil conservation, flood control, and recreational development along the shore lines. Hildner, now a Monsignor, supported the new proposal along with other prominent citizens such as Congressman Clarence Cannon.[1]

In his more directly priestly ministry, Monsignor Hildner served the entire Franklin County in the capacity of vicar foraine and dean of Franklin County. That deanery

Schooling sold over half a million copies. As the publishing program of magazines, pamphlets, and Sunday bulletins grew, Father Miller developed a large editorial center and a priory on the old Benjamin O'Fallon estate in Jefferson County, not far south of the Meramec River.

When changes followed Vatican II, Father Miller and his successors did not go down as so many Catholic publishers — by either tying totally to the past, or leaping to the future with revolutionary ideas and a dramatic change of format. The Liguorian Press kept its old readers, brought them along gradually to the new with a constant explanation of the changes that Vatican II brought to the Church. Thus by the time of the late sixties, the *Liguorian* was to be the largest non-organizational magazine published by Catholics in the country with the circulation of over 460,000. Only the Knights of Columbus magazine, *Columbia*, had a greater circulation.

When Jesuit Fathers decided to end their publishing program begun by Father Lord, the Liguori Publishing House took over and continued the publication of the many successful Queen's Work titles that had endured over the years. The Archdiocese of Saint Louis thus remained one of the leading Catholic pamphlet publishing centers in the entire nation.

Council of Catholic Youth

The Archdiocesan Council of Catholic Youth, under the successive direction of Monsignor Lloyd Sullivan and Monsignor Louis Meyer, promoted a variety of activities — religious, social, cultural, education, and athletic. The council sponsored leadership training institutes, vocation projects, musicals, one-act play festivals, speech and essay contests, roller and ice skating parties, bowling tourneys, and a wide program of competitive athletics.[4]

In late November and early December 1955, the local council hosted the National Catholic Youth Council annual convention. Thirteen hundred delegates from forty-seven different dioceses, accompanied four archbishops and twenty-five bishops to the city. Sixteen thousand young people participated in the High Mass offered by Archbishop Ritter in the Kiel Auditorium on December 1.

Former President Harry S. Truman had received three thousand invitations to speak that fall. Since he wanted, above all, to reach the youth of the land, he accepted the archbishop's invitation to address the Catholic youth convention. "I hope one day one of you will be president," Mr. Truman said. A newspaper commentator remarked that this was perhaps the first time a president had uttered these words to an entirely Catholic audience.[5]

The Saint Louis Council of Youth took a consistent part in the national program and frequently assumed the lead with the versatility of its program. In 1960 Elinor Engelhard, a counsellor at Don Bosco Camp for girls near Pevely, Missouri, and a freshman at Fontbonne College from St. Anthony's parish, won top prize in a nationwide essay contest sponsored by the National Catholic Camping Association.[6] A year later, Dennis Donnelly, a sophomore at Saint Louis University from St. Mary Magdalen's parish, won first place in the young adults' section of the NCCY oratorical contest. Robert Joplin, ACCY program coordinator, and religious chairman of the NCCY, left the Saint Louis Catholic Youth office in the summer of 1961 after four years of service, to become executive secretary of the National Council in Washington.[7] In 1962, Betty

Deckert, ACCY vice-president, a student at Notre Dame High School in Saint Louis, won first prize in the national speech contest. She gave a ten minute prepared speech on the 1961 bishops' statement and a four minute *extempore* speech on Pope John's famous encyclical *Mater et Magistra*.[8]

Occasionally the moderator of the youth program, Monsignor Lloyd Sullivan, expressed concern for the over-emphasis on the athletic part of the program in the ACCY's public image.[9] In spite of the wide range of youth programs sponsored by the council, most publicity went to athletics or social gatherings at such teen towns as the one at Monsignor Sullivan's own Epiphany parish. Sometimes, however, athletic excellence simply demanded attention, for instance, the success in soccer.

Under the direction of Robert Guelker, athletic director of the ACCY, ten thousand young Saint Louisans participated in a soccer program unequalled in the entire country. In 1958, Guelker discussed with Robert Stewart, athletic director at Saint Louis University, the possibility of collegiate soccer. During that year, Guelker fielded a soccer team of Saint Louis University students on a club basis. The team went through the entire season undefeated. The following year soccer became a varsity sport at Saint Louis University. Simultaneously the National Collegiate Athletic Association made soccer a permanent part of its program. The national championship stood at the end of the road.

Coach Guelker enjoyed the enviable position of having known all the candidates for the team from their early years and had available a group of talented players. Local people were not amazed that both players and coaches came from Saint Louis. Other coaches were astounded. One went so far as to doubt that any coach could build a winning team without foreign imports. Soccer at other schools had an international flavor. In fact, the coach who made the preceding remark put eight foreigners on his starting eleven. The Saint Louis team was more than entirely American; it was entirely Saint Louisan.

Under Guelker's direction the Saint Louis University took part in the NCAA play-offs every year. Five times, in 1959, 1960, 1962, 1963, and 1965, the Billikens won the national championship. In seven seasons Coach Guelker won eighty-eight; lost six and tied two. Harry Keough succeeded him and kept up the championship tradition. Rightly *Sports Illustrated* magazine called Saint Louis University "the elite school in collegiate soccer."[10]

The Catholic Youth Council, of course, was not set up simply to train soccer players. Its purpose was wider even than its athletic program and it did fulfill all its purposes; but this one dramatic result deserves special attention. It served as a tribute to the many outstanding soccer players, to the directors — priests and laymen — of the Catholic Youth Council, to Catholic teachers, especially the Christian Brothers, who for so long had promoted soccer among their students, and to the pastors who promoted the sport among the young men of their parishes.

Steel and Concrete Evidence of Progress

The City of Saint Louis had long been dreaming by the river. But in the post World War II era, the city began to move ahead. The early thirties had seen the levelling of buildings three blocks back from the levee between Washington and Spruce in preparation for a national memorial to President Jefferson's purchase of Louisiana and the resultant westward expansion of the nation. Outstanding architects of various nations submitted designs for a fitting memorial. The judges chose the soaring catenary arch of Finnish architect, Eero Saarinen. At the same time, the blocks in front of the City Hall and the Union Station became lovely inner-city parks.

During the terms of Mayor Raymond Tucker, the city launched one of the largest redevelopment programs in the nation. Bulldozers levelled almost every structure from Twenty Second Street to Grand Avenue in the five blocks immediately north of the Mill Creek Valley. Saint Louis University sought to expand into the westernmost blocks of this area, where General Daniel Frost had set up Camp Jackson for the state militia in 1861. But the school had to fight a lawsuit to insure its right to do so. Interestingly, General Frost's daughter, Mrs. Samuel Fordyce, contributed the money to purchase the new property that gained the title the Frost Campus.

At the same time, the other Catholic colleges of the Saint Louis area moved ahead. Fontbonne and Webster expanded their facilities. Maryville moved to an entirely new location in the west county. The Augustinian Fathers opened an academy for boys in the old Maryville on Nebraska at Meramec. The Jesuits began DeSmet High.

The Mercy Sisters opened a new novitiate in Frontenac, and devoted the former convent in Webster Groves to retreat and sister retirement purposes, and laid plans for a new St. John's Mercy Hospital on Ballas Road. The Josephites set up a residence for retired nuns at Nazareth in South County. The Sisters of the Incarnate Word enlarged their hospital at Grand and Lafayette. Among new congregations, the Redemptoristines opened a convent at Liguori in Jefferson County, the Medical Missionaries a House of Studies on South Grand, and Poor Clares moved to Oakville, the Benedictines of Perpetual Adoration to Morganford Road just beyond the city limits, and the Maryknoll Sisters opened a western novitiate in Valley Park.

Among the men's religious orders that came to the archdiocese in Archbishop Ritter's years, the English Benedictines opened the Priory School in the west county; the American Benedictines from Conception Abbey began Pius X Monastery. The Mill Hill, Holy Family, and Maryknoll Fathers, and the Servants of the Paraclete set up houses of studies. During Archbishop Ritter's time, twenty-five orders of men and fifty-four orders of women had residences in the diocese.

In 1956, the archdiocese purchased the De Soto Hotel on Locust Street in downtown Saint Louis and converted it into a residence for older people. The Franciscan Sisters of Mary conducted this senior citizens' center that bore the name Alverne Hotel. In 1958, Archbishop Ritter converted a large apartment unit at 4540 Lindell into a home for retired priests. The Congregation of the Sacerdotal Fraternity staffed this new institution.

The archdiocese began a high school department in the Kenrick Seminary complex in 1957, and opened Cardinal Glennon College in the former preparatory seminary building. This allowed an enlargement of the student body to include seminarians from the eight dioceses of Missouri and Kansas and four or five others during the ensuing terms.[11]

Two new Catholic buildings made architectural headlines in the succeeding years. Interestingly both were circular structures. The Priory Church appeared on the cover of several national building magazines. The new chancery, in the forty-fourth block of Lindell, stood two doors west of the new Cathedral.[12]

Retreat Movement Advances

The retreat movement, long a vigorous religious force in the archdiocese, moved ahead during these years. The Cenacle for women, now on Spoede Road and Conway Road, and the White House for men on the Mississippi bluffs south of Jefferson Barracks, continued to have capacity crowds for retreats throughout the year. The Cenacle also sponsored study clubs and other religious programs.

The Passionist Fathers began Our Lady's Retreat House at Warrenton, Missouri. The Christian Brothers at Vaugirard Retreat House near Cedar Hill, Missouri, specialized in retreats for young people. When the Sisters of Mercy opened a new novitiate in Frontenac, Missouri, they turned part of their former novitiate, St. Joseph's Convent of Mercy in Webster Groves, to retreats for women and girls. The Passionist Nuns sponsored retreats for women and girls at their convent in west Saint Louis County. The Jesuit Fathers of Saint Louis University used the Fordyce Estate in Hazelwood, as a retreat for varieties of groups. At St. Joseph's Church in downtown Saint Louis, retired Bishop David Hickey, S.J., sponsored "open" retreats for working men who could not get to one of the closed retreat houses.

The Benedictine Monks of St. Pius X Monastery near Pevely, Missouri, pioneered in a new type of retreat. They

CYO Director Bob Guelker coached Saint Louis University teams to the NCAA soccer championship five times. All players had taken part in the local CYO program.

The visitor senses the infinity of God on entering St. Anselm's, the Benedictine Priory Church in St. Louis County, one of many modern churches built during the time of Cardinal Ritter. (Photo St. Louis Review)

opened a contemporary lodge-like guest house in ,1961, and began married couples retreats. Under the direction of Father Anselm Ginter, O.S.B., the Family Life Center developed a less rigidly structured weekend program than the other retreat houses. It concerned itself less with an individual's personal relationship with God, and more with the entire context wherein he worked out his salvation. Several monks conducted a marriage counselling program and a family life education service.

In this way between four and five hundred married couples could make a retreat each year. The Benedictine Monks also scheduled common interest group retreats — divorcees, widows, clergymen, high school students. But the Christian family remained the core apostolate of the St. Pius X Monastery.[13]

The Cardinal Mindszenty Foundation

During 1956 and 1957 a group of Saint Louis area Catholic women, including Phyllis Schlafly, Kay Dougherty, and Eleanor Schlafly, sponsored a series of lectures on communism. At these meetings they met Father C. S. Dunker, Vincentian Missionary in China for twenty years, and prisoner of the Chinese Reds for two years (1949-1951).

From their mutual discussions, on the need of education on communism, Father Dunker and Miss Eleanor Schlafly decided to set up a society for this purpose in June, 1958. They named their association for Joseph Cardinal Mindszenty, primate of Hungary, who had suffered eight years of imprisonment at the hands of the communists until released by young Hungarian Freedom Fighters in 1956. When Russian tanks rolled into Budapest, he chose to remain behind the Iron Curtain and accepted the hospitality of the U.S. Embassy. He thus remained a symbol of opposition to communism.

The Cardinal Mindszenty Foundation set educational goals. It provided copies of reports and documents on communism at minimal cost. It encouraged study groups, much like the great books discussions so popular at that time. It conducted seminars for the general public; and sent out a monthly news bulletin on communism from its Delmar Boulevard offices. All officers of the organization agreed to work without pay. The Dougherty Real Estate Company provided office space.[14] The foundation developed a professional staff and was able to call on a large group of volunteer workers.

Early in 1959, *Our Sunday Visitor* carried an article on the Cardinal Mindszenty Foundation.[15] As a result, individuals in other cities became interested. After a few years with only a Saint Louis base, centers of the foundation grew up in Houston, Los Angeles, Columbus, Chicago, Philadelphia, and other cities. The foundation promoted a radio program, "Dangers of Apathy," that went over 368 stations in thirty-two states.[16]

Although the foundation directs its efforts primarily at the education of Catholics, it does not confine its work to members of the Church. It retains close ties, however, with the Church. When its original spiritual director, Father Dunker, went to Taiwan as superior of the Vincentian Fathers, the foundation set up an advisory council that consisted of two Chinese cardinals, six bishops and fifteen priests, including Father Dunker. Each of these had personal experience with the communist apparatus.[17]

The Cardinal Mindszenty Foundation, then, sought exclusively educational goals and never entered the field of social reform. It's main work remained the expose of communist aims and methods throughout the world. It had no distinct effect on the Archdiocese of Saint Louis that it did not have on other archdioceses. But it was another example of the zeal and versatility of Saint Louis Catholics.

Citizens for Educational Freedom

The writings of Marquette University's political scientist, Father Virgil Blum, on the rights of children in independent schools, stimulated a group of Saint Louis parents to organize the Citizens for Educational Freedom in 1959. Father Blum's proposition was simple: the states voted educational benefits for children; but, at the same time, insisted that these children must go to a particular school system to enjoy these benefits. Yet the courts had repeatedly ruled that the state could not force a citizen to give up one right to enjoy another. Father Blum felt that this practice would ultimately lead to a unhealthy monopoly in American education.

After tentative meetings at various homes, the group consisting of Martin and Mae Duggan, Vincent Corley, James Bick, and others, began to meet regularly at the Queen's Work on South Grand. They gained the attention of Judge Anthony Daly of Madison County, Illinois, who had written in a vein similar to Father Blum. Judge Daly coined the term "the non-religious ingredients of education," and claimed these areas deserved state support. Judge Daly gave his strong support to the movement until his untimely death. As a result of careful discussion, the group drew up a constitution and a plan of action for the Citizens for Educational Freedom. To allay the fears of some Negro groups, the CEF leaders invited a prominent black lawyer, David Grant, a parochial school parent but not a Catholic, to join in the actual drawing up of the constitution. Grant advised a wording similar to the phrasing of the courts on integration.

The CEF published a regular newsletter, provided speakers for appropriate occasions, and promoted helpful legislation in various states. In spite of the sound Americanism of their program, and their obvious excellent purpose, the CEF promoters met sometimes surprising opposition. Many pastors wanted no state interference with "their schools." Suburban Catholics had no problems; and hesitated to involve themselves in the issues facing less fortunate Catholics. Many "liberals" felt that the inclusion of the independent school issue in projected legislation would hold back the more universal cause of federal aid to education. Gauche tactics of some CEF promoters alienated still others: such as high pressure methods, overemotional appeals and propaganda, and the injection of CEF issues into the agenda of other meetings without invitation.[18] To some who might otherwise have been sympathetic, facets of CEF propaganda suggested a "ghetto mentality" at a time when American Catholics were turning away from ghettos. In spite of these obstacles, the basic rationality of the program prevailed. The organization spread.

Within three years, one hundred and fifty chapters of the CEF existed in twenty states. It chose as the chairman of its twenty-six-member national board of trustees an Iowa banker, Glenn Andreas. Andreas was a member of the Christian Reformed Church, even though the bulk of the members were Catholics — a natural development in view of the greater concern of Catholics for parochial and other independent schools. In July 1962, the CEF hired a Saint Louis lawyer, David LaDriere, as full-time executive secretary.

In a feature article in the *St. Louis Review* early in 1963, Glen Goellner described the workings of CEF and interviewed its executive secretary. In answer to the objection that the type of aid the CEF envisioned would fragment American schools, LaDriere saw no indication that many religious groups would start their own school systems. The real danger, he believed, lay in the possibility that growing educational costs and rising taxes would force the closing of all independent schools. He warned:

Unless the current trend is halted, all except the children of the wealthy will end up in state institutions. This will be done in the name of democracy and in the name of church-state separation. We will have accomplished by economic means what the Supreme Court has prohibited.[19]

Interestingly, over the years, the CEF has less public success in the founding state of Missouri than in many neighbors to the north and east.

The Growth of Catholic Schools

During the years of Archbishop Ritter, the Catholic school population of the archdiocese doubled. Forty-five new parish schools had gone up during these years. By 1961 there were 210 elementary schools with 87,000 students. The secondary school enrollment was 28,000. Thus the entire enrollment reached 115,000 students. At the same time the lay teachers rose from 48 to 802.[20]

In early 1962 the archdiocese assumed responsibility for the elementary schools and set up a school board of twenty-five pastors — thirteen chosen by the archbishop, and twelve elected by their fellow pastors. The school board had three standing committees: 1. ways and means, to handle teacher salaries; 2. building and sites, to consider applications for the erection of new elementary schools or additions to old ones; 3. instruction and spiritual life, to deal with curriculum and teacher certification.[21]

The archdiocesan office handled teacher placement and the hiring of lay teachers with a view to the total good of the archdiocese rather than the specific good of an individual parish. At the time, the increase in school population rose out of proportion to the number of Sister-teachers. Far more lay teachers joined the Catholic school system. The school office froze enrollments at the 115,000 mark.[22]

The school office also set up its own office of teacher certification. It granted permanent certification to those with college degrees, 120 credit hours of recognized college credits, or fifteen years of teaching experience in the archdiocese. It granted temporary certification to those with a minimum of sixteen hours of college credits or ten years parochial teaching experience. The temporary certificates were valid for three years while the teacher continued to work towards the degree. The school board hoped in this way to develop a greater uniformity of instructional quality throughout the archdiocese. It balanced the quality of instruction in the well-to-do suburban parishes and the inner-city parishes and thus provided great help to the Negro apostolate.

But the new program had disadvantages as well as advantages. The program tended towards overcentralization. Certainly it gave little attention to the notion of subsidiarity. Some of the schools lost the distinctive administrative characteristics of an earlier time. Among the advantages were these: a greater uniformity throughout the archdiocese; wider planning that looked to a fair treatment of all; and an expertise in relating local developments to the wider educational picture throughout the nation.

A program of great value to Catholic education in the archdiocese and in the nation at large grew up in the early 1950's: the Sister Formation Movement. Nuns of the area played their part in its development. One of these, Sister Bertrande Meyers, D.C., had previously studied the academic preparation of Sisters in conjunction with her doctoral program at Saint Louis University. Sheed and Ward published her findings in a book entitled *The Education of Sisters* (1940). This book helped to alert religious groups to the need of a more systematic educational program for young Sisters. As a result many groups sent their junior Sisters through several years of college or university before their first teaching assignment. The Daughters of Charity, under the impetus of Sister Bertrande and others, set up a program exclusively for nuns at Marillac College, adjoining their provincial headquarters in suburban Saint Louis. Marillac College gradually came to gather students and faculty members of other religious orders and congregations. One out-of-state congregation even set up its novitiate on the college grounds.

Chapter 40

The Church and the Wide-Wide World

A New Pope Names a New Cardinal

When the cardinals chose the elderly Angelo Cardinal Roncalli, Patriarch of Venice, as Pope in October, 1958, most observers throughout the world looked upon him as an interim Pope, a fatherly old gentleman who would guide the destinies of the Church until such a time as a younger man would be ready for the post. Almost immediately, however, Pope John came through as a warm, vibrant human being, especially at Christmas-time when he visited the prisoners in Rome. Shortly after the new year, he startled the world by calling an ecumenic council to work toward the reuniting of all Christians.

The Church in the United States at the time was perhaps the most highly organized church that the world had ever seen. But it was a walled citadel, a defensive-minded enclave in the midst of a large Protestant or religiously uncommitted population. It was a haven of security. Those who followed its formalities could find salvation at the end of life. Even some of the more open-minded American church leaders took a pessimistic view of the wider ecumenic movement. Rumors spread of this or that change in the offing. People began to hear a new word from Pope John's lips, *aggiornamento*, an expression that had no equivalent in English but conveyed the notion of updating the Church in accidental things to meet the modern world and its special spirit. Bishops went to Rome to work on preliminary meetings for the council, but curial officials seemed to drag their heels.

Before the council opened its sessions, Pope John enlarged the college of cardinals to eighty-five — the highest number in history. He named four new members on December 16, 1960: Saint Louis' Archbishop Joseph Elmer Ritter, the archbishops of Caracas, Venezuela, and Bogota, Colombia, and a Roman curial official who had experience in Latin-American affairs. Since Cardinal Ritter had taken the lead among North American archbishops in his concern for Latin America, and his three new colleagues had Latin American ties, many observers felt this interest was a deciding factor in Pope John's decision. Cardinal Ritter himself believed that the honor was a tribute to the archdiocese itself. Others believed it a more personal honor. Most likely all threads contributed. The Saint Louis cardinal received his red hat at a public consistory on January 19, 1961.

When he returned to Saint Louis, the entire community honored him with a dinner on February 10, 1961. Newly inaugurated President John Fitzgerald Kennedy sent his greetings. Governor John M. Dalton praised the deep religious spirit of Saint Louis' archbishop. The new cardinal himself seemed to enjoy particularly the whimsical remark of TV and sports personality Joe Garagiola. At least he repeated the words several times in public and private in the ensuing months. Garagiola remarked that with the baseball Cardinals under Busch Brewery ownership and the football Cardinals partially controlled by

Pope John places the red biretta on the head of Cardinal Ritter while M[onsignors Dante and Nasalli Rocca assist.

Falstaff, it was nice to have a cardinal in Saint Louis not sponsored by a brewing company.

The next few years of Cardinal Ritter's career centered around the great ecumenical council of the twentieth century, Vatican II. Much of what Cardinal Ritter did there belonged more properly to his own personal biography and to the history of the universal Church. But many causes he fought for in Rome, he also promoted in his administration of the Saint Louis archdiocese.

The Second Vatican Council

When Pope John XXIII summoned the bishops of the world to Rome for the Second Vatican Council, Cardinal Ritter expressed the American mind well with the words, "We went to Rome to find out what Rome wanted. Only after we got there did we learn that we should do something more than listen."[1] Describing more directly his own approach, Cardinal Ritter was to say two years later: "When I went to the Council in 1962, I hadn't the least idea of taking an active part in it."[2]

These dramatic statements referred more properly to the preliminary meetings than to the council itself. An Indianopolis friend, Father Raymond Bosler, editor of the archdiocesan paper, the *Criterion*, proved especially effective in persuading Cardinal Ritter to take an active part in proceedings. He pointed out the example of Kenrick at Vatican I. He urged him to read Mansi's *History of the Councils* — a work that devoted much attention to the work of Kenrick.[3]

Always an avid reader, Ritter usually made no evening appointments and reserved this time for quiet reading and reflection. He had always read the London *Tablet* that came by air mail, and, once he became a cardinal, he received a daily copy of the *Osservatore Romano*. He read materials in English, Latin, Italian, and German. Occasionally he would send a magazine article, with personal annotations, to someone he thought might enjoy it or profit from reading it.

He had a love for and an amateur knowledge of Church history, especially of the early missionaries of the middle West, such as Bishop Flaget and Father Nerinckx. Now he delved more deeply into Church controversies. He readily discussed what he thought the Fathers ought to do at the council with such men as editors Fathers Raymond Bosler and Daniel Moore, with Monsignor William Baum of Kansas City, and also with his theological advisers for the council, Monsignor Joseph W. Baker, a canon lawyer, and Very Reverend Nicholas Persich, C.M., who was to accept reappointment as rector of Kenrick Seminary shortly before the opening of the council.[4]

Appointed to the Central Commission in 1962, a half year before the official opening of the council, Ritter went to Rome with three major concerns: 1. the nature of the Church; 2. religious liberty; 3. the liturgy. At one of these preliminary meetings, a German cardinal urged Ritter and another midwestern archbishop to be spokesmen for the United States. Ritter read carefully all preliminary documents and commented on almost all issues. He understood the inner workings of the Church. He knew many of the European bishops, including most Italian cardinals, and had warm personal relationships with them — even those he differed with sharply as the discussions proceeded.

When the council began in October, 1962, Pope John wanted positive decisions for renewal with a compassionate understanding of current trends. The initial indication that the Holy Father was to get such new approaches came at the first general congregation of October 13. Two north European cardinals, Lienart of Lille, and Frings of Cologne, asked a delay in the voting on the members of the permanent commissions so that the fathers might get to know the men for whom they were voting. Back at Vatican I in 1870, Archbishop Kenrick of Saint Louis was among those who had sought this in vain. This time, with Pope John's support, the motion carried.

The council fathers began the discussion on the proposals relating to liturgy and to revelation. Cardinal Ritter gave his first major speech on the *schema* or statement on revelation. "What a tedious and unrealistic attitude it betrayed toward the Word of God which we call the Scriptures," he said. "It must be rejected."[5] The cardinal of Saint Louis found himself with an outstanding international team of dissenting prelates. An historian of the council, Joseph Ratzinger, wrote:

Without prior agreement, Cardinals Lienart [France], Frings [Germany], Leger [Canada], Koenig [Austria], Alfrink [Holland], Suenens [Belgium], Ritter [U.S.A.], and Bea [Germany], each from his own point of view, delivered sharp criticisms of the *schema*, something surprising to both its authors and its opponents.[6]

To give the opposition an even more world-wide flavor, Melchite Patriarch Maximos IV Saigh of Antioch, Archbishop Albert Soegijipranata of Indonesia,[7] Archbishop J. B. Zoa of Camerun, in the name of the African bishops, and Cardinal Gracias of India, condemned the *schema*.[8] The original proposal obviously reflected an outmoded view. Pope John intervened. He appointed a new commission of experts to draw up a fresh statement.[9]

Much of the remainder of the first session proved simply a bridge to the second session. The council fathers discussed communications media, church unity, and the Church itself. Cardinal Ritter spoke on this last topic, emphasizing particularly the responsibility of the laity and calling for a clear statement on freedom of conscience — matters not to come up for extended discussion until later sessions.[10]

Though the first session had not debated at length the question of ecumenism, Cardinal Ritter came home convinced that the ecumenical spirit was vital and necessary for Christianity. In his early years in Saint Louis, he had been regularly cooperative with members of other religious denominations in specific projects for social and civic welfare. But he tended to shy away from interfaith discussions, such as the programs promoted by the National Conference of Christians and Jews. He came to recognize that times had changed. He changed with them. When he returned from Rome, he took action in his own archdiocese. In February, 1963, he addressed religious leaders of churches and synagogues throughout the area at the Saint Louis Advertising Club and answered their questions on ecumenism and related topics.

In the spring of 1963, four Protestant Episcopal leaders, Bishop Lichtenberger, George Cadigan, Very Reverend Dr. Clifford Morehouse of New York, president of the Episcopal House of Deputies, and Reverend W. Murray Kenney of Saint Mark's Church in Saint Louis, invited Cardinal Ritter to address a major session of the convention of the Protestant Episcopal Church of the nation scheduled for October of the following year in Saint Louis. In an unprecedented act of mutual esteem the four Episcopal divines asked the cardinal's blessing. He granted their request and then said he would be honored if they gave him their blessing.[11]

Bishop Cadigan was to relate this incident to a predominantly Catholic audience at Maryville College a year later, as a member of a panel on ecumenism. The other participants were: Mother Patricia Barrett, R.C.S.J., of Maryville, President Robert Davidson of Westminister College, and Dom Columba Cary-Elwes, O.S.B., of the Saint Louis Priory.[12] Bishop Cadigan emphasized the need of true union. "I think this is what we're all concerned about," he said, "nothing less than organic unity."[13]

Cardinal Ritter spoke often on the ecumenic spirit between the first and second sessions of the council. He remarked on one occasion:

No one can foresee when unity will be brought about. It is pretty much in the hands of God. I believe that the Council and the more ecumenic spirit on the part of the non-Catholic is creating a climate which will enable the Holy Spirit to do His work. Virtually everyone now is aware of the need for union. Different groups have different ideas about how this should be done, of course, but with prayers and desire, no one can say that unity will not be accomplished in the near future. Surely the world situation religiously will hasten unity. Political, social, and economic pressures also may hasten unity.

As an Episcopalian clergyman from Washington said recently, "it is possible that the Council will force the Protestants to face the challenge that is being made." It is not intended as a challenge, of course, but is so developing that we can no longer hide behind our prejudices. We have got to face each other and discuss our differences — this is so essential to the peace of the world. A united Christendom is so vitally needed. The fact that Christendom has been divided may account for its weakness and the world situation somewhat.[14]

Cardinal Ritter's openminded understanding of his "separated brethren" extended also to his fellow Catholics who might not receive a warm welcome elsewhere. The Archdiocese of Los Angeles lowered the "Iron Curtain" in front of the young Swiss priest-theologian Hans Kung, "the most talked-about priest of the decade." Cardinal Ritter invited clergymen of all faiths to hear Kung at Glennon College on April 20, 1963. The cardinal himself sat in an audience that included Reverend Dr. Alfred Fuerbringer, president of Concordia Seminary, and Ven. Charles F. Rehkopf, executive secretary of the Protestant Episcopal diocese of Missouri.[15] Father Kung had addressed the National Catholic Education Convention at the Kiel Auditorium the previous day.[16] In an interview in Saint Louis, he spoke on the Saint Louis archbishop's part in the first session of the council: "Cardinal Ritter will be mentioned in the history of the Council for his leadership of the American Hierarchy at the time of the theological discussion over the scheme on revelation."[17]

Along with his growing interest in ecumenism, Cardinal Ritter continued his long-standing concern for civil rights issues, at the time in the forefront of American life. Five hundred priests of the Saint Louis region held a three-day pastoral institute on human rights. Cardinal Ritter set up an Archdiocesan Commission on Human Rights and ordered pastors throughout the archdiocese to begin seminars for laymen patterned on the clergy institute. He urged sermons; but much more he urged action. At a press conference at the end of the institute, he expressed his sense of outrage at the death by dynamite of four Negro girls in a church in Birmingham, Alabama.[18]

In an article in *Marriage* magazine, Cardinal Ritter urged all Catholics to make up for their past failures by going out of their way to help Negroes in the present.[19] Members of the clergy began to show their concern for racial justice by taking part in civil rights demonstrations. Cardinal Ritter said that his priests needed no special permission from the chancery to take part in such demonstrations, if they conscientiously believed that this was necessary to advance the cause of human and civil rights.[20] He sent a representative to the services held for the Reverend James Reeb, an integrationist minister beaten to death by a white mob.[21]

Pope Paul Reconvenes the Council

Seven months after the first session of the council, on June 3, 1963, Pope John died. Many wondered what course the council would take. Part of the Italian press, for instance, presumed an indefinite adjournment. Cardinal Ritter returned to Rome to become the first cardinal archbishop of Saint Louis to participate in a papal election. The choice of Archbishop Giovanni Baptista Montini of Milan, a friend of Pope John, lifted this uncertainty. His leadership meant more than a mere continuation. It brought a new beginning.

In a reception for curial officials on September 21, shortly before the council reconvened, Paul invited the council to deal with curial reform and consider the creation of a special senate to represent the world's episcopate.[22] The new Pope presented to the fathers on their arrival in Rome a revised set of statutes that called for a governing board of four moderators, a strengthening of the individual commissions at the expense of their chairmen, an opportunity for all council fathers to submit items for discussion (something Kenrick had vainly sought at Vatican I), and the admission of laymen as auditors.[23] On September 29, the new Pope addressed the reconvened council. He touched the hearts of all with his remarks on their deceased Holy Father. Then he formulated a four-point program: the Church's reinterpretation of its own nature, the renewal of the Church, the reestablishment of unity among Christians, the Church's dialogue with contemporary man.[24]

Cardinal Ritter appreciated the ecumenic spirit of the new Holy Father's remarks. The Saint Louis archbishop saw the revised text on ecumenism as the end of the counter reformation. "It obliges us to make a thorough examination of conscience," he said. "Likewise, it puts us under obligation to hasten the desirable day of unity by fervent prayer, example, and study."[25]

A week later, Ritter returned to the same topic:

It should be pointed out [in the *Schema*] how the unity which is the goal of all ecumenism is a fundamental principle of the ecumenical movement. For this reason the *Schema* should work out a real concept of unity. Our basic inaspiration must be pastoral. We are not only issuing a decree, but are also expected to provide it with an effective stimulus for action. The goal to be achieved is the principle of all motion.

We have with our separated brethren common desires and common activities. We should present unity not merely as a goal of inestimable value, but in such a way as to show disunion as an evil of equal magnitude. Chapter One presents a concept of unity which only Catholics can recognize. In her present state, the Church is far from the realization of the full perfection which belongs to her nature. Separation and division in the ranks of Christians are a scandal to the world.[26]

The eminently practical approach of Cardinal Ritter appeared in two statements he made during the October debates. On October 3, he called for the restoration to preaching of its basic importance — a position put in the background by necessary reforms at Trent.[27] On October 14, he insisted that the basic issue in the discussion of the diaconate was whether "it is to be restored, is necessary, and is useful."[28] The fathers should discuss related questions later.[29]

Cardinal Ritter had hoped to speak in favor of the diaconate in the name of all American bishops. Missionary bishops, especially those from Latin America, had asked for its restoration. Some American bishops favored it for mission lands. Cardinal Ritter was open to its application even for the United States. But seaboard American prelates opposed his speaking for the entire American hierarchy.[30]

Commentators divided the Council Fathers into two camps, oversimplifying them as "liberals" and "conservatives." Shortly, they had placed Cardinal Ritter along with Albert Cardinal Meyer of Chicago in the liberal camp. Actually, Cardinal Meyer had a definitely conservative outlook and Cardinal Ritter a moderate one. Yet in the vortex of discussion at the council, both of these outstanding midwestern prelates saw the need of assuming a leadership for the United States that some of the better known cardinals, such as Francis Cardinal Spellman, had failed to assume.

Twice that same November, 1963, Cardinal Ritter differed sharply with his American colleagues, Cardinals Spellman and McIntyre, and even, on one occasion, with his fellow mid-westerner, Cardinal Meyer of Chicago. In

Cardinal Ritter, accompanied by Monsignor Joseph Baker and flanked by Cardinal Rugumbwa, enter Saint Peter's for the opening of the Vatican Council.

spite of Pope Paul's recommendation, the archbishop of New York felt that it was not the bishops' function to criticize the Roman Curia. Ritter, on the contrary, insisted that "the Council Fathers should speak of the relationship of the bishops with the Roman Pontiff, not of relationships with the Roman Curia, since this organ does not exist except as a delegate of the Pope. It does not have autonomous existence."[31] Ritter wanted the council to remind the Curia that it is solely an instrument of the papacy.

In the discussion of juridical powers for the national bishops' conference, Cardinal McIntyre argued:

No one knows better than the Pope how to provide for the needs of the Church. His natural talents are elevated by supernatural protection which make him the one best qualified to understand problems and find their solutions. Why put strictures on him through the adoption of juridical character for national conferences?[32]

But Cardinal Meyer of Chicago saw an opposite danger. He thought juridical decisions by national episcopal conferences would restrict the freedom of the individual bishop.

Cardinal Ritter spoke immediately after. He believed that the national conferences of bishops would do for a nation what the council was doing for the entire Church, and that decisions of the national conference had to have binding force in order to promote the total welfare of the Church in a given country. Ritter stated:

National conferences are essential for any effective apostolate in the church. . . . All of us know how frequently unanimity is required in order to achieve a purpose and to provide support for individual bishops — not only in things directly concerned with the salvation of souls, but also in regard to social and moral problems.

National conferences with juridical power will promote decentralization because according to the principle of subsidiarity, when problems are solved on a local level the central authority has no need to intervene. . . . National conferences have nothing contrary to the nature of the episcopate. Thus they do not interpose a new body between the bishops and the pope.[33]

The schema on Christian unity had five chapters: 1. principles of ecumenism; 2. implementation; 3. Christians separated from the Catholic Church; 4. the attitude of Catholics towards non-Christians and particularly the Jews; 5. religious freedom. Many fathers wanted to eliminate one or the other. Cardinal Ritter insisted that they discuss all of them.[34]

Religious liberty became a prime concern of Cardinal Ritter. On November 18, 1963, he stated that a declaration on this topic should proceed "from solid theological principles: namely, one, the absolute freedom of the act of faith; two, the inviolability of human conscience; and three, the incompetency of any civil government to interpret the gospel of Christ, with consequent independence of the Church from civil authority in the accomplishment of its mission."[35] This view directly opposed the traditional position of most Italian and Spanish Church leaders.

When Archbishop Felici announced the tragic death of President Kennedy and a solemn funeral service to be held at St. John Lateran at 5:00 p.m. that afternoon, Cardinal Ritter answered in the name of his countrymen. He thanked all the fathers for their expressions of condolence and their promise of prayers. "Where charity and mutual consideration are not in possession of the human heart," he stated, "there can only be hate of which this untimely death is one of the fruits."[36]

Throughout the archdiocese, as in the rest of the saddened nation, and in so many other countries of the world, priests held memorial services for the assassinated president. Father Nicholas Schneider of Holy Cross Parish made a compilation of the religious views of President Kennedy that B. Herder Book Company was to publish a short time later as a lasting memorial to the first Catholic chief executive of the country.

Meanwhile in Rome, the second session of Vatican II drew to a close. When the fathers of the council voted final approval of the constitution on the sacred liturgy, Cardinal Ritter expanded his primary concern for better preaching. He came back from Rome intent on enriching the archdiocese.

He said after his return:

The Mass is a community affair. It can never be an individual affair. It is always the whole Church. It is not only the universal Church, but the Church here in this parish. It is their assembly, their coming together to worship the Heavenly Father with Christ and through Christ. In turn with that worship, Christ through the Holy Spirit, brings untold graces to us, awakening our faith, strengthening our faith and our love, our commitment to Him, to our fellowmen. . . .

I want all the people to be a part. I want it to be an active participation – a full participation. And furthermore, I want the priests to carry out the directive of the constitution – that they have a homily, a sermon. They should address the people on the gospel, on the Scriptures – give them the message that is meant for them to have on that particular day.[37]

Archdiocese and City Celebrate the Bicentennial

As the city approached its two hundredth anniversary in February, 1964, it looked forward with renewed hope. In one of his first public appearances outside of Washington after taking office at the tragic assassination of John Fitzgerald Kennedy, President Lyndon B. Johnson visited Saint Louis. He landed at the lovely Saint Louis airport, acclaimed one of the most beautiful in the country, on February 14, 1964. The Mark Twain Expressway took him to the riverfront.

He stood on the spot where Pierre Laclede had founded the city two hundred years before. He saw the site where a representative of the French government had officially handed over to delegates of President Thomas Jefferson the Territory of Louisiana in 1804. The two arms of the Jefferson Memorial Gateway Arch, to commemorate that historic event, reached towards the sky. The president viewed the Old Court House, scene of the original Dred Scot Decision. He passed the old cathedral of Bishop Rosati. Once hidden by factories and business houses, the riverfront Cathedral now stood out in all its early glory. The archdiocese had undertaken extensive renovation of the building, as part of the riverfront restoration.

President Johnson passed the area at the south end of the downtown business district where the new Busch Memorial Stadium was under construction, thanks to the energy of August A. Busch, Jr., beer and baseball executive, and other businessmen of the city. The president rode through the Mill Creek area, in the process of rebuilding, to the new section of the Saint Louis University campus. He planted a maple tree to stand as a symbol of the renewed life of the entire area. He spoke within view

of several new buildings under construction: a classroom building to bear Cardinal Ritter's name, the Monsanto Chemical Building, the Busch Memorial Student Center, a tribute to the Busch family and its business affiliates, and, a few blocks farther south, the David P. Wohl Mental Health Clinic.

As the entire city celebrated, the archdiocese commemorated the founding of Saint Louis with a series of Masses of thanksgiving and other religious ceremonies. The Archdiocesan Bureau of Information planned a bicentennial series of historical booklets, with Father John F. Bannon, S.J., as general editor. Father Peter J. Rahill, historian of the archdiocese, wrote the initial booklet entitled "Catholic Beginnings in Saint Louis." The present writer contributed the second in the series, a booklet entitled "The Catholic Ancestry of Saint Louis." Other historians wrote articles of interest in religious history for the occasion. Franciscan historian, Father Marion Habig, for instance, described the career of Father Luke Collet, a French Recollect on the mission of colonial Illinois. Although retired at the time and of extreme old age, Father Collet may well have said Mass for the original settlers of Saint Louis.

The spirit of the bicentennial offered great hope for the city and the archdiocese.

World-Wide Ecumenism

The council fathers did not give the final touches to the decree on ecumenism at the second session. But shortly after its closing Pope Paul paid a dramatic visit to the Holy Land and greeted the Orthodox Patriarch Athenagoras. In this aura of good will thus generated, Cardinal Ritter proceeded to appoint an archdiocesan commission on ecumenicism on March 19, 1964. He himself served as chairman, Monsignor Baker as vice-chairman, and Reverend Raymond Rustige as secretary. Three priests, Monsignor Edward T. O'Meara, Reverend Joseph Dwyer, and Reverend Robert Peet, and three lay members of the archdiocesan councils, Parker R. Bowman, Paul L. Watson, and Mrs. Andrew Reis, formed the commission.[38] The group met regularly to work out guidelines for the future.

As the council progressed, a true revolution took place in the minds of the Catholic people. Before, most had looked on the Church primarily as an organization. Now they saw it both as an organization and as the body of Christ that it was. They came to use more and more the conciliar term "people of God." Before, in a defensive spirit, they had thought little of total Christian reunion, looking only to an individual conversion here and there; now they saw the ultimate vision of a reunion of all who believed in Jesus Christ. Before they had prayed their rosaries privately during Mass; now they began to participate. All this did not come easily. Rome reacted by standing still; others rushed headlong into a variety of practices of questionable merit or validity. But the spirit of Pope John moved in the archdiocese.

During the National Liturgical Week, held in Saint Louis, in August, 1964, Cardinal Ritter authorized the use of the vernacular, even though the permission for it to be used generally did not come until fall of that year.[39]

The second session of the council had begun on a note of optimism that had carried over from the first session, but ended in a more somber atmosphere. The third session followed this pattern. It reached its highlight early, with the vote on the chapter on collegiality. Following in tradition of his predecessor, Archbishop Peter Richard Kenrick, Cardinal Ritter strongly endorsed the doctrine.

Collegiality, however, was not the subject of what many considered Cardinal Ritter's best speech at the council. A few days before the vote on collegiality, he spoke eloquently on the relations of Christians and Jews. "A fine example of decisiveness," Monsignor John Osterreicher called Ritter's speech, in his official commentary.[40] Cardinal Ritter said:

> This declaration ... quite clearly meets a need of our time. I speak of a need, not of some political or national pressure to be evaded or appeased, nor of some human approval to be sought for, but simply of a century's old injustice that cries aloud for reparation. For many centuries we Christians have been guilty of error and injustice towards the Jews ... even ecclesiastical documents have charged the Jewish people with the suffering and death of Christ. In prayers they were called "the perfidious," the deicidal people who once called down upon themselves the blood of the Saviour. We who are gathered here in this Ecumenical Council have today been given an opportunity to root out such errors and injustices and to make reparation. ... The schema is ... a good start in this direction. Jews and Christians are in a special way vessels of divine love and a powerful unity of love and respect should therefore prevail between us and them. This spirit of love ... should shine out more strongly in this declaration.[41]

Cardinal Ritter objected vigorously to references about the *conversion* of the Jews. He pointed out that the text did not speak of the Moslems and pagans in this way. He wanted no offensive wording; but, instead, at the end of the document, a paragraph expressing hope for the ultimate union of all men.[42]

In the debate on the lay apostolate, Cardinal Ritter called for a complete revision of the *schema* for three reasons: its juridical tone, its favoritism toward official Catholic Action to the detriment of other apostolic forms, and its patronizing and clerical spirit. It seemed to suggest, he felt, that "the highest role of the laity was to aid the clergy and not to pursue its own proper role."[43] He asked for a clear theological basis of the lay apostolate.[44]

In the discussion of the *schema* on Christian education, Cardinal Ritter insisted on freedom of parents to select schools of their choice, and freedom of operation in the schools. He remarked:

> Within their own walls, Catholic schools must be models of Christian freedom in their administration, their teaching and particularly in the inter-personal relationships among the teachers, pupils and parents. ... Our schools and their professors and students must pursue the truth boldly and freely without fear.[45]

The document on education, he insisted, "should emphasize the fact that Catholic schools by their very nature must be a substantial benefit to the entire community where they serve and to society itself." They do not exist to serve "narrow sectarian purposes nor to protect the self-interest of the Church ... they stand as an expression of the free choice and liberal sacrifice not only of parents, but of priests, religious, and devoted laymen and laywomen, for God and country as well as for families in the Church itself."[46]

Ritter also approved a more humane and ecumenic approach to the legislation on mixed marriages.[47]

In the first session of the council, the Church fathers of Central Europe had taken the lead, with the missionary bishops, the majority of Latin Americans, and some North Americans, like the Saint Louis archbishop, following their lead. Now in the third session, the American episcopate, led chiefly by Cardinal Meyer of Chicago, mounted its first broad offensive in the debate on religious liberty. The Americans challenged a position taken by the Italian and Spanish episcopate that had outlived whatever usefulness and validity it had ever had. The bishops of the British Empire, of the mission countries, and some of the Latin Americans, joined the North American campaign. Conciliar historian Ratzinger wrote:

> In a critical hour, council leadership passed from Europe to the young Churches of America and of the mission countries. It was now as never before unmistakably clear that the Church had become an international Church, drawing on the treasures of all nations and showing the meaning of plurality within the unity of the Church.[48]

Unfortunately, an adequate declaration of religious liberty did not come to a vote before the close of the session, in spite of Council Secretary-General Archbishop Pericle Felici's promise of November 18, 1964. The next day's meeting — the second of the last of the council's third session — exploded in confusion and controversy. Eugene Cardinal Tisserant, dean of the council presidency, announced that the session would hold no vote on the question. Taken by surprise, Albert Cardinal Meyer of Chicago, one of the council presidents, left his seat and gathered a group of bishops around him, including Cardinals Ritter, Leger, and Alfrink.[49] Their protest brought the assurance of a vote at the next session. On his return to Saint Louis, Cardinal Ritter openly discussed the feeling of frustration that faced the proponents of the liberty declaration.

Ecumenic Guidelines in the Archdiocese

Shortly after his return from Rome in December, 1964, Cardinal Ritter attended the Fourth Annual Dialogue between ministers and priests under the auspices of the Archdiocesan Commission on Ecumenism. Monsignor William Baum of the Kansas City (Missouri) diocese, an expert at Vatican II, gave the featured address at Kenrick Seminary on December 14. One hundred and thirty-six clergymen of the Lutheran, Anglican, and other denominations joined with ninety-two priests in a frank exchange. In his brief greetings that evening, the cardinal reflected the open spirit of the meeting. He acknowledged Catholic neglect of Scriptures and urged his Protestant brethren to a greater concern for the Eucharist. He called the conciliar document on ecumenism "a remarkable decree."[50]

Two months later, 125 Protestant seminarians gathered at Kenrick for the first all-seminarian ecumenic convocation in the history of the archdiocese.[51]

A week later, with the approval of His Eminence, the Commission on Ecumenism issued a directory of guidelines to the clergy of the archdiocese. It had many highlights. Priests could join ministerial alliances and associations, if they wished, and should acquaint themselves with the clergy of other denominations in the neighborhood where each worked. The directory encouraged joint prayer for unity, both in Catholic churches and churches of other Christian confessions, especially on ecumenical occasions, unity octaves, and certain national holidays. Priests could accept invitations to preach at other Christian churches on the occasion of prayers for unity and could invite clergymen of other Christian confessions to preach in the Catholic churches on such occasions. If members of other Christian congregations privately approached a priest for confession or communion, with the customary dispositions required of Catholics, the priest should accept his spirit of good will. Likewise if anyone asked a priest to anoint him when in danger of death, the priest should follow the norms of charity. Priests, further, could officiate at the funeral services of members of other Christian denominations at funeral parlors or in the home or at the graveside when the family requested that he did so.

The directory closed with important words on ecumenism:

> An awareness of ecumenical reality leads us to recognize that the baptized and practicing members of other Christian churches should not be regarded as proper subjects for proselytizing activity. With the literally millions of unchurched in this country and in the world, sound theology must lead us to the conclusion that our witness and preaching must be directed towards those who have not in any manner acknowledged Christ as Lord and Saviour.[52]

The directory suggested that a proper attitude in this last regard would be a symbol of the sincerity of the Catholic participation in the ecumenical movement. Taking into consideration the needs of charity and the desire for ecumenic dialogue, it set down guidelines for the attendance of Catholics at Protestant services. In general, the directory encouraged priests and laymen to become better acquainted with the beliefs and practices of other Christian communions. To bring this about, it suggested the invitation of a clergyman of another Christian denomination to a Catholic study club or parish group to explain the beliefs and attitudes of his congregation. It encouraged, lastly, dialogue by qualified groups of Catholics with members of other Christian communions.

The two and one half years since the beginning of Vatican II had changed the outlook of Catholics in a dramatic way. Catholics of Saint Louis had always had relatives, friends, or neighbors who belonged to other Christian denominations. Catholics understood their neighbors' outlook and recognized their sincerity. Catholics and Protestants worked and played together. They belonged to the same associations. Quite often, however, Church law prevented a type of religious dialogue and discussion that might have been mutually beneficial. A few years before, the common attitude among Catholics found expression in the placard: "All roads lead to Rome! Come home brothers!" Slowly a new feeling grew that all Christians were moving, with adjustments on both sides, towards a point of unity in the future.

In the exhilaration of conciliar openness, many felt that the hopes for the Church were higher than at any time since the thirteenth century. But the Church in the United States and in Saint Louis in particular did not move ahead with consistency in implementing the spirit of Vatican II. With Cardinal Ritter in attendance on March 12, 1965, the Clergy Conference of the archdiocese explored ways of implementing in the parishes the liturgical changes recommended by the council. In spite of this, some dragged their heels in matters of church worship; while others rushed headlong into new experiments without thought for tradition, reverence, or the meaning of religious action.

Top-Heavy Bureaucracy Suddenly Outdated

Cardinal Ritter had developed an amazing administrative structure in place of the less-organized procedures of earlier times. This organization was, in fact, one of his distinct achievements. The archdiocese had commissions on finances, parish boundaries, buildings, ecumenism, human rights, sacred liturgy, sacred music, sacred art, insurance, vigilance, schools, an orphans' board, a seminary board, a conference on rural life and home missions, a priests' mutual benefit society, an office of radio and television apostolate, a conference commission, and a board for direction of sodalities. Individual priests served as directors of Catholic hospitals, the priests' purgatorial society, the archdiocesan cemeteries, the Apostoleship of Prayer, the Priests Eucharistic League, the Family Life Bureau, vocation development, the councils of Catholic men, women, and youth, Christian doctrine, the St. Vincent de Paul Society, and the Holy Name Society.

In this long list of personnel were one Marianist, one Jesuit, one Vincentian, a Sister of St. Joseph, and a Notre Dame Sister on the school board, another Sister of St. Joseph on the commission for sacred music, two laymen and one laywoman on the ecumenic commission, one layman each on the commissions on human rights and sacred music, two laymen on the school board, and two laymen on the orphans' board. The remainder of the countless individuals were members of the archdiocesan clergy. Only the school board had a lay president. The cardinal himself chaired the commission on ecumenism, the archdiocesan orphans' board, the diocesan seminary board, the archdiocesan rural and home missions conference. Bishop Gottwald chaired the commissions on sacred liturgy, sacred music, and sacred art. Several monsignors participated in the work of three or four commissions, and sometimes served as executive secretaries of more than one.[53]

During the years when Cardinal Ritter spent considerable time in Rome, it became steadily clearer that this vast machinery of the Church in Saint Louis depended entirely on his initiative. He had given much leeway of action to his various administrative heads. They functioned freely within their sphere. But they did not initiate policy. When Cardinal Ritter was away, they failed to move in any fresh directions — except in ecumenical and liturgical matters — even though the council called for such. Further, no lay person had any real area of decision-making.

Cardinal Ritter took a stance at Vatican II that called for greater freedom, subsidiarity, and local decision making. The whole notion of collegiality demanded more cooperative, mature, and free action by individuals on various levels. In promoting this trend in Rome — good thing that it was — the cardinal was psychologically undercutting the intense centralization prevailing throughout the American Church, and the complex bureaucracy of his own archdiocese.

"Little Council"

While Cardinal Ritter was in Rome for the third session of the council in the fall of 1964, a group of thirty Catholic priests and laymen had discussed the possibility of a grass roots effort to gain from dialogue some of the results the bishops gained in Rome. Out of this informal gathering, a plan took shape. The group drew up a blueprint for a "Little Council." When the cardinal returned from Rome, he met with the group and encouraged them to go ahead. In January they submitted their plan.

After some weeks, the cardinal rejected the plan in a letter to the pastor who had served as chairman of the meetings. Ritter wanted more emphasis on the parishes, a more simplified plan of renewal, and a greater involvement of the official lay organizations of the archdiocese.[54]

Cardinal Ritter meets with leaders of the Archdiocesan Council of Catholic Woman: (from left) Mrs. Frank Fehlig (Elizabeth), 1st vice-president; Mrs. John C. Hamm (Pat), 2nd vice-president; Mrs. Charles T. Dougherty (Dolores), president; Cardinal Ritter; Mrs. Louis H. Gummersbach (Catherine), treasurer; Mrs. John E. Drury (Doris), secretary; (seated) Mrs. Paul C. Reid (Kathryn), past president.

The "Little Council" hoped to meet with the cardinal again before he left for Rome. Unfortunately, a break occurred in communications. Without doubt, the group did not reflect a total cross-section of the archdiocese. They were interested individuals, rather than a true grass-roots representative. But such representation was probably not feasible. On some occasions members of the "Little Council" seemed to insist that whatever they decided to do was what Vatican II wanted. Not all of them were judicious in their actions or remarks. But that did not excuse a campaign of name-calling that arose against them. Some opponents, in fact, seemed to think that "open season on the Little Council" extended throughout the year.

Whatever its failings, the original "Little Council" had given a voice to many articulate individuals in the city. It seemed unfortunate that it did not get to see the cardinal before he left for Rome. Many Catholic lay people felt that a wall had dropped between themselves and the cardinal shortly before he left for the last session of the Vatican Council. Many came to believe that the very man who urged Cardinal Ritter to take a progressive stance in Rome, relative to the major issues in the Church, now recommended caution in regard to the implementation of these programs within the archdiocese.

In late August, 1965, however, the archdiocese stated that thorough study had to precede the formation of the Saint Louis Archdiocesan Assembly, or "Little Council."[55] The announcement by-passed the already existing body. Before Cardinal Ritter left for the final session of the council in September, he prepared a letter for the pastors to read on Sunday, September 12. In it, he affirmed once again his determination to have a "Little Council" in the archdiocese to parallel the one in Rome. He urged his pastors to inaugurate study groups in every parish on the decrees of Vatican II. He announced special orientation sessions for the clergy in theology, catechetics, liturgy, and Scripture to begin in the fall. He sent the pastors a sixteen-step plan for the renewal of the diocese in the spirit of Vatican II.[56]

This plan for renewal anticipated most dioceses of the country. A liberal Catholic weekly called it "the most ambitious attempt in the United States to extend the concept of archdiocesan collegiality into the grass roots,"[57] and stated that the Cardinal's plan contained an estimated seventy percent of the suggestions of the "Little Council."[58] Many feared, however, that it too strongly reflected the already top-heavy archdiocesan structure. And in by-passing the existing "Little Council," it seemed to reject some of the most concerned individuals in the archdiocese.

Close of the Council

The fourth and final session of the Vatican Council that began in late summer, 1965, and closed on December 8, 1965, was a triumph for the progressive spirit within the Church. Cardinal Ritter saw programs come to fruition that he had worked for throughout the sessions.

In the debate on religious liberty, he gave unqualified support on September 16, 1965. He believed that charity, justice, and consistency demanded its endorsement. Charity required that the council do something for those suffering from religious persecution. Justice required reparation for past acts against the freedom of others. Consistency demanded support for the declaration on religious liberty in view of the flavor of certain passages in the decrees on ecumenism, and the Church. Ritter concluded with a warning: if the fathers failed to approve the religious liberty document, they ran "the risk of being numbered among the enemies of the gospel."[59] The last session approved the document on religious liberty as well as those on the Church in the modern world, on the priestly ministry, and on the missions. Cardinal Ritter rightly felt, as did much of the archdiocese, that the council of Popes John and Paul had done far more than men hoped.

At the last session, on December 8, 1965, three cardinals, Agaganian of Armenia, Gracias of India, and Ritter of America, presented six youngsters from six continents, as representatives of the youth of the world, to the Holy Father, Pope Paul VI. The choice of Cardinal Ritter was a great tribute.

What then could be an evaluation of the work of Cardinal Ritter in "The Great Event of the Twentieth Century"? In his book, *The New Pentecost*, Editor Vincent Yzermans discusses some of the north European churchmen and then goes on to say, "Other men, of course, were outstanding. The respect shown Cardinal Meyer of Chicago and Cardinal Ritter of Saint Louis whenever they rose to speak was equaled only by the recognition they received wherever they went."[60]

Xavier Rynne in *Letters from Vatican City* goes even farther. "Cardinal Ritter, the cheerful dynamic Archbishop of Saint Louis, for all the apparent simplicity of his approach, turned out to be the outstanding American prelate at the Council."[61]

In a tribute to Cardinal Ritter, Monsignor Frederick R. McManus of the canon law faculty of the Catholic University of America and director of the U.S. Bishops Committee on Liturgy, had this to say:

In the Council he spoke consistently and effectively for the progress that prevailed, for episcopal collegiality and responsibility. To take one example, he offered the formulation which guarantees the bishop's pastoral office; instead of waiting for faculties and dispensations from the Pope, the bishop has his own pastoral responsibility fully recognized unless the Pope reserves a decision to himself. Thus a law was changed and more important a whole attitude and approach changed.

Few bishops reared in another generation and in other ways have grasped and welcomed the renewal as had the great Cardinal. A strong spokesman in the Council, he has been above all else open and willing, with a spirit much younger bishops and priests can emulate. A kind of supernatural instinct has made him ready to accept change and also to initiate it — as a part of the true role of the bishop in the Church.[62]

Chapter 41

Council Aftermath

Aggiornamento *at Home*

The *aggiornamento* of Pope John caught most American Catholics psychologically unprepared. They had defended beleaguered citadels; now they were to go out and bring salvation to all the world. They had left the Bible to Protestants; now they continually heard the Word of God and came to see their own poor grasp of the Scriptures. They had performed many actions, like eating fish on Friday, partially to show their distinctiveness from the various Protestant groups; now they were to pursue ecumenic dialogue with their "separated brethren." They had presumed something sacred in the Latin language; now they attended an English liturgy and understood the words. They had sometimes overemphasized the awe and mystery of the Holy Mass; now the priest faced them at the altar and they answered his prayers. They had thought of Christian living as a cut-and-dried routine of prayers and devotions and sound parish living; now they were told that they were on pilgrimage through life, like the Jews of old going through the desert to the promised land. They had waited for the Church to pronounce on all moral questions; now they were told to form their own consciences. They had looked on the Church as the same everywhere; and now they found variations from diocese to diocese.

Some accepted the new with joy; some clung to the old in dismay at the changes. Almost at once polarization set in throughout the nation.

Since Cardinal Ritter had opened his mind toward the new in Rome, many presumed that the Saint Louis archdiocese would lead the way in implementing the decrees of Vatican II at home. The cardinal had welcomed the progressive theologian Hans Kung to Saint Louis. The Commission on Ecumenism had issued a most flexible program of dealing with those of other denominations. Monsignor Hellriegel and others had prepared many people of the archdiocese for liturgical change. Priests and seminarians had carried on inter-faith dialogues with clergymen and students of other persuasions. Saint Louis had long been religiously open to the new.

When Cardinal Ritter returned from Rome at the end of the council, he spoke of the dialogue conference as the means of implementing the new spirit.[1] Twenty-six hundred archdiocesan study groups would meet as part of this Operation Renewal.[2] In the cardinal's plan, the paper structure was truly remarkable, but amazingly top-heavy. Perhaps he did not realize how much the vast complexity depended on his own decisions.

During the next year (1966), the *St. Louis Review* carried regular articles on facets of Operation Renewal: the election of delegates from parishes and deaneries, appointments by the cardinal, the election and appointment of priest delegates, and the choice of representatives of various orders.[3] The next phase of Operation Renewal got underway in mid-October of the same year. By March of 1967, under the deputy general secretariate of Father Robert Kaletta, the organization made over a hundred proposals for renewal in the archdiocese.[4] The delegates had debated such topics as the responsibility of laymen, the question of Mass stipends, pastoral visits to hospitals, the hiring of lay administrators, the abolishment of women's headress in church, and the establishment of parish advisory boards and building commissions. The parish councils asked that contractors and suppliers in each parish be allowed to make bids on parochial construction and called for an end to special collections, for simplicity in church design, and for a greater responsibility for assistant pastors. One recommendation would have subdivided each parish into sections with an associate pastor having a special care of each.[5] These recommendations looked almost exclusively to parish concerns. Many of them were fine. Given the parochial orientation of the program, the limitations of scope did not surprise anyone. Operation Renewal scheduled its next phase for the following month (April, 1967).[6]

Cardinal Ritter had stated that the American bishops had gone to the council to find out what Rome wanted. They stayed to learn and participate. So the average American layman had faced the new age unaware of the depths of controversy. They knew little of the long-enduring liberal-conservative struggle within the Church and the some-times high-handed methods of the Roman Curia in bringing about what American Catholics had believed was a freely arrived at uniformity of view.

To them the Church had already answered all questions. They did not know that repression had sometimes prevented many sincere Catholics from asking honest questions. And so when new ideas came into view on the liturgy, on scripture, on the nature of the Church and its relationship to the modern world, on the relations with people who professed other creeds, they did not have the tools to keep up with a new world aborning. They latched on to external things — such as the new garb of nuns, the goatees of some young priests, the kiss of peace at Mass, or the witness of inner-city apostolates — and made these seem, either with approval or disapproval, the reform of John XXIII.

It had become clear that Operation Renewal's efforts offered something on the parochial level; but other levels of operation were mandatory. The archdiocese should have called on its abundance of talent for planning on a diocesan-wide basis. A "Big Council" of the top intellectual lay and clerical leaders should have met to promote the reforms of Vatican II on the regional level. This would have included leaders in business, education, communications, the professions, civil administration, religious administration — every area of influence. The archdiocese boasted experts in liturgy, philosophy, sociology, history, communications, art, church music, scripture, ecumenics, and other fields, who were willing to use their energies in the great challenges of the time. But the call never came. Great energies remained unchannelled.

Part of the delegation of the Archdiocesan Commission on Human Rights leaving for Atlanta to attend the Martin Luther King funeral: (from top of ramp) Rev. Jerome Brzakowski, S.V.D., dean Richard Childress of the Saint Louis University School of Law, and Rev. Paul E. Gopaul, S.S.E.; (from left) Louis T. McKinnie, Rev. Anthony Siebert, James Smith, Sister Estelle, C.S.J., and Sister Hilda Brickus, S.S.M. (Photograph by St. Louis Review.)

Academic Advances and Changes

The archdiocese and the nation saw new developments in various areas of Church life. In preparation for the post-Vatican II age of the Church, the Catholic University of America and the McGraw-Hill Book Company planned a *New Catholic Encyclopedia*. The chief editors came from the staff and faculty of the Catholic University of America in Washington. No Saint Louisan occupied a central position in this project as Conde Pallen had done with the original *Catholic Encyclopedia*. Only Francis J. Guentner of the Department of Music of Saint Louis University contributed an extensive list of articles comparable numerically to those of Father Souvay and Monsignor Holweck in the ealier work. Leo C. Brown, professor of economics of Saint Louis University, at the time temporarily residing at the Cambridge School of Social Studies in Massachusetts, served as staff editor for social sciences. Scholars of the archdiocese wrote for the new work that came out in 1967. Peter Rahill, archdiocesan historian, wrote on church history topics. The list of contributors included Monsignor Vincent Naes, Fathers Ralph Bayard, C.M., and Stafford Poole, C.M., Mother Louise Callan of Maryville College, and many Saint Louis University professors, among them Drs. Charles T. Dougherty, James Collins, and Thomas P. Neill, and Fathers John F. Bannon, Lucius F. Cervantes, Francis Petru, Walter Ong, and George Klubertanz.

The *Catholic Encyclopedia* was not the only major scholarly concern in Saint Louis at this time, however. In late summer of the city's bicentennial year (1964), Saint Louis University had purchased the former Coronado Hotel as a residence for theology students of various orders and dioceses. At the same time the president of Saint Mary's College in Kansas, the Saint Louis University's School of Divinity, announced that within a few years, the theological faculty would move back to Saint Louis whence it had gone in 1931. Students of the Servite Order and of the Montfort Congregation resided in the east wing of the Coronado Hotel at the beginning of the 1965-1966 school year. The Conventual Franciscans

set up a residence on the property purchased from the Helpers of the Holy Souls on Washington about eight blocks from the campus. Other religious orders and congregations began to look to Saint Louis. History professors of the university faculty taught at Kenrick Seminary. Greater cooperation between the two institutions followed.

With the University's School of Theology scheduled for the city campus, the archdiocese laid plans to participate in the development of a theological center. Father Robert Coerver, C.M., rector of Kenrick Seminary, announced that third and fourth year theology students at Kenrick would take some courses at Saint Louis University. This would allow them a choice of degree areas, provide opportunity for faculty exchanges, and bring closer association between seminary and university. Father Coerver described this move as "part of an amalgamation of seminaries that is taking place throughout the country." It would give "a chance to develop mature priests, who will gain a realistic view of the world in which they will serve. The bishops of the twelve dioceses who send seminarians to Kenrick," Father Coerver stated, "have given 'enthusiastic support' to the new affiliation."[7] With the impetus of Vatican II, the university saw bright prospects for theological and ecumenic studies.

The city's bicentennial celebration had hardly finished when Saint Louis University approached its one hundred and fiftieth anniversary with plans for a year-long celebration. In the previous twelve years, it had added many new buildings in its medical center on South Grand, in the old campus on North Grand, and especially in the expanded section of the north campus east of Grand in the Mill Creek redevelopment area. Here, thanks to a gift of Mrs. Harriet Fordyce, Saint Louis University now had adequate room for expansion.

At this time, for a variety of reasons, both to clarify the status of their students with regard to government grants, and also to give lay people a greater say in the once totally religious control of higher education, various Catholic colleges and universities throughout the country began to look for new relationships between the sponsoring religious order and the total institution. Webster College, for instance, put its religious teachers, the Sisters of Loretto, on a salary basis similar to that of lay teachers on the same academic level in September, 1966; and a short time later announced the setting up of a lay board of trustees with control no longer vested in the Sisters of Loretto. Webster College did not require that the president be a Sister of Loretto. When President Jacqueline Grennan sought separation from her religious institute shortly after, but remained president of the college, this disassociation came sooner than expected.

In early 1967 President Paul Reinert of Saint Louis University announced that Saint Louis University was enlarging its board of trustees to include eighteen lay members along with ten members of the Jesuit order. Since the university had gained its charter in 1832, every trustee had been a member of the Society of Jesus. The lay members of the board could include alumni and non-alumni, educators and non-educators, affiliates of various religious denominations. Daniel Schafly, a member of the Saint Louis Board of Education, accepted the chairmanship of the enlarged board of trustees.

At the first conferral of degrees after the announcement of the enlargement of the board of trustees, Chairman Daniel L. Schlafly read from the by-laws:

1. the University will be publicly identified as a Catholic university and a Jesuit university; 2. the University will be motivated by the moral, spiritual, and religious inspirations and values of the Judaeo-Christian traditions; 3. the University will be guided by the spiritual and intellectual ideas of the Society of Jesus.[8]

The president of the university would be a Jesuit.

Fontbonne College followed the pattern of Saint Louis University rather than of Webster, by expanding its board of trustees to include lay people but keeping the presidency in the hands of a Sister of St. Joseph and keeping its close identification with the ideals of the order and the Church that had nurtured it.

Ritter's Last Days

What, in brief, was the Church in Saint Louis and the rest of the world trying to do in the late 1960's? On a world-wide scale, the Church was trying to free herself from outmoded social patterns of the past, to distinguish the good from the bad trends of modern civilization, and to bring about a mutual enrichment of Church and society.

In the seventeenth and eighteenth centuries, the Church had so embedded itself in the absolutist and class conscious social structure of Europe that revolt against the old order meant also revolt against the Church and her beliefs. Instead of analyzing objectively the basic ideas — so many of them fundamentally Christian — of the incoming political and social order of Europe, the Church of the mid-nineteenth century had issued only condemnations. Once the mother and teacher of Europe, the Church had become alien and hostile to a civilization her children had brought into being.

The Church in America, on the other hand, had begun in a climate of freedom. In spite of periods of nativism and prejudice, and its own minority status, it had grown strong in an atmosphere unlike that of contemporary Europe. Consistent with its background, the American Church had brought its greatest weight in the council to bear in the discussions of human liberty.

Vatican II had considered almost every issue of significance in Christian history, and pointed out answers. Catholic sociologist Thomas F. O'Dea, in *The Catholic Crisis*, summarized the great challenge to Catholicism in the post-Vatican II age in these words:

Can Catholicism confront the consequences, intellectual and spiritual, of modern developments in sciences and scholarship, and in political, social and economic life, and adapt to them, and still preserve its own lively sense of God's reality and presence? . . . Can it shed forms evolved historically, and find new modes of thought, expression, and participation relevant to the new age which is advancing upon us? . . . Can it do so and evolve the new form of organization and presence . . . requisite to its mission in tomorrow's world?[9]

Although neither cardinal nor people put the matter so succinctly, that is what they were trying to do. The task never could have been easy. Extremism on every issue — ecumenism, liturgy, Church music, retreats, devotion to Our Lady, seminary studies, everything — made the issues more embattled. In his effort to hold the middle of the road, Cardinal Ritter did not always place himself in the same progressive stance he had assumed during Vatican II. People came to read every message from the chancery in a liberal-conservative context. When the cardinal wrote a letter condemning certain forms of unauthorized liturgical innovation,[10] liberals wondered why he did not also reprove unauthorized retention of old practices. In the growingly embattled spirit of the times, routine changes

and appointments took on a significance they sometimes did not have in reality.

A newspaper feature by Edward A. Higgins of the *Post-Dispatch* quoted local Catholics who saw in the assignment of three young priests a growing conservative ascendancy. Higgins praised the *St. Louis Review*, the archdiocesan newspaper. He heard liberals give glum predictions for its future. He did not expect the cardinal to interfere with its publication; but stated a "liberal" surmise that the *Review* "would revert to being the archdiocese's official bulletin board, as many priests and laymen believe it should have been all along."[11] As Higgins expected, the cardinal did not move against the *Review*.

Besides implementing the decrees of Vatican II, Cardinal Ritter had to carry out the routine administration of a large archdiocese, and, in fact, catch up with the business that had remained undone while he was in Rome. In a televised interview in May, 1967, he spoke on various aspects of education. He contrasted the educational climate at the time of the Third Plenary Council of Baltimore — when the American bishops called for a parochial school in each parish — and the current picture, and concluded: "The vast parochial school system existing in the Church would not be started if it were proposed at the present time."[12] He noted the pluralistic atmosphere of contemporary life, the impossibility of educating every child in a Catholic school, and the costs of maintaining schools.[13]

When asked about the new board of trustees of Saint Louis University and the status of the Catholic University of America, he commented in general:

Lay ability . . . surely should improve the qualities of a school. I think it is reciprocal. Perhaps a clergyman or a bishop or some bishops on a board would add something, but I don't think it's too good to have exclusively bishops, or exclusively priests or exclusively religious. The University is serving not only the Church but the community.[14]

Collegiate affairs at Webster College came steadily into the news, as President Jacqueline Grennan initiated pro-

Rev. Joseph McNicholas gives communion at the Boy Scout field Mass. (Photograph by St. Louis Review.)

The lunette on the east wall of the Great Cathedral recalls Cardinal Ritter's leadership in the fields of integration and ecumenism. (John Wm. Nagel Photo)

grams that seemed to suggest that Webster College was no longer a Catholic institution, but merely an institution with a Catholic and Lorettine "presence." An article in *Look* magazine for May 30, 1967, alleged heated confrontations between the archdiocesan authorities and the administrators of Webster College and proved embarrassing to both.[15] A subsequent issue of *Look* carried a demur of Miss Grennan. She also wrote to the cardinal that the article deeply disturbed her and spoke reassuringly that the Webster College of the future would be a real grace and credit to the Church.[16]

As Cardinal Ritter celebrated his golden jubilee in the priesthood and approached his seventy-fifth birthday — it would have been July 20, 1967 — he prepared to retire. This decision would have accorded with the decree of Pope Paul of August, 1966, that implemented the spirit and decisions of Vatican II on the tenure of office of bishops. Cardinal Ritter tendered his resignation through the apostolic delegate, Archbishop Egidio Vagnozzi.[17] Since the Pope had previously refused the resignations of such prelates as Cardinals Spellman of the United States, Ottaviani of Italy, and Frings of West Germany, Ritter strongly requested that the Pope allow him to retire. He intended to work in a country parish.[18]

Before his seventy-fifth birthday came, however, Cardinal Ritter suffered a heart attack in early June, 1967. "His heart is just failing from all the strain," his personal physician, Dr. C. G. Vournas stated.[19] It was his first critical illness. A second attack proved fatal. He died peacefully, Saturday June 10, 1967.[20]

Archiepiscopal Epitath

Eulogies and condolences on the death of Joseph Cardinal Ritter from local, state, national, and international civic and religious leaders stressed his interest in the ecumenic movement, civil rights, and renewal of the Church, along with the simplicity of his own personal style of life.

Certainly the two most publicly recognized achievements of his career as archbishop of Saint Louis were his desegregation of the schools in 1947, and his progressive leadership at Vatican II. But he did other things at home that did not often come to the attention of the wider community. He opened three new churches each year he served the city. He built among his people a strong sense of the universality of the Church, with his vigorous support of the Society for the Propagation of the Faith[21] and his inaugural of a Latin American mission in Bolivia. His concern for the spiritual development of the people of the archdiocese showed itself in many ways, particularly in the retreat movement. He continued and expanded an already well-developed program of Catholic education. He totally organized the archdiocese, concluding a program begun by Chancellor Cody in the late Glennon years. He built up a vast machinery with commissions and chairmen, and gave these chairmen leeway to perform their tasks. He brought the many organizations of Catholic Saint Louis into the framework of the various national councils of Catholic men, women, and youth.

He wanted a greater sense of lay responsibility. But he never forced lay decisioning on the pastors. As Vatican II moved along, he did not have time to come up with a plan to decentralize the church in Saint Louis, in a way comparable to the decentralization he looked for in the universal Church.

Ritter lacked the flamboyance of Du Bourg, but had a greater sense of orderly progress than Du Bourg had. He had the unsophisticated simplicity and the rapport with his fellow bishops that Rosati had, but lacked the warm at-homeness with the ordinary man that had marked the first bishop of Saint Louis. He had a similar concern for the spiritual, but a far greater business sense and a flock more ready to contribute to good causes. Ritter did not have the theological background and acumen of Peter Richard Kenrick, but he was open to new ideas, and he participated in a council that was more ready to hear his ideas and suggestions than the embattled assembly that Kenrick attended.

Like Kain, Ritter had distinguished shoes to fill. He proved more successful in filling them. Ritter did not have the oratorical skill, the grand manner, or the handsome physique of Cardinal Glennon, but he matched the Irish patriarch in his building prowess and in his parochial expansion. While not the heroic figure among local Catholics that Glennon was, Ritter called forth a warmer personal reaction among Jews and Protestants and among Negroes — Catholic or Protestant — than Cardinal Glennon evoked.

Ritter's record overshadowed his personality.

Troubled Waters

American Catholics still moved through turbulent times during 1967, while Saint Louisans wondered who their new archbishop might be. They, too, shared the uncertainties of the post-Vatican II era.

Changes gripped the air. These changes affected accidentals of course, not substantials. But in the inflexible thinking of many, the Latin language in the Mass had been as important as the Consecration.

Pre-Vatican II Catholics had emphasized the Mass as a sacrifice; the Council also recalled that it was a banquet, and stressed anew the importance of receiving Communion.

Men came to look on mortal sin not as a specific failing against a commandment, but as a rejection of God's love, "a fundamental option" for evil. Confession lines dwindled, while Communions increased.

Many Catholics, clergy and laity, were unready for the changes. Instead of taking the lead with a sure hand, and establishing priorities, giving immediate concern to some matters and holding action on others, most bishops hesitated. Saint Louis, at the time, had no archbishop, through the last half of 1967.

The parochial schools, too, faced serious changes in outlook and actualities. Some observers advanced the theory that the Catholic school reflected the beleaguered citadel

At the death of Cardinal Ritter, many Saint Louisans thought of their own former pastors serving the Church elsewhere, such as Bishop Charles Helmsing of Kansas City, Mo., or Bishop Mark Carroll of Wichita, shown here receiving the crosier from Cardinal Ritter.

approach to religious life no longer consistent with the more ecumenic days ahead.

The cost of separate schools created a major burden on Catholics. Programs of federal aid that went almost exclusively to public schools imposed an added hardship on parents and teachers.

At the same time, the decline in religious vocations, the return to lay life of so many members of religious congregations and the expansion of other apostolates by orders involved in education, decimated the staffs of many schools. Not unexpectedly, fewer novices entered. Seminary enrollment was dropping dramatically.

The issues facing Catholic colleges and universities differed from the secondary and elementary Catholic education pattern. Universities were trying to establish their freedom to function, independently of the ecclesiastical structure, at the very time when the church authorities were loosening restrictions. In the name of academic excellence, many Catholic educators were idolizing and imitating the secular academic establishment, rather than emphasizing their own distinct Catholic contribution.

To add further confusion, as colleges needed State and federal aid in order to perform their tasks, they had to de-emphasize their distinctly denominational aspects in order to gain that aid. It was as if it were necessary to become secularized in order to continue Catholic in name.

At the same time, the religious orders who sponsored these Catholic colleges were finally coming to grips with the necessity of giving lay people a greater place in the administration and direction of the schools. Many feared the move from cleric to lay control might lead to a loss of religious identification—as has been the case with the great Protestant institutions of the last century.

On the positive side, the imminent return of the Saint Louis University School of Theology to the city, advocated by Archbishop Ritter back in 1949, the probable enrollment of seminarians of many religious orders, and the co-operation with Kenrick Seminary, gave promise of making Saint Louis "the Louvain of the Midwest," a major theological center.

Throughout the nation, an uncertainty began to shake the cock-sure approach to the future that had marked the American manner. The Vietnam War helped bring on this malaise. Growing opposition to the war led to riots equal in vehemence, though not in destructiveness to those of the black militants.

The nation began to see widespread drug abuse, heard "rock and roll" music at its loudest, and watched the "hippies"—the drifting and disoriented young people of the time—gather for mass drug and music parties.

The only major positive note for the country came from the National Aeronautics and Space Agency. The anticipated moon launch before 1970 held that timetable set by President Kennedy early in the decade.

In spite of unresolved aspects of the Civil Rights struggle, Saint Louis Blacks continued their peaceful approach to improving race relations during that long hot summer of 1967 when tensions shook so many American cities.

The general spirit of the city far outshone that of the country. Under the energetic and glad-handing leadership of Mayor A. J. Cervantes, the city saw action as well as controversy. The Gateway Arch, topped out two years before, had now been completed, and welcomed its first visitors on July 24, 1967, a month after Archbishop Ritter died, and spurred a complex of new buildings that changed the aspect of the city at the river.

PART VIII

John J. Carberry:
Marian Advocate (1968-1980)

Cardinal Carberry blesses a little child after Mass at the Old Cathedral. (Photograph by Eldon Arteaga).

The smiles of the Archdiocesan Development Fund Council reflect its appreciation of the generosity and cooperation of Saint Louis Catholics in the 1979 campaign: Seated (L. to R.) R. Emmet Kelly, M.D., Henry J. Elmendorf, General Chairman; Cardinal Carberry; James A. Corrigan; Standing: Msgr. Lloyd Sullivan, Bishop George J. Gottwald; Bishop John M. Wurm; Harry F. Harrington; Daniel F. Sheehan, Sr.; Bishop Charles Koester; David Blanton, Jr.; James F. Bussman; Joseph H. Vatterott; Oliver Parks; Gene Jantzen; and Msgr. Rowland E. Gannon. (Photograph by Saint Louis Review).

Chapter 42

Placid Bridging

Thousands of Missourians gather for the inter-denominational Pro-Life rally at the Old Courthouse on October 21, 1973. Shortly afterward, a national newspaper called Missouri the leading Pro-Life state in the Union.

Missouri Citizens for Life of various denominations and of all ages walk in protest in front of the Abortion Mill on the northeast corner of Euclid and West Pine on May Day 1979. (Review Photo)

Achievements

The long wait in River City came to an end on February 21, 1968, when Pope Paul VI appointed Bishop John J. Carberry of Columbus, Ohio, Archbishop of Saint Louis.

The son of James J. Carberry and Mary O'Keefe, John Joseph Carberry was born in Brooklyn, New York, on July 31, 1904. Educated at Cathedral College Seminary in Brooklyn and at the North American College in Rome, he was ordained in the eternal city in July 1929. After a quarter of a century experience in pastoral ministry and Marriage Tribunal work in the diocese in Brooklyn, he became Coadjutor Bishop of Lafayette, Indiana in 1956, and Bishop the following year. Transferred to Columbus, Ohio, in 1965, he took part in ecumenic affairs, a concern that won him the "Pastor of Pastors" Award from the Ohio Council of Churches in January 1968. A month later Pope Paul VI transferred him to Saint Louis, and, a year afterward named him Cardinal.

As Archbishop of Saint Louis, John J. Carberry made his presence felt in four areas: financial sure-footedness, spiritual reconciliation, the pro-life campaign and leader-ship among the bishops. His predecessor had died suddenly while his parish and high school expansion programs were still underway. Under Cardinal Carberry, the archdiocese carried these to a conclusion.

To assess financial needs and to plan fund-raising efforts, Cardinal Carberry approved the formation of an Archdiocesan Development Council with prominent businessmen as well as leading clerics. The generosity of the Catholics of Saint Louis moved the annual fund-raising figure from slightly over a million and a half to beyond the three million mark in five years.

In facing the uncertainties stemming from Vatican II, Cardinal Carberry "stressed strong devotion to Our Lady and love and loyalty to the Pope,"[1] but gave little long-range guidance. He tended to restrain the liberals, but to put up with the conservatives who tarried in implementing conciliar changes. He did, however, approve such new activities as the marriage encounter program in 1974 and the charismatic movement in 1975. He supported the Citizens for Educational Freedom, founded in Saint Louis in 1959, and the Institute for Theological Encounter with Science and Technology, also based in Saint Louis.

When the Supreme Court issued its abortion decision early in 1973 Cardinal Carberry put the archdiocese strongly in the forefront of the pro-life forces. In February 1973 he issued a pastoral on the rights of the unborn, and a month later he set up an Archdiocesan Pro-Life Committee. Soon the archdiocese won recognition as one of the strongest pro-life centers in the nation. At a city-wide pro-life rally, he shared the platform with the Reverend Jacob Preus, President of the Lutheran Church-Missouri Synod.

Cardinal Carberry's greatest acclaim came, however, from his fellow bishops. They elected him three successive times as an American delegate to the World Synod of Bishops, in 1972, 1974, and 1976. They admired his diligent study of the background of ths issues, his forthrightness in asserting his views.

The Congregation for Religious and Secular Institutes named Cardinal Carberry chairman of the Special Commission for Contemplative Nuns in March 1972. In the fall of 1974, his fellow American bishops elected him vice president of their National Conference.

He took part, finally, in two papal elections that chose Popes John Paul I and John Paul II in 1978.

During his middle years in Saint Louis, Cardinal Carberry rivaled the American government in setting up commissions. Except in the strongly manned Development Board, many participants felt that the Cardinal did not give these groups the power to make decisions.

On March 25, 1969, the first anniversary of his own ordination, Archbishop Carberry ordained Joseph McNicholas as auxiliary bishop. After he ordained Charles Koester as auxiliary bishop on September 11, 1971, he divided responsibility between them and Bishop George Gottwald.

When Pope Paul VI named Bishop Joseph McNicholas head of the Diocese of Springfield in Illinois, he raised Father John N. Wurm to the episcopacy. The new auxiliary bishop divided his time between his duties as pastor of the Old Cathedral and chancellor of the archdiocese.

During the Carberry years, three Catholic mayors, A. J. Cervantes, John Poelker and James Conway, varied greatly in style, but all served the city well, guiding it through troublesome times for the nation. The first woman elected to the House of Representatives from Missouri, back in 1952, Leonor Kretzer Sullivan, won reelection regularly for a quarter of a century, and gained great acclaim as a consumer advocate and a distinguished member of Congress.

During Mrs. Sullivan's later terms, two other Catholics, Robert Young of St. Ann's and William Clay of Saint Louis, represented the other districts of the metropolitan area. During this period, a redistricting of the state placed the outer reaches of north Saint Louis County in the northeast Congressional district. Harold L. Volkmer, a Catholic from Hannibal, won this post in 1978.

Missouri's first Catholic Governor, Joseph Teasdale, appointed Professor Joseph Simeone of Saint Louis University's School of Law to the Missouri Supreme Court. Other outstanding Catholics served on the bench, including former presidents of the Board of Aldermen, Donald Gunn, and Paul Simon. Many state legislators belonged to various parishes in the archdiocese.

The prevailing religious spirit of the people showed itself in the active spiritual life of the established parishes, in the retreat movement, and in continued concern for Catholic education. Such archdiocesan organizations as the Radio and Television Office continued their effective work. Many parishes that had seemed destined for decline came back strong. Several factors influenced this recovery: a program

of area days, such as Bevo Day, and the Badenfest; renewed interest in the neighborhoods, and therefore in the parish as a social institution; privately and publicly organized restoration plans, and the wise leadership of community organizers and parish priests.

The apostolate of black Catholics continued to advance under the leadership of Monsignor John Shocklee, a large group of dedicated young priests, including two Blacks, Herbert Harrison of the archdiocese, and Chester Gaiter, Jesuit pastor at St. Matthews, and loyal and generous lay people. A survey by interview of the religious background of black Catholics presented an inspirational story.[2]

The archdiocese opened six new parishes during Cardinal Carberry's 12 years: Christ, Prince of Peace, in Manchester in 1971; Mary, Mother of the Church, in Mattese in 1971; Queen of All Saints in Oakville in 1972; St. John Bosco in Creve Coeur in 1972, St. Elizabeth Ann Seton in St. Charles in 1975, and finally St. Patrick's, diagonally behind the Cervantes Convention Center in downtown Saint Louis in 1979. These parishes did not plan to open schools.

At the same time, the archdiocese had to board up, tear down or consolidate a number of city churches. Another, St. Joseph's Shrine, seemed destined for the "headache ball." It stood only six blocks from the site of a projected new St. Patrick's Church in the revitalized Convention Center area.

The Landmarks Society of Saint Louis made a study of St. Joseph's, the only baroque-style church still standing in the city. A report, submitted to the society by architect Ted Wofford, stressed the unique qualities of the structure and urged its restoration on architectural, historical and religious grounds. The suburban papers carried a full front page feature on the historic church, emphasizing the authentic miracle there. A group of interested citizens formed under the name of the Friends of St. Joseph's.

In one of his last acts as Archbishop, Cardinal Carberry authorized the start of a new church and expressed willingness to give St. Joseph's to a responsible group.

While the archdiocese planned no schools in the new parishes and had to close some inner-city schools, parochial education took an unexpected turn in the national consciousness. The details of this upsurge appear in the history of education in the archdiocese, FROM ONE GENERATION TO THE NEXT, authorized by the Archdiocesan School Board to commemorate the 75th anniversary convention of the National Catholic Education Association, held in Saint Louis in 1978.[3] Important factors in this revitalization were the early and orderly integration of Saint Louis parochial schools; the dedication and high qualifications of religious and lay teachers and administrators and the retention of high academic and disciplinary goals.[4] Uncertain of their future at the outset of Cardinal Carberry's years, the parochial schools had won high esteem by the time of his retirement. At the end of 1980, 500 religious teachers and 1,612 lay teachers taught 48,000 students in 178 schools.

St. Joseph's Institute for the deaf ranked among the top three institutions in the country.

The 34 Catholic high schools, with an enrollment of 19,750 continued to flourish. The teaching staffs included 377 religious and 833 lay teachers. Among new institutions, coeducational John F. Kennedy, an Archdiocesan High School, and De Smet High for boys opened in west county; and Cor Jesu moved from "the Hill" to a new location in southwest county. One city high school, Xavier, a highly successful integrated school for girls closed its doors, as well as seven other private, parochial or archdiocesan highs.

Webster College moved steadily away from a religious identification. Maryville College changed its course; and Saint Louis University paused. Fontbonne and St. Mary's of O'Fallon appeared to cling more firmly to the traditional educational goals of its Sister Founders. Newman College opened in Normandy with a traditional educational program, while Notre Dame College closed, perhaps prematurely, on its lovely terrace above the Mississippi.

The high hopes for the School of Divinity at St. Louis University that might have made the city a center of theological learning comparable to Louvain in Belgium succumbed to a series of administrative blunders, not only in its internal policies and within the Jesuit family and the university community, but equally notable and fatal in relations with the archdiocesan authorities, as James E. Adams described so well in a newspaper article that local historians praised for its grasp of the total picture.[5]

The Dogmatic Constitution on the Church, promulgated by the Fathers of Vatican II restored the permanent deaconate, and authorized its conferment on "men of mature age, even those in the married state." Following this recommendation, Cardinal Carberry ordained twelve men deacons for the archdiocese on January 29, 1977, and an even larger class in 1978.

In retrospect, people found Cardinal Carberry more friendly in chance meetings than his predecessor; but more difficult in arranging a formal appointment–even in an emergency. He grew up in an area where coastal Catholic attitudes prevailed. Such Catholic scholars, as Professor George Devine of Seton Hall, refer to them as "clerical top-heaviness" and "over-concern for external continuity" in contrast to the "receptivity to change in the heartland."[6]

Besides his Brooklyn up-bringing, the new archbishop boasted a Roman education none of his predecessors could claim. He showed a thoroughly Roman orientation. In the tradition of Archbishop Kenrick, Cardinal Ritter fought for a clear definition of religious liberty at Vatican II, and challenged curial centralization; with Archbishop Carberry all ideas seemed to require a Roman origin for validity.

Cardinal Carberry came to Saint Louis in the times of agitation, disturbance and militancy that swept the entire nation in the late sixties. The Church, too, had its own fourfold crisis: of vocations, of authority, of faith, and of identity. By the middle of his term the whole nation moved more calmly, and the Church walked with more certainty.

Cardinal Carberry left to his successor a diocese fairly sound financially, with a group of thriving parishes and schools that were winning respect and esteem long overdue in American life, and an inner-city that had begun to fight back and look toward restoration after years of deterioration. Above all, he left a dedicated people.

He submitted his resignation to Pope John Paul II on his 75th birthday, July 31, 1979.

Cardinal Carberry traveled to Milwaukee to invest Knights and Ladies of the Holy Sepulchre: At the left are Rev. Bernard H. Sanheinrich and Dr. and Mrs. Joseph O'Donnell. On the right are Dr. and Mrs. John T. Lawton and Msgr. Fenton J. Runge.

Chapter 43

The Changing Climate of City and Nation (1945-80)

By the time of the appointment of Archbishop John May in March 1980, the city and the nation differed amazingly from the post-WWII period when Archbishop Ritter came from Indianapolis in 1946. The government had grown during the Depression with the setting up of agencies and offices designed to help people survive and after Pearl Harbor to further the war effort. Instead of declining after the war, these agencies endured and continued to expand throughout the succeeding years. The central government unwittingly created a sense of dependency among many poor.

Great changes marked the next thirty five years. Three decisions of the Supreme Court greatly affected the lives of citizens. In the New Jersey School-bus Case of 1947 the Court declared in effect that the United States was a secular, not a religious country. The Warren Decision of 1954 ruled out school segregation and triggered a long struggle for racial justice. Roe-vs-Wade made abortion a "right" and polarized the country. The "Sexual Revolution" and the reaction to the Vietnam War shook the nation.

At the time of Archbishop Ritter's arrival in 1946, the average veteran was pursuing his education under the GI Bill, marrying and settling down in business or on the family farm. The corner grocery, bakery and pharmacy were still the norm in the area. Agri-business and nation-wide chains loomed like clouds on the horizon that might bring nourishing rain or devastating hail. By 1980 they had all but swept away their individual competitors.

These thirty-five years between 1945 and 1980 also saw a tremendous change in the status of the American working man. Early in the century an outstanding labor leader, John Mitchell, had stated that the majority of members of his union were Catholic. This assertion proved true in many of the unions, centered as they were in the industrial cities of the north and east where the Catholic population in the working class was great.

In spite of the efforts of Presidents Theodore Roosevelt and Woodrow Wilson, labor unions had tottered until the Depression of 1929. The Norris-LaGuardia Act of the following year gave some legal support to organized labor. In 1931 Pope Pius XI issued a new encyclical letter on social justice that reiterated the message of *Rerum Novarum* of Leo XIII. It reaffirmed labor's right to organize, and denounced class warfare. It called for a contract of partnership so that the laboring man might gain a share in ownership, management, or profits.

The New Deal brought further labor legislation and renewed vitality to the labor movement. Alongside the staid and conservative craft unions of the American Federation of Labor, the Congress of Industrial Organizations developed among steel, auto, and clothing workers. Philip Murray, the Catholic head of the steelworkers, became head of the CIO in 1940. War brought an end to the Depression and new opportunities for the American workers.

In good times, management and labor cooperated, but no contract of partnership, as recommended by *Quadragesimo Anno*, developed. The AFL and the CIO united under George Meany, a Catholic, but looked in no new directions, such as organizing the workers in consumer cooperatives.

Gradually white collar union members such as teachers and retail clerks came to match the blue collar workers of the old AFL and the young CIO. Early in the century only one third of the union members worked for the government. As time went on, the percentage approached forty. Solidarity of labor began to crack. Workers who found it necessary to strike could not depend on the solidarity of the working classes. An entire generation grew up that knew only good times. The young people of the Sixties and Seventies had little sympathy with the cause of the worker. In turn, many sons of workingmen, thanks to the G.I. Bill, were now doctors, lawyers, and businessmen. Unions ebbed.

When baseball players were neighbors and fellow parishioners, not transient millionaires, five members of the World Champion Cardinals of 1946 conducted a Christmas tree lot for a local charity. Left to right: Del Wilber, Dick Sisler, Terry Moore, Stan Musial and Red Schoendienst. (Mercantile Library Collection.)

Rev. John Aloysius Melloh presents the Michael Mathis Award to Msgr. Martin Hellriegel for his outstanding contribution to the renewal of pastoral liturgy in the United States. (Review Photo)

Archbishop John Glennon had ruled for almost a half-century with a strong but inconspicuous hand and minimal delegation. He established few diocesan boards. These few merely carried out his decisions. Archbishop Ritter saw the need of wider input and a dispersal of responsibility. He set up many agencies according to the pattern of the National Catholic Welfare Council, such as the Archdiocesan Council of Catholic Youth under the leadership of Msgr. Lloyd Sullivan. By the time of Cardinal Ritter's death, according to the Archdiocesan Yearbook, thirty eight commissions averaged ten members each. Close to four hundred men and women took part in these committees.

By the time of Archbishop May's arrival in March 1980, the agitation and disruption that had marked the late Sixties and Seventies had given way to a business-as-usual attitude. The city continued to decline in population but the percentage of illegitimacy and one-parent families rose like the temperature in mid-August. Many young people lived together without the approval of the Chancery or the Recorder of Deeds. St. Louis County grew, as did the adjoining counties of Jefferson and St. Charles. Vincent Schoemehl was Mayor of the City, and Gene McNary Commissioner of the County. Few people from the county came into the city except to the Busch Stadium, the Jefferson Memorial Arch, the Powell Symphony Hall, the Missouri Botanical Garden, or the newly renovated Union Station.

The "Running Redbirds," managed by "Whitey" Herzog, filled the Stadium regularly on the way to three pennants and one championship in the decade ahead. The football Cardinals flew to Phoenix. The Arch contin-

ued to lure an average of three million visitors a year. Leonard Slatkin brought the St. Louis Symphony Orchestra to unprecedented heights. Peter Hamilton Raven added new features to the world-leading botanical center, a gift from Henry Shaw to his fellow citizens. The new Union Station made people realize that downtown St. Louis still breathed after dark even if there was no game at Busch.

The north side of the city continued to decline. Business moved elsewhere. Housing deteriorated. New houses went down even faster. Weeds grew on the twenty blocks where the thirty-three eleven-story apartments had held a mere twenty years. The project bore the names of two outstanding individuals, Lt. Wendell Pruitt of the U.S. Army Air Corps, an heroic black pilot in WWII, and the Hon. William Igoe, northside Congressman during WWI. The city government found it necessary to close the once prestigious Homer G. Philipps Hospital.

The south side of the city held firm over the years, but housing authorities and private charitable agencies sometimes pursued policies that lessened the sense of security that had once pervaded the area. These agencies often moved many one-parent tenant families into a stable family area of resident-owners. Black residents of Carondelet questioned these policies as strongly as whites. Courts shuttled students around the city, and later to the county also, in a questionable attempt to bring "racial balance." These decisions showed little regard for educational values or community concerns. The chief beneficiary seemed to be the county high school football teams. They now had as many fast running backs as the city schools. Cleveland High, once a

Father Charles Koester (soon to be named auxiliary bishop) quizzed eighth graders at St. Joan of Arc's Parish School on their catechism lessons. (Review Photo)

college preparatory school with a strong academic record, became a military school. Only Sumner among city public high schools was able to keep alive its outstanding tradition.

The State of Missouri continued to hold the unofficial title as the leading Pro-Life state in the Union. Both senators, Thomas Eagleton, Democrat, and John Danforth, Republican, were strong Pro-Life advocates as were successive governors Christopher Bond and John Ashcroft, both Republicans.

In the religious sphere the exuberance that followed Vatican II had waned, like an avalanche that had run its course. The Church had made many gestures of reconciliation toward our "separated brethren," but found few matching signs. Catholics gave greater attention to the Sacred Scriptures, but found few Protestants concerned about those passages Catholics cherished: Christ's plea for the unity of his followers, and his building his church on Peter the Rock. A few Protestants simply felt that Catholics were finally catching up with them. Some still thought of the Pope as anti-Christ but were less open in asserting this belief.

Some Catholics misinterpreted the ecumenical spirit and came to believe that all religions were equally good.

The tallest and best known of the 1987 class of Permanent Deacons was "Easy Ed" Macauley, Billiken All-American and star with the Boston Celtics and the St. Louis Hawks in the NBA...Center, rear row.

They lost their sense of the need to seek the truth. Convert-making went the way of pew-rent.

Under the leadership of such pastors at liturgist Msgr. Martin Hellriegel at Holy Cross in Baden and the support of dedicated Religious, especially Sisters of the Precious Blood of O'Fallon, many Catholics were ready for such innovations as greater participation in the Mass, a wider choice of Scripture readings, and the introduction of English into the fore-part of the Mass.

Unfortunately, in many places the liturgical light-rail got off the worship track. Familiar religious music ended in archival vaults, devotion to the Blessed Sacrament waned, and the tabernacle found a hidden place in numerous churches. Many individuals looked on Holy Mass merely as a banquet and forgot that the Council Fathers had spoken of the Mass as a sacrifice. Fortunately, attendance at Sunday Mass remained high.

Many priests and Religious asked laicization. Vocations declined drastically. Zealous young people looked to temporary volunteer apostolates especially in developing countries. In the Catholic School System, with the departure of a great number of nun-teachers in the late 1960s and the decline in vocations, many parochial schools found difficulty recruiting teachers. The number of parochial schools dropped from 10,879 in 1965 to 8,149 in 1980 and the enrollment of 5 million went down to 3.2 million. But to the surprise of all but a few sociologists who studied the real trends and tendencies, interest in Catholic education grew stronger.

As the number of nuns and religious men available for teaching declined sharply, more lay teachers moved into the classrooms and the administrative offices. The pay might be less than in public education but the basic attitudes of the system made teaching a more pleasant experience. Gradually, it became clearer that the Catholic populace, no longer predominantly poor immigrants but now mostly prosperous middle-class citizens, wanted a religious education for their children such as they themselves had enjoyed.

In the meantime, the urban American public school, once Protestant-oriented in fact though not in the mind of the law, had become so secularized, and in many places actually anti-religious, that many Protestants, especially Baptists, began to open their own schools. Lutherans had long supported parochial schools. Mainline Protestants of wealth had always sent their children to private academies that abounded near big cities.

The courts of the nation had given to public schools responsibilities no educational system could be expected to handle: to lead communities in bringing about better race relations.

All the while parochial schools continued their educational traditions, and innovated in two areas. Even though Catholics formed a minority in many former slave areas, they pioneered in integration in such states as Missouri, Arkansas, Alabama, and North Carolina. In many cities of the nation they opened their inner-city schools to black Protestant children whose parents wanted a more traditional education.

Catholic educators woke up one morning to find that their schools were winning acclaim as institutions that kept the fundamental values of order, discipline, and regular progress. Strangely, this change stemmed not from a theological viewpoint but from the educational philosophy of the Catholic schools that had rejected the false premises of the French philosopher Jean Jaques Rousseau. His unstable views questioning authority and the nature of the child weakened so many public school systems.

The fight for justice in the schools had ceased to be a Catholic versus Protestant struggle, but a dispute between parents who believed in religious education and an assortment of secularists.

The educational picture on the college and university levels was different. In the early decades of this century, most of the Catholic colleges and universities, situated in metropolitan areas, inconspicuously but determinedly taught the sons and daughters of immigrants and prepared them for Christian marriage and for careers in many fields. The parents of these students and the lay and religious teachers who staffed these schools made great sacrifices in the interest of Catholic education.

After World War II, the G.I. Bill brought thousands of veterans to the college of their choice. Great numbers chose Catholic institutions. Enthusiasm long gripped the college campuses.

Vatican II had brought many new attitudes. Even though a major factor in the success of Catholic colleges was the loyalty of parents and students to Mother Church, Catholic educators in the mid-1960s sought to sever ties with religious authorities, claiming academic autonomy. Some educational theorists held that the schools did not really belong to the religious societies that founded them.

The members of religious orders who ran these schools began at that time to invite lay persons to their boards, sometimes choosing members without reference to the spirit and purposes of the school. As a result, in a fifteen-year period between 1965 and 1980, ninety colleges, among them Webster and Maryville in suburban St. Louis, begun by religious women and funded principally by Catholics, lost their Catholic identity.

A number of inner-city parishes closed and others consolidated. The question arose regularly: what should be done with these unneeded church buildings? Two historic churches, St. Joseph's on the city's near northside and St. Ferdinand's in Florissant, won status as "historic landmarks." Friends of those institutions sought to preserve them as shrines.

Such was the climate of city and nation when Archbishop John L. May arrived in the spring of 1980.

PART IX

John L. May:
Calm Midwesterner (1980-1992)

The Serra International, one of the few Catholic organizations that began on either coast, had as its main purpose the promotion of vocations to the priesthood and religious life. Annually, the local Serrans sponsored a benefit day at a country club, entitled "Beat the Bishop." In this photograph Archbishop May takes a practice swing before accepting the challenge. (Review photo)

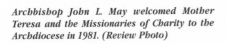

Archbishop John L. May welcomed Mother Teresa and the Missionaries of Charity to the Archdiocese in 1981. (Review Photo)

Chapter 44

The Time of Archbishop John May
in St. Louis (1980-1992)

In the sermon at his installation on March 25, 1980, Archbishop John L. May said, "I come not as a scholar, an orator, or an administrator...I come to live among you...a father and pastor...in the midst of his people as one who serves."[1] As his people heard these remarks and recalled the stories of his previous years in Chicago and Mobile, they welcomed an archbishop imbued with the traditions of the American heartland whence he had come and the Archdiocese where the Holy Father had sent him.

The son of Peter M. and Catherine Allare May, the new archbishop was born on March 31, 1922 in Evanston, Illinois. He attended St. Nicholas School in Evanston, Quigley Preparatory Seminary and St. Mary of the Lake Seminary in Mundelein, earning M.A. and S.T.L. degrees.

Chicago's archbishop Samuel Cardinal Stritch ordained him on May 3, 1947. He served as assistant pastor and hospital chaplain for a few years and then became the General Secretary and President of the Catholic Extension Society. He taught at St. Gregory's High School and Loyola University and served on the Archdiocesan Marriage Tribunal. On June 21, 1967, Pope Paul VI named him Auxiliary Bishop of Chicago. Two years later he became Bishop of Mobile.

He started a number of parishes and two new schools, dedicated a dozen churches and consolidated two high schools. He approved the Council of Priests, introduced the liturgical reforms of Vatican II and began the new rite of reconciliation. He set up a Pastoral Council, supported the Pro-Life Movement, set a limited time of tenure for pastors and continued the program of permanent deacons.[2]

During his early days in St. Louis, Archbishop May granted an interview to the editors of the *Review*. He stressed two issues, "I am extremely committed to a strong Catholic system of education...I would hope that the archdiocese would continue to be leader in the pro-life field." In the area of civil leadership he promised to "work with people of good will for the rights and welfare of individuals who didn't have anyone to speak for them." He spoke strongly also on the question of ecumenism. "I do not think we're convinced," he said, "especially on the grassroots level, of the importance of continuing to work for Christian unity, as Jesus prayed that we might be one."[3]

Archbishop May sent a signal to the people of St. Louis by moving the archiepiscopal residence from suburban Ladue back to the stone mansion on the southwest corner of Lindell and Taylor where Archbishop Glennon had resided. That he could bring along his few possessions in the back of a pickup truck sent a further message to the people. Like Glennon, he walked to his office across the street and down the block. Unlike his predecessor, he needed no chauffeur, no limousine. He drove his own moderate-sized care.

When he met people on Lindell, as he often did, he was friendly and easy to approach. People of other faiths often spoke to their Catholic neighbors, "I saw your bishop today as he walked down the street." An anonymous St. Louisan, queried by a *Review* writer, put the feelings of his fellow Catholics in these words, "He (Archbishop May) felt at home with us and we felt at home with him."[4]

He was not a great pulpit orator like John Glennon, nor an outstanding theologian like Peter Richard Kenrick, but like Joseph Rosati, an accessible pastor. He had a frank, open expression, but not the welcoming smile of Cardinal Carberry. His homilies were informative rather than inspiring. He spoke clearly with some unexpected accenting, even in the prayers at mass. After mass, he greeted members of the congregation in the vestibule – a practice just coming in at the time.

After his installation, Archbishop May invited members of his flock to write him and voice their attitudes about their religious situation. Many did. Further, each complaint had a matching defense. The correspondence proved excessive and he had to discontinue it. Nonetheless, people felt they had access to the top. While the bulk of the Catholic people reflected the easygoing conservatism of the city, some priests and lay people, who had felt the Archdiocese had marked time since Vatican II, expected more evident collegiality in decision-making. No dramatic changes came.

As editor of *Extension* magazine for many years in Chicago, young Father May learned to write fluently and with humor. He had won the first place award from the Catholic Press Association in 1965 for his article on the Second Vatican Council. On his arrival in St. Louis he decided to write a weekly column for the St. Louis *Review* as well as an occasional pastoral letter. In these columns he promoted Catholic education, ecumenism, religious vocations, public morality, while opposing the arms race, efforts to liberalize abortion laws, violence, easy handgun possession and similar current issues. He usually ended with a humorous story. Few of these stories were shop-worn or "corny."

National newspapers rated Missouri the strongest pro-life state in the Union. Cardinal Carberry had joined with Protestant leaders in public demonstrations against abortion. At the same time, some protesters violated laws and went to jail in several cities to dramatize their horror of abortion. As a result the courts began to harass those who demonstrated against abortion clinics. Archbishop May stated his attitude clearly shortly after his arrival, "I yield to no one in my abhorrence to abortion...At the same time I do not believe that incurring arrest by violating the just laws of a municipality is the best strategy."[5] In short, he wanted a strong pro-life stance from the archdiocese. Those who wished to picket or protest should do so in a peaceful and legal manner.

Archbishop May lauded the great leadership role of Catholic women as directors of hospitals and presidents of colleges – an achievement neither matched nor recognized by secular society. Many religious orders and congregations of women were bigger than dioceses or larger corporations, he pointed out, and "women guide and govern them."[6] Consistent with this view, he appointed Sister Mary Ann Eckhoff, SSND, Director of the Archdiocesan Education office.

Archbishop May's term in St. Louis occurred during a period of great concern for "Women's History." Yet most of these stories recalled the achievement of American women without mentioning Mother Seton, religious founder, or Philippine Duchesne, the pioneer woman educator of the trans-Mississippi. Countless histories of the Civil War failed to mention that the only trained nurses at the outset of the conflict were Catholic nuns. Even feminist historians ignored nuns. Joanna L. Stratton's, *Pioneer Women*, for instance, lists 832 names. Not one is a nun.[7]

With the arrival of John May, St. Louis had a retired archbishop living in the community for the first time since 1895. At that time a lack of rapport between Archbishop Peter R. Kenrick and his successor Archbishop John Kain had caused uncertainties. In this century both Cardinals Glennon and Ritter had died while in office. What would be the relationship between Cardinal Carberry and his successor? An interviewer asked the new archbishop what activities he had in mind for his predecessor. "Whatever the Cardinal wants to do," Archbishop May responded, "I will be happy to have him do it." Mutual esteem keyed their relationships.

During his first year in St. Louis, Archbishop May accepted an invitation from the Jewish Congregation, Shaare Emeth (Gates of Truth), to the dedication of its new building in West St. Louis County. Founded in 1866, Shaare Emeth was the oldest "Reform" congregation in the city. He also joined the bishops of three Lutheran Churches in a pastoral letter commemorating the 450th anniversary of the "Augsburg Confession." This was a statement drawn up in 1530 by the humanist, Melanchthon, a follower of Luther, at the demand of the Catholic Emperor, Charles V, as basis for Lutheran-Catholic dialog. It could still serve in that way.

A department of Saint Louis University scheduled a talk by the avant-garde theologian and former professor at the Catholic University of America, Rev. Charles E. Curran. A number of individuals protested the University's invitation. Archbishop May stated his belief that communities of scholars found on university campuses are appropriate sites for a discussion of controversial issues.

Saint Louis University took a dramatic step forward a year later by welcoming the Aquinas Institute of the Dominican Fathers that had formerly made its home in Dubuque, Iowa. As it had done for most of the century, the University could boast once again of a School of Divinity.

By remaining in Midtown, when so many other institutions fled westward, the University anchored the area. Laclede Town several blocks east proved a disaster, but Powell Hall, the Fox Theatre and Sheldon Memorial took new life. Later on, under the leadership of Father Lawrence Biondi, the University undertook a program of campus beautification that made it a show place.

Archbishop May inaugurated a highly organized discussion program called RENEW under the direction of Fathers John Jay Hughes, historian, and William Scheib, pastor, and Sister Mary Ann Klohr, C.S.J., school principal. RENEW set out to introduce the average parishioner to the total vision of the Church called for by the Fathers of Vatican II. The only complaint that surfaced about this fine program was that it should have taken place shortly after the Council.

Archbishop May continued the initiatives of his predecessors. Under the leadership of John Cardinal Glennon, the Archdiocese had built the Great Cathedral on Lindell and began the installation of an amazing display of mosaic art. During the May years, the archdiocese brought this work to completion with half-domes of the Resurrection and the Descent of the Holy Spirit, and lunettes of Cardinal Ritter's achievements and the work of the missionaries of the past and present. Various artists had designed sections. Mosaicist Arno Heuduck, who had worked with his father Paul on the earlier mosaics, carried out the design of the artists who conceived the various sections.

In spite of rising costs that resulted in a nationwide drop in enrollment from six million to three million in Catholic schools, Archbishop May continued the archdiocesan tradition of emphasizing Catholic education. The Archdiocese opened nine new schools, expanded nineteen and consolidated others. As a service to the community, it kept open many inner city schools even though the majority of their black students were of other denominations.

A task force of the Archdiocesan Board of Education offered forty recommendations for the continued health of the Catholic educational enterprise. Major firms of the region assisted in the Today and Tomorrow Fund for scholarships, faculty support, and enhanced programs. An instance of the success of the Catholic educational program was the fact that more than ninety percent of seniors at Catholic high schools in the Archdiocese went on to college.

Archbishop Ritter had taken a dramatic step in leading the way in racial integration in the former slave states of the nation. Archbishop May continued the steady advance in race relations. During his years in Mobile, he had joined the Knights of St. Peter Claver, a fraternal order of black Catholic men. He had, in fact, dealt more personally with members of the black community there than Archbishop Ritter had done in Indianapolis or St. Louis. He so encouraged the Mobile branch of the Knights of St. Peter Claver that the members conferred on him its Fourth Degree. Grand Knight James M. Seals of Council Number One, the founding branch of the Society, said of Bishop May, "He was a godsend to the Mobile community."[8] That the entire Mobile community shared the feelings of Grand Knight Seals shows clearly in the action of the people at the time of Bishop May's departure. At his departure the Catholics in Mobile pledged one million dollars to Catholic Charities in his honor.[9]

In St. Louis Archbishop May continued his membership in the Knights of St. Peter Claver and reaffirmed the forward-looking policies of his predecessors. He went a step further in emphasizing a multi-cultural pattern in education. He welcomed the archdiocese's first black bishop, Father Terry Stieb, Provincial Superior of the Society of Divine Word.

Auxiliary Bishop John Wurm left his office in the chancery, by that time officially "The Catholic Center," to become Bishop of Belleville, Illinois. The Archdiocesan Superintendent of Schools, Msgr. John Leibricht, became Bishop of Springfield-Cape Girardeau and *Review* editor Edward O'Donnell became Auxiliary Bishop and Chancellor of St. Louis. Later Father Paul Zipfel was also consecrated Auxiliary Bishop.

In the document on the Church, the Fathers of the Second Vatican Council spoke of the diaconate, as "a ministry of service." The deacons could administer baptism, dispense the Eucharist, bless marriages, bring Viaticum to the dying, read sacred Scripture to the faithful, instruct and exhort the people and officiate at burial services. Responding to parochial needs, Archbishop May ordained an average of more than twelve permanent deacons a year during his twelve years in St. Louis.

Archbishop May had a few liturgical directions, both for those who wanted continual change and those who accepted no change whatsoever. As to the former, in the days of stoles and chasubles of various colors and design, Archbishop May prescribed a standard "archdiocesan chasuble." He recommended the silver or gold plated metal chalice over those made of crockery. He called for a continuation of the traditional silence in church and the genuflection before the Blessed Sacrament. To those who considered all changes suspicious, he asked, "Doesn't it seem natural that we Catholics would reach out to one another in a gesture of charity and unity just before going up the aisle together to receive the Body of the Lord?" He recommended wider use of Communion under both species.

Every year the Serra Club sponsored a benefit golf match at one of the local clubs. The Archbishop encouraged the Serrans in their work for the promotion of vocations. When he accepted the challenge to compete in the golf match, the tournament directors gave the name "Beat the Bishop" to the enjoyable proceedings. The golf scores made their way immediately into the "secret" files at the Archives.

The members of the St. Vincent de Paul Society renewed their double promise to practice virtue in their private lives and to assist their neighbor by direct action. As they prepared for the sesquicentennial of the Society in America, they found that many secular charitable institutions had begun to follow their tradition of personal involvement in helping the needy.

The Cardinal Ritter Institute, an archdiocesan agency, served the elderly. Our Lady of Life opened on property formerly belonging to Kenrick Seminary. The Catholic Charities Office, under the direction of Msgr. Robert Slattery, started various centers for the disadvantaged: the Catholic Commission on Housing and the Catholic Community Services. Many parishes and neighborhood groups organized to improve their areas. Sister Marie Charles, C.S.J., developed such a program for the Carondelet area. In recognition, the city named a park along the Mississippi River in her honor.

Church historian Father Timothy Dolan supervised changes and consolidations of the archdiocesan seminaries. The Kenrick Seminary building became a Pastoral Center for archdiocesan offices, retreats and meetings. The school itself joined with Glennon College to form Kenrick-Glennon Seminary in the former Glennon building. Prep-North, near the Florissant City Hall in St. Thomas Parish, closed its doors. The students moved to Prep-South on the Shrewsbury campus.

Many individuals of the Archdiocese, lay and religious, men and women, lived heroic Christ-like lives. Four pioneers of the first half of the last century received consideration for sainthood: Philippine Duchesne of the Religious of the Sacred Heart, Vincentians Father Felix De Andreis and Bishop Joseph Rosati, and the previously unmentioned Jesuit Peter Arnoudt, spiritual director and writer of a religious classic, whose cause was promoted in his native Belgium.[10] The causes of the three men stalled. Pope John Paul II declared Mother Duchesne a saint in 1988. Hundreds of St. Louis citizens made a pilgrimage to Rome on that occasion.

During the last two-thirds of the 1980s, Archbishop May had many duties outside of St. Louis, as Vice President (1983-86) and then President (1986-89) of the National Conference of Catholic Bishops. In one of his first duties in 1984, he chaired a study committee on the proposed Equal Rights Amendment. An out-state Missouri bishop recommended enactment. Archbishop May saw good and bad in the proposal and urged his fellow bishops to remain neutral on the issue. The majority of bishops approved his stand.

When ERA dropped from the headlines, AIDS took its place. Archbishop May recommended a more positive action in this matter. Even though many individuals looked on the AIDS epidemic as divine retribution, Archbishop May chose to leave the judgment to God. People with AIDS needed help and the Archbishop proposed an inter-faith effort to help those afflicted. He also urged a frank and open facing of the problem of pedophilia among priests. Many others thought that the ostrich pointed to the proper approach.

As the years advanced, expenditures rose. By the late 1980s, the Archdiocese faced a persistent budget deficit. Close to fifty percent of the parishes could not meet expenses. Some parishes faced midnight: either close or consolidate. Besides the closing and consolidating of various parishes, many urged the curtailment of many programs. This presented serious difficulties. Many were doing indispensable work. Archbishop May announced a hiring freeze and a moratorium on new building. Further action on the financial front seemed mandatory.

When inner city parishes that had lost their parishioners had to be closed, the Archbishop held back the "headache ball." He believed that the transference of these houses of worship to black congregations displayed a true Christian spirit.

To commemorate the Archbishop's 25th year as a bishop in 1992, Father John J. Hughes selected and edited many of the prelate's writings. The Liguori Press published this collection in a 343-page book entitled *With Staff and Pen*. Even a short reading gives a clear understanding of why John May won awards from the Catholic Press Association. It offers inspirational and informative reading. This was only one of the fine Liguori Press publications that guided Catholics throughout the nation.

The University of Missouri Press undertook the publication of a Dictionary of Missouri Biography. At the same time, the Oxford University Press planned a similar set of volumes to tell the story of the men and women who contributed to the growth and development of the nation. Several historians of the archdiocese wrote accounts of the many men and women who had their part in the growth and development of the state and the nation. Many of these notable historic figures were members of the Archdiocese.

When planning began for the Archbishop's 25th episcopal jubilee on November 22, 1992, he asked that it be an archdiocesan-wide celebration, with young people participating extensively. Before that day came, however, brain cancer struck the jubilarian. The people of the city prayed that he would have the strength to accept their demonstration of appreciation.

He was able to walk into the Arena assisted by Msgr. Bernard Sanheinrich and Father George J. Lucas. Thousands of Catholics came from all corners of the ten county archdiocese for the memorable occasion. Bishop O'Donnell, Administrator of the Archdiocese, read the homily the Archbishop had written. Archbishop May had his wish in that six hundred young people assisted as choir members, lectors, musicians, ushers, and intercession leaders. Logistically, the jubilee followed a master plan. Spiritually, the people of St. Louis gave a warm-hearted thanks to their Archbishop for his twelve years among them.

During those years he had guided the Archdiocese along an established course rather than into new directions. He made no landmark decisions, as Archbishop Kenrick had done in 1861 by maintaining neutrality in a divided state during the Civil War or Archbishop Ritter did in 1947 by integrating the parochial schools. Instead Archbishop May continued the fine initiatives of earlier years: Catholic education, parochial expansion, improved race relations, Pro-Life programs interdenominational dialog, and support of the missions, especially in La Paz, Bolivia. Priests of the Archdiocese labored there, and where Bishop Morgan Casey was Auxiliary Bishop, a position held earlier by another missionary from the Archdiocese Bishop Andrew Schierhoff.

Archbishop May confers with his auxiliaries: from the left: Bishop Terry Stieb, Edward O'Donnell, Paul A. Zipfel, George Gottwald and Charles R. Koester. (Review Photo)

The Archdiocese held Renew Sunday in September 1982. (Review Photo)

Epilogue –
Archbishop Justin Rigali:
Nearing A New Millennium

While all his predecessors had served in another American diocese before taking office in St. Louis, Archbishop Justin Rigali came directly from Rome where he had held various diplomatic and administrative posts under three Popes. The first far-westerner to lead the Church in St. Louis, the Archbishop had gone to Rome from Los Angeles shortly after his ordination in April 1961 to finish his doctorate in canon law at the Pontifical Gregorian University and to study at the pontifical Ecclesiastical Academy, a training school for Vatican diplomats.

After serving four years in the nunciature in Madagascar, he assisted Popes Paul VI, John Paul I and John Paul II as Director of the English language section of the Secretariat of State. Pope John Paul II ordained him titular Archbishop of Bolsena, Sept. 14, 1985, the year he became President of the Pontifical Ecclesiastical Academy. In 1989 he became Secretary of the Congregation of Bishops and early in 1990 Secretary of the College of Cardinals.

In January 1994 Pope John Paul II named him Archbishop of St. Louis. Bernadin Cardinal Gantin came from Rome to grace the new archbishop's installation in the Cathedral of Saint Louis on March 16, 1994. Eight American cardinals, the largest number ever officiating in any ceremony in St. Louis, added splendor to the gathering.

In his inaugural address, Archbishop Rigali greeted the many dignitaries and welcomed the presence of Orthodox and other Christians with whom the Church continued to exchange views, looking to reunion. "The wisdom of God, so dynamically presented in the Hebrew Scriptures," he said, "remained the basis for exchange with those of the Jewish faith. With our Muslim brethren, we honor the living God."

He pledged to work with civil authorities and private institutions in promoting human rights, to continue the strong Pro-Life efforts of his predecessors and to promote sound values in the areas of morality, education and family life.

Formidable challenges faced the new Archbishop. He had to act promptly and decisively on the temporary assignments Bishop O'Donnell had made during his fourteen months as administrator of the archdiocese. The Archbishop needed to stabilize the financial situation while continuing an extensive array of services rendered by archdiocesan offices.

City churches had lost their flocks to "white flight," and at the same time the archdiocese had to build new churches in subdivisions in West St. Louis County, St. Charles and Jefferson Counties. In the area east of Grand and north of Delmar, five parishes had recently closed down, due to unsound federal housing policies. One of the parishes, hoping to survive, sought government backing for a housing project of its own, only to be turned down for not having a "population mix." Few Catholics remained in the northwest quadrant of the city, west of Grand and north of Delmar, where fifteen parishes flourished fifty years before. Many church buildings lost their Catholic identity. Some kept schools going for predominantly Protestant pupils. Individual apostles, such as Mother Flora of the Convent Helpers, made converts, but no imaginative evangelistic program attempted to reach the adult newcomers.

Flourishing parishes on the South Side suffered, too. They felt the pressure of "forced busing" and the introduction of an abundance of government-sponsored tenants and dysfunctional families in once stable neighborhoods of home-owners. Catholics in parishes east of Grand and south of I-44 felt threatened. With each new plan to bus public school children, more white Protestant parents fled across the River Des Peres, leaving Catholics and Lutherans to hold their neighborhoods together.

In another area, too, the Archdiocese suffered. Vocations to the religious life, once so plentiful in St. Louis, dwindled. Several congregations had no novices. Would the schools and hospitals founded and developed by these congregations be able to keep their traditional Catholic spirit with fewer members to give the institutions stability? Were the busy members of these groups giving serious thought to this issue?

Before he could get well established in his residence on Lindell, the new Archbishop received a call that one of the most loved churches of the city, St. Anthony of Padua, the Franciscan-staffed parish on Meramec in South St. Louis, had caught fire. He visited the scene and offered support and encouragement to the Pastor and the people. They set out immediately to rebuild. He next visited Sacred Heart Parish in Valley Park that feared the spring run-off. Fortunately, the rising waters of 1994 did not match the flood of the century that had overwhelmed countless farms, homes and businesses during the previous year. He visited many other areas of the city and the ten counties of the archdiocese.

Archbishop Rigali decided to continue his predecessor's custom of writing a weekly column in the Review. He chose as his subjects the documents of our present Holy Father. He encouraged the wide use of the new *Catechism of the Church* and made copies available for all the priests.

The new Archbishop announced new members of his administrative team. Among them, Monsignor Richard F. Stika became Chancellor, and Very Rev. Joseph F. Naumann, Vicar General along with Bishop Paul Zipfel and the new Auxiliary Bishop Edward K. Braxton, formerly of the Archdiocese of Chicago. Bishop Edward J.

O'Donnell, who had handled the administration of the archdiocese so well during the fourteen months after the retirement of Archbishop May, left St. Louis to become Bishop of Lafayette, Louisiana.

George Henry, a former principal, succeeded Sister Mary Ann Eckhoff, SSND, as Superintendent of Education. Father Dennis M. Delaney became editor of the Review.

The St. Vincent de Paul Society prepared for the one-hundred and fiftieth anniversary of the founding of the first American conference in St. Louis back in 1845. Fittingly, the men and women of all American conferences gathered in St. Louis in September 1995 to celebrate the occasion. The National Spiritual Adviser of the Society, St. Louis' former auxiliary, Bishop Terry Stieb, transferred to Memphis, gave the keynote address.

Robert O'Donnell and Debbie Estopare of the St. Vincent de Paul office invited Father Donald W. Ramson, retiring President of the Kenrick Seminary and the present writer to prepare a memorial book for the anniversary. The contents included a sketch of the city at the time of the foundation, biographies of the pioneers who formed the first unit and the development beyond Cathedral Parish to the other parishes of the city. To mark, further, the anniversary celebration, the Society enlarged its Exchange Depot in the building to the east of its office on Forest Park Boulevard. Robert O'Reilly succeeded Robert Gronemeyer as president of the Metropolitan Central Council.

With so many offices, committees, councils and foundations in the archdiocese serving the needs of people so well, the budget soared over the years. The archdiocese drew up long-range plans "to stay in the black."

In an Advent message in 1995 Archbishop Rigali emphasized devotion to the Real Presence of the Lord in the Eucharist. The tabernacle should hold a prominent and beautifully decorated place, suitable for prayer. The parishes should hold extended periods of exposition on the Feast of Corpus Christi. The Archbishop recommended benediction and short periods of exposition at suitable times, Forty Hours' Devotion, and perpetual exposition in those religious communities and other pious associations that observe the devotion in accordance with their constitutions.

In September 1996, diocesan priests under the leadership of Rector-president George J. Lucas, the former Chancellor, took over the direction of Kenrick-Glennon Seminary. The Vincentian Fathers terminated their splendid years of service at the Seminary.

Bishop Du Bourg had invited the Vincentians to work in Missouri when he came as Bishop of Louisiana Territory in 1818. One of these Vincentians, Father Joseph Rosati, taught seminarians and lay students at St. Mary's in Perryville before becoming Bishop of St. Louis. The Vincentians continued in seminary education in the area through the succeeding century and three quarters. Archbishop Rigali and Vincentian Provincial John Gagnepain mutually announced the change. In greeting the fifty three seminarians shortly before his installation as Rector-President, Monsignor Lucas stressed this willingness to learn, openness to new attitudes, simplicity of life style, generosity to others, and respect for their integrity.

As the Archdiocese looked forward to its 150th anniversary in 1997 and the universal Church prepared for the coming of the Third Millennium of Christianity, the Archbishop called clergy, religious and laity to look forward with the hope that our Holy Father Pope John Paul II so ardently insisted all should have on this occasion.

Archbishop Justin Rigali taking a peaceful stroll by the Cathedral.

Three- and four-year olds welcome Archbishop Rigali at an orphanage in Cochabamba. Sister Joyce Schramm is one of seven Precious Blood Sisters of O'Fallon who work with Bolivian orphans. Standing behind the Archbishop is Msgr. Bernard H. Sandheinrich archdiocesan mission director.

Source Material

The main deposit of materials of value for this study was, not unexpectedly, the Saint Louis Archdiocesan Archives. Here one can find Rosati's carefully kept correspondence and diary, some letters of Du Bourg and such early missionary priests as Edmund Saulnier, the financial records of Kenrick, the correspondence of later archbishops, and some letters of other priests. The remainder of Kenrick's correspondence is scattered: in the Archives of the University of Notre Dame (especially his correspondence with Archbishop Edward Purcell of Cincinnati), in the Irish college in Rome, in the Seminary at Maynooth in Ireland, in the archives of the archdioceses of Philadelphia and Baltimore (especially his correspondence with his brother, Francis Patrick Kenrick), and in the Archives of the Propaganda in Rome. Materials on the Vincentians are available at Saint Mary's Seminary in Perryville and at the Archives of the Congregation of the Mission in Paris. Jesuit materials are at the Missouri Province Archives, including correspondence of the early missionaries, formerly available only at Woodstock College in Maryland. The Archives of the Mullen Library at the Catholic University of America contain the Powderly Papers, of use in the study of the relationships of the archdiocese and the Knights of Labor. Some of the early letters of Du Bourg are in the Archives at the Saint Louis Cathedral in New Orleans. Some of the records of the Cathedral of Saint Louis in Saint Louis appear in book form; others are available at the old cathedral or the chancery. Members of the St. Louis Catholic Archivists Association direct twenty-one religious archives open for research, in the St. Louis area. The archives of the Archdiocese are at Kenrick Seminary in Suburban St. Louis.

Supplementary Bibliography

Among recent books on the history of the Catholic Church in this country, the present writer's *American Catholic Heritage: Stories of Growth* (Kansas City: Sheed & Ward 1991) gives more attention to the Archdiocese of St. Louis than any other. The author writes from a midwestern vantage. He gives proper space to the French residents of the Mississippi Valley, to the significant place of the Archdiocese of St. Louis in the nineteenth century, and that of Chicago in the twentieth. He discusses the many church initiatives that grew up in the Midwest. Among older books in his four volume work, *The Catholic Church in the United States* (New York: John G. Shea, 1886-1892), John Gilmary Shea gives greater space to the Archdiocese of Saint Louis since it had a relatively more significant place in the period he discussed in his fourth volume (1843-1866).

Among the many histories of Missouri that bring out aspects of Church development, David March, *The History of Missouri*, 4 vols. (New York: Lewis Historical Publishing Company, 1967) serves a helpful purpose especially since it is the most recent at this time. Floyd C. Schomaker, *Missouri Day by Day*, 2 vols. (Columbia, Missouri, 1943), is a mine of historical information on events and personalities of the state arranged according to the day of the year when the event occurred. Louis Houck, *A History of Missouri from the Earliest Exploration and Settlement Until the Admission of the State into the Union*, 3 vols. (Chicago: R. R. Donnelly & Sons, 1908) is most helpful for the colonial and the territorial periods. Duane Meyer, *The Heritage of Missouri - a History* (Saint Louis: State Publishing Company, 1963), is an up-to-date, comprehensive, one-volume history of the state, with extensive and excellent, but unannotated bibliographies.

Two histories of the city served well for their times: J. Thomas Scharf, *History of Saint Louis, City and County*, 2 vols. (Philadelphia, Louis H. Everts and Co., 1883) and Frederick Louis Billon, *The Annals of Saint Louis in Its Early Days Under The French and Spanish Dominations* (Saint Louis, 1886). A most helpful short book is Charles E. Peterson's *Saint Louis: Building a Creole Capital* (Saint Louis: Saint Louis Historical Society, 1949). Two books of essays, edited by John Francis McDermott, *The French in the Mississippi Valley* (Urbana: University of Illinois Press, 1965) and *Frenchmen and French Ways in the Mississippi Valley* (Urbana: University of Illinois Press, 1969) give much background material of interest on early Saint Louis development.

In the period after World War I, Monsignors John Rothensteiner and Frederick Holweck, and Fathers Charles Souvay, C.M., and Gilbert Garraghan, S.J., and others, wrote a considerable number of articles on archdiocesan affairs in the five volumes of the *Saint Louis Catholic Historical Review*, the *Illinois Catholic Historical Review*, and *The Catholic Historical Review*. The work of these men culminated in John Rothensteiner's History of the Archdiocese of Saint Louis, 2 vols. (Saint Louis: Blackwell Wielandy Co., 1927), a lode of historical wealth. A fine account of Church origins in Saint Louis is Peter Rahill's *Catholic Beginnings in Saint Louis* (Saint Louis, 1964). Paul C. Schulte's *The Catholic Heritage of Saint Louis, A History of the Old Cathedral Parish* (Saint Louis, 1934) leans heavily on the work of John Rothensteiner in telling the interesting story of this Mother Church of the Upper Mississippi Valley. Gregory Franzwa brought the story of the old cathedral up to date with a popular account at the time of the bicentennial of Saint Louis (Saint Louis, 1965).

Many histories of religious orders shed light on the wider history of the archdiocese. Such were Gilbert J. Garraghan's monumental *The Jesuits of the Middle United States*, 3 vols. (New York: America Press, 1938), Marion Habig's *Heralds of the King* (Chicago: Franciscan Herald Press, 1958), Brother Hubert Gerard, F.S.C.'s *Mississippi Vista: The Brothers of the Christian Schools in the Midwest*, 1849-1949 (Winona: St. Mary's College Press, 1948), Sister Lilliana Owens, *Loretto on the Old Frontier* (1823-1864) (Saint Louis, 1965), and Sister Dolorita Dougherty's *Sisters of Saint Joseph of Carondelet* (Saint Louis: B. Herder Book Company, 1966).

Writers have given limited attention to the stories of the archbishops or bishops of Saint Louis. Only Easterly's *Life of Rosati* (Washington, 1942) is an adequate historical appraisal of a career of a Saint Louis bishop in book length. The section on Peter Richard Kenrick in John J. O'Shea's *The Two Kenricks* (Philadelphia: John J. McVey, 1904) is triumphal in tone. James Johnson's booklet on Joseph Cardinal Ritter gives many facts of the Saint Louis prelate's career up to 1964, the third session of Vatican II. It does not intend to be a final and authoritative appraisal. The present writer has a chapter "The Personality and Influence of Louis William Valentine Du Bourg: Bishop of "Louisiana and the Floridas' 1776-1833," in J. R. McDermott's *French Men and French Ways in the Mississippi Valley*, pp. 43-55. A factual account of the Saint Louis years of Bishop Du Bourg is Peter J. Rahill's "The Saint Louis Episcopacy of L. W. Du Bourg" in *Records of American Catholic Historical Society*, 78, no. 2 (June 1966), pp. 67-98. Father Nicholas Schneider has presented a readable account of *The Life of John Cardinal Glennon* (Liquori, Missouri: Liquori Press, 1972). His last section is especially valuable.

Mary Constance Smith collected extensive factual data on many Saint Louis priests in *Our Pastors in Calvary* (1854-1924) (Saint Louis, 1924). Bishop John J. Hogan gives much information on the Church in outstate Missouri in *On the Mission in Missouri* (Kansas City, 1892); Canon John O'Hanlon of Ireland recalled personalities and events of his years in Saint Louis (1843-1853) in *Life and Scenery in Missouri* (Dublin, 1890); Sister Mary Gilbert Kelly, O.P., devoted considerable attention to colonies in Missouri and Illinois, at the time part of the Saint Louis diocese, in *Catholic Immigrant Colonization Projects in the United States*, 1815-1860 (New York, 1939). Biographies of other American bishops proved most helpful, especially these: Peter Guilday, *The Life and Times of John Carroll, Archbishop of Baltimore*, 1735-1815 (New York: Encyclopedia Press, 1922); *The Life and Times of John England: First Bishop of Charleston*, 1786-1842, 2 vols. (New York: America Press, 1927); John Tracy Ellis, *The Life of James Cardinal Gibbons, Archbishop of Baltimore*, 1834-1921, 2 vols. (Milwaukee: Bruce Publishing Company, 1952); James H. Moynihan, *The Life of Archbishop John Ireland* (New York: Harper and Brothers, 1953); Hugh T. Nolan, *The Most Rev. Francis Patrick Kenrick, Third Bishop of Philadelphia* (1830-1851) (Washington, 1948); and M.M. Hoffman, *The Church Founders of the Northwest* (Milwaukee: Bruce Publishing Company, 1937), Bishops Matthias Loras of Dubuque and Joseph Cretin of St. Paul. Joseph Bernard Code gives biographical data on the bishops of the country to 1940 in *Dictionary of the American Hierarchy* (New York: 1940). Ralph Bayard, C.M., Lone Star Vanguard, *The Catholic Reoccupation of Texas*, 1828-1848 (Saint Louis: The Vincentian Press, 1945), tells the stories of Father Timon and Odin in their years in Saint Louis and on the Texas mission, and also gives much of the history of the Vincentians at the time.

Louise Callan, R.S.C.J., *Life of Philippine Duchesne, Frontier Missionary of the Sacred Heart*, 1769-1852 (Westminster: Newman Press, 1957) combines the story of Mother Philippine and the early years of the Religious of the Sacred Heart in the Saint Louis archdiocese.

Among specialized histories, one of the most helpful is Colman J. Barry, O.S.B., *The Catholic Church and the German Americans* (Milwaukee: Bruce Publishing Company, 1953). Daniel T. McColgan described the Saint Louis origins of the St. Vincent de Paul Society in *A Century of Charity: The First One Hundred Years of the St. Vincent de Paul Society in the United States* (Milwaukee: Bruce Publishing Company, 1951). Ray A. Billington's *The Protestant Crusade*, 1800-1860 (New York: The Macmillan Company, 1938) will long remain the authoritative study of nativism before the Civil War. An important recent book,

Philip Gleason's *The Conservative Reformers: German American Catholics and the Social Order* (Notre Dame: University of Notre Dame Press, 1968) tells of the *Central Verein* and its great leaders. *The Dictionary of American Biography* contains fine sketches of Philippine Duchesne, Joseph Rosati, Louis W.V. Du Bourg, Felix DeAndreis, Charles Van Quickenborne, Pierre Jean DeSmet, Peter Verhaegen, James Van De Velde, Peter Richard Kenrick, and David Phelan. Noteworthy among articles in the *New Catholic Encyclopedia* are those on Bishop Du Bourg, Cardinal Glennon, and the Saint Louis archdiocese, by Peter Rahill; on Bishop Rosati, by Frederick J. Easterly, C.M.; on Archbishop Ryan, by Joseph T. Durkin; on Peter De Smet, by W.L. Davis; on Archbishop Kenrick and Monsignor Holweck, by John J. Leibricht; on Fathers Phelan and Verhaegen, by Martin F. Hasting; on Father Souvay, by Newman C. Eberhardt; and Fathers Van Quickenborne and Edward Garesche, by Edward R. Vollmar.

A number of Saint Louis University theses and dissertations proved most helpful: Daniel M. Hogan's "The Catholic Church and the Negroes of Saint Louis" (1955); John T. White's "Survey of the Organized Work of the Catholic Church Among the Negroes in Saint Louis District" (1937); Sister Marie Felicity Hanratty's "A Study in Early Irish Contributions to the Growth of Saint Louis 1804-1840" (1933); Alice Cochran's "The Saga of an Irish Immigrant Family: The Descendants of John Mullanphy" (1958); Virgil C. Blum's "The German Element in Saint Louis 1859-1861" (1945); Walter J. Galus' "History of the Catholic Italians in Saint Louis" (1936); Clement S. Mihanovich's "Americanization of the Croats in Saint Louis, Missouri, During the Past Thirty Years" (1936); Fenton J. Runge's "National Parishes in the City of Saint Louis" (1955); George McHugh's "Political Nativism in Saint Louis 1840-1857" (1939), Donald Molitor's "The History of Glennonville and Adjacent Catholic Colonization Ventures in Southeast Missouri: A Study in Changing Rural-Urban Patterns, 1905-1947" (1965); Margaret LoPiccolo Sullivan's "Newpaper Attitudes Towards Saint Louis Minorities 1900-1923" (1968); Margaret Webster's "History of Catholic Hospitals in Saint Louis" (1968); Sister Isadore Lennon, R.S.H., "Social History of the Sisters of Mercy in Saint Louis" (1934); and Marie Mueller's "Parish Jubilee Booklets: A Problem in Historiography" (1952). Three recent works of great importance for a study of St. Louis Catholicism are Gary Mormino's *Immigrants on the Hill: Italian-Americans in St. Louis*, 1882-1892, (Champaign: University of Illinois Press, 1986); Faherty-Oliver's *Religious Roots of Black Catholics in St. Louis* (Florissant: St. Stanislaus Museum, 1977); and S. J. Miller, "Peter Richard Kenrick: Archbishop of St. Louis," in *Records of the American Catholic Historical Society of Philadelphia*, Vol. 84, No. 1-3, March June, 1973, a study of the theological views of the leading American theologian in the hierarchy.

The present author discussed the relations of Father O'Leary and the Knights of Labor in "The Clergyman and Labor Progess: Cornelius O'Leary and the Knights of Labor," *Labor History* 11, no. 2 (Spring 1970): 175-189. He explored bigotry in Saint Louis in "Nativism and Midwestern Education: The Experience of Saint Louis University, 1832-1856," *The History of Education Quarterly* (Winter 1968): 447-458. In other recent periodical literature, Father Stafford Poole, C.M., described the story of Saint Mary's College and Seminary in Perryville in *The Missouri Historical Review* 65, no. 1 (October 1970): 1-22.

Notes

ABBREVIATIONS

ACM — Archives of the Congregation of the Mission, Paris.
BAA — Baltimore Archdiocesan Archives
FCV — Files of the *Central Verein*
KFL — Kenrick-Frenaye Correspondence
LUND — Library of the University of Notre Dame
Md. Prov. Arch. — Maryland Province Archives-Jesuit Order
Mo. Gaz. — *Missouri Gazette*
Mo. Prov. Arch. — Missouri Province Archives-Jesuit Order
SLAA — Saint Louis Archdiocesan Archives
SLU Arch — Saint Louis University Archives
SLCHR — *Saint Louis Catholic Historical Review*

Introduction

1. John Gunther, *Inside U.S.A.* (New York: Harper & Brothers, 1947), p. 353.

I. SAINT LOUIS: FRONTIER PARISH

1. *The Dream of Pierre Laclede*

1. For a more complete view of the personality and significance of the founder of Saint Louis, see John Francis McDermott, "Myths and Realities Concerning the Founding of Saint Louis," in a volume edited by John Francis McDermott, *The French in the Mississippi Valley* (Urbana: University of Illinois Press, 1965), pp. 1-15.

2. Chouteau later became chief clerk of Maxent & Co., and still later executor of Laclede's affairs. That anyone could consider a fourteen-year-old boy co-founder of a city is preposterous, except in that wide sense that all with Laclede at the time were "co-founders." In his mature years he gradually became a continually more distinguished member and finally leader of the community. See John Francis McDermott, ed., "Auguste Chouteau: First Citizen of Upper Louisiana," in *Frenchmen and French Ways in the Mississippi Valley* (Urbana: University of Illinois Press, 1969), pp. 1-13.

3. "Fragment of Col. Auguste Chouteau's Narrative of the settlement of St. Louis," in *Missouri Historical Collections* 4, 4 (1911): pp. 352-353. Chouteau wrote: "And he named it Saint Louis, in honor of Louis XV, whose subject he expected to remain for a long time . . . ."

4. Clarence W. Alvord, *The Illinois Country, 1673-1818* (Springfield: Illinois Centennial Commission, 1920), p. 218.

5. Frederick Louis Billon, *Annals of St. Louis in its Early Days Under the French and Spanish Dominations* (St. Louis: Printed for the author, 1886), pp. 17, 20, 29, 45. See also Louis Houck, *A History of Missouri* (Chicago: R. R. Donnelley & Sons, Company, 1908), 2: 12.

6. Billon, *Annals of St. Louis*, p. 27; Houck, *A History of Missouri* 2:17-18. On social conditions in early Saint Louis, see Charles E. Peterson, *Colonial St. Louis: Building a Creole Capital* (Saint Louis: Missouri Historical Society, 1949).

7. Alvord, *Illinois Country*, p. 195.

8. Billon, *Annals of St. Louis*, pp. 76, 95.

9. Jean Delanglez, S.J., *The French Jesuits in Lower Louisiana* (Washington: The Catholic University of America, 1935), pp. 495-515.

10. Charles H. Metzger, S.J., "Sebastian Louis Meurin," *Illinois Catholic Historical Review* 3, no. 3 (Jan. 1921): 253-259.

11. Ibid., 3, no. 4 (Apr. 1921): 371-372.

12. Parish Records of the Church of Saint Louis, in Old Cathedral Archives. A copy of Collet's Index to these records and those of the Church in Carondelet is in the Pius XII Library, St. Louis. See also, Billon, *Annals of St. Louis*, p. 79; and John Rothen-steiner, *History of the Archdiocese of St. Louis* (St. Louis: Blackwell Wielandy Co., 1927), 1: 102. A mine of information on parish development and personnel, but uneven, and not always presented in the wider focus of American Church history.

13. Billon, *Annals of St. Louis*, p. 98.

14. Parish Records of the Church of Saint Louis.

15. Alvord, *Illinois Country*, p. 318. Philippe Rocheblave, a Frenchman by birth, commanded at Ste. Genevieve during the early years of the Spanish domination. Later he quarrelled with the Spanish, fled across the Mississippi, and entered the British service at Kaskaskia. He was hardly the man to criticize Meurin for lacking loyalty to Spain.

16. Parish Records of the Church of Saint Louis. See also Houck, *A History of Missouri*, pp. 306-307.

17. Rothensteiner, *History of the Archdiocese* 1: 107.

18. Ibid., 1: 108.

19. Ibid., 1: 142-143.

20. Billon, *Annals of St. Louis*, p. 140; see also J. Thomas Scharf, *History of Saint Louis City and County* (Philadelphia: Louis H. Everts and Co., 1883), p. 1640.

21. Parish Records of the Church of Saint Louis; see also Rothensteiner, 1: 145.

22. Billon, *Annals of St. Louis*, p. 140.

23. Houck, *A History of Missouri* 2: 29.

24. Parish Records of the Church of Saint Louis.

25. Billon, *Annals of St. Louis* 1: 79; Scharf, *History of Saint Louis*, p. 305.

26. Billon, *Annals of St. Louis* 1: 102.

27. Ibid., 1: 303.

28. Samuel Knox Wilson, "Bishop Briand and the American Revolution," *The Catholic Historical Review* 19, no. 2 (July 1933): 143-144.

29. Joseph P. Donnelly, S.J., "Pierre Gibault and the Critical Period of the Illinois Country, 1768-78," in McDermott, *The French in the Mississippi Valley*, pp. 81-91.

30. J. B. Culemans, "Catholic Explorers and Pioneers of Illinois," *The Catholic Historical Review* 4, no. 2 (July 1918): 167.

31. Houck, *A History of Missouri* 2: 38.

32. John Rothensteiner, "Paul de Saint Pierre, The First German-American Priest of the West," *The Catholic Historical Review* 5, nos. 2-3 (July-Oct. 1919): 195-222. (Hereafter *Cath. Hist. Rev.*)

33. *Illinois Historical Collections* 1: 588, 592.

34. *American Catholic Historical Researches* 23: 203-239.

35. Ibid., pp. 217-218.

36. Ibid., pp. 218-219.

37. Ibid., pp. 221-223.

38. *Decree of the Propaganda*, quoted in the *Records* of the American Catholic Historical Society of Philadelphia 18: 162.

39. *American Catholic Historical Researches* 23: 223-225.

40. Rothensteiner, *History of the Archdiocese* 1: 182-183. See also *Cath. Hist. Rev.* 5, nos. 2-3: 220-222.

41. Rothensteiner, *History of the Archdiocese* 1: 184, 186.

2. River Valley Reunited

1. Rothensteiner, *History of the Archdiocese* 1: 152-154. Father Bernard's only extant letter, written to his Superior in New Orleans in 1787, is in the Library of the University of Notre Dame. (Hereafter LUND.)

2. Ibid., 1: 155.

3. Parish Records of the Church of Saint Louis (The Old Cathedral).

4. Perez to Miro, quoted in Louis Houck, *The Spanish Regime in Missouri* (Chicago: R. R. Donnelley & Sons, 1909), 2: 223. Houck misdates this letter Nov. 9, 1797. In his *A History of Missouri* 2: 309, he gives the date as 1789. This was the time of Father Le Dru's pastorate (1789-1794), of Miro's governorship (1785-1791) (Houck, *The Spanish Regime* 1: 208 n.) and Perez' lieutenant-governorship (1788-1793) (Ibid., 2: 224 n.).

5. Parish Records of the Church of Saint Louis. See also Rothensteiner, *History of the Archdiocese* 1: 212.

6. Trudeau to Carondelet, Oct. 7, 1792, in Houck, *The Spanish Regime* 1: 351. Abraham Nasatir and Noel Loomis combined on a fine account of the exploits and explorations of Vial, entitled *Pedro Vial and the Roads to Santa Fe* (Norman: University of Oklahoma Press, 1967).

7. Quoted by Bishop Penalver in a letter to the governor, Don Manuel Gayoso de Lemos, Feb. 14, 1798, in Houck, *The Spanish Regime* 2: 222.

8. Ibid.

9. Trudeau's Report of 1798, in Houck, *The Spanish Regime* 2: 248-250.

10. Rothensteiner, *History of the Archdiocese* 1: 202-204.

11. Houck, *A History of Missouri* 2: 311.

12. Ibid., 3: 365.

13. Hassett to Carroll, Dec. 23, 1803, in Baltimore Cathedral Archives, Case 4-D 5. (Hereafter BCA.)

14. Archives of the Propaganda, Rome, Letters, 289, F. 356.

15. Walsh to Catholics of New Orleans, Mar. 27, 1805, BCA, Case 11-B 3.

16. Archives of the Propaganda, Particular congregations, 145, F. 95-96.

17. Castillon to Carroll, Apr. 12, 1805, in BCA, Case 2-L 8.

18. BCA, Case 2-W 3.

19. BCA, 4-E 7.

20. BCA, Case 5-E 7.

21. With its relatively larger Creole population, New Orleans, by way of contrast, saw a slower development of rapport between the Creoles and the Anglo-American newcomers.

22. Dorothy Garesche Holland, "St. Louis Families from the French West Indies," in McDermott, *The French in the Mississippi Valley*, pp. 40-58.

23. Scharf, *History of Saint Louis* 2: 1641.

24. Gilbert Garraghan, S.J., "The Trappists of Monks Mound," *Illinois Catholic Historical Review* 8, no. 1 (July 1925): 106-135.

25. Ibid., pp. 113-114.

26. Ibid., p. 144.

27. Ibid., pp. 115-119.

28. Ibid., pp. 119-124. See also Gilbert Garraghan, *Chapters in Frontier History* (Milwaukee: Bruce Publishing Co., 1933), pp. 94-135.

29. Sarah Guitar and Floyd Shoemaker, "The Missouri Chronicle, 1673-1924," *The Missouri Historical Review* 19 (1925): 215.

30. For a thorough look at the career of Father James Maxwell, confer John Rothensteiner, "Father James Maxwell of Ste.

Genevieve," *Saint Louis Catholic Historical Review* 4 (1922): 3. (Hereafter *SLCHR*.)

31. John Rothensteiner, "The Northeastern Part of the Diocese of St. Louis Under Bishop Rosati," *Illinois Catholic Historical Review* 2, no. 2 (Oct. 1919): 181.

32. John Reynolds, *My Own Times* (Illinois, 1855), p. 183.

II. LOUIS W. V. DU BOURG:
PROMOTIONAL PRELATE (1815-1825)

3. A Prince-Bishop of the Old Regime

1. John C. Fitzpatrick, *Diaries of George Washington, 1748-1789* (Boston: Houghton Mufflin, 1925), 4: 280. For a more close look at the life of Bishop Du Bourg, see Peter J. Rahill, 'The St. Louis Episcopacy of L. William Du Bourg, in *Records* of the American Catholic Historical Society, 78, no. 2 (June 1966): 67-98; and William Barnaby Faherty, "The Personality and Influence of Louis William Valentine Du Bourg: Bishop of Louisiana and the Floridas (1776-1833)," in J. F. McDermott, ed., *Frenchmen and French Ways in the Mississippi Valley*, pp. 43-55.

2. Charles Herbermann, *The Sulpicians in the United States* (New York: The Encyclopedia Press, 1916), pp. 94-95.

3. *Memorial Volume of the Centenary of St. Mary's Seminary* (Baltimore, 1891), passim.

4. Peter Guilday, *The Life and Times of John Carroll* (New York: The Encyclopedia Press, 1922), 2: 583. Chapter 24 of this fine work, entitled "Archbishop Carroll's Extra-diocesan Jurisdiction," gives valuable background material on the relationships of Bishop Du Bourg and Archbishop Carroll and the creation of the first American see west of the Mississippi.

5. *Metropolitan Catholic Almanac and Laity's Directory, 1839* (Baltimore, 1839), pp. 51ff. This issue of the *Directory* contains an account of the main events of Bishop Du Bourg's career.

6. Herbermann, *Sulpicians in the United States*, p. 222.

7. *Catholic Directory*, 1839, pp. 53-55.

8. Carroll to Du Bourg, Baltimore, August 1812, quoting the Pontifical Brief of Apr. 6, 1808. *The Catholic Historical Review* 4: 56 n., carried these two documents.

9. Martin Spalding, *Sketches of the Life, Times, and Character of the Rt. Rev. Benedict Joseph Flaget* (Louisville: Webb and Lavering, 1855), pp. 163-164. See also Charles Souvay, C.M., "A Centennial of the Church in St. Louis," in the *Catholic Historical Review* 4, no. 11: 61.

10. Du Bourg to Carroll, Feb. 29, 1813, in the Shea Collection, Georgetown University Archives, Washington, D.C.

11. Du Bourg to Carroll, Apr. 29, 1813, Georgetown University Archives.

12. Spalding, *Sketches*, passim. When Spalding wrote his life of Flaget in 1855 all of this journal was available to him. Since that time large sections have disappeared.

13. Flaget's Journal, June 18, 1814, quoted in Spalding, *Sketches*, p. 132.

14. Ibid., July 4, 1814.

15. Spalding, *Sketches*, p. 133.

16. Flaget's Journal, Aug. 3, 1814.

17. Ibid., Sept. 14, 1814.

18. Archives of the Propaganda, Letters, 296, F. 248.

19. Du Bourg to Dugnani, Apr. 11, 1816, in the Archives of the Propaganda, Rome, 1 LC, Code 3, F. 369.

20. Ibid.

21. Ibid.

22. Du Bourg to De Andreis, Apr. 24, 1816, in Saint Louis Archdiocesan Archives. (Hereafter SLAA.)

23. Ibid.

24. Du Bourg to Dunagni, June 24, 1816, in Archives of the Propaganda, LC, Code 3, Ff. 372-373.

25. Flaget to Olivier, Feb. 8, 1816, in SLAA.

26. Flaget to Neale, June 26, 1816, in *American Catholic Historical Researches* 19: 108-109.

27. Ibid.

28. Letter of Du Bourg, Dec. 28, 1816. Archives of the Propaganda, LC, Code 3, Ff. 387-388.

29. De Andreis to Sicardi, Jan. 5, 1817; quoted in Joseph Rosati, *Life of Felix de Andreis* (Saint Louis: B. Herder, 1900), p. 154.

4. Bourbon Bishop on the American Frontier

1. *Annales de la Propagation de la Foi* 2: 331.

2. *Bulletin des Ecoles Chretiennes* (Nov. 1907): 370.

3. Brother Angelus Gabriel, F.S.C., *The Christian Brothers in the United States, 1848-1948* (New York: The Declan X. McMullen Company, 1949), p. 50.

4. Letter to Propaganda, June 16, 1817, Archives of the Propaganda, LC., Code 3, F. 453.

5. *Annales de la Propagation de la Foi* 2: 334-335.

6. Rosati, *Life of Felix de Andreis* p. 169.

7. Ibid., pp. 170-171.

8. Ibid., pp. 172-173.

9. Ella M. Frick, ed., "Diary of Father Marie Joseph Dunand," *Records of the American Catholic Historical Society* 27 (1916): 49-50.

10. Letter of Father A. Blanc, *Annales de la Propagation de la Foi* 2:36.

11. De Andreis to Sicardi, Feb. 24, 1818, quoted in Rosati, *Life of Felix de Andreis*, p. 182.

12. Charles Souvay, C.M., *Catholic Historical Review* 4, no. 1 (Apr. 1918): 66-69.

13. Marechal to Gradwell, June 24, 1823, in Thomas A. Hughes, *History of the Society of Jesus in North America, Colonial and Federal* (New York, 1907-1917), Documents, 2: 1018-1019.

14. Louise Callen, R.C.S.J., *Philippine Duchesne* (Westminster: Newman Press, 1957), p. 305. Thorough and authoritative.

15. Du Bourg's Cathedral Account Book, in SLAA.

16. *Catalogus Cleri Diocesis S. Ludovici*, A.D. 1818, p. 23, in SLAA.

17. Du Bourg to Dugnani, Feb. 16, 1819, in *SLCHR* 1, no. 3 (Apr. 1919): 190.

18. *Missouri Gazette and Public Advertiser* 11 (Oct. 23, 1818): 525. (Hereafter *Mo. Gaz.*.)

19. *SLCHR* 1, no. 1 (Oct. 1918).

20. Pratte to Rosati, Dec. 23, 1818, quoted in *SLCHR* 5 (1923): 132-133.

21. Brother Angelus Gabriel, *Christian Brothers in the United States*, p. 53.

22. John Paxton, *The Saint Louis Directory and Register* (St. Louis: printed for the publisher, 1821), p. 261 of 1854-1855 supplementary reprint.

23. Parish Account Book, p. 21, in SLAA.

24. Ibid., passim.

25. *Mo. Gaz.*, 11 (Sept. 11, 1819).

26. Ibid.

27. Timon to Rosati, June 1, 1822, in LUND.

28. *Mo. Gaz.*, 12 (Dec. 8, 1819): 584.

29. Ibid., 12 (Aug. 23, 1820): 621.

30. Ibid., 13 (Oct. 3, 1820): 624.

31. Ibid., 13 (Oct. 18, 1820): 629.

32. Paxton, *Saint Louis Directory*, p. 261.

33. Circular Letter of John C. Calhoun, Sept. 3, 1818, Re: Indian Schools, in the Archives of the Missouri Province, Pius XII Library, Saint Louis University. See also *Mo. Gaz.* 12 (Feb. 23, 1820): 595.

34. Edwin W. Hemphill, editor of the Calhoun Papers, to Dr. R. Adams, Feb. 21, 1966; copy in SLU Archives.

35. *Annales de la Propagation de la Foi* 1: 438, 482.

36. Louis W. Du Bourg, ed., *Officia Propria pro Diocesi Ludovicensi* (Saint Louis: James Cummings, 1821).

37. Ibid., p. 2.

5. New Orleans Beckons

1. Du Bourg to Dugnani, Feb. 16, 1819, in *SLCHR* 1 (1919): 190. Also Du Bourg to Litta, May 12, 1819, in *SLCHR* 1 (1919): 191-196.

2. Propaganda to Du Bourg, Aug. 20, 1820, *SLCHR* 2 (1920): 51.

3. De Sedella to Du Bourg, Jan. 2, 1819, in the Archives of the Cathedral of New Orleans.

4. Gilbert Garraghan, *The Jesuits in the Middle United States* (New York: America Press, 1938), 1: 367. (This three-volume work is an authoritative guide to the history of an order that worked in the Saint Louis area since 1823.) See also Edward J. Hickey, *The Society for the Propagation of the Faith, 1822-1922* (Washington, 1922).

5. Du Bourg to Fontana, May 8, 1821, in *SLCHR* 5 (1923): 32.

6. Consalvi to Du Bourg, Jan. 11, 1822, in *SLCHR* 2 (1920): 211.

7. *SLCHR* 2 (1920): 138.

8. Ibid.

9. Du Bourg to Borgna, Feb. 27, 1823, *SLCHR* 3 (1921): 123.

10. Ibid.

11. Brother Angelus Gabriel, *Christian Brothers in the United States*, p. 55.

12. *U.S. Catholic Miscellany*, Charleston, S.C., 3, no. 2 (1824): 43-46.

13. Du Bourg to Rosati, letters from July 16 to Sept. 23, 1822, in SLAA.

14. Paxton, *Saint Louis Directory*.

15. *Enquirer* (Saint Louis), Sept. 2, 1822.

16. Ibid.

17. Du Bourg's Cathedral Account Book, in SLAA.

18. *The St. Louis Assessment Book of 1820* showed that Auguste Chouteau, the richest man in the city at the time, had a total estate valued at $76,600; Pierre Chouteau's estate reached $15,160, and Bernard Pratte's $9,800. (Reprinted in *St. Louis Globe-Democrat*, 1893.)

19. Paul Schulte, *The Catholic Heritage of Saint Louis* (Saint Louis, 1934), pp. 115-119. This generally solid study of the old cathedral parish of Saint Louis leaned heavily on Rothensteiner; the fiscal material in this present section used extensively Du Bourg's Cathedral Account Book, in SLAA.

20. Rosati to the Secretary of the Propagation of the Faith, Saint Louis, Apr. 23, 1830, in SLAA.

21. Elihu Shepard, *Autobiography* (Saint Louis: George Knapp and Co., 1869), p. 103.

22. *Registrum Ecclesiae St. Ludovici*, in SLAA.

23. *Missouri Republican* 2 (1823-1824): *passim*.

24. Resolution of the Mayor and the Board of Aldermen, City of Saint Louis, Sept. 10, 1825 (Microfilm Dept. Code F, 488).

25. Outline of Career of Edmund Saulnier in SLAA.

26. *Missouri Republican* 3154, Mar. 7, 1825.

27. Baptismal Register, St. Ferdinand's Parish, Florissant, Missouri.

28. Du Bourg to Fontana, Feb. 24, 1821, in *SLCHR* 2 (1920): 136.

29. Calhoun to Du Bourg, Feb. 20, 1823, *Calhoun Papers*, FC in DNA, 72 E 392.

30. Du Bourg to Marechal, Mar. 6, 1823, in BAA.

31. Du Bourg to Borgna, Feb. 27, 1823, in *SLCHR* 2 (1921): p. 123.

32. Du Bourg to Calhoun, Mar. 17, 1823; *Calhoun Papers*, LS in DNA 77.

33. Du Bourg to his brother, Mar. 17, 1823, in Records of the American Catholic Historical Society 14: 149.

34. Agreement of Mar. 19, 1823, in the Archives of the Missouri Province of the Jesuit order, Pius XII Library, Saint Louis, Missouri.

35. Calhoun to Du Bourg, Mar. 21, 1823: *Calhoun Papers*, FC in DNA, 72.

36. Quoted in Garraghan, *Jesuits in the Middle United States*, 1: 58.

37. Marechal to Gradwell, June 24, 1823, in Hughes, *History of the Society of Jesus*, 1, 2: 1018-1019.

38. Walter Hill, S.J., *Historical Sketches* (unpublished), p. 34, in the Archives of the Missouri Province.

39. Father Peter Kenney, official Visitor of the Jesuit missions in the United States, reported to the Father General in 1832 that he had never known Jesuit superiors as severe as Van Quickenborne, and his successor De Theux (Peter Kenney to John Roothaan, Saint Louis, Feb. 22, 1832, in Jesuit General Archives in Rome; copy in Folder 491 in Cudahy Memorial Library, Loyola University, Chicago). Father John Elet wrote to the superior in Maryland: "The government of Rev. Father Van Quickenborne is deemed by all his subjects intolerable" (Elet to Dzierozynski, Florissant, Aug. 29, 1830, 3, M, 11, in Maryland Province Archives, Woodstock College, Woodstock, Md.). Elet later became president of Saint Louis University and vice-provincial of Missouri.

40. Bishop Du Bourg complained in 1825 that Van Quickenborne was evasive and silent in a way the bishop did not expect of a Jesuit. The bishop wanted to ordain several of the Jesuit theology students. Van Quickenborne hesitated. "He constantly eluded the question," Du Bourg wrote: "and now he writes me that the thing does not depend on him, without telling me on whom it does depend." (Du Bourg to Dzierozynski, July 10, 1825, in Md. Prov. Arch., 30, 2, 7.)
Van Quickenborne's treatment of De Theux, the Belgian nobleman and distinguished priest sent out to help him at Florissant, could only have resulted in ill-feeling between De Theux and the other men not yet ordained (Van Quickenborne to Dzierozynski, Florissant, Nov. 29, 1827, in Md. Prov. Arch., 30, Q, 11).
The young Jesuits frequently complained of the confusing set-up in the administration of the mission (Elet to Dzierozynski, undated, presumably Dec. 1828, in Md. Prov. Arch., 30, P, 10; De Smet to Verhaegen, Florissant, May 2, 1830; 30, M, 8; Verhaegen to Dzierozynski, Saint Louis, Aug. 20, 1830, 30, M, 9).

41. Du Bourg to the Jesuit superior in Maryland, Nov. 27, 1823, in Mo. Prov. Arch., 30, M, 8.

42. Du Bourg to Dzierozynski, Jan. 7, 1824, Georgetown University Archives; Van Quickenborne to Dzierozynski, Jan. 1, 1824, in Md. Prov. Arch., 30, T, 1.

43. Letters of Edmund Saulnier, passim, in SLAA.

6. Du Bourg Withdraws from Missouri

1. Rosati to Consalvi, Apr. 2, 1823, in *SLCHR* 3 (1921): 313 n.

2. Pius VII to Bishop-elect Rosati, July 14, 1823, in SLAA.

3. Diary of Bishop Rosati, Dec. 6, 1823, in SLAA. The Diary of Bishop Rosati is one of the most valuable ecclesiastical records of the midwestern Church in his time.

4. Nerinckx to Rosati, Jan. 2, 1824, in SLAA.

5. *U.S. Catholic Miscellany*, Charleston, S.C., 3, no. 2 (1824): 43-46.

6. Rosati to his brother, Mar. 29, 1824, in SLAA.

7. Rosati to Baccari, July 14, 1824, in SLAA.

8. *Catholic Historical Review* 3, no. 2 (July 1917): 177.

9. Diary of Bishop Rosati, Aug. 16, 1825, in SLAA.

10. Ibid., Nov. 27, 1825.

11. Du Bourg to Dzierozynski, July 10, 1825, in Md. Prov. Arch., Folder 30, Z, 7.

12. Du Bourg to Dzierozynski, Oct. 24, 1825, in Md. Prov. Arch., Folder 30, Z, 8.

13. Diary of Bishop Rosati, Nov. 25, 1825, in SLAA.

14. Flaget to Baccari, Jan. 1, 1826, in SLAA.

15. Du Bourg to Caprano, undated, but presumably in early 1826, *SLCHR* 2 (1920): 209-211; and Du Bourg to Caprano, Feb. 27, 1826, *SLCHR* 3 (1921): 206-207.

16. Rosati to Portier, Mar. 10, 1826, *SLCHR* 4 (1922): 180.

17. Du Bourg to Dzierozynski, July 10, 1825, in Md. Prov. Arch.

18. Diary of Bishop Rosati, Jan. 29, 1826, and Mar. 11, 1826, in SLAA.

19. Ibid.

20. Ibid., Apr. 20, 23, 1826.

21. Du Bourg to Rosati, May 11, 1826, in SLAA.

22. Saulnier to Rosati, June 6, 1826, in SLAA.

23. Petitioners to Rosati, Aug. 27, 1826, in SLAA.

24. Rosati to the Trustees, Sept. 1, 1826, in SLAA.

25. Diary of Bishop Rosati, Sept. 12, 1826, in SLAA.

26. Ralph Bayard, *Lonestar Vanguard, The Catholic Reoccupation of Texas (1838-1848)* (Saint Louis: The Vincentian Press, 1945), p. 11. Gives insights into the lives of Fathers John Timon and John Odin, Vincentians who worked in Saint Louis and became bishops elsewhere.

27. Saulnier to Rosati, Sept. 12, 1826, in SLAA.

28. Rosati to Baccari, Nov. 17, 1826, in SLAA.

29. Ibid.

30. Spalding, *Sketches*, pp. 280-281.

31. *Apostolic Brief*, Mar. 20, 1827, in SLAA.

32. Rosati to Cappellari, July 14, 1827, in SLAA.

33. Rosati to Du Bourg, Sept. 14, 1828, in St. Mary's (Perryville) Archives; also *SLCHR* 4 (1922): 192.

34. Van Quickenborne to Dzierozynski, Nov. 17, 1828, in Md. Prov. Arch.

35. Van Quickenborne to Fortis, Sept. 9, 1830, and Dzierozynski to Fortis, May 10, 1827, in the Jesuit General Archives in Rome.

III. ROSATI: SAINTLY PASTOR (1827-1843)

7. *A Missionary Bishop Lays Plans*

1. Shepard, *Autobiography*, p. 103.

2. *Ninth Census, The Statistics of the Population of the United States* (Washington: Government Printing Office, 1872), 1: 194.

3. Peter Guilday, *The Life and Times of John England, The First Bishop of Charleston, 1786-1842* (New York: The America Press, 1927), 1: 7. The author describes the career of an influential American bishop, a close friend of Rosati; and, incidentally, describes the development of the American Church in England's time.

4. Callan, *Philippine Duchesne*, p. 455.

5. Cholleton to Rosati, May 27, 1827, in SLAA.

6. Paul Beckwith, *Creoles of Saint Louis* (Saint Louis: Nixon-Jones Printing Co., 1893), p. 136.

7. Rosati to Mother M. Augustine, Oct. 14, 1828, in SLAA.

8. Rosati to Mother Augustine, Nov. 27, 1828, in the Archives of the Sisters of Charity, Emmitsburg, Md.

9. John Darby, *Personal Recollections* (Saint Louis: G. I. Jones and Co., 1880), p. 258.

10. Garraghan, *Jesuits in the Middle United States* 1: 210.

11. Verhaegen, "Narrative of the Church of St. Charles," Archives of the Missouri Jesuit Province, Saint Louis. For a complete discussion of Verhaegen's career, confer William B. Faherty, S.J., "Peter Verhaegen: Pioneer Missouri Educator and Church Administrator," *Missouri Historical Review* 60, no. 4 (July 1966): 407-415.

12. Garraghan, *Jesuits in the Middle United States* 1, 212 n.

13. *Annales de la Propagation de la Foi* 3: 572.

14. Saulnier to Rosati, Feb. 24, 1829 in SLAA. The Chouteau donation at the funeral was three dollars and a half.

15. Peter Guilday, *Life and Times of John England* 2: 396.

16. Rosati to England, Dec. 7, 1826, in SLAA.

17. Quoted in full in Peter Guilday, ed., *National Pastorals of the American Hierarchy*, 1792-1919 (n.p., 1923), pp. 18-19.

18. Rosati to Van Quickenborne, Dec. 29, 1829, Abstracts of Correspondence, book 6, no. 223, in SLAA.

19. Rosati to Bishop Lartique of Montreal, June 10, 1828, Abstracts of Correspondence, book 5, no. 142, in SLAA.

20. Rosati to Le Saulnier, Feb. 24 and Sept. 15, 1826, Abstracts of Correspondence, book 1, no. 25118, in SLAA.

8. *The Bishop Moves to Saint Louis*

1. Rosati to Cardinal Cappellari, July 14, 1827, *Epistolae ad Emos. Cardinales de Propaganda Fide*, no. 10.

2. Rosati to Salhorgne, May 26, 1830, Archives of the Congregation of the Mission, Paris, France. The author leaned heavily on the earlier researches of Frederick J. Easterly (*Life of Rt. Rev. Joseph Rosati* [Washington: Catholic University Press, 1942]). He was able to pay only a short visit to the central headquarters of the Congregation of the Mission in Paris.

3. Rosati to Cholleton, Jan. 24, 1830, *Annales de la Propagation de la Foi* 4: 593-595.

4. *Leopoldine Reports* 1, passim. (A bound copy is in the Library of the Catholic University of America.)

5. Rosati to the Leopoldine Foundation, Mar. 10, 1830, in *Leopoldine Reports* 1: 28-35.

6. Ibid.

7. Rosati to the Secretary of the Propagation of the Faith, Saint Louis, Apr. 23, 1830, in SLAA.

8. Rosati's Account Book, 1831, in SLAA.

9. Rosati to Du Bourg, Sept. 11, 1832, in *Annales de la Propagation de la Foi* 7: 108-112.

10. *Leopoldine Reports* 7: 17-23.

11. Rosati's Account Book, 1831, in SLAA.

12. Kenrick's Account Book, p. 74, in SLAA.

13. Diary of Bishop Rosati, Oct. 22, 1832, in SLAA.

14. Benjamin J. Webb, *The Centenary of Catholicity in Kentucky* (Louisville: Charles Rogers, 1884), pp. 298-302.

15. *Missouri Republican*, Oct. 27, 1829.

16. Letter of Peter Poursine, Feb. 1, 1879, cited in Walter Hill, S.J., *Historical Sketch of the Saint Louis University* (Saint Louis: Patrick Fox, Publisher, 1879), p. 41.

17. Walsh to George Fenwick, Jan. 14, 1830, in Md. Prov. Arch., 30, M, 2.

18. *Mrs. Royall's Southern Tour*, 1830-1831 (Washington: Royall, 1830-1831), p. 155.

19. Ibid.

20. Ibid., p. 156.

21. Memorial left with the Superior of the Mission, S.J. by Reverend Father Peter Kenney, Visitor of the Missions of the Society of Jesus in the United States, passim, in Missouri Prov. Arch.

22. Rosati to Pedicini, May 13, 1832, in SLAA.

23. Garraghan, *Jesuits in the Middle United States* 1: 306.

24. Missouri, Senate, *Journal*, 7th General Assembly, 1st sess., 1833: 123.

25. Rosati to Mother Madeline Augustine, Nov. 4, 1832; Abstracts of Correspondence, book 8, no. 256, in SLAA.

26. Quoted in *Illinois Catholic Historical Review* 1: 362.

27. Eccleston to Rosati, 1835, passim, in SLAA.

28. England to Rosati, Jan. 14, 1833, in SLAA.

29. Peter Guilday, *A History of the Councils of Baltimore* (1791-1884) (New York: The Macmillan Company, 1932), p. 106.

30. Rosati to Nozo, Feb. 28, 1833, Archives of the Congregation of the Mission, Paris.

31. Guilday, *History of the Councils of Baltimore*, p. 106.

9. *A Surprising Surge of Nativism*

1. Ray Allen Billington, *The Protestant Crusade, A Study of the Origins of American Nativism* (New York: The Macmillan Co., 1938), p. 1. This is the authoritative study of nativism before the Civil War.

2. Ibid., pp. 10-24.

3. Ibid., p. 118.

4. Ibid., p. 120.

5. Ibid., p. 121.

6. Paul J. Foik, *Pioneer Catholic Journalism* (New York: U.S. Catholic Historical Society, 1930), pp. 75-93; 100-119; 159-180. Foik devotes a short chapter of two pages (Chap. 16, pp. 128-129) to *The Shepherd of the Valley* and other Catholic journalistic efforts in Saint Louis.

7. *The Shepherd of the Valley* 1, no. 1 (July 7, 1832): passim.

8. Quoted in *The Shepherd of the Valley* 1, no. 25 (Dec. 29, 1832).

9. Ibid., 1, no. 46 (May 25, 1833).

10. Quoted, Ibid., 1, no. 15 (Oct. 13, 1832).

11. Memorial of Visitation of 1832-1833, in Mo. Prov. Arch.

12. *The Shepherd of the Valley* 1, no. 8 (Aug. 25, 1832).

13. Ibid., 1, no. 46 (May 25, 1833).

14. Ibid., 1, no. 40 (Apr. 13, 1833).

15. Ibid., 2, no. 2 (Sept. 27, 1833).

16. Ibid., 2, no. 32 (Apr. 25, 1834).

17. Ibid., 2, no. 2 (Sept. 27, 1832).

18. Ibid., 2, no. 38 (June 6, 1834); 2, no. 39 (June 13, 1834); 2, no. 40 (June 20, 1834).

19. Ibid., 2, no. 31 (Sept. 20, 1833).

20. Ibid.

21. *U.S. Catholic Miscellany* 13, no. 4 (1832): 31.

22. *The Observer*, Sept. 3, 1835; Sept. 24, 1835; Oct. 1, 1835; Oct. 22, 1835; Dec. 31, 1835; Jan 7, 1836; Aug. 10. 1836. For a scholarly analysis of this aspect of Lovejoy's life, confer Jasper Cross, "Elijah Lovejoy as an Anti-Catholic," in the *Records* of the American Catholic Historical Society of Philadelphia 60, no. 3 (Sept. 1951): 172-180.

23. Cited in *U.S. Catholic Miscellany* 11, no. 28 (Jan. 7, 1832).

24. *Catholic Telegraph* (Cincinnati), Mar. 24, 1832, quoted in *U.S. Catholic Miscellany* 11, no. 41 (Apr. 7, 1832).

25. Rosati to Pedicini, Jan. 4, 1833, in SLAA.

26. Rosati to Franzoni, Nov. 27, 1837, in SLAA.

27. Roothaan to Blanc, June 1838, in Jesuit General Archives in Rome.

28. Rosati to Franzoni, Nov. 25, 1837, in SLAA.

29. *Illinois Catholic Historical Review* 2 (1919): 412.

30. Diary of Bishop Rosati, Apr. 1833, passim, in SLAA.

31. St. Cyr to Rosati, June 4, 1833, in SLAA.

32. Gilbert Garraghan, *The Catholic Church in Chicago, 1673-1871* (Chicago: Loyola University Press, 1921), p. 61.

33. Bruté to Rosati, Oct. 1834, in SLAA.

34. Roux to Rosati, Mar. 11, 1834, in SLAA.

35. Gilbert Garraghan, *Catholic Beginnings in Kansas City, Missouri* (Chicago: Loyola University Press, 1920), pp. 35, 85.

36. F. G. Holweck, "The Beginnings of the Church in Little Rock," *The Catholic Historical Review* 6, no. 2 (July 1920): 157.

37. Ibid., p. 163.

38. Ibid., p. 166.

39. *Leopoldine Reports* 8: 17-23.

40. Ibid., 9: 1-7.

41. *The Shepherd of the Valley*, Nov. 1, 1834.

42. Diary of Bishop Rosati, Apr. 7, 1835, in SLAA.

43. Diary of Bishop Rosati, Sept. 22, 1835, in SLAA.

44. Rosati to Du Bourg, 1832, in SLAA.

45. Rosati's Account Book, in SLAA.

46. Rosati's Account Book, in SLAA.

47. Theodore Roemer, O.F.M. Cap., *The Leopoldine Foundation and the United States (1829-1839)* (New York: The United States Catholic Historical Society, 1933), p. 156.

48. Rosati to Blanc, Aug. 22, 1836, in SLAA.

49. Ibid.

50. Ibid.

10. Religious Institutes Develop

1. *Mémorié Addressé à M. Le Supérieur Général de la congrégation de la Mission, Vers la Fin du Mois d'Aout 1835, Concernant Nos Establisements du Missouri, Diocese de St. Louis — Par M. Odin*, Archives of the Congregation of the Mission, Paris. (Hereafter ACM.)

2. Etienne to Timon, Sept. 4, 1835, in the ms. collections of the Library of the University of Notre Dame. (Hereafter LUND.)

3. Rosati to Timon, Nov. 8, 1835, LUND.

4. Rosati to Timon, Dec. 6, 1835, LUND.

5. Bayard, *Lonestar Vanguard*, p. 11.

6. Rosati to Franzoni, May 9, 1835, in SLAA.

7. Rosati to Nozo, Feb. 28, 1836, ACM.

8. Odin to Nozo, Dec. 10, 1836. LUND.

9. Nozo to Timon, Apr. 8, 1837, LUND.

10. Bayard, *Lonestar Vanguard*, p. 13.

11. Ibid.

12. *Catalog* (1834), Saint Louis University, passim.

13. Ibid.

14. *Saint Louis University Consultors and Minutes*, p. 12, in Saint Louis Room of Pius XII Library.

15. *St. Louis Medical Society Proceedings* 1: 17.

16. Edmund Flagg, *The Far West* (New York: Harper and Brothers, 1838), 1: 142.

17. *Catalog* (1834), Saint Louis University, p. 70.

18. U.S., Congress, Senate, *Congressional Globe*, 25th Congress, 2d sess., 1838, 4, pt. 430.

19. John Darby, *Personal Recollections*, p. 260.

20. Charles Dickens, *American Notes* (London: Chapman and Hall, 1900), p. 204.

21. Cholleton to Rosati, May 27, 1827, in SLAA.

22. Sister M. Aloysia to Mother Agatha Guthrie, Nov. 3, 1890, Generalate Archives of the Sisters of St. Joseph.

23. Sister Dolorita Marie Dougherty, C.S.J., et al., *Sisters of St. Joseph of Carondelet* (Saint Louis: B. Herder Book Company, 1966), p. 53.

24. Countess de la Rochejacquelin to Bishop Rosati, June 10, 1835, in SLAA.

25. Memoirs of Sister St. Protais Debollie, General Archives of the Sisters of St. Joseph.

26. Saulnier to Rosati, Feb. 9, 1838, in SLAA.

27. *Missouri Session Laws*, p. 334.

28. Sister Delphine Fontbonne, Letter of resignation, General Archives of the Sisters of St. Joseph, Saint Louis.

29. Guilday, *History of the Councils of Baltimore*, pp. 112-119.

30. Loras to Rosati, Dec. 27, 1837, in SLAA.

31. Ibid.

32. M. M. Hoffmann, *The Church Founders of the Northwest* (Milwaukee: Bruce, 1937), pp. 104-105.

33. Samuel Mazzuchelli, O.P., *Memoirs of a Missionary Apostolic*, translated by Sister Mary Benedicta, O.P. (Chicago, 1915), p. 239.

11. Missions in a Melting Pot

1. F. G. Holweck, "Abbe Joseph Anthony Lutz" in *SLCHR* 5 (1923): 183-204.

2. *Leopoldine Reports* 11: 33-36.

3. Ibid., 12: 45-51.

4. Ibid., 12: 52-57.

5. Rosati, Instructions to Mr. Philip LeDuc, April 1840, in SLAA. LeDuc added his observations to the Bishop's entry.

6. Fenwick to Rosati, Nov. 6, 1837, in SLAA.

7. Sr. Mary Gilbert Kelly, O.P., *Catholic Immigration Colonization Projects in the United States, 1815-1860* (New York: U.S. Catholic Historical Society, 1939), pp. 85-87.

8. Diary of Bishop Rosati, Oct. 21, 1838, in SLAA.

9. Kelly, *Catholic Immigration*, p. 44.

10. Verhaegen to Rosati, Nov. 17, 1837, in SLAA.

11. Rosati to Timon, Oct. 20, 1838, in SLAA; Diary of Bishop Rosati, Oct. 14, 1838, in SLAA.

12. F. G. Holweck, "Public Places of Worship in Saint Louis," *Saint Louis Catholic Historical Review* 4 (1922): 9-11.

13. Rosati to Nozo, Sept. 7, 1838, in ACM.

14. Rosati to Timon, Jan. 10, 1842, in LUND.

15. Lefevere to Rosati, Dec. 26, 1837, in SLAA.

16. Rosati to Timon, Oct. 20, 1838, in SLAA.

17. Callan, *Philippine Duchesne*, pp. 628-635.

12. The Diocese Faces the 1840's

1. Rosati to Nozo, Sept. 7, 1838, ACM.

2. *Compendium of the Sixth Census, Missouri* (Washington: Blair and Rives, 1841), p. 90.

3. *Metropolitan Catholic Almanac and Laity's Directory for the Year of Our Lord, 1840* (Baltimore: Fielding Lucas, Jr., 1840), pp. 160-161. (Father Verhaegen's personal copy of the book is in the Saint Louis Room, Pius XII Library.)

4. Ibid., pp. 109-111.

5. Ibid., p. 115.

6. Ibid., pp. 85-86.

7. Ibid., p. 149.

8. Ibid., p. 152.

9. Rosati to Timon, Nov. 14, 1840, LUND.

10. Rosati to Timon, Nov. 14, 1840, LUND.

11. Bayard, *Lonestar Vanguard*, p. 99.

12. Ibid., p. 29.

13. Rosati to Fransoni, Nov. 27, 1838, in SLAA.

14. Nozo to Timon, May 25, 1839, in LUND.

15. Timon to Etienne, Sept. 8, 1839, in ACM.

16. Bayard, *Lonestar Vanguard* p. 103.

17. Etienne to Timon, Dec. 19, 1839, in LUND.

18. Timon to Nozo, June 16, 1840, in ACM.

19. Timon to Nozo, Apr. 19, 1840, in ACM.

20. Diary of Bishop Rosati, Apr. 17, 1840, in SLAA.

21. Rosati to Franzoni, Sept. 1839, in SLAA.

22. *Decretum erectionis Vice-Provinciae*, in Mo. Prov. Arch.

23. Verhaegen to Rosati, Mar. 13, 1840, in SLAA.

24. Diary of Bishop Rosati, Apr. 26, 1840.

25. Verhaegen to Roothaan, Mar. 18, 1840, in Jesuit General Archives, Rome.

26. Verhaegen to Rosati, 1840-1841, in SLAA.

27. Verhaegen to Rosati, Dec. 16, 1840, in SLAA.

28. Diary of Bishop Rosati, May 27, 1840, in SLAA.

29. Rosati to Timon, Dec. 18, 1840, in SLAA.

30. Rosati to Purcell, Nov. 3, 1840, in LUND.

31. Guilday, *History of the Councils of Baltimore*, p. 149.

32. Amleto Cicognani, *Sanctity in America* (Paterson: St. Anthony Guild Press, 1941).

**IV. PETER RICHARD KENRICK:
THE LION OF SAINT LOUIS (1843-1895)**

13. Kenrick as Coadjutor

1. *The Catholic Calendar and Laity's Directory for the Year of Our Lord 1834* (Baltimore: Fielding Lucas, Jr., 1834), p. 75.

2. George Pare, *The Catholic Church in Detroit, 1701-1888* (Detroit: The Gabriel Richard Press, 1951), p. 435.

3. *Records of the American Catholic Historical Society* 6: 295.

4. James L. Pillar, *The Catholic Church in Mississippi, 1837-1865* (New Orleans: Hauser Press, 1964), p. 3, n.

5. Rothensteiner, *History of the Archdiocese* 1: 796.

6. Peter Richard Kenrick (hereafter PRK) to Purcell, Feb. 2, 1842, in LUND. The references will refer interchangeably to "PRK" or "Kenrick." The last name used alone will never refer to the Saint Louis prelate's brother, Francis Patrick Kenrick, bishop of Philadelphia and later archbishop of Baltimore. Gratefully, the author acknowledges the thorough researches of Professor S. J. Miller of Boston College in Kenrick materials in the Archives of the University of Notre Dame, at the Irish College, and the Archives of the Propaganda in Rome, at the Seminary of Maynooth in Ireland and in the Archives of the Archdioceses of Baltimore and Philadelphia.

7. Ibid. Also Kenrick's *Account Book*, p. 74, in SLAA.

8. PRK to Purcell, Mar. 2, 1842; Sept. 30, 1842, LUND.

9. Francis Patrick Kenrick (hereafter FPK) to PRK, Jan. 10, 1842, in *Kenrick-Frenaye Correspondence* (hereafter *KFL*) (Philadelphia, 1920), pp. 138-141.

10. Ibid.

11. PRK to Rosati, Feb. 20, 1842, in SLAA.

12. PRK to Rosati, Aug. 31, 1842, in SLAA.

13. Ibid.

14. FPK to PRK, July 20, 1842, in *KFL*, p. 151.

15. PRK to Father Louis Deluol, S.S., Feb. 23, 1842; copy in the Archives of the Saint Louis Province of the Daughters of Charity.

16. Statement in the Archives of the Saint Louis Province of the Daughters of Charity.

17. Sister Benedicta, D.C., to Deluol, May 31, 1843, in the Archives of the Saint Louis Province of the Daughters of Charity.

18. PRK to Purcell, Aug. 28, 1842, in LUND.

19. E. J. Goodwin, M.D., *A History of Medicine in Saint Louis*, (Saint Louis: W. L. Smith, 1905), p. 146. (*Encyclopedia of the History of Missouri* [Saint Louis: Southern, 1899], 3: 13, 14.)

20. John Hogan, *Thoughts About Saint Louis* (Saint Louis: 1854), p. 12.

21. *St. Louis Republican*, July 15, 1843.

22. John Gilmary Shea, *A History of the Catholic Church in the United States, 1844-1866* (New York: John G. Shea, 1892), 11: 215.

23. F. G. Holweck, "Public Places of Worship in Saint Louis," *SLCHR* 4 (1922): 7 ff.

24. Rosati to Blanc, July 23, 1841, in LUND.

25. PRK to Rosati, Feb. 20, 1842, in SLAA.

26. *Catholic Directory*, 1843, p. 87.

27. PRK to Purcell, Jan., 1843, in LUND.

28. *Catholic Directory*, 1844, p. 105.

29. PRK to Purcell, Aug. 28, 1842, in LUND.

30. PRK to Purcell, Mar. 27, 1843, in LUND.

31. PRK to Purcell, Mar. 7, 1843, in LUND.

32. *The Catholic Cabinet and Chronicle of Religious Intelligence* 1, no. 1 (May 1843).

33. FPK to PRK, Aug. 2, 1843, in *KFL*, p. 168.

34. *The Catholic Cabinet* 1, no. 12 (Apr. 1844).

35. Ibid., 1, no. 4 (Aug. 1843).

36. FPK to PRK, Aug. 2, 1843, in *KFL*, p. 169; Nov. 15, 1843, in *KFL*, p. 176.

37. FPK to PRK, Dec. 4, 1843, in *KFL*, p. 178.

38. *The Catholic Cabinet* 3, no. 2 (July 1843).

39. Garraghan, *Jesuits in the Middle United States* 1:318, 327, 335, 496.

40. Unidentified newspaper clipping in SLAA, on the occasion of Kenrick's death.

41. Van de Velde to Kenrick, Feb. 28, 1850, in Mo. Prov. Arch.

42. *St. Louis Post-Dispatch*, Sept. 15, 1893.

43. Spalding to Purcell, Apr. 6, 1868, in LUND.

44. Patrick Ryan, "Archbishop Kenrick's Jubilee," quoted in John J. O'Shea, *The Two Kenricks* (Philadelphia: John J. McVey, 1904), p. 350. O'Shea's work is triumphalist rather than objective; but it includes a number of quotations and some facts of value.

45. [William Walsh?], *Life of Most Rev. Peter Richard Kenrick, D.D.* (Saint Louis: Catholic Publishing Co., 1891), p. 60.

46. Walsh, *Life of Kenrick*, p. 59.

47. Patrick Ryan, "Archbishop Kenrick s Jubilee," p. 356.

48. Walsh, *Life of Kenrick*, p. 63.

49. Ibid.

50. Patrick Ryan, "Funeral Sermon of Archbishop Kenrick," in O'Shea, *The Two Kenricks*, p. 350.

51. Ibid., p. 406

52. Unidentified newspaper clipping in SLAA, from time of Kenrick's death.

53. Bertha May Ivory, *Fifty Years a Bishop* (Saint Louis, 1891), p. 9. A chatty pamphlet with a few stories not found elsewhere.

54. O'Shea, *The Two Kenricks*, p. 417.

55. Governor David Francis, "Greetings to Archbishop Kenrick," quoted in O'Shea, *The Two Kenricks*, p. 382.

56. Walsh, *Life of Kenrick* p. 54.

14. The Lion in Spring

1. Kenrick's *Account Book*, pp. 73, 83, in SLAA. Kenrick kept careful and detailed accounts, not only of the business transactions involved in these buildings and rentals, but of all donations to the Church of Saint Louis, and the use thereof; and, later on, of the entire People's Bank that he conducted for immigrants after the death of Father Heim (see Chapter 16).

2. Kenrick to Purcell, Feb. 17, 1843, in LUND.

3. Ibid.

4. *The Catholic Cabinet* 1, no. 1 (May 1843).

5. Ibid.

6. Kenrick to Timon, May 13, 1844, in SLAA.

7. Ibid.

8. *The Catholic Cabinet* 2, no. 10 (Feb. 1845), p. 634.

9. Sister Benedicta to Deluol, May 31, 1843, in the Archives of the Saint Louis Province of the Daughters of Charity.

10. *The Catholic Cabinet* 2, no. 1 (May 1844), p. 60.

11. Kenrick to Milde, Dec. 10, 1844. in *Berichte de Leopoldinen Stiftung, Heft* 18, pp. 6-14.

12. Ibid.

13. *Community Annals*, p. 279; in Archives of the Sisters of St. Joseph of Carondelet, Frontenac, Missouri.

14. Ibid., pp. 283-284.

15. FPK to PRK, Jan. 1, 1846, *KFL*, p. 220.

16. *Catholic News-Letter*, July 11, 1846.

17. Ibid., Sept. 12, 1846.

18. *Missouri Session Laws*, 1847, Sections 1-5, pp. 103-104.

19. FPK to PRK, Jan. 25, 1846, in *KFL*, p. 221.

20. Ibid., p. 221, n.

21. Sister Mary Lucinda Savage, *The Congregation of St. Joseph of Carondelet* (Saint Louis: B. Herder Book Company, 1923), pp. 65-66.

22. *Catholic News-Letter* 1, no. 1 (Nov. 22, 1845).

23. Ibid., passim.

24. Ibid., passim.

25. Ibid., July 11, 1847.

26. Ibid., Apr. 1, 1848.

27. Kenrick, Pastoral Letter, Sept. 14, 1846, in SLAA.

28. Kenrick, Pastoral Letter, Sept. 1, 1850, in SLAA.

29. Guilday, *History of the Councils of Baltimore*, pp. 143-153.

30. PRK to Franzoni, July 24, 1846, in the Archives of the Propagation of the Faith, Rome.

31. PRK to FPK, Nov. 20, 1846, in the Baltimore Archdiocesan Archives (Hereafter BAA).

32. Daniel T. McColgan, *A Century of Charity: The First One Hundred Years of the Society of St. Vincent de Paul in the United States* (Milwaukee: Bruce, 1951), p. 44.

33. Ibid., p. 45.

34. Report of Timon to Sturchi, Mar. 26, 1846, in ACM. In Paris, Timon to the General Council of the Society of St. Vincent de Paul, Oct. 8, 1848, in ACM.

35. McColgan, *Century of Charity*, p. 80.

36. Proceedings of the Particular Council, Saint Louis, Missouri, Dec. 19, 1860, quoted in *History of the St. Vincent de Paul Society in Saint Louis, Missouri* (Carondelet: LaSalle Press, 1861), p. 3. See also McColgan, *Century of Charity*, pp. 63-64.

37. McColgan, *Century of Charity*, pp. 65-69.

38. J. Thomas Scharf, *History of Saint Louis City and County* (Philadelphia: Louis H. Everts and Co., 1883), p. 1759.

39. Ibid., p. 1766.

15. The Midwest's First Archdiocese

1. FPK to Franzoni, May 24, 1848, *KFL*, p. 278.

2. Kenrick to Choiselat-Gallien, Saint Louis, Dec. 3, 1847, in the transcripts of the Propagation, in LUND.

3. Ibid.

4. PRK to Spalding, July 2, 1864, in BAA.

5. PRK to FPK, Jan. 8, 1852, in BAA.

6. Kenrick to Barnabo, July 2, 1860, in the Archives of the Propagation of the Faith, Rome.

7. Diary of Bishop Rosati, Nov. 16, 1838, in SLAA.

8. F. G. Holweck, "Abbe Joseph Anthony Lutz," in *SLCHR* 5 (1923), p. 201.

9. Kenrick to Purcell, Saint Louis, May 16, 1848, in LUND.

10. Kenrick to McMasters, Saint Louis, Oct. 7, 1849, in LUND.

11. Elet to Roothaan, Saint Louis, Jan. 14, 1850, Mo. Prov. Arch.

12. Ibid.

13. De Smet to Van de Velde, Saint Louis, [1850], in Mo. Prov. Arch.

14. Van de Velde to Kenrick, Chicago, Feb. 28, 1850, in Mo. Prov. Arch.

15. PRK to Purcell, Oct. 17, 1855, in LUND.

16. Purcell to Blanc, Apr. 12, 1841, in LUND.

17. PRK to Spalding, Nov. 7, 1864, in BAA.

18. PRK to FPK, July 9, 1846, in BAA.

19. Billington, *Protestant Crusade*, p. 167.

20. Ibid., p. 168.

21. Ibid., p. 224.

22. Ibid., p. 230.

23. Ibid., pp. 231-232.

24. John O'Hanlon, *Life and Scenery in Missouri* (Dublin, 1890), pp. 92-93. (Father O'Hanlon was an eye-witness of the events he describes.)

25. *SLU Charter and Minutes*, p. 70, in SLU Arch.

26. Ibid., p. 73.

27. *Lenten Pastoral*, Saint Louis, Feb. 2, 1849, in SLAA.

28. O'Hanlon, *Life and Scenery in Missouri*, passim.

29. Kenrick, *Pastoral*, Feb. 1849, in SLAA.

30. Ibid.

31. *Decrees* of Synod of 1850, in SLAA.

32. *Pastoral*, Feb. 2, 1849, in SLAA.

33. Records of the American Catholic Historical Society, 30: 343.

34. Rothensteiner, *History of the Archdiocese* 2: 454.

16. The Expansive Fifties

1. Hubert Gerard, F.S.C., *Mississippi Vista: The Brothers of the Christian Schools in the Midwest, 1849-1949* (Winona: St. Mary's College Press, 1948), p. 104.

2. Angelus Gabriel, F.S.C., *The Christian Brothers in the United States, 1848-1948* (New York: Declan X. McMullen, 1947), p. 175.

3. Gerard, *Mississippi Vista*, Chronological List of Schools, p. 269.

4. "Total List of Depositors," p. 1 (among Kenrick's *Account Books*, in SLAA.

5. Kenrick's *Account Books* (1850-58), pp. 44, 78, 79, 183, in SLAA.

6. While most other papers of Kenrick are missing from the chancery Archives, Kenrick's financial accounts are extensive and presumably complete (SLAA).

7. Kenrick's *Account Books, Personal Accounts* (1850-58), Index of depositers, in SLAA.

8. Kenrick's *Special Account Book* (1855-58), p. 335, in SLAA.

9. Ibid., p. 339.

10. Ibid.

11. Ibid., p. 341.

12. Ibid., p. 339.

13. Ibid., p. 345.

14. Ibid., passim.

15. Ibid.

16. Ibid.

17. Kenrick's *Account Books* for August 1857 show an undesignated loan of $50,000. Rothensteiner lists it as $150,000. (Rothensteiner, *History of the Archdiocese* 2: 150.) The City Records for 1857 are not available.

18. PRK to Cullen, Saint Louis, Oct. 18, 1848, Irish College Transcripts, in LUND.

19. PRK to Choiselat-Gallien, Saint Louis, Sept. 18, 1850, in LUND.

20. "The Statistics of the Population of the United States," *Ninth Census* (Washington: Government Printing Office, 1872), 1: 194.

21. Ibid.

22. Kenrick to Purcell, Saint Louis, Nov. 9, 1853, in LUND.

23. Rothensteiner, *History of the Archdiocese* 2: 181-182.

24. Ibid.

25. Andrew Mudd, *History of Millwood and St. Alphonsus Parish* (1927), passim.

26. *Catholic Directory*, 1850, pp. 168-173.

27. Ibid., pp. 174-180.

28. Ibid., pp. 180-185.

29. Ibid., pp. 99-102.

30. Ibid., 112-119.

31. Ibid., pp. 85-92.

32. *The Shepherd of the Valley*, Mar. 27, 1852. Sister M. Lilliana Owens, S.L., wrote a brochure, *St. Louis Catholic Journalism Prior to the Civil War* (Saint Louis: Central Bureau, 1964). Professor Jaspar Cross discussed the political views of the *Shepherd* and other local Catholic publications during this period, in "The St. Louis Catholic Press and Political Issues, 1845-1861," in *Records* of the American Catholic Historical Society (Philadelphia) 80, no. 4 (Dec. 1969).

33. *The Shepherd of the Valley*, July 5, 1851.

34. John Gilmary Shea carried Bakewell's speech in full in *History of the Catholic Church* 4: 606-607.

35. *Shepherd of the Valley*, Nov. 22, 1851.

36. Ibid., Apr. 10, 1852.

37. Ibid., June 11, 1854.

38. Scharf, *History of Saint Louis* 1: 945.

39. *Litterae Annuae*, SLU, 1854, in SLU Arch.

40. *Missouri Republican*, Feb. 1856 (Undated clipping in SLU Scrapbook).

41. Kenrick to Purcell, May 2, 1848, in LUND.

42. Ibid.

43. FPK to PRK, Jan. 2, 1852, in BAA.

44. FPK to PRK, May 24, 1848, in *KFL*, p. 277.

45. Bishop Francis Patrick Kenrick condemned the slave trade, the enslavement of individuals and groups, and the unjust treatment of slaves; he praised men who freed slaves with proper provision for their well-being; but he did not hold it as necessarily "unjust to hold the descendants of these slaves in slavery, a condition in which they are born and are not able to leave." Hugh P. Nolan, *The Most Reverend Francis Patrick Kenrick, Third Bishop of Philadelphia, 1830-1851* (Philadelphia: American Catholic Historical Society, 1948), pp. 241-42.

46. Guilday, *History of the Councils of Baltimore*, p. 182.

47. Ibid.

48. Cretin to Loras, Dec. 28, 1855, in Dubuque Archdiocesan Archives.

49. PRK to Purcell, Oct. 17, 1855, in LUND.

50. Barnabo to Kenrick, Feb. 17, 1857, in *Collectio Lacensis* 3, 311; *Concilium Provincia St. Ludovici*, 306.

17. Continued Growth

1. *Catholic Directory*, 1854.

2. FPK to PRK, Jan. 25, 1858, in *KFL*, pp. 407-408.

3. Kenrick's *Account Books*, Thornton Estate, p. 28, in SLAA.

4. Ibid., pp. 34-37.

5. Ibid., p. 31. Doran Killian edited the *Western Banner*. Like its predecessors, it succumbed after two years. Bound copies of the *Western Banner* are in the Saint Louis Room, Pius XII Library.

6. Ibid., p. 39.

7. Ibid., p. 71.

8. *Court Records*, Will of John Thornton, Mar. 1861, in the Saint Louis City Hall.

9. De Smet to Beckx, May 13, 1856, in the Jesuit General Archives in Rome.

10. Alexander Garesche to Brownson, Nov. 23, 1853, in LUND.

11. *Western Banner*, Dec. 11, 1858.

12. McColgan, *Century of Charity*, p. 146.

13. Ibid., p. 77.

14. *St. Louis Globe-Democrat*, Aug. 28, 1932.

15. John J. Hogan, *On the Mission in Missouri* (Kansas City, 1892), pp. 7-8.

16. Ibid., p. 47.

17. Ibid., pp. 94 ff.

18. Rothensteiner, *History of the Archdiocese,* 2: 64.

18. Civil War Divides an Archdiocese

1. "Agriculture," *U.S. Census Report* (1860), pp. 233-234.

2. *Ninth Census* 1: 194.

3. *Kenrick Correspondence*, Kenrick Seminary, Saint Louis, quoted in Sister Mary Emmanuel White, R.S.M., *Archbishop Peter Kenrick and the Civil War* (Saint Louis, 1948), pp. 58-59.

4. *Missouri Republican*, May 15, 1861.

5. Frank P. Blair to De Smet, June 7, 1861, in the Mo. Prov. Arch.

6. Garraghan, *Jesuits in the Middle United States* 2: 150.

7. P. J. Ryan, "Most Reverend Peter Richard Kenrick, D.D.," *American Catholic Quarterly Review* 21 (1896): 426.

8. *American Catholic Ecclesiastical Review* 7, no. 6 (Dec. 1897): 643.

9. Rothensteiner, *History of the Archdiocese* 2: 213.

10. Parish Records, Basilica of St. John the Evangelist.

11. For further information on this matter, see *Catholic Historical Review* 16 (Apr. 1930): 18.

12. Murphy to Beckx, Oct. 12, May 17, 1861, in Jesuit General Archives, Rome.

13. De Smet to Joseph Van Jersel, Feb. 1863, in *De Smet Papers* 4: 1439, in SLU Arch.

14. Garraghan, *Jesuits in the Middle United States* 2: 158.

15. Keller to Beckx, Oct. 12, 1864, in Jesuit General Archives, Rome.

16. Linton to Brownson, Oct. 16, 1861, in LUND.

17. *Records* of Appointments, Hospital Chaplains, A.G.O. Confederate Archives, Missouri Division, 51.

18. *Journal*, Missouri State Convention, Saint Louis, 1862, pp. 14-15.

19. PRK to FPK, Saint Louis, Aug. 22, 1862, in BAA.

20. Elder, *The Bishop's Letter Book*, no. 10 (1864-66): 449, in SLAA.

21. Hogan, *Mission in Missouri*, pp. 128-134. Confer the *Missouri Republican*, July 30, 1865, for Kenrick's letter against the Drake Oath.

22. Missouri *vs.* Cummings, 36, Missouri (1865) 1614 ff.

23. Kenrick *vs.* Cole, et al., *Missouri Reports* 26: 85.

24. John J. Hogan, "Kenrick Jubilee Sermon," quoted in O'Shea, *Two Kenricks*, p. 364.

19. Lion Rampant

1. Kenrick to Spalding, Saint Louis, Jan. 6, 1865, in BAA.

2. Kenrick to Spalding, Saint Louis, May 16, 1866, in BAA.

3. PRK to Spalding, May 22, 1866, in BAA.

4. Kenrick's *Account Books* pp. 39, 75 ff., in SLAA.

5. John Lancaster Spalding, *Life of the Most Reverend M. J. Spalding, D.D., Archbishop of Baltimore* (New York: 1878), pp. 298-300.

6. James Hennessey, S.J., "The Baltimore Council of 1866: An American Syllabus," in *Records* of the American Catholic Historical Society of Philadelphia, 76, no. 3 (Sept. 1965), p. 166.

7. Ibid., p. 171.

8. Archives of the Propagation of the Faith, *Acta* 232 (1867), p. 407, *Congregatio Private Extraordinaria*.

9. Quoted in Eduardo Misch, *The American Bishops and the Negro from the Civil War to the Third Plenary Council of Baltimore (1865-1884)* (Rome: Gregorian University, 1968), p. 46.

10. Ibid., pp. 46-47.

11. Kenrick to Ryan, Rome, June 15, 1870, in SLAA.

12. Guilday, *History of the Councils of Baltimore*, p. 215.

13. J. L. Spalding, *Life of M. J. Spalding*, p. 305.

14. Ibid., p. 220.

15. Letter of Cardinal Cullen, quoted in Spalding, *Life of M. J. Spalding*, pp. 317-318.

16. Quoted in Guilday, *History of the Councils of Baltimore*, p. 220.

17. *Western Watchman*, Dec. 18, 1886. Early in 1879, Bishop Peter J. Baltes of Alton, Illinois, published a pamphlet that condemned Phelan for attempting "to weaken and undermine the authority of the American episcopate." Bishop Baltes claimed that the Saint Louis archbishop did not countenance Phelan's paper. The Alton bishop seemingly intended the pamphlet for circulation among his own people. Not unexpectedly, Saint Louis readers obtained copies (*St. Louis Globe-Democrat*, Feb. 19, 1879).

18. *Western Watchman*, 1886, passim.

19. *Western Watchman*, Sept. 23, 1915.

20. *Western Watchman*, May 18, 1893.

21. Rothensteiner, *History of the Archdiocese* 2: 350.

22. *Times*, May 7, 1877 to Nov. 20, 1878.

23. *Ninth Census*, 1: 194.

24. PRK to the Roman Catholics of Saint Louis, quoted in Rothensteiner, *History of the Archdiocese* 2: 460.

25. Ryan to Abbot Smith, Saint Louis, Sept. 15, 1871, Microfilm 64, in the Archives of St. John's University, Collegeville, Minnesota. Abbot Bernard Smith, O.S.B., served as consultor for three congregations of the Roman Curia, first pro-rector of the North American College in Rome, and Roman agent for a large number of English, Irish, Canadian, Australian, and American Churchmen from the early 1840's to his death in 1892. His incoming American letters numbered 3,168. Bishop Patrick Ryan of Saint Louis was one of his correspondents.

26. *Life of Most Reverend Peter Richard Kenrick, D.D.* (Saint Louis: Catholic Publishing Co., 1891), p. 33.

27. Rothensteiner, *History of the Archdiocese*, 2: 645.

28. Kenrick to Spalding, Sept. 6, 1868, in BAA.

29. Barnabo to Kenrick, Dec. 1, 1869, in the Archives of the Propagation of the Faith.

30. James Gibbons, *Retrospect of Fifty Years* (Baltimore: John Murphy Co., 1916), 1: 32.

31. Spalding to Dupanloup, May 1870, draft in BAA, 39-N-10.

32. Kenrick to Spalding, Apr. 21, 1870, BAA, 36-A-L-10.

33. James Hennessey, *The First Vatican Council: The American Experience* (New York: Herder and Herder, 1963), p. 39. An appreciative appraisal of Kenrick's stand at Vatican I. With permission of the publisher.

34. Cuthbert Butler, *The Vatican Council* (London: Longmans, Green & Co., 1930), 1: 245.

35. *World Almanac* (1886), pp. 32-33.

36. For the complete text of the *Concio*, see Raymond J. Clancy, "American Prelates at the Vatican Council," in *Historical Records and Studies* (New York: The United States Catholic Historical Society, 1937), Appendix V, 28: 93-131.

37. Clancy, "American Prelates at the Vatican Council," p. 97.

38. Ibid., passim.

39. Patrick Ryan, "Archbishop Kenrick's Jubilee Sermon," *American Catholic Quarterly Review* 21 (1896): 410.

40. Butler, *Vatican Council* 2: 158-159.

41. Ibid., 2: 176.

42. Hennessey, *First Vatican Council*, p. 328.

43. *Western Watchman*, Mar. 15, 1896.

44. Larne to Icard, Rome, July 20, 1870, quoted in Hennessey, *First Vatican Council*, p. 315.

45. McCloskey to Smith, Louisville, Sept. 23, 1870, in *Smith Papers*, Collegeville, Minn.

46. Luigi Cardinal Bilio refers to the matter in his *Diary*, quoted in Hennessey, *First Vatican Council*, p. 316, but there seems to be no extant copy of such a letter.

47. *Western Watchman*, Jan. 7, 1871.

48. Kenrick to Barnabo, Saint Louis, Jan. 13, 1871, in G. D. Mansi, et al. *Sacrorum conciliorum nova et amplissima collectio* (Paris: Welter, 1907), 53: 955.

49. *The New Catholic Encyclopedia*, 14: 561.

50. De Angelis to Hogan, Rome, Oct. 15, 1870, in the Archives of the Diocese of Kansas City, Mo.; mentioned in Mansi, *Sacrorum conciliorum nova et amplissima collectio*, 53:955.

51. Kenrick to Acton, Saint Louis, Mar. 29, 1871, quoted in Schulte, *Der Altkatholizismus* (Giessen, 1887), pp. 267 ff.

52. *Western Watchman*, Mar. 22, 1896.

53. Ryan to Smith, Saint Louis, Sept. 15, 1871, in *Smith Papers*.

54. Hennessey, *First Vatican Council*, pp. 322-323.

55. Ryan to Smith, Saint Louis, Sept. 15, 1871, in *Smith Papers*.

56. Constantine Smith, *Catholic Standard and Times*, Mar. 23, 1896.

57. *Western Watchman*, Mar. 15, 1896.

20. Patrick J. Ryan: All But Archbishop

1. Constantine Smith, *Catholic Standard and Times*, Mar. 23, 1896.

2. Ryan to Smith, Sept. 15, 1871, in *Smith Papers*.

3. Prefect to Kenrick, Rome, Jan. 29, 1872, in the Propagation of the Faith Archives.

4. Kenrick's *Account Book*, p. 77, in SLAA.

5. Panken to Zealand, July 14, 1873, in Mo. Prov. Arch.

6. Bayley to Purcell, May 14, 1873, in LUND.

7. Peter Leo Johnson, *Halcyon Days: The Story of St. Francis Seminary, Milwaukee, 1856-1956* (Milwaukee: The Bruce Publishing Company, 1956).

8. Rothensteiner, *History of the Archdiocese* 2: 654.

9. SLCHR 1 (1919): 13.

10. Ibid., p. 11.

11. *Western Watchman*, May 10, 1879.

12. F. G. Holweck, "The Historical Archives of the Archdiocese of Saint Louis," *SLCHR* 1 (1919): 25.

13. *Globe-Democrat*, Dec. 17, 1877.

14. Ibid., Dec. 18, 1877.

15. Jim Allee Hart, *A History of the St. Louis Globe-Democrat* (Columbia: University of Missouri Press, 1961), p. 137.

16. *Globe-Democrat*, Dec. 23, 1877.

17. Ibid.

18. Ibid.

19. Ibid., Dec. 24, 1877.

20. Ibid.

21. Ibid., Dec. 25, 1877.

22. Ibid., Dec. 27, 1877.

23. Ibid., Dec. 28, 1877.

24. Ibid.

25. Ibid., Dec. 29, 1877.

26. Ibid., Dec. 30, 1877.

27. Ibid., Jan. 3, 1878.

28. Ibid., Jan. 4, 1878.

29. Ibid., Jan. 5, 1878.

30. Ibid., Jan. 6, 1878.

31. Ibid., Jan. 7, 1878.

32. Ibid., Jan. 6, 1878.

33. Ibid., Jan. 8, 1878.

34. Ibid., Jan. 9, 1878.

35. Ibid., Jan. 14, 1878.

36. Ibid., Jan. 15, 1878.

37. Ibid., Jan. 16, 1878.

38. Ibid., Jan. 21, 1878.

39. Ibid., Jan. 22, 23, 24, 28, 29, 1878.

40. Ibid., Feb. 7, 1878.

41. Ibid., Jan. 10, 1878.

42. Hart, *History of the St. Louis Globe-Democrat*, p. 137.

43. The correspondence relating to the creation of St. Francis Xavier Parish was amazingly extensive. Confer SLU Archives.

44. Ryan to Smith, Saint Louis, June 29, 1878, in *Smith Papers*.

45. Ryan to Smith, Saint Louis, Nov. 27, 1789, in *Smith Papers*.

46. Ryan to Smith, Saint Louis, Jan. 19, 1880, in *Smith Papers*.

47. Ryan to Smith, Saint Louis, Mar. 4, 1884, in *Smith Papers*.

48. Peter Paul Cahensly, *Der St. Raphaelsverein zum Schutze katholischer deutscher Auswanderer* (Freiburg im Breisgau, 1900), p. 28.

49. William B. Faherty, *Better the Dream: Saint Louis University and Community* (Saint Louis: Saint Louis University, 1968), p. 182.

50. *Western Watchman*, June 7, 1884.

51. Map of St. Francis Xavier's Parish, in Archbishop Kenrick's own hand, in SLU Arch.

52. *Western Watchman*, June 14, 1884.

53. Ibid., Dec. 24, 1893.

54. Ibid.

55. Ibid.

56. Marion A. Habig, O.F.M., *Heralds of the King, the Franciscans of the Saint Louis-Chicago Province, 1858-1958* (Chicago: Franciscan Herald Press, 1958), p. 132.

57. *Western Watchman*, Aug. 11, 1883.

58. Ryan file, in SLAA.

59. *Western Watchman*, June 14, 1884.

60. *Freeman's Journal and Catholic Register* (New York), Aug. 1884.

61. *Western Watchman*, Mar. 15, 1896.

62. *The New Catholic Encyclopedia* 12: 768.

63. *Western Watchman*, Mar. 15, 1896.

64. Ryan, "Archbishop Kenrick's Jubilee," quoted in Shea, *Two Kenricks*, p. 356.

65. Gleeson File, in SLAA.

66. *Western Watchman*, June 7, 1884.

67. Bertha May Ivory, *Fifty Years a Bishop* (Saint Louis, 1891), p. 15.

68. *Decree* of the Propaganda, Mar. 4, 1884, copy in SLAA.

69. *Western Watchman*, June 7, 1884. The priest then went west to Colorado, whither misfortune followed him. A Saint Louis layman wrote Bishop Machebeuf accusing him of a new instance of unpriestly conduct. The Secretary of the Denver prelate received a vague answer from Archbishop Kenrick; then wrote to Chancellor Van der Sanden for a more complete appraisal of the entire matter (Raverdy to Van der Sanden, Apr. 6, 1885, in SLAA), Van der Sanden's investigation of this second charge brought out a melodramatic story that suggested at least a lack of prudence on the priest's part (Callahan Deposition, Apr. 14, 1885, in SLAA). The priest worked in three towns in Colorado, then in Pendleton, Oregon, where he died on Jan. 13, 1890 (Priests' File, in SLAA).

70. *Western Watchman*, July 19, 1884.

71. Ibid., Aug. 23, 1884.

72. Ibid.

73. P.W.T. to Phelan, in *Western Watchman*, Aug. 30, 1884.

74. Ibid., June 14, 1886.

75. Ibid., Sept. 6, 1884.

76. Ibid., Sept. 4, 1886.

21. Kenrick Resumes Control

1. *American Catholic Quarterly Review* 8 (July 1883): 524.

2. Ibid., p. 525.

3. Ibid.

4. Ibid.

5. Habig, *Heralds of the King*, p. 478.

6. Colman J. Barry, O.S.B., *The Catholic Church and German-Americans* (Milwaukee: Bruce Publishing Co., 1953), p. 53.

7. *Western Watchman*, Aug. 9, 1884.

8. Ibid.

9. Barry, *Catholic Church and German-Americans*, p. 54.

10. Muehlsiepen to Gibbons, Saint Louis, Oct. 20, 1884, in BAA, 78-R-18.

11. Gibbons to Corrigan, Baltimore, Oct. 21, 1884, in the Archives of the Archdiocese of New York.

12. Ryan to Gibbons, Philadelphia, Oct. 22, 1884, in BAA, 78-S-32.

13. *Letterbook of James Gibbons*, Oct. 23, 1884, in BAA.

14. *Letterbook of James Gibbons*, Dec. 17, 1886, in BAA.

15. *Acta et decreta concilii plenarii Baltimorensis tertii* (Baltimore, 1884), p. cii.

16. Walsh, *Life of Kenrick*, p. 39.

17. *Western Watchman*, June 5, 1886.

18. Ibid., June 12, 1886.

19. Ibid., June 19, 1886.

20. Ibid., June 26, 1886.

21. Quoted, Ibid., June 26, 1886.

22. Ibid., Sept. 4, 1886.

23. Ibid., Sept. 4, 1886.

24. Ibid., passim, 1886.

22. Catholics in Controversy

1. Rothensteiner, *History of the Archdiocese* 2: 526.

2. Henry J. Browne, *The Catholic Church and the Knights of Labor* (Washington: The Catholic University of America Press, 1949), passim.

3. Browne, *Catholic Church and the Knights of Labor*, pp. 108-109.

4. John Tracy Ellis, *The Life of Cardinal Gibbons*, 2 vols. (Milwaukee: Bruce Publishing Co., 1952), 1: 495-497.

5. *Globe-Democrat*, May 13, 1886.

6. *St. Louis Post-Dispatch* Apr. 2, 1886.

7. *Globe-Democrat*, Apr. 2, 1886.

8. *O'Leary to Powderly*, De Soto, Sept. 20, 1886, in *Powderly Papers*, in the Mullen Library, the Catholic University of America, Washington, D.C.

9. *Post-Dispatch*, Apr. 3, Apr. 9, 1886.

10. U.S., Congress, House, *Investigation of Labor Troubles in Missouri, Arkansas, Kansas, Texas and Illinois*, House of Representatives Report 4174, 49th Congress, 2d sess., 1887, pp. 468-469.

11. House Report, 4174, pp. 470-473.

12. *Western Watchman*, Apr. 24, 1886.

13. Ibid., May 1, 1886.

14. *Post-Dispatch*, Apr. 7, 1886.

15. Records of St. Rose of Lima's Church, De Soto, Missouri.

16. *Western Watchman*, Sept. 4, 1886.

17. O'Leary to Powderly, Saint Louis, Apr. 4, 1887, in *Powderly Papers*.

18. *Connecticut Catholic*, Nov. 20, 1886.

19. Browne, *Catholic Church and the Knights of Labor*, p. 222.

20. Powderly to O'Leary, Scranton, Sept. 27, 1886, in *Powderly Papers*.

22. Ibid.

23. Ryan to Corrigan, Philadelphia, Apr. 21, 1886, in Archives of the Archdiocese of New York.

24. Ibid.

25. Browne, *Catholic Church and the Knights of Labor*, p. 217.

26. *Western Watchman*, Sept. 11, 1886.

27. Ibid., Aug. 28, 1886.

28. Browne, *Catholic Church and the Knights of Labor*, p. 212.

29. O'Leary to Powderly, Jan. 23, 1877, in *Powderly Papers*. O'Leary heard the story of the Kenrick-Hoxie meeting from Father John J. Hennessey, Pastor of St. John's Church in Saint Louis, where Kenrick resided at the time. Hennessey, incidentally became bishop of Wichita in 1889 (O'Leary to Powderly, Mar. 30, 1887, in *Powderly Papers*).

30. O'Leary to Powderly, Jan. 23, 1877, in *Powderly Papers*.

31. Records of St. Rose of Lima parish, De Soto, Missouri, p. 379.

32. "A McGlynn Case in Saint Louis," *New York Sun*, Apr. 5, 1887.

33. Powderly to O'Leary, Scranton, Apr. 6, 1887, in *Powderly Papers*.

34. Powderly to Gibbons, June 30, 1887, in BAA, 82-W-9. The author wishes to acknowledge extensive use of the materials of Monsignor John Tracy Ellis in the relationships of Cardinal Gibbons with the Knights of Labor and with Archbishop John J. Kain of Saint Louis. (See Ellis, *Life of Cardinal Gibbons*.)

35. Ibid.

36. Ellis, *Life of Cardinal Gibbons* 1: 521-524.

37. *Globe-Democrat* Oct. 4, 1887.

38. O'Leary to Powderly, Saint Louis, June 4, 1888, in *Powderly Papers*.

39. Rothensteiner, *History of the Archdiocese* 2: 526.

40. Terrence V. Powderly, *The Path I Trod*, ed. by Harry J. Carman, *et al.* (New York, 1940), p. 380.

41. Gerald P. Fogarty, S.J., "Denis J. O'Connell: Americanist Agent to the Vatican 1885-1903" (Ph.D. diss., Yale University, 1969), p. 61. In this work, Fogarty gives a penetrating and surprisingly balanced view of the late nineteenth century struggles within the American Church.

42. Philip Gleason, *The Conservative Reformers: German-American Catholics and the Social Order* (Notre Dame: Notre Dame University Press, 1968), p. 32. Gleason presents the social reform work of the *Central Verein*, and especially of Frederick Kenkel. With permission of the publisher.

43. Fogarty, "Americanist Agent to the Vatican," p. 62.

44. Ibid., p. 61.

45. Ibid., p. 62.

46. Barry, *Catholic Church and German-Americans*, p. 51.

47. Simeone to Gibbons, Rome, June 8, 1887, BAA, 88-S-5.

48. *Catholic Universe*, Jan. 12, 1888.

49. Barry, *Catholic Church and German-Americans*, pp. 98-99.

50. New York *Herald*, Aug. 3, 1887.

51. *Report* of Rt. Rev. Henry Muehlsiepen of the Leo House Committee, Archives of the Leo House, Feb. 25, 1888.

52. Barry, *Catholic Church and German-Americans*, p. 107.

53. Ibid., pp. 112-116.

54. O'Connell to Ireland, Rome, June 11, 1891, in Archives of the Archdiocese of St. Paul.

55. Barry, *Catholic Church and German-Americans*, p. 137.

56. Kain to Gibbons, Wheeling, May 18, 1891, in BAA, unclassified.

57. New York *Herald*, June 1, 1891.

58. St. Paul *Pioneer Press*, June 12, 1891.

59. Ireland to Gibbons, St. Paul, May 30, 1891, in BAA, unclassified.

60. New York *Times*, May 31, 1891.

61. *Church Progress*, June 13, 1891.

62. *Westliche Post*, June 21, 1891.

63. *Associated Press*, June 13, 1891.

64. Fogarty, "Americanist Agent in the Vatican," pp. 99-100.

65. New York *Herald*, Dec. 13, 1892.

66. John Conway, "Cahenslyism versus Americanism," in *The Review of Reviews* 6, no. 32 (Aug. 1892): 45.

67. Ibid., p. 45.

68. Ibid., p. 43.

69. Gleason, *Conservative Reformers*, passim.

23. The Saint Louis Lion in Winter

1. David Spalding, C.F.X., treats this question thoroughly in his article, "The Negro Catholic Congresses, 1889-1884," *Catholic Historical Review* 55, no. 3 (Oct. 1969): 337-357.

2. Albert S. Foley, *God's Men of Color* (New York: Farrar, Strauss & Co., 1955), p. 33 n.

3. A. J. Faust, "The Congress of Colored Catholics," *The Catholic World* 49 (Apr. 1889): 94-103.

4. Spalding, "Negro Catholic Congresses," pp. 343-344.

5. Ryan to Gibbons, Feb. 17, 1891, in BAA.

6. Gibbons to Leo XIII, May 18, 1891, in BAA.

7. Quoted in Rothensteiner, *History of the Archdiocese* 2: 572-573.

8. Ibid.

9. Hogan, "Kenrick's Jubilee Sermon," p. 360.

10. Ibid.

11. Minutes of the meeting of the archbishops in Saint Louis, Nov. 29, 1891, in BAA.

12. Kain to Simeone, Wheeling, Dec. 17, 1891, in BAA, 89-F-1.

13. Ireland to Gibbons, St. Paul, Dec. 28, 1891, in BAA, 89-G-3.

14. Kain to [?], Wheeling, Feb. 17, 1892, in Catholic University Letter File.

15. *The Washington Post*, quoted in *Western Watchman*, Dec. 24, 1893.

16. Gibbons to Simeone, Dec. 29, 1891, in BAA.

17. Rudolph J. Meyer, "Memorandum," *Acta Consultorium, Provinciae Missourianae* (Apr. 26, 1888), in Archives of the Missouri Jesuit Province, Saint Louis.

18. Thomas Hughes, "Letter of June 29, 1890," *Woodstock Letters* 19, no. 3 (1890): 294.

19. Gibbons to Kenrick, Nov. 20, 1892, in BAA.

20. Personal testimony of Father Thomas Lynam of Saint Louis, a parishioner and protege of Father James McCabe, to the author, Jan. 24, 1967.

21. Saint Louis Priests to Gibbons, Nov. 14, 1892, in SLAA.

22. *Western Watchman*, Dec. 4, 1892.

23. *Circular*, Nov. 17, 1892, in SLAA.

24. Gibbons to Scannel, Dec. 12, 1892, in BAA.

25. Scannel to Gibbons, Dec. 16, 1892, in BAA.

26. Kain to Gibbons, Dec. 17, 1892, 90-V-4, in BAA.

27. Gibbons to Ledochowski, Dec. 27, 1892, in BAA.

28. Rothensteiner, *History of the Archdiocese* 2: 582.

V. JOHN J. KAIN: "JOURNEYMAN" BETWEEN GIANTS (1895-1903)

24. In the Shadow of the Lion

1. *Catholic Mirror*, July 8, 1865.

2. Gibbons to Bayley, Richmond, July 22, 1874, 41-S-5 in BAA.

3. Kain to Gibbons, Harpers Ferry, Feb. 16, 1875, 72-T-3, BAA.

4. Gibbons to Bayley, Richmond, Jan. 19, 1876, 40-G-1, BAA.

5. Ellis, *Life of Cardinal Gibbons* 1: 142.

6. Kain to Gibbons, Wheeling, Apr. 7, 1876, 72-V-8, BAA.

7. Ellis, *Life of Cardinal Gibbons* 1: 142.

8. Kain to Gibbons, Wheeling, Apr. 15, 1878, 73-Q-12, BAA.

9. Gibbons, *Diary*, Mar. 11-13, 1880, p. 139, BAA.

10. *Conciliar Plenarii Baltimorensis III. Acta et Decreta*, passim.

11. Guilday, *History of the Councils of Baltimore*, pp. 221-249.

12. Zwierlein, Frederick J., *Life and Letters of Bishop McQuaid* (Rochester, 1925), 1: 152.

13. Gibbons, *Diary*, Oct. 20, 1886, pp. 210-211, in BAA.

14. *Catholic Mirror*, Apr. 2, 1887.

15. Kain to Gibbons, Wheeling, Apr. 4, 1887, 82-P-5, in BAA.

16. Powderly to Kain, Mar. 14, 1888, in the *Powderly Papers*.

17. Kain to O'Connell, Wheeling, Apr. 23, 1888, in Archives of the Diocese of Richmond.

18. Simeone to Gibbons, Rome, Dec. 17, 1890, 98-E-9, BAA.

19. Gibbons, *Diary*, Jan. 16, 1891, p. 250, in BAA.

20. Kain to [?], Wheeling, May 19, 1892, in Catholic University Archives.

21. Ibid.

22. *Western Watchman*, Oct. 17, 1903.

23. Kain to Van der Sanden, Wheeling, July 26, 1893, in SLAA.

24. Van der Sanden to Kain, Aug. 3, 1893, in SLAA.

25. *Western Watchman*, Aug. 13, 1893.

26. Ibid., Sept. 3, 1893.

27. Ibid., Oct. 1, 1893.

28. Ibid.

29. Ibid.

30. Ibid., Sept. 10, 1893.

31. Ibid., Sept. 17, 1893.

32. *Globe-Democrat*, Sept. 15, 1893.

33. *Chronicle*, Sept. 16, 1893.

34. *Sunday Mirror*, Sept. 17, 1893.

35. *Globe-Democrat*, Sept. 15, 1893.

36. *Sunday Mirror*, Sept. 17, 1893.

37. Ibid.

38. *Western Watchman*, Sept. 17, 1893.

39. *Post-Dispatch*, Sept. 15, 1893.

40. Kain to Gibbons, Saint Louis, Sept. 26, 27, 1893, 91-W-5, in BAA.

41. Ryan to Gibbons, Philadelphia, Sept. 27, 1893, 91-W-7, in BAA.

42. Kain to Gibbons, Saint Louis, Dec. 18, 1893, 92-V-6, in BAA.

43. Gibbons to Ledochowski, Baltimore, Dec. 22, 1893 (copy), 92-W-2/1, in BAA.

44. Kain to Gibbons, Jan. 15, 1894, 93-A-8, in BAA.

45. Ledochowski to Gibbons, Rome, Jan. 13, 1894, 93-A-7, in BAA.

46. Kain to Van der Sanden, Dec. 26, 1893, in SLAA.

47. Kain to Phelan, Feb. 17, 1894, in SLAA.

48. Kain to Van der Sanden, Feb. 17, 1894, in SLAA.

49. Quoted in "David Phelan," *The Dictionary of American Biography*, 14: 521. Since the use of this reference by historian Richard Purcell, some enterprising "Defender of Archbishops" tore this and other pages of unpleasant memory out of the almost complete copy of the *Western Watchman* at Kenrick Seminary.

50. Kain to Clergy, Mar. 15, 1894, in SLAA.

51. Ibid.

52. *Phelan's Apology*, Mar. 30, 1894. Chancellor Van der Sanden attests that the letter is in Kain's handwriting; the annotations Phelan's, in SLAA.

53. Kain to Clergy, Apr. 28, 1894, in SLAA.

54. Humphrey Desmond, *The A.P.A. Movement* (Washington: The New Century Press, 1912), passim.

55. Washington Gladden, "The Anti-Catholic Crusade," *The Century Magazine* 47 [new series 25] (Mar. 1894): 794.

56. Desmond, *A.P.A. Movement*, p. 63.

57. Ibid., p. 18.

58. *Western Watchman*, Aug. 22, 1895.

59. Collins to Walsh, Nov. 1, 1948, in SLU Arch.

60. *Western Watchman*, Aug. 19, 1894, p. 8; Aug. 26, 1894, p. 5; Sept. 2, 1894, pp. 1-8.

61. Ibid., Sept. 9, 1894, p. 4.

62. Ibid., Sept. 20, 1894.

63. Ibid., Sept. 6, 1894.

25. Kain Becomes Archbishop

1. Kain to Ledochowski, May 3, 1895, in SLAA.

2. Ledochowski to Kain, May 25, 1895, in SLAA.

3. Decree of Cardinal Ledochowski, June 10, 1895, in SLAA.

4. Documents relating to the court proceedings of July 27, 1895, in SLAA.

5. Reyburn, Frost, Foy, A. Lee, and J. F. Lee to Kain, Aug. 28, 1895, in SLAA.

6. *Western Watchman*, Mar. 15, 1896.

7. Ivory, *Fifty Years a Bishop*, p. 20.

8. Fanny Smith to Kain, Dec. 30, 1895; Mary Anne McMahon to Kain, Mar. 20, 1896; Susan Eustace Myers to Kain, July 8, 1896; O'Hanlon to Kain, Mar. 13, 1897; Lucy Eustace Gormley to Kain, Mar. 22, 1897; Kain to Gormley, Apr. 3, 1897; Gormley to Kain, May 18, 1897; Gormley to Kain, June 16, 1897; Geraldine Eustace Gerard to Kain, Aug. 22, 1897; John Cleary to Kain, Oct., 1897, in SLAA.

9. *Catholic Directory*, 1893, p. 441.

10. *Catholic Directory*, 1895, p. 178.

11. *Financial Record*, in SLAA.

12. Personal recollections of Rev. Thomas Lynam of Saint Louis, a parishioner and protege of Father James McCabe, to the author, Jan. 24, 1967.

13. *Western Watchman*, Oct. 17, 1903. Italics the author's not Phelan's.

14. Rothensteiner, *History of the Archdiocese* 2: 601.

15. Ibid., 2: 601-602.

16. *Western Watchman*, Mar. 15, 1896.

17. Ibid., Mar. 15, 1896.

18. Van der Sanden to City Rectors, Mar. 6, 1896, in SLAA.

19. *Western Watchman*, Mar. 8, 1896.

20. Ibid.

21. Ibid.

22. *American Catholic Quarterly Review* 21 (1896): 425.

26. In "Tornado Alley"

1. *Church Progress*, May 16, 1896.

2. Ibid.

3. Ibid.

4. *American Catholic Ecclesiastical Review* 7, no. 6 (Dec. 1897): 643.

5. *Western Watchman*, Sept. 13, 1896.

6. *American Ecclesiastical Review* 5, no. 4 (Oct. 1896): 431.

7. *American Ecclesiastical Review* 5, no. 5 (Nov. 1896): 545-547.

8. Margaret LoPiccolo Sullivan, *Newspaper Attitudes Towards Saint Louis Minorities, 1900-1923* (Ph.D. diss. Saint Louis University, 1968).

9. *Western Watchman*, Sept. 13, 1896.

10. Pastoral letter of Archbishop Kain, Oct. 28, 1896, in SLAA.

11. Ibid.

12. *Western Watchman*, Oct. 3, 1903.

13. Ibid.

14. *Star*, Nov. 13, 1896.

15. Ibid.

16. Kain to Garrigan, Saint Louis, Jan. 2, 1897, in Catholic University Archives.

17. Rothensteiner, *History of the Archdiocese* 2: 458.

18. *Star*, May 29, 1897.

19. *Post-Dispatch*, June 12, 1897.

20. Ibid.

21. Ibid.

22. Ibid.

23. Rothensteiner, *History of the Archdiocese* 2: 583-584.

24. *Church Progress*, Oct. 15, 1889.

25. Kain to Tuohy, Dec. 11, 1894.

26. Tuohy to Kain, Feb. 20, 1896.

27. Ibid.

28. Kain to Tuohy, Oct. 2, 1896, in SLAA.

29. *Post-Dispatch*, May 2, 1897.

30. Tuohy to Kain, July 16, 1897, in SLAA.

31. *Globe-Democrat*, Nov. 23, 1897.

32. *Republic*, Jan. 14, 1898.

33. *Globe-Democrat*, Mar. 17, 1898.

34. *Republic*, Mar. 19, 1898.

35. *Globe-Democrat*, Apr. 13, 1898.

36. *Globe-Democrat*, Feb. 3, 1899.

37. Martinelli to Kain, Aug. 29, 1898, in SLAA.

38. Kain to Martinelli, Sept. 1, 1898, in SLAA.

39. Sebastian to Kain, Sept. 3, 1898, in SLAA.

40. *Globe-Democrat*, Feb. 3, 1899.

41. Thomas T. McAvoy, C.S.C., *A History of the Catholic Church in the United States* (Notre Dame: University of Notre Dame Press, 1969), p. 333.

42. Ibid., p. 334.

43. *Review*, 1899, passim.

44. *Review* 6, no. 1 (Mar. 23, 1899).

45. Kain to Preuss, Mar. 28, 1899, quoted in *Review* 6, no. 3 (Apr. 6, 1899).

46. Ibid.

47. Kain to Magnien, Apr. 8, 1899, xeroxed copy in SLAA.

48. Ibid.

49. *Dictionary of American Biography*, ("Chopin") 4: 90; ("Finn") 6: 392; ("Reedy") 15: 463.

50. J. P. Curtiss, ed., *American Catholic Who's Who* (Saint Louis: B. Herder Book Company, 1911), p. 204.

51. Richard H. Potter, "Kate Chopin Checklist," *Bulletin* of the Missouri Historical Society 26, no. 4, Part 1 (July 1970): 312-313.

52. *The Cambridge History of American Literature* (New York: The Macmillan Co., 1944), 2: 390.

53. Ibid., pp. 390-391.

54. William Marion Reedy, "Reflections," *The Mirror* 14 (Aug. 25, 1904): 1.

27. Kain's Late Years

1. Annals of Sts. Peter and Paul's, 1897. Provincial Archives, Maryhurst Normal, Kirkwood, Missouri.

2. Gerard, *Mississippi Vista*, pp. 118-119.

3. Marshall S. Snow, *Higher Education in Missouri*, Circular of Information, #21. Ed. by Herbert B. Adams, United States Bureau of Education (Washington: 1901), p. 166. The edition is not available in the Library of Congress or the Library of the Dept. of Health, Education & Welfare.

4. Ibid., p. 165.

5. Kain to Gibbons, Saint Louis, Mar. 14, 1898, 96-E-3, in BAA.

6. Ledochowski to Gibbons, Jan. 11, 1900, 98-A-7 / 1 in BAA.

7. Papers of Incorporation, Saint Louis Roman Catholic Theological Seminary in SLAA.

8. *Pastors*, Nov. 8, 1902, in SLAA.

9. *Missouri House Bill*, No. 210, 41st General Assembly, 1901. A copy is in SLU Arch.

10. Ibid.

11. Copy in the SLU Arch.

12. Lightholder to Rogers, City of Jefferson, Jan. 23, 1901, in SLU Arch.

13. *Church Progress*, Feb. 2, 1901.

14. Ibid.

15. *Star*, Apr. 15, 1901.

16. Walter John Galus, C.R., "The History of the Catholic Italians in Saint Louis" (M.A. thesis, Saint Louis University, 1936), p. 81.

17. *Western Watchman*, Feb. 18, 1900.

18. Ibid., Apr. 29, 1900.

19. Ibid.

20. Ibid., Jan. 24, 1901.

21. *Republic*, Nov. 3, 1902.

22. Kain to Tannrath, various dates, 1899, in SLAA.

23. Kain to priests, Apr. 2, 1900, in SLAA.

24. Van der Sanden to priests, Mar. 1, 1900, in SLAA.

25. Kain to Tannrath, Aug. 21, 1900, in SLAA.

26. Kain to pastors, Feb. 15, 1901, in SLAA.

27. Kain to pastors, May 25, 1901, in SLAA.

28. "Tentative Program," Eucharistic Congress, 1901.

29. "Program," Eucharistic Congress, Oct. 16, 1901.

30. Phelan to priests, Apr. 27, 1902, in SLAA.

31. Kain File, SLAA.

32. Tannrath to Gibbons, Saint Louis, Oct. 4, 1902, in SLAA.

33. Boyson to Gibbons, Saint Louis, Oct. 8, 1902, in BAA, 100-B-4.

34. Gibbons to Gotti, Baltimore, Oct. 22, 1902, copy in French, in BAA, 100-C-2.

35. Glennon to Dennis O'Connell, Jan. 21, 1903, in the Mullen Library Archives, Catholic University of America.

36. Riordan to Gibbons, Jan. 19, 1903, in BAA, 100-G-5.

37. Gibbons to Giotto, Jan. 22, 1903, in BAA, 100-G-6.

38. *Western Watchman*, Dec. 16, 1915.

VI. JOHN J. GLENNON: ELOQUENT BUILDER (1903-1946)

28. The West Awakens

1. *Recollections* of John J. Glennon, as told to Joseph Donovan, C.M., in SLAA.

2. Glennon to O'Connell, Saint Louis, May 25, 1903, in Catholic University Archives.

3. *Fleur-de-Lis* 4 (1902-03): p. 289.

4. Rothensteiner, *History of the Archdiocese* 2: 637.

5. "Invitation," Glennon Reception, May 5, 1904, in the papers of Howard Benoist; Xerox copy in author's possession.

6. Undated newspaper clippings, 1904, in Benoist Scrapbook.

7. Minutes of the Meeting of the Archbishops, Apr. 14, 1904, 101-E, in BAA.

8. Ibid., May 4, 1905, 102-K in BAA.

9. Glennon to O'Connell, Saint Louis, Feb. 24, 1904, in Catholic University Archives.

10. Report of the NCEA Convention, July 1904, p. 81.

11. Ibid., pp. 39-59.

12. Ibid., p. 52.

13. Glennon to Gibbons, Saint Louis, Jan. 27, 1904, 101-B, in BAA.

14. Colman J. Barry, O.S.B., *The Catholic University of America, 1903-1909* (Washington: The Catholic University of America Press, 1950), p. 123.

15. Barry, *Catholic University of America*, p. 210.

16. Ibid., pp. 212-213.

17. Ibid., p. 177.

18. Minutes of the Meetings of the Board of Trustees of the Catholic University of America, Nov. 16, 1907, in the Mullen Library.

19. Barry, *Catholic University of America*, p. 244.

20. Ellis, *Life of Cardinal Gibbons* 2: 203.

21. Rothensteiner, *History of the Archdiocese* 2: 401.

22. Constance Smith, *Our Pastors in Calvary* (Saint Louis, 1924), p. 135.

23. Ibid.

24. *Catholic Directory*, 1906, p. 160.

25. Ibid., 1907, p. 167, 176.

26. Ibid., 1908, p. 179.

27. Ibid., 1909, p. 178.

28. Ibid., 1913, p. 202.

29. Ibid., 1917, p. 1127.

30. Ibid., p. 187.

31. Ibid., 1918, p. 189.

32. Monsignor Martin Hellriegel, *Recollections*.

33. Records of Apostolic Missionary Band, in SLAA.

29. Builder, Colonizer, Orator

1. Charles Souvay, C.M., *The Cathedrals of Saint Louis* (Saint Louis, n.d.), pp. 30-31.

2. Barry, *Catholic Church and German-Americans*, p. 258.

3. Donald Molitor, "The History of Glennonville and Adjacent Catholic Colonization Ventures in Southeast Missouri: A Study in Changing Rural-Urban Patterns, 1905-1947" (M.A. thesis, Saint Louis University, 1965).

4. Ibid., p. 120.

5. *Post-Dispatch*, Dec. 24, 1945.

6. Quoted in Rothensteiner, *History of the Archdiocese* 2: 719.

7. Glennon to Gramann, May 19, 1909, in the Kenkel Correspondence, in LUND.

8. *Republic*, June 4, 1919.

9. Sermon, Sept. 1916, in SLAA.

10. *Globe-Democrat*, Jan. 17, 1914.

11. Quoted in the *Star-Times*, Dec. 24, 1945.

12. *Globe-Democrat*, Oct. 8, 1917.

13. Ibid., Dec. 21, 1930.

30. Archdiocesan Development

1. *Western Watchman*, Sept. 6, 1884.

2. *The Catholic Encyclopedia and its Makers* (New York: The Encyclopedia Press, 1917), p. 133.

3. Ibid., p. 79.

4. Ibid., p. 55.

5. Ibid., pp. 163-164.

6. Ibid., p. 63.

7. *Church Progress*, Sept. 6, 1928.

8. *Republic*, June 1910.

9. Report of the Proceedings and Addresses of the 16th Annual Meeting of the Catholic Educational Association, Saint Louis, Mo., 16 (1919), p. 43.

10. *Republic*, June 1910.

11. *Church Progress*, June 23, 1919.

12. *Oriflamme*, Oct. 1918.

13. Sister Mary Arthur (Elizabeth) Kolmer, Ad.PP.S., "John Cardinal Glennon's Contribution to the Catholic Secondary Education in Saint Louis," *Social Justice Review* 60, nos. 2-5 (Apr.-Sept. 1967), p. 172.

14. *Oriflamme*, Oct. 1938.

15. Glennon to Garthoeffner, Aug. 16, 1911, in the Archdiocesan Office of Education.

16. Aloysius Garthoeffner, "Catholic Free High Schools — A Statement," Oct. 5, 1911, p. 3.

17. Report of the Catholic High School Association, 1913.

18. Minutes of the Catholic High School Association, 2: 47.

19. Kolmer, "Glennon's Contribution to Catholic Secondary Education," p. 97.

20. *Post-Dispatch*, Sept. 1911.

21. Garthoeffner to McDevitt, July 12, 1911, in the Archdiocesan Office of Education.

22. Kolmer, "Glennon's Contribution to Catholic Secondary Education," p. 64.

23. *Western Watchman*, Nov. 19, 1911.

24. *Church Progress*, June 20, 1912.

25. Saint Louis County Recorder of Deeds, Apr. 18, 1912, Book 293, p. 406.

26. *Western Watchman*, Dec. 4, 1913.

27. *Globe-Democrat*, Sept. 21, 1930.

28. Sister M. Lilliana Owens, S.L., *Loretto in Missouri* (Saint Louis: B. Herder Book Co., 1965), p. 138.

29. Faherty, *Better the Dream*, p. 278.

31. Last Look at Nationalities

1. "The Social Reform Activities of the Central Bureau, 1909-1917," *Social Justice Review* 54 (Dec. 1961, Jan. 1962): 263, 301-304.

2. Philip Gleason, "An Immigrant Group's Interest in Progressive Reform: the Case of the German-American Catholics," *American Historical Review* 72, no. 2 (Dec. 1967): 369.

3. Ibid., p. 378-379.

4. McAvoy, *History of the Catholic Church*, p. 399.

5. *Western Watchman*, June 30, 1904.

6. Ibid., Aug. 9, 1906.

7. Ibid., Nov. 30, 1913.

8. Galus, "History of the Catholic Italians," p. 184.

9. *Globe-Democrat*, Nov. 27, 1927.

10. Clement Mihanovich, *Americanization of the Croats in Saint Louis, Mo. during the Last Thirty Years* (M.A. thesis, Saint Louis University, 1936).

11. *Globe-Democrat*, Oct. 7, 1934.

12. Ibid., Feb. 8, 1931.

13. Daniel T. Kelleher, "Saint Louis 1916 Residential Segregation Ordinance," *Bulletin of the Missouri Historical Society 26*, no. 3 (Apr. 1970): 245-246. This article discusses the question thoroughly and soundly.

14. *Post-Dispatch*, Nov. 6, 1917.

15. Kelleher, "Residential Segregation Ordinance," p. 248.

16. Glennon to Fumasoni-Biondi, Saint Louis, Feb. 18, 1927, in SLAA.

17. Ibid.

18. *Glennon Papers*, Speech of May 30, 1915, in SLAA.

19. Kenkel to Dietz, Oct. 24, 1914, quoted in Edward Cuddy, "Pan-Germanism and American Catholicism," *Catholic Historical Review* 54, no. 3 (Oct. 1968), p. 451.

20. Cuddy, "Pan-Germanism," p. 434.

21. Ibid., p. 433.

22. Ibid., p. 448.

23. Formal Invitation to Requiem Mass for Emperor Franz Joseph, in the papers of Howard Benoist of Saint Louis. Xerox copy in author's files.

24. Rothensteiner, *History of the Archdiocese*, 2: 713.

25. Ibid.

26. *Globe-Democrat*, Mar. 8, 1931.

27. Ibid., Nov. 23, 1930.

28. *Irish-American*, Mar. 1, 1919.

29. *Post-Dispatch*, Nov. 12, 1923.

32. Organizations Galore

1. *SLCHR* 1: 14.

2. Ibid., passim.

3. Rothensteiner, *History of the Archdiocese* 1: vii.

4. W. C. Ruoff to J. B. Turner, May 8, 1919, in the Archives of the Laymen's Retreat League, Saint Louis.

5. Minutes of the Meeting of the Saint Louis University Trustees, May 17, 1924, in the Archives of the Saint Louis University.

6. Testimony of Father Laurence Chiuminatto, Director of White House Retreat, quoted in Faherty, *Better the Dream*, p. 276.

7. *Globe-Democrat*, May 29, 1927.

8. Ibid., May 5, 1929.

9. Ibid., May 24, 1931.

10. Ibid., Oct. 21, 1928.

11. Ibid., Dec. 20, 1931.

12. Ibid., Dec. 7, 1930.

13. For a historical analysis and evaluation of the work of Father Daniel A. Lord and the Queen's Work, see William B. Faherty, S.J., "The Queen's Work: Fifty Years," in *Woodstock Letters* 92 (Apr. 1963): 99-114.

14. O'Hara to Kenkel, Aug. 14, 1923, in the Files of the *Central Verein* (hereafter FCV).

15. O'Hara to Kenkel, July 31, 1923, in FCV.

16. O'Hara to Brockland, Aug. 14, 1923, in FCV.

17. Glennon to Brockland, Oct. 25, 1923, in FCV.

18. Dana C. Jennings, "Priest of Many Names Saves Soil and Souls," *Catholic Rural Life Magazine*, Apr. 1960.

19. Habig, *Heralds of the King*, p. 445.

20. Ibid., p. 437.

21. Ibid., p. 262.

22. Ibid., pp. 443-444.

33. Internal Expansion in the Twenties

1. "History of the House, 1922-1948," Christian Brothers College, Archives, Saint Louis, Missouri.

2. *Globe-Democrat*, Feb. 14, 1932.

3. Copies of these two pamphlets are in SLAA.

4. Recollections of Rev. Paul Ritchie in the possession of his sister, Mrs. Mary Connell.

5. *Globe-Democrat*, May 14, 1905.

6. Ibid., May 15, 1905.

7. *Post-Dispatch*, Apr. 6, 1907.

8. *Baltimore Sun*, Aug. 8, 1909.

9. *Republic*, Aug. 21, 1917.

10. *New York Times*, Dec. 23, 1918.

11. Gibbons to Glennon, July 12, 1920, in SLAA.

12. *Annual Reports*, 1926-1928, Archives of the Motherhouse of the Sisters of Saint Mary, Saint Louis, Missouri.

13. Glennon to Schwitalla, Saint Louis, Oct. 2, 1925; copy in SLAA.

14. Guidelines on the Corporate College System, copy in SLAA.

15. *History of the Archdiocese of Saint Louis* (Saint Louis: The Western Watchman Publishing Co., 1924), p. 3.

16. *Sunday Watchman*, Diocesan Centennial Number, Aug. 8, 1926.

17. Ibid., pp. 15-32.

18. Ibid., pp. 37-45.

19. Oliver H. Hoss, "Col. Nicholas Bell," *History of the Archdiocese of Saint Louis*, pp. 26-28; *Sunday Watchman*, Aug. 8, 1926, p. 110.

20. Rothensteiner, *History of the Archdiocese* 2: 759.

21. Ibid., 2: 760.

22. Ibid., 2: 763.

23. *Globe-Democrat*, June 16, 1935.

24. Quoted in *SLCHR* 5 (1923): 94.

25. *Globe-Democrat*, Oct. 5, 1930.

26. Ibid., June 17, 1934.

27. Ibid., Dec. 13, 1931.

28. Ibid., May 15, 1932.

29. *Catholic Directory*, 1930, p. 182, pp. 292-293.

30. Ibid., pp. 77-78.

31. Ibid., pp. 80-81; 182.

34: Parochial Activities

1. Marie Mueller, "Parish Jubilee Booklets: A Problem in Historiography" (M.A. thesis, Saint Louis University, 1952).

2. Anna D. Cook, *History of St. Rose's Church* (Saint Louis: Mangan Press, 1910).

3. *St. Boniface Parish, the Record of the Growth of a Mustard Seed* (Saint Louis: Wellington Printery, 1935).

4. Mueller, "Problem in Historiography," p. 87.

5. Ibid., p. 78.

6. *St. Lawrence O'Toole Parish Journal* 1 (1913) to 5 (1917).

7. *Globe-Democrat*, Apr. 22, 1928.

8. Ibid., Nov. 18, 1928.

9. Ibid., Dec. 21, 1930.

10. Ibid., July 21, 1929.

11. Ibid., Feb. 11, 1934.

12. Ibid., Nov. 8, 1931.

13. Ibid., Oct. 4, 1931.

14. Ibid., Jan. 24, 1932.

15. Ibid., June 11, 1933.

16. Ibid., Feb. 3, 1929.

17. Ibid., Sept. 1, 1929.

18. Ibid., Mar. 16, 1930.

19. Ibid., Dec. 31, 1933.

20. Ibid., Feb. 5, 1928.

21. Ibid., May 22, 1927.

22. Ibid., May 5, 1929.

23. Ibid., Dec. 27, 1931.

24. Ibid., Dec. 11, 1932.

25. Ibid., May 7, 1933.

26. Ibid., Oct. 5, 1930.

27. Ibid., June 5, 1932.

28. Ibid., Dec. 25, 1937.

29. Ibid., Nov. 27, 1932.

30. Ibid., Apr. 2, 1933.

31. Ibid., July 5, 1934.

32. William Markoe, "Memoirs," in author's personal files.

33. Ibid.

34. *The Chronicle* 3, no. 1 (Jan. 1930).

35. Ibid., passim.

36. Ibid., 4, no. 11 (Nov. 1931): pp. 656-658.

37. *Interracial Review* 5, no. 11 (Nov. 1932).

38. Ibid., 6, no. 1 (Jan. 3, 1933), pp. 12-13.

39. Ibid., 7, no. 8 (Sept. 1934), p. 106.

40. John T. White, *Survey of Organized Catholic Activities Among the Negroes in the Saint Louis District 1917-1937* (M.A. thesis, Saint Louis University, 1937), p. 2.

41. Joseph P. Donovan, C.M., "Is This the Long Looked For Church Society?" *American Ecclesiastical Review* 86, no. 3 (Mar. 1932), p. 245.

42. N. Schall to the Editor, *American Ecclesiastical Review* 86, no. 4 (Apr. 1932), pp. 424-425.

43. Donovan, "Is This the Long Looked For Church Society?" pp. 245 ff.

44. Files of the Legion of Mary, Saint Louis *Senatus*, Legion of Mary Office, Saint Louis, Missouri.

45. Cecily Halleck, *The Legion of Mary* (New York: Thomas J. Crowell Company, 1950), p. 101. For some unaccountable reason, the author hesitates to identify individuals by their proper names preferring "an American Vincentian," or "an Irish businessman."

46. Frank Duff, *The Spirit of the Legion of Mary* (Glasgow: John S. Burns and Sons, 1956), pp. 126-128.

35. Advances Despite the Depression

1. Joseph Husslein, "A University in Print," *Jesuit Bulletin* 15, no. 4 (Apr. 1936): 2.

2. Quoted, Ibid.

3. Quoted, Ibid.

4. *Jesuit Bulletin* 26 (Feb. 1947): 4.

5. Testimony of Joseph J. Lotharius, publications director, Bruce Publishing Co., in author's files.

6. *Between the Lines*, Spring 1944.

7. Unpublished statement of William Holub, in author's files.

8. "Recollections" of Father James Conway, Lexington, Missouri.

9. Glennon to Hellriegel, Oct. 14, 1926, in the personal papers of Msgr. Hellriegel.

10. *Worship,* passim.

11. Glennon to Ellard, Apr. 23, 1941, in SLAA.

12. Glennon to Hellriegel, Feb. 28, 1945, in SLAA.

13. Donovan to Hellriegel, Oct. 1, 1945, in SLAA.

14. Personal Papers of Sister Anna Joseph, C.S.J.

15. Ibid.

16. James Rorty, "How Saint Louis Broke the Race Barrier," *Ave Maria*, reprint no. 101.

17. Sister Ann Adelaide, C.S.J., "A Follow-Up Study of the Vocational Adjustment of Saint Joseph High School Graduates," (M.A. thesis, Saint Louis University, 1950).

18. Floyd Hunter, *Top Leadership, U.S.A.* (Chapel Hill: University of North Carolina Press, 1959), p. 20.

19. Sister Mary Joseph, S.L., *Gallery of Living Catholic Authors* (Webster Groves, 1945), passim.

20. Glennon to pastors, Dec. 27, 1940, in SLAA.

21. Saint Louis *Register* files.

22. Saint Louis *Register*, Jan. 3, 1941.

23. Ibid., Feb. 24, 1941.

24. Glennon to pastors, Dec. 31, 1942, in SLAA.

25. *Register*, Jan. 8, 1943.

26. *Register* files.

27. *Register*, Jan. 5, 1943.

36. World War II and After

1. *Register*, Dec. 24, 1941.

2. Cody to Clergy Conference, Saint Louis, Aug. 14, 1944, in files of the conference.

3. Blair to Donovan, Jefferson City, June 22, 1943, copy in the files of the Catholic Interracial Council of Saint Louis.

4. Council Minutes, Sisters of Loretto, July 11, 1943, in Archives of the Loretto Motherhouse, Nerinx, Kentucky.

5. Correspondence file, Archives of the Loretto Motherhouse.

6. Priests to Glennon, Saint Louis, July 12, 1943; copy in the files of the Clergy Conference.

7. Donovan to Mother Edwarda, Saint Louis, Sept. 7, 1943, in the Archives of Loretto Motherhouse.

8. Council Minutes of the Sisters of Loretto, Sept. 20, 1943, in the Archives of the Loretto Motherhouse.

9. Glennon to Molloy, Dec. 7, 1943, in the files of the Clergy Conference.

10. Ibid.

11. Pittsburgh *Courier*, Feb. 5, 1944.

12. *Post-Dispatch*, Feb. 12, 1944.

13. Johnson to Heithaus, Washington, Mar. 4, 1944, in SLU Arch.

14. Symington to Heithaus, Saint Louis, 1944, in the SLU Arch.

15. Ibid.

16. Molloy to Heithaus, Feb. 22, 1944, in SLU Arch.

17. Holloran to Heithaus, Saint Louis, Feb. 16, 1944; Heithaus to Zuercher, Dec. 18, 1944, in SLU Arch.

18. Rorty, "How Saint Louis Broke the Race Barrier."

19. *Register*, Sept. 29, 1944.

20. Ibid.

21. *Oriflamme*, Nov. 1944.

22. Radio Address, Oct. 29, 1944, in SLAA.

23. *Register*, Nov. 3, 1944.

24. Ibid., Dec. 15, 1944.

25. Ibid., Mar. 15, 1946.

26. Ibid.

27. Ibid.

28. *Social Justice Review* 37 (Jan. 1945): 323.

29. Ellis, *Life of Cardinal Gibbons* 2: 649.

30. James H. Moynihan, *The Life of Archbishop John Ireland* (New York: Harper and Brothers, 1953), p. 385.

VII. JOSEPH ELMER RITTER: ORGANIZER, INTEGRATOR, ECUMENIST (1946-1967)

37. Ritter to Saint Louis

1. Martin Duggan, "The Red Hat," in the *Globe-Democrat Magazine*, June 22, 1961, p. 6.

2. Justin L. Faherty, "The Life Story of Joseph E. Ritter," *Globe-Democrat Magazine*, Dec. 4, 1955, p. 5.

3. Ibid., p. 18.

4. *The Midwestern Post* 2, no. 33 (Nov. 24, 1944): 1.

5. Duggan, "Red Hat," p. 6.

6. Files of the Catholic Interracial Council, Saint Louis.

7. Integration File in SLAA.

8. Robert Donner, "Cardinal Ritter: Welcoming the Future," *The Sign* (Mar. 1963): 17.

9. Justin Faherty, "Life Story of Ritter," p. 11. The author could not locate such a letter in the Glennon files.

10. Con Keliher, "Meeting New Challenges," *Register*, Oct. 5, 1956, p. 15.

11. Testimony of Msgr. Joseph Baker to the author.

12. *Review*, July 14, 1961.

13. *Register*, Oct. 5, 1956.

14. Justin Faherty, "Life Story of Ritter," p. 18.

15. *Globe-Democrat*, Jan. 1, 1948.

16. Hamilton Thornton, "The Lay Apostolate," *Register*, Oct. 5, 1956.

17. Robert L. Burnes, "A Positive Program for Youth," *Register*, Oct. 5, 1956.

18. Harry B. Wilson, "Catholic Action in the Community," *Register*, Oct. 5, 1956.

19. Thornton, "The Lay Apostolate."

20. *Review*, Aug. 16, 1957.

21. Ibid., Sept. 28, 1962.

38. Domestic Development

1. Con Keliher, "Meeting New Challenges."

2. Virgil A. Kelly, "The See of Saint Louis," *The Catholic Market* (Apr. 1963): 5 (Reprint).

3. Duggan, "Red Hat," p. 6.

4. Ibid., p. 11.

5. *Review*, May 3, 1957.

6. Ibid., Aug. 9, 1957.

7. *Register*, Oct. 5, 1956.

8. *Review*, July 14, 1961.

9. James Johnson, *Joseph Cardinal Ritter* (Notre Dame: Notre Dame Press, 1964), p. 25.

10. Martin Duggan, "One Faith for All," *Register*, Oct. 5, 1956.

11. *Review*, Feb. 1, 1957.

12. *Register*, July 6, 1956.

13. Ibid.

14. *Globe-Democrat*, Jan. 1, 1955.

15. *Register*, June 3, 1955.

16. Ibid., Mar. 2, 1956.

17. *Review*, Feb. 1, 1957.

18. Ibid.

19. *Register*, Dec. 24, 1941.

20. *Review*, May 31, 1957.

21. Ibid., Aug. 16, 1957.

22. Ibid.

23. Ibid., Sept. 13, 1957.

24. Ibid., July 12, 1957.

25. Ibid., Apr. 26, 1963.

26. Ibid., May 21, 1959.

27. Ibid., May 20, 1960.

28. Ibid., May 26, 1961. During 1960 also, Brother Lawrence J. Gonner, S.M., began a series of articles on the Catholic Press in Saint Louis. He listed twenty-six papers printed in the city in various languages, French, English, German, and Bohemian (Ibid., Apr. 8, 1960).

29. Ibid., May 24, 1963.

30. Rorty, "How Saint Louis Broke the Race Barrier."

31. Ibid.

32. Testimony of Mr. Clifford Powts, Supervisor of the Retail Sales Department at the Queen's Work, 1956-62, to the author.

33. Rorty, "How Saint Louis Broke the Race Barrier."

34. Quoted in *Register*, Oct. 5, 1956.

39. Personalities and Progress

1. *Washington Missourian*, Apr. 27, 1967.

2. Dana C. Jennings, "Priest of Many Names Saves Soil and Souls," *Catholic Rural Life Magazine*, Apr. 1960.

3. "The Passing of a Giant," *Liguorian*, Jan. 1970, p. 32.

4. *Review*, passim.

5. *Register*, Dec. 9, 1955.

6. *Review*, Nov. 1, 1960.

7. Ibid., June 16, 1961.

8. Ibid., Apr. 27, 1962.

9. Ibid., June 9, 1961.

10. Joe Jares, "U.S.F. wins one for the U.N.," *Sports Illustrated* 25 (Dec. 12, 1966): 24.

11. *Review*, Oct. 6, 1961.

12. Ibid., Nov. 10, 1961.

13. Ibid., June 19, 1970.

14. *Globe-Democrat*, Jan. 22, 1960.

15. *Our Sunday Visitor*, Jan. 1959.

16. *Globe-Democrat*, Mar. 21, 1969.

17. Ibid.

18. *Review*, Jan. 11, 1963.

19. Ibid., Jan. 11, 1963.

20. Very Rev. Msgr. James D. Curtin, "The Catholic Schools of Saint Louis," *Catholic School Journal* 63, no. 4 (Apr. 1963): 31-32.

21. Ibid.

22. Ibid.

40. The Church and the Wide-Wide World

1. Cardinal Ritter, Speech at the Pius XII Library, Sept. 1963.

2. *Review*, Dec. 18, 1964.

3. Testimony of Msgr. Joseph Baker to the author.

4. *Review*, Sept. 28, 1962.

5. Xavier Rynne, *Letters from Vatican City* (New York: Farrar, Strauss and Co., 1963), p. 148.

6. Joseph Ratzinger, *Theological Highlights of Vatican II* (New York: Paulist Press, 1966), p. 22.

7. Robert B. Kaiser, *Pope, Council and World — the Story of Vatican II* (New York: Macmillan Co., 1963), pp. 169-170.

8. Rynne, *Letters from Vatican City*, pp. 158-160.

9. Ratzinger, "Theological Highlights," p. 25.

10. Rynne, *Letters from Vatican City*, p. 217.

11. *Now* 8, no. 6 (June 1963), a xeroxed copy of Bishop Cadigan's article is in the files of the *St. Louis Review*.

12. *Review*, Jan. 24, 1964.

13. *Now*, Feb. 1964.

14. Quoted in Johnson, *Cardinal Ritter*, p. 38.

15. *Review*, Apr. 26, 1963.

16. Ibid.

17. Ibid.

18. Johnson, *Cardinal Ritter*, p. 21. With permission of the publisher.

19. *Marriage*, Oct. 1963.

20. Johnson, *Cardinal Ritter*, p. 21.

21. *Social Justice Review* 60, no. 4 (July-Aug. 1967), 140.

22. Ratzinger, "Theological Highlights," p. 34.

23. Ibid., pp. 36-39.

24. Ibid., pp. 41-42.

25. Johnson, *Cardinal Ritter*, p. 39.

26. Ibid., pp. 40-41.

27. *Council Day Book*, Vatican II, Sessions I and II (Washington: NCWC, 1965), p. 159.

28. Ibid., p. 181.

29. Ibid.

30. Johnson, *Cardinal Ritter*, p. 46.

31. *Council Day Book*, Sessions I and II, p. 239.

32. Johnson, *Cardinal Ritter*, p. 43.

33. *Council Day Book*, Sessions I and II, p. 256.

34. Ibid., p. 271.

35. Johnson, *Cardinal Ritter*, p. 39.

36. *Council Day Book*, Sessions I and II, p. 301.

37. *Review*, Aug. 1964.

38. Ibid., Mar. 20, 1964.

39. *Social Justice Review* 60, no. 4 (July-Aug. 1967), p. 140.

40. John Osterreicher, *Commentary on the Documents of Vatican II* (New York: Herder and Herder, 1969), 3: 68.

41. Ibid.

42. *Council Day Book*, Session III, p. 67.

43. Ibid.

44. Ibid.

45. Ibid., p. 272.

46. Ibid.

47. Ibid., pp. 297, 298.

48. Ratzinger, "Theological Highlights," p. 97.

49. *Council Day Book*, Session II, p. 285.

50. *Review*, Dec. 18, 1964.

51. Ibid., Feb. 12, 1965.

52. *Archdiocesan Directory on Ecumenism* (Saint Louis, 1965), p. 16.

53. *Yearbook of the Archdiocese of Saint Louis*, 1965, passim.

54. *National Catholic Reporter*, Oct. 27, 1965.

55. *Review*, Aug. 27, 1965.

56. Ibid., Sept. 17, 1965.

57. *National Catholic Reporter*, Oct. 27, 1965.

58. Ibid.

59. *Council Day Book*, Session IV, p. 19.

60. Vincent Yzermans, *A New Pentecost* (Westminister: Newman, 1963), p. 234.

61. Rynne, *Letters from Vatican City*, p. 148.

62. Frederick R. McManus, "The Role of the Bishop," *Review*, April 28, 1967.

41. Council Aftermath

1. *Review*, Dec. 18, 1965.

2. *Globe-Democrat*, Dec. 5, 1965.

3. *Review*, passim, especially Mar. 4, 1966; May 20, 1966; June 24, 1966.

4. Ibid., Mar. 24, 1967.

5. Ibid., Mar. 17, 24, 1967.

6. Ibid.

7. Ibid., Sept. 15, 1967.

8. Address of Daniel L. Schafly, June 3, 1967, in SLU Arch.

9. Thomas F. O'Dea, *The Catholic Crisis* (Boston: The Beacon Press, 1968), pp. 10, 250. With the permission of the publisher.

10. *Post-Dispatch*, Nov. 20, 1966.

11. Ibid.

12. *Review*, May 12, 1967.

13. Ibid.

14. Ibid.

15. *Look*, May 30, 1967.

16. *Review*, May 19, 1967.

17. *Vagnozzi to Ritter* Feb. 1967, in SLAA.

18. Testimony of Msgr. Joseph Baker to the author.

19. Review, June 16, 1967.

20. Ibid.

21. Edward T. O'Meara, New York, O'Meara to Medgyesi-Mitschang, Sept. 18, 1968, in the author's files.

VIII: JOHN JOSEPH CARBERRY: MARIAN ADVOCATE

42. Placid Bridging

1. *Review*, October 26, 1979.

2. William B. Faherty and Madeline Oliver, *Religious Roots* of Black Catholics of Saint Louis. (Saint Louis: 1977).

3. William B. Faherty, *From One Generation to the Next*. (Saint Louis: Archdiocesan Education Office, 1978).

4. Ibid, passim.

5. St. Louis *Post-Dispatch*, February 2, 1975, 16-G.

6. George Devine, *American Catholicism*, Englewood Cliffs: Prentice-Hall, 1975, pp. 100-103.

IX: JOHN L. MAY: CALM MIDWESTERNER

44. The Time of Archbishop May in St. Louis.

1. *Review*, March 28, 1980 E-1.

2. Ibid., passim. April 15, 1994, Section 2, p. 3.

3. Ibid., March 28, 1980, C-2.

4. Ibid.

5. Ibid.

6. Ibid., March 28, 1980, C-1.

7. Joanna L. Straton, *Pioneer Woman*, New York, Simon and Schuster, 1981.

8. *Review*, March 28, 1980, B-6.

9. *Review*, March 28, 1980, C-6.

10. "Arnoudt File, in *Belgian Jesuit Archives*, Louvain, Belgium.

A crowd of Saint Louisans listens as Cardinal Carberry welcomes newly arriving Archbishop John May at the Saint Louis Airport: Seated: (L. to R.) Archbishop May, Mayor James Conway, Senator Thomas Eagleton, Mrs. Conway, County Commissioner Gene McNary, and Bishop John M. Wurm. (Photograph by Saint Louis Review).

Acknowledgments

The author wishes to thank historians Joseph P. Donnelly, S.J., Monsignor John Tracy Ellis, Ralph Bayard, C.M., and Professor S.J. Miller; stylistic evaluator NiNi Harris; photographers Robert Arteaga, Eldon Arteaga, Richard Finke and Ralph Frese; typists Rita Kwapiszeski, Gwen Miller, Mary Struckel, Bonnie Vaux, Barbara Middleton and Suzie Poole; proofreader Nancy Merz; artists Edna Suermann, Roscoe Misselhorn and Sheila Harris; and librarians Ann Hurley, Jeanne Rohner, Joan Way, John Waide, Noel Hollebeck, and Sister Teresa Maria Eagan, C.S.J.

Archbishop Justin Rigali commissioned this third edition. Msgr. Richard F. Stika approved the publishing plan of John Kiske. Msgr. Dennis M. Delaney, Editor of the *Review*, worked with the publisher and the author.

Members of the St. Vincent de Paul Society from all over the country met in October 1995, at the Old Cathedral, the site of the first meeting in American, one hundred and fifty years before.

Very Rev. Edward K. Braxton, Auxiliary Bishop of St. Louis, discusses educational problems with Sister Emily Orf, C.PP.S., of Assumption School in O'Fallon and Sister Donna Marie Kist, C.PP.S., of St. Angnes School in Bloomsdale, and Ms. Ellen Ryan of the school office.

Joseph Mueller, National President of the St. Vincent de Paul Society, confers with Robert Gronemeyer, President of the local unit, in preparation for the 150th anniversary of the Society in America.

Brother Bonaventure Thelen (shown on the left in this mural) began the Alexian Health Ministry in America after the Civil War. The Brothers opened their hospital on South Broadway in 1869.

Index

Index — Part VIII

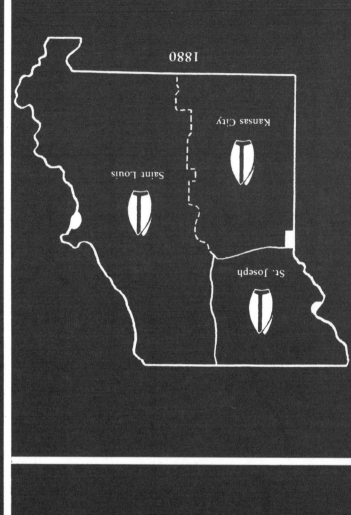

THE ECCLESIASTICAL MIDWEST —

MISSOURI DIOCESES

1868

1880

Saint Louis

St. Joseph

Kansas City

ECCLESIASTICAL PROVINCES

Carved out in whole or in part from the original area actually served by the bishop of Saint Louis in 1826.

A. Saint Louis (1847)
B. Milwaukee (1875)
C. Chicago (1880)
D. St. Paul (1888)
E. Dubuque (1893)
F. Denver (1942)
G. Omaha (1945)
H. Kansas City, Kansas (1962)
I. Oklahoma City (1973)

Saint Louis Archdiocese 1966